WHY NOT TORTURE TERRORISTS?

Why Not Torture Terrorists?

Library
01254 292120

Please return this book on or before the last date below

OXFORD
UNIVERSITY PRESS

Great Clarendon Street, Oxford OX2 6DP

Oxford University Press is a department of the University of Oxford.
It furthers the University's objective of excellence in research, scholarship,
and education by publishing worldwide in

Oxford   New York

Auckland Cape Town Dar es Salaam Hong Kong Karachi
Kuala Lumpur Madrid Melbourne Mexico City Nairobi
New Delhi Shanghai Taipei Toronto

With offices in

Argentina Austria Brazil Chile Czech Republic France Greece
Guatemala Hungary Italy Japan Poland Portugal Singapore
South Korea Switzerland Thailand Turkey Ukraine Vietnam

Oxford is a registered trade mark of Oxford University Press
in the UK and in certain other countries

Published in the United States
by Oxford University Press Inc., New York

British Library Cataloguing in Publication Data

Data available

Library of Congress Cataloguing in Publication Data

Data available

Typeset by Newgen Imaging Systems (P) Ltd., Chennai, India
Printed in Great Britain
on acid-free paper by
Biddles Ltd, King's Lynn

ISBN 978–0–19–954091–4

1 3 5 7 9 10 8 6 4 2

To my family,

With love, absolutely.

Special Dedication

A special dedication must, I feel, be made to the staff of the Public Committee Against Torture in Israel (PCATI) who work tirelessly to protect the rights of Palestinian terrorist suspects, and did so during the darkest days of the *Intifadah*. Suicide bombers were then, at any given time, targeting civilians in Israel generally, and in Jerusalem, where PCATI is based, in particular. In dozens of cases their murderous plots succeeded; hundreds of civilians died. But while many, including human rights organizations, chose in the circumstances to give the issue of torture a wide berth, PCATI staff endeavoured to protect from torture every single human being, even 'ticking bomb' terrorists, for all they knew.

I believe that these and similar activists elsewhere are the real heroes of the 'war on terror'. And they wield our most formidable weapon against the evil that is terrorism—our humanity.

Foreword

When Amnesty International began its first worldwide campaign against torture in 1973, I had just become its first legal officer. As its Report on Torture that year affirmed, international law already reflected the norm contained in Art 5 of the Universal Declaration of Human Rights: 'No-one shall be subjected to torture or to cruel, inhuman or degrading treatment or punishment.' Nevertheless, it was feared that there might be room for legal manoeuvre by those wishing to defend torture or similar ill-treatment, and there were those willing to defend the use of torture in certain circumstances.

Many of the international normative developments over the next decade and a half were aimed at closing down the wiggle room for legal ingenuity in circumventing the prohibition, the 1984 UN Convention against Torture being the most prominent. The expectation was that the clarity and comprehensiveness of the law—no torture, by any authority, against any individual, in any circumstances, anywhere in the world—would also put paid to any lingering moral-philosophical doubts.

For a while, this objective was broadly achieved. Torture still happened, but not generally under colour of law. Rather it was denied. Since the atrocity of 11 September 2001, the issues have been resurrected. While no government has sought to challenge the prohibition as such, spurious legal loopholes have been concocted and some commentators have reopened the case for legalized torture. Even government officials have opined that some of the protections offered detainees by the Geneva Conventions of 12 August 1949 are 'quaint' or that questioning resort to simulated drowning in a 'ticking bomb' situation is a 'no-brainer'.

The time could not, then, have been more propitious for Yuval Ginbar's magisterial riposte to those who would confront terrorists with methods that betray the values they are supposed to be defending. Based on his PhD thesis for the University of Essex, the book examines minutely the arguments that have been deployed either to challenge the absolute prohibition of torture/ill-treatment or to find escape routes round it.

He first looks at the moral-philosophical arguments, of which the ticking bomb scenario is at once the most seductive and the most misleading. Importantly, he looks at the arguments both in the private sphere ('What would you as an individual do?') and in the public sphere ('What should the state do?'). The two are often equated but the issues are very different. He goes on to address the legal issues, including the legal implications of allowing possible exceptions to the absolute prohibition, notably the defence of necessity.

The discussion takes the arguments of the torture advocates/apologists head on and with intellectual power. It is no criticism of his argument that he tells us vividly what the various anodyne-sounding torture techniques involve in pain and suffering and the dehumanization of all concerned. It is not easy reading, but it is essential to understanding what the torture advocates/apologists are asking us to require officials to do to others (and themselves) in our name.

Written lucidly, accessibly and passionately, Dr Ginbar's book is a work of thoroughly-researched, meticulous scholarship. It is a rare work of both international law and legal philosophy. It is written for and deserves to be read by all those lawyers, judges, moral philosophers, political theorists and media pundits, as well as political leaders, who have ventured to doubt whether the torture/ill-treatment prohibition should remain absolute. This book should put their doubts to rest. It will also be useful to human rights advocates needing to confront the doubters.

Professor Sir Nigel Rodley
University of Essex
October 2007

Acknowledgements

Originally written in the guise of a PhD thesis at the Department of Law, University of Essex, this work is actually an attempt to chart, in academic form, a personal journey which I had for a long time felt the need to make. It started back in the mid-1990s, when I worked for an Israeli human rights NGO, and it became clear to me that the incantation and re-incantation of the absolute prohibition of torture in international law is insufficient when it comes to convincing potential victims of suicide bombings that torture must never by practiced.

But while I was slowly setting sail, as it were, at the turn of the twenty-first century, the world, audaciously, embarked upon its own journey rather than wait for mine to conclude. Within a few years, especially as a result of the USA's response to the terrorist attacks on its territory on 11 September 2001, the 'ticking bomb situation' was transformed from an obscure philosophers' imaginary scenario deemed worthy of legal consideration only in Israel, to one frequently invoked in legal parlance as well as media discussions and academic writings throughout the world. No less importantly, it became a standard justification for actual torture practices. All of which (or at least, in view of the uncontrollable deluge of material which these developments have left in their wake, the salient features of which), I have tried to address here.

Research for this study was completed in early 2006, but wherever possible I have taken account of further developments.

The following is a partial list of those to whom I owe gratitude, though none, of course, bears any responsibility for any flaws within this study:

My PhD supervisor, Professor Sir Nigel Rodley for his counsel, his wisdom, his encouragement and his patience; Professors Sheldon Leader, Tom Sorell, and Daniel Statman for their useful comments, especially on Part I.

As noted, I combined work on this study with human rights work, to the benefit, I hope, of both. As a result, certain texts included in this book were originally written for B'Tselem, the Public Committee Against Torture in Israel, Amnesty International and joint documents involving other organizations. In all these cases, I benefited greatly from comments, changes and additions made by my colleagues—too many to mention by name—for which I am grateful. Rob Freer made specific, extremely helpful comments on the chapter on the US model of 'quasi-legalized' torture.

I am also grateful to the various institutions and organizations which have supported me financially, including the University of Essex, the Anglo-Jewish Association (AJA) and the FCO.

I would also like to thank Maria Heed at the Department of Law for her invaluable assistance.

My gratitude and love for my family deserve a cliché—they go beyond what words can express.

Finally I would like to mention Khardol.

Contents

IV. LEGALIZING TORTURE 2—THREE ISSUES

V. CONCLUSIONS

Table of Cases

Note: This table is arranged in alphabetical order of case names rather than adjudicating bodies.

INTERNATIONAL (INCLUDING REGIONAL)

NATIONAL

Australia

Canada

Germany

Israel

United States of America

Table of Treaties and Statutes

NATIONAL

Argentina

India

Israel and the Occupied Palestinian Territories

Germany

United Kingdom

United States of America

List of Abbreviations and General Notes

CAT	(UN) Committee Against Torture
CUP	Cambridge University Press
DoD	Department of Defense (USA)
(DoD/N)	Defence of duress/necessity
DoJ	Department of Justice (USA)
DoN	'Defence of necessity'
E	Ethica (a moral/state agent)
HRC	(UN) Human Rights Committee
IC	Innocent civilians
ICCPR	International Covenant on Civil and Political Rights
ICLQ	International and Comparative Law Quarterly
ILC	International Law Commission
OUP	Oxford University Press
V	Vicious (a terrorist)

Notes

1. Unless otherwise indicated, all translations from Hebrew and Arabic are mine.
2. I have chosen a stricter transliteration of Arabic words and names than is commonly used (eg Qur'an, Usamah, al-Qa'idah rather than Koran, Osama, Al Qaeda).
3. Some publishing houses work from two, three or more cities. I have chosen to mention, for the sake of brevity, only the first city referred to in the publication.

Introduction

> During the hearing at the High Court of Justice, the judges pressured Adv.
> Rosenthal to clarify whether an interrogator would be allowed to use force
> when a 'ticking bomb' is considered. Justice Heshin illustrated: 'supposing
> a bomb was planted inside the Shalom Tower [a multi-storey building in the
> heart of Tel-Aviv], and the interrogee knows. It will explode in two hours.
> It is impossible to evacuate people out of the building. What do I do in such
> a situation?' Rosenthal refused to admit that in such a situation it would be
> permissible to use force during interrogation. Heshin responded: 'this is the
> most extreme immoral position I have ever heard. A thousand people are
> about to die, and you propose to do nothing?'[1]

Should twenty-first century democratic states facing terrorism use torture in the
interrogation of terrorists suspects, at least in extreme, 'ticking bomb situations'?
This study leads to this question, and attempts to answer it.

A 'ticking bomb situation' (TBS) is, as in the scenario described by Justice
Heshin, where the torture of a terrorist suspect seems to be the only means of
obtaining urgently-needed information crucial for the thwarting of planned terrorist attacks which, if carried out, are likely to kill many innocent civilians.

In this book, I will approach the TBS question from three interrelated angles:
as a question of private morality; as a question of public, applied morality (or
'practice'); and as a question of law, modifying the scenario slightly to suit each
context. I will address what I consider to be the most important issues raised by
approaching the question from each of these angles.

The choice of the word 'should' in the original question and of the particular
angles from which to address it, reflect this study's orientation. Laws prohibit torture
everywhere. But should they? Where appropriate I will analyse the law as it currently
stands, but ultimately I will ask (and try to answer) whether this prohibition must
remain in its current, absolute form. This is a meta-legal question, and so this study
will need assume the form of a moral-philosophical debate, a discussion of applied
ethics, or a human rights NGO report, as often as that of a legal analysis.

Part I examines torture in a TBS as a question of 'pure' private morality: by
private I mean that it is a lone, non-official individual who faces the terrorist and
the dilemma. By 'pure' I mean a laboratory-type situation where the would-be

---

[1] HCJ 8049/96 *Muhammad 'Abd al- 'Aziz Hamdan v the General Security Service*, hearing
of 14 November 1996, as described by the Israeli newspaper *Haaretz* (15 November 1996). In
December 1996, Adv Rosenthal confirmed to the present writer (henceforth: I, me etc) that these
were in fact Justice Heshin's words.

torturer's actions will have no 'ripple effects' on society, the law, and so on, and that she knows the facts with absolute certainty: the person is definitely a 'knowledgeable' terrorist, the bomb has definitely been planted, torture—and only torture—will definitely thwart the planned explosion and avoid the massive death toll which would otherwise result.

If the question ultimately concerns states in the real, uncertain world, why choose the doubly-unlikely scenario of a situation free of uncertainties and a choice faced by a private individual?

My answer is five-fold. Firstly, presenting extreme, 'pure' scenarios is a legitimate, oft-used technique in ethical debates—we will encounter a few illustrations in the discussion below. Charles Krauthammer, who makes this point convincingly, concludes that once the justifiability of torture in extreme situations is established in principle, 'all that's left to haggle about is the price'.[2] This is essentially true, albeit oversimplified, as even accepting both this argument and (at least *arguendo*) the justifiability of torture in the 'pure' scenario, it can—and will—be argued that the price may nevertheless be too high once torture is used by officials in the real world.

Secondly, humans can never be 100 per cent sure of the future, and writers have come up with scenarios that are clearly, perhaps deliberately, absurd, such as terrorist bombs that 'will kill hundreds of millions of people'.[3] However, it can reasonably be claimed that, particularly in states facing frequent terrorist attacks, situations similar to a 'pure' TBS have indeed taken place, and more importantly, that situations not departing from the 'pure' TBS enough to change its basic moral contours are possible. In fact, one state has actually provided statistics according to which dozens of 'ticking bomb' situations (so named) requiring the use of torture (not so named) to save lives occurred during each of two consecutive years. Backed as they are by the State Attorney (in individual cases) and based, in both instances, on confidential state information, I for one have no means of refuting these claims.

Thirdly, at least one state, and several writers, have opted for what I call 'eat-your-cake-and-have-it' solutions, or models; one involves preserving an absolute legal prohibition on torture, but with individual interrogators who torture granted immunity if the situation is judged, *ex post*, to have been a TBS. In these cases, the state and its laws purport to withdraw into the shadows during the TBS, leaving an individual to face a private dilemma. Whether such withdrawal is possible will be among the issues addressed in later Parts of this book.

Fourthly, I will argue (in Part II) that in extreme situations, no two moralities exist—one for individuals, one for states—so the dilemma is one and the same (see more below).

---

[2] Charles Krauthammer, 'It's time to be honest about doing terrible things', *The Weekly Standard* (5 December 2006).

[3] KE Himma, 'Assessing the Prohibition Against Torture' in SP Lee (ed) *Intervention, Terrorism and Torture: Contemporary Challenges to Just War Theory* (Dordrecht: Springer, 2007) 235–48, 238.

Finally, a TBS is where the torture-justifying argument is at its strongest, and being an anti-torture absolutist,[4] it is only fair that I allow the rival view the opportunity to 'give it its best shot'.

In Part I, I hope to facilitate, using a 'pure', private TBS, a 'clean' discussion of the moral[5] question which is essentially, I believe, whether the morality of human action should ultimately be open-ended or be constrained by some form of absolutism, however minimal, with emergencies setting the scene for such '*ultimum*'. More specifically, the question is whether the prevention of a catastrophe involving 'disastrous consequences' justifies resort to torture—or whether torture must, morally, be prohibited absolutely, regardless of the consequences. In other words, should a person facing this choice essentially compare the pain of the dead, wounded and bereaved innocent civilians which will result from the explosion of the bomb with that of the terrorist being tortured, or should she consider the immorality of one human being torturing another to be an inherent, unassailable immorality, which cannot, can *never*, yield to such 'cost-benefit' calculations?

Examining these issues will require a discussion of certain general theories of ethics and the controversy among them, before taking the issue of torture as a case in point. I believe it is impossible to offer a thesis on torture in a TBS without addressing what is perhaps the most enduring 'clash of the Titans' among ethicists—utilitarianism versus deontology. However, this will be done only to the extent necessary to answer the question posed. In order to provide my (negative) answer to the 'pure' moral question, it would suffice, I will submit, to use an idea, or a device, which I call 'minimal absolutism', rather than a whole new (or old) theory of morality or ethics. My discussion of the debate around moral absolutism, namely the question of whether or not there are moral 'no-go' areas (ie acts that no-one may ever perform) and attempt to show that the position denying any and all absolute prohibitions is untenable, will produce the logical 'minimal absolutist' conclusion, namely that there must be at least one type of act that is, morally, prohibited absolutely. Next I will argue that torture is, logically, the candidate *par excellence* for such absolute prohibition and, in much greater detail, that this conclusion holds beyond the confines of logic, through a discussion of what the act of torture means and entails, and an analysis of the moral situation in which each of the 'participants' in the TBS scenario would find themselves— the torturer, the tortured terrorist, and the innocent civilians who would be the victims of the bomb, should it explode.

That there are no two different sets of morality, or ethics, for private and public life respectively, at least as regards extreme situations, needs logically to be established for the examination of the 'pure' private case to be relevant to the

---

[4] Whatever descriptions fit this book, the reader will very soon discover that 'a thriller' is not among them.

[5] For the sake of simplicity, I have chosen to use 'moral' and 'ethical' interchangeably.

actions of states (or agents of states). This is done at the beginning of Part II. This Part then recasts the moral question in two significant ways: as a question facing a state rather than an individual; and as a question posed in the world as we know it rather than in a 'pure', doubt-free environment. The first change will entail the addition of society-wide and long-term repercussions of actions to our considerations; the second will mean that other issues, blocked artificially out of the scenario in Part I to ensure its 'purity', such as uncertainty as to the facts and the generally murky nature of real-life situations, will now have to be taken into account.

The bulk of Part II is devoted to an analysis of what happens once a state has opted to allow torturing in TBSs. Since such an option entails, as is shown in Part I, the adoption of a utilitarian morality in the case of extreme situations (or at least in this particular one), Part II mostly examines utilitarian, or what is termed popularly 'slippery slope', dangers of allowing state agents to torture, be it only in a TBS. The 'slippery slope' argument against torture is essentially that once allowed, torture will spread far beyond TBSs, and that society and indeed the international community will be adversely affected by its introduction in a host of other ways, to the extent that allowing torture in TBSs may actually cause more harm than good. This will be done by examining both theoretical 'slippery slope' implications of state resort to torture and those which have emerged from the real practice of states that have resorted to anti-terrorist torture in the twentieth and early twenty-first centuries. The discussion will first focus on 'slippery slope' dangers relating to the immediate context of interrogations, including the difficulties of how to determine issues such as the immediacy of the need to torture; certainty as to the facts; and deciding whom to torture; as well as the effectiveness of torture in comparison to humane interrogation methods. Then the broader, society-wide and worldwide dangers of opting for torture will be examined and illustrated, including that torture, once introduced, would inevitably be institutionalized, necessitating the training and involvement of a wide array of professionals; that it would legitimize other inhumane methods in fighting terrorism; that it would legitimize the torture of other, non-terrorist suspects; that it would have the effect of prolonging and exacerbating conflicts; and that legalizing interrogational torture in TBSs at international law would make violations of the ban on (other) torture well-nigh impossible to condemn and detect, let alone stop. Abu Ghraib is the obvious recent example, but others will also be provided. The overarching question of whether, as a society (and a world) we should give governments the power to do *anything* with a human being under their control if the stakes are high enough will be addressed in the conclusion of this Part.

Parts III and IV focus on the legal aspect, or aspects, of states practicing or allowing torture in TBSs or similar situations. This will be done, first, through examining models of legalized torture, in one case the more cautious term 'quasi-legalized torture' has been preferred. The models to be examined, in Part III are:

- the Landau model in Israel;
- the 'torture warrants' model;
- the High Court of Justice (HCJ) model in Israel;
- the 'high-value detainee' (HVD) model in the USA's 'war on terror'.

Of these, the second one is also the only model that is theoretical, namely, that has only been suggested by writers rather than actually implemented by any state, although I will submit that the Landau model did in fact function, to an extent, also as a 'torture warrants' model. The other three models are 'real life' ones: the Landau model, was set out in a document adopted by the Israeli government in 1987, which established methods for interrogating suspected terrorists and outlined the legal (and moral) framework within which they were practised in Israel between 1987–1999; the HCJ model, which succeeded the Landau model following a ruling by Israel's Supreme Court, sitting as High Court of Justice (HCJ) and applied in that country between the date of the ruling, in September 1999, and the time at which this study was completed; and the USA's model of 'quasi-legalized torture' in the interrogation of detainees, to be applied, in theory, only to HVDs captured during the 'war on terror' that it declared in the wake of the 11 September 2001 terrorist attacks on its territory.

The two Israeli models have, I will submit, legalized torture in all but name, and certainly did so in practice, including legal practice. For the Landau model, legalization occurred through Supreme Court rulings supporting, and even praising, the system in general and allowing the specific, torturous techniques permitted under it to be carried out. For the HCJ model, legalization occurred through the 1999 Supreme Court ruling, which determined that torturers (not so named) in a TBS may be exempt from criminal liability and even prosecution, and setting up a system where, on the one hand, dozens, if not hundreds (or, by now, even more), have been tortured while, on the other, not a single torturer has been prosecuted. Both models relied, legally, on the 'defence of necessity' (DoN), the former as a basis for the compilation of detailed instructions on how to use physical and psychological 'pressure' during the interrogation of terrorists, the latter, as a plea available *ex post facto* to the 'individual interrogator' who decided to torture in a TBS.

The HVD model is far less clear, much more diffuse, and has been constantly changing. It originally combined a great deal of secrecy; Presidential decrees stripping certain detained terrorist suspects of any legal protection, including the right to 'humane treatment'; a series of memoranda by Ministry of Justice and Defense lawyers, two of them explicitly declaring that the President has power under the US Constitution to order torture during war, that the defences of 'necessity' and 'self-defence' applied to those who torture, and that torture was limited to the most extreme acts while 'cruel, inhuman or degrading treatment' need not be criminalized, thus allowing for most of the interrogation methods envisaged by these memoranda; and, at least for a while, acceptance by the (lower) federal courts that the treatment of foreign detainees by US officials on foreign soil was beyond their jurisprudence. In practice, this led to the composition of elaborate lists of interrogation techniques, applied widely, probably too widely, and probably excessively (in the model's own terms) in the USA's various detention centres around the globe. Later, the veil of secrecy over much of this model was lifted; the Supreme Court ruled that federal courts had jurisdiction over at least those detained in Guantánamo Bay and that international humanitarian law applies to them; some of the memoranda were withdrawn and replaced; the President declared that he would not allow, let alone order, torture, and he even signed new laws prohibiting the use of cruel, inhuman or degrading treatment in the interrogation of any person under US control. The new laws, however, granted sweeping *ex post* immunity from prosecution to 'good faith' torture. Moreover, in 2007 a model of 'quasi-legalized torture' prevails, in the continued detention of hundreds beyond the full reach of the law, and the continued CIA program under which HVDs may be held in total isolation in secret, incommunicado detention for months and years, with a variety of other methods used in their interrogation. These practices are clearly unlawful, indeed torturous (at least with the accumulation of time and methods) under international law, but perfectly legal under US law (or at least the administration's interpretation thereof). US courts have so far been reluctant to challenge this interpretation, and these practices.

The discussion of the models will not be purely theoretical and legal—it will also provide detailed descriptions of the models' practical aspects, including the interrogation methods used in each model and the extent to which torture was used beyond the restrictions which the models purported to impose.

What I consider to be the salient legal questions arising from the models examined will be addressed in some detail, in Part IV. In another 'eat-your-cake-and-have-it' position some states—and writers—have advocated that you can 'coerce' terrorists into providing life-saving information without torturing, indeed without breaking international law at all. In view of this, the 'definitional' aspects of methods of interrogation used under the models ('torture lite', 'moderate physical pressure' and the like) and the scope of the international legal ban on torture and other cruel, inhuman or degrading treatment or punishment will first be examined. Next the 'defence of necessity', already mentioned here, will be analysed in detail. This humble criminal law defence became the cornerstone of the two Israeli models, has formed a part, albeit hitherto a passive (or secret?) one, of the US HVD model, and has been recommended by several theorists as the ideal solution for the TBS dilemma. Moreover, in its torture-justifying form the 'defence of necessity' fully and explicitly reflects the 'lesser evil' moral view of the torture-justifying ethicists. I will therefore examine the question of whether the 'defence of necessity', as it now stands at both the domestic and international levels can provide the key to justifiably torturing terrorists in TBSs and saving the innocent while avoiding the 'slippery slope' and other long-term, society-wide and global dangers described in Part II. Finally, the question of the compatibility of the 'defence of necessity' model with the realities of states facing terrorism at the beginning of the twenty-first century will be addressed.

In concluding this study I will attempt to show how the different angles from which the torture in a TBS question have been examined may be seen as mutually complementary.

This study definitely takes sides—it presents and defends a very clear thesis: an absolute opposition to the use of torture (and other ill-treatment) under any circumstances and a total rejection of any attempt to justify or legalize its use. Nevertheless, I have made every effort to do so while presenting other views and arguments fairly and respectfully.

PART I

PRIVATE MORALITY: IS IT MORALLY JUSTIFIABLE FOR AN INDIVIDUAL TO TORTURE A TERRORIST IN ORDER TO SAVE MANY INNOCENT LIVES?

1

Part I—Introduction

A. The Problem Defined

Ethica,[1] a private individual, has just captured and bound a *terrorist*, *Vicious*, who has planted a time-bomb in a *crowded marketplace*, or has just sent a fellow terrorist, consciously and intentionally, on a suicide bombing mission there.[2] The bomb is set, or planned, to explode in a few hours, and kill many *innocent civilians*. Is it morally *justifiable* for Ethica to *torture* Vicious, if this is the only way to get him to reveal the location of the bomb (or the suicide bomber), and thereby save the lives of all those people?

This example, in one version or another,[3] has been widely used by philosophers, to the extent that it was described as 'a standard philosopher's example'[4] by one writer, and as 'a particular kind of hackneyed modern example'[5] by another. It has also been invoked in several legal cases and materials, almost all of them in Israel.[6] Since the attacks on the USA on 11 September 2001, it has been the subject of a much wider debate.

In discussing this question, in addition to the above scenario, I will presume as given (ie if and only if), a string of descriptions and definitions, moral convictions, and facts relating to it. These will be necessary to keep the discussion as clear and simple as is possible; to maintain its focus, by avoiding going into issues not essential to this discussion; to protect as far as is possible the 'purity' of the case; and to ensure, the above notwithstanding, a smooth transition from the 'pure' private and theoretical case to the messy, public and practical—and eventually legal—cases in subsequent Parts.

---

[1] All terms italicized in this paragraph are defined or explained below.

[2] There is no moral (or for that matter legal) distinction between the culpability of a person who plants a bomb and one who consciously and intentionally sends another to plant (or explode with) one.

[3] See the Annex for some examples of 'ticking bomb' scenarios. The most important variations, ie the 'ticking bomb' being nuclear, and the person whose torture is required being innocent, will be discussed later in this Part, as well as (in the case of the former variation), in the conclusions of Part II.

[4] H Shue, 'Torture' 7 *Philosophy and Public Affairs* 124 (1978) 141. This article was reproduced in S Levinson (ed), *Torture: A Collection* (Oxford: OUP, 2004) 47–60.

[5] Lincoln Allison, 'The Utilitarian Ethics of Punishment and Torture' in Lincoln Allison (ed), *The Utilitarian Response: The Contemporary Viability of Utilitarian Political Philosophy* (London: Sage, 1990) 9–29, 23.

[6] See below, especially Part III.

B. Descriptions and Definitions

As a general rule, I will stick to definitions and descriptions which are of an undisputed, non-contentious, 'hard core of settled meaning'[7] type.

'Ethica' 'Ethica' (E) is a private individual, namely one not acting in any official capacity, with any authority or under any instructions for such situations. Ethica is a moral agent—she is a sane adult, possessing a conception of good and a sense of justice, and capable of bringing those to bear in the circumstances. What we believe she should or should not do is what we believe every person should or should not do under similar circumstances.[8] The extreme situation notwithstanding, she has enough strength of character to make a proper moral choice. As noted above, however, we do not expect her, with the time-bomb ticking away, to make complex long-term and wide-ranging moral considerations. In the words of Justice Holmes:

Detached reflection cannot be demanded in the presence of an uplifted knife.[9]

E's moral considerations will thus, by and large, be confined to the here and now, to those who would be immediately affected by her decision: Vicious, the innocent civilians, and herself.[10]

While the 'innocent civilians' (see below) would probably, but not necessarily, be her fellow-citizens, E is not worried that any of those near and dear to her may be harmed by the bomb. Nor is she in any personal danger. In other words, we assume E is not acting under anything that could be construed as 'diminished mental capacity' or duress (owing to personal, hence emotional involvement) and that her motivation in trying to save the innocent civilians is altruistic in the wider sense of the word.

'Terrorism, terrorist' 'Terrorism, terrorist' means here a policy of, or (respectively) a person wilfully engaged in, attacks deliberately targeting civilians, men

---

[7] HLA Hart, 'Positivism and the Separation of Law and Morals' in RM Dworkin (ed), *The Philosophy of Law* (Oxford: OUP, 1977) 17–37, *passim*, eg 29. A philosopher, Bernard Williams, equated legal and ethical premises on this point: '... [in legal debates] there has to be a shared understanding of some core or central cases to make these disputes about hard cases possible. To some extent this must be equally so within the less formal structures of ethical discussions...' (*idem, Ethics and the Limits of Philosophy* (London: Fontana, 1985) 96).

[8] Daniel Statman writes: 'An agent in a moral dilemma, searching for the right answer, is not just deliberating about what he or she will do, but about what ought to be done (probably by any agent in similar circumstances), on the basis of moral principles and values.' See *idem*, 'Hard Cases and Moral Dilemmas' 15 *Law and Philosophy* 117 (1996) 119. For a discussion of what a 'moral agent' is, or the qualities such a person should possess, see eg T Regan, 'Introduction' in *idem* (ed), *Matters of Life and Death* (3rd edn, New York: McGraw-Hill, 1993) 1–29, 8–11; J Rawls, *A Theory of Justice* (revised edn, Oxford: OUP, 1999) eg 11–12, 17. I have generally followed the latter here.

[9] *Brown v US*, 256 US 335 (1921) 343.

[10] I am aware that even the discussion here assumes much more time and mental composure than could be reasonably expected from a person in a real emergency.

women and children, whose only 'culpability' is, say, their perceived ethnic, religious or national identity, in an effort to kill them to forward some political or ideological aim, the nature—or, for that matter, the morality—of which is irrelevant here. This is, again, a deliberately 'hard core of settled meaning' definition, aimed at facilitating the negative 'moral conviction' regarding it below, by excluding 'grey areas' concerning the morality of which there may not be wide agreement.[11]

'Vicious' 'Vicious' (V) is a terrorist, as defined above. He is a sane adult who, by planting the bomb, or sending his fellow-terrorist, consciously seeks to kill as many of the innocent civilians as possible for some political aim.

'Innocent civilians' The 'innocent civilians' (IC) are men, women and children who have been selected by V at random. V does not know the identity of any of those people, and is targeting them because he assumes that, in the place and time chosen, there will be many of them, and that they would generally belong to, say, the ethnic group he considers as enemies, or wishes to terrorize, or the killing of whom would best serve his purpose etc. By 'innocent' is meant that no pertinent moral blame can be attached to these people.[12]

'The crowded marketplace' 'The crowded marketplace' was similarly selected by V solely because it serves his terrorist purposes best: it is crowded at that particular time, the bomb could be hidden well (or the suicide bomber would blend in with the crowd well), escape routes exist, and so on. It has no characteristics that would provide any possible justification for the act, other than the terrorist ones. Obviously, 'marketplace' is perfectly interchangeable with 'railway station,' 'city centre,' 'skyscraper', and so on.

'Torture' 'Torture' means 'any act by which severe pain or suffering, whether physical or mental, is intentionally inflicted on a person', in our case for the purpose of 'obtaining from him information'. This definition is taken from Art 1(1) of the UN Convention against Torture and Other Cruel, Inhuman or Degrading

---

[11] According to the Terrorism Research Centre (<http://www.terrorism.com>, accessed 28 May 2002), the FBI defines terrorism as '…the unlawful use of force or violence against persons or property to intimidate or coerce a government, the civilian population, or any segment thereof, in furtherance of political or social objectives'. This is somewhat too wide for our purposes, and includes the notion of 'unlawfulness', which is unsuitable here. For other definitions of terrorism and discussions thereof see eg C Greaty (ed), *Terrorism* (Aldershot, Hants: Dartmouth, 1996) Part I; M Walzer, *Just and Unjust Wars: A Moral Argument with Historical Illustrations* (New York: Basic Books, 1997) 197–8; C Walker, *The Prevention of Terrorism in British Law* (Manchester: Manchester University Press, 1992) 7–10. For a discussion of attempts to define 'terrorism' in international law see eg H Duffy, *The 'War on Terror' and the Framework of International Law* (Cambridge: CUP, 2005) 18–41. At the time this study was prepared for publication, in mid-2007, there was still no internationally agreed definition of terrorism.

[12] The random nature of the attack may result in individuals to whom 'pertinent moral blame' may be attached (say, soldiers in a vicious occupying army) also becoming its victims, but such coincidence would not, for that very reason, alter the picture meaningfully.

Treatment or Punishment.[13] For the purposes of this part of the discussion, however, the requirement of official involvement included therein has been omitted. This definition, while from a legal source, is I believe unproblematic, as it sits quite easily with philosophers' definitions of 'torture' in the core sense of the word.[14]

'Justifiable' 'Justifiable' is used to clarify two points. One concerns the question of whether E *'ought* to' torture V or torture in this case is (if at all) merely 'permissible'.[15] I believe that imposing a moral *duty* to torture seems far reaching, and addressing the general question of how much a person is morally bound to take upon him/herself for the sake of others is not essential to the issue on hand. 'Justifiable' indicates vindication, rightness, even praiseworthiness of an act, but does not go so far as to impose a duty to act, and here we are thus content with finding out whether the 'softer' requirement of permissibility is fulfilled.[16] In other words, the question of whether for E to torture V is justifiable, therefore morally permissible, will be addressed, while the question of whether it is E's moral *duty* to torture V will not. Rather (this is admittedly determined in anticipation of likely arguments), it will be up to the 'opposition' to claim that such torture is *un*justifiable, therefore *im*permissible.

Secondly, 'justifiable' indicates that it would be right for *any* moral agent to act in a given way in the given situation, the aim being to exclude any personal or particular factors that would move us to forgive, or in legal terms to 'excuse' E for having made a morally *wrong* decision.[17]

C. Moral Convictions

Torture (as defined above) is an immoral act, at least under most circumstances. Even those who would justify it in a TBS would consider it only a necessary, or

---

[13] UNGA res 39/46, 10 December 1984, entered into force 26 June 1987. For text of human rights treaties see eg Office of the United Nations High Commissioner for Human Rights, *Human Rights: A Compilation of International Instruments*, vol 1 (First Part) (New York: UN 2002) and the Office's website <http://www.ohchr.org>. The question of what constitutes torture under international law is discussed in Part IV, Ch 18.

[14] B Paskins, 'What's Wrong with Torture?' 2 *Brit J Int'l Studies* 138 (1976), 146. Compare, for instance, Paskins' own 'core' definition: 'Torture is the systematic and deliberate infliction of acute pain in any form by one person on another, or on a third person, in order to accomplish the purpose of the first against the will or interest of the second' (*ibid,* 139). By Paskins' own admission, this definition was 'adapted from' Amnesty International, *Report on Torture* (2nd edn, London: Duckworth, 1975) 31.

[15] The distinction between the two is at the heart of Judith Jarvis Thomson's forceful argument in 'A Defence of Abortion' in P Singer (ed), *Applied Ethics* (Oxford: OUP, 1986) 37–56. Discussing a TBS, Daniel Statman takes the approach I am following here (*idem,* 'The Absoluteness of the Prohibition Against Torture' [Hebrew] 4 *Mishpat u-Mimshal* 161 (1997), n 26, p 172).

[16] This is in line with Charles Fried's concept of 'right': 'When something is said to be right, this does not mean invariably that it must be done, but perhaps only that it may be done, that is, that it is not wrong' (*idem, Right and Wrong* (Cambridge, Mass: Harvard University Press, 1978) 9).

[17] The legal issue of justification and excuse will be discussed in Part IV, Ch 19.

lesser, evil in those circumstances rather than an act which would be acceptable, say, to force V to disclose where he has hidden E's stolen car.

The act of terrorism (as defined above) is morally wrong at least under most circumstances. It is immaterial, for our purposes, whether we consider it wrong because we believe *any* such act to be wrong, or merely that this particular act is wrong. It follows that preventing that act, at least under most circumstances, is morally right, if the means to do so are.

D. Facts

E is capable of torturing V in a way that would 'extract' the vital information out of him. Now this is one quality of E that is not morally straightforward. Should a 'moral agent' have that capacity? Can a person with that capacity be a moral agent? These questions will form part of the discussion.

E knows with absolute certainty, or conversely must, under the circumstances accept as a given, that unless she tortures V, the bomb will explode, and the IC would die or be injured. She similarly knows or must assume with absolute certainty that if she does torture him, he will give the life-saving information, the bomb will be diffused or the bomber neutralized, and those lives saved.

To sum up, the discussion presumes that V, a terrorist, has intentionally embarked on what we consider to be an immoral and unjustifiable act of mass murder. The only, and (it must be assumed) certain, way to prevent it from happening would be for E, a moral agent, to commit an act which, at least in most other cases, we consider an evil too—namely to torture him. The question then is whether it would be morally justifiable, in the circumstances, for her to do so.

The question posed here may be complex, as may be the various ways of addressing it, but E's answer must, eventually, be a simple yes or no.

E. Methodology

In discussing the question posed in the title of this Part and putting forward my response to it, the scope will be kept limited; positions put forward will be required to maintain strict logical form; a dialogic, conversational style will be used; and an open, eclectic approach to content will be adopted. This choice will now be briefly defended, the subsequent discussion itself providing the full defence. The full explanation of the concepts of 'minimal absolutism' and 'slippery surface' which are introduced here, will also wait for that discussion.

As to scope, I will describe, but refrain from offering solutions to, one of moral philosophy's great ethical debates and the one most relevant to our topic—consequentialism (or utilitarianism) versus deontology—limiting the discussion to those issues that need to be addressed in order to answer the question on hand,

and then offering the narrowest moral position ('minimal absolutism') needed to defend a negative answer.

As to form, there is little need to explain that a moral position must be logically sound, that is, it must be consistent and avoid untenable inner tensions, contradictions and absurdities. I will attack the torture-justifying view for such flaws, point to the actual scope of their position (through what I call 'slippery surface' arguments) and defend the minimal absolutist idea in general, and the view that, within it, torture is the ideal candidate for an absolute moral prohibition in particular, as logically flawless.

However, while formal—in the case in point legal—aspects of the torture in a TBS question are discussed at length, in Parts III and IV, this study was largely motivated by the miserable failure of 'form' to lay the question it poses to rest. The fact that there is a formal (legal) prohibition on torture which, as will be shown here too, is clearly and unequivocally absolute, and the fact that human rights lawyers can display an impressive, indeed impeccable, array of treaties, provisions, customary rules and case-law to prove this, have simply not been enough to uphold the prohibition—not even in principle, let alone in practice. Not least, in my view, because many—including members of the government, academics and the wider public—support a general ban on torture, but are not convinced that this ban should be absolute, and specifically, in the context of twenty-first century international terrorism, that it should extend to 'ticking bomb' situations.

As to style, I believe that the failure just referred to dictates a discussion which, while remaining academic and not compromising on formal requirements, is able, at least potentially, to reach as many as possible of those unconvinced (or not sufficiently convinced) by formal argument. I have therefore opted, in this Part, and to a lesser extent in those which follow, to use a dialogic, conversational style of writing, which addresses the reader not only as a consumer of academic material, but as a full human being: a son or daughter, a parent, a friend, a potential victim of terrorist attacks, a potential torturer and a potential victim of torture. Hence, for instance, the extensive use of examples, detailed accounts of terrorist attacks and of torture, rhetorical questions and real-life dilemmas, as well as the use of 'I'—the first person singular, rather than the passive form or terms such as 'the present author'. This must not be confused with a 'keep it simple' style, which the subject matter simply does not allow.

As to content, and in tandem with the above, I have adopted an open, eclectic, 'anything goes' approach, to what is a valid moral argument. The last expression is not to be understood literally, of course—the illogical, the purely emotive, the incontrovertibly atrocious are deemed inadmissible here, save when their presence is used to show a *weakness* in an argument. However, I will not attempt to establish an elaborate structure within which all arguments and examples fit like pieces in a puzzle to create a perfect whole. Instead, I will allow as arguments everything that will, or may, persuade a reasonable person, a moral agent, of the morality (or immorality) of views discussed or put forward within this debate. My approach to content may therefore be described as 'intuitionist' in the Rawlsian sense or in an even looser one, but it is justified, I believe, by a combination of the tempering effect produced by the logical framework to which it must conform, and the aforementioned failure of exclusive reliance on the formal.

Finally, the words of John Rawls, at the outset of his momentous work, express the nature of my own invitation to a dialogue within this much more modest undertaking:

For the purposes of this book, the views of the author and the reader are the only ones that count. The opinions of others are used only to clear our own heads.[18]

---

[18] Rawls, *supra* n 8, 42. For Rawls' discussion of intuitionism see *ibid*, 30–40.

2

The Wider Moral Issue: Do Consequences or 'No Go Areas' Determine What is Ethical in an Extreme Situation?

The general question which Ethica should answer is, I propose, whether ultimately her decision should be determined by consequences or by an absolute moral prohibition. This question, apart from being the obvious one, is also at the heart of the legal controversy which will be considered in Parts III and IV. Other moral questions will be considered to the extent that they contribute to the discussion of this question.

Before continuing, it will be necessary to examine the various moral theories which have had a say on the matter, so that their reasoning may be properly understood.

A. Introduction—the Consequences

Ethica (E) compares the consequences of the two avenues of action available to her. As noted earlier, she will limit herself to the immediate future and to those immediately affected, namely herself, Vicious (V) and the innocent civilians (IC), although she would probably go slightly beyond the latter, to include their families.[19]

This task is not contentious, nor is it particularly difficult. E's likely considerations are set in the table below:

Person/s affected	If E tortures V	If E does not torture V
E	E has to undergo the painful, possibly traumatic, experience of severely hurting another human being who is at her mercy.	The bomb explodes, and E has to undergo the painful, possibly traumatic, experience of learning about the deaths and injuries among the IC, as well as the pain of their families, and may well suffer acute guilt for not having saved the IC when she could have.

(Continued)

[19] I suggest, however, that she would not go further, to consider V's fellow terrorists, or the IC's compatriots etc, the line being drawn between those affected personally, or intimately, and those affected in a more detached sense. Friends and acquaintances of various shades of closeness would form the intermediate level, but will be similarly ignored, as including them would add complication and little else.

Table (*Continued*)

Person/s affected	If E tortures V	If E does not torture V
V	V has to undergo severe pain and suffering—until he discloses the life-saving information.	V's health remains intact, and he possibly learns with satisfaction of the success of his mission.
IC	The lives and health of the IC remain intact, and they can continue leading their normal lives.	The bomb explodes, many die, many others are injured, some of them experiencing severe pain and suffering—possibly for life. Families of victims also undergo severe, and for some life-long suffering.

Following is the same table depicting 'gains' (+) and 'losses' (−) in terms of consequences (and how many times (denoted by '×') each participant would incur them)—setting aside, for the moment, the question of exactly *how much* pain or pleasure are incurred, or avoided, in each case:

Person/s affected	If E tortures V	If E does not torture V
E	− (× one)	− (× one)
V	− (× one)	+ (× one)
IC	+ (× many)	− (× many)
Total	+ (× many bar 2)	− (× many bar 1)

Taking the enormous quantitative disparity into account, E's conclusions are similarly non-contentious: clearly the immediate overall consequences of her decision not to torture V will be much worse than the consequences of torturing him. E realizes that she herself is in for a raw deal no matter what she decides, and leaves aside, for now, the question of which option will leave *her* better (or less badly) off. V would be the only clear beneficiary of a decision not to torture him. However, the suffering he would avoid, and the pleasure he would enjoy if not tortured, pale in comparison to the many deaths, injuries and instances of suffering in that case. In all likelihood, some will suffer serious injuries such as the loss of a limb or blindness—or will suffer severely in other ways for the rest of their lives. In addition, families of the victims will be heart-broken.

Following are two real-life examples of these consequences.

New York, 11 September 2001[20]

Collected by reporters for The New York Times, these last words give human form to an all but invisible strand of this stark, public catastrophe: the advancing destruction across the top 19 floors of the north tower and the top 33 of the south, where loss of life was most severe on Sept. 11. Of the 2,823 believed dead in the attack on New York, at least 1,946, or 69 percent, were killed on those upper floors, an analysis by The Times has found. [...]

The evidence strongly suggests that 1,100 or more people in or above the impact zones survived the initial crashes, roughly 300 in the south tower and 800 in the north. Many of those lived until their building collapsed.

In both towers, scores of people lost chances to escape. Some paused to make one more phone call; others, to pick up a forgotten purse; still others, to perform tasks like freeing people from elevators, tending the injured or comforting the distraught.

At least 37 people, and probably well over 50, can be seen jumping or falling from the north tower. [...]

Then, below the thick black smoke and through clouds of pulverized plaster, she [Mary Jos] gradually noticed something worse. The 78th floor sky lobby, which minutes before had been bustling with office workers unsure whether to leave the building or go back to work, was now filled with motionless bodies.

The ceilings, the walls, the windows, the sky lobby information kiosk, even the marble that graced the elevator banks—everything was smashed as the second hijacked plane dipped its left wingtip into the 78th floor.

In an instant, the witnesses say, they encountered a brilliant light, a blast of hot air and a shock wave that knocked over everything. Lying amid the deathly silence, burned and bleeding, Mary Jos had a single thought: her husband. 'I am not going to die,' she said, remembering her words. [...]

As Ms. Wein came to, she had her own battered body to deal with: her right arm was broken, three ribs were cracked and her right lung had been punctured. In other words, she was lucky. All around her were people with horrific injuries, dead or close to it. Ms. Wein yelled out for her boss, Mr. Kestenbaum. When she found him, she said, he was expressionless, motionless, silent. Ms. Hagerty, who had joked about the cats at home, showed no signs of life when a colleague, Ed Nicholls, saw her. And Richard Gabrielle, another Aon colleague, was pinned to the ground, his legs apparently broken by marble that had fallen on them. [...]

Another phone call was under way nearby. Edmund McNally, director of technology for Fiduciary, called his wife, Liz, as the floor began buckling. Mr. McNally hastily recited his life insurance policies and employee bonus programs. 'He said that I meant the world to him and he loved me,' Mrs. McNally said, and they exchanged what they thought were their last goodbyes.

Then Mrs. McNally's phone rang again. Her husband sheepishly reported that he had booked them on a trip to Rome for her 40th birthday. 'He said, "Liz, you have to cancel that,"' Mrs. McNally said. [...]

---

[20] J Dwyer, E Lipton, K Flynn, J Glanz and F Fessenden, 'Fighting to Live as the Towers Died' *New York Times* (26 May 2002).

Sean Rooney called Beverly Eckert. They had met at a high school dance in Buffalo, when they were both 16. They had just turned 50 together.

He had tried to go down but was stymied, then had climbed 30 floors or so to the locked roof. Now he wanted to plot a way out, so he had his wife describe the fire's location from the TV pictures. He could not fathom why the roof was locked, she said. She urged him to try again while she dialled 911 on another line. He put the phone down, then returned minutes later, saying the roof door would not budge. He had pounded on it.

'He was worried about the flames,' Ms. Eckert recalled. 'I kept telling him they weren't anywhere near him. He said, but the windows were hot. His breathing was becoming more labored.'

Ceilings were caving in. Floors were buckling. Phone calls were being cut off. He was alone in a room filling with smoke. They said goodbye.

'He was telling me he loved me.'

'Then you could hear the loud explosion.'

Jerusalem, 3 March 2002[21]

At least nine people were killed, including two 1-year-old infants and a 10-year-old boy, and 57 others were wounded last night, when a Palestinian suicide bomber blew himself up in a crowd of people making their way home from a synagogue in Jerusalem's Beit Yisrael neighborhood.

Four people were in critical condition last night at Jerusalem's Hadassah-University Hospital at Ein Kerem, including an unconscious seven-year-old boy suffering from second degree burns. [. . .]

The explosion hurled passersby dozens of meters away, amid huge balls of fire. The small side street was littered with pieces of flesh and articles of clothing. A nearby parked car—whose gas tank was apparently set off by the blast, leading to initial reports of a car-bombing—lay completely gutted, as the smell of burned metal and human flesh pervaded the air in the blackened street. [. . .]

'The scene was of a horror unimaginable: babies dead on the street, children burned and bleeding,' said Aviva Nachmani, who was staying at the guesthouse celebrating her son's Bar-Mitzvah. Her son escaped unharmed.

'I saw an empty baby carriage, with the infant lying dead on the street,' said Shlomo, an eyewitness from the nearby Meir Yeshiva. A middle-aged man lay on the ground, his arm nearly severed from his body, he recalled. 'He kept crying out: "Please—save my arm, save my arm." [. . .]

Shrilly Biton, 19, had just left the Mahane Yisrael Yeshiva's guest house, whose stone walls were stained with blood, heading to her car when the blast went off. 'I saw people flying in the air, my own brother' said Biton, lightly wounded in the attack, as she was wheeled away on a stretcher.

The site of the attack had been targeted before. Last February, a car bomb ripped through a side street in the neighborhood just meters away from last night's attack, but

---

[21] E Lefkovits, 'Suicide bomber kills nine in Jerusalem' *Jerusalem Post* (3 March, 2002). One of the injured, a 17-year-old boy, remained for months in intensive care and died of his wounds on 19 June 2002. See *Haaretz* (20 June 2002).

miraculously failed to cause any serious injury that time. Last night a sign affixed to the site last year could still be seen reading: 'A great miracle happened here.'

The huge disparity of consequences, or of suffering, incurred by the tortured terrorist on the one hand and the innocent civilian victims on the other has for some writers been sufficient to conclude, without further explanation, that torture in such circumstances would be the moral thing to do. Thus Steven Lukes writes:

...the obligation, and thus the right, can always be legitimately overridden, in certain circumstances. Consider some promising candidates for absolute status. Take first, the right not to be tortured. Suppose you have captured someone who knows where the bomb is that will blow up a crowded airport which there is no time to clear.[22]

Lukes' discussion of the matter ends abruptly here—he considers the mere mention of the TBS example as laying his case to rest. Daniel Statman similarly writes, having described a (nuclear) TBS, which would cause 'tens of thousands of deaths and injuries':

Is it not obvious that under these circumstances it is our supreme moral duty to find the bomb and neutralise it, even if this involves torturing? My point of departure will be that the answer to this question is positive, and hardly anyone would dispute this.[23]

Statman relies on 'our strong intuitions',[24] and elaborates no further.[25] I will assume, however, that E is willing at least to consider a diagonally opposing argument (which, it could be argued, rests on no less strong intuitions), namely that from the moral point of view, torture is absolutely prohibited, regardless of the consequences.

At this point the debate does become complex, and warrants a general, albeit brief description of the two views of morality which have been locking horns on the issue of what Immanuel Kant called 'the supreme principle of morality'[26] for the past two centuries at least: consequentialism and deontology. This is a

---

[22] S Lukes, *Marxism and Morality* (Oxford: Clarendon Press, 1985) 67. Many years later, Lukes devoted an article to the question of torture, liberal democracies and terrorism. Approaching the issue from the 'dirty hands' angle (an angle discussed in Part II, Ch 8), Lukes first 'agrees' that an absolute prohibition should be combined with effective executive discretion in TBSs, but then, expressing mistrust in liberal democratic governments' self-restraint, seems to hint at support for an absolute prohibition. It is not entirely clear to me whether or not this denotes a change of mind as to the 'pure' moral question discussed here. See S Lukes, 'Liberal Democratic Torture' 36 *British J of Political Science* 1 (2005).

[23] Statman, *supra* n 15, 171.

[24] *Ibid*, 178.

[25] Later in the essay, Statman briefly provides (utilitarian) reasoning for his support for such torture, one 'related to measuring the conflicting evils' (*ibid*, 192). This places him alongside other deontologists with 'a disastrous consequences clause' for which see *infra*, Ch 3, Section B.

[26] Immanuel Kant, *The Moral Law: Groundwork for the Metaphysics of Morals*, trans HJ Paton (2nd edn, London: Routledge, 1991) 57/xiii (here, and henceforth, the first page number denotes the number in Paton's translation, the second the number in the second edition of Kant's original work—in this case in Kant's preface).

debate about what moral principle, or principles, should guide human action, and within it is the debate on the narrower question relevant to the discussion here—what should guide people's actions in extreme circumstances, of which the TBS is one. As will be seen, not all deontologists would object to torture in a TBS, nor would all consequentialists allow it. Nevertheless, the split is chiefly along the consequentialist/deontologist divide.

Far from attempting a thorough, let alone exhaustive description of the two moral views, I will confine myself at this stage to 'textbook' definitions and brief explanations, in effect sketching the skeletons and leaving the flesh to be added on later, when we return to E and her specific predicament.

B. Consequentialism and Utilitarianism

Consequentialists hold that determining whether an act is morally right or wrong depends on a single question: whether the consequences of the act will be better or worse than all other possible acts. In a simplified form, consequentialism holds, according to Shelly Kagan, that:

…in any given choice situation, the agent is morally required to perform the act with the best consequences.[27]

Pettit defines the 'consequentialist answer' as:

The answer, roughly, that the right option in any choice is that which produces the goods, that which promotes expected, neutral value.[28]

There is much debate as to what 'best consequences' or 'goods' means. Of particular interest (explained below) for our purposes is a brand of consequentialism called utilitarianism. For utilitarians, 'best consequences' are defined as maximum utility. There is also much debate as to what 'utility' means. In classical utilitarianism, known also as 'hedonistic utilitarianism', utility is equated with happiness, and disutility with pain. One of the 'founding fathers' of utilitarianism, John S Mill, described the theory thus:

The creed that accepts as the foundation of morals, Utility, or the Greatest Happiness Principle, holds that actions are right in proportion as they tend to promote happiness,

[27] S Kagan, *Normative Ethics* (Boulder, Colorado: Westview, 1998) 61. Practically every study which addresses ethical questions includes a definition, a description or an argument on one or more of the terms discussed here. I have therefore chosen, almost at random, those definitions I have found useful.

[28] P Pettit, 'The Consequentialist Perspective' in P Pettit, M W Baron and M Slote, *Three Methods of Ethics* (Malden, Mass: Blackwell, 1997) 92–174, 92. For other definitions of consequentialism see eg GEM Anscombe, 'Modern Moral Philosophy' 33 *Philosophy* 1 (1958), 9, 12; A Isenberg, 'Deontology and the Ethics of Lying' in JJ Thomson and G Dworkin (eds), *Ethics* (New York: Harper and Row, 1968) 163–185, 163.

wrong as they tend to produce the reverse of happiness. By happiness is intended pleasure, and the absence of pain; by unhappiness, pain, and the privation of pleasure.[29]

A more recent utilitarian writer, William Shaw, explains further:

Actions can have both good and bad results... the 'greatest happiness principle' does not tell us to choose the action that has as part of its outcome the single effect with more happiness than any other effect we might have produced. Rather, it tells us to choose that action whose net outcome, taking into account all of its effects is the happiest (or least unhappy).[30]

Because the consequences that are the subject of the moral debate about torture and ticking bombs are chiefly pain and death, and the disagreement revolves around whether it is justified to produce pain in order to avoid greater pain and death, consequentialists participating in it, whatever their wider views are, would in this context often operate within the utilitarian domain, and evoke hedonistic utilitarian moral claims.

When deciding whether or not to perform a certain action, under certain circumstances, a utilitarian will consider the good and bad results, namely the pleasure and pain that the action will bring about—much in the same way as I have done regarding torture in a TBS in the tables above. The utilitarian will then sum up the overall pain and pleasure, and opt for the action which will result in maximum pleasure, or minimum pain. Utilitarians or consequentialists with a more complex, or pluralist view of 'utility', 'goods' or 'consequences' may add the value of factors such as rules, intentions, acceptance, desire satisfaction, preference satisfaction and even the intrinsic value of actions. However, they will still seek the same type of 'bottom-line', by assigning each factor (in the circumstances) a certain weight or value; then calculating the cumulative 'positive' value of the action and its cumulative 'negative' value; and finally summating the two. An action may be described as putatively moral where such calculation yields a 'positive' bottom line, but ultimately, choosing the right (moral) action, is opting for that action which compares favourably to all other possible actions (in the circumstances), thus *maximizing* utility, or bringing about the *best* consequences, which may be the least bad ones.

---

[29] JS Mill, *Utilitarianism* (1863) Ch II. See eg in HB Acton (ed) *Utilitarianism, Liberty, Representative Government* (London: JM Dent & Sons, 1972) 1–61, Ch II, 6. Another 'founding father', Jeremy Bentham, described the 'principle of utility' as one that '... approves or disapproves of every action whatsoever, according to the tendency which it appears to have to augment or diminish the happiness of the party whose interest is in question... if that party be the community in general, then the happiness of the community: if a particular individual, then the happiness of that individual' (*idem, An Introduction to the Principles of Morals and Legislation* (new edn, 1823) (Oxford: Clarendon, 1879) Ch 1, paras 2–3). For other definitions see eg H Sidgwick, *The Methods of Ethics* (4th edn, London: Macmillan, 1890) Book IV, Ch 1, §1, 409; J Harrison, 'Utilitarianism, Universalisation, and Our Duty to be Just' in JJ Thomson and G Dworkin (eds), *Ethics* (New York: Harper and Row, 1968) 76–103, 76, 78, 93; A Sen, 'Plural Utility' 81 *Proceedings of the Aristotelian Society* 193 (1980–81), 207.

[30] WH Shaw, *Contemporary Ethics: Taking Account of Utilitarianism* (Malden, Mass: Blackwell, 1999) 12.

C. Deontology, Kantianism

Taken literally, a deontologist is someone who believes that a moral person should act out of a sense of duty (the Greek word for 'duty' is *deon*). Unlike consequentialism or utilitarianism, however, deontology does not hinge on a single principle—in fact, it cannot even be described as a single doctrine or theory at all, and therefore does not lend itself easily to definitions. Many of the attempts to define deontology (some of which follow) tend to do so by contrasting it with consequentialism.

JL Mackie described 'a deontological system' in 'a very broad sense' as,

... a moral system built not round the notion of some goal that is to be attained but rather round the notions of rules or principles of action or duties or rights or virtues, or some combination of these...[31]

Rawls defines his 'justice as fairness' theory as a 'deontological theory' in a negative way, ie as being 'non-teleological' (ie not goal-oriented) or as:

... one that either does not specify the good independently from the right, or does not interpret the right as maximizing the good.[32]

Kagan, while conceding that 'there is nothing like a standard or received definition of the term (deontology)', explains its main tenets as follows:

... deontologists, unlike consequentialists, believe in the existence of constraints, which erect moral barriers to the promotion of the good... in particular, certain factors make it morally impermissible to perform an act, even though that act would have the best result.[33]

Clearly the most influential deontological theory is that of Immanuel Kant (1724–1804). Moreover, he was an absolutist,[34] which is particularly significant for our purposes.

Kant was a deontologist in the literal sense. He argued[35] that a good action is one performed only for the sake of duty—the duty to obey the (moral) law, and not for the sake of results. The moral law is 'encoded' in the form of a categorical

---

[31] JL Mackie, *Ethics: Inventing Right and Wrong* (London: Penguin Books, 1990) 149.

[32] Rawls, *supra* n 8, 28.

[33] Kagan, *supra* n 27, 73–4. Kagan is, obviously, adopting Robert Nozick's notion of 'side constraints' for the sake of this definition. See R Nozick, *Anarchy, State and Utopia* (Oxford: Blackwell, 1974) Ch 3. For other definitions of deontology see eg Regan, *supra* n 8, 17–18; Isenberg, *supra* n 28, 163; Fried, *supra* n 16, 8.

[34] This term will be discussed in detail below, in Ch 4.

[35] Mainly in his (details are of translations I use here) *Groundwork of the Metaphysics of Morals*, *supra* n 26; *The Metaphysics of Morals*, trans M Gregor (Cambridge: CUP, 1991); *Critique of Practical Reason*, trans LW Beck (3rd edn, New York: Macmillan, 1993). Secondary sources are, again, too numerous to mention, but for the present purposes it should be noted that practically every translation of Kant's works includes useful introductions and explanatory notes. Works

(ie unconditional) imperative.[36] It does not, however, come from without; rather, it is the product of the good will of every individual, autonomous, rational being. A human (or other rational) being's will is good, indeed absolutely good, indeed the only thing good-in-itself, once it is free—that is, unhindered by fears, desires, regard for results or any other 'inclination' (its only subjective quality being reverence of the moral law), so that s/he will consider an action on the sole basis of reason. A person possessing such good will would inevitably arrive at the morally right decision, that is, one in line with the categorical imperative. Moral choice is thus arrived at when the most private (a person's will) meets the most universal (reason).

Kant offered three main formulae for the categorical imperative:

[1] Act only on that maxim[37] through which you can at the same time will that it should become a universal law... [2] Act in such a way that you always treat humanity, whether in your own person or in the person of any other, never simply as a means, but always at the same time as an end... [3] A rational being must always regard himself as making laws in a kingdom of ends[38] which is possible through freedom of the will...[39]

To make it simpler, I would propose[40] that a Kantian agent, confronting a given situation, would choose the morally right course of action by ensuring: (1) that it would be right for *all* human beings to act similarly in similar circumstances; (2) that the action does not involve the sheer exploitation[41] of any human being (oneself included), for whatever purpose; and (3) that in determining the above, all human beings are considered as having their own ends, and being similarly capable of making moral choices. The subjectively-chosen course of action

I have used will be mentioned when cited. It is doubtful whether the brief summary here can possibly do justice to a theory as complex as Kant's.

[36] Kant defines an imperative as 'a rule the representation of which *makes* necessary an action that is subjectively contingent and thus represents the subject as one that must be *constrained* (necessitated) to conform to the rule' in *idem, The Metaphysics of Morals, ibid*, 49.

[37] A 'maxim' is defined as 'a subjective principle of action' (*Groundwork of the Metaphysics of Morals supra* n 26, 84/51 (n)).

[38] 'Kingdom' is defined as 'a systematic union of different rational beings under common laws' (*ibid*, 95/74). (Footnote added.)

[39] For these formulae see *ibid*, 84/52; 91/66–7; 95/75, respectively. In between, Kant provides an array of alternative versions of these formulae, as well as a few other formulae, which may be described as secondary.

[40] This is my own interpretation, and is offered by way of illustration and explanation only.

[41] DD Raphael provides a useful example: I may be using a carpenter as a means to an end by hiring him to put up bookshelves for me, but by doing this through a freely-agreed transaction, and by paying him fairly, I treat him also as an end, ie cater for his goals as well as for my own. If, on the other hand, I acquired a slave for that purpose, I would be treating him as a mere means—what I have called 'sheer exploitation'. See DD Raphael, *Moral Philosophy* (2nd edn, Oxford: OUP, 1994) 56–7. Kant himself comes close to providing this example in 'On the Common Saying: "This May be True in Theory, but it does not Apply in Practice"' in *idem, Political Writings*, trans HB Nisbet, Hans Reiss (ed) (2nd edn, Cambridge: CUP, 1991) 61–92, 76. To avoid possible Marxist objections to this example (although at the risk of attracting others), I will add another one: fully consensual sex between adults, however casual, would be of the 'treating one also as an end' type, while rape would constitute 'treating one merely as a means'.

(through a 'maxim') is thus justified not by any 'inclinations', that is, feelings or interests the agent may have for—or against—it, but rather through its reconciliation with rational, universal, 'objective' considerations.

Kant, and deontologists in general, anchor the morality of human actions in the human being him/herself,[42] and in a special responsibility s/he has for his/her freely-chosen actions, which renders the nature of such an action the only, or (for some such theorists) the paramount determinant of its morality.

***

Surely, the consequentialist would say, when our actions affect other human beings[43] it is their—our—good, or well-being, that we should have in mind. An action—any action—must be right, and cannot be wrong, if, in the circumstances, it results in enhanced, indeed maximized human happiness, pleasure, satisfaction, etc, or if it minimizes their opposites. We must consider every single person equally, and do that which would overall be best for everyone.

Surely, the deontologist would say, when our actions affect other human beings we must act from our own humanity. We must always examine the nature of our actions, to ensure that they address the humanity of every person our action affects. Only persons are ends in themselves, and we must never sacrifice them, never use a human being as a mere pawn, a means of production—not even the mass-production—of good, happiness, or any other end.

And so the battle rages on.[44]

Coming back to the particular issue, I will now put forward the consequentialist and deontological arguments regarding torture in a TBS.

---

[42] The consequentialist/deontological rift is sometimes described in terms of 'agent-neutral' versus 'agent-relative' values, respectively. See eg RG Frey, 'Introduction: Utilitarianism and Persons' in *idem* (ed), *Utility and Rights* (Oxford: Basil Blackwell, 1985) 3–19.

[43] The question of whether, or to what extent, (other) animals come into the debate over ethics is irrelevant to our particular issue.

[44] Practically every deontologist who writes about ethics generally (and often those addressing specific ethical issues) has a bash at consequentialism, and vice versa. For collections of such mutual bashing see eg (arranged chronologically): B Williams and JJC Smart, *Utilitarianism: For and Against* (Cambridge: CUP, 1973; RG Frey (ed), *supra* n 42; S Scheffler (ed), *Consequentialism and its Critics* (Oxford: OUP, 1988); J Clover (ed), *Utilitarianism and Its Critics* (New York and London: Macmillan, 1990); JG Haber (ed), *Absolutism and its Consequentialist Critics* (Lanham, MD: Rowan and Littlefield, 1994); Baron *et al*, *supra* n 28.

3

Consequentialist Argument for Torturing in a Ticking Bomb Situation

The consequentialist argument for torturing Vicious (V) practically stares Ethica (E) in the face. She can easily imagine what would happen if the bomb exploded, having watched the aftermath of similar explosions in the media: the mutilated bodies, the blood, the screams of the injured, the wailing of children—helpless, suffering, dying— and the agony of the families. Why should the well-being of one single person—and the cause of all this suffering at that—be more important than the well-being of so many others? E can also imagine the suffering V would endure if she tortures him. She is convinced that torturing a human being—any human being—is an awful thing to do. But surely, if it is the only way to avoid an occurrence by far more awful, it must be done?

A. Consequentialist Arguments for Torture by Consequentialists

Bentham, considering an imagined case where the torture of one was necessary to stop the torture of many, put forward the consequentialist argument in the following way:

> To say nothing of wisdom, could any pretence be made so much as to the praise of blind and vulgar humanity, by the man who to save one criminal, should determine to abandon a 100 innocent persons to the same fate?[45]

Justifying torture in our private and pure TBS, consequentialists in general and utilitarians in particular seem to shed off some of the main weaknesses their general ethical theories are often accused of having. Thus the difficulty of assessing the future consequences of one's actions in an uncertain and complex world does not exist here *ex hypothesi*.[46] The criticism that the consequentialist way of

---

[45] J Bentham, Mss Box 74.b, 429 (27 May 1804), reprinted in WL Twining and E Twining, 'Bentham on Torture' 24(3) *Northern Ireland Legal Quarterly* 305 (1973) 347, fn 3. For the full scenario, see Annex.

[46] For a discussion of this difficulty see eg GE Moore, *Principia Ethica* (Cambridge: CUP, 1960) Ch 5, paras 99–100, 162–167; JJC Smart, 'An Outline of a System of Utilitarian Ethics' in Smart and Williams (eds), *supra* n 44, 1–76, esp 30–42; J Fishkin, 'Utilitarianism versus Human

'comparing human goods is rather like dividing apples by oranges'[47] is not convincing here, as there is the possibility of reasonably comparable physical and mental suffering on both horns of the dilemma. The claim that maximization of utility, or of other neutral values, may be at loggerheads with principles of distributive justice[48] is similarly irrelevant here: there is no doubt that both 'average' and 'overall' pain and suffering total much more on the side of the IC.

Like Bentham, the vast majority of the consequentialists justifying torture in a TBS therefore rely heavily on a consequentialist comparison of outcomes, opting for the 'lesser evil'. This is true for theorists as it is for those addressing concrete situations. During the Battle of Algiers in the late 1950s, Father Delarue, the chaplain of the 10th French Parachute Division, wrote in a note published by the French *Students' Review* in Algiers:

Faced with a choice between two evils, either to cause temporary suffering to a bandit taken in the act who in any case deserves to die, or to leave numbers of innocent people to be massacred by his criminal's gang, when it could be destroyed as a result of his information, there can be no hesitation in choosing the lesser of the two evils, in an effective but not sadistic interrogation.[49]

Leon Sheleff states that in such situation:

If time is of the essence and if the safety of innocent lives is at stake, an argument might be made that an exception be allowed when simple utilitarian stock-taking indicates the undeniable advantages that would accrue to the potential victims at the expense of the pain and suffering inflicted on an accomplice before the fact of the crime [...] in unique situations of emergency there may be a need to make a utilitarian accounting of evil against evil.[50]

Rights' 1(2) *Social Philosophy and Policy* 103 (Spring 1984); Shaw, *supra* n 30, 12–16. The issue of uncertainty in our context will be discussed in Part II, Ch 9, Section D(1)(a).

[47] G Grisez and R Shaw, 'Persons, Means and Ends' in Haber (ed), *supra* n 44, 21–28, 23. This is the common argument of incommensurability, ie that a calculus of consequences is unworkable in determining an action's morality, as there is no reasonable single scale of 'human goods' such as pain, disappointment, humiliation, comfort, sexual pleasure, love etc. For a discussion of this argument see eg *ibid*, 22–5; Frey, *supra* n 42, 10–16; J Griffin, 'Toward a Substantive Theory of Rights', *ibid*, 137–160, especially 156–8.

[48] Rawls discusses, and rejects, utilitarian approaches to the allocation of goods throughout his *A Theory of Justice*, *supra* n 8. For the approaches of the 'founding fathers' of utilitarianism to problems of distributive justice see eg Bentham, *supra* n 29, Ch IV; Mill, *supra* n 29, Ch V; Sidgwick, *supra* n 29, Book IV, Ch 1.

[49] Quoted in P Videl-Naquet, *Torture: Cancer of Democracy, France and Algeria, 1954–62*, trans B Richard (Baltimore: Penguin Books, 1963) 51.

[50] LS Sheleff, *Ultimate Penalties: Capital Punishment, Life Imprisonment, Physical Torture* (Columbus: Ohio State University Press, 1987) 305, 308, respectively. Sheleff repeated this argument in 'Maximizing Good and Minimizing Evil—On the Landau Commission's Report, Terrorism and Torture' [Hebrew] 1 *Plilim* (1990) 185 and in 'The Need to Defend the Honest Truth: Legal Agonies on the Subject of the Use of Torture' [Hebrew] 17 *Mehqarei Mishpat* 459 (2002). In a similar vain, Robert Gerstein concludes a somewhat inconsistent discussion of the right not to be tortured in general, and in a TBS in particular, by stating that '[i]t would therefore have to be a very extreme case indeed that would justify resort to torture' (*idem*, 'Do Terrorists Have Rights?' in DC Rapoport and Y Alexander (eds), *The Morality of Terrorism* (New York: Pergamon Press, 1982) 290–307, 298).

The Landau Commission of Enquiry in Israel makes this argument more graphic:

The choice is, clearly and simply: must we accept the offence of assault associated with slapping an interrogee's face, or threatening him, in order to make him speak and expose the hiding place of explosives designed to be used in carrying out a massive terrorist attack against a civilian population, and thus avert the great evil about to happen? The answer for that is obvious.[51]

'Everything depends on weighing the evils against each other', the Commission concludes.[52]

A similar justification was made in the 1970s by 'one colonel from a Western Great Power', as an eminent international legal expert, Antonio Cassese, recounts:

…at the Geneva Diplomatic talks (1974–77) to update the 1949 Geneva Conventions, one colonel from a Western Great Power told another negotiator off the record that he had sometimes found himself in the position of having an enemy prisoner tortured, knowing that that prisoner could supply essential information for saving a whole battalion. 'I was aware of the inhumanity of what I had ordered,' said the Colonel, 'but against that one man's suffering, an enemy into the bargain, was the safety of hundreds of my men. For me they weighed heavier in the balance.'[53]

Applying this logic to a hypothetical scenario where torture would have prevented the terrorist attacks of 11 September 2001 in the USA, Alan Dershowitz makes a similar point:

The simple cost-benefit analysis for employing such nonlethal torture seems overwhelming: it is surely better to inflict nonlethal pain on one guilty terrorist who is illegally withholding information needed to prevent an act of terrorism than to permit a large number of innocent victims to die.[54]

In the same context, and contemplating the danger of even more devastating terrorist attacks, Steve Chapman argues:

No one could possibly justify sacrificing millions of lives to spare a murderous psychopath a brief spell of intense pain, which he can end by his own choice. When the threat is

---

[51] *Report of the Commission of Inquiry in the matter of Interrogation Methods of the General Security Service regarding Hostile Terrorist Activity*, First Part (Jerusalem: October 1987), para 3.15, p 52. For extensive excerpts of the Government Press Office translation (not used here) see 23 *Is L Rev* 146 (1989). The Commission was headed by former President of the Supreme Court, Moshe Landau. The 'Landau Model' of legalized torture is discussed in Part III.

[52] *Ibid*, para 3.16.

[53] A Cassese, 'The Savage States: Torture in the 1980's' in *idem, Human Rights in a Changing World* (Cambridge: Polity Press, 1990) 105. Cassese follows his discussion of this case by giving a (fictitious) TBS as a further example of to the kind of 'problems that have to be faced head on' by democratic societies.

[54] AM Dershowitz, *Why Terrorism Works: understanding the threat, responding to the challenge* (New Haven: Yale University Press, 2002) 143. See similarly RA Posner, 'Torture, Terrorism and Interrogation' in Levinson (ed), *supra* n 4, 291–298, 293–4. Dershowitz proceeds to state that his 'simple cost-benefit analysis' would be 'limited by acceptable principles of morality', 147. I will argue that his construction is logically untenable, *infra* Ch 5, Section A.

so gigantic and the solution so simple, we are all in the camp of the Shakespeare character who said, 'There is no virtue like necessity.'[55]

More generally, consequentialists of various persuasions argue that saving the lives of many innocent persons justifies sacrificing the one, or few. Thus for David Cummiskey, the equality of humans dictates such sacrifice:

By emphasizing solely the one who must bear the cost if we act, we fail to sufficiently respect and take account of the many other separate persons, each with only one life, who will bear the cost of our inaction. If one truly believes that all rational beings have an equal value, then the rational solution to such a dilemma involves maximally promoting the lives and liberties of as many rational beings as possible.[56]

Sidgwick argues that disasters must be prevented even at the cost of departing from convictions which are generally utility-maximizing, and the consequent 'moral deterioration' when:

... considering whether we shall influence another to act contrary to his conviction as to what is right. A utilitarian would decide the question by weighing the external felicific consequences of the particular right act against the infelicific results to be apprehended hereafter from the moral deterioration of the person whose conscientious convictions were overborne by other motives: unless the former effects were very important he would certainly regard the danger to character as the greater: but if the other's mistaken sense of duty threatened to cause a grave disaster, he would not hesitate to overbear it by any motives which it was his power to apply.[57]

Allison brings this line of argument back to torture in a TBS:

... for a utilitarian, the problem of torture is this: a sense of security from torture is of endemic benefit to society, but particular acts of torture can also produce great benefits. Can those benefits ever outweigh the harm done to the sense of security? It would be morally attractive, and convenient, if the answer were a universal 'no'. But such an answer is not plausible. Even a strong belief about the dis-utility of the fear of torture combined with a similar strength of belief in the corrupting effects of the practice of torture cannot contradict the possibility that a single act might have benefits which outweigh the dis-benefits. The possibility is enhanced when we consider that the act might be kept secret and the balance further tilted towards torture when man-made nuclear

---

[55] S Chapman, 'Should we use torture to stop terrorism?' *Chicago Tribune* (1 November 2001).

[56] D Cummiskey, *Kantian Consequentialism* (New York and Oxford: OUP, 1996) 145. Amartya Sen reaches similar conclusions from a rights-consequentialist view: see *idem*, 'Rights and Agency' in Scheffler (ed), *supra* n 44, 188–223. See similarly, for what may be termed 'rights-utilitarianism', Griffin, *supra* n 47.

[57] Sidgwick, *supra* n 29, Book IV, Ch 3, §2, 427–8. Most consequentialists believe, to a lesser or greater extent, in the value of upholding convictions and rules, but at the same time argue that in extreme circumstances these may be broken. See eg J Austin, *The Province of Jurisprudence Determined* (1832), ed WE Rumble (Cambridge: CUP, 1995), Lecture II, 38–57; Smart, *supra* n 46; RB Brandt, 'Utilitarianism and the Rules of War' in M Cohen, T Nagel and T Scanlon (eds), *War and Moral Responsibility* (Princeton: Princeton University Press, 1974) 25–45; RM Hare, 'Rules of War and Moral Reasoning' *ibid*, 46–61.

and environmental catastrophes are considered. A naive equation of universal rules and proper consequentialist judgements, amounting to a pious hope that the dilemma could never be real, is less credible even than it was.[58]

B. Consequentialist Arguments for Torture in a TBS by Deontologists with a 'Disastrous Consequences' Clause[59]

Support for torture in a TBS is by no means confined to straightforward consequentialists. Quite a few deontologist theorists who in most circumstances would vehemently oppose the consequentialist justification for actions such as torture seem, when it comes to a TBS (and similar extreme, or 'catastrophic' situations), to cave in under the enormity of the looming disaster and endorse such actions.[60] The endorsement by these non-absolutist deontologists of torture in a TBS stems from their rejection of 'moral absolutism' (or 'moral deontological absolutism'). Moral absolutism ('absolutism' on its own will also be used here) is central to our discussion here, and warrants some elaboration before discussing their arguments.

1. The argument about torturing in a TBS as an argument about an absolutist moral position

Grisez and Shaw describe the basic question concerning moral absolutism, and stress (rightly, I believe) its importance:

...is any action whatsoever allowable, at least in certain circumstances? Or are there actions which it is never morally right to perform? What is at issue here is far removed

---

[58] Allison, *supra* n 5, 24. I must confess that I couldn't quite understand how Allison proposes to keep the 'act' of torture secret, short of holding the terrorist totally 'incommunicado' for the rest of his life, or dumping him, Mafia-style, into the river; *cf* S Levinson, ' "Precommitment" and "Post-Commitment": The Ban on Torture in the Wake of September 11' 81 *Texas L Rev* 2013 (2003) 2042–3. Allison's comment on the danger of nuclear and environmental terrorism carries more weight, and will be discussed in Part II.

[59] This term was coined by DW Brock in 'Recent Work in Utilitarianism' 10 *Am Phil Quart* 241 (1973) 251, fn 13. Brock claims that 'any deontological theory which is at all plausible must have some form' of such clause (*ibid*). MS Moore calls his view in support of torture in a TBS 'threshold deontology' in *idem*, 'Torture and the Balance of Evils,' 23 *Israel L Rev* 280 (1989). The article was later published, unchanged, in *idem*, *Placing Blame: A General Theory of the Criminal Law* (Oxford: Clarendon Press, 1997) 669–736. See also L Alexander, 'Deontology at the Threshold' 37 *San Diego L R* 893 (2000); and the discussion by EA Posner and A Vermeule, 'Should Coercive Interrogation Be Legal?' *U of Chicago Public Law Working Paper No 84*, March 2005, 6–8. I have preferred Brock's definition, as it clearly points to the centrality of the 'consequences' element.

[60] It should be stressed that we are still within the confines of a 'pure' TBS. As will be seen in Part II, not all of those deontologists (or, for that matter, consequentialists) who would support torture in the pure theoretical case would necessarily do the same in practical contexts, indeed in *any* practical context.

from idle speculation. This is one of the most burning ethical questions of our times, a matter of far-reaching practical ramifications for individual and social life.[61]

I will use here Joram Haber's simple definition of 'moral absolutism' as:

…the theory according to which there are certain kinds of actions that are absolutely wrong; actions that could never be right whatever the consequences.[62]

To clarify further—the kind of absolutism we are debating here is what Alan Gewirth calls 'rule absolutism,' ie where the act whose absolute prohibition[63] is in question is specific, so that a specific rule can be stated describing (and proscribing) the act, but without such description being so specific as to use proper names and other individual expressions, which Gewirth terms 'individual absolutism' (as in 'Mary Smith must never marry Peter Jones'). On the other hand, such rule must be general, but not to the extent that it would consist only of some moral principle of a very high degree of generality (which Gewirth terms 'principle absolutism', as in the Golden Rule, Kant's 'categorical imperative' or 'maximizing utility').[64]

I believe that it is quite safe to describe the argument that E must not torture V in the TBS scenario presented in the opening section of this Part as a 'rule absolutist' view: in light of the fact that it prohibits torture in the most extreme of circumstances, it *a fortiori* amounts to arguing 'never torture', that is, never perform an act of the kind defined in that opening section. This prohibition is at once specific, covering a well-defined (and unfortunately well-recognized) act-type, but not to the extent of becoming 'individual absolutism';[65] and it is

---

[61] Grisez and Shaw, *supra* n 47, 21.

[62] JG Haber, 'Introduction' in *idem* (ed), *supra* n 44, 1–13, 1. For other definitions see eg Mackie, *supra* n 31, 159; Griffin, *supra* n 47, 152–3; S Scheffler, *The Rejection of Consequentialism: A Philosophical Investigation of the Considerations Underlying Rival Moral Conceptions* (Oxford: Clarendon, 1982) 85. And see my discussion immediately below. MS Moore includes in his definition of the 'simple absolutist view' the requirement that absolutist prohibitions be '…applicable to what we indirectly cause as well as what we directly do through our action, applicable to what we allow to happen as well as what we make happen' (*supra* n 59, 298). I would submit, however, that these requirements are too wide, and would in certain circumstances (for instance in Bentham's example, *supra*, text accompanying n 45, where one must either torture someone or that someone would torture others) put an absolutist agent *a priori* in an impossible position, of being duty-bound both to refrain from performing a certain act and to perform that very act in order to avoid allowing it to be performed by another.

[63] I believe it is not essential here to address the question of whether there could be absolute moral duties of the *positive* type, ie 'you must always do X, whatever the consequences', as the positive duty to help people in danger, which is in conflict with the prohibition on torture in our scenario, is seldom, if ever, described in such absolute terms. This does not deny supporters of torture in a TBS the option of arguing that in such a situation E's duty to save the IC is superior to her duty not to torture V (which of course means that the latter duty is not absolute). The idea that certain moral, or human *rights* are absolute, imposing on others an absolute duty, eg never to torture, is also relevant, of course, but for our purposes the difference between an absolute duty not to torture and an absolute right not to be tortured is not crucial.

[64] A Gewirth, 'Are There Any Absolute Rights?' 31(122) *Philosophical Quarterly* 1 (Jan 1981) 3–4. Gewirth is discussing absolute *rights* rather than prohibitions on acts, so I have made certain modifications, but have by and large kept to his line of reasoning.

[65] Bearing in mind, of course, that E and V are mere symbols.

general, being applicable to a wide range of situations (and actions), but not to the extent of becoming 'principle absolutism'.[66]

2. The arguments

The typical anti-absolutist argument by deontologists (in this case by HJ McCloskey), is that '[o]nly the most weighty utilitarian considerations can justify overriding such a basic, important right as the right to life ...'[67] but such considerations *can* override basic rights, or basic moral prohibitions. These deontologists distinguish 'normal' situations, or even difficult ones where the scale of a potential negative outcome is relatively small, from situations where 'horrendous consequences'[68] may follow if deontological prohibitions are strictly adhered to.

In Thomas Nagel's words:

While not every conflict between absolutism and utilitarianism creates an insoluble dilemma, and while it is certainly right to adhere to absolutist restrictions unless the utilitarian considerations favoring violation are overpoweringly weighty and extremely certain—nevertheless, when that special condition is met, it may become impossible to adhere to an absolutist position.[69]

David Ross gives the following example to justify his anti-absolutist '*prima facie* duties' theory:

The interests of the society may sometimes be so deeply involved as to make it right to punish an innocent man 'that the whole nation perish not.' But then the *prima facie* duty of consulting the general interest has proven more obligatory than the perfectly distinct *prima facie* duty of respecting the rights.[70]

Fried makes a very similar argument:

...we can imagine extreme cases where killing an innocent person may save a whole nation. In such cases it seems fanatical to maintain the absoluteness of the judgment, to do right even if the heavens will in fact fall. And so the catastrophic may cause the absoluteness of right and wrong to yield.[71]

Michael Moore, whose discussion focuses to a large extent on a TBS, similarly argues:

Despite my non-consequentialist views on morality, I can't accept the Kantian [ie absolutist] line. It just isn't true that one should allow a nuclear war rather than

---

[66] Thus avoiding the danger of trivialization, as described by Statman, when an 'act-type' description is burdened with exceptions and specifications to the extent that the difference between the absolutist and non-absolutist becomes blurred. See *idem, supra* n 15, 168.

[67] HJ McCloskey, 'Respect for Human Moral Rights versus Maximizing Good' in Frey (ed), *supra* n 42, 121–136, 134.

[68] This term is used by MS Moore, *supra* n 59, eg 341–2.

[69] T Nagel, *Mortal Questions* (Cambridge: CUP, 1985) 55.

[70] D Ross, *The Right and the Good* (Oxford: Clarendon, 1930) 61.

[71] Fried, *supra* n 16, 10.

killing or torturing an innocent person. It isn't even true that one should allow the destruction of a sizeable city by a terrorist nuclear device rather than kill or torture an innocent person. To prevent such extraordinary harms extreme actions seem to me to be justified.[72]

C. Consequentialist and Deontological Views Supporting Torture in a TBS as a Unified Argument

So far I have cited arguments by consequentialists and by non-absolutist deontologists for torture in a TBS separately. However, I would submit that once we have established first that a TBS constitutes the kind of disastrous or catastrophic circumstances in which moral prohibitions applicable in most situations must, according to *both* these views, give way—which is undisputed; and secondly that our discussion is confined to these very circumstances, there is no longer any justification for keeping this separation here. We are now moving towards the issue of whether consequences or 'no go areas' are to determine what is ethical in an extreme situation.[73] Now deontologists with 'disastrous consequences' clauses offer no rationale for torturing in the 'ultimate' circumstances of a TBS that is distinct from the one provided by consequentialists.[74] Fried makes an attempt to do this. He follows the passage, quoted above,[75] in which he indicates that killing the innocent would be justified to avoid a catastrophe, with the argument that:

...even then it would be a non sequitur to argue (as consequentialists are fond of doing) that this proves that judgments of right and wrong are always a matter of degree, depending on the relative goods to be attained and harms to be avoided. I believe, on the contrary, that the concept of the catastrophic is a distinct concept of the situations in which the usual categories of judgment (including the category of right and wrong) no longer apply.[76]

---

[72] MS Moore, *supra* n 59, 328. See similarly Shue, *supra* n 4, 141. Shue describes an imaginary nuclear TBS to justify his view (see Annex), which is in turn cited by Statman, another deontologist supporting torture in a pure TBS. See *supra*, text accompanying n 23. Note, however, that Shue later modified his position (albeit not regarding a purely theoretical TBS). See *idem*, 'Torture in Dreamland: Disposing of the Ticking Bomb' 37 *Case W Res J Int'l L* 231 (2006).

[73] The united front suggested here is limited to this particular discussion. Regarding issues such as responsibility and intentionality, consequentialists and *all* deontologists stand sharply divided.

[74] Alexander makes a strong case against 'threshold deontology' in general, concentrating on the incapability of this approach either to justify a point at which 'things become their opposites', ie wrong becomes right, or survive without establishing, and justifying such a point. See *idem*, *supra* n 59, quotation from p 912. This wider issue is, however, beyond the scope of this study.

[75] Text accompanying n 71.

[76] Fried, *supra* n 16, 10.

However, neither he nor Williams, who argues along similar lines,[77] come up with alternative, non-consequentialist 'categories of judgment' for otherwise immoral actions in such circumstances, and we are thus left with 'catastrophe,' ie the disastrous *consequences*, as their sole justification. Other deontologists, such as M Moore and Statman, explain that consequences always play a role in a deontologist's considerations, and that in the face of a catastrophe, this role becomes dominant,[78] which supports the point I am making here. What such deontologists would argue to distance themselves from consequentialists is, first, that (using Fried's words) 'judgments of right and wrong' are not *'always* a matter of degree', in fact that they are not so in *most* circumstances. This, however, does not concern as here because, as noted, we are not dealing with 'most' circumstances. Secondly, they may claim, as M Moore does, that:

A consequentialist is committed by her moral theory to saying that torture of one person is justified whenever it is necessary to prevent the torture of two or more.[79]

This, however, is an oversimplification. When it comes to justifying extreme acts such as torture, sophisticated consequentialists would be very reluctant to break an established, value-maximizing rule prohibiting such acts. Thus Pettit, the consequentialist, argues that torture could only be justified in rare circumstances indeed, using the very same adjective and noun, 'horrendous' and 'consequences' to describe the consequences to be avoided in those rare justifying circumstances,[80] which M Moore the deontologist uses.[81]

I conclude that for the purposes of this Part at least, in discussing the absolutist and anti-absolutist views on torture, this basic division is the only one that need concern us.

***

To recapitulate, the consequentialists would try to convince E that since the outcome of her not torturing V would be horrendous, involving so much human suffering—death, mutilation, loss of loved ones—it must override the reasons, important as they may be, for her not to cause much pain and suffering to one single person, ie V. Many deontologists, who would normally oppose

---

[77] See eg B Williams, 'A Critique of Utilitarianism' in B Williams and JJC Smart, *supra* n 44, 77–150, 92.

[78] MS Moore, *supra* n 59, 331; Statman, *supra* n 15, 172. Statman adds, *ibid,* that the duty not to torture is overridden in a TBS by the duty to 'prevent negative consequences' but obviously it is the scale of these consequences that gives the latter duty the overriding strength it would lack in normal circumstances.

[79] MS Moore, *ibid,* 330.

[80] P Pettit, 'Consequentialism' in P Singer (ed), *A Companion to Ethics* (Oxford: Blackwell, 1999) 230–240, 234.

[81] See *supra*, text accompanying nn 68 and 72.

consequentialist reasoning of this type, even regarding acts which may bring about better overall results, have joined their rivals in this particular case. They would tell E that the enormity of the disaster which the IC are facing justifies putting aside any other moral considerations. While in arguing so, such deontologists accept what could be termed consequentialist side-constraints on their morality, as they do not offer a unique deontological justification for torturing in a TBS, the very fact that they make such a concession attests to the strength of consequentialist reasoning in this case.

4

The Minimal Absolutist Approach I: Anti-absolutism as Morally Untenable

A. The Idea of Minimal Absolutism

It has emerged from the foregoing discussion that those who oppose torture in a pure TBS would have to clear two hurdles. The first is the principled argument rejecting moral absolutism, the second (assuming the first is cleared) is the argument rejecting a specific absolute moral prohibition on torture.

To clear the first hurdle, our anti-torture absolutist is not required to defend any comprehensive absolutist moral theory, such as Kantianism or Catholicism. Nor does s/he have to defend a long list of absolute prohibitions. The task at this stage is confined to defending what I would call 'minimal absolutism'.

Minimal absolutism is the moral view that *certain acts must be prohibited absolutely,* namely that *they must never be performed, whatever the consequences.*

While this description is not essentially different from Haber's definition of 'moral absolutism',[82] the term 'minimal absolutism' is introduced to steer the discussion away from all-embracing moral theories, and keep it, to the extent possible, in the realm of specific acts. Minimal absolutism makes minimal theoretical demands. Logically it is the narrowest form of rejecting the view that any, or all acts may be justified to prevent disastrous consequences. Where the anti-absolutist view claims, as it must, that 0 (zero) acts must never be performed, minimal absolutism claims that ≥1 acts must never be performed.

Minimal absolutism does not address the issue of the relations between absolute moral prohibitions and wider morality—whether such prohibitions must dictate all or most of our moral behaviour; whether they form 'side constraints', namely a sort of casing, or outer boundaries within which behaviour may be determined by other moral views; or whether they constitute no more than small, isolated, haphazardly located islands in a vast sea, which they affect only in the rare occasions where behavioural waves attempt to break through their flood-barriers, only to find them invincible. All that minimal absolutism argues is that some acts must never be performed. This, however, is a 'hard core' view,

---

[82] Haber, *supra* n 62.

in that it claims that such absolutism is a *sine qua non* for any theory of human action to be morally (and logically) sound.

Before going into the minimal absolutist arguments, it may be useful to examine various 'candidates' for acts worthy of absolute moral prohibition. This, I believe, will set the scene for the difficult task that the minimal absolutist faces, even without the need to defend a full-fledged moral theory.

B. Questionable Candidate Acts for Absolute Moral Prohibition

Moral absolutism, even in its minimal version, is not easy to defend. It brings to mind the kind of zealots who would prohibit a 12-year-old rape victim from taking the 'morning after' pill or, at the beginning of the twenty-first century, the refusal of the Catholic Church to recommend the use of condoms in sub-Saharan Africa, even between spouses, as a means of slowing down the catastrophic spread of HIV/AIDS.[83] In December 2002, a UK columnist wrote of 'Osama bin Laden and his army of medieval absolutists'.[84]

Many of us may believe that we would never, and *should* never choose to murder, molest, rape, torture, deeply humiliate or be grossly unjust or unkind towards other people. However, many, if not all of the items on this list may raise problems of definition and scope, thus in fact limiting the actual applicability of such prohibitions, possibly, in some cases, beyond the 'lower' boundaries of 'rule absolutism'. In addition, our experience has taught us that we cannot always comply with some of those prohibitions absolutely. To this philosophers have added cases, mostly imagined ones, which may further weaken our confidence in the 'absoluteness' of such prohibitions.

Following are discussions of three act-types which have been put forward as candidates for absolute moral prohibition.

1. Lying

In a short article, Kant stated categorically that one has a moral duty of refusing to lie to a murderer who asks whether a person pursued by him is hiding in one's home.[85] Kant is indeed convincing in questioning the scenario's claim of offering

---

[83] In July 2000, the UK International Development Secretary, Clare Short, speaking at the thirteenth international AIDS conference in Durban, South Africa, attacked the Roman Catholic church for being a 'burden' in the fight against AIDS because of its refusal to help distribute condoms. See S Bosley, 'Aids vaccine for Africa to begin human trials', *The Guardian* (12 July 2000). The UK (Labour) government, naturally, distanced itself from Ms Short's remarks. The issue of HIV/AIDS will be discussed further below, in Section C(1)(c).

[84] J Freedland, 'Use brains, not brawn', *The Guardian* (4 December 2002).

[85] Kant, 'On a Supposed Right to Lie from Altruistic Motives' in *Critique of Practical Reason and Other Writings in Moral Philosophy*, trans and ed LW Beck (Chicago: University of Chicago Press, 1967) 346–350.

only the choice between lying and having the murderer kill the fugitive, as is John Finnis, referring to the same type of dilemma, in doubting 'the likelihood that the pursuing axeman or Nazi is willing to be blocked or deflected by the householder's response'.[86]

However, it cannot be convincingly argued that hiding a fugitive could be undertaken without a strong likelihood that telling lies may be involved—not only, say, lying to the Gestapo but also to one's anti-Semitic neighbour—or grocer.

James Rachels[87] describes a real-life case where 'lie or the fugitives under your care will die' was exactly the simple, unavoidable choice—that of Dutch fishermen who shipped Jewish refugees to safety in England during World War II. When stopped by Nazi patrol-boats, and asked about their cargo, destination, and so on, they had the choice of lying (convincingly) or for the refugees, and themselves, to be killed.

Facing such a choice, Kant's view that refusing to lie is the moral one, as '[t]o be truthful in all declarations . . . is a sacred and absolutely commanding decree of reason, limited by no expediency'[88] is, to my mind, less convincing, as are the similar positions of Thomas Aquinas[89] and Finnis.[90]

In view of the inevitability (in the fishermen's case), or strong probability (in the fugitive's case) of the need to lie, the right choice for a true Kantian or Thomist may ironically be to deny fugitives shelter, or refuse to ship them to safety, leaving these tasks to someone less scrupulous. This irony would reflect not only a consequentialist criticism, but also what many of us would intuitively feel—that being ready to lie under such circumstances would not constitute a fundamental moral wrong (or, indeed, a moral wrong at all) while a refusal to help a fugitive, certainly on these grounds, would.

Beyond this, a moral view which combines legitimating resort to self-defence[91] and (just) war[92]—both of which inevitably involve ruses of various kinds—with denying similar legitimacy to resort to lying seems to suffer from considerable inner tensions.

By way of accommodation, Aquinas and Finnis offer a provision, in both cases, for 'some forms of equivocal expression and mental reservation'.[93] Thus in the

---

[86] J Finnis, *Aquinas: Moral, Political and Legal Theory* (Oxford: OUP, 1998) 160.

[87] J Rachels, 'On Moral Absolutism' in Haber (ed), *supra* n 44, 199–215, 210, and see his discussion, *passim*.

[88] Kant, *supra* n 85, 348.

[89] St Thomas Aquinas (1225–1274), *Summa Theologica*, Second and Revised Edition, 1920, literally translated by Fathers of the English Dominican Province, <http://www.newadvent.org/summa/>, accessed 21 October 2007, second part of the second part, question 110, article 3. Henceforth this work will be referred to in the following manner: II-II, q 110, art 3. 'Ad' plus a number will denote a response to a numbered objection.

[90] Who explains and defends Aquinas' position, *supra* n 86, 154–170.

[91] See eg Aquinas, *supra* n 89, II-II, q 64, art 7.

[92] See eg Aquinas, *ibid*, II-II, q 40, art 1; Kant, 'Perpetual Peace: A Philosophical Sketch' (1795), in *idem*, *Political Writings, supra* n 41, 93–130, 96.

[93] Finnis, *supra* n 86, 159–60, *cf* Aquinas, *ibid*, II-II, q 70, art 1, ad 1; q 110, art 3, ad 3. Kant supports equivocation only to a very limited extent, see 'Ethical Duties towards Others: Truthfulness'

case of the fugitive, we could give an answer that the Gestapo would understand as denying that we are hiding anyone, but on a different 'reading' (reflecting the truth) there is no such denial. Similarly, fleeing the enemy and luring it to an ambush does not constitute lying, as what we are doing is 'not...an act of communication' but rather a real act the intentions of which are hidden.[94] In other words, communicating a falsehood, even to your enemy, is a lie, therefore always wrong, while hiding the truth, at least under such circumstances, is not.

To my mind the line between the two seems too thin to constitute a credible watershed between right and wrong, certainly an absolute wrong. In war, does painting your face constitute hiding the truth or communicating to the enemy that you are, say, part of the foliage? In another situation, of self-defence, this absolutist position would presumably allow us to distract a murderous assailant by telling him: 'there's a policeman behind you' (meaning: somewhere behind you, in the village, the county, the world, there is a policeman)—which would constitute an equivocation—but preclude us from saying: 'there's a policeman *right* behind you' (a lie). Pointing a toy gun at the murderer and saying: 'drop the knife or I'll shoot' would under this view only be allowed with the kind of toy that actually discharges something.

Moreover, Aquinas, Kant and Finnis would have, for consistency's sake, to preclude us, when facing an attacker, from pretending that we are turning to the right while intending to duck to the left, as this also is clearly, to use Kant's definition, 'an intentional untruthful declaration',[95] albeit a non-verbal one.[96] I conclude that lying may seem a problematic candidate for an absolute moral prohibition.[97]

---

in *idem*, *Lectures on Ethics*, trans L Infield (Indianapolis, Indiana: Hackett Publishing, 1980) 224–235, 229.

[94] Finnis, *ibid*, 158–9, Aquinas, *ibid*, II-II, q 40, art 3; *cf* q 69, art 2.

[95] 'On a Supposed Right to Lie...', *supra* n 85, 347.

[96] Just as it would be a lie, in Kant's scenario, to shake my head to indicate 'no' to the murderer, when 'yes' is the true answer. See similarly Aquinas, *supra* n 89, II-II, q 110, art 1, ad 2.

[97] A case may nevertheless be made for an absolute prohibition on lying, the scope of which is limited—presumably through defining the kind of situations and relationships within which our duty not to lie is absolute. Kant states that 'truthfulness is a duty which must be regarded as the ground of all duties based on contract' ('On a supposed Right to Lie...' *supra* n 85, 348). However, this may lead us to ask about the kind of 'contract' we have with the murderer or the Gestapo. To my mind, Kant was more convincing in applying the 'contractual' approach to lying, and answering this question, when, a decade before writing 'On a Supposed Right to Lie...', he himself suggested a more lenient view, using the (apparently interchangeable) concepts of 'a false statement' and 'a white lie'. Regarding the former, Kant states: 'I may make a false statement (*falsiloquium*) when my purpose is to hide from another what is in my mind and *when the latter can assume that such is my purpose*, his own purpose being to make a wrong use of the truth. Thus, for instance, if my enemy takes me by the throat and asks where I keep my money, I need not tell him the truth, because he will abuse it, and my untruth is not a lie (*mendacium*) because the thief knows full well that I will not, if I can help it, tell him the truth and that he has no right to demand it of me' ('Ethical Duties towards Others: Truthfulness', *supra* n 93, 227). (Emphasis added.)

On the similar concept of 'a white lie' Kant states the following: 'The misuse of a declaration extorted by force justifies me in defending myself. [...] The forcing of a statement from me under

2. Breaking a promise

This is another favourite target for attacks by anti-absolutists—often in conjunction with the issue of lying. I would clarify that not keeping a promise here denotes *changing one's mind* about keeping it. Making a *false* promise is just a form of lying.[98]

Here, however, those anti-absolutist theorists seem to overlook the distinction between promises as theoretical concepts and their meaning in real life. There is an oft-raised example, initially cited by Ross,[99] claiming that an absolutist would let a person drown when she could easily save him because she has promised a friend to meet him for dinner at a particular hour. Critics of absolutism invoking this and similar examples seem to overlook a feature of promises which is obvious in everyday life: we often talk in codes and shortcuts, and most of our real-life promises have in-built escape clauses. Suppose you told your friend: 'I promise to come to dinner at eight, but only if my child doesn't fall ill, my mother doesn't have an accident, a person doesn't drown right in front of my eyes…' to ensure that you would not be breaking your promise should any of these contingencies materialize. Your friend would probably respond with: 'Forget about dinner, you need some rest. Have you considered therapy?' This is because such 'waivers' in fact exist, in implied but universally understood form, in our everyday promises, and there is no need to express them orally, lest all our promises resemble some monstrous legal document.

conditions which convince me that improper use would be made of it is the only case in which I can be justified in telling a white lie.' (*ibid*, 228).

One could argue, from a 'contractual' approach, that there are situations, such as self-defence, hiding fugitives and war (for a 'good faith' approach to lying in war see eg Major JM Mattox, US Army, 'The Moral Status of Military Deception,' *Joint Services Conference on Professional Ethics*, Springfield, Virginia, 27–28 January 2000, <http://www.usafa.edu/isme/JSCOPE00/Mattox00.html>, accessed 12 November 2007)—as well as games, the arts and, say, the preparation of a surprise party, where certain lies are both expected and accepted by all concerned, and should therefore not fall under an absolute prohibition.

A minimal absolutist view of lying that allows us to hide fugitives, defend ourselves etc may similarly build on Finnis' own argument that 'Those who lie to the Gestapo enter, so far forth, into the Nazis' politics of manipulation' (at 160). While this is clearly true, it is equally true that those who take up arms against the Gestapo enter, so far forth, into the Nazis' politics of violence. Neither Aquinas nor Finnis, nor yet Kant (at least not regarding people under foreign occupation) would condemn such action, but they all would nevertheless advocate a 'so far *and no further*' approach; they would, in other words, place limits, including absolute ones, upon our use of violence in this or any other type of armed conflict (see eg Kant, 'Perpetual Peace', *supra* n 92, 96–7)—and the same could be true of lying.

For a discussion of lying as an absolute prohibition see also eg Isenberg, *supra* n 28; Harrison, *supra* n 29, 92–103; Sidgwick, *supra* n 29, Book IV, Ch 3, *passim*; Kant, *Groundwork*, *supra* n 26, 67–8/18–19, 82–3/48–9, 91–2/67–8 (all on making false promises).

[98] For a discussion see eg D Hume, *A Treatise of Human Nature* (1739–1740), (2nd edn, Oxford: Clarendon, 1978), Bk III, Sec V, 516–525; Ross, *supra* n 70, 18; Raphael, *supra* n 41, 19–22; Allison, *supra* n 5, 26; Smart, *supra* n 44, 43–4; Harrison, Sidgwick, *ibid*.

[99] *Ibid*.

Imagine, conversely, telling your friend: 'I promise to come to dinner at eight even if my child falls ill, my mother has an accident or a person drowns in front of my eyes.' Surely the friend's reaction would be a similar urge for you to seek professional help.

In view of the fact that arguments to this effect were made very early, eg by Aquinas (an obvious absolutist), who stated that a person is not obliged to keep his or her promise 'if circumstances have changed with regard to persons and the business in hand',[100] this oversight by critics is curious.

To sum, the vast majority of our real-life promises are conditional rather than absolute, or to use Kant's terms, the duty to keep them is hypothetical rather than categorical, thus anti-absolutists are in effect bursting here into an open door.[101]

3. Killing/murdering

This is, perhaps, the most serious candidate, outside torture, for an absolute moral prohibition, and has been a favourite among philosophers. The imaginary cases put forth by philosophers often feature a dilemma caused by a situation in which many would die unless one, often innocent, person dies, or more acutely—unless the moral agent kills one, innocent person.

Here are two famous examples.[102]

(a) The sheriff, the 'Negro', and the mob

This example was provided by HJ McCloskey (a long time ago, hence the now unacceptable terminology):

Suppose that a sheriff were faced with the choice of either framing a Negro for a rape that had aroused hostility to the Negroes (a particular Negro generally being believed to be guilty but whom the sheriff knows not to be guilty)—and thus preventing serious anti-Negro riots which would probably lead to some loss of life and increased hatred of each other by whites and Negroes—or hunting for the guilty person and thereby allowing the anti-Negro riots to occur, while doing the best he can to combat them.[103]

---

[100] Aquinas, *supra* n 89, II-II, q 110, art 3, ad 5. Aquinas cites an even earlier authority, Seneca.

[101] It should be emphasized, however, that *some* of our real-life promises are indeed absolute. Thus most Western couples getting married promise each other to 'forsake *all* others' rather than to only be faithful pending the arrival of an extremely attractive person (and a few even manage to *keep* this promise). More strongly—if you promise to be at the hospital within the hour, so that you can donate a kidney to save the life of your child or mother, you would surely keep that promise, and would not stop even to save a drowning person. I believe that, as in the case of lying, it may still be possible to define promises of such narrower, minimal absolutist scope in terms that fall under 'rule absolutism' but attempting this is beyond the scope of the present study. *Cf* Mackie's position, *infra* n 230.

[102] An amazing number of such examples, some later used and developed by others, are sketched by P Foot, 'The Problem of Abortion and the Doctrine of Double Effect' in *idem, Virtues and Vices and Other Essays on Moral Philosophy* (Oxford: Basil Blackwell, 1978) 19–32. For a short compilation of such cases see also Gewirth, *supra* n 64, 1, n 1.

[103] HJ McCloskey, 'An Examination of Restricted Utilitarianism' 66 *Philosophical Review* 466 (1957) 468–9.

(b) *The trolley problem*

Judith Jarvis Thompson has devoted a well-known study to the problem she originally described thus:

Suppose you are the driver of a trolley. The trolley rounds a bend, and there come into view ahead five track workmen, who have been repairing the track. The track goes through a bit of a valley at that point, and the sides are steep, so you must stop the trolley if you are to avoid running the five men down. You step on the brakes, but alas they don't work. Now you suddenly see a spur of track leading off to the right. You can turn the trolley into it, and thus save the five men on the straight track ahead. Unfortunately... there is one track workman on that spur of track. He can no more get off the track in time than the five can, so you will kill him if you turn the trolley onto him. Is it morally permissible for you to turn the trolley?[104]

While the two cases above may be rejected as exceptions to an absolutist moral prohibition of murder by absolutists who would not play the numbers game (a view strongly echoed in this Part), the following examples are less amenable to such principled opposition. Many of us could imagine killing a loved one who is moribund, and is suffering immensely, or has mentally deteriorated to a point where he or she has completely lost his or her personhood, character or dignity—especially if this was the explicit wish of that loved person. Others have even actually done so. In September 2000, when this text was first written, the local North Essex daily newspaper carried the following story, summarized here:

On 8 January 2000, Pensioner Leslie Parsons, 83, shot his 87-year-old wife, Dorothy, and killed her at their daughter's home in Thorpe-le-Soken. He then shot himself in the head three times but survived.

They had been married for 62 years. She had suffered of Alzheimer's disease, and when, in the words of Martin Lavett, mitigating (as cited by the *Evening Gazette*) 'the sight of his wife deteriorating from a woman into the shell of a human being became too much for him,' he killed her and attempted to kill himself.

Judge Brian Watling QC convicted Parsons of manslaughter on grounds of diminished responsibility, to which he had admitted, and put him on probation for three

---

[104] JJ Thomson, 'The Trolley Problem' 94 *Yale L J* 1395 (1985) 1395. Jarvis Thomson actually centres on a version of this story where the agent is the 'bystander at the switch', ie someone who has no official or professional responsibility for what happens on the track. She cites Foot, *supra* n 102, as the source of this story. There is an earlier (and even less likely) version of this dilemma in the writings of a prominent modern Jewish scholar, Avraham Kareliz, or 'Hazon Ish' (1878–1953), who argues that diverting an arrow about to kill many so that it would kill one may be permissible under Jewish law. Hazon Ish contrasts this with delivering a person ('a soul from Israel' in his words) to the enemies, so that they would kill him but spare many, which would be impermissible. See a strong criticism of this view by RB Rabinovich-Te'omim, 'Extradition to the Custody of Gentiles' [Hebrew] 7 *Noam* 366 (1973–4) (where the former source is cited) 367.

years. He said: 'this must be one of the most tragic cases the courts have ever had to consider.'[105]

Two days later, the UK media, and the Appeals Court, were engaged in a heated debate over a case which, while real, resembles the imaginary philosophers' scenarios, described by Lord Justice Ward as follows:

Jodie and Mary[106] are conjoined twins. They each have their own brain, heart and lungs and other vital organs and they each have arms and legs. They are joined at the lower abdomen. Whilst not underplaying the surgical complexities, they can be successfully separated. But the operation will kill the weaker twin, Mary. That is because her lungs and heart are too deficient to oxygenate and pump blood through her body. Had she been born a singleton, she would not have been viable and resuscitation would have been abandoned. She would have died shortly after her birth. She is alive only because a common artery enables her sister, who is stronger, to circulate life sustaining oxygenated blood for both of them. Separation would require the clamping and then the severing of that common artery. Within minutes of doing so Mary will die. Yet if the operation does not take place, both will die within three to six months, or perhaps a little longer, because Jodie's heart will eventually fail. The parents cannot bring themselves to consent to the operation. The twins are equal in their eyes and they cannot agree to kill one even to save the other. As devout Roman Catholics they sincerely believe that it is God's will that their children are afflicted as they are and they must be left in God's hands. The doctors are convinced they can carry out the operation so as to give Jodie a life which will be worthwhile. So the hospital sought a declaration that the operation may be lawfully carried out. Johnson J. granted it on 25th August 2000. The parents applied to us for permission to appeal against his order. We have given that permission and this is my judgment on their appeal.[107]

* * *

Whatever we may think of Mr Parsons or the medical staff at St. Mary's Hospital, few of us would condemn them as callous murderers, and the courts seem to have found ways to avoid punishing the former severely, and rendering the lethal but life-saving operation permissible in the latter case.

Both philosophical and real-life cases thus show that putative absolute prohibitions, while attractive in pure theory, may be problematic and even doubtful when applied in specific, extreme circumstances. Not, however, I will submit, to the extent that the very idea of any absolute prohibition is destroyed. I will now turn to defend the view that such prohibitions are both possible and necessary, starting by attacking its rival—anti-absolutism.

---

[105] 'Man shot wife to end their misery' *Colchester and North Essex Evening Gazette* (20 September 2000).

[106] Ward LJ is not using the children's real names. (Footnote added.)

[107] *Re A (Children) (Conjoined Twins: Surgical Separation)* [2000] 4 All ER 961, per Ward LJ, I (introduction). The case is further discussed in Part IV, especially in Ch 19, Section A(2)(b).

C. The Argument for Moral 'No Go Areas'

1. Slippery slope, slippery surface

The 'negative' onslaught of the minimal absolutist on anti-absolutism is largely composed of the type of argument I will call 'slippery surface,' as distinct from the better-known 'slippery slope' type. Both terms, and the difference between them, need some explanation.

The often-used 'slippery slope' argument is of the type 'if you perform act A_1, justifying it by its desirable result R_1, you will also, inevitably, bring about undesirable results R_2, R_3, R_4 etc'. Thus opponents of the death penalty often claim that it inevitably leads to the execution of the innocent, and opponents of euthanasia argue that legalizing it would inevitably lead to the killing, indeed murder, of those who do not wish to die.

The argument is, in such cases, that even assuming an act to be justified in a given case, it is impossible in practice to erect an efficient wedge which would allow the production of its desired results while barring the undesired ones, and this has the effect of overriding the justification for the original act.

The 'slippery slope' is thus a *consequentialist* argument against act A_1, claiming that performing it would inevitably lead to much worse overall consequences[108] than its supporters have anticipated. At the outset of this Part, I have, *ex hypothesi*, ruled out such arguments (ie on certainty and long-term or wider consequences) here, but they will obviously figure prominently when the 'real' and 'public' TBS case is discussed.

The 'slippery surface' argument is of the type 'if you justify act A_1, you must also, inevitably, justify acts A_2, A_3, and A_4.' For example, critics of the view that deterrence, on its own, is a necessary and sufficient justification for punishment, have argued that it is just as right, under that view, to punish an innocent person who is believed by would-be criminals to be guilty as it is to punish a guilty person. My argument above against a general, absolute prohibition of lying, to wit, that it drastically limits one's right to self-defence, is of the same type.

The claim, in such cases, is that no morally relevant distinction exists between given acts, therefore justifying one of them is impossible without justifying the others, which in turn calls the very justification of the original act into question.

The 'slippery surface' is thus a *logical*, or *casuistic* argument (ie an argument about scope, or logical boundaries) against act A_1, claiming that its supporters are inevitably forced to either withdraw their support or to justify additional acts, to which they may be opposed.

---

[108] Obviously, the fact that performing an act could have consequences beyond those deemed positive is not in itself sufficient to convince its consequentialist supporters to change their minds about justifying it. Thus for the pro-euthanasia consequentialists, the undesired death of, say, one or two persons for every million 'desired' deaths may not suffice to override their support for its legalization. However, at some (quantitative) point a consequentialist would turn from supporter to opponent.

2. Preliminary objections—anti-absolutism as an absolutist view

It will be recalled that moral absolutism was described by various members of the united anti-absolutist front of consequentialists and deontologists with 'disastrous consequences clauses' as 'blind and vulgar humanity',[109] and in the specific case of torture in a TBS, of being 'the most extreme immoral position',[110] to which may now be added, for example, an 'inflexibility [that] leads to an unfeeling disregard for other people',[111] 'indefensible rigidity in some extreme cases',[112] being 'hypocritical' and 'cold hearted',[113] and the charge that absolutism would prohibit 'the violation of a restriction even if a violation were the only way to prevent a genocidal catastrophe...'.[114] Perhaps the favourite adjective among anti-absolutists describing their opponents, both in the general context and in the specific TBS one, is 'fanatical'.[115]

Scheffler goes further, to illustrate the extremes to which, in his view, a moral absolutist must go:

In order to be an absolutist, it is not enough to hold that it would be impermissible to torture one child to death even if that would produce universal happiness. One must also hold that it would be impermissible to torture one child to death even if that were the only way to prevent, say, everyone else in the world being tortured to death.[116]

I would submit, however, that even setting aside the considerable practical difficulties that Scheffler's example presents (torturing *everyone* in the world—bar one child—to death would necessarily involve either sophisticated robotics or the enlisting of extra-terrestrials), this is where the principled anti-absolutist argument runs into serious difficulties.

In order to reject minimal absolutism, it is the anti-absolutist who must, logically, go to extreme lengths, and reject every single putative absolute prohibition.

---

[109] Bentham, *supra*, text accompanying n 45.

[110] Justice Heshin of the Israeli Supreme Court, *supra*, Introduction, text accompanying n 1. To which could be added Allison's accusing a policeman who would not torture the terrorist in a TBS of 'a combination of cowardice and self-indulgence', *supra* n 5, 11.

[111] Rachels, *supra* n 87, 208.

[112] Mackie, *supra* n 31, 167.

[113] O Gross, 'Are torture warrants warranted? Pragmatic absolutism and official disobedience' 88 *Minn L Rev* 1481 (2004) 1511. Gross uses the same term in *idem*, 'The Prohibition on Torture and the Limits of the Law' in Levinson (ed), *supra* n 4, 229–253, 237; and in O Gross and FN Aoláin, *Law in Times of Crisis: Emergency Powers in Theory and Practice* (Cambridge: CUP, 2006) 283.

[114] Scheffler, *supra* n 62, 86.

[115] Fried, *supra*, text accompanying n 71. To which he adds that 'the term absolute certainly has a nasty, pervasive ring to it...' (*ibid*, 15). Posner and Vermeule also use 'fanatical' to describe those who would condemn torture ('coercive interrogation') in a TBS. See *supra* n 59, 5. Levinson cites Fried's use of 'fanatical' and similar views approvingly (*supra* n 58, 2033); on that basis he may be classified as a deontologist with a 'disastrous consequences' clause, though his basic moral line is not clear to me.

[116] Scheffler, *supra* n 62, p 86, n 3. I apologize to the reader for the increasing violence (as well as absurdity) of some of the examples from now on—it is dictated by the subject matter. At any rate, all that is being spilt here is ink.

This is exactly what Jonathan Bennett does, in what, I submit, is the only logically sound formulation of the anti-absolutist view:

My arguments will tell equally against *any* principle of the form 'It would always be wrong to X [X being an act], whatever the consequences of not doing so'.[117] [Emphasis added.]

It should, first, be noted that by using the term 'any', Bennett is presenting nothing short of an 'absolutist anti-absolutist' view. I submit that logically, the idea of minimal absolutism can indeed only be rejected by an opposing *absolutist* view; to wit: the argument that some acts must *never* be allowed, no matter what the consequences, can only be countered by the argument that to prevent some ('disastrous') consequences, *any* act, namely *all* acts, that would prevent it must be allowed, the sole proviso being that in preventing such catastrophe these acts would not cause an even greater one.

This exposes the anti-absolutist view to many of the weaknesses it attributes to moral absolutism. Using Bennett's formula, and 'slippery surface' arguments and illustrations, Scheffler's argument could easily be turned on its head, as could his example. Bennett, Scheffler and, I submit, anyone else rejecting minimal absolutism in principle, would have to *reject* an absolute prohibition of the type 'it would always be wrong to torture everyone in the world to death, whatever the consequences of doing so'.

Now the anti-absolutist could counter that this is, in effect, the exception that proves the rule, and that any act with consequences *short* of the total (and painful) destruction of human life on earth cannot be prohibited absolutely, if refraining from performing it would result in such total destruction.[118] Under this view, however, it would still be right to actually *commit* the very 'genocidal catastrophes' (for example, wiping out a small nation in order to save the rest of humanity[119]) which Scheffler[120] can only accuse absolutists of *failing to prevent*.

But even when discussing individual, private acts, the 'never say never'[121] argument of the anti-absolutists may at times seem tenuous.

---

[117] J Bennett, 'Whatever the Consequences' in Thomson and Dworkin (eds), *supra* n 28, 211–236, 214.

[118] I am not sure that this is a wholly unrealistic debate, what with an all-out nuclear war still a possibility, and global environmental catastrophes possible or even, some argue, in the making.

[119] Or, to use Scheffler's example, torturing 'only' a quarter of the world's population to death so that the other three quarters may survive. This may actually support the *opposite* conclusion—that, at least on a theoretical level, even the survival of humanity is not necessarily a good basis for anti-absolutist permissiveness: in an imagined situation where humanity could only survive if people were to inflict perpetual, horrible and universal suffering on one another, it may be morally preferable to let humanity perish. On a less apocalyptic scale, a nation may wonder whether it should go to absolutely any length to ensure its survival, or whether, some point, it should prefer to 'perish' (or at least surrender) rather than commit certain atrocities without which it cannot survive or prevail.

[120] *Supra*, text accompanying n 116.

[121] My son (eleven years old at the time this was first written) and I like to refer to this aphorism as 'never say never—oops!'

Suppose you are a father and your seven-year-old son has been told about another father who beat his eight-year-old child severely for every real or perceived misdemeanour. You have never beaten your child but he, apparently believing that this has something to do with reaching the age of eight, asks you apprehensively: 'You won't ever do this to me Dad, will you?' Now a minimal absolutist parent who considers severely beating one's children by way of punishment an act worthy of an absolute prohibition would have no trouble whatsoever in answering the child: 'No, I'll never ever do this to you, no matter what.' On the other hand, the anti-absolutist, if he is truthful, would have to respond with something like: 'I would only do this to you under the most extreme circumstances',[122] adding perhaps that such circumstances would be so extreme as to be almost purely theoretical. Somehow, even with the added clarification, this does not strike me as having quite the same reassuring effect on the child. He now feels—actually *knows*—that his father has in himself the capacity, propensity, even readiness (however remote) for punitive violence against him. Indeed, the term 'fanatical' may seem, in this case, to describe the anti-absolutist more accurately than it would the minimal absolutist.

Of course, being what he is, the anti-absolutist father could simply lie to his son. However, the choice between lying to your children about your basic moral beliefs, and leaving them unsure at to whether or not they are always safe from your punitive violence must worry any parent, be they consequentialist, deontologist or whatever. Would it not be preferable, and would not the vast majority of parents rightly prefer, to declare a solemn, *absolute* vow *never* to punish their children by beating them, at least not severely—*and* mean it?[123]

Mythology, and to a much lesser extent history, are replete with stories of heroes(?) who risked their loved ones,[124] and even actually killed them[125] for some high ideal, such as obeying God's command or ensuring victory for their

[122] See eg Pettit, *supra* n 28, 154, who, referring to the value of 'promoting the confidence of children in their parents' argues that a 'parent would have to be very effective, and would have to be pretty sure of being very effective indeed, in order to be able to justify the neglect of their own children in the name of promoting that value elsewhere'. While convincingly pointing out the improbability of such action being justified, Pettit nevertheless would seem, by implication, to accept, or at least not rule out, the idea that it may be morally justified to beat one's son severely so that, say, millions of other parents would realize how wrong this form of punishment is.

[123] In contrast, it would appear much easier to explain to your child that some acts must never be performed, eg by telling him/her that while you would do almost everything to save his/her life, you would not kill, say, his/her mother, father or sister—just as you would not kill that child to save any of them. It must be conceded, however, that explaining why you would not torture a terrorist who would otherwise kill your child may not be as easy, especially since one would hesitate to explain fully to a child what torture means.

[124] Eg the biblical story of Abraham and Isaac, Genesis 22, the similar Qur'anic story of Ibrahim and Isma'il, 37 (a-Saffat): 102–111; and some versions of the story of Agamemnon and Iphigenia, eg Euripides, *Iphigenia at Aulis* eg in *Euripides:10 Plays*, trans Paul Roche (New York: Signet Classics, 1998) 215–276.

[125] Eg the Biblical story of Jephte and his daughter; Judges 11; and other versions of the story of Iphigenia, eg in Aeschylus, 'Agamemnon' (ca 458 BC) in *idem, The Oresteia*, trans I Johnston (Arlington, Va: Richer Resource Publications 2007) 7–70. Note that according to the Chorus, Agamemnon sacrificed his daughter having 'strapped on the harsh yoke of necessity'. *Ibid*, 15.

nation. However, it is unlikely that most people in the real, modern world would condone, let alone admire such behaviour. Nor, I would submit, should they. The example also shows what is often overlooked—that while the anti-absolutists would do everything to ensure that extreme acts would indeed be performed only in extreme situations, they may not always be able to prevent their own approval of such acts, however restricted, from casting a dark shadow over their lives, even their everyday lives.

3. More candidate acts for absolute moral prohibition

It has transpired that anti-absolutists would have us believe that we should morally be ready, at least in pure theory, to break each and every one of our intuitive prohibitions, and, moreover, any other possible absolute prohibition we could ever imagine—the anti-absolutist's only condition being that violating the prohibition would result in the avoidance of an adequately horrible disaster.[126] In other words, anti-absolutists claim that any act, and to be precise *absolutely* any act, may be justified if a large enough catastrophe is looming.

To counter such claims further, let us consider three other acts which may be better candidates for an absolute prohibition than the ones discussed above.

(a) *Torturing babies to death for fun*

Judith Jarvis Thomson provides this obvious candidate for an absolutely prohibited act: 'One ought not to torture babies to death for fun.'[127] Treating the 'absoluteness' of the prohibition in this case as self-evident, she goes on to say,

...surely [this] is true. It is not merely true that other things being equal one ought not torture babies to death for fun; one just plain ought not do it, no matter what the circumstances.[128]

However, the anti-absolutists, it should be remembered, must reject *any* absolute prohibition of an act which claims to hold 'no matter what the circumstances'. Applying Bennett's anti-absolutist formula to the case in point, their argument,

...will tell equally against... [the] principle... '*It would always be wrong to torture babies to death for fun*, whatever the consequences of not doing so.'[129] [Italicized words mine.]

Perhaps we could construe such arguments by imagining a scenario in which we introduce circumstances surrounding the basic act (torturing babies for fun) as

---

[126] To be more precise—the disaster avoided would have befallen a large number of people, much larger than the number of those who would suffer from the performance of the putatively prohibited act.

[127] JJ Thomson, *The Realm of Rights* (Cambridge, Mass: Harvard University Press, 1990) 18.

[128] *Ibid*. Note also her subsequent apology (*ibid*): 'Overheated examples in ethics are tiresome (one feels one's lapels are being clutched), and I apologize for this one. Still, if what is wanted is places where morality meshes with the world, then melodrama is useful...'.

[129] See *supra* n 117 and accompanying text.

described by Jarvis Thompson, that will eventually turn such torturing into a 'disaster-preventing' act.

Would the act become moral, or any less immoral, if we added that not one but ten men will do the torturing, immensely enjoying themselves? What if we added that the baby is not suffering from the torture—say it has just been born in an irreversible vegetative state combined with a totally dysfunctional nervous system, and its doctors are unanimous both that it cannot feel a thing, and that it would die in a matter of days anyway? What if we added that three hundred thousand murderous paedophiles all around the globe will watch the torture on the net and have the time of their lives? What if we added that the torturers (and net viewers) are ready to pay the baby's abjectly poor parents millions, thus saving them and the baby's very large family from a life of poverty, or even from starvation?

What if we added, finally, that of the three hundred thousand murderous paedophiles, at least one per cent (ie three thousand) are likely—indeed certain—to cancel plans to go out and actually abduct and torture babies to death for fun, preferring to stay in front of their computer screens and enjoy the torture vicariously and safely, so that thousands of children will be saved from torture and death by the torture and death of that single, unfeeling, moribund child?[130]

I must admit that the very conjuring of such possibilities has made my skin crawl. Many of us would feel that a person has to be a morally suspect to even *entertain* the idea that the introduction of such factors could affect the morality of this act.

But consider the views of the anti-absolutist theorists on this case. Practically all, maybe absolutely all of them would dismiss any suggestion that the first four circumstantial elements I have added would in any way tilt the moral balance in favour of torturing the baby. These elements were put in place, to a large extent, to set the stage for the fifth and final element, although they may also point to the problems, indeed dangers, of determining the morality of an act through (or solely through) agent-neutral value calculations.

However, when that fifth element is added, and faced with the possibility of preventing a catastrophe, ie the suffering and death of thousands of children, by torturing the one to death, anti-absolutists are, I submit, on a moral 'slippery surface' which simply would not allow them to both deny that such torturing must be prohibited and maintain their principled anti-absolutist stand.

The consistent anti-absolutist must (albeit grudgingly) join the 'ayes' for justifying the torturing of the baby to death for fun once it becomes clear that such torture is a catastrophe-preventing act.

---

[130] We could even imagine that the paedophile is actually trying to do something 'good': aware of the evil of his ways, he nevertheless wants to use his perversion to save as many children as he can by torturing that one baby. Only he can carry out the act for it to be authentic, otherwise (ie without the 'for fun' bit) those watching cannot be convinced to abandon their murderous plans.

Scheffler, as we have seen, takes this very stand,[131] and the same would surely be true regarding other anti-absolutists, such as Bentham[132] and M Moore. The latter states:

Only the most horrendous of consequences could justify the torture of those who neither caused a threat or serious harm nor become a part of such threat by refusing to remove it.[133]

Surely, the torturing to death of three thousand babies amounts to such 'most horrendous of consequences'. Otherwise justifications for torture in a TBS would exclude even the prevention of the terrorist attacks of 11 September 2001.

Two principled minimal absolutist arguments against anti-absolutism may be derived from the above scenario.

(i) Moral corruption

A serious problem lies in this very process of gradual turnover. It is a process of moral corruption.[134] Such a process is inevitable when one considers it right, at *any* given point, however remote, to allow consequences to override our moral aversion to certain acts. In Nagel's words:

Many people feel . . . that something has gone seriously wrong when certain measures are admitted into consideration in the first place. The fundamental mistake is made there, rather than at the point where the overall benefit of some monstrous measure is judged to outweigh its disadvantages, and it is adopted.[135]

A principled anti-absolutist must admit every single act, including the worst atrocities imaginable, into consideration. As we have seen, such moral corruption may affect a person's life, or at least inner life, not only in extreme situations but in everyday ones as well. Visiting friends and seeing their child, one would often say something like: 'that's a really cute little child you've got there'. Under the anti-absolutist view, it would be *morally legitimate* for a moral agent to have the following thought, or calculation (apologies for what follows): 'Under what circumstances would I (or worse—the friends) be *justified* in torturing this child? I wonder what method would be best?'

---

[131] See *supra* n 117 and accompanying text.

[132] See *supra* n 45 and accompanying text.

[133] MS Moore, *supra* n 59, 333. Moore goes on to argue, rightly to my mind, that the likelihood of the need to such torture arising is extremely 'remote'. Likelihood, however, is not the issue here. A very similar moral view is taken by M Levin, 'Torture and Other Extreme Measures Taken for the General Good: Further Reflections on a Philosophical Problem' in P Suedfeld (ed), *Psychology and Torture* (New York: Hemisphere Publishing, 1990) 89–98.

[134] For this point see eg Anscombe, who, discussing the Sheriff's case (for which see *supra*, text accompanying n 103) argues the following: '. . . if someone really thinks, *in advance*, that it is open to question whether such an action as procuring the judicial execution of the innocent should be quite excluded from consideration—I do not want to argue with him; he shows a corrupt mind' (*idem, supra* n 28, 17). (Footnote omitted.)

[135] Nagel, *supra* n 69, 58.

Now it could be argued that this very corruption may serve as a consequentialist reason *not* to allow such thoughts, and such actions, *ever* to take place—but this, of course, would be abandoning the anti-absolutist stand.

I should add that my point is not, of course, that anti-absolutists actually walk around their friends' houses entertaining such thoughts—it is, rather, that there is nothing in their moral view which would reject such entertaining, at least not in a 'pure' scenario subjected to the same criteria as the 'pure' TBS.

(ii) Moral enslavement

The anti-absolutist view of the TBS actually provides us with another set of circumstances in which we should (under that view) reject an absolute prohibition on torturing babies to death for fun. Such a scenario is suggested by Haber, who explains that for consequentialists (ie anti-absolutists), 'torturing a child is morally permissible':

> ...if the consequences of not torturing children are desperate enough (eg, a terrorist will detonate a bomb in a crowded arena unless you torture an innocent child)...[136]

Thus if Vicious is not Ethica's prisoner but is, rather, free, and negotiating the terms for neutralizing the bomb, it is clear from the above discussion that Scheffler, Bentham, Michael Moore, Michael Levin, Posner and any other principled anti-absolutists must logically justify allowing, or even performing such torture.

Even in our original TBS, the terrorist may be described as 'negotiating' the terms under which *Ethica* would allow, indeed perform, torture.

Thus the terrorist, has, under the anti-absolutist approach, full control over what *we* should morally do; the terrorist dictates *our* moral choice—as long as it does not involve a catastrophe worse (or much worse) than the one that the terrorist is threatening us with.

The very essence of morality—the agent's *freedom* to choose, namely to consider circumstances, emotions, beliefs, intuitions, values, and arrive at her own moral conclusions and response—has been denied her. In extreme circumstances, the moral agent has become, under the anti-absolutist view, a moral slave. Her only option is to obey the commands, *any* commands, of a moral master—even if he is, in fact *precisely because* he is —a moral monster.[137]

(b) Death penalty for minor offences and cruel death penalty in the West

The similarities between the debate on capital punishment and that surrounding torture in a TBS were illustrated by Ernest van den Haag who, having spoken

---

[136] Haber, *supra* n 62, 3.
[137] *Cf* Foot, *supra* n 102, 25.

to several prominent 'abolitionists', went on to report, and then 'infer' the following:

Each [of the abolitionists] told me that, even if every execution were to deter a hundred murders, he would oppose it. I infer that, to these abolitionist leaders, the life of every murderer is more valuable than the lives of a hundred prospective victims...[138]

However, such similarities are not our concern here. My argument here is that, in the moral and legal debate for and against the death penalty in the West,[139] especially in the USA, there are two points on which both sides agree, and where consequently both sides, not just one, are absolutist: they agree, first, that *the death penalty may only be imposed, if at all, for the most serious crimes*, and secondly, that *criminals must never be executed in ways designed to cause suffering*, beyond what the USA Supreme Court termed 'the necessary suffering involved in any method employed to extinguish life humanely'.[140]

Historically, of course, this has not been the case. People were executed for 'crimes' such as pick-pocketing petty sums and 'being in the company of gypsies'.[141] Now the death penalty has been abolished in the vast majority of the democratic states, and where retained, it is limited to the worst crimes in the law books, such as murder. The chances of this changing significantly, say that an epidemic of petty theft prompts lawmakers in the USA or elsewhere to allow courts to sentence shoplifters or pickpockets to death, are very slim indeed. In other words, there is a consensus, both on the moral-theoretical and the legal-practical levels, around an *absolutist prohibition* on punishing petty crimes with death. This point is obvious, and below I will concentrate on the second one.

Ancient and not-so-ancient methods of execution in the West historically included burning, boiling, disembowelling, maiming and drowning.[142] In other words they were often torturous, designed specifically to make the doomed criminal suffer severely before dying. At the turn of the twenty-first century, methods

---

[138] E van den Haag, 'The Death Penalty Once More' in HA Bedau (ed), *The Death Penalty in America: Current Controversies* (New York: OUP, 1997) 445–456, 450.

[139] See generally, eg Amnesty International, *When the State kills...: The Death Penalty v. Human Rights*, AI Index: ACT 51/07/89 (London, 1989); Bedau (ed), *ibid*; *idem, The Case against Death Penalty*, <http://www.soci.niu.edu/~critcrim/dp/dppapers/aclu.antidp>, accessed 25 October 2007; F Carrington, *Neither Cruel nor Unusual: The Case for Capital Punishment* (New Rochelle, NY: Arlington 1978); HH Haines, *Against Capital Punishment: The Anti-Death Penalty Movement in America, 1972–1994* (New York: OUP, 1996); P Hodgkinson and A Rutherford (eds), *Capital Punishment: Global Issues and Prospects* (Winchester: Waterside Press, 1996); LP Pojman and J Reiman, *The Death Penalty: For and Against* (Lanham, MD: Rowman & Littlefield, 1998); WA Schabas, *The Death Penalty As Cruel Treatment and Torture: Capital Punishment Challenged in World Courts* (Boston: Northeastern University Press, 1996); T Sorell, *Moral Theory and Capital Punishment* (Oxford: Basil Blackwell, 1987).

[140] *Louisiana ex rel Francis v Resweber*, 329 US 464 (1947).

[141] J Górecki, *Capital Punishment: Criminal Law and Social Evolution* (New York: Columbia University Press, 1983) 60.

[142] See eg *ibid*; J Laurence, *A History of Capital Punishment: with Special Reference to Capital Punishment in Great Britain* (London: Sampson Low, Marston & Co, no date).

of execution either designed to, or at any rate sure to cause suffering in the process of carrying them out (notably stoning and crushing to death) still existed in some countries.[143]

In contrast, William Schabas describes the situation in the vast majority of modern states thus:

In distinction with earlier times, there appears to be virtually unanimous agreement in modern systems of criminal law that the method [of execution] should attempt to avoid undue suffering.[144]

The legal debate surrounding the death penalty in the USA has to a large extent (and the moral debate to a lesser extent) concentrated on the issue of whether this or that—or *any*—method of or procedure leading to execution constitutes 'cruel and unusual punishment' prohibited by the Eighth Amendment to the US Constitution. Those supporting the death penalty do so, like van den Haag, only 'provided it be done in a nontorturous manner',[145] and in the courts they have claimed that the death penalty was not cruel, rather than that it was *right*, or legal, for it to be cruel. Thus in the 1970s, the death penalty in the USA, to use Herbert H Haines'[146] words, fell[147] and rose[148] on the issue of whether or not the death penalty, either *per se* or in the particular physical and legal circumstances, was 'cruel and unusual'.

Thus anti-cruelty absolutists battled, and still battle other anti-cruelty absolutists, the disagreement between them being only (regarding this aspect) about whether that particular penalty inevitably involves cruelty; but there is a consensus that penalties should not involve cruelty, whatever the consequences.

Now it may be argued that this last addition, 'whatever the consequences', is excessive. What if an extreme situation arises where the execution of certain

---

[143] See eg Amnesty International, *Afghanistan: Cruel, inhuman or degrading treatment or punishment*, AI Index: ASA 11/015/1999 (London: 1 November 1999) (including a piece on five men convicted of sodomy who were sentenced to death by crushing a wall on them); Amnesty International Urgent Action (on a 15-year-old Iranian girl sentenced to stoning), AI Index: MDE 13/006/2001 (London: 18 January 2001); Amnesty International, *Iran: stonings should stop*, AI Index MDE 13/024/2001 ((11 July 2001) on the execution by stoning of a woman for 'adultery' on that same day); Amnesty International, *Iran: Death Sentences of juvenile offenders and stoning sentences continue to be passed*, Press release (20 October 2005) <http://news.amnesty.org/index/ ENGMDE130632005>, accessed 25 November 2005 (including the case of a woman sentenced to death by stoning for 'adultery').

[144] Schabas, *supra* n 139, 200.

[145] Van den Haag, *supra* n 138, 454.

[146] Haines, *supra* n 139, Chapter 1.

[147] Following the Supreme Court decision in *Furman v Georgia*, 408 US 238 (1972). Part of the 'cruelty' or 'unusualness' lay in the fact that death penalty was imposed arbitrarily or, in the words of Justice Stewart, was 'so wantonly and so freakishly imposed'. Some of the concurring Justices, but not all, considered the very penalty of death to be 'cruel and unusual punishment'. These facts do not affect my basic claim that cruelty in one form or another (or the absence thereof) was at issue here.

[148] Following the Supreme Court decision in *Gregg v Georgia*, 428 US 153 (1976).

criminals in a cruel manner is the only way to deter people from committing some heinous crimes that may result in the death of thousands or millions?

My answer is twofold: First, such arguments are simply absent from the writings of those Western theorists who support the death penalty—whether they argue from a utilitarian point of view, like van den Haag or Kantian, like Sorell. The former writes, *inter alia*:

Still, is it [the death penalty] repulsive? Torture, however well deserved now is repulsive to us. But torture is an artifact. Death is not, since nature has placed us all under sentence of death. Capital punishment, in John Stuart Mill's phrase, only 'hastens death'—which is what the murderer did to his victim. I find nothing repulsive in hastening the murderer's death, provided it be done in a nonturtorous manner.

[…] To believe that capital punishment is too severe for any act, one must believe that there can be no act horrible enough to deserve death. I find this belief difficult to understand. I should readily impose the death penalty on a Hitler or a Stalin, or on anyone who does what they did, albeit on a smaller scale.[149]

What is clear from this is that van den Haag would not support torturous death as punishment even for 'a Hitler or a Stalin'. In other words, he is an absolutist.

Elaborating his 'Kantian approach', Sorell argues that Kant's view of a person's,

…'inherent personality' rules out arbitrary and 'infamous' forms of treatment…the criminal is still an object of respect and cannot be used by anyone else merely as a means.[150]

Sorell devotes a chapter to the question of whether or not death penalty is 'cruel and unusual,' and answers in the negative, rather than claim justification for cruelty.[151] Discussing the utilitarian approach to the issue, and its 'deterrence' justification of punishment, Sorell argues that 'the thinking behind deterrence can be understood to have a built-in break on increasing severity' which would also rule out cruel executions.[152]

Secondly, as the possibility of a court in the West sentencing a person to penalties hitherto not provided for in the law books is a distinctly remote one indeed, so in practice the principle of 'non-cruel' death is likely to work at least until after the next emergency. Empirically, horrendous crimes and extreme emergencies, both in the USA and worldwide, have so far shown the principle of 'no cruel executions' to be very resilient.

---

[149] Van den Haag, *supra* n 138, 453–4. Van den Haag's argument invites the criticism that doing certain things to a person may be wrong, regardless of whether or not that person deserves them. If a Hitler or a Stalin were to accidentally suffer horribly, say if he were to boil to death, we may think he deserved such fate, without this morally obliging, or even allowing us or our state, to boil his kind.

[150] Sorell, *supra* n 139, 133.

[151] *Ibid*, Ch 5.

[152] *Ibid*, 106.

The period when this was first written, mid-September 2001, was tragically an appropriate time to make this point. It was only a few months after the execution of Timothy McVeigh, convicted for the murder of 168 people in a bomb attack in Oklahoma City in 1995,[153] and only a few days after the terrorist attacks which destroyed the twin towers in New York and part of the Pentagon in Washington, killing thousands. McVeigh was executed by chemical injection, namely through a method understood by the US legal system to be 'non-cruel', despite the enormity of his crime.

In the immediate wake of 9/11, there were several calls on the internet to torture Usamah Bin Laden, who was suspected of masterminding the attacks. Following is one of the 'cleaner' examples, which was posted on the *New York Daily News* Yankees web forum:

Being a Red Sox fan I hate to have to say it but...I am rooting for the Yankees to win the World Series this year. After the final out of the World Series the Federal Government has a surprise for Yankee fans. They have Osama Bin Laden in custody and he gets tossed onto the field at Yankee Stadium. The NY crowd gets to slowly torture him to death and Vince McMahon gets the Pay Per View rights.[154]

However, it is safe to conclude that no *serious* suggestions to reintroduce torturous executions (such as attempts to change US law—which in this case would have to include its Constitution) have been made, even in immediate response to 'black Tuesday'. Despite the fact that the 'war on terrorism' is still ongoing as these words are being written, I believe it is similarly safe to assume no such suggestions *will* be made either, and that if Mr Bin Laden were to be extradited or captured, he would face no such or similar punishment.

On a global scale, the international tribunals for Former Yugoslavia and Rwanda and the International Criminal Court, have all been denied, by their statutes, the authority to sentence people to death,[155] let alone cruel death. These courts, it should be remembered, are established to try those who have perpetrated or master-minded the worst crimes, and on a large scale, such as mass-murders, rape, torture and genocide.

It could still be argued that future developments now impossible to predict may nevertheless change all this some time in the future. Such argument is

---

[153] McVeigh was executed in an Indiana federal prison on 1 June 2001. See eg Reuters report, 12 June 2001, 6:03 AM PT, <http://www.zdnet.com/zdfeeds/msncobrand/news/0,13622,2773428-hud00025nshm3,00.html>, accessed 17 September 2001.

[154] Posted by 'ORSF' at the *New York Daily News Yankees Webforum*, <http://www.webforums.com/forums/f-read/msa110.11.html>, on Saturday, 15 September 2001, accessed 20 September 2001.

[155] See Article 24 of the Statute of the International Criminal Tribunal for the former Yugoslavia (an updated version of the Statute is available at <http://www.un.org/icty/legaldoc-e/index-t.htm>); Article 23 of the Statute of the International Criminal Tribunal for Rwanda <http://www.ictr.org>; Article 77 of the Rome Statute of the International Criminal Court <http://www.un.org/law/icc/statute/romefra.htm>. In the two former cases the Statutes state explicitly that 'The penalty imposed by the Trial Chamber shall be limited to imprisonment.'

impossible to refute, and I would therefore concede that 'never' or 'whatever the consequences' here are true on the practical level and of the foreseeable future rather than fully covering all theoretical possibilities. I doubt, however, that this weakens the argument considerably.

All of which comes to show that minimal absolutism actually works, backed by moral, political and legislative consensus, in the real world and in more-or-less civilized countries. Following is another illustration of this assertion.

(c)   Waiving consent when experimenting on human subjects in order to find a vaccine for HIV/AIDS

(i)   Introduction: HIV/AIDS, experiments on humans, 'informed consent'

HIV (human immunodeficiency virus) is the aetiological agent (that is, the cause) of acquired immunodeficiency syndrome (AIDS).[156] This virus attacks T-4 white blood cells. It is a retrovirus, namely has only RNA, but once in the cell, it copies itself into DNA, 'penetrates' the cell's DNA, and attaches itself onto it, replicating itself thousands of times within the cell (while constantly changing in the process), and eventually destroying it. The subsequent spread of the virus into other cells, in the same way, may lead to a considerable weakening of the body's immune system, and thus to enhanced vulnerability to a range of infections and cancers. HIV is most commonly passed during sexual intercourse,[157] but also through needle-sharing, blood-transmissions and other blood-borne paths.

By the end of 2006, more than 25 million people had died of AIDS since 1981.[158] The UN's AIDS/HIV agency (UNAIDS) and the World Health Organisation (WHO) have estimated that in December 2006, about 39.5 million people were living with HIV, 2.3 million of them children under the age of 15. About 4.3 million were infected with the virus in 2006, half a million of them children. About 2.9 million died of AIDS in 2006, some 380,000 of them children.[159] The organizations stated that '[p]romising developments have been seen in recent years'. Nevertheless, they concluded that 'the number of people living with HIV continues to grow, as does the number of deaths due to AIDS'.[160]

---

[156] A simple and clear explanation regarding HIV/AIDS was provided by the World AIDS Day website, <http://www.worldaidsday.org/difference/findout.cfm>, accessed 27 November 2001; Thomas Kerns, *Ethical Issues in HIV Vaccine Trials* (London: Macmillan, 1997) Ch 5. I have used the online edition <http://home.myuw.net/tkerns/MyUWsite/evtsite/evt-toc.html>, accessed 4 December 2001. The dilemma posed here concerns attempts to circumvent the requirement for informed consent of a few to save the live of many rather than, for instance, to maximize *profits*, which is a serious problem but outside the remit of the discussion here. On this problem see eg J-P Chippaux, 'Pharmaceutical colonialism in Africa' *Le Monde Diplomatique* (English Edition), August 2005.

[157] 86 per cent, according to Kerns, *ibid*, Ch 7.1.

[158] See eg the website of Avert, a UK-based international HIV/AIDS charity, <http://www.avert.org/worldstats.htm>, accessed 25 April 2007.

[159] UNAIDS/WHO, 'AIDS epidemic update December 2006' <http://data.unaids.org/pub/EpiReport/2006/2006_EpiUpdate_en.pdf>, accessed 26 April 2007, 1, and see tables on pages 2; 64–7

[160] *Ibid*, 3.

For over two decades scientists had tried to find treatments for the disease. In the modern era, the development of new vaccines and cures is a lengthy, costly and highly regulated process. This is especially true regarding the clinical testing of a new vaccine, involving human subjects.

While computer models, cultures and animals could be used at the initial stages of testing (the ethics of animal testing will not be addressed here), at the beginning of the twenty-first century the safety and efficiency of a vaccine or drug designed for humans ultimately could only be determined by subjecting it to tests involving human subjects.

Testing a new vaccine on human subjects is done in three main phases:[161]

- Phase I—to determine the vaccine's safety.
- Phase II—to determine its immunogenicity (namely the capacity to induce an immune response).
- Phase III—to determine its effectiveness in providing protection from infection or disease.

Experiments on humans are regulated nationally and internationally. Our focus here is on one of the principal ethical requirements, which according to the USA National Bioethics Advisory Commission 'is reflected in all published national and international codes, regulations, and guidelines pertaining to research ethics'[162]—that of 'informed consent' by anyone taking part in such experiments (or by that person's legally authorized representative, for instance in the case of children). This requirement means, in the words of one international instrument, that the 'subjects must be volunteers and informed participants in the research project'.[163]

The concept of 'informed consent' is not straightforward.[164] It is not even absolute overall, admitting of certain exceptions, notably in what may be called *de*

---

[161] See eg Kerns, *supra* n 156, 8.1; Christine Grady, *The Search for an AIDS Vaccine: Ethical Issues in the Development and Testing of a Preventive HIV Vaccine* (Bloomington and Indianapolis: Indiana University Press, 1995) 148.

[162] National Bioethics Advisory Commission [USA], *Ethical and Policy Issues in Research Involving Human Participants, Volume I: Report and Recommendations of the National Bioethics Advisory Commission,* April 2001. The Commission was established by a Presidential Executive Order in 1995, and submitted its report in 2001. See <http://bioethics.georgetown.edu/nbac/pubs.html>, accessed 15 December 2001.

[163] Article 20 of the World Medical Association Declaration of Helsinki: Ethical Principles for Medical Research Involving Human Subjects. The Declaration was adopted by the 18th WMA General Assembly Helsinki, Finland, June 1964 and underwent several amendments in subsequent WMA General Assemblies. For text see eg <http://www.wma.net/e/policy/b3.htm>, accessed 25 October 2007. See similarly article 1 of the Nuremberg Code, developed by the post-World-War II military tribunals in response to Nazi experiments ('The voluntary consent of the human subject is absolutely essential'), *Trials of War Criminals before the Nuremberg Military Tribunals under Control Council Law No 10,* Vol 2, Washington, DC, US Government Printing Office, 1949, 181–182, reprinted *ibid;* Art 7 of the International Covenant on Civil and Political Rights, UNGA res 2200 A (XXI) adopted 16 December 1966, entered into force 23 March 1976.

[164] Henry Beecher contends that often 'Consent in any fully informed sense may not be obtainable.' He nevertheless hastens to add that such consent '. . . remains a goal toward which one must

minimis cases, namely where a legally authorized ethical review body has determined, *inter alia*, that the potential harm is minimal,[165] therapeutic intervention is not required and waiving consent is necessary for the research (eg when awareness by the subject may jeopardize the experiment);[166] and, more contentiously, in cases of 'emergency research', ie where, *inter alia*, the prospective subject is in a life-threatening situation, neither the subject (for instance, being unconscious) nor his or her representative (if absent, or owing to lack of time) can give consent, and there is no viable alternative way of saving that person's life.[167]

Our focus here, however, is on the core of the concept, or requirement, of 'informed consent' for participation in medical experiments, namely outside personal emergencies and above *de minimis* risk: that only adults of sound mind, each of whom is offered all the necessary information and whose full consent has been sought before participation, may be the subject of such experiments. And here there seems to be a consensus around an absolute prohibition on waiving such consent.

This has not always been the case. The twentieth century saw the most horrific of experiments on non-consenting humans, during what Grady interestingly calls '"the utilitarian" era of human-subjects research'.[168] That era saw not only

---

strive for sociologic, ethical and clear-cut legal reasons. There is no choice in the matter.' See *idem*, 'Ethics and Clinical Research' in H Kuhse and P Singer (eds), *Bioethics: An Anthology* (Oxford: Blackwell 1999) 421–426, 422. On informed consent see also eg TL Beauchamp and JF Childress, *Principles of Biomedical Ethics*, 4th edn (New York: OUP, 1994), Ch 3; Grady, *supra* n 161, 134–140; Kerns, *supra* n 156, Ch 14–16; and sources cited below.

[165] The US government's 'Institutional Review Board Guidebook' defines 'minimal risk' as '... where the probability and magnitude of harm or discomfort anticipated in the proposed research are not greater, in and of themselves, than those ordinarily encountered in daily life or during the performance of routine physical or psychological examinations or tests'. Thus for example 'the risk of drawing a small amount of blood from a healthy individual for research purposes is no greater than the risk of doing so as part of routine physical examination'. See the Glossary in Office for Human Research Protections, US Department of Human Health and Services, *Institutional Review Board Guidebook*, <http://www.hhs.gov/ohrp/irb/irb_guidebook.htm>, accessed 25 October 2007.

[166] See eg Art 2.1(c) of the *Tri-Council Policy Statement: Ethical Conduct for Research Involving Humans*, prepared jointly by the Canadian Medical Research Council (MRC), the Natural Sciences and Engineering Research Council (NSERC), and the Social Sciences and Humanities Research Council (SSHRC) <http://www.ncehr.medical.org/english/code_2/apdx02.html>, accessed 12 November 2007.

[167] See eg *ibid*, Art 2.8; and the US Food and Drug Administration regulations, 21 CFR 50.23 (revised as of 1 April 2000) <http://www.access.gpo.gov/nara/cfr/waisidx_00/21cfr50_00.html>, accessed 11 December 2001. For a discussion see eg N Fost, 'Waived Consent for Emergency Research' 24(2&3) *Am J Law Med* 163 (1998). For criticism of the FDA's approach see eg EN Kraybill and BS Bauer, 'Can Community Consultation Substitute for Informed Consent in Emergency Medicine Research?' in NMP King, GE Henderson and J Stein (eds), *Beyond Regulations: Ethics in Human Subjects Research* (Chapel Hill and London: University of North Carolina Press, 1999) 191–198; JP Browder, 'Can Community Consultation Substitute for Informed Consent in Emergency Medicine Research? A Response' *ibid*, 199–203; NMP King, 'Medical Research: Using a New Paradigm Where the Old Might Do' *ibid*, 204–212.

[168] Grady, *supra* n 161, 34.

the well-known experiments that Nazi doctors carried out on prisoners,[169] and the lesser-known (in the West) experiments that Japanese doctors carried out on prisoners during World War II,[170] but also non-consensual experiments in democratic societies—for instance, in the USA, the Tuskegee experiments in the 1930s (where black men were injected with syphilis without consenting and were subsequently left untreated),[171] and the injection of eighteen men, women, and children with plutonium by doctors working with the Manhattan Project, again without their consent or even knowledge (the cover-up lasting for no less than forty years).[172]

Nor can it be claimed, even remotely, that the search for vaccines and cures for HIV/AIDS has been devoid of ethical controversy. For instance, the placebo-controlled trial of Zidovudine (AZT) was abandoned—first, in effect, by subjects and then by the researchers, the use of a placebo arm in a test involving desperate, moribund AIDS patients being the cause in both cases. According to Udo Schüklenk and Carlton Hogan's (somewhat self-contradictory) account:

It was revealed...that soon after the beginning of this trial, patients had their capsules analyzed by chemists to find out who was randomized into the placebo arm. Patients who received the active agent started sharing their drug with those who got a placebo. The trial effectively became unblinded and was not placebo controlled. It was aborted prematurely because 19 patients died in the placebo arm compared to only 1 in the Zidovudine arm.[173]

Similarly controversial have been issues such as choosing, preparing and interacting with groups, or communities, where phase III trials for HIV vaccines are to

---

[169] See eg G Annas and M Grodin (eds), *The Nazi Doctors and the Nuremberg Code: Human Rights in Human Experimentation* (Oxford: OUP, 1992); AL Caplan (ed), *When Medicine Went Mad: Bioethics and the Holocaust* (Totowa, NJ: Humana Press, 1992); RJ Lifton, *The Nazi Doctors: Medical Killing and the Psychology of Genocide* (London: Macmillan, 1986); Robert Proctor, *Racial Hygiene: Medicine under the Nazis* (Cambridge, Mass: Harvard University Press, 1989). Some Nazi doctors actually justified their experiments citing the need to alleviate human suffering and as a 'lesser evil'. This is briefly discussed in Part IV, Ch 19, Section B(1)(b).

[170] See eg S Harris, *Factories of Death: Japanese Biological Warfare 1932–45 and the American Cover-up* (New York: Routledge, 1994); P Williams and D Wallace, *Unit 731: Japan's Secret Biological Warfare in World War II* (New York: The Free Press, 1989).

[171] See eg JH Jones, *Bad Blood: The Tuskegee Syphilis Experiment* (New York: Free Press, 1993); B Roy, 'The Tuskegee Syphilis Experiment: Biotechnology and the Administrative State' 87(1) *J Nat Med Ass* 56 (1995). According to the latter source, the main aim of the experiment was to provide researchers with a steady supply of blood for developing new syphilis tests, some of which became highly profitable commercial products marketed worldwide.

[172] See E Welsome, *The Plutonium Files: America's Secret Medical Experiments During the Cold War* (New York: Delacorte Press, 1999).

[173] U Schüklenk and C Hogan, 'Patient Access to Experimental Drugs and AIDS Clinical Trial Designs: Ethical Issues' in Kuhse and Singer (eds), *supra* n 164, 441–448, 441. See also Beauchamp and Childress, *supra* n 164, 301–2, 446–7, who conclude (at 447) that 'As a result of this trial... [in subsequent research of treatments for HIV/AIDS] placebo controlled trials must be considered unethical, at least for certain groups of patients.'

be conducted,[174] and trials in developing countries.[175] The fact is, nevertheless, that while the requirement of 'informed consent' features prominently in practically all debates around these issues, there have been no serious arguments for compromising on this requirement in view of the enormity of the crisis, let alone waiving it altogether.[176]

(ii) Why not waive the consent of a few to save the lives of many?
There is thus an absolute ban on waiving 'informed consent' in HIV vaccine trials—it is never waived, whatever the consequences. All the above essentially goes to show that the minimal absolutist position here is firmly grounded in actual ethical policies. These will now be described in terms relevant to our wider topic:

1. The HIV/AIDS global pandemic constitutes a real-life, ongoing catastrophe at least as large, severe and urgent as any TBS, theoretical or otherwise, may harbour.
2. Notwithstanding this, efforts to develop a vaccine or a cure for HIV/AIDS have not (at least so far) involved waiving this ban in order to speed up the process and thus save many lives.

Let us turn the latter fact around while we move into the realm of moral speculation. Suppose *Dr Ethica*, a leading scientific researcher, decided to test a new antiretroviral vaccine on non-consenting human subjects—either during phases I or II of clinical trials (phase III involves large numbers of subjects) or indeed earlier, instead of trying the vaccine first on animals.[177]

Developing a vaccine for HIV/AIDS is indisputably a very long process, and while trials on candidate vaccines have been conducted since the early 1990s, at

---

[174] See eg L Blanchard, 'Community Assessment and Perception: Preparation for HIV Vaccine Efficacy Trials' in King, Henderson and Stein (eds), *supra* n 167, 85–94; RP Strauss, 'Community Advisory Board—Investigator Relationships in Community-Based HIV/AIDS Research' *ibid*, 94–101; KA Wailoo, 'Research Partnerships and People "at Risk": HIV Vaccine Efficacy Trials and African American Communities' *ibid*, 102–107.

[175] See eg S Loue, *Legal and Ethical Aspects of HIV-Related Research* (New York and London: Plenum Press, 1995), 40–42; Grady, *supra* n 161, 120; U Schüklenk, 'Protecting the Vulnerable: Testing Times for Clinical Research Ethics' <http://www.wits.ac.za/bioethics/res.htm>, accessed 10 November 2001. See also sources and discussion *infra*, in the next section.

[176] Absence of this kind is difficult to prove, but here are two attempts: Kerns writes: 'That the principle of requiring informed consent from each individual research subject does and should apply, virtually all ethicists (including those from developing nations) do seem to believe.' (*supra* n 156, Ch 16). Kerns does not point to any exceptions. An issue of the Journal of Medical Ethics wholly devoted to 'The impact of AIDS on medical ethics'—26(1) *J Med Ethics* (2000)—similarly lacks a single call to waive, or even consider waiving, 'informed consent' in this context.

[177] The main reason why vaccines are first tested on animals is, of course, to minimize risk to humans. The result is, however, that much time is spent (put over-simply) on finding a 'suitable' animal, 'adapting' both the disease and the animal to 'suit' one another, then, once a vaccine is developed, on 'readapting' it to suite humans, that is, to ensure that it is both effective and safe for humans. On the particular difficulties of animal testing in the case of HIV, 'a uniquely human infection', see eg KM Boyd, R Higgs and AJ Pinching, 'An AIDS lexicon' 26(1) *J Med Ethics* 66 (2000). The quotation is from p 75.

the beginning of the twenty-first century they were unlikely to be completed for quite a few years. This is how the International AIDS Vaccine Initiative (IAVI) described the situation in mid-2006:

As of June 2006, there are close to 30 ongoing trials with preventive HIV vaccine candidates in approximately two dozen countries, with advanced testing now taking place or planned for several candidates. [...] Other Phase I and II studies of preventive HIV vaccines currently under way also stand to significantly inform the field in coming years.[178]

Dr Ethica justifies her actions by claiming that they are necessary[179] to prevent 'disastrous consequences'.[180]

Which leads us back to the first factual claim, namely that the scope, urgency and severity of the HIV/AIDS crisis is comparable, indeed exceeds, that of our TBS. Let us assume, quite conservatively, that Dr Ethica's use of human guinea pigs in trying a promising candidate vaccine would save the scientific world one hundred days of research.[181] In other words, with her experiments, a safe and effective vaccine for HIV/AIDS will be available to the population one hundred days earlier than without them. The annual death toll of around three million means that every day, some eight thousand people die.[182] This means that shortening global research time by two hours would save over 650 people—more than the deadliest terrorist bomb has so far killed. Shortening it by one day would save more than twice as many lives as those lost on 11 September 2001. If Dr Ethica can indeed wipe 100 days off the global research timetable, she will have saved the lives of some 800,000 people—a population which only a large nuclear bomb can destroy.

Grady does note that:

...proving efficacy may set the stage for suggesting radical alternatives in HIV to the normal processes of proving efficacy...Among the suggestions are to recruit volunteers willing to be artificially challenged with live virus; to test death-row inmates; to recruit a susceptible African village to be vaccinated (without telling them it is 'experimental'); not to offer any counselling or education about risk reduction, to test multiple candidates on

---

[178] IAVI website <http://www.iavi.org/viewpage.cfm?aid=12>, accessed 6 April 2007.

[179] At the beginning of the twenty-first century, other means of prevention and cure have proven insufficient to reduce global mortality from AIDS on the scale described here, thus it was widely agreed that, in Grady's words 'The development of a safe and effective vaccine against this virus is an urgent social good and priority, with potentially great benefits for the global society.' See *supra* n 161, 7.

[180] See the discussion *supra*, Ch 3, Section B(2).

[181] This would be true even if the particular trial fails, as in this case time saved on 'dead ends' could then be allocated to more promising candidates.

[182] This figure was used, for instance, by the then UN Secretary General Kofi Annan in the run up to International AIDS Day in 2001: 'Every day more than 8,000 people die of AIDS. Every hour almost 600 people become infected. Every minute a child dies of the virus. Just as life—and death—goes on after September 11, so must we continue our fight against the HIV/AIDS epidemic.' (*idem*, 'No Letting Up on AIDS' *Washington Post* (29 November 2001) A33). The statistics cited *supra*, text accompanying nn 158–160, show that this figure has not changed significantly since.

a large scale now, without further data, in order to obtain answers; or to give up the entire endeavor as too costly and complicated and therefore not practical or worth doing.[183]

But she hastens to add the following:

Although there can be a place for radical approaches to difficult problems, none of these suggestions is an acceptable solution because each of them shows profound disrespect for the communities and individuals who would be involved in the research.[184]

Nor have any of the 'radical approaches' been accepted or even seriously considered, let alone implemented—no real-life Dr Ethicas have emerged. By and large, ethical requirements have been adhered to during vaccine tests, and there certainly have been no deliberate or explicit attempt to waive the requirement of 'informed consent'.[185] Campaigners for the development of anti-HIV/AIDS vaccines have been tirelessly calling for more resources to be allocated and more efforts to be made by governments, corporations and individuals to research into vaccines and cures for HIV/AIDS. An IAVI petition reads, *inter alia*:

We call for support of human trials of vaccines, and we salute trial volunteers, the unsung heroes of vaccine development.[186]

However, I am not aware of any organization calling on governments or on the pharmaceutical industry to waive the requirement of 'informed consent' in vaccine trials. In fact the opposite is true. A case in point were the regional workshops sponsored by UNAIDS in Brazil, Thailand and Uganda—all 'developing' countries (and regions) with sizeable HIV/AIDS problems, which took place in 1998, and discussed 'ethical issues in preventative HIV vaccine trials'. Most participants were local and included 'lawyers, activists, social scientists, ethicists, vaccine scientists, epidemiologists, people working in nongovernmental organizations (NGOs), people living with HIV/AIDS, and people working in health policy'.[187]

---

[183] Grady, *supra* n 161, 107. See also Kerns' account of allegations regarding early trials on HIV vaccines, *supra* n 156, Ch 16(2). Kerns adds that if any allegations were found to have merit, the research concerned 'would then be out of business'.

[184] *Ibid.*

[185] Professor Steven Hale of Georgia Perimeter College, Georgia, USA, has compiled a website which he entitled 'Resources on Nonconsensual Human Experimentation' <http://www.gpc.edu/~shale/humanities/composition/assignments/experiment.html>, accessed 25 October 2007—it includes no links specifically devoted to experiments on vaccines or cures for HIV/AIDS. I reiterate that I am not addressing here circumvention attempts by pharmaceutical companies for profit maximizing, which are carried out (if they are) surreptitiously and are not justified on moral grounds. See *supra* n 159.

[186] IAVI petition, prepared for presentation at the XIV International AIDS Conference, July 2002 in Barcelona <http://www.iavi.org/callforaction/>, accessed 10 January 2002.

[187] The workshops took place in April 1998. For the full report see *UNAIDS Sponsored Regional Workshops to Discuss Ethical Issues in Preventative HIV Vaccine Trials: UNAIDS Report*, UNAIDS/00.036 E (Geneva, September 2000). The report is also available on <http://data.unaids.org/Publications/IRC-pub04/una00-36_en.pdf>, accessed 18 October 2007. The quotation is from the introduction.

All three workshops reported a 'consensus' to the effect that '[n]othing can substitute for individual informed consent'.[188]

In short there is a dearth, perhaps indeed an *absence* of either ethicists calling for 'informed consent' to be waived during trials of vaccines of HIV/AIDS, or researchers waiving such consent in practice. There is, in other words, a wall-to-wall absolutist prohibition on waiving 'informed consent' whatever the consequences, these being not imagined or potential but a real, unfolding, horrendous catastrophe.

Before inferring any 'slippery surface' conclusions from the above, the minimal absolutist should counter arguments that the HIV/AIDS vaccine situation and the TBS are different in at least two crucial aspects.

One such argument could be that whereas Vicious is clearly the cause of the danger to be averted by Ethica torturing him, Dr Ethica would be harming innocent people.

My response is, first, that this is not an anti-absolutist argument—it amounts to claiming that certain things must never be done to *innocent* persons, whatever the consequences—which is, of course, an *absolutist* position. The anti-absolutist position is, it will be recalled, that some consequences are so very bad (or, rather, very bad for so many) that their prevention justifies resorting to *any* means (short of those likely to cause bad consequences in comparable quantities), obviously including harming the innocent.[189] The possibility of limiting the absolutist prohibition to harming the innocent, which would still allow torturing Vicious in our TBS, will be discussed below.[190] Here, at any rate, the issue could be averted if Dr Ethica were to adopt one of the 'radical approaches' and choose her human guinea pigs from among guilty persons—say 'death-row inmates'—convicted murderers, rapists etc, or possibly from among pimps who knowingly exploit HIV-positive prostitutes and do not provide them with condoms—in which case she would be using those *materially* guilty of the spread of the disease in order to save its victims.[191]

Another argument might be that we risk losing much more by trying vaccines for HIV on non-consenting human subjects than by torturing Vicious in a TBS, as more persons must of necessity be involved in the former case, both as researchers and as subjects; long-established, value-maximizing ethical standards be compromised etc, so that even if utility is maximized in the short run, great dangers

---

[188] The words of the report of the workshop in Brazil, *ibid*, 10. See similarly under 'consensus' in the report of the workshops in Thailand, 18, and in Uganda, 25–6.

[189] See *supra* n 133 and accompanying text.

[190] Chapter 5, Section A.

[191] Such behaviour would not satisfy the 'highly subjective *mens rea*' justification for criminalization laid down by Janet Dine and Bob Watt, which requires that causing HIV infection be actually the aim of the agent, rather than a mere result, albeit a foreseeable one, of his actions. It might, however, reach the much lower threshold for their 'public health' justification of 'public nuisance' criminalization at common law. See J Dine and B Watt, 'The Transmission of Disease during Consensual Sexual Activity and the Concept of Associative Autonomy' [1998] 4 *Web JCLI* <http://webjcli.ncl.ac.uk/1998/issue4/watt4.html>, accessed 12 October 2001.

may lurk in the longer run, or, to use James Bailey's words, '[o]ur suspicions of forthcoming exploitation should be raised'.[192] Similar claims, however, could be made regarding torture—certainly in real-life situations, namely in Bailey's land of 'Imperfectia', (which is the real world, discussed in Part II below), and I did emphasize at the outset of this discussion of a 'pure, private TBS' that 'we do not expect her [Ethica], with the time-bomb ticking away, to make complex long-term and wide-ranging moral considerations'.[193] With 8,000 people dying every day, Dr Ethica should similarly be exempt from making such considerations, and certain countries might claim that unless they can stop the pandemic, there will be no long-term for them at all.

The argument here is, in 'slippery surface' terms, that just as the anti-minimal-absolutist would tell Ethica: 'thousands will surely die unless you torture', so s/he must tell Dr Ethica, at the beginning of the twenty-first century: 'thousands will surely die unless you experiment on non-consenting humans.' Both statements are factually true—one within the term of our scenario, the other in actual reality. And yet, as noted, and in stark contrast to the debate surrounding the TBS case, the invocation of such facts as justification for waiving 'informed consent' is virtually absent from both professional and lay debates on the ethics of developing a vaccine for HIV.

There are certainly differences between a TBS and the HIV/AIDS pandemic. These are not, however, to be found in the degrees of 'disastrousness' of the consequences, nor in the urgency of the need to prevent them, nor yet in the potential benefit of exploiting humans for such prevention.

Two related notes will now be made. First, even in the face of terrorist threats of humongous proportions, that of biological warfare, the US FDA preferred, in May 2002, to approve the use of antidotes to substances such as smallpox or nerve gas without testing them first on humans as to their efficacy, thus in effect waving phases II and III of experiments, over waiving the ethical requirement of 'informed consent', say, through 'volunteering' detained *al-Qa'idah* suspects for those experiments.[194]

Secondly, Jean Maria Arrigo shows that the 'slippery surface' reverse of the situation described here is also true, namely that allowing torture and allowing experimentation on humans go hand in hand, in theory but also in practice:

Another unintended consequence of biomedical research on torture is the opportunity for secret, illegal research on human subjects for other purposes. Administrators of

---

[192] JW Bailey, *Utilitarianism, Institutions and Justice* (New York: OUP, 1997) 152.
[193] *Supra*, Ch 1, Section B.
[194] A Pollack and WJ Broad, 'Bioterrorism: Anti-Terror Drugs Get Test Shortcut' *New York Times* (31 May 2002). The article explains the decision, *inter alia*, by the following: 'The F.D.A. could allow the use of unproven drugs as experiments. But that requires informed consent of each person treated, which might be hard to obtain in an emergency after a biological or chemical attack, Dr. Woodcock [of the FDA] said. The new rule sprang in part from a controversy that arose when the military tried to have the informed consent rule waived so it could give botulism vaccine and a nerve gas antidote to soldiers in the Persian Gulf war.'

torture interrogation programs cannot prevent alternative uses by their own biomedical scientists, who have negotiating power over valuable resources. Historically, government-sponsored ethics investigations of the CIA's mind control Project MKULTRA and the Department of Energy's radiation studies exposed extraneous, excessive, and criminal human subjects research.[195]

The minimal absolutist position is consistent in its refusal—its *total* refusal—to 'show profound disrespect for…communities and individuals',[196] namely, in Kant's terms, to turn humans—*any* humans—into mere tools, however useful and beneficial that may prove to be. This refusal may be a loose common denominator for the minimal absolutist stand not only in these two cases but also in the case of torturing a baby to death for fun, punishing by cruel death, and other 'no-go' areas. 'Loose', however, must be the operative word here, as a full discussion of criteria for minimal absolutist prohibitions is beyond the scope of this study.

***

It would clearly be a logical fallacy (or in Moore's terms a 'naturalistic fallacy'[197]) to infer from the mere fact that some acts are never performed that they *should* never be. However, that fact, especially taken within the wide modern, democratic and international contexts in which such minimalist absolute prohibitions are applied, does go some way towards undermining a view of absolutism as being the exclusive domain of fanatical, uncaring and inhumane individuals, groups or governments. In addition, their discussion shows that in certain circumstances it is actually the anti-absolutists who might be accused of the same.

4. Recapitulating: the minimal absolutist arguments generally

Minimal absolutism is the 'bare-boned' moral view that certain acts must never be performed, whatever the consequences. The arguments presented so far have sought to counter the principled attack by anti-absolutists on this view.

One does not need to oppose minimal absolutism to acknowledge that absolutist positions may be very dangerous. They may indeed involve the fanaticism, indefensible rigidity or inhumanity that critics accuse absolutists of having. Both philosophical and real-life cases discussed here have shown that even promising putative absolute prohibitions, including on lying, breaking promises and killing, while attractive in pure theory, may be problematic and even doubtful when applied to specific, extreme circumstances.

---

[195] JM Arrigo, 'A Utilitarian Argument Against Torture Interrogation of Terrorists' 10(3) *Science and Engineering Ethics* 543 (2004) 552.

[196] Grady, *supra* n 161.

[197] Moore, *supra* n 46, Ch 3.

It may be at least as dangerous, however, to reject absolute prohibitions on *any* act whatsoever. The discussion has exposed the following dangers, or weaknesses, of the anti-absolutist view:

- *Justifying atrocities*: While anti-absolutist views may, in certain, immediate circumstances,[198] enable the prevention of catastrophes which minimal absolutists would not, the former would actually *commit*, or justify the commission, of the worst atrocities, even on a large scale (such as mass-murder), provided this was the only way to prevent a horrendous catastrophe (such as murder on an even larger scale). In other words, the kind of disaster which a minimal absolutist may *allow* to happen, by refusing to perform certain acts (although they would always oppose atrocities), could actually be the intended, desired and justified result of an anti-absolutist's actions, for the sake of avoiding a (much) greater disaster.

- *Moral enslavement:* In the face of a looming catastrophe, the anti-absolutist loses his or her freedom to make a moral choice. A terrorist such as Vicious, or any monstrosity—human or otherwise—may, through the threat of a disaster (such as by planting a bomb) or the promise of averting one (such as finding a vaccine for HIV/AIDS or distracting murderous paedophiles) actually dictate what the moral thing to do—or at least what the morally justifiable thing to do—must be. In extreme situations, the anti-absolutist is thus a slave to the whims of a moral monster, precisely *because* the latter is one.

- *Moral corruption:* A principled anti-absolutist must admit every single act, including the worst atrocities imaginable, into moral consideration. Most of us may want to steer away from a person who weighs the pros and cons of torturing our children, murdering our parents, raping our partners and the like, as we may find their thought processes revolting, if not threatening, and may find their insistence that they would only resort to such actions in extremely rare situations a less than satisfactory reassurance.

Minimal absolutism does not purport to create a general theory, or a system of absolute prohibitions, such as 'mortal sins' or 'categorical imperatives', and this may save it from some of the accusations of general fanaticism and rigidity. To

---

[198] It could be argued that minimal absolutist persons, societies or international systems are less likely to produce 'horrendous catastrophes' in the first place than non-absolutist ones. In the words of Alan Donagan 'While it repudiates escape clauses by which its precepts may be violated if the consequences are "bad enough," traditional moral theory does not concede that the consequences of generally accepting such an escape clause would be better than those of rejecting it' *idem, The Theory of Morality* (Chicago: University of Chicago Press, 1977) 207.

This could be the kind of ironic twist which would justify absolutism on consequentialist grounds, and which Sidgwick may have approved of, at least in a society not composed wholly of 'enlightened utilitarians' (see *supra* n 29, Book IV, Ch 5, §§2–4), and seems to be similarly reflected in GE Moore's brand of 'utilitarian rule-absolutism'. The latter states that '…though we may be sure that there are cases where the rule should be broken, we can never know which those cases are, and ought, therefore, never to break it' (*supra* n 46, Ch 5, para 99, 162–3).

counter such accusations further, three real-life absolute prohibition have been discussed—on the death penalty for minor offences, on punishment by torturous death and on waiving 'informed consent' in clinical trials of new HIV/AIDS vaccines.

Even the most ardent supporters of the death penalty in the West do not call for the reintroduction of the death penalty for pickpocketing or of torturous methods of execution, not even for 'a Hitler or a Stalin'—nor for a Bin Laden. Even members of communities which have suffered immensely from the HIV/AIDS pandemic, and are likely to suffer much more (as communities and, for each member, possibly as an individual) do not call for ethical 'shortcuts' that would save the lives of many thousands, or millions—not even in a year like 2007, when the AIDS death toll on any single day was more than double the number of victims of terrorism on 11 September 2001.

The principled anti-absolutists are on a slippery surface. For their view to hold, they would need to call for the reintroduction into the law-books of tortuous punishments, just in case (or once) someone far worse than Hitler or Stalin needs to be punished or deterred; they would need to call for people (possibly certain criminals) to be coerced into participating in HIV vaccine tests; they would need to be prepared to justify actions such as the torture of a baby to death for fun, rape, murder, racism, slavery, the use of weapons of mass destruction, bombing civilians and, of course, acts of terrorism—you name it, the principled anti-absolutist must justify it, providing that the gap between the harm caused by such acts and that which they seek to prevent is wide enough.

Such a morality, the minimal absolutists would argue, is one disastrous consequence only *they* can prevent.

5. Justifying terrorism—the anti-absolutist's 'to torture or not to torture' dilemma

All of this leads to an additional dilemma which Ethica would face if she chooses to adopt anti-absolutism: she cannot rule out the possibility that Vicious' planned terrorist act is a *moral* one, in what would then be her terms. Moral justifications for terrorism very seldom, if ever, point to the terrorist attacks being good in themselves, regardless of context. Thus for the leader of the HAMAS movement in Palestine in early 2003, Sheikh Ahmad Yassin, who openly supported terrorist attacks (within the 'hard-core of settled meaning' used here) by his movement, '[i]t is a cause of true sorrow...if children are killed' in such attacks.[199] Rather, it is the extreme circumstances, the need to confront, prevent or deter a greater evil that is almost invariably relied upon. The 'military' wing of HAMAS, ''Izz al-Din al-Qassam Brigades', justified its terrorist operations in terms of maintaining 'a

---

[199] J Passow, 'Warlord of the Jihad' *The Sunday Times Magazine* (26 January 2003) 25–29, 27. Yassin goes on to say: 'Let them stop killing our children, and then we'll stop killing theirs' (*ibid*).

balance of deterrence' with Israel. Thus an article posted on the 'Brigades'' web-site at the end of May 2002 stated, *inter alia*, the following:

The balance of deterrence called for by the HAMAS movement necessitates powerful retaliation for the [Israeli] Occupation's crimes and massacres which do not distinguish between civilians, combatants, old men, women and infants, whose blood is still flowing. The best retaliation for the enemy's strikes against all our towns and the demolition of our homes is striking deep into their territory, reaching them and making them taste their own medicine. [...] the issue does not essentially need explication or proof, as the heroes of the Resistance who blow their own bodies and attain martyrdom strive to enable the Palestinian People to live honourably, and in doing so they serve the most noble of national causes...[200]

'Deterrence' could reasonably mean, in anti-absolutist terms, 'preventing greater evil'—for which suicide bombing could be the only means available to the terrorist, just as torture is the only one available to Ethica. 'Enabling the Palestinian People to live honourably' may be interpreted as promoting a situation where no further blood of 'civilians...old men, women and infants' is spilled on either side.[201]

Acts of terrorism have also been openly justified as part of a state's war against 'terrorists'. Roger Trinquier, outlining his 'French view of counterinsurgency', says the following on the proper management of 'maquis actions', ie the operation of local guerrilla units loyal to the 'counterinsurgency' forces in 'enemy territory' (when 'terrorists' have bases in neighbouring countries):

Maquis action begins immediately with the dismantling of the local administration. The maquis leader...establishes himself as the ultimate authority in this area and puts an end to any action of the local police or gendarmerie that interferes with his activity. A few well-calculated *acts of sabotage and terrorism* will then compel any reluctant citizens to give the required cooperation.[202] [Emphasis added.]

As Barak Cohen sums up this point, 'the very rationale used to justify torture, *mutatis mutandis*, justifies terrorism'.[203] If the death of the innocent civilians

---

[200] 'Martyrdom-Seeking Operations between Israeli Conspiracies and Palestinian Successes' [Arabic] 'Izz al-Din al-Qassam Brigades website <http://www.qassam.net/tagrer/taqreer2002/05_2002/taqree25_05_02.htm>, accessed 31 May 2002. The term 'martyrdom-seeking operations' (*amaliyyat istishhadiyyah*) refers mostly to what are known in the West as 'suicide bombings'. A statement by the 'Brigades' following a terrorist attack which killed 21 people and injured about 120 on 1 June 2001 similarly spoke of 'attaining a balance of deterrence and terror'. See <http://www.qassam.org/byanat/byanat2001/04_06_2001.htm>, accessed 18 February 2002.

[201] In terms not acceptable to most Israelis, ie the establishment of an orthodox Islamic state throughout Palestine/Israel, but the political issue is not the point here.

[202] R Trinquier, *Modern Warfare: A French View of Counterinsurgency*, trans Daniel Lee (London: Pall Mall Press, 1964) 108. Trinquier uses the term 'terrorists' to denote the 'enemy' throughout the book. Naturally, Trinquier also supports the torture of 'terrorists', (see *infra* n 218 and accompanying text) and having served under General Jacques Massu during the 'Battle of Algiers' in 1956–7, actually practised what he preached.

[203] B Cohen, 'Democracy and the Mis-Rule of Law: The Israeli Legal System's Failure to Prevent Torture in the Occupied Territories' 12 *Ind Int'l & Comp L Rev* 75 (2001) 90.

from V's bomb can prevent the death of a much greater number (or arguably even a marginally greater number) of innocent civilians, then an anti-absolutist E must not only refrain from torturing V, she must not do *anything at all* that could prevent the bomb from exploding, even if she does know where it was planted and how to defuse it. Under this view she may, conceivably, go as far as to help V in carrying out his greater-catastrophe-preventing act. Otherwise logically-consistent anti-absolutists must brand her just as 'cold hearted' or 'fanatical'[204] as if she were to refuse torturing V in our original scenario.

***

Anti-absolutism slides on a slippery surface that takes it to places where I doubt most of its proponents would want to find themselves, both regarding fantastic scenarios and real-life situations depicted here. And as shown, the purely theoretical affects real life, even everyday life. In contrast, I submit, it could reasonably be claimed, following the discussion here, that minimal absolutism is a viable position logically and is implemented in practice. This, I believe, is sufficient to enable us to turn now and examine the question of whether, accepting that some acts must be prohibited absolutely, torture should be one such act.

---

[204] See *supra* nn 109–115. And see for this point *infra*, Ch 5, Section E.

5

The Minimal Absolutist Approach II: Arguments for an Absolute Prohibition on Torture

And when a man sees that the God in himself is the same God in all that is, he hurts not himself by hurting others: then he goes indeed to the highest Path.

The Bhagavad Gita, Ch 13, § 28[205]

A. Introduction

Much has been written about the evils of torture, but the near-consensus about such evils, and the fact there is little that I can add to the considerable literature in this regard[206] render detailed recounting unnecessary. But here I need to establish that torture is evil enough to warrant a place among the 'one or more' acts which, minimal absolutism contends, must never be performed, not even to prevent a horrendous catastrophe.

I will attempt to do this through logical and 'slippery surface' arguments backed by illustrations, regarding each of the components of Ethica's situation and moral predicament. These are the act itself and the three 'categories' of persons involved, namely torturing; the torturer (Ethica); the tortured (Vicious); and his would-be victims—the innocent civilians.

B. The Act—Torture

There is little need to convince most of us (including all theorists mentioned here) that torture is wrong, at least in the vast majority of circumstances, and this has

---

[205] *The Bhagavad Gita*, trans Huan Mascaró (London: Penguin Books, 1962).

[206] Which includes human rights reports, court cases and personal accounts too numerous to list here, as well as most of the anti-torture literature cited above and below. For general works see eg P DuBois, *Torture and Truth* (New York: Routledge, 1991); D Luban, 'Liberalism, Torture, and the Ticking Bomb' 91 *Virginia L Rev* 1425 (2005); R Maran, *Torture: the Role of Ideology in the French-Algerian* War (New York: Praeger, 1989); K Millett, *The Politics of Cruelty: An essay on the literature of political imprisonment* (London: Penguin Books, 1995); El Scarry, *The Body in Pain* (New York: OUP, 1985) Ch 1; Videl-Naquet, *supra* n 49.

been assumed here as a given.[207] What we are looking for now is, rather, a more elusive property—that which makes it an *absolute* evil, namely not just wrong, but so wrong that it must never be done, not even when torturing an evil man is the only way to save many innocent lives that he intended to take.

I propose, following the minimal absolutist argument so far, that torturing a person is an absolutely evil act because it is both an evil act and an absolute one. That torture is evil is, as stated, a given here. It is also virtually undisputed; this near-consensus is manifested, for instance, by the absolutist prohibition of torturous executions in the West, discussed above, which entails that punishment by torture is not to be meted out even to 'a Hitler or a Stalin',[208] and the fact that pro-torture ethicists insist that in a TBS, torture must cease the minute the life-saving information has been provided[209]—the disagreement is only on whether torture could sometimes be a *necessary*, or lesser, evil. A view that torture is good, either intrinsically or 'only' to the extent that it is not overweighed by a greater good, may logically be put forward, but such view would be too far removed from the kind of moral assumptions at the basis of this discussion to make a meaningful dialogue with those holding it possible.

The act of torturing is absolute, in that it epitomizes, and in fact contains every and *any* harm that one person can inflict upon another; this point is succinctly illustrated in Aristophanes' *Frogs*: when Xanthias proposes that 'his slave' (who is, actually, Dionysus) be tortured, and is asked what he has in mind, he replies: 'Why, anything!'[210] This is precisely what, by justifying the torture of a person, we justify—doing absolutely anything unto him or her. No act of torment is so harmful, painful or cruel as to go beyond the boundaries of torture, as torture knows no such boundaries. This point will be illustrated below.

This quality of 'absoluteness' inherent in the view justifying torture could, regarding a TBS, be shown by a simple logical formula:

Moral justification for torture in a TBS (1): In a TBS, ie where torturing V is the only means of preventing a bomb exploding and causing death, injury and grief to many innocent civilians (IC),
If:

(a) torturing a person, V, in a TBS is justified as a 'hugely lesser evil,' in view of the enormous gap between the amount of suffering that would be incurred by

---

[207] See *supra*, Ch 1, Section C.

[208] *Supra* nn 149–150 and accompanying text.

[209] See eg Bentham, 'Of Torture', *Bentham Manuscripts, University College London* 46/63–70, reprinted by Twining and Twining, *supra* n 45, 308–320, 311; Shue, *supra* n 4, 134. This position often takes the form of the argument that the tortured is not totally helpless, as he can stop the torture at any time by providing the information. See eg KE Himma, 'Assessing the Prohibition Against Torture' in SP Lee (ed), *Intervention, Terrorism, and Torture: Contemporary Challenges to Just War Theory* (Dordrecht: Springer, 2007) 235–248, 242.

[210] Aristophanes, 'Frogs' (ca 405 BC), trans RH Webb in M Hadas (ed), *The Complete Plays of Aristophanes* (New York: Bantam Books, 1962) 366–415, 389. Xanthias goes on to name suggested methods, including 'the wheel, the whip…skin him alive!' He subsequently adds: 'No lashing with a leek or onion top!' but this is not a morally-induced qualification—Xanthias only wishes to avoid bringing tears to his own eyes.

V, if tortured, on the one hand, and by the IC, if the bomb were to explode, on the other;

and

(b) no amount of suffering by V, a single person, could bridge, or even significantly reduce, that gap;[211]

it follows inevitably that:

(c) any means of torturing V, causing him any amount of suffering, in a TBS is justified, provided that it is aimed solely[212] at obtaining the life-saving information.

In other words, torture in a TBS provides the case *par excellence* for the general argument, made earlier in this Part, that an anti-absolutist must justify committing the worst atrocities, as long as this is done to prevent atrocities befalling a much larger number of persons. Once accepted, however, this strength-in-numbers argument, applied to torture in a TBS, weakens, indeed nullifies, any reservations we may have to the use of *any* means of torture, provided it produces the desired results. In 1972, writing a minority report within the report of a British commission of enquiry set to examine the legality (and for that matter morality) of 'moderate' physical and psychological techniques of interrogation used by British forces against suspected terrorist detainees in Northern Ireland during the previous year, Lord Gardiner made this point forcefully:

If it is to be made legal to employ methods not now legal against a man whom the police believe to have, but who may not have, information which the police desire to obtain, I, like many of our witnesses, have searched for, but have been unable to find, either in logic or in morals, any limit to the degree of ill-treatment to be legalised. The only logical limit to the degree of ill-treatment to be legalised would appear to be whatever degree of ill treatment proves to be necessary to get the information out of him, which would include, if necessary, extreme torture.[213]

Richard A Posner, a supporter of torture in a TBS, echoes Lord Gardiner's assessment of the choice on hand, arguing that in such a situation, 'as much pressure as it takes' should be allowed—and applied.[214] Even the idea of starting with relatively moderate means and escalating the torture gradually[215] may,

---

[211] See *supra*, Ch 2, Section A.

[212] This wording is used exclude purely sadistic torture excessive of the necessary.

[213] *Report of the Committee of Privy Counsellors appointed to consider authorized procedures for the interrogation of persons suspected of terrorism*, Cmmd No 4901 (Lord Parker of Waddington, Chairman, 1972), para 20(2) of the minority report. See the discussion in Part III, Ch 16.

[214] R Posner, *supra* n 54, 293. M Bagaric and J Clarke similarly support the view that in a TBS '*all* means should be used to extract the information' (emphasis added). See *idem*, 'Not Enough Official Torture in the World? The Circumstances in which Torture is Morally Justifiable' 39 *U of San Francisco L Rev* 581 (2005) 583–4.

[215] See eg Bentham, *supra* n 209, 314 ('Rule 7'). In an Israeli court case, the State, defending regulations for applying means of interrogation including what it called 'a moderate measure of

with the bomb ticking away (or the suicide bomber getting ever closer to his target), be applied for a brief time only, beyond which it may prove an unaffordable luxury.

Justifying torture in a TBS thus sets the scene for legitimizing the worst imaginable—and unimaginable—things one human being can inflict upon another. Three examples will now be discussed in the abstract (but as will be seen later, they are unfortunately far from being divorced from reality).

First, the debate around whether torture is less or more wrong, morally, than murder[216] is irrelevant here: while the death of Vicious before he discloses the whereabouts of his ticking bomb would mean a catastrophic failure for Ethica, his death *following* such disclosure would be no more than an extremely regrettable accident in an otherwise successful operation. As an evil, his death too would pale, under the torture-justifying view, in comparison to the amount of deaths and injuries thus prevented. The methods she would use may therefore be ultimately lethal, provided that death does not precede disclosure. That death under torture in a TBS is not unforeseeable is acknowledged, for instance, by Bagaric and Julie Clarke.[217] On a much less theoretical level, Trinquier argues that when undergoing interrogation, a terrorist refusing to give 'the information requested... must face the suffering, and perhaps the death he has heretofore managed to avoid'.[218]

A second example is that of rape. Rape is clearly one of the worst acts imaginable. However, E, searching for the most efficient ways of getting V to talk, might find the option of raping him quite attractive. Carried out (apologies) properly, rape would combine low-intensity physical pain—thus avoiding the dangers of

---

physical pressure' stated the following: '...the new regulations made clear that the interrogator must act gradually, namely, he must first conduct the interrogation without applying exceptional measures. Only once the interrogator is convinced that without applying measures enumerated in these regulations, the required information cannot be obtained, would he be allowed to apply during interrogation an exceptional measure of pressure detailed within the regulations' (HCJ 2581/91 *Murad 'Adnan Salahat and the Public Committee Against Torture in Israel v The Government of Israel et al*, Affidavit by Head of the GSS, 25 April 1993, para 17). It should be noted that the regulations and guidelines in question concerned the interrogation of 'terrorists' in a much wider array of situations than a TBS. See Part III, Ch 12.

[216] Amihud Gil'ad, who advocates an absolutist prohibition on torture, nevertheless grades it second to murder: 'There is a hierarchy among moral imperatives, and the most binding one is: 'thou shalt not murder!' Within this hierarchy I would place below it, in second place, the prohibition on torture' (*idem*, 'An Absolute Moral Imperative: Torturing is Prohibited' [Hebrew] 4 *Mishpat u-Mimshal* 425 (1998), 427).

In contrast, Sheleff calls the chapter in his book where he discusses, *inter alia*, torture (Ch 11 of *Ultimate Penalties*, *supra* n 50), 'Worse than Death'. Fr Heinz Hunke and Justin Ellis, writing on torture by South African forces during their war in Namibia in the late 1970s, state the following: 'Torture is worse than killing: it is the temporary annihilation of a human person in his/her uniqueness as a person' (*idem*, *Torture—a Cancer in Our Society* (London: the Catholic Institute for International Relations and the British Council of Churches, 1978) 11).

See also F Hampson, 'Torture' in PB Clarke and A Linzey (eds), *Dictionary of Ethics, Theology and Society* (London and New York: Routledge, 1996) 829–831, *passim*; Shue, *supra* n 4, 125–6.

[217] Bagaric and Clarke, *supra* n 214, 584.

[218] Trinquier, *supra* n 202, 21–2.

premature loss of consciousness or sanity and death, inherent in harsh physical methods—with intense humiliation, which is a powerful tool for breaking a person's will. Ideally, stripping him, placing him in the right position and similarly ominous measures—perhaps of the type used in Abu Ghraib (discussed in the following Parts), may suffice to convince V to talk. The disgust that the reader would probably feel (and the writer certainly does) at this kind of reasoning, let alone this kind of interrogational technique, is what this section aims at: to show, by means of evocation: the depth of inhumanity to which those who justify torture in a TBS must, by the very logic of their justification (to avoid the alternative, 'blind and vulgar humanity'[219]) be prepared to sink.

But what, thirdly, about the possibility of torturing V by threatening to torture, or actually torturing, an innocent person he deeply cares for?[220] Supposing that V, evil man that he is, took his young daughter with him on his deadly mission, to avoid suspicion,[221] and she too is now under E's control. Supposing also that E knows that torturing V directly is far less likely to produce results, as he is very tough and determined, and nothing but extremely painful measures which would run a high risk of death or loss of consciousness or sanity would break him.[222] She also knows, however, that V genuinely cares for his daughter. Like rape, torturing the daughter—and torturing V by torturing her—combine the advantages of great effectiveness with a low-level risk of 'losing' V prematurely.

In such a situation, the anti-absolutist view *dictates* that torturing the daughter is justified—again, no amount of pain that this double-torture may produce can be more than a quantitative fraction of the pain that dozens, or hundreds of dead and wounded men, women and children and their close relatives would suffer should V's bomb explode.

---

[219] Bentham, *supra*, text accompanying n 45.

[220] It should be stressed that this, and what follows, are not a journey down the 'slippery slope'—the scenarios evoked remain squarely within the parameters of the basic 'quantity of suffering gap'—justification for torture in a TBS, attacking its *qualitative* value, rather than trying to narrow it. They are thus strictly of the 'slippery surface' type. In contrast, arguments that proponents of torture in a TBS must be ready to justify the torture of 10, 20 or 30 persons to save 40 would have had the effect of narrowing that very quantitative gap, changing, or eroding the abovementioned parameters and thus constituting consequentialist, or 'slippery slope' type, arguments. To avoid approaching any 'grey areas' between the two types of argument, I will strictly confine myself here to a maximum of three people, including V himself and Ethica (to allow for the suffering she may undergo, either through having to torture others, or for allowing V to torture her, discussed below) being used to induce him to talk—the reader should contrast their suffering with that of dozens, hundreds or thousands of IC, if the bomb were to explode. For a discussion of 'slippery slope' and 'slippery surface' arguments see *supra*, Ch 4, Section C(1).

[221] This point is made by Luban, *supra* n 206, 1144. Alistair Horne recounts how on 30 September 1956, an Algerian member of the FLN, Samia Lakhari, went to place a bomb in a cafeteria frequented by European students in Algiers accompanied by her mother. See *idem, A Savage War of Peace: Algeria 1954–1962* (London: Papermac 1987) 186.

[222] For this point see Sheleff, 'The Need to Defend the Honest Truth' *supra* n 50, 473. And see Part II, Ch 9, Section D(1)(d) for examples of detainees resisting torture, even unto death.

In other words, the anti-absolutist formula is in fact wider in application than our initial wording may suggest. We should now revise it, by way of clarification, as follows:

Moral justification for torture in a TBS (2): In a TBS, ie where torturing V is the only means of preventing a bomb exploding and causing death, injury and grief to many innocent civilians (IC),

If,

(a) torturing a person, V, in a TBS is justified as a 'hugely lesser evil', in view of the enormous gap between the amount of suffering that would be incurred by V (and another person), if tortured, on the one hand, and by the IC, if the bomb were to explode, on the other;

and

(b) no amount of suffering by any one or two persons could bridge, or even significantly reduce, that gap;

it follows inevitably that

(c) any means of torture, causing V and any other person (such as his innocent beloved one) any amount of suffering in a TBS is justified, provided that the torture of both is aimed solely at obtaining the life-saving information.

1. Torturing the innocent—beyond the (consequentialist) pale?

Some may find the above point hard to digest. Many of those intuitively supportive of torture in a TBS may feel that it is the evil nature of this person (and/or his act), his callous readiness to murder and injure a great number of innocent people, that allows us to perform an otherwise abominable act against him. The idea, in this context, of us harming an innocent person seems almost self-contradictory. Should the moral approach not combine a permission to torture the terrorist in a TBS with an absolute, whatever-the-consequences prohibition on harming the innocent? Put differently, would it not be logical to allow the use of any means whatsoever to save the innocent from harm, with the exception of harming the innocent?

There is no denying that the innocence of the person potentially at the receiving end of a violent act must be a formidable moral barrier against performing it. However, innocence cannot shield V's daughter from those who would torture her father: this is due to the fact that the only justifications for V's torture, within what I have defined as our paradigmatic 'moral convictions',[223] are consequentialist, that is, essentially and ultimately *quantitative*. We have seen, in

---

[223] *Supra*, Ch 1, Section C.

Chapter 3, that theorists supporting such torture have either been consequentialists or else non-consequentialists who abandoned, within that limited context,
their principled positions and adopted consequentialist, pain-minimizing moral
reasoning.

An argument allowing the torture of a 'guilty' person but not of an innocent
one cannot rest on consequentialist reasoning—at least not in extreme situations
where 'disastrous consequences' are at stake. As noted, one could go outside the
aforementioned 'moral convictions' and claim that torturing a person is *not* morally wrong at all, not even *prima facie* wrong, but in this case there could be nothing wrong with torturing an innocent person either.

Theories which suggest levels of moral reasoning, or more complex consequentialist reasoning, such as Hare's 'intuitive' and 'critical' levels,[224] or
Mackie's 'rule-right-duty-disposition utilitarianism'[225] cannot be of much use
to V's daughter either, as these theories (beyond considerable differences) are,
again, consequentialist—at least where it counts for our purposes. Both these
theories, and similar ones,[226] may approve of, or even advocate, instilling a
moral ban on torture—or maybe only the torture of the innocent—in people's
minds, and promulgating such a ban in laws. This may mean that Ethica would
be excused if she were to act 'intuitively' (in Hare's sense) in deference to the ban
and not torture Vicious, or if she tortured him but not his daughter. However,
our concern here is with whether it would be *justifiable* for her to torture either
of them, and this question must be answered on Hare's second level, that of
'critical moral thinking' (ie by the 'archangel' rather than the 'prole'), regarding
which Hare states the following:

> ...the logical apparatus of universal prescriptivism, if we understand what we are say-
> ing when we make moral judgments, will lead us in critical thinking (without relying
> on any substantial moral intuitions) to make judgements which are the same as a careful
> act-utilitarian would make.[227]

---

[224] See eg RM Hare, *Moral Thinking: Its Levels, Method, and Point* (Oxford: Clarendon, 1981)
and more recently his *Sorting Out Ethics* (Oxford: Clarendon Press, 1997), especially chs 1, 7 and 8,
and the very brief elaboration below.

[225] See especially his *Ethics: Inventing Right and Wrong*, *supra* n 31. The quotation is from p 200.
Mackie is, essentially, an ethical 'realist', claiming that there in fact is no intrinsic moral right or
wrong. He therefore rejects both classical utilitarianism and Kantianism, proposing instead an
all-round 'utilitarianism' which weighs into its calculus factors such as special interests or relations, rights and virtues. As shown above (*supra* n 112 and accompanying text) and immediately
below, his anti-absolutist 'bottom line' renders him, for our limited purposes, indistinguishable
from other supporters of torture in a TBS.

[226] Of the 'rule-utilitarian' or 'rule-consequentialist' variety, ie those proposing, like John
Austin, that 'Utility should be the test of our conduct, ultimately, but not immediately: the immediate test of the rules to which our conduct would conform, but not the immediate test of specific or individual actions. Our rules would be fashioned on utility; our conduct, on our rules'
(*supra* n 57, 49, and see the other sources there). This prescription is not, according to most rule-
consequentialists, an absolute one.

[227] Hare, *Moral Thinking...*, *supra* n 224, 42–3. For the concepts of 'the archangel and the
prole' see Ch 3.

As a 'careful act-utilitarian', Hare believes that moral absolutism leads to impasse in sorting out moral conflicts[228] and that 'the implications of consistent absolutism are unacceptable'.[229]

Mackie similarly argues that:

The most plausible absolute prohibitions must be violated where strict adherence to them would result in disaster.[230]

V's daughter cannot, therefore, find shelter from torture with the anti-absolutists, whose arguments are either consistently or ultimately consequentialist. This point may be illustrated further through considering the views of two supporters of torture in a TBS. Dershowitz, admitting the dangers of using a 'single-case utilitarian justification' for torture in a TBS, as it 'has no inherent limiting principle', proposes the introduction of 'constraints' which 'can come from rule utilitarianism or other principles of morality, such as the prohibition against deliberately punishing the innocent'.[231] However, Dershowitz does not offer any elaboration of these other principles, or justification for such 'absolutist' prohibition; the only type of moral consideration he consistently supports is a consequentialist 'cost-benefit analysis'.[232] Such analysis does not—and *cannot*—provide a moral basis for preferring the well-being of one person (however innocent) to that of hundreds, or thousands. Dershowitz's 'constraint' may therefore be viewed as a *technical* barrier against 'slippery slope' dangers (for which see Part II); however, he introduces it without subjecting (utilitarian) rule and (absolutist) exception to the same scrutiny. The inconsistency becomes even more pronounced when Dershowitz recommends that Israel resort to 'bulldozing an entire [evacuated Palestinian] village' in response to terrorist attacks[233]—clearly a deliberate punishment of many innocents.

Sheleff does attempt to provide a reason for torturing a terrorist but not his family:

It is precisely because of the severity of the extraordinary [interrogation] methods...that using them against innocent persons is absolutely prohibited (even if they are members

---

[228] *Ibid*, 32.

[229] Hare, *supra* n 57, 60.

[230] Mackie, *supra* n 31, 168. Mackie makes an interesting exception regarding agreements: '...it is important to have the notion of agreements with different degrees of bindingness or solemnity—some which contain, as it were, the implied clause "provided that no strong reason for doing otherwise turns up", and others on which one can rely no matter what happens' (*ibid*, 183–4). Mackie later explains the need for absolutely reliable agreements, especially between states (184–5), but does not reconcile it with his anti-absolutist approach.

[231] Dershowitz, *supra* n 54, 146.

[232] Dershowitz, *ibid*, 143, 148. Dershowitz seems to go as far as to imply that 'cost-benefit analysis' is *exhaustive* of moral consideration. Having justified torture in a TBS on the basis of such analysis without considering alternative moral approaches, he feels safe in concluding that 'In the end, absolute opposition to torture—even nonlethal torture in the ticking bomb case—may rest more on historical and aesthetic considerations than on moral or logical ones' (*ibid*, 148).

[233] See Dershowitz, *ibid*, 177. Sheleff opposes house demolitions, but does not rule out resorting to them as a 'lesser evil'. See 'Maximizing Good and Minimizing Evil...' *supra* n 50, fn 40, p 197. This issue will be discussed in detail in Part II, Ch 9, Section D(2)(b).

of the terrorist's family or his friends), the reason being that they are not capable of bringing about an end to the interrogation, because they do not possess the sought after information.[234]

I submit that this will not do either. The 'stock-taking' or 'analysis' that Sheleff, Dershowitz and other supporters of torture in a TBS, advocate would, in the present scenario, inevitably involve a quantitative comparison of the potential suffering of a single innocent civilian (V's daughter) with that of the dozens, hundreds or thousands of equally innocent civilians who would be killed, maimed or traumatized if V's bomb were to explode, one which the former simply cannot win. Clearly the IC are just as incapable as V's daughter is of 'bringing about an end to the interrogation', so there is nothing in the utilitarian or wider consequentialist views to set her apart, morally, from them: quantities (of pain) must prevail. 'Careful' utilitarians (or other consequentialists) would certainly take the daughter's innocence—or rather the consequences of torturing an innocent girl—into account, in addition to V's culpability, the 'severity' of the act of torture, the consequences of breaking a generally value-maximizing rule, the added emotional difficulty of torturing an innocent and other relevant values.[235] All of this may lead them to argue, for instance, that whereas saving ten, or twenty, ICs would suffice to justify the torture of V, it would take fifty, or one hundred potential victims to justify the torture of his daughter.[236] However, they cannot succumb fully (that is, absolutely) to their reluctance to justify the torture of an innocent person: no matter how many values, preferences, rules, rights, and dispositions we may pile up on V's daughter's side of the consequentialist scales, as long as we *use* such scales, the moral weight of her innocence may be counterbalanced, and eventually overwhelmed, by the number of victims (with their own innocence, rights, etc) on the opposite side.

As we have seen, the 'slippery surface' argument about torturing innocent loved ones was not invented by anti-torture absolutists: other ethicists supporting torture in a TBS have been courageous enough to follow their position (albeit reluctantly) to its logical conclusion, namely that the 'prevention of a horrendous catastrophe' justification for torturing a terrorist in a TBS must extend to the torture of an innocent person.[237] One such ethicist, Levin, explicitly considered,

---

[234] Sheleff, 'The Need to Defend the Honest Truth…' *supra* n 50, 474.

[235] They could even 'factor in' the heavier weight of suffering caused directly by one's intended act when compared to suffering caused by another's.

[236] Sheleff's point about not torturing the innocent may be explained by the fact that he makes it when discussing a specific (and real) case where torture was used in a (failed) attempt to save 'only' one person. The case is discussed in Part IV, Ch 18, Section B.

[237] For this view generally see eg Cummiskey, Sen and Griffin, *supra* n 56 and accompanying text. For specific justifications of torturing the innocent see Michael Moore, *supra* n 133; Scheffler, *supra* n 114, respectively, and accompanying texts. In Moore's text, his anguish at conceding that the innocent may be tortured is almost palpable but, unlike Sheleff and Dershowitz, he at least acknowledges this inescapable logical outcome of his line of reasoning.

and approved, torturing a terrorist's family members in a (nuclear) TBS. In his own words he:

...defended torture as a permissible tool of interrogation in certain emergencies, such as that created by a terrorist refusing to disclose where an atomic bomb is planted...I subsequently extended this defense to the torture of the terrorist's innocent wife and children should timely disclosure require such measures.[238]

Of course (apologies), rape could prove a very effective torturing tool in this scenario too (and this, unfortunately, is not a mere theoretical construct[239]), as could murder (especially if there are several members of the terrorist's family at the torturer's disposal).[240]

V's daughter can only find shelter from torture in minimal (or other) absolutist views which prohibit torture under any circumstances.[241]

2. The self-defence variation

The half-hearted attempts by some theorists to justify torture in a TBS as a measure of 'self-defence' (including the defence of others)—in the moral sense, the legal one or both, are a variation of the attempt to spare the innocent from torture, and will now be considered briefly.[242]

These attempts have been half-hearted because the idea that a bound, immobilized prisoner is the attacker while another, for instance sticking needles under that

---

[238] Levin, *supra* n 133, 89. Levin cites *idem*, 'The case for Torture' in *Newsweek* (17 June 1982) 13 (see Annex for his ticking bomb scenario), and an interview with J Spieler in *Penthouse* (October 1982) 132–181, and devotes the rest of his article to defending this view. He uses a 'liberty-maximizing' and aggression-minimizing justification for torture in a TBS, which is not essentially different from other consequentialist justifications considered here. See, in stark contrast, Marcy Strauss' invocation of the same scenario to argue for an absolute prohibition on torture, *idem*, 'Torture' *Loyola-LA Public Law Research Paper* No 2003–7, January 2003, 273–4.

[239] Lisa M Kois describes such use of rape (in the real world) as follows: 'Rape is used as a form of torture not only directly against the rape victim but also against male family members who are forced to witness the rape of their wives, sisters, partners, daughters or mothers.' This is sometimes done in the way that would seem 'applicable' to our scenario (if the 'partners' in what follows are suicide bombers), which Kois calls '... the "impossible choice scenario", whereby a detainee is presented with an impossible choice between two equally horrifying alternatives: for example, either tell "us" (the state, through the torturer) where "your" (the political prisoner) partners are hiding or we will rape your wife...' (*idem*, 'Dance, Sister, Dance!' in B Dunér (ed), *An End to Torture: Strategies for its Eradication* (London: Zed Books, 1998) 85–108, 94–5).

[240] A Sri Lankan interrogator told Hoffman how he shot dead one detainee to get two others to talk (*idem*, 'A nasty business' 289 (1) *The Atlantic Monthly* 49 (January 2002) 52). See Annex 1.

[241] It is only in such theories that innocents will find shelter *in all circumstances* from other acts, which absolutists do justify when taken against the guilty—for instance punishment: where the stakes are high and, say, punitive measures against the innocent are proven to be the only efficient way to deter criminals, or, specifically, terrorists (and thus prevent a catastrophe), consequentialist reasoning would work in much the same way as it does regarding torture—and for torture itself as deterrent. This point will be discussed further in Part II, Ch 9, Section D(2)(b).

[242] See, in addition to the sources cited here, those cited in the brief discussion of attempts to justify torture in a TBS on *legal* 'self-defence' grounds *infra*, Part IV, Ch 19, Section A(1).

prisoner's fingernails, is acting in self-defence defies common sense, in addition to exceeding the logical boundaries of the self-defence rationale. The justification for the use of force in self-defence ends where the attacker ceases to use force, namely surrenders—but without such surrender, and the interrogator gaining full control over the interrogee, torture cannot begin. This argument has therefore not been used often. It was rejected even by some of those supporting torture in a TBS.[243]

Moreover, while referring to the concept of 'self-defence,' writers invoking it as justification for torture have actually tended (or been forced) to steer that concept away from its original meaning and towards the 'lesser evil' justification. Thus Paskins wraps up his 'self-defence' argument by stating that,

... weighed against the deaths of millions from a nuclear explosion, the effects on the torturer would be anything but an utterly insignificant factor.[244]

Bagaric and Clarke argue that:

...torture—in the circumstances that we indicate is morally permissible—is in fact a manifestation of the right to self-defense, which extends to the right to defend another.[245]

However, they combine this position with a utilitarian justification of interrogational torture:

...torture is morally defensible in certain circumstances, mainly when more grave harm can be avoided by using torture as an interrogation device.[246]

The similar 'stretching' of the legal concept of 'self-defence' towards a 'defence of necessity' ('lesser evil') one is described in Part IV. The result in both cases has been the blurring of any meaningful distinctions between the two concepts, rendering a detailed separate discussion unnecessary, the arguments above being valid equally against this variation.

3. Some examples

It must first be stressed, again, that while our discussion may be theoretical, the means and methods of torture mentioned here—including rape, torture resulting in death, and torturing members of the 'target victim's' family (including children[247])—are unfortunately far from being so. What follows are three cases

---

[243] See eg MS Moore, *supra* n 59, 320–5; Shue, *supra* n 4, 130.

[244] Paskins, *supra* n 14, 143.

[245] Bagaric and Clarke, *supra* n 214, 603.

[246] *Ibid,* 583. Punishing and torturing the innocent are also defended on these grounds. See eg 607–9; 612.

[247] In a book published by Amnesty International, Mike Jempson states that the organization 'has evidence that children are sometimes tortured or threatened with torture as a means of persuading a relative to co-operate with security forces.' See *idem,* 'Torture Worldwide' in D Forest (ed), *A Glimpse of Hell* (London: Cassell and Amnesty International 1996) 46–86, 60.

which I personally found particularly demonstrative of the evils of torture. The minimal absolutist argument against torture here is that those supporting torture in a TBS cannot condemn any of the acts described bellow, *just for what they are in themselves*—at most, they can condemn them conditionally, or 'prima facie'. Otherwise they must suspend final judgment regarding the morality of these acts until they are satisfied either that a TBS was involved or that it was not.

1. Dr Jamal Muhammad Mussa 'Amer[248]

The policeman took me along the corridors, until we passed a door with a curtain immediately behind it. He closed the door. On the floor was a pile of stinking sacks, beside them a large plastic bag containing garbage... The policeman all the time spoke Hebrew, slowly. I told him I didn't understand. He said in Arabic 'You're a donkey. You're a professor and you don't understand Hebrew?' He spoke excellent Arabic. He released one hand and held the handcuffs. He told me to pick up a sack from the floor. I took a sack, and he yelled at me to put the sack on my head. I have a big head and it was very tight. In addition, the sack was made of material like army fatigues, but the part that was on the crown of the head was of some other material, harder and restricting. The sack is a dreadful thing—there is nothing worse. Better to be beaten for 24 hours than to have the sack on you. The sack is narrow, and it is difficult to breathe. You sweat and the sweat trickles over your entire body. Three fluids combine on your body—sweat, snot from your nose and saliva from your mouth—and your hands are not free to wipe them away. And of course the sack is used by one prisoner after another. I never received a clean sack. Once the sack was particularly dreadful. I am 100% certain that it had been in the toilet, for there was a smell of excrement. I asked a guard... to give me another sack. His response was like that of the interrogators: he beat and kicked me, and said 'What, you think I'm your servant?' and went on to curse me using language that I can't repeat. He refused to change the sack.

[...]

The policeman made me sit down, on a thing that they call a chair, but its real name is an instrument of torture. It stands about 20 centimetres high, the width of the seat is less than an A4-sized plank of wood, and it is tipped forward. There is a small backrest to the chair, about the same size as the seat. The chair itself is something like a rabbit—the back legs are long and the front ones short. There is a piece of iron with a hole in it projecting from the floor. A rope runs through the hole, tying the chair leg to the iron bar.

[...]

The policeman told me to lower my hands, he undid the handcuffs, and then bound my hands, behind my back, tying them to the chair, one hand in front of the chair's back,

---

[248] This is part of a testimony taken by Yuval Ginbar and Marwah Jabara-Tibi at Bir Zeit University in the West Bank on 25 March 1998 and by Yuval Ginbar at 'Orient House', East Jerusalem, on 2 April 1998. Interrogation testimony no 62 on file at B'Tselem, the Israeli Information center for Human Rights in the Occupied Territories. Sarah Menobla did the original translation into English, from which I have strayed on occasion.

It would be futile to claim that my personal involvement played no part in choosing this particular case. Nevertheless, there is an 'objective' reason for including this testimony here, namely to show how dreadful 'moderate', 'torture lite', or 'stress and duress' torture techniques can also be. For more on the Landau system under which 'Amer's interrogation was conducted see Part III, Ch 8.

one behind it. If you try to stretch yourself because your shoulders are aching badly, you tighten the handcuffs and your hands swell up. In the first 24 hours my hands swelled badly and I began to bleed in the places where the handcuffs had been...Inside the sack your head is hot and you sweat, while your feet are frozen...Loud music was played in the corridor, with a throbbing beat, which doesn't let you sleep at all. It was a song with English words, something like 'Nobody Can Help You,' which they played over and over again. Occasionally there was a break, and you could hear people screaming as they were beaten 'Ya Allah, oooh, that hurts' and so on.

I sat for 48 hours on that chair. Every so often someone would come and say to me 'You're still alive! You don't want to get out of this situation?' Each time it was a different person. My hands swelled up, I lost all sensation in my legs, my body was stiff, and it was impossible to sleep because of the music, the shouting and the cold—all combined.

[...]

The worst of all was when [interrogators] 'Abu Hatem' and 'Shawki' would grab their genitals (they didn't undress), and come up to me and say 'Suck, you dog, suck'. I tried to get away from them as best I could, but of course I couldn't move, as I was tied to the chair. They actually physically touched my mouth with their genitals. Afterwards they would say, 'Enjoyed it? Enjoyed it? Now your wife has men who do the same thing to her.'

[...]

They used the 'Karmaza' or 'Kambaz.' This involves kneeling on your toes. It would kill my knees. You're not allowed to touch the floor, you're not allowed to sit down. After 40 minutes you're screaming in agony. You feel you're going to explode. The interrogator would be reading a newspaper and now and then he'd speak 'Come on, say something, confess to something, anything, even a lie. Something that you did against the State of Israel'...When they saw that I was about to collapse the interrogators would come in. One of them would hold me by the chest, another from behind, so that I wouldn't fall, either forwards or backwards. Another one pushed me downwards, on my head. You feel as though you're going to split in two.

2. Şükran Aydın[249]

Mrs Şükran Aydın...was born in 1976. At the time of the events in issue she was 17 years old and living with her parents in the village of Tasit...

[...]

The applicant alleges that, on arrival at the gendarmerie headquarters, she was separated from her father and her sister-in-law. At some stage she was taken upstairs to a room which she later referred to as the 'torture room'. There she was stripped of her clothes, put into a car tyre and spun round and round. She was beaten and sprayed with cold water from high-pressure jets. At a later stage she was taken clothed but blindfolded to an interrogation room. With the door of the room locked, an individual in military clothing

---

[249] *Aydin v Turkey*, European Court of Human Rights, *Reports* 1997-VI (57/1996/676/866), Judgment of 25 September 1997 paras 13, 20. The Court accepted Mrs Aydın's version of the facts (contested by Turkey), and concluded that 'the accumulation of acts of physical and mental violence inflicted on the applicant and the especially cruel act of rape to which she was subjected' amounted to torture, adding that 'the Court would have reached this conclusion on either of these grounds taken separately' (*ibid*, para 86). Seven judges disagreed with the finding of torture, but they all disputed the applicant's factual claims.

forcibly removed her clothes, laid her on her back and raped her. By the time he had finished she was in severe pain and covered in blood. She was ordered to get dressed and subsequently taken to another room. According to the applicant, she was later brought back to the room where she had been raped. She was beaten for about an hour by several persons who warned her not to report on what they had done to her.

3. *'Susana' (a fictional account)*[250]

Near the wall was the man who had been tortured in the water tank the previous day. He was naked and his hands had been bound to the same shackles he was wearing on his ankles, forcing him into a fetal position. I was strapped to another bed. The lieutenant asked the man about an attack on a particular army base. When the man didn't answer, the lieutenant began to call out several names. The prisoner remained silent. The lieutenant became impatient. As he pronounced each name he kicked the prisoner all over his body. He obtained nothing but groans and left.

After a short while, the lieutenant returned. In one hand he carried a motor oil can open at one end and in the other hand he held a paper bag. I heard strange squeaks and scratching coming from the bag.

The lieutenant was accompanied by a man I had never seen before who was carrying a blow torch and a fine metal rod about eighteen inches long.

Those who were torturing me obviously knew the purpose of the items being brought because they immediately joined the lieutenant and became as children with new toys. They went over to the prisoner and carried him to the center bed. With ropes and chains, he was bound to the bed so tightly that his back arched.

'Now I know you'll talk, you son of a bitch,' muttered the lieutenant while drilling a small hole through the bottom of the can. The other man handed him the metal rod which the lieutenant tested to see if it would go easily through the opening.

He then placed the opening of the paper bag over the open end of the can, and I realized in terror what had been in the bag—a rat that scuttled into the can.

The hairs of my body stood on end; I trembled. The lieutenant placed the open end of the can against the man's anus, using broad strips of adhesive tapes to hold it in place.

I shook at the sound of the rodent clawing against the interior of the container and squeaking furiously and loud.

Desperation was clearly marked on the man's faced as he writhed violently.

'Talk, you son of a whore. Where is your leader?'

'Who the fuck planned the attack?'

---

[250] O Rivabella, *Requiem for a Woman's Soul* (Hammondsworth, Middlesex: Penguin Books, 1987) 47–9. This is an extract from the diaries of 'Susana', tortured in an unnamed South American dictatorship, as read by a priest, who eventually loses his mind. Note also that it is clearly not only the man who is being tortured, but also the two women present. The terrorist—the person from whom the vital information is needed—could in that scenario be any of the three.

While this description is a work of fiction, the method of torture described here was in fact used in the 1970s by the military dictatorship in Rivabella's homeland, Argentina, where it was known as the 'rectoscope'. This method was described by a former detainee as consisting of '... inserting a tube into the victim's anus or into a woman's vagina, then letting a rat into the tube. The rodent would try to get out by gnawing at the victim's internal parts.' See the Argentine National Commission of the Disappeared, *Nunca Mas (Never Again)* (London: Faber and Faber, 1986) 72. The quotation is from a testimony by Daniel Eduardo Fernández (file No 1131), who had been detained at 'Club Atlético' secret detention centre in August 1977.

The man groaned a couple of times but didn't say a word.

The lieutenant gave a signal to the man who came with him, who struck a match and lit the blow torch. After adjusting the flame, he slowly heated the metal rod until it became red hot at the tip. He gave it to the lieutenant who walked to the prisoner and carefully inserted it into the bottom of the can.

The intense heat made the rat go mad; its scratching became wilder as it searched frantically for a way out.

The prisoner began to scream for the first time since he had been under torture and to writhe so violently as to scare the rat even more.

Luisa [another prisoner] was shrieking. I was beside myself. The torturers turned up the volume of a radio and continued to watch the man's convulsions, mesmerized by his suffering.

Three times the lieutenant heated the rod. Luisa fainted. The man became motionless. I realized that the rat had suffocated inside the man's intestines. The horror drove me into unconsciousness...

When I awoke I turned immediately toward the center bed. The man's body was still there. There was a streak of blackish blood in the crack of his buttocks, around which were the rabid toothmarks of the rat, whose hairless tail protruded from his anus.

'Kill me!' I began to scream in rage.

From the other bed, Luisa burst into the frenzied laughter of the insane.

'These fucking bitches, take them away!' shouted the lieutenant.

***

I submit that if torture in a TBS is morally justified, then it is logically unavoidable that every single one of the above types of torture, as well as those described in all human rights reports, court cases, memoirs of victims, historical research, fiction and so on is a moral act in the proper circumstances. This perhaps helps to explain why combinations of justifying the coercion of detainees and placing restrictions on coercive methods have never worked in practice.[251]

Once this unlimited, or 'absolute' scope of torture is acknowledged, and the anti-absolutist position is rejected, I submit that another logical conclusion becomes inevitable—that the anti-torture minimal absolutist can (logically) rest his or her case: If

(a) anti-absolutism is rejected, and therefore, necessarily, there must be at least one type of act that no human being may ever carry out upon another

and

(b) moral justification of torture is licence for one human being to carry out absolutely any act upon another

it follows inevitably that

---

[251] This is discussed, from various angles, in the following Parts.

(c) torture is a type of act (ie is or is inclusive of an act, or acts) that one human being may never carry out upon another.

However, as has already been stated, I believe that it would have been wrong to confine the discussion to the purely formal.

C. The Actor—the Torturer

The lead interrogator...had given me specific instructions: I was to deprive the detainee of sleep during my 12-hour shift by opening his cell every hour, forcing him to stand in a corner and stripping him of his clothes. Three years later the tables have turned. It is rare that I sleep through the night without a visit from this man. His memory harasses me as I once harassed him...I failed to disobey a meritless order, I failed to protect a prisoner in my custody, and I failed to uphold the standards of human decency. Instead, I intimidated, degraded and humiliated a man who could not defend himself. I compromised my values. I will never forgive myself.[252]

The main anti-torture argument here is that anyone ready to, and capable of justifying (or actually carrying out?) all of the above and more, or, to put it more bluntly, anyone who has read the above descriptions not as a list of unspeakable horrors but rather as, potentially, a manual for action (just, albeit regrettable)—cannot, to that extent, be good. To quote James Cargile, these are the sort of,

...actions which someone possessing the dispositions characteristic of a good man could not possibly perform in any circumstances.[253]

To an extent we are now moving, temporarily, from the morality of the act to the morality of the person, which would lead us away from both deontological and consequentialist moral views and into the realm of virtue ethics.[254]

[252] E Fair, 'An Iraq Interrogator's Nightmare' *Washington Post* (9 February 2007) A19.

[253] J Cargile, 'On Consequentialism' 29 *Analysis* 78 (1969), 87. For a consequentialist criticism of this approach see RG Frey, 'What a Good Man Can Bring Himself to Do' in Haber (ed), *supra* n 44, 109–117. Frey counters Cargile's reliance on sympathetic feelings for happiness rather convincingly, to my mind, but in doing so he seems more at ease with a scenario where amputating his friend's gangrenous leg is the only way of saving him (at 114–115) than with one closer to our subject—where torturing a baby is the only way to save 20 people from dying, which he leaves essentially unresolved (116).

[254] Very roughly speaking, virtue ethics are rooted in Aristotle's view of morality, expressed especially in Book II of his *Nichomachean Ethics*, as grounded in the quest for desire-controlling 'states of character' (at II.5) ideal for human flourishing (in both the individual and societal meanings of this term). Aristotle saw each such 'state' (discussed in detail in III.6–IV.9) as 'a mean relative to us' between extremes, both of which are 'vices' (at II.6). See Aristotle, *The Nichomachean Ethics*, trans D Ross, revised by JL Ackrill and JO Urmson (Oxford: OUP 1998). Modern virtue ethicists have, to varying degrees, modified, or revised Aristotle's theory (with the issue of virtue as a mean often criticized), but most have maintained his 'focus...on the virtuous individual and on those inner traits, dispositions and motives that qualify her as being virtuous.' See M Slote, 'Virtue Ethics' in Baron *et al*, *supra* n 28, 175–238, 177. For modern discussions of virtue ethics see eg M Slote, *From Morality to Virtue* (New York: OUP, 1992); P Foot, 'Virtues and Vices,' in

What kind of a human being must one be in order to be able to torture a terrorist efficiently? What traits of character does E need in order to carry out what Page DuBois called 'the calculated infliction of human agony'?[255] Vicious is defenceless, and totally at her mercy. She must suppress any feelings of human compassion. If V screams, she must reject the human urge to help him, to alleviate his pain, she must instead concentrate on inflicting it—on judging whether, or to what extent, the scream indicates effective use of the method on hand; whether, assuming V is still not talking, it would be worthwhile at that point to increase his suffering slightly or sharply; whether to apply the electrodes (and if so, to what part of his body); whether to use the sack, (apologies) the rat, rape, the daughter, or rape of the daughter. All this must be coolly calculated and carefully carried out, with meticulous weighing of the dangers, the success in causing pain, V's physical and psychological composition and so on. While Aristotle, in whose society torture was an institutionalized practice enshrined in law,[256] may have seen much of the above as perfectly reasonable (to the extent that it was applied to slaves), it is doubtful whether most of us would consider the kind of personality needed to carry out such acts as commendable.

The anti-torture absolutist's claim that there is something fundamentally wrong about the character of a torturer is put in a way I found very forceful by a torture victim, who turned his thoughts, in the midst of his agony, to his tormentors. Georgios-Alexandros Mangakis, a Greek prisoner under the military dictatorship there, wrote:

I have experienced the fate of a victim. I have seen the torturer's face at close quarters. It was in a worse condition than my own bleeding, livid face. The torturer's was distorted by a kind of twitching that had nothing human about it. He was in such a state of tension that he had an expression very similar to those we see on Chinese masks; I am not exaggerating. It is not an easy thing to torture people. It requires inner participation. In this situation,

---

idem, supra n 102, 1–18; A MacIntyre, *After Virtue* (2nd edn, Notre Dame: University of Notre Dame Press, 1984); G Pence, 'Virtue Theory' in Singer (ed), *supra* n 80, 249–258; G Trianosky, 'What is Virtue Ethics All About?' 27 *Am Phil Quart* 335 (1990). While it may be argued that virtue ethics could provide a useful angle, distinct both from the deontological and consequentialist, from which to tackle all aspects of the question posed in this work, and should therefore have been introduced earlier, I have preferred to limit this strand's 'application' to the particular issue of the torturer's character, principally because the focus of that wider discussion is necessarily on *an act*, which value theory is relatively less equipped to address. In addition, character traits and other virtues do not translate easily into legal discourse, to which this debate must lead. See, however, Steve Buckler's analysis of limitations on executive power from an essentially virtue ethical stand, *infra*, Part II, Ch 8, Section E.

[255] DuBois, *supra* n 206, 3. On the character of torturers see eg RD Crelinsten, and AJ Schmid, *The Politics of Pain: Torturers and Their Masters* (Boulder, Col: Westview Press, 1995); J Glover, *Humanity: a moral history of the twentieth century* (London: Pimlico, 2001) 33–7; E Sottas, 'Perpetrators of Torture' in Dunér (ed), *supra* n 239, 62–84; E Staub, 'The Psychology and Culture of Torture and Torturers' in P Suedfeld (ed), *Psychology and Torture* (New York: Hemisphere Publishing, 1990) 49–88; F de Zulueta, 'The Torturers' in Forest (ed), *supra* n 247, 87–103.

[256] On torture in ancient Greece see eg B Innes, *A History of Torture* (New York: St Martin's Press, 1998) 12–17; E Peters, *Torture* (Expanded ed, Pennsylvania: University of Pennsylvania Press, 1996) 11–18.

I turned out to be the lucky one. I was humiliated. I did not humiliate others. I was simply bearing a profoundly unhappy humanity in my aching entrails. Whereas the men who humiliate you must first humiliate the notion of humanity within themselves. Never mind if they strut around in their uniforms, swollen with the knowledge that they can control the suffering, sleeplessness, hunger and despair of their fellow human beings, intoxicated with the power in their hands. Their intoxication is nothing other than the degradation of humanity. The ultimate degradation. They have had to pay dearly for my torments. I wasn't the one in the worst position. I was simply a man who moaned because he was in great pain. I prefer that. At this moment I am deprived of the joy of seeing children going to school or playing in the park. Whereas they have to look their own children in the face.[257]

Those supporting torture in a TBS would challenge the applicability of the above to our scenario by arguing that in a TBS, it was through torture alone that many people could go home safely to their children, and for many children to escape death, injury, disability or (sometimes and) life without parents, siblings or both.

They will, moreover, argue that even assuming that such characterization did apply to the torturer in a TBS, it would be right for Ethica to become a torturer: she would thereby be gallantly sacrificing her own peace of mind for the sake of others. In contrast, it is the character of those who would *not* torture in a TBS, preferring their own 'moral purity'[258] to the lives and well-being of so many people that is called into question. In the words of Allison:

The term 'morally unhinged' would, perhaps, be too strong to apply to a policeman who would not be prepared to torture a potential source of information on a terrorist atrocity, but confusion and moral cowardice might be reasonable accusations, depending on the exact circumstances.[259]

Debating a moral dilemma in an imaginary 'kill one innocent or many will die' case,[260] Kai Nielsen similarly accuses the absolutist ('moral conservative' to use his term) of 'moral evasiveness':

... because rather than steeling himself to do what in normal circumstances would be a horrible and vile act but in this circumstance is a harsh moral necessity, he allows, when he has the power to prevent it, a situation which is still many times worse. He tries to keep his 'moral purity' and avoid 'dirty hands' at the price of utter moral failure and what

---

[257] G-A Mangakis, *Letter to Europeans* (1973). Quoted in Twining and Twining, *supra* n 45, 355.
    See also a poem by an Algerian prisoner, Leila Djabali, 'For My Torturer, Lieutenant D...' trans by A Barrows, in H Cronyn, R McKane and S Watts (eds), *Voices of Conscience: Poetry from Opposition* (North Shield, Northumberland: Iron Press, 1995) 193.

[258] Kant, for instance, speaks often in terms such as 'the maxim of striving towards moral purity'. While acknowledging that such purity may in practice be an unattainable ideal, he warns that using this as pretext to base action on anything other than this maxim would be 'the death of all morality'. See *idem*, 'On the Common Saying...' *supra* n 41, 69.

[259] Allison, *supra* n 5, 26. MS Moore similarly talks of '... a narcissistic preoccupation with your own "virtue"—that is, the "virtue" you could have if the world were ideal and did not present you with such awful choices' (*idem, supra* n 59, 329). Bentham's wrath at absolutists' 'blind and vulgar humanity' *supra*, text accompanying n 45, is of the same variety of criticism.

[260] Where the only way to save potholers trapped in a cave is to blow up an innocent fat man stuck at its only entrance and blocking it. For a description of similar cases see Ch 4, Section B(3).

Kierkegaard called 'double-mindedness.'[261] It is understandable that people should act in this morally evasive way but this does not make it right.[262]

This argument, however, contains a serious logical flaw, as pointed out by Nagel:

> ...the notion that one might sacrifice one's moral integrity justifiably, in the service of a sufficiently worth end, is an incoherent notion. For if one were justified in making such a sacrifice (or even morally required to make it), then one would not be sacrificing one's moral integrity by adopting that course: one would be preserving it.[263]

Thus in the TBS, if the moral thing for E to do is torture V, his daughter, or both, then by torturing she would actually be *preserving* her 'moral purity' rather than tainting it, while it is by *refraining* from torturing them that she would acquire 'dirty hands'.

These objections, however, raise another question—that of E's moral priorities. For supporters of torture in a TBS, it is obvious that E's foremost duty in the circumstances is to save the lives and well-being of the IC, which she is in a unique position to do.

I propose to start examining this question from two seemingly uncontroversial premises. The first is that E, as a moral agent, has a general duty to help the IC—her endangered fellow humans, although the scope of this duty may be a matter of contention.[264]

The second premise is that E, as a moral agent, has moral duties towards both others and herself. This was neatly put in Ibsen's *A Doll's House*, in the following (fragment of a) dialogue between Nora and her husband, Helmer:

HELMER. To forsake your home, your husband, and your children! And you don't consider what the world will say.

NORA. I can pay no heed to that. I only know that I must do it.

HELMER. This is monstrous! Can you forsake your holiest duties in this way?

NORA. What do you consider my holiest duties?

HELMER. Do I need to tell you that? Your duties to your husband and your children.

NORA. I have other duties equally sacred.

HELMER. Impossible! What duties do you mean?

NORA. My duties towards myself.[265]

---

[261] For this concept see S Kierkegaard, *Purity of Heart is to Will One Thing* (1847), trans D Steere (New York: Harper & Row, 1958). Footnote added. To my mind, Kierkegaard's 'double-mindedness' refers, rather, to making choices out of extra-moral motives, which would apply to Nielsen's characterization of the absolutist only in circular fashion.

[262] K Nielsen, 'Against Moral Conservatism' in Haber (ed), *supra* n 44, 161–173, 172. For a different, but still essentially consequentialist view of this issue see TE Hill Jr, 'Moral Purity and the Lesser Evil' 66 *The Monist* 213 (1983).

[263] Nagel, *supra* n 69, 63.

[264] Obviously, the discussion here would be pointless without this premise, and unnecessary if the matter of its scope were uncontroversial.

[265] H Ibsen, *A Doll's House*, trans W Archer (Studio City, Ca: Players Press 1993), Act 3.

If we are to shun extreme views of what moral living should include, namely those advocating constant self-sacrifice for the sake of others[266] on the one hand, and those admitting no 'duty of care' whatsoever[267] on the other, we would probably arrive at Nagel's middle-of-the-road formula for the duty to care for others which, given the wide margins it leaves to interpretation, may be accepted by ethicists of most persuasions:

...we ought to care for others as much as we can consistent with a reasonable concern for the quality of our own lives.[268]

I would submit, however, that the view justifying torture in a TBS leaves no room at all for the would-be torturer to fulfil her 'duties towards herself' or show any concern whatsoever for 'the quality of her own life'. These are not merely set aside or compromised—they are *nullified*. According to the torture-justifying view she may, if need be, sacrifice her life, but that is relatively easy. She would also be justified, as we have seen, in using each of the torture methods described above, and any others, on V or on his innocent daughter.

The 'slippery surface' does not stop there. Ethica is equally justified in doing anything—including the worst things imaginable—to *herself*. If torturing another person is not self-destructive enough,[269] E is also justified—in a scenario where he is out of grasp and able to demand this—in allowing V to torture her in any way he may think of, if he reliably promises that afterwards he would tell her where the bomb, or the suicide bomber, is—or pass this information to someone else capable of saving the lives of the IC if she dies, faints or loses her sanity. As noted above,[270] anti-absolutists, who see torturing in a TBS as morally justified, in effect give the terrorist full mastery over the question of what act is morally justified go prevent his attack, and correspondingly deny the moral agent (ie the torturer) any control over that question. As long as the numbers of those tortured are, comparatively,

---

[266] This is a criticism often directed at utilitarians—that if their constant duty is to maximize utility, there is very little else they are morally allowed to do. See eg S Smilansky, 'Who Should a Utilitarian Be?' No. 44 *Iyyun, The Jerusalem Philosophical Quarterly* 91 (1995); S Wolf, 'Moral Saints,' 79(8) *Journal of Philosophy* 419 (August 1982).

I believe, however, that sophisticated utilitarian views convincingly refute this argument, by citing utilitarian reasons for not being wholly altruistic. As Austin famously remarked 'Though he approves of love because it accords with his principle, he is far from maintaining that the general good ought to be the motive of the lover. It was never contended that the lover should kiss his mistress with an eye to a common weal' (*idem, supra* n 57, 97). See also eg Pettit, *supra* n 28, 92–102; Shaw, *supra* n 30, 265.

[267] This corresponds at least to the more crude versions of 'moral egoism', for which see eg T Hobbes, *The Leviathan* (1651), ed JCA Gaskin (New York: OUP, 1996), especially The First Part ('of Man'); K Baier, 'Egoism' in Singer (ed), *supra* n 80, 197–204; E Barcalow, *Moral Philosophy: Theories and Ethics* (2nd edn, Belmont, Ca: Wadsworth Publishing Company, 1998) Ch 4.

[268] T Nagel, 'World Poverty' in Singer (ed), *ibid*, 273–283, 282. I believe that Nagel is also right in saying that even this formula 'would still constitute a challenge to most of us' (*ibid*).

[269] Nagel's argument for the logical incoherence of the 'anti-moral purity' position, *supra* n 263 and accompanying text, is not relevant to the argument here, as we are now concerned with preserving, or sacrificing, Ethica's life, limb and personality rather than her 'moral purity'.

[270] This is the 'moral enslavement' argument, see *supra*, Ch 4, Sections C(3)(a) and C(4).

very small, E would fit neatly and safely into my second formulation of the justification for torture in a TBS instead of—or in addition to—V and his daughter. She herself thus has no say in determining what is morally justifiable for her to do and what is not. Since only V can stop his torture (by talking), anything done to him, to his daughter, *or* to E herself, is right while he refuses to disclose the life-saving information (as a means of ending that refusal).

Ethica's own sense of self, her dignity, her moral, religious or other beliefs, her bodily integrity, every single component of her personality[271]—all these count for nothing. Taking them into consideration in a TBS would be 'cold hearted',[272] 'unfeeling disregard for other people'.[273] They all must go, if necessary, because however painful the loss of any or all of them may be, it can never get anywhere close to the amount of pain that the exploding bomb would cause. And note—these losses, this nullifying of self, may or may *not* be temporary: even if the experience causes her life-long harm, loss of sanity, of limbs, of life itself—it is still justifiable in view of the disastrous (and similarly long-term or permanent) consequences to be avoided.

To put it more simply—those supporting torture in a TBS do not care for E at all. All they are interested in is the life-saving information, for which she, like V, is a mere vehicle. Nothing that she does, nothing that is done to her, could upset the 'balance of evils' that for them tilts so heavily in favour of torturing. She is totally dispensable. What they require from the torturer in a TBS is not self-sacrifice—it is self-effacement.

When Nora is told by Helmer, continuing the dialogue quoted above, that '[b]efore all else' she is 'a wife and a mother', she replies:

That I no longer believe. I believe that before all else I am a human being, just as much as you are—or at least that I should try to become one.[274]

Jean-Paul Sartre, echoing Ibsen (perhaps consciously), writes the following on the French policies of torture in Algiers in the late 1950s:

…if there is no precipice of inhumanity over which nations and men will not throw themselves, then, why, in fact, do we go to so much trouble to become, or to remain, human?[275]

Instead, to avoid 'reasonable accusations' such as 'moral cowardice',[276] Ethica must become, and possibly remain, a torturer, and if that clashes with her personality, she

---

[271] Logically one could add 'her own beloved ones'. I have, however, preferred throughout to steer away from Ethica's own beloved ones, so as to keep the discussion within the more abstract sphere of care for one's neighbour. For a hypothetical case where torture of an agent's own mother is balanced against the demise of a whole city see Gewirth, *supra* n 64.

[272] O Gross, *supra*, text accompanying n 113.

[273] Rachels, *supra* n 87, 208.

[274] Ibsen, *supra* n 265.

[275] J-P Sartre, 'A Victory' (originally 'Une Victoire' published in *L'Express*, preface in H Alleg, *The Question*, trans J Calder (London: John Calder, 1958) 11–28, 13–14. Peters uses these last words ('to become, or to remain, human') for the title of his concluding chapter in *Torture, supra* n 256, 141–87.

[276] Allison, *supra* n 259 and accompanying text.

must become a non-person, a non-Ethica. It cannot be right, the anti-torture absolut-ist would claim, for a moral agent to torture, to thereby 'injure in himself the essence of humanity',[277] or, to use Sartre's words, to fling oneself over the 'precipice of inhumanity', down to the absolute bottom of its abyss—not even to prevent a horrendous catastrophe.

D. The Terrorist

Vicious is an evil man. He would murder, maim and traumatize as many people as he can to promote his goal—a goal to the attainment of which these people are not an obstacle, but rather a mere tool.

Does he deserve to suffer? Perhaps. Has he forfeited every single right as a human being? Few would openly claim this.[278] The only reason he is being tor-tured is that he refuses to give the vital information, and treatment of him as a fully-fledged human being (albeit, presumably, a prisoner) would be resumed as soon as he speaks, which is in his own hands.

However, it would be difficult for those supporting torture in a TBS to point out which aspect of his treatment as a human being has *not* been suspended, which aspect of his human dignity is still upheld whilst he is being tortured. During torture, every single conceivable fundamental human or moral right is being trampled upon. Everything that Dr 'Amer, Ms Aydın or the unnamed man in 'Susana's' diaries underwent he too must undergo and, if needed, more. If needed, he may also be forced to suffer everything that Ethica must suffer,[279] with the added burden that he faces an even more limited choice—between tor-ture and betrayal. As Shue has pointed out,

> ...compliance [with the torturers] means, in a word, betrayal, betrayal of one's ideal and one's comrades. The possibility of betrayal cannot be counted as an escape. Undoubtedly some ideals are vicious and some friends are partners in crime—this can be true of either the government, the opposition, or both. Nevertheless, a betrayal is no escape for a dedicated member of either a government or its opposition, who cannot collaborate with-out denying his or her highest values.[280]

---

[277] P-H Simon, *Contre la Torture* (Paris: 1957), quoted by Horne, *supra* n 221, 206.

[278] One example is Michael L Gross, who writes: 'The terrorist who recognizes no intrinsic value in the life of his victim, who takes advantage and abuses his innocence for his own pur-poses, forfeits his own moral status as a human being. He may then find his own human dignity stripped away and his body subject to abuse' (*idem*, 'Regulating Torture in a Democracy: Death and Indignity in Israel' 36(3) *Polity* 367 (2004) 382).

[279] This includes the agonies of the torturer—E could torture V by forcing him to torture others. This is yet again, unfortunately, not a mere theoretical construction. Thus an Amnesty International report on Sri Lanka mentions the following, within a long (and dreadful) list of torture methods being used by 'members of [Sri Lanka's] security forces in the south' in the late 1980s: 'Men and women prisoners have reportedly been raped, and male prisoners have said that they were forced to sexually abuse women prisoners' (Amnesty International, *Sri Lanka: Extrajudicial Executions, 'Disappearances' and torture, 1987 to 1990*, AI Index ASA 37/21/90 (London: 1990) 39).

[280] Shue, *supra* n 4, 135.

It is, again, the absoluteness of the suffering allowable, the totality of the denial of any and every right that is disturbing. As in the case of the torturer, described above, there is no guarantee whatsoever that this is temporary only—while the torture-justifying moral view ensures that the torture itself would cease once the information has been disclosed (or the bomb has exploded), there is nothing in it that would limit torture to those methods with short-lived effects only.[281]

Why should anything that befalls a thoroughly evil person disturb us at all? A possible answer, not to be pursued here, would be to stretch the minimal absolutist view into the realm of *positive* duties,[282] to include an absolute duty to respect the dignity of every human being, regardless of his or her character or actions, as well as, needless to add, the consequences of doing so. For our purposes, however, the present version of a negative minimal absolutist argument against torture, with its onus on the act and its implications for the would-be torturer's duties rather than on the would-be victim's rights is sufficient. Nevertheless, the 'artifact' criterion suggested by van den Haag for distinguishing between torture (as punishment), of which he disapproves, even in the case of 'a Hitler or a Stalin', and the death penalty, which he supports,[283] may point us in that 'positive' direction, as may the seemingly awkward criterion that Nagel suggests for distinguishing killing, which may sometimes be justified, from torture, which may not:

One could *even* say, as one bayonets an enemy soldier, 'it's either you or me.' But one cannot really say while torturing a prisoner, 'You understand, I have to pull out your fingernails because it is absolutely essential that we have the names of your confederates'; nor can one say to the victims of Hiroshima, 'You understand, we have to incinerate you to provide the Japanese government with an incentive to surrender.'[284]

E. The Innocent Civilians

Though I am indebted I shall not pay with my blood
I shall run from forest to forest with the wild monkeys
howling my horror, because maybe
One day you will murder me

Avraham Halfi, from 'Because maybe you'[285]

---

[281] On this point see further in Part IV, Ch 18.

[282] For a discussion of the differences between positive and negative moral duties and an argument for the supremacy of the latter see Foot, *supra* n 102.

[283] See *supra* n 145 and accompanying text.

[284] Nagel, *supra* n 69, 67–8. Mordechai Kremnitzer and Re'em Segev, considering limits on the 'lesser evil defence' (which is the legal version of the consequentialist justification for torture in a TBS) similarly argue: '… when harm to a person is absolute from his point of view, it is totally impossible to demand of him legitimately to accept the act as justifiable, and accordingly the justification for the lesser evil defence evaporates' (*idem*, 'The Application of Force in the Course of GSS Interrogations—A Lesser Evil?' [Hebrew] 4 *Mishpat u-Mimshal* 667 (1998) 709).

[285] In *idem*, *New and Old* [Hebrew] (Tel-Aviv: 'Eqed, 1977) 83.

The men, women and children innocently going about their business in the crowded marketplace appear to be the main concern of those advocating torture in a TBS. The life and well-being of every single one among the IC is what prompts them to justify such an extreme act when it is necessary to save them. Harold Rudolph, in justifying such torture, makes this point:

It is precisely because utilitarians hold the lives of every individual as sacred that they justify action that will protect the lives of the greater number of individuals when faced with the harrowing duty of having to choose between two evils.[286]

The anti-torture absolutist would point, however, to two problems within the torture-justifying view in this regard. First, the overwhelming power of numbers would also mean, logically,[287] that in a scenario where Vicious is just a sadist, not within Ethica's grasp, and the only way to get him to disclose the place of the bomb is to give him a baby, a young man, an aging woman or a dentist for him to torture, then Ethica, as a moral agent, would have to search the general, civilian population, namely those very same IC, for the required victim. She would have to abduct that person and present him or her for V to torture. The scenario is, obviously, so 'fantastic' that it may be deemed too much so for this argument to have any impact in the real world, where the threat of terrorist attacks by sadists demanding victims for torture is hardly the foremost danger facing humanity.

Out of this purely theoretical example would, however, emerges a point that is valid for this theoretical debate but may also have implications in the real world—that under the torture-justifying view, no one is safe from torture, death or any other harm if the stakes are high enough and his or her suffering or death are the only means of averting catastrophe.

But even the IC as a whole are not entirely immune from atrocities under the torture-justifying view—not even from V's ticking bomb. As argued above,[288] a view justifying torture in a TBS to prevent a catastrophe cannot rule out the possibility that a terrorist operation may itself be justified if it prevents a greater catastrophe. Thus another scenario is envisaged by Twining and Twining who, applying Bentham's thoughts on torture to a modern-day TBS, cite the following as one of the conditions without which torture in such a situation *cannot* be justified:

There are reasonable grounds for believing that the torturing will not have consequences (eg retaliation by X's [the terrorist's] friends) which would be worse than the damage likely to result from the bomb going off.[289]

---

[286] H Rudolph, *Security, Terrorism, Torture: Detainees' Rights in South Africa and Israel: A Comparative Study* (Cape Town: Juta, 1984) 219.

[287] See the discussion on 'torturing babies to death for fun' *supra*, Ch 4, Section C(1)(a).

[288] *Supra*, Ch 4, Section C(5).

[289] Twining and Twining, *supra* n 45, 347. Sheleff supports this reasoning in both sources cited *supra* n 50, pp 307 and 218, respectively.

If such retaliation is reasonably possible, E must not torture V. This is, again, the only logical conclusion to be drawn from the 'disastrous consequences' justification for torture. In either of these cases, for Rudolph and others of this view, 'the lives of every individual' among the IC is only worth saving if a larger number of IC is not waiting in the wings as a target for attack, at which point all 'sacredness' evaporates from their lives, and like a swarm of angry bees flies off and lands on that larger crowd, whose lives have now assumed sacredness. As to the smaller group of IC—they have now become dispensable, like V, his daughter, E and individual members of the public before them.

Morality of extreme situations under the view justifying torture in a TBS thus resembles the lives of buffalos in the savannah—as long as you stick to the herd, your belonging to the many will protect you from harm, as 'there is safety in numbers'. To be precise, however, there is safety *only* in numbers: if you dare stray, or through some misfortune find yourself alone, you are doomed—the predators of anti-absolutism are lurking in the tall grass and will, circumstances necessitating, pounce on you and devour you whole (or worse, in the case of torture, they will consume you slowly and agonizingly). To be even more precise, you must also make sure that you are part of a large enough herd, because those predators would have no qualms in obliterating a whole herd (or at least allowing such obliteration) if the well-being of a larger one is at stake. What is perhaps most disturbing is that these predators are actually your fellow 'buffalos'.

The anti-torture minimal absolutist, in contrast, offers very little by way of grand theories, but can assure you of one thing—torture is never justified, and your friends, if they are minimal absolutists, will never consider you, your child, your partner or anyone else, either as a would-be victim for their (or anyone's) torture or as one who would justifiably torture them—or anyone. Nor, for that matter, would a minimal absolutist consider anyone as a justifiable—or 'allowable'[290]—target for a terrorist attack.

---

[290] Within minimal absolutist limits, of course, that is to the extent that the rejection of 'allowing' such attacks does not itself involve a breach of a minimal absolutist prohibition.

I would also note that I am assuming here, throughout, that a terrorist attack is also a worthy candidate for a minimal absolutist prohibition. While this assumption is not defended here *per se*, it flows logically—in a 'reverse slippery surface' manner, if you will—from the defence of an absolute prohibition on torture.

6

Part I—Conclusions

Ethica, a private individual, has just captured and bound a terrorist, Vicious, who has planted a time-bomb in a crowded marketplace, or has just sent his fellow terrorist on a suicide bombing mission there. The bomb is set to detonate in a few hours, and the resulting explosion will kill many innocent civilians. Is it morally justifiable for Ethica to torture Vicious, if this is the only way to get him to reveal the location of the bomb (or the suicide bomber), and thereby save the lives of all those people?

The view supporting torture in such a 'ticking bomb situation' (TBS) and the view opposing it are essentially simple, but understanding them fully has necessitated a long and complex journey. I will first offer a brief summary of the debate so far, before drawing what I see as the necessary conclusions.

Both views on torture in a TBS reflect strong intuitions and rely on well-established, comprehensive, age-old moral theories, for which the TBS has usually served as just a case in point, one theoretical cannon-ball among the many that ethicists have for generations hurled at each other's reasoned fortifications in an effort to weaken, and eventually demolish them, before these issues gained prominence in the wake of 9/11.

This particular case in point has, for understandable reasons, been much more popular among those who see the morality of an act as contingent upon its consequences (consequentialists) than among those who look to the nature of the act itself, and its relation to one's duties towards self and others (deontologists).

Placing this particular, extreme dilemma at the centre of attention has resulted in some shifting loyalties, notably a considerable defection of deontologists to the consequentialist camp which, they emphasize, by no means indicates acceptance of consequentialist reasoning as a whole, only an acknowledgment of the overwhelming moral weight of numbers in such extreme, rare circumstances.[291]

This is not surprising—the argument for torture in a TBS is more straightforward, and its intuitive appeal more obvious: there is an evil man on one the one hand, innocent people in large numbers—who are his intended victims—on the other, and a moral agent has to decide whether or not to harm the single evil one so as to save the many innocents. The choice, to many, seems clear. Torture, all

---

[291] But see the discussion of the claimed rarity of TBSs in reality at the beginning of the twenty-first century *infra*, in the conclusions of both Part II and Part IV.

would readily agree, is an abominable act, but where it is the only means of preventing disastrous consequences, such as death, injury and grief on a large scale,
many believe that it must be resorted to, however reluctantly.

The opposing position rejects torture under any circumstances. I have put forward an idea, or a concept, which I call minimal absolutism, that encompasses
this and other absolutist prohibitions without attempting to defend every candidate for such prohibition, or to tie those it does defend to any comprehensive
moral theory. Unlike (at least some) wider absolutist theories, minimal absolutism
cannot therefore be accused of at least *general* rigidity or fanaticism. Moreover,
absolutist prohibitions may—and do—work in the real world, as shown by our
discussion of the death penalty for minor offences and torturous death penalty
in the West and on the waiving of informed consent during experiments for the
development of a vaccine for HIV/AIDS worldwide. They work even when they
clearly entail, as in the latter case, a horrendous catastrophe far greater than even
the most vicious and 'quantitatively' costly terrorist attack the world has either
known or is likely to know.

Parenthetically I would add that it is tempting to incorporate the minimal
absolutist rejection of torture into more general absolutist theories. It may be
argued, for instance, that even accepting Kant's categorical imperatives to be
mere formal frameworks within which what is moral in practice may vary with
circumstances, torture is the one (or just one) case where form and content are in
total, watertight concurrence, leaving no room for variation. An absolute prohibition on torture could also, arguably, be a good candidate for what people would
reach agreement on beyond Rawls' 'veil of ignorance',[292] and being quite narrow
would neatly fit at the top of what he calls the 'lexical order' of the principles they
would agree upon.[293]

However, none of this would be simple, let alone short, and all of it, I submit
again, is beyond what is necessary and sufficient for the purposes of this study,
and specifically for defending the position that torture is one act that is never
morally justifiable.

Anti-torture absolutists would claim that the overwhelming strength of the
'numbers' in the torture-justifying argument is also its moral downfall. This is
apparent even in the arguments of torture-justifying ethicists—they do raise
other, *qualitative* arguments, such as the terrorist's responsibility for his own suffering under torture and the need to distinguish between torturing a terrorist and
torturing an innocent person. However, the 'disastrous consequences' argument
is so powerful that, like the moral equivalent of a tsunami, it destroys all before

---

[292] See Rawls, *supra* n 8, Ch I §3; Ch III; *passim*. Luban uses the 'veil of ignorance' to argue
for the need for 'rock bottom protections' against arbitrary and lengthy loss of liberty under anti-
terrorism laws, which would surely apply equally to protection against torture. See *idem*, 'Eight
Fallacies About Liberty and Security' in RA Wilson (ed), *Human Rights in the 'War on Terror'*
(Cambridge: CUP, 2005) 242–257 (the quotation is from p 244).

[293] Rawls, *ibid*, 37–8.

it, so the consistent among these ethicists wind up conceding that if the catastrophe to be avoided is horrendous enough, the torture of innocent persons, such as members of the terrorist's family, would also be justified as a way of forcing the terrorist to disclose the life-saving information. This means you, me, her brother, his daughter are, potentially, either inflictors or victims of justified torture.

Even, however, when it is 'only' the terrorist who is being tortured, it is difficult for many of us to read the accounts of unimaginable cruelty inflicted by one human being on another and consider them to be, under certain circumstances, morally justifiable, and the torturer as possessing the characteristics of a moral person. After all, this aspect of morality is essentially about what you would and would not do to yourself and to your neighbour, including your vicious neighbour, in one situation or another.

Having said all that, would we not prefer the kind of neighbour who tells us: 'In hard times, I would do anything possible to save you'? The trouble is, those justifying torture in a TBS cannot in good conscience (or good logic) say this. At best they can say: 'In hard times, I would do anything possible to save you, providing that you are one of many would-be victims', which is somewhat less heart-warming, let alone comforting, especially if you think, in addition, of the kind of atrocities your neighbour is morally capable of committing in the process. Moreover, the neighbour has stepped unto a 'slippery surface' which forces that person to also say: 'I would do unto *anybody*—yourself and myself included—the worst things imaginable to save many innocent people.' The TBS, in all likelihood, will not reach your neighbourhood, but you are stuck with a potential torturer living next door.

In essence, the torture-justifying view creates (to use another metaphor) *a moral black hole*, one that may be small in diameter, admitting only one or two victims at a time, but the depths of inhumanity which it allows and justifies are unfathomable—enough to swallow our morality, our humanity, whole.

In contrast, a neighbour opposing torture absolutely, believing that morality necessarily involves *some* limits (beyond numerical ones) on human behaviour, could tell you: 'In hard times, I would do anything humanly possible to save you.'

PART II

PUBLIC, PRACTICAL MORALITY: IS IT MORALLY JUSTIFIABLE FOR A STATE TO TORTURE IN ORDER TO SAVE MANY INNOCENT LIVES?

7

Part II—Introduction

A. The Problem Defined

Described in a format similar to that used in Part I, the Part II version of the dilemma is as follows:

Agent Ethica,[1] a police interrogator in *a state facing terrorism*, is questioning a *detained terrorist suspect*, Vicious, who, *she is certain*, possesses information the disclosure of which is *urgently* needed to thwart a planned (and *imminent*) terrorist attack which would kill many *innocent civilians*. If she is similarly certain that *torture* is the only means of making him disclose that information, is it *morally justifiable* for the state to instruct, or at least *allow* Agent Ethica to torture Vicious?

There are two main differences between this version of the moral dilemma and the one discussed in Part I. First, the dilemma faced by a private person, a moral agent, in Part I is now faced by a state agent acting under official instructions, therefore by the state itself.[2] This will entail the addition of society-wide and long-term repercussions of actions to our considerations. Secondly, I am now posing it in the world as we know it at the time this study is being written—the beginning of the twenty-first century, so that other issues, blocked artificially in Part I out of the scenario to ensure its 'purity', such as uncertainty as to the facts[3] and the generally murky nature of real-life situations, will now have to be taken into account.

Jean Maria Arrigo's 'double-barrelled' version of our essential question, which she poses in terms of 'program design', is of relevance here:

According to studies the quintessential element of program design and implementation is a sound causal model relating input to output. Can we put (only) key terrorists into the torture chamber and put out at the other end timely and true knowledge of terrorist plans? Can just a little bit of torture interrogation cause just a little bit of harm to a democratic society?[4]

---

[1] All terms italicized in this paragraph are defined or explained below. The private names I have assigned the interrogator and the terrorist will not be used here as frequently as in Part I.

[2] There is a twist to this last point in the 'defence of necessity' models of legalized torture as well as in theoretical 'ex post' torture facilitating proposals, all discussed in Parts III and IV.

[3] See Part I, Ch 1, Section D.

[4] JM Arrigo, 'A Utilitarian Argument Against Torture Interrogation of Terrorists' 10(3) *Science and Engineering Ethics* 543 (2004) 545 (footnote omitted).

B. Descriptions and Definitions

- *'Agent Ethica' (AE)* is, as an agent of the state, following instructions and, as noted, our focus is now on the morality of those instructions rather than on Ethica herself.

- *'A state* facing *terrorism'* is used to ensure that the discussion involves a state whose society and leadership have had time to consider the moral issues on hand, and have taken the necessary steps to ensure that AE knows what her orders are for this situation. Thus we need not concern ourselves with the kind of spur-of-the-moment improvisations to which agents of a state for which a TBS is a new, unforeseen, unprepared-for situation must resort, and which essentially revert the dilemma back to the individual agent (but see further under 'allow' below). As for the nature of that state—to avoid a lengthy discussion I will describe it as a democracy at the beginning of the twenty-first century and leave it at that.

- *'A detained terrorist suspect'*: 'terrorism' and 'terrorist' will be used in the same sense as in Part I; 'detained' and 'suspect' need to be added in light of both the uncertainties and the institutions that have now been introduced.

- *'She is certain'* replaces the absolute, objective certainty regarding facts in Part I. Her certainty, however, is not altogether subjective, being that of a professional. It must apply to each and all of the factual assumptions which follow, namely not only that Vicious possesses information, but that its disclosure would thwart an attack, that the attack is imminent, that the attack would kill many innocent civilians, that no means other (or less inhuman) than torture would make Vicious disclose the information, and that torturing him would. Instructing, or allowing torture in circumstances where there is less than reasonable belief regarding any of these elements would push the scenario onto a 'slippery slope.'[5]

- *'Urgently, imminent'*: the question of whether the attack has to be imminent or it is sufficient for the information to be urgently needed to justify torture is a matter of both moral and legal debate, and will accordingly be discussed both here and in Parts III and IV.

- *'The innocent civilians'*: as in Part I, but with the added proviso that the state in question has a moral obligation to protect them as they are within the territory, or otherwise under the jurisdiction[6] of that state.

---

[5] Or further down it, depending on one's view.

[6] This term should be understood, at this stage, in the moral sense, ie denoting some moral responsibility of the state for those persons, rather than the legal sense, whether or not the two are synonymous.

- *'Morally justifiable'*: as in Part I, but it will be argued that the moral obligation cited immediately above entails a *duty* on the state to use all morally justifiable means at its disposal to protect the innocent civilians.

- *'Allow'* is used to provide for the case of Israel, whose Supreme Court (as noted) deferred the decision back to the individual interrogator, and for similar suggestions made (but not applied, so far) in the USA and by certain theorists. Even this, however, is a decision taken by society through its judiciary (see further under 'torture').

- *'Torture'* in this Part means '. . . any act by which severe pain or suffering, whether physical or mental, is intentionally inflicted on a person for such purposes as obtaining from him or a third person information or a confession, punishing him for an act he or a third person has committed or is suspected of having committed, or intimidating or coercing him or a third person, or for any reason based on discrimination of any kind, when such pain or suffering is inflicted by or at the instigation of or with the consent or acquiescence of a public official or other person acting in an official capacity. It does not include pain or suffering arising only from, inherent in or incidental to lawful sanctions.'[7] Thus we now use the full definition of the UN Convention Against Torture. The introduction of state involvement in the act of torture, omitted in Part I, is necessitated by the redirection of our focus onto the public sphere.

I propose to discuss in this Part what I consider the two main questions raised by the changes made to the TBS scenario. First, whether transferring the 'torture in a TBS' moral dilemma from the private to the public sphere *in itself* calls for a different moral solution. This question will be addressed in Chapter 8. The second question, to be addressed in Chapter 9, is whether, setting all else aside and assuming torture in a TBS to be morally justified—obviously against the position advocated in this study—states can torture in 'ticking bomb situations' while keeping both torture and the direct and indirect harm it may cause to a morally acceptable level, or else must slide down an inevitable, and intolerable 'slippery slope.' Other, non-'slippery slope' dangers, including 'slippery surface' ones that arise in this context, will also be considered.

---

[7] UN Convention Against Torture And Other Cruel, Inhuman Or Degrading Treatment Or Punishment, Art 1(1) UNGA res 39/46, 10 December 1984, entered into force 26 June 1987. (Henceforth: UN Convention Against Torture.)

For human rights treaties generally see eg Office of the High Commissioner for Human Rights, *Human Rights: A Compilation of International Instruments* (2 volumes, New York and Geneva: UN 1997) and that Office's website, <http://www.ohchr.org>.

This is not the only internationally—or nationally—recognized definition, but here too it would serve as a convenient and uncontroversial tool; the 'grey areas' around this definition, to the extent that such exist, will be discussed in Part IV, Ch 18.

8

Is there a 'Public Morality' that is Distinct from 'Private Morality'?

A. Preliminary Remarks

As in the previous Part, we are dealing in this chapter with, as it were, the 'tip' of a large moral issue rather than the whole of it. That large issue concerns the applicability of private morality to the public sphere, or the differences and similarities between moral behaviour in the two spheres; however, for our purposes we need only address the issue of public morality in extreme situations, and the question of whether or not, in such situations, acts of states should be limited by the kind of moral constraints debated in the previous Part.

Michael Walzer actually uses a TBS as a 'dramatic example' of his view that 'a particular act of government... may be exactly the right thing to do in utilitarian terms [of which Walzer, generally a non-utilitarian, approves in such circumstances] and yet leave the man who does it guilty of a moral wrong':[8]

> ...the first decision the new leader faces is this: he is asked to authorize the torture of a captured rebel leader who knows or probably knows the location of a number of bombs hidden in apartment buildings around the city, set to go off within the next twenty-four hours. He orders the man tortured, convinced that he must do so for the sake of the people who might otherwise die in the explosions—even though he believes that torture is wrong, indeed abominable, not just sometimes but always. He has expressed this belief often and angrily during his own campaign; the rest of us took it as a sign of his goodness. How should we regard him now? (How should he regard himself?)[9]

Walzer answers that we should regard the leader approvingly (as long as he is willing 'to acknowledge and bear... his guilt'):

> Here is the moral politician: it is by his dirty hands that we know him. If he were a moral man and nothing else, his hands would not be dirty; if he were a politician and nothing else, he would pretend that they were clean.[10]

---

[8] M Walzer, 'Political Action: The Problem of Dirty Hands' in M Cohen, T Nagel and T Scanlon (eds), *War and Moral Responsibility* (Princeton: Princeton University Press, 1974) 62–82, 58, 63 respectively.

[9] *Ibid*, 69.

[10] *Ibid*. I am puzzled by the practical aspect of Walzer's argument: How are 'we', the modern voters, who by and large see our leaders only through the media, in often carefully orchestrated

Another supporter of torture in a TBS, Lincoln Allison,[11] makes this point in even blunter terms:

Indeed, it is when we move from the sphere of private decisions...to formal political leadership, that we would least welcome the preservation of moral integrity. Whereas there is doubt about the meaning of utilitarianism...in private action, there is no doubt about what governments should do. They exist to maximise the benefits to the population and their role requires them to kill people, both in war and in the distribution and regulation of public expenditure. The politician who will not have blood on his hands, who will not seriously contemplate a Hiroshima, a Dresden or a *Belgrano* (irrespective of which of these was actually decided rightly) is no use to us.[12]

It should be emphasized that Walzer and Allison share neither the same views on the overall merits of utilitarianism nor on what is worthy of 'serious contemplation' in times of war.[13] They do, however, share the view that governments may justifiably resort to acts such as torture in a TBS on the basis of utilitarian calculations, regardless of their weight in private morality.

Walzer, and many others writing on the relations between private and public morality, have done so while examining the Machiavellian idea that 'it is necessary for a prince who wishes to maintain his position to learn how not to be good'[14] which modern theorists have termed the 'dirty hands' dilemma.[15] Much of the 'dirty hands' debate covers these relations, but some of it revolves around the issue of the individual leader's character and personal way of handling the tension between his/her private and public moral duties. I propose, however, to set that last issue aside here. We will assume that leaders confronting a TBS work within boundaries set by society through its institutions rather than that leaders may step outside *any* boundaries in such situations—even the view of the US administration in the wake of the 9/11 terrorist attacks, that the President may order the torturing of terrorists during war (see Part III, Chapter 15) conforms to this view, as it was argued on grounds of the US Constitution, namely that such authority was essentially granted by the US people. Otherwise we would be drawn back to discussing some type of personal morality, and render any examination

---

appearances, to 'know' that a particular leader is sincerely feeling 'guilt'? After all, many a Machiavellian leader would happily shed (public) tears of remorse if that is all it takes to swing 'liberal' voters to their side while luring the 'hardliners' by their actions. Paradoxically, it is in the *private* sphere that Walzer's 'dirty hands' criterion may be of some value, as we are much more capable of distinguishing true feelings from false, manipulative manifestations thereof in people with whom we interact directly.

[11] See Part I, Ch 3, n 58; Ch 5, n 259 and accompanying texts.

[12] L Allison, 'The Utilitarian Ethics of Punishment and Torture,' in *idem* (ed), *The Utilitarian Response: The Contemporary Viability of Utilitarian Political Philosophy* (London: Sage 1990) 9–29, 12.

[13] For Walzer's views on the latter subject see his well-known *Just and Unjust Wars: A Moral Argument with Historical illustrations* (New York: Basic Books, 1997).

[14] N Machiavelli, *The Prince* (1532), trans P Bondanella (Oxford: OUP, 1984), Ch XV.

[15] After a play by that name by JP Sartre, *Les Mains sales* (1948). For an English translation (by L Abel) see eg in *idem*, *No Exit and Other Plays: Dirty Hands, The Flies, The Respectful Prostitute* (New York: Vintage Books, 1989).

of the legal aspect of torturing in a TBS superfluous. Conversely, accepting that such boundaries exist need not necessarily tie our leaders' hands in the situation under consideration: we may, and arguably *should*, empower our leaders, as the US administration saw itself empowered, to use any means necessary (or at least to torture[16]) to save the nation, or the innocent civilians, in a TBS and similar emergencies—but the focus here will not be on what occupies our leaders' or agents' minds in a TBS, but rather on whether or not we should empower them to torture in such a situation.

In other words, and more specifically—the question in this section is whether, in a TBS, we think that our state may (and at times must) act, through its agent (Agent Ethica), differently from the way we think that an individual (Ethica of Part I) should act in a similar situation.

Why not avoid the whole 'headache' by keeping the absolute prohibition but allowing individuals, whether leaders or interrogators, who break it in TBSs to escape prosecution, or punishment, in retrospect? This 'keep-your-cake-and-have-it' approach, a prominent variety of which is the current Israeli model, will be touched upon here, but discussed in greater length at the following Parts.

B. The Main Differences Between the Private and Public Spheres

Theorists discussing the tensions between morality in the private and in the public spheres generally,[17] have by and large agreed that the following are the

---

[16] The difference as to responsibility between actually torturing and ordering that others torture should, I submit, be ignored, as it is morally negligible. Legally, it is nonexistent—see eg Rome Statute of the International Criminal Court (A/CONF.183/9), Arts 25(1)–25(3).

[17] See eg Allison, *supra* n 12; SI Benn, 'Private and Public Morality: Clean Living and Dirty Hands' in *idem* and GF Gaus (eds), *Public and Private in Social Life* (London: Croom Helm, 1983) 155–181; Steve Buckler, *Dirty Hands: The Problem of Political Morality* (Aldershot Hants: Avebury, 1993); CAJ Coady, 'Politics and the Problem of Dirty Hands,' in P Singer (ed) *A Companion to Ethics* (Malden, Mass: Blackwell, 1993) 373–383; BC Van Fraassen, 'Values and the Heart's Command' in CW Gowans (ed), *Moral Dilemmas* (New York and Oxford: OUP, 1987) 138–153, especially 142–7; SA Garrett, 'Political Leadership and "Dirty Hands": Winston Churchill and the City Bombing of Germany' in CJ Nolan (ed), *Ethics and Statecraft: The Moral Dimension of International Affairs* (Westport, Conn: Greenwood Press, 1995) 75–91; SA Garrett, *Conscience and Power: An Examination of Dirty Hands and Political Leadership* (New York: St Martin's Press, 1996); S Hampshire, 'Public and Private Morality' in *idem* (ed), *Public and Private Morality* (Cambridge: CUP, 1978) 23–53; S Hampshire, *Innocence and Experience* (Cambridge, Mass: Harvard University Press, 1989), Ch 5; WL LaCroix, *War and International Ethics: Tradition and Today* (Lahmand, MD: University Press of America, 1988), especially Ch 13(II); T Nagel, 'Ruthlessness in Public Life' in Hampshire (ed), *Public and Private Morality* (CUP, 1978) 75–91; T Sorell, *Moral Theory and Anomaly* (Oxford: Blackwell, 2000), Ch 4; Walzer, *supra* n 8.

For a thorough analysis of the differences between public and private morality in the specific context of torture in a TBS see M Kremnitzer and R Segev, 'The Application of Force in the Course of GSS Interrogations—A Lesser Evil?' [Hebrew] 4 *Mishpat u-Mimshal* 667 (1998) 702–707.

main differences between actions within the two, leading to such tensions and, arguably, to two different 'moralities':

1. *Representation:* A person acting within the public sphere—and especially those acting for a state, is not only acting on her own behalf (as she would within the private sphere), but is, rather, representing the public and acting for their interests as a whole.

2. *Numbers:* Actions within the public sphere both involve and impact on much larger numbers of people.

3. *Impersonality and impartiality:* Actions within the public sphere are impersonal, and must be impartial, avoiding the kind of inter-personal commitments and preferences which figure prominently in our private lives.

4. *Violence:* Actions within the public sphere often involve violence or the threat of violence, whereas in the private sphere they seldom do.

5. *Consequences:* To an extent as a further claim, and to an extent as a conclusion drawn from those cited above, it is argued that actions within the public sphere are more often, and to a greater degree, oriented toward consequences.

Here are a few examples of arguments using these points (in addition to the two already cited).

Stuart Hampshire emphasizes the fifth point, claiming a frequent need for leaders to choose 'between two evils'—that is, two evil consequences:

The exercise of reason in public affairs is distinguished from its normal use in private life by its negativity; it seems unavoidable that, in the exercise of political power, one should very often, perhaps usually, be choosing between two evils, and trying to prevent the greater misery and the worse injustice. A government is required to improvise in the emergencies which are bound to occur in the unceasing struggle for power between states and between parties and social groups within states. An innocent interlude is not to be expected by anyone who possesses real political power.[18]

Steve Buckler takes the issue termed 'representation' here as the source of what characterizes action within the public (in this case political) sphere:

Politics consists in activity in the light of collective concerns. In view of this, it will have distinctive features: it will place a strong emphasis upon consequences, it will often

---

[18] Hampshire, *Innocence and Experience, ibid,* 172. In the spirit of his anti-theory view, Hampshire later adds the following: 'A philosopher in his study is in no position to lay down rules for justified murders and reasonable treachery. Nor can one determine *a priori* what degree of achievement outweighs what degrees of inhumanity in the means employed. Once again the philosophical point to be recorded is that there is no completeness and no perfection to be found in morality.' (*ibid,* 177). This presumes, questionably to my mind, agreement that there are such things as 'justified murders . . . reasonable treachery' etc, and that the acceptability of 'inhumanity in the means' may always be determined by the sole criterion of 'achievement'. Hampshire also fails to address the fact that legislators, diplomats, generals and politicians have, in their own 'studies', or parlours, placed *a priori* restrictions on certain actions by leaders, states and agents thereof, regardless of such actions' consequential 'weight'. This point will be discussed below.

involve judgment of an acutely impersonal sort and it will be bound up with questions of power and appearances...Questions about means and ends become prominent and judgements of expedience become a principal characteristic of the political standpoint.[19]

Thomas Nagel discusses the implications of the 'impersonality' of public action:

The impersonality suitable for public action has two aspects: it implies both a heightened concern for results and a stricter requirement of impartiality. It warrants methods usually excluded for private individuals, and sometimes it licences ruthlessness.[20]

Tom Sorell brings the discussion closer to our angle of the subject, considering institutional and what may be termed 'extra-institutional'[21] methods of dealing with emergencies, which he links to the issue of numbers:

Other institutions exist to cope with types of public emergency that collective experience has shown to be severe and not entirely preventable. Thus there are established, politically controlled bodies to deal with military invasion, with disease, with threats from the extremes of weather...But to deal with the actions of dangerous people across the board, other measures and institutions, perhaps less public and more questionable, may also have to be contemplated. Thus, if it is a moral requirement on governments that they be ready for terrorism or that they act to contain aggressive regimes abroad, it may also be a moral requirement that governments be ready to carry out assassinations or acts of sabotage, if there is reason to believe that the danger can be met in no other way. Action that might seem unthinkable to individual agents in danger may have to be considered seriously by the authorities if thousands are at risk.[22]

There is, however, no universal agreement regarding these differences, and certainly not regarding their significance. CAJ Coady, for instance, attacks every one of the points of difference listed above, at least to the extent that they imply different moral standards. Thus countering the argument that, in his words, the '"necessity" to manipulate, lie, betray, steal or kill may arise in private life occasionally but is it much more *frequent* in politics'[23] (corresponding to point 4 above), he argues, rather convincingly to my mind, that:

Politics may be very bland as, I imagine, in Monaco, and private life can be a maelstrom of agonizing conflicts, as in a black ghetto or an Ethiopian village during famine.[24]

---

[19] Buckler, *supra* n 17, 146.

[20] Nagel, *supra* n 17, 82.

[21] Bernard Williams uses the term 'structured and unstructured violence' in the same context. See *idem*, 'Politics and Moral Character' in Hampshire (ed), *supra* n 17, 55–73, 71.

[22] Sorell, *supra* n 17, 74–5. Sorell later writes, in a manner similar to Walzer: 'A more likely source of paradox is the following. As a ruler or member of a government, an individual must always be ready to authorise killing or torture if the threat to public safety is big enough; but in private life the very same person should be very averse to doing anything of the kind...' (*ibid*, 100–101). Like Hampshire, Sorell seems to make far-reaching moral presumptions ('must always be ready') which, I submit, cannot be taken as self-evident or axiomatic.

[23] Coady, *supra* n 17, 376.

[24] *Ibid*.

Allison's contention that the 'politician who will not have blood on his hands, who will not seriously contemplate a Hiroshima, a Dresden or a *Belgrano*...is no use to us'[25] is thus questionable in contemporary Monaco, and even in a state much more involved in international politics and violence, like the United Kingdom, we may wonder, even on utilitarian grounds, whether voters must, as Allison seems to suggest, *always* prefer, as it were, a Churchill to an Atlee.

Regarding the issue of representation (point 1 above), Coady argues the following:

> ...representation, by itself, does not do much to alter one's moral stature; it extends one's powers and capabilities, though it also restricts them in various ways, but the question of moral limits and freedoms will be largely a matter for ordinary moral assessment of the institutional purposes for which these powers have been created.[26]

It may also be argued that impartiality (point 3) is often morally required in the private sphere as well; for instance—few would call into question the moral duty of a parent taking his or her child and the child's friend to a theme park to be as impartial as a public servant in the allocation of goods (such as sweets and drinks) and the provision of services (such as piggybacks) between the two.

C. The 'Quantitative' Aspects

As a first step in analysing the relevance of the discussion above to our topic I propose that, in view of this topic's limited scope within the general private/public morality debate, we set aside one aspect much discussed in that general debate, the aspect of frequency—as reflected in the argument that moral issues in the public sphere *more often* involve large numbers of people, violence and huge consequences than they do in private life. Regardless of whether, or to what extent, this is true or significant for that general debate, our concern here, both under the Part I and the Part II scenarios, has been solely with a kind of situation *already* defined as an emergency involving violence, large numbers of people and dire consequences.

Other 'quantitative' aspects may be similarly set aside, but in a more qualified manner. Regarding the issues of numbers and consequences, I submit that utilitarians, other consequentialists and deontologists with a 'disastrous consequences' clause[27] justifying torture in a distinctly public TBS have in fact relied on the 'lesser evil' argument discussed in Part I rather than elicited any principled justification from the very fact that the scene was played out in the private rather than the public sphere. At first glance it may seem that Walzer, Allison and

---

[25] *Supra*, text accompanying n 12.
[26] Coady, *supra* n 17, 377.
[27] See Part I, Ch 3.

Sorell take exception to this view, all claiming that, specifically in emergencies, different moral approaches are needed in the two spheres.[28] It is clear from their own words, however, that they are simply making a consequentialist argument about likely circumstances rather than a principled (or an otherwise principled) one. Allison explicitly evokes utilitarian reasons;[29] while Sorell, as stated, argues that 'a ruler... must always be ready to authorize killing or torture *if the threat to public safety is big enough*'[30] (emphasis added). Therefore the other passage by Sorell quoted above[31] should be understood as arguing that it is the difference between *one* 'individual agent' being 'in danger' and '*thousands* being at risk' that renders certain, otherwise 'unthinkable' actions worthy of consideration, rather than the fact that such actions are considered by the 'authorities.' Put differently, in the unlikely event that (as in our 'pure, theoretical' scenario in Part I) an 'individual' needs to act where 'the threat to public safety is big enough' as 'thousands are at risk', Sorell, it appears, would have the agent consider the same extreme actions applying the same moral criteria. There is also nothing to suggest that Walzer, who is, generally, not a consequentialist but whose ideal leader would nevertheless order a terrorist tortured 'for the sake of the people who might otherwise die in the explosions'[32] would counsel a private moral agent in an identical situation to act differently. At any rate, none of the three provides any alternative, or additional, justification.

The fact that torture, or similar actions, have to be considered by a state may nevertheless have greater consequences, and consequences for a greater number of people, than would action by an individual. This is an effect of my first point, namely that of representation, coupled by our search for a solution for a 'state facing terrorism', entailing a need for policies rather than one-off improvisations.[33] That a state decides to adopt torture as one of its tools of governance—even in rare cases—will surely have a deeper and wider effect on that society (and possibly on others) than a decision by one of its private citizens to torture one terrorist.

D. 'Non-quantitative' Aspects

Beyond the concept of 'the divine rights of kings,' one could find a kind of sweeping principled *ex officio*—or *raison d'état*—justification for actions which a leader

---

[28] See *supra*, texts accompanying nn 9–10, 12 and 22, respectively.

[29] Allison describes the purpose of his essay as 'to re-develop and defend a utilitarian system of ethics defined as a system which is consequentialist, aggregate and sensualist...' *supra* n 12, 9. For Walzer see text accompanying n 8.

[30] Sorell, *supra* n 22.

[31] *Supra*, text accompanying n 22.

[32] See *supra* n 9 and accompanying text.

[33] See *supra*, Ch 7, Section A.

may carry out and individual persons may not in the writings of some (but obviously not all[34]) early 'social contractarians'. Thomas Hobbes[35] and, arguably, Immanuel Kant,[36] seem to view social contracts as granting leaders, or sovereigns, unlimited authority, and the citizenry no right to oppose it.[37]

However, while all save anarchists agree that the state, through its officials, should have powers that ordinary citizens should not, notably a near-monopoly

---

[34] John Locke, for instance, states simply, that 'Where-ever law ends, tyranny begins' and infers that a tyrant 'may be opposed'. See *idem, Two Treatises of Government* (1690) (Cambridge: CUP, 1988), Book II, Ch XVIII, sec 202. John Austin gives the general duty to obey governments, but the right, nevertheless, to rebel against a bad one as an example of his rule-utilitarian view whereby in most cases, 'Our rules would be fashioned on utility; our conduct, on our rules', but in certain circumstances of 'comparatively rare occurrence', rules must be abandoned and we must 'calculate *specific* consequences to the best of our ability'. See *idem, The Province of Jurisprudence Determined* (1832), ed WE Rumble (Cambridge: CUP, 1995), Lecture II, 49, 52, 53, respectively.

[35] Hobbes writes '…because the right of bearing the person of them all is given to him they make sovereign, by covenant only of one to another, and not of him to any of them, there can happen no breach of covenant on the part of the sovereign; and consequently none of his subjects, by any pretence of forfeiture, can be freed from his subjection. […] nothing the sovereign representative can do to a subject, on what pretence soever, can properly be called injustice or injury; because every subject is author of every act the sovereign doth, so that he never wanteth right to any thing, otherwise than as he himself is the subject of God, and bound thereby to observe the laws of nature' (T Hobbes, *The Leviathan* (1651) ed JCA Gaskin (New York: OUP 1996), Chapters XVIII, XX, respectively).

[36] Kant, whose views are generally more 'democratic' than those of Hobbes, nevertheless writes: '…the power of the state to put the law into effect is also *irresistible,* and no rightfully established commonwealth can exist without a force of this kind to suppress all internal resistance. For such resistance would be dictated by a maxim which, if it became general, would destroy the whole civil constitution and put an end to the only state in which men can possess rights.

It thus follows that all resistance against the supreme legislative power, all incitement of the subjects to violent expressions of discontent, all defiance which breaks out into rebellion, is the greatest and most punishable crime in a commonwealth, for it destroys its very foundations. This prohibition is absolute. And even if the power of the state or its agent, the head of state, has violated the original contract by authorising the government to act tyrannically, and has thereby, in the eyes of the subject, forfeited the right to legislate, the subject is still not entitled to offer counter-resistance. The reason for this is that the people, under an existing civil constitution, has no longer any right to judge how the constitution should be administered.' (I Kant, 'On the Common Saying: "This May be True in Theory, but it does not Apply in Practice"' in *idem, Political Writings,* trans HB Nisbet, ed H Reiss (2nd edn, Cambridge: CUP, 1991) 61–92, 81). In a footnote (81–2) Kant also argues, *inter alia,* that '…it might be necessary for someone to betray someone else, even if their relationship were that of father and son, in order to preserve the state from catastrophe. This preservation of the state from evil is an absolute duty, while the preservation of the individual is merely a relative duty (i.e. it applies only if he is not guilty of a crime against the state).' Since Kant does not seem to limit this principle, eg to when the said state has not 'violated the original contract', I find the possible combination of the two ideas a rather chilling prospect.

[37] An earlier writer, St Thomas Aquinas (1225–1274), reaches, from a different starting point (the state as 'public authority acting for the common good'), a similar view on the sovereign's unique powers—see for instance his explanation of why only public officials are allowed 'to kill [intentionally] a man who has sinned' *idem, Summa Theologica,* trans by the Fathers of the English Dominican Province (1947) Benzinger Brothers Inc, Hypertext Version 1995, 1996 New Advent Inc, <http://www.newadvent.org/summa>, accessed 18 May 2001, second part of the second part, question 64, article 3. See similarly E Anscombe, 'War and Murder' in JG Haber (ed), *Absolutism and its Consequentialist Critics* (Lanham, MD: Rowan and Littlefield, 1994) 29–40, especially 29–32.

on the use of force; the idea of unlimited authority of a sovereign is not relevant here. As stated, we are assuming a 'democracy at the beginning of the twenty-first century' as a given,[38] which means a more democratic modern state (or perhaps a more modern democratic state) than Kant, and certainly Aquinas and Hobbes, advocated.

In addition, in virtually all contemporary states, democratic or otherwise, official conduct in emergencies is regulated by specific laws and orders. Events like the terrorist attacks on the USA in 11 September 2001 are met by a flurry of new legislation in many countries, which almost invariably granted governments added powers, but seldom, if ever, unlimited ones.[39] This suggests, I believe, a *range* of considerations and justifications *within* the sovereign's reasons for action, therefore a mere assertion of the sovereign's limitless powers by virtue of it being a sovereign would not suffice. For these reasons, this view will also be set aside. Nevertheless, a *legal* argument that a ruler in a certain state may, by virtue of his or her constitutional powers, have the authority to order the torture of terrorist suspects during war was indeed put forward in the aftermath of the aforementioned event, and it will be discussed in Part III.

In contrast, another difference between the two scenarios stemming from the fact that officials are acting as representatives must, I submit, be taken into account. In Part I we limited ourselves to questions of whether torturing the terrorist in a TBS would be morally *permissible* to Ethica, the moral agent.[40] However, as Agent Ethica, a police interrogator acting for the state, she is—like the state itself—under an *obligation* to defend her fellow citizens, an obligation which is closely connected to the state's monopoly on violence, imprisonment etc, and is similarly uncontroversial. Now, the state must do all that is permissible (and within constraints such as budget, availability of equipment and staff, and so on) to defend its citizens. In other words, the police force, unlike the private citizen, is by definition 'a good Samaritan', denied the option to forego the use of permissible means that are at its disposal.

Finally, a note on the issue of impartiality—we should bear in mind that the moral agent of Part I, Ethica, though a private individual, was facing a 'public-type' emergency not only because of the numbers of people involved, but also in the sense that in defining the problem it was determined that neither herself nor her own, private loved ones or crucial interests were endangered.[41] This means that morally she had no justification for being any less impartial in her considerations than a public agent. From this angle too, there is therefore little separating the two scenarios.

---

[38] See Ch 7, Section A.

[39] For such legislation see eg the reports submitted by states to the UN Security Council's Anti-Terrorism Committee, established under resolution 1373 of 28 September 2001, on the Committee's website, <http://www.un.org/Docs/sc/committees/1373>, accessed 21 November 2002.

[40] See Part I, Ch 1, Section B.

[41] See *ibid.*

E. Unlimited Powers for Governments in Emergencies—For and Against

I have concluded that, to the extent that contemporary writers so inclined address the issue of *why* leaders of states should be allowed to order acts such as torture, they justify it on consequentialist grounds, namely on the need to cause a 'lesser evil' in order to prevent a (much) greater one from happening. This is in line with anti-absolutist moral reasoning, discussed in Part I. I will now present two more examples of such anti-absolutist consequentialist positions, this time centring on large-scale, intentional killings of civilians during war, but will then make a brief comment questioning the applicability of theoretical consequentialist anti-absolutism in the real-life context of this Part, before citing arguments against unlimited powers for leaders and governments, even in emergencies.

RB Brandt, applying his rule-utilitarian views to the laws of war, suggests that:

It is conceivable that ideal rules of war would include one rule to the effect that *anything* is allowable, if necessary to prevent *absolute catastrophe*.[42] (Emphases added.)

More concretely—and, it appears, less strictly—Brandt proposes the following:

A proper (not ideally precise) rule for such operations [as 'area bombing of the kind practised in Hamburg' in WWII, mentioned immediately above] might be: substantial destruction of lives and property of enemy civilians is permissible only when there is good evidence that it will significantly enhance the prospect of victory.[43]

RM Hare, applying his not-dissimilar 'two-level morality' to the conduct of states in war, emphasizes the need to inculcate deontological morality in general, and the laws of war in particular, unto citizens and soldiers.[44] However, in rare, extreme circumstances, namely 'where there is a strong indication that the situation is so peculiar that the application of the general principle is unlikely to be for the best,'[45] his second level, which he here describes as 'specific rule-utilitarianism' comes into play. At such times, rules must be broken and reshaped, under what is essentially a straightforward act-utilitarian calculation. Thus in conclusion, Hare more than hints at his support for the destruction of Hiroshima by a nuclear bomb in 1945, stating that,

---

[42] RB Brandt, 'Utilitarianism and the Rules of War' in M Cohen, T Nagel and T Scanlon (eds), *War and Moral Responsibility* (Princeton: Princeton University Press, 1974) 25–45, 27.

[43] *Ibid*, 36. Brandt distinguishes between 'wars like World War II, where the stakes are very high' (*ibid*) and where such rules would apply, and lower-stake wars, where he proposes somewhat different utility-based rules. Brand also emphasises that 'we know enough about how bombing affects civilian morale to know that such bombing could be justified only rarely, if at all' (*ibid*, 39).

[44] RM Hare, 'Rules of War and Moral Reasoning' in Marshall, Cohen, Nagel and Scanlon (eds), *supra* n 42, 46–61, 53–57. See the brief discussion of his theory in Part I, Ch 5, Section B.

[45] *Ibid*, 57.

I would include more people [than Nagel, who opposes the Hiroshima bombing] in the class of those whose sufferings are relevant to our moral decisions (for example, in the Hiroshima case, those that will die if the war is not ended quickly, as well as those actually killed in the bombing).[46]

Brandt, Hare and Allison would theoretically allow our leaders to do *anything* if the stakes are high enough. However, in the real world, they may not be the anti-absolutists that they are in theory. At the risk of sounding demagogic I will pose the following question: would Allison, for instance, insist that 'the politician who...will not seriously contemplate a Hiroshima, a Dresden *or an Auschwitz* is no use to us'? (words in italics added)[47] Would Brandt or Hare? I doubt very much that any of them would, nor do I think that they would need to abandon their utilitarian convictions in order to reject such a suggestion. I therefore submit that where public policy in the real world is concerned, there may be room for utility-based minimal absolutism. This point will be discussed further in the specific context of torture.

Many other writers, including some who generally point to differences between morality in the private and the public spheres, emphasize that neither are these differences to be taken too far, nor should public morality be considered limitless, even in emergencies.

Thus Nagel, having stressed the 'heightened concern for results' in public action,[48] goes on to qualify that position:

But not everything is permitted. Restrictions on the treatment of individuals continue to operate from a public point of view, and they cannot be implemented entirely by the courts. One of the hardest lines to draw in public policy is the one that defines where the ends stop justifying the means. If results were the only basis for public morality then it would be possible to justify anything, including torture and massacre, in the service of sufficiently large interests. Whether the limits are drawn by specific constitutional protections or not, the strongest constraints of individual morality will continue to limit what can be publicly justified even by extremely powerful consequentialist reasons.[49]

Buckler, who analysis the problem of 'dirty hands' from an essentially virtue ethical standpoint, reaches the conclusion that this problem should be limited to those deeds which are not 'monstrous':

...we might want to insist that, despite its autonomous standpoint, politics can itself embody a value which is the source of noncontingent obligations and which may give a moral centre of gravity to the practice of politics.

---

[46] *Ibid*, 61. For a similar justification, by the US Secretary of State for War at the time, see Henry L Stimson, 'The Decision to Use the Atomic Bomb' in Amy Gutmann and Dennis Thompson (eds), *Ethics & Politics: Cases and Comments* (Chicago: Nelson-Hall Publishers, 1984) 4–15.

[47] *Cf supra*, n 12 and accompanying text.

[48] See text accompanying n 20.

[49] Nagel, *supra* n 17, 89.

Buckler goes on to talk of 'broad limits to the practice of politics' which are set by 'a definition of what it is to be a moral person, to be possessed of a moral character and identity'. Struggling to 'itemize' these limits, Buckler nevertheless provides good, and relevant, clues:

There may be some evils with which we simply cannot collude no matter what the collective benefit, or the collective risk of noncollusion (—are there any risks that would justify collusion with a state engaged in genocide?). Again, there may also be deeds which become horrific because of their scale (torture would seem to fall into this category).

Buckler goes on to argue that dirty hands is a dilemma within these boundaries, not exceeding them:

...the crux will lie in the difference between that which is morally undesirable and that which is unacceptable because it is monstrous...And we need not think of this as purely personal limit: acting so as to jeopardize one's moral identity is equally to cut oneself off from others, from the moral community within which we can construe ourselves and be recognized by others as moral persons.[50]

Garrett reflects on the citizen's right and duty to place moral limits on leaders' conduct:

...the morally sensitive citizen has not only a right but even a duty to suggest that in terms of certain basic values the credo for the statesman should be 'thus far and no farther.'...we say to the statesman that we accept your doing things that would be abhorrent if done in private life, but that this grant of freedom to be sometimes wicked is not unbounded. Even here, moreover, there can be a utilitarian aspect in our message.[51]

In Part III, the possibility of leaders having unfettered powers during emergencies, and specifically to order the torture of terrorists, will be revisited.

F. Conclusion: Private Versus Public—the Main Moral Similarities and Differences

The discussion above shows, I believe, that the crux of the arguments for and against torturing in a TBS is not to be found in the question of whether the would-be torturer is acting in a private or public capacity. In fact, practically all the theorists cited both here and in Part I have debated torture in a TBS as a dilemma faced by an official interrogator rather than a private person, but have done so within the terms of general moral or ethical debate, rather than limiting it to 'public policy' issues. Similarly, examples discussed in Chapter 4 such as 'the sheriff, the "negro" and the mob'; 'Jodie and Mary'; a torturous death penalty; and waiving consent when testing HIV/AIDS vaccines on humans are all clearly

---

[50] Buckler, *supra* n 17, 40, 99, 149.
[51] Garrett, *supra* n 17, 49.

public policy issues, and yet the moral debate regarding them revolves mainly around general ethical principles rather than those specific to the public arena. As in Part I, the principal moral question here is whether the morality of human action is, ultimately, open-ended or constrained by some form of absolutism, however minimal, with emergencies setting the scene for such *'ultimum'*. More specifically, the question is whether the prevention of a 'disastrous catastrophe' justifies torture, or whether torture should be absolutely prohibited regardless of the consequences.

Nevertheless, the switch from the private to the public arena does have significant repercussions for the moral debate, stemming mainly from three of the five putative differences between actions within the private and public spheres discussed in this section:

• *Representation:* The shift from a private individual to an agent who acts on behalf of society as a whole entails a positive moral duty to protect the innocent civilians, through whatever means society in our democratic state deems permissible.

• *Numbers, consequences:* While the immediate scenario, hence the number of persons immediately affected by it, remain essentially the same, a decision by a democratic state to use torture, however rarely, as a tool of policy, would have much wider effects, on a much larger number of people, than would a single act of torture by an individual. Such effects, I will later claim, would be felt from the moment such a state takes this decision, rather than only after a decision to actually torture a person has been taken.

9

'Slippery Slope' and Other Dangers

We have now arrived at the second—and main—question that this Part aims to address: setting all else aside and assuming (for me, obviously, without conviction) that torture in a TBS could be morally justified, whether states can torture in a TBS while limiting torture only to such (or comparable) situations, or else slide inevitably down a morally unacceptable 'slippery slope'. Are there, in other words, *consequentialist* reasons for placing certain absolute prohibitions, in this case on torture, at least on state actions? This question will be addressed once two comments are made, on the issue of the idle bystander, necessitated by the shift from the 'laboratory' case to the 'real life' one; and on the limits of the 'slippery slope' debate.

A. Preliminary Remarks: the Issue of the Idle Bystander

It will be recalled that an Israeli Supreme Court Judge, Mishael Heshin, accused a human rights lawyer who defended an absolute prohibition on torture, even in an imaginary TBS, as follows:

> ...this is the most extreme immoral position I have ever heard. A thousand people are about to die, and you propose to do nothing?[52]

Along similar lines, Michael S Moore argues:

> The...interrogator must choose for others who will pay the costs for his decision if he *decides not to act*, a cost he does not have to bear...[53] [Emphasis added.]

In Part I there was, *ex hypothesi*, only one way to prevent the bomb from exploding—to torture Vicious, therefore the stark choice was indeed between torturing and doing 'nothing,' or standing 'idly by'. However, in the present scenario, namely in a real-life public case, an accusation along the lines posed by Justice

[52] HCJ 8049/96 *Muhammad 'Abd al-'Aziz Hamdan v the General Security Service*, hearing of 14 November 1996, as described by the Israeli newspaper *Haaretz* (15 November 1996) A full quotation of his words may be found in the Introduction to this book.
[53] MS Moore, 'Torture and the Balance of Evils' 23 *Israel L Rev* 280 (1989) 329. See similarly LS Sheleff, *Ultimate Penalties: Capital Punishment, Life Imprisonment, Physical Torture* (Columbus: Ohio State University Press, 1987) 306.

Heshin, MS Moore and Sheleff would have been misleading: a variety of arguably efficient non-torturous means could be used in the interrogation of the terrorist, and torturing him is only *presumed*—but not guaranteed—to be the *most*
efficient one. In carrying out its duties, a state often, and legitimately, opts for a
means which, within the immediate context, is less than ideal. Among the reasons for this may be budgetary or humanpower constraints, priorities, internal
or external politics and even ethical considerations. Such factors affect decisions
on matters as diverse as acceptable road-safety levels, provision of hospital equipment, and the purchase and even use of weapons and other means by which a
state protects its citizens.

Moreover, whereas in Part I Ethica faced Vicious and his bomb all by herself,
in a real-life public case where there is a threat of an imminent terrorist attack the
state will operate on a variety of levels concurrently with the terrorist's interrogation: roadblocks will be set up, police will patrol vulnerable areas, citizens are
alerted, intelligence-gathering operations are mounted or intensified, and more.
In this Part too, it is assumed that unless the terrorist is tortured, the bomb will in
all likelihood explode, but here it cannot be argued that where a state decides not
to torture, it stands idly by while the blood of its citizens is being shed. Nor can it
even be claimed that all such a state does is make symbolic, ineffective gestures:
As will be seen, non-violent interrogations are often effective, as are the other
anti-terrorist means such as those described above; each could, and in fact has,[54]
prevented terrorist bombs from exploding, and they are only assumed here to be
insufficient, or less effective than torture.

In a real-life TBS, those supporting torture cannot therefore claim themselves
to be the good Samaritan, while the anti-torture absolutists play the part of the
priest or the Levite.[55] The issue here too is whether or not, to use Sheleff's words,
'*any* means is justified' (emphasis added)[56] in helping the needy in question, not
whether to help them or to 'pass by on the other side'.[57]

B. Preliminary Remarks: the Limits of the 'Slippery Slope' Debate

In Part I, I described the 'slippery slope' argument as a consequentialist one, of
the type 'if you perform act A_1, justifying it by its desirable result R_1, you will also,

---

[54] Following are three real-life examples, all from Israel during the first half of 2002. 19 February
2002: a bus driver prevented a suicide attack by pushing a would-be suicide bomber out of the bus.
4 May 2002: a surprise police roadblock stopped a car which was loaded with explosives. The two
would-be suicide bombers tried to escape, were shot at and some of the explosives exploded, killing
both. 24 May 2002: a security guard at a Tel Aviv nightclub shot at a would-be suicide bomber,
whose bomb then exploded outside the club, the terrorist being the only fatality.
See eg *Haaretz*, 20 February 2002, 5 May 2002 and 24 May 2002, respectively.

[55] See *New Testament*, Luke 10: 30–37.

[56] Sheleff, *supra* n 53, 476.

[57] As the priest and the Levite did in the parable, *supra* n 55, verses 31 and 32.

inevitably, bring about undesirable results R_2, R_3, R_4 etc'. Applied to our topic, the 'slippery slope' argument is that even assuming torture to be theoretically justified in a TBS, it is impossible in practice to erect an efficient wedge which would allow the production of its justified results while barring the unjustified ones, to the extent that the latter ultimately have, in the consequentialists' own terms, the effect of overriding the original justification for torture.

In other words, the 'slippery slope' argument is that torturing in a TBS would inevitably lead to much worse overall consequences than its supporters have anticipated, so much so that an absolute prohibition on torture would actually achieve better overall results, even for a state facing terrorism.

Four comments will now be made, setting out the limits, as I see them, of what a discussion of the 'slippery slopes' of torture may reasonably achieve. First, in the real world, a certain slide down 'slippery slopes' occurs inevitably. Alan Dershowitz tries to refute this in our specific context:

An appropriate response to the slippery slope is to build in a principled break. For example, if nonlethal torture were legally limited to convicted terrorists who had knowledge of future massive terrorist attacks, were given immunity, and still refused to provide the information, there might still be objections to the use of torture, but they would have to go beyond the slippery slope argument.[58]

Dershowitz is apparently making a theoretical point rather than a practical suggestion, as under such a system torture would not be permissible in situations where he himself consistently advocates its use, namely where a *'suspect* had information needed to prevent an imminent terrorist attack'[59] (emphasis added). At any rate, I submit that even his theoretical point is in practice untenable, because where a system which has adopted that 'principled break' is faced with cases of urgently needed information, enormous pressures are likely to build up on the prosecution, judges and juries. For example, there may be pressure for trials to be swift, so that suspects may quickly become 'convicted terrorists' and thus 'qualify' for torture. Alternatively, there may be a desire for suspected terrorists to be convicted of light-weight but easy-(and quick)-to-prove 'terrorist' crimes. More generally, there may be pressure on the legislature and courts to expand the definitions of such crimes and expedite procedures for processing cases under them—all so that suspects may speedily and easily be convicted of 'terrorism', and their torture commence. In addition, there are serious 'slippery slopes' dangers in determining what constitutes 'knowledge', 'future', and 'massive'.

However, that a certain extent—or amount—of undesirable consequences is unavoidable when states act does not automatically render such acts immoral.

---

[58] AM Dershowitz, *Why Terrorism Works: understanding the threat, responding to the challenge* (New Haven: Yale University Press, 2002) 147.

[59] *Ibid*, 158, and see the example he gives, discussed *infra*, text accompanying n 80. For a similar criticism see SF Kreimer, 'Too Close to the Rack and the Screw: Constitutional constraints on torture' 6 *Univ of Penn J of Const L* 278 (2003) 321.

There are, for instance, no just wars without civilians being mistakenly or unintentionally killed, nor is there any justice system that does not, from time to time, erroneously convict and punish innocent persons. Most of us would nevertheless accept as morally justifiable the establishment and operation of institutions such as armed forces, courts and prisons. Ronald Dworkin's argument against the claim that euthanasia would necessarily lead to 'Nazi eugenics' may also be relevant here:

That ['slippery slope'] argument also loses its bite once we understand that legalizing *no* euthanasia is itself harmful to many people, then we realize that doing our best to draw and maintain a defensible line, acknowledging and trying to guard against the risk that others will draw the line differently in the future, is better than abandoning those people altogether. There are dangers both in legalizing and refusing to legalize, the rival dangers must be balanced, and neither should be ignored.[60]

To be effective, the 'slippery slope' argument must therefore be, as noted, not merely that an act may have some undesirable consequences, but that no 'defensible line' can in practice be drawn (or maintained) to prevent undesired consequences 'heavy' enough to *outweigh* the desired ones.

Which brings us to the second comment: while the theoretical consequentialist formula—judging an act as moral or immoral by weighing its positive and negative consequences—is fairly straightforward, we do not enjoy in this Part the luxury of comparing essentially identical values, namely human suffering, as we did in Part I.[61] In its simplest form, the 'slippery slope' argument against torture was put forward by Amnesty International in a worldwide report on torture:

From the point of view of society, the argument of torturing 'just once' does not hold. Once justified and allowed for the narrower purpose of combating political violence, torture will almost inevitably be used for a wider range of purposes against an increasing proportion of the population.[62]

More recently, *The Economist* phrased the same argument in its Opinion column as follows:

Even if you allow, as many will not, that torture might be justified under the most extreme circumstances, it would be difficult to confine its use to those very rare cases. Any system that allowed torture in tightly controlled situations would risk eroding into wider use.[63]

---

[60] R Dworkin, *Life's Dominion: An Argument about Abortion and Euthanasia* (London: HarperCollins, 1993) 197–8.

[61] See Part I, Ch 3, Section A.

[62] Amnesty International, *Torture in the Eighties*, AI Index: ACT 04/01/84 (London: 1984) 7. As will be seen below, Amnesty International's own reports point to 'slippery slope' dangers beyond the issue of how many are being tortured and the purposes for which this is done.

[63] 'Opinion: Is torture ever justified?' *The Economist* (9 January 2003).

However, the absolutist 'slippery slope' argument against torture is not confined to claims that many innocent persons will suffer torture alongside terrorists.[64] Rather, it covers a wide range of other claims, regarding the involvement—and possible corruption—of a vast array of social institutions, including the judicial and medical professions; long-term negative affects on wider conflicts within the context of which terrorism—and torture, take place; the weakening of international mechanisms for the protection of human rights; and more. It will be obvious that not only are such alleged results very difficult to compare, quantitatively, with the suffering of the innocent civilian victims of terrorist attacks, some of the claimed negative results cannot be neatly 'synthesized' and set apart from other causes and effects within situations that are invariably complex and often unclear.

Thirdly, unless these differences can be reconciled (I will not attempt such reconciliation here), the debate around the acceptable price society may pay for life-saving torture is likely to be conducted in more general terms. Near-absolutists may accept only a very narrow margin of mistakes and excesses, while advocates of 'zero tolerance for terrorism' may consider wide-ranging 'collateral damage', including the torture of a considerable number of innocent persons and even some harm to individual freedoms, democratic institutions and international agreements, as heavy but necessary sacrifices for a good cause. I see little point in attempting here to establish an acceptable price-tag for torture in a TBS.

Finally, even in the unlikely event that agreement could be reached on all of the above points, this would not suffice to resolve the issue of the 'slippery slopes' of torture on the theoretical level. The reason for this insufficiency is logical: it cannot be proven exhaustively that a certain system would in reality provide watertight protection against (further, intolerably) undesired consequences, but neither can the possibility of devising such a system be ruled out exhaustively: if the failure of one 'anti-slippery slope' model could be proven, this would still leave open the logical possibility of introducing an inexhaustible number of either improvements to that model, or alternative ones.

One conclusion of this theoretical treatment of 'slippery slope' dangers of states torturing in TBSs is thus already clear at its inception: they exist, but it is impossible to determine conclusively either whether 'slippery slope' damage can be limited to an acceptable degree or what that degree should be. It will be left for Parts III and IV to shed some further—but still not conclusive—light on these issues with a more *empirical* (including legal) debate on whether theoretical and real-life models of limited anti-terrorist torture may (or did) achieve, by and large, what they set out to do, or whether they would (or did) result in much wider damage than they had originally foreseen or considered acceptable.

---

[64] In contrast, perhaps, to the debate surrounding the death penalty in the West, although that debate too obviously has other 'slippery slope' aspects as well as non-consequentialist ones. See Part I, Ch 4, Section C(3)(b).

With these remarks in mind, arguments for an absolutist position against torture on societal (and international) grounds will now be put forward.

C. General Arguments for Anti-torture 'Practical Absolutism' on 'Slippery Slope' Grounds—Some Examples

Germain Grisez and Russell Shaw, who are moral absolutists, outline the practical dangers of states implementing non-absolutist policies:

If there are no absolute responsibilities, there are no inalienable rights. If it were true that any action, no matter what, is permitted in certain circumstances, then no good intrinsic to the person would be safe from invasion and suppression, provided the justifying circumstances existed. This is true even in regard to ethical theories which propose the existence of virtual absolutes: norms which proponents of such theories say they can hardly conceive as being in practice subject to violation... [but] others less idealistic are quite able to imagine, and find, just the circumstances in which people can be sacrificed to the attainment of ulterior ends.[65]

When it comes to torture or other extreme acts by governments in the *real* world, minimal (and other) absolutists are not as isolated as they were in Part I. It has already been shown, and will be further shown below, that many theorists believe it realistically possible to limit torture, by and large, to TBSs, or at least to serious terrorist suspects. However, others, who would support torture in a 'pure', imagined TBS, consider the 'slippery slope' dangers of trying to apply their view in practice daunting enough to warrant anti-torture 'practical absolutism' on utilitarian grounds. Thus LW Sumner, in his discussion of 'consequentialist rights', makes a consequentialist argument for an absolute right to freedom from torture:

It may well be true of all rights that their violation will sometimes best promote our basic goals. And it may also be true of most rights that the policy of sometimes permitting their violation will best promote our basic goals. But in other cases we might do better to raise an insurmountable threshold against goal-based considerations even though we think that sometimes these considerations would justify violating the right. This might be so if the exceptional cases are likely to be extremely rare and if allowing ourselves direct appeal to our goal will lead us to violate the right in many non-exceptional cases. Where these conditions are satisfied the additional gains we might realize in the extraordinary cases would be vastly outweighed by the additional losses we would sustain in the ordinary cases, so that we will do better overall to deny ourselves a goal-based override. A plausible instance of this is the claim-right not to be subjected to torture. The case for rendering this right dispensable rests on exceedingly unlikely scenarios in which large numbers of lives could be saved if some vital piece of information were extracted from an unwilling subject. The real practice of torture, however, has nothing to do with these cases. It is

---

[65] G Grisez and R Shaw, 'Persons, Means and Ends' in Haber (ed), *supra* n 37, 21–28, 25.

quite believable that the price we must pay in order to contain the ordinary practice of torture is to condemn it even in extraordinary cases. If so, then there is a consequentialist case for rendering this right absolute.[66]

Michael Ignatieff similarly combines what is essentially a consequentialist view with a call for an absolute ban on torture. However, Ignatieff tries to get around the moral and legal problems by rejecting 'physical torture' while justifying the use of 'non-physical' methods such as sleep deprivation which, he claims 'would amount to coercion, rather than torture,' relying on 'some evidence that physical duress is unnecessary where interrogators are skilled and persistent'.[67] Ignatieff's position thus claims to avoid both the negative consequences of torture *and* those of terrorist attacks occurring, and is therefore less principled than Sumner's. The idea that torture must be physical defies common sense and, as will be seen in Part IV, this type of evasion is not possible in law or practice either.

Daniel Statman, a deontologist with a 'disastrous consequences' clause that would allow for torture in a 'pure' TBS,[68] concludes an extensive discussion of the theoretical 'slippery slope' and other practical dangers of permitting torture in a TBS with the following:

The moral danger involved in torture is so great, and the moral benefit so doubtful, that in practice torture should be considered as prohibited absolutely.[69]

Barrie Paskins, who also supports the torture of a terrorist in a 'pure', imagined nuclear TBS,[70] makes a *threshold* 'slippery slope' argument, namely that the very minute we shift from theory to reality, insoluble problems of making 'notional distinctions' arise which render torture absolutely impermissible, as the real-life situation is one of '*a priori* uncertainty':

We can imagine and describe cases in which we would think torture justified and unjustified. We can state the grounds on which we are making the discrimination. But what we cannot do is this: *we cannot provide for ourselves, or for those who must act for us in real situations any way of making our notional distinctions in reality.* What might be claimed about

---

[66] LW Sumner, *The Moral Foundation of Rights* (Oxford: Clarendon, 1987) 212–3. For (rule) utilitarian reasons for 'practical absolutism' see also Part I, Ch 4, Section C(4).

[67] See *idem, The Lesser Evil: Political Ethics in an Age of Terror,* (Edinburgh: Edinburgh University Press, 2005) 136, 8, 138 and 141, respectively.

[68] Daniel Statman, 'The Absoluteness of the Prohibition Against Torture' [Hebrew] 4 *Mishpat u-Mimshal* 161 (1997). See Part I, ch 4, section B.

[69] *Ibid,* 195. See similarly WL Twining and E Twining, 'Bentham on Torture' 24(3) *Northern Ireland Legal Quarterly* 305 (1973) 307.

[70] B Paskins, 'What's Wrong with Torture?' 2 *Brit J Int'l Studies* 138 (1976) 141–2. Paskins invokes, in addition to the usual consequentialist reasons (at 142), 'the just war tradition' (141) to justify such torture—an argument which is factually problematic, as this 'tradition' has, at least since the middle of the nineteenth century, included an absolute ban on inhumane treatment of prisoners, regardless of how unjust *their* war is or how much life-saving information they possess. This point is made by Daniel Statman, *ibid,* 183. For Paskins' views on torture see also W Twining and B Paskins, 'Torture and Philosophy' 52 (Supp) *Proceedings of the Aristotelian Society* 143 (1978) 169–94.

the imaginary example is not that something significantly analogous could not occur but that in reality we cannot enable those who must act to recognize the case for what it is and other cases, by contrast, for what they are. In a real situation we can never be certain that the case in hand is of this kind rather than another. A too vivid imagination blinds us to the dust of war that drifts into the interrogation centre.

If this is agreed, then a moral conclusion is readily derived. We agree that torture is always a terrible thing. You must not do a terrible thing unless you have a very good chance indeed of knowing what you are doing. But in any real case where torture is in question you cannot have a good chance of knowing what you are doing. Hence torture is always wrong.[71]

Consequentialists may accept Paskins' argument but counter that, at least where the question is one of policy and the stakes are high, a state may justifiably do 'terrible things' even *without* a good chance of knowing whether each one of them is justified, as long as the overall result is that thousands of lives are saved. This is, however, an admission not only that unjustified torture may occur through accident or negligence, but that unjustified torture is inherent in the very decision to adopt torture as a matter of policy, so that even strict adherence to instructions and restrictions would result in a toss-of-the-dice mixture of justified and unjustified torture.

D. Specific 'Slippery Slope' and Other Dangers

In what follows, I will list the main practical dangers (and, on occasion, related principled ones) inherent in the introduction of torture as an instrument of state, even in limited, 'ticking bomb' cases. In view of the excellent and virtually exhaustive discussions of these issues by Statman, Kremnitzer and Segev, Arrigo and David Luban,[72] I will to a considerable extent follow their arguments. I will first discuss the main dangers present within the immediate context of torturing in a TBS, before turning to wider, societal and international contexts.

While the majority of these dangers are of the 'slippery slope' type, two others are not, consisting instead of 'slippery surface' dangers relevant to torture in the public sphere. The practical dangers involving the issue of effectiveness and alternatives are not, strictly speaking, 'slippery slope' dangers either. They have all been lumped together for the sake of simplicity, and where a danger is discussed which is of a 'slippery surface' nature, this will be noted.

---

[71] Paskins, 'What's Wrong With Torture?' (*ibid*, 144). The term '*a priori* uncertainty' is used on p 146.

[72] M Kremnitzer, 'The Landau Commission Report—Was the Security Service Subordinated to the Law, or the Law to the "Needs" of the Security Service?' 23 *Israel L Rev* 216 (1989); Kremnitzer and Segev, *supra* n 17; Statman, *supra* n 70; Arrigo, *supra* n 4; D Luban, 'Liberalism, Torture, and the Ticking Bomb' 91 *Virginia L Rev* 1425 (2005).

1. The immediate context

(a) Problems of certainty

Statman lists the areas of possible uncertainty that must be cleared before justified torture can take place:

Since torture is one of the most severe and shocking acts, from the moral point of view, an extremely heavy onus of proof rests on the shoulders of whoever seeks to justify it. He must know with certainty that a bomb really exists (despite the fact that no one saw it besides the terrorists); that it will explode if we do not defuse it (that the terrorists have been sufficiently professional); that it really can be defused (that it will not explode the minute it is handled); that the person in our possession does indeed know where the bomb is (perhaps he was compartmentalized out, or perhaps they moved the bomb to another location when they heard that he had been captured); that if we torture him he would provide the needed information (and not die first, or keep silent, or provide false information); that if he provides the information we will be able to defuse the bomb (it will not be too late); and that there is no other way to discover the bomb (for instance, using sophisticated electronic methods); and so on.[73]

As Statman points out, this extensive list is nevertheless a partial one. In cases of a suicide bomber, additional uncertainties arise, such as whether the bomber actually got to the designated place, did not get 'cold feet', and so on.

In real-life situations the uncertainty regarding facts even blurs the moral requirement of ceasing the torture the minute the information is revealed, so important to Bentham that he included it in his very definition of torture,[74] and thus the claim, that, in Henry Shue's words:

... interrogational torture does have a built-in end-point: when the information has been obtained, the torture has accomplished its purpose and need not be continued.[75]

While true in theory, in reality the point at which can we be satisfied that 'the information has been obtained' may be elusive. Shue himself concludes that,

Any keeping of the tacit bargain to stop when compliance has been as complete as possible would likely be undercut by uncertainty about when the fullest possible compliance had occurred.[76]

---

[73] Statman, *ibid*, 173. See also Kremnitzer, *ibid*, 252–3, Kremnitzer and Segev, *ibid*, 712–721; Luban, *ibid*, 1442.

[74] This definition reads: 'Torture, as I understand it, is where a person is made to suffer any violent pain of body in order to compel him to do something or to desist from doing something which done or desisted from the penal application is immediately made to cease.' J Bentham, 'Of Torture' *Bentham Manuscripts, University College London* 46/63–70, reprinted by Twining and Twining, *supra* n 69, 309. See similarly *idem*, 'Of Compulsion and herein of Torture, *Bentham Manuscripts, University College London* 46/56–62, *ibid*, 320–337, 324 (rule 13); L Sheleff, 'Maximising Good and Minimising Evil—On the Landau Commission's Report, Terrorism and Torture' [Hebrew]1 *Plilim* 185 (1990) 209.

[75] H Shue, 'Torture' 7 *Philosophy and Public Affairs* 124 (1978) 134.

[76] *Ibid*, 135.

Jean-Paul Sartre makes the same argument in more poetic terms:

...whether the victim talks or whether he dies under his agony, the secret that he cannot tell is always somewhere else and out of reach. It is the executioner who becomes Sisyphus. If he puts *the question* at all, he will have to continue for ever.[77]

I will now elaborate this point: If Vicious the terrorist has revealed to Agent Ethica what he says is the location of a bomb or suicide bomber about to explode, does she stop torturing him while she and her colleagues ascertain the truth of his information, or does she continue, just in case it is not true?[78] Even once she has ascertained the truth, there may still be good reasons to carry on torturing: Supposing, for instance, that Agent Ethica tortured Vicious, he gave her information about a bomb placed in a restaurant, and that information proved true. Should officials now, while evacuating the restaurant, go on torturing Vicious, just in case his plan did not involve a simple TBS, but a *combined* terrorist operation, such as the one in Bali, Indonesia, on 12 October 2002, where a small bomb exploded in front of a disco and a much larger one exploded nearby, and shortly afterwards, possibly designed to kill many of those who were running for safety?[79]

Or, to use Dershowitz's example—supposing we tortured Zacarias Moussawi, apparently a member of the terrorist group which later, on 11 September 2001, would carry out the attacks in the USA shortly after he had been detained, a few weeks prior to the attacks, by the Immigration and Naturalization Service.[80] Supposing he then gave us information about a small '*al-Qai'idah*' 'sleeper cell', complete with a cash of explosives, somewhere in the USA, and that information proved to be true. If torture were to cease then, it would not have prevented the 9/11 attacks. The same would probably be true if he were, on 11 September, to disclose the details of one of the highjack-and-suicide plots but not the others.

To be absolutely sure that a terrorist has provided us with all the urgently needed, life-saving information he possesses, our state-administered torture in many, if not most real-life situations would have to go *beyond* the disclosure of a single place where a single bomb or suicide bomber has been planned to explode, and beyond ascertaining the truth of such initial information; it would have to continue until we are convinced that he really does have no further life-saving information to reveal. If Mr Moussawi had told us, early on 11 September, after much torturing, that four planes were to be highjacked and flown into key

---

[77] J-P Sartre, 'A Victory' (originally 'Une Victoire' published in *L'Express*), Preface in H Alleg, *The Question*, trans J Calder (London: John Calder 1958) 11–28, 23.

[78] *Cf* Luban, *supra* n 72, 1442–3. On the possibility of the terrorist lying under torture until it is too late see also *infra*, Ch 9, Section D(1)(d).

[79] I took this account from A Sipress and E Nakashima, 'Death Toll in Bali Attack Rises to 188; Most Victims Were Foreigners; Terror Network Suspected', *Washington Post* (14 October 2002).

[80] See Dershowitz, *supra* n 58, 142–3. See similarly *idem*, 'Tortured Reasoning' in S Levinson (ed), *Torture: A Collection* (Oxford: OUP, 2004) 257–280, 264.

buildings, how were we to know that there was no fifth plane, or sixth? Could we have ceased his torture, and potentially risked the lives of thousands of innocent persons in, say, the Empire State Building in New York, the Sears Tower in Chicago or the Bank of America Plaza in Atlanta? The conclusion must be that the 'built-in end-point' is fuzzy at best, and may in fact be reached only when we are torturing a person for information he does not possess, namely what is, by all accounts, *unjustified* torture.

(b) Problems of immediacy

The requirement that the bomb will *soon* explode is at the heart of the TBS scenario. Indeed, that 'time is of the essence';[81] the 'attack now appeared to be imminent';[82] or '[t]here is no time to evacuate the innocent people'[83] often feature as a *sine qua non* component for the justifiability of resorting to torture.

This is not, however, a moral requirement *per se*; rather, it is a secondary, or 'facilitator' requirement to the main one—that of choosing the lesser evil. As long as there is time for other, less drastic (therefore less evil) measures to be used, torture should not be, but by the same logic, if there is no viable alternative—even where there *is* time—resort to torture would be justified.

Kremnitzer and Segev, discussing the requirement of immediacy in the context of the availability of the legal 'defence of necessity',[84] ('lesser evil defence') to torturers, make a similar point while addressing the argument that the need for 'immediacy of action' (where action must be taken immediately to prevent a non-immediate danger from materializing) is sufficient to make that defence available, rather than 'immediacy of the danger':

... the importance of the requirement for immediacy of action in the defence of necessity stems mainly from its role as a significant indication of two related conditions, the importance of whose existence is uncontroversial: the certainty of the danger's materialisation and the need for the act, namely the impossibility of preventing the danger from materialising by other means. The necessity for immediate action is a central indicator for the certainty of the danger, which, in turn, is the main indication of the need for the act.[85]

This wider concept of the immediacy requirement has led some advocates of torture in a TBS to stretch the time-frame within which torture may be justified beyond the imminent, or Justice Heshin's two hours.[86] The 'judicial torture warrant' systems advocated by Sheleff, Dershowitz and Levinson necessarily entail

---

[81] Sheleff, *Ultimate Penalties...supra* n 53, 305.
[82] Dershowitz, *supra* n 58, 143.
[83] Shue, *supra* n 75, 141. See also Annex, *passim*, for the immediacy component in similar such scenarios.
[84] This is discussed in Part III, Chs 8 and 10 and IV, Ch 19, *passim*.
[85] Kremnitzer and Segev, *supra* n 17, 717.
[86] See *supra* n 52.

adding time for the judges to deliberate the case and issue the warrant. Similarly, the documents setting out the two Israeli models[87] both extended the applicability of the 'lesser evil' justification (or, in legal terms, the defence of necessity) for torture[88] far beyond the immediate:

The report of the Landau Commission of Inquiry in Israel, which established its first legalized torture system, having cited a 'ticking bomb' case, states the following:

...when the clock wired to the explosive charge is already ticking, what difference does it make, in terms of the necessity to act, whether the charge is certain to be detonated in five minutes or in five days?[89]

In its principled ruling in 1999, in what I call here the *Israel Torture* case, the Israeli Supreme Court stated:

...we are prepared to accept...that the 'necessity' exception is likely to arise in instances of 'ticking time bombs', and that the immediate need ('necessary in an immediate manner'[90] for the preservation of human life) refers to the imminent nature of the act rather than that of the danger. Hence, the imminence criteria is satisfied even if the bomb is set to explode in a few days, or perhaps even after a few weeks, provided the danger is certain to materialize and there is no alternative means of preventing its materialization. In other words, there exists a concrete level of imminent danger of the explosion's occurrence...[91]

The USA has held suspected terrorists for months and years in secret locations within an interrogation plan that, in the words of its President 'saved innocent lives by helping us stop new attacks',[92] apparently reflecting a similar view.

As Kremnitzer and Segev point out, however:

If the immediacy of action is deemed sufficient, and action against non-immediate dangers is permitted, an opening is created for committing unnecessary acts aimed at preventing obscure, uncertain dangers as...only rarely is a danger that is not immediate certain to materialise, and accordingly, there is usually no assurance that an act designed to prevent a danger which is not certain is indeed necessary.[93]

---

[87] All three models are discussed in Part III.

[88] Naturally, neither used this term but both, as will be seen, did in effect allow it. See Part III, Chs 2 and 4.

[89] Commission of Inquiry into the Methods of Investigation of the General Security Service Regarding Hostile Terrorist Activities, *Report* (Part 1) (Jerusalem: October 1987) para 3.15.

[90] The Court is quoting from the provision for the defence (or 'exception') of necessity in Israel's Penal Code, S 34(11). (Footnote added.)

[91] HCJ 5100/94 *The Public Committee Against Torture in Israel v the Government of Israel et al*, PD 53(4) 817, ruling of 6 September 1999 (henceforth: *Israel Torture* case), para 34.

[92] 'President Discusses Creation of Military Commissions to Try Suspected Terrorists' 6 September 2006 <http://www.whitehouse.gov/news/releases/2006/09/20060906–3.html>, accessed 10 October 2006. See further in Part III, Ch 15.

[93] Kremnitzer and Segev, *supra* n 17, 718.

(c) Deciding whom to torture

Amnesty International makes the case about an ever-widening circle of candidates for torture:

History shows that torture is never limited to 'just once': 'just once' becomes once again—becomes a practice and finally an institution. As soon as . . . use is permitted once, as for example in one of the extreme circumstances like a bomb, it is logical to use it on people who might plant bombs, or on people who might think of planting bombs, or on people who defend the kind of person who might think of planting bombs.[94]

Many of the worst and bloodiest terrorist attacks in the late twentieth and early twenty-first centuries—for instance in the USA, Iraq, Israel and Indonesia (Bali)—have been carried out by suicide bombers. This means that once the attacker has been arrested and disarmed, there is no longer a TBS, as he and the 'ticking bomb' are one. Those interrogated in such cases are therefore not as directly connected to the act as in the 'classic' TBS. If we torture persons who intended to carry out terrorist attacks and may know of other such attacks, or persons involved in an attack but not in carrying it out, we are already, to an extent, on a 'slippery slope' as to who should be tortured.

Further down the line, since the element of immediacy, as seen above, is conceived in terms of need for action rather than of danger, an interrogator, facing an interrogee in search of an elusive terrorist cell in the making, is likely to consider the following: if I do not torture now, today, this first link in the information-chain (who is perhaps a moderate political activist refusing to provide information on non-violent groups, which is likely to lead to information on more extremist political groups, and so on), the entire complicated and drawn-out process of exposing the terrorist cell will be delayed by a day or two, which could be the crucial difference between preventing the explosion and reaching the cell too late.

Luban provides a real-life example of this logic:

In the Argentinian Dirty War, the tortures began because terrorist cells had a policy of fleeing when one of their members had disappeared for forty-eight hours, leaving authorities two days to wring the information out of the captive.[95]

Especially acute, in this context, is the prospect of torturing the innocent. Unlike in Part I, or even in the scenario just described, here the added danger exists of torturing also innocent persons where such torture contributes *nothing* to revealing the life-saving information. The trouble is, there is nothing in the torture procedure to separate those who are totally innocent, and void of any useful information, from the totally culpable and knowledgeable. The authorities' treatment of people whose

---

[94] Amnesty International, *Report on Torture* (2nd edn, London: Duckworth, 1975) 23.
[95] Luban, *supra* n 74, 1447.

liberty it has suspended or deprived is thus profoundly affected; essentially such treatment is—or must be—designed specifically to target suspects or criminals while avoiding any harm, even the harm involved in detention, to the innocent. Thus a person would be detained or charged only as long as there is *prima facie* evidence against him/her and s/he should be punished only if such evidence proves sufficient—any such steps are halted the moment his/her innocence is established. Once torture in a TBS has begun, however, the situation is the absolute reverse.

Statman explains this point:

One of the problems which deciding that the person who is the object of torture does in fact possess the required information creates, is that usually this person is the only source, or at least the only authoritative source, capable of denying that. But once we have determined that he is a legitimate candidate for torture, this possibility no longer exists: even if the person shouts that he does not have the information till he is blue in the face, this would, for the interrogators, only prove that he should be beaten more severely. If he provides false information, this would be proof that he is trying to mislead the interrogators and evidence, again, that more force is needed to break him down. In other words, the moment we allow torture in order to extract vital information from a certain person, if we are wrong and he does not possess the required information, he has no way of proving this and stopping the torture, and the moral horror associated (by all accounts) with torturing a person without justification continually increases.[96]

Writing in the context of the debate around the use of torture by the USA in its 'war against terror' following the 11 September 2001 terrorist attacks, Patricia J Williams makes a related point:

While fully acknowledging the stakes of this new war, I worry that this righteous lawlessness is not new but has been practiced in oppressed communities for years. It is a habit that has produced cynicism, riots and bloodshed. The always urgently felt convenience of torture has left us with civic calamities ranging from Abner Louima in New York City to Jacobo Timerman in Argentina to Alexander Solzhenitsyn in the Soviet Union—all victims of physical force and mental manipulation, all people who were 'known' to know something.[97]

In this context, the statistics which Arrigo provides on the rate of acquittals to criminal charges for serious crimes in the USA are relevant. According to Arrigo, between two and three out of every four charged are acquitted. As Arrigo points out, the torture-to-acquittals rate would be much higher under a torture interrogation program, where judicial safeguards would be absent.[98]

Lubin, addressing the same issue, adds another 'statistical' angle:

The authorities know there may be a bomb plot in the offing, and they have captured a man who may know something about it, but may not. Torture him? How much? For weeks? For months? The chances are considerable that you are torturing a man with

---

[96] Statman, *supra* n 70, 173–4.
[97] PJ Williams, 'Any Means Necessary', *The Nation* (26 November 2001).
[98] Arrigo, supra n 4, 22–3.

nothing to tell you. If he doesn't talk, does that mean it's time to stop, or time to ramp up the level of torture? How likely does it have to be that he knows something important? Fifty-fifty? Thirty-seventy? Will one out of a hundred suffice to land him on the waterboard?[99]

(d) Effectiveness and alternatives

It would be futile to argue that interrogational torture is never effective in the immediate sense. It would, however, be equally futile to claim that it always is, or that it is always the most efficient way of extracting information.

Torture may be particularly inefficient in the 'classic' TBS, where the bomb is due to go off in a matter of a few hours or less. As Nigel Rodley has argued:

The reality is that the usual sort of circumstances that is given—for example, the nuclear bomb that is going to go off in twenty minutes—is a load of rubbish. First of all, the individual will know the bomb is going to go off in twenty minutes and can last twenty minutes. Second of all, all he has to do is send the person somewhere else for that twenty minutes until the bomb goes off.[100]

This could be equally true in Justice Heshin's two-hours scenario.

That the suspect may send interrogators on a wild goose chase is but one reason why torture may be ineffective. Another obvious one, mentioned by Sheleff, that 'the interrogee would pass out, be severely injured and need medical treatment or even die',[101] was discussed in Part I.[102] Avoiding such dangers would require stepping onto the 'slippery slope' of professional involvement, to be discussed in the next section. Another problematic 'solution', mentioned (but rejected) by Sheleff, is to torture the detainee's relatives, also discussed in Part I.[103]

A related problem is pointed out by Kremnitzer:

The existence of the license to employ physical pressure...is also liable to constitute a negative incentive regarding the development and perfection of non-violent means of interrogation, and thus to reduce the effectiveness of the interrogation and increase the number of cases in which resource is made to physical pressure. What is supposed to be...a last resort may become—out of considerations of efficiency and economy in personnel and time—the first method tried.[104]

While Kremnitzer writes in the context of the Landau Commission's wide view as to who should undergo 'physical pressure', the same may to a large extent be

---

[99] Luban, *supra* n 72, 1442.

[100] N Rodley, 'The Prohibition of Torture and How to Make it Effective' *Proceedings of a seminar on Israel and international human rights law: the issue of torture*, 9 June 1995 (Jerusalem: Center for Human Rights, the Hebrew University of Jerusalem, 1995) 5–32, 25–6. Sheleff concedes this point. See *idem, Ultimate Penalties...supra* n 53, 478.

[101] *Ibid*, 473.

[102] I added the possibility of loss of sanity.

[103] *Ibid*; Sheleff, *Ultimate Penalties...*, *supra* n 53. And see my argument there that Sheleff's 'lesser evil' justification for torture in a TBS contradicts his rejection of torturing the innocent.

[104] Kremnitzer, *supra* n 72, 254.

true in a stricter regime. Torture is allotted, by its very designation as a means of last resort, a special place at the top of the (perceived) efficiency hierarchy of interrogation methods. When the stakes are (or may be) high enough and time is (or may be) crucial, interrogators are unlikely to risk a catastrophe by 'playing around' with means perceived as less efficient, inefficient or slow.

Worse still, a 1963 CIA manual makes an observation, which is also supported by reason, that may complicate decisions as to using other means first:

> If an interrogatee is caused to suffer pain rather late in the interrogation process and after other tactics have failed, he is almost certain to conclude that the interrogator is becoming desperate. He may then decide that if he can just hold out against this final assault, he will win the struggle and his freedom. And he is likely to be right. Interrogatees who have withstood pain are more difficult to handle by other methods. The effect has been not to repress the subject but to restore his confidence and maturity.[105]

It may be safer, then, to start straight up with torture, namely to make it a *first* rather than last resort, but this would mean a clash, even within the consequentialist reasoning, between the requirement of efficiency and that of ensuring that there are 'no alternative means of preventing' the danger.[106]

On the other hand, once torture is resorted to, it would be extremely hard, if not impossible, to return (if torture has failed), to humane methods of interrogation, as the latter are based on dialogue, even on trust. Cyril Cunningham, who served as Senior Psychologist engaged, during World War II and beyond, in prisoner of war intelligence on behalf of the British government, made this point, and praised the efficiency of humane means of interrogation, during the debate in Britain over the use of physical interrogation methods against suspected members of the Irish Republican Army in Northern Ireland in 1971. Cunningham stated that '[i]f the Royal Ulster Constabulary, or indeed the Army, is using the methods reported, they are being singularly stupid and unimaginative', blaming 'commanders and politicians who, in their ignorance, continue to regard interrogation simply as a hostile questioning by people whose only qualification is a loud voice and an overbearing manner'. He added, in brackets: 'The best interrogator I ever met, the one who trained me, had the demeanour of an unctuous parson' and concludes:

> A variety of 'backdoor' methods are available, all of which *depend for their effectiveness* upon the avoidance of brutality in any form.[107] [Emphasis added.]

---

[105] CIA document entitled 'KUBARK Counterintelligence Interrogation,' July 1963, see eg <http://www.gwu.edu/~nsarchiv/NSAEBB/NSAEBB27/01–01.htm>, accessed 12 November 2007. For the rather disturbing history of the development of this document, including through the use of 'uninformed, nonconsenting experimental subjects,' see R Lemov, 'The Birth of Soft Torture: CIA interrogation techniques—a history', *Slate*, 16 November 2005 <http://www.slate.com/id/2130301/>, accessed 18 November 2005.

[106] The words of Israel's Supreme Court, *supra*, text accompanying n 91.

[107] Letter to *The Times*, 25 November 1971. I am thankful to Amnesty International for pointing to this source and the next one.

In the same context, L St Clare Grondona, Commandant of the British Combined Services Detailed Interrogation Centre (CSDIC) during World War II, discussed the use and effectiveness of non-torturous methods in the interrogation of German POWs:

In the early stages [of the second World War] all our 'guests' (and they were invariably so termed) were survivors from either shot-down aircraft or destroyed submarines—usually truculent Nazis cockily confident that it was only a matter of time before Hitler had crushed Britain, with world domination in prospect. They possessed valuable information of which it was our job to extract as much as possible; but always with proper regard to the Geneva Convention.

So it was that our interrogators (then and thereafter) had to be as wily as they were resourceful. The methods they used were processes of 'painless extraction' seasoned with legitimate guile. More often than not a 'guest' would be unaware that he had given useful data. Courtesy was extended to every prisoner so long as his behaviour warranted this—and it usually did. Comfortable quarters were provided, and prisoners' fare was precisely the same as for British personnel.

It is the simple truth to say that if one of our interrogators had suggested submitting any prisoner to *any* form of physical duress (which would certainly not have been permitted) he would have been a laughing-stock among his colleagues. Nevertheless, the 'intelligence' we obtained (all the items of which were carefully correlated) was of inestimable value.

In this regard it may suffice to say that, had it not been for the information elicited by the CSDIC, it might have been London and not Hiroshima that was devastated by the first atom bomb.[108]

The Petitioners in *Israel Torture* case, having quoted the above statement, added that:

It is thus clear that even during a full-scale war, in the desperate struggle against the Nazi enemy, and even facing the menacing 'ticking' of an atomic bomb, the British meticulously maintained humane methods of interrogation, and to an impressive effect.[109]

Even a former head of the Interrogation Department in Israel's Genera Security Service (GSS), Zvi Aharoni, questioned the 'irreplaceablility' of torture when

---

[108] Letter to *The Times*, 27 November 1971. In November 2005, *The Guardian* reported, based on official documents 'discovered in the National Archives' that during World War II another secret service, MI19, tortured German prisoners in a secret centre in the heart of London. See I Cobain, 'Secrets of the London Cage' *The Guardian* (12 November 2005). This later report does not necessary belie the statements quoted above—it seems that, as in other states, different forces, or services, worked according to different rules. However, it does point to the fragility of factual assertions in a field where secrecy is so pervasive. This factor probably works both ways.

[109] *Israel Torture* case, *supra* n 91, *Supplementary Statement by the Respondents*, 17 May 1998, para D(3). Having written this part of the Statement, which was submitted to the Court by Advocates Leah Tzemel and Allegra Pacheco for the Public Committee Against Torture in Israel, I hesitantly point to an English translation of this and other documents relating to the case, made hastily when the case was still being considered, and which has not been used here: A Pacheco (ed and trans), *The Case Against Torture in Israel: A Compilation of Petitions, Briefs and Other Documents Submitted to the Israeli High Court of Justice* (Jerusalem, The Public Committee Against Torture in Israel, 1999).

commenting, in 1997, on that body's later resort to torture in the interrogation of suspected terrorists:

I took part in building the internal security service and I was proud of it, of everything we did. Today I'm disgusted by it. Let me tell you one thing, when I was head of the interrogation department, nobody could touch a prisoner. Sure, you could do all kinds of tricks, you could bug them, listen in on their conversations. But beating them? Torturing them?
    And today not only is it being done, it's legal. Arabs can be tortured. It's legal and in my country.[110]

In the context of the 'war on terror' at the beginning of the 21st Century, it was reported that the Saudi security forces, not renowned for their humane interrogation methods, have nevertheless found that some *al-Qai'idah* suspects could be made to cooperate through the use of clerics who spoke to them and convinced them that their ways were un-Islamic.[111]

    The US administration's claims regarding the efficiency interrogation methods used in its 'war on terror' have been seriously challenged as well, not least from within the US intelligence community. According to investigative reporter Katherine Eban, crucial information from Abu Zuaydah, the first prominent *al-Qa'idah* leader captured after 9/11, was obtained by FBI agents who, rather than torturing him, 'had been nursing his wounds and cleaning him after he'd soiled himself'. She adds:

America learned the truth of how 9/11 was organized because a detainee had come to trust his captors after they treated him humanely.[112]

    The official—indeed Presidential—version is that Abu Zubaydah then refused to talk any further, 'so the CIA used an alternative set of procedures'.[113] However, according to Eban's research, the CIA elbowed in, at its Directors' orders. She adds:

While the [CIA] methods were certainly unorthodox, there is little evidence they were necessary, given the success of the rapport-building approach until that point.[114]

Eban cites several intelligence experts who argue that the CIA's methods, described in detail in Part III, are unprofessional, unnecessary and have, in the words of an Air

---

[110] Interview in *The Guardian* (16 July 1997).
[111] 'Saudi interrogators use Koran to connect with captives', CNN website, 1 December 2003, <http://www.cnn.com>, accessed 2 December 2003.
[112] Katherine Eban, 'Rorschach and Awe' *Vanity Fair* website <http://www.vanityfair.com/politics/features/2007/07/torture200707?printable=true&currentPage=all> 17 July 2007, accessed 18 July 2007.
[113] George W Bush, quoted in 'President Discusses Creation of Military Commissions to Try Suspected Terrorists' 6 September 2006 <http://www.whitehouse.gov/news/releases/2006/09/20060906-3.html>, accessed 10 October 2006. One such method is described *infra*, text accompanying n 222.
[114] Eban, *supra* n 112.

Force Reserve colonel and expert in human-intelligence operations, 'caused more harm to American national security than they'll ever understand'.[115] Elsewhere psychologists and other specialists, commissioned by the US Intelligence Science Board were similarly critical of these interrogation methods in particular, and of torturous methods in general. For example, Randy Borum, described as 'a Behavioral Science Consultant on counterintelligence and national security issues' who often provides advice to the US intelligence community, wrote:

The potential mechanisms and effects of using coercive techniques or torture for gaining accurate, useful information from an uncooperative source are much more complex than is commonly assumed. There is little or no research to indicate whether such techniques succeed in the manner and contexts in which they are applied. Anecdotal accounts and opinions based on personal experiences are mixed, but the preponderance of reports seems to weigh against their effectiveness. [...] Psychological theory and some (indirectly) related research suggest that coercion or pressure can actually *increase* a source's resistance and determination not to comply.[116]

Aside from the tortured suspect lying or losing his life, consciousness or sanity, there is the possibility that he would not break under torture, and refuse to speak despite it.

Historically, resistance to torture has not been confined to saints and famous heroes. Lisa Silverman tells the story of two 'ordinary' men in eighteenth century Toulouse, when torture was carried out as part of legal procedures in capital cases. Jean Bourdil[117] was accused of participating in the murder of two soldiers in 1726, his sword having been found blooded. He insisted that he was innocent and that he had lent the sword to a friend. Bourdil underwent repeated torture, including the use, on five occasions, of the *question d'eau*, which, according to Silverman, consisted of the following:

...fastening the wrists of the accused to an iron ring bolted into the wall at waist height, and the feet to another ring embedded in the floor, thus extending the prisoner's body to its full length at a slant. Trestles of varying heights were then wedged under the prisoner's back, forcing a further extension of the body. Finally, his face covered by a linen napkin, water was forced down his throat through a cow's horn, as much as sixteen liters at a time.[118]

---

[115] *Ibid*. The Colonel, Steve Kleinman, was referring directly to the 'architects' of these methods. For his professional views see also eg Steven M Kleinman, 'Barriers to Success: Critical Challenges in Developing a New Educing Information Paradigm' in Intelligence Science Board, *Educing Information Interrogation: Science and Art*, Washington, DC: National Defense Intelligence College, 2006), <http://www.fas.org/irp/dni/educing.pdf>, accessed 16 January 2007, 235–266.
[116] Randy Borum, 'Approaching Truth: Behavioral Science Lessons on Educing Information from Human Sources' *ibid*, 17–44, 35. The description of Borum's field of expertise is provided at xxvii.
[117] L Silverman, *Tortured Subjects: Pain, Truth and the Body in Early Modern France* (Chicago and London: the University of Chicago Press, 2001) 28–49.
[118] See *ibid*, 46, and 46–7 for a description of other torture methods used at that time in France.

All this was to no avail—Bourdil refused to either confess the murder or point out to the murderers or alleged accomplices. The local *parlement* eventually sentenced him to serve in the King's galleys in perpetuity, overturning the magistrate's decision to break him on the wheel.

In 1762, Jean Calas,[119] whose son had probably committed suicide, and the family having reported to the investigating magistrate that he had been murdered, to avoid the humiliating procedures reserved for those who committed suicide (the body being dragged naked through the streets, then exhibited in a gibbet), was himself accused of murdering his son. He was convicted, sentenced to death and tortured on the wheel before his execution, in order to reveal the names of his accomplices. Silberman recounts:

Under torture, Calas failed to confess to the crime himself and failed to implicate others, maintaining what many contemporary observers saw as a heroic silence.[120]

Voltaire, touched and enraged by this case, launched a public campaign which resulted, eventually (1765) in Calas' posthumous acquittal.

Modern history and mythology are replete with tales of persons who were tortured but refused to confess, denounce their faith or provide information. To name but three twentieth century examples—Milovan Djilas was tortured for being a Communist in Yugoslavia in the 1930s, and for not being a good enough Communist under Tito in the 1950s and 1960s;[121] Hannah Senesh, a Hungarian Jew who escaped to Palestine, but in 1943 volunteered to parachute for the Royal Air Force back into Nazi-occupied Europe to help prisoners of war and Jewish civilians escape, was caught and tortured by the Nazis;[122] and Henry Alleg, who had edited a left-wing magazine in Algiers, was caught and tortured by the French paratroopers in 1957.[123] All three, and many others,[124] withstood torture by the most brutal—and efficient—interrogators.

---

[119] *Ibid*, 157–9.

[120] *Ibid*, 157–8.

[121] M Djilas, *Of Prisons and Ideas*, trans MB Petrovitch (San Diego, Cal: Harcourt Brace Jovanovich Publishers, 1986).

[122] See eg P Hay, *Ordinary Heroes: The Life and Death of Chana Szenesh, Israel's National Heroine* (New York: Paragon House, 1989) and the Hanna Senesh Legacy Foundation website, <http://www.hannahsenesh.org.il/>, accessed 13 January 2003.

[123] H Alleg, *supra* n 77. Alleg himself writes of the resilience of other prisoners, for instance the following: 'On the other side of the wall, in the wing reserved for women, there are young girls of whom not one has given way . . . [six names follow] and others: undressed, beaten, insulted by sadistic torturers, they too have been submitted to the water and the electricity. Each one of us here knows of the martyrdom of Annick Castel, raped by a parachutist and who, believing herself pregnant, thought only to die' (*ibid*, 35–6).

[124] The following three examples were picked off the internet during one day in early 2003. *Vladan Popovic*, a Serb who worked for the anti-Nazi resistance in Yugoslavia, was caught in 1943 by local fascists, tortured, but refused to give any information and eventually died of his wounds (US Holocaust Memory Museum website <http://www.ushmm.org/museum>). *Ignatius Kung*, who was consecrated Bishop of Shanghai in 1950, was arrested and tortured by the Communist authorities but refused to relinquish his faith. See the Catholic Educator's Resource Centre website, <http://www.catholiceducation.org/>. *Captain Humbert Roque ('Rocky') Versace* of the US army

Such resilience is not, unfortunately, limited to one side's heroes. In the Israeli-Palestinian context, Yaacov Perry, who headed the GSS between 1988 and 1995, describes a HAMAS member who, despite 'intensive' interrogation, did 'not provide a single piece of new information'. Perry adds, almost in admiration:

This is easy to understand. Only people with a strong character, like him, can fill the position he held in Hamas. Such people can bear any discomfort and withstand any pressure, any temptation, during interrogation.[125]

More recently 'P', a GSS interrogator, when asked by an Israeli journalist about torturing in situations 'defined as ticking bombs', replied, *inter alia*:

Here you use all possible manipulations up to shaking and beating, and you will beat the hell out of him. To say that it always succeeds?—it doesn't.[126]

This may in turn encourage the torture of lesser terrorists, as Malise Ruthven explains:

. . . the hardened guerrilla or terrorist who continuously flirts with death and even welcomes it is perhaps the least likely of men to speak under torture. Like the Cappadocian bandits, members of underground organizations may learn the techniques of resistance. In practice, then, torture will be most efficacious against the 'softer' targets—the 'fellow-travellers' or sympathizers rather than the militant operators.[127]

2. The wider context—torture, society and beyond

A state facing terrorism—such as, in mid-2007, the USA, Iraq, Israel and Afghanistan[128]—are in what may be termed a 'wider ticking bomb situation', namely one where it is safe to assume that, *at any given moment*, hostile organizations are at some stage of recruiting, training, preparing, planning or executing a terrorist attack against their citizens, and those attacks would be carried out unless thwarted by security services. In the real 'war on terror', time is *always* of the essence. If torture is considered a legitimate weapon in this war, albeit within a limited stretch of the battlefield, as it were, such a state would be effected both in its conduct of the 'war' and further afield.

---

was captured, while wounded, by the Viet Cong in Vietnam in 1963. He was tortured, but refused to give any information and resisted his captors' attempts to indoctrinate him. He was executed in 1965. See eg 'Rocky the Reactionary', one of many websites dedicated to his memory, <http://www.homeofheroes.com/profiles/profiles_versace.html>. All websites accessed 13 January 2003.

[125] Y Perry, *Strike First*, [Hebrew] (Tel Aviv: Keshet, 1999) 166.

[126] A Navon, 'Stories from the Interrogation Rooms' [Hebrew] *Maariv Weekend Supplement* (5 July 2002). The first quotation is from the question.

[127] M Ruthven, *Torture: The Grand Conspiracy*, (London: Weidenfeld and Nicolson, 1978) 297.

[128] As noted (see Part I, Ch 1, Section B), terrorism is defined here by the means it uses (attacks on civilians) rather than by the cause in the service of which they are used. The Palestinians for instance could, to my mind, make quite a convincing argument that they were themselves facing Israeli (state) terrorism, but were not included here since the discussion is confined to *states* facing terrorism.

(a) Persons involved in torturing (the 'institutionalization' trap)[129]

> 19.45: The doctor checked the detainee. The doctor looked at the detainee's
> back to ensure there were no abrasions from sitting in the metal chair for
> long periods of time. The doctor said everything was good.[130]

It is undisputed, and has already been stated, that the 'representation' aspect of
public action includes a duty by states to defend their citizens by all acceptable
and reasonable means. Some institutional implications of deeming torture such a
means will now be considered.

In one sense, there is a profound difference between the moral position of
an individual facing an unforeseeable emergency and that of a state facing a
foreseeable one: we may, for instance, praise a private individual who, although
unable to swim, managed to improvise a lifeboat, using a plank, and saved a
drowning person, but would certainly not claim that individuals have a moral
duty to learn either to swim or to improvise lifeboats, just in case they face
such a situation. In contrast, in recognized swimming areas we certainly do
expect the authorities to place (or to ensure that there be placed) qualified lifeguards who can swim, and who therefore need no improvisation in order to stay
afloat. Furthermore, in affluent societies we also expect our lifeguards to have
access to proper boats, resuscitation equipment, and so on—and to be trained
to use them properly. In other words, where situations which may endanger the
public are known and are likely to occur, an authority *must* be prepared and
must act professionally to save lives whereas an individual *may* improvise and
volunteer.

Kremnitzer and Segev explain this point:

> …while an individual may find himself in many emergencies which are, for him, unfore-
> seeable, every authority deals with a specific area regarding which it has expertise; this
> places the authority's personnel in an entirely different position as far as being prepared
> for the situation is concerned.

This distinction is particularly apparent when at issue are actions by the security
authorities, which by their nature are designed to deal with situations that a private person faces only in rare cases, if ever. In the vast majority of cases it would therefore be
true only of an individual that he is facing an unforeseeable emergency, which necessitates swift action without the possibility of thought and planning in advance. […] The

---

[129] I am elaborating here on Twining and Twining's concept, see *supra* n 69, 348–9. For three
excellent elaborations (to my mind), from different angles, of this 'trap' see Arrigo, *supra* n 4, who
describes what she calls 'dragnet torture'; Luban, *supra* n 72, who calls it 'torture as an organized
social practice'; and Henry Shue, the gist of whose argument is echoed in Chapter 20. See *idem*,
'Torture in Dreamland: Disposing of the Ticking Bomb' 37 *Case West Res J Int'l L* 231 (2006). See
also Dershowitz, *supra* n 58, 163.

[130] 'Interrogation Log, Detainee 063' [Muhammad al-Qahtani, interrogated at Guantánamo
Bay, Cuba] at 61, entry for 26 December 2002. The log was obtained by Time magazine, <http://
www.time.com/time/2006/log/log.pdf>, accessed 22 June 2006. The case is described *infra*, Part
III, Ch 15, Section E.

possibility to plan the authority's action exists in every situation which recurs, and is thus foreseeable...[131]

Those charged with protecting us against terrorist attacks should be resourceful in unforeseen situations, but, no less importantly, must be *trained and equipped* for situations which *are* foreseeable. Here we are assuming, *ex hypothesi*, a 'state facing terrorism' where a TBS is a foreseeable situation.[132] If torturous interrogation methods are legitimate (and considered vital) in such situations, we would demand that anti-terrorist forces should include interrogators who are trained and equipped to use such methods professionally, just as we would demand, for instance, that such forces should include trained and equipped snipers or bomb-diffusion squads. Amateur torture in interrogation may result either in the terrorist detainee refusing to divulge the vital information, or else in him losing his consciousness, sanity or life—in all of which cases the bomb will probably go off and the innocent people whose lives the state must defend will die. In a society which holds torture in a TBS to be legitimate, amateur, ill-equipped torturers would be no more acceptable than combat soldiers who cannot shoot (and do not have guns), police patrolmen and women who cannot drive (and do not have cars), firemen and women who cannot work the hose (and do not have firefighting equipment) etc.

I would therefore submit that, in a state facing terrorism, the pro-torture reasoning inevitably calls for sending in professionals: for example, martial arts experts (perhaps assisted by neurologists) would teach interrogators where and how to hit a detainee in order to achieve the desired effect. And for such interrogations to be truly efficient, other physicians must be attached to our crack interrogation unit, as people are not physiologically uniform, and minute-by-minute monitoring is required, to ensure that the right (or exact) amount of pain is administered. Similarly, psychologists or psychiatrists must be on the scene, to advise interrogators as to the methods that would be most efficient against the particular individual, and monitor the effect of the methods used on the terrorist's willpower, endurance and sanity. Where the use of methods described in Part I, such as rape, electric shocks, and so on, is deemed unavoidable, properly trained and equipped staff should similarly be available. The same is true

---

[131] Kremnitzer and Segev, *supra* n 17, 706. There is a comparable difference between a *state* surprised by a sudden, unpredictable terrorist attack and one which has been defined here as 'a state facing terrorism', which the following analogy may illustrate: Emergency services in Sweden are expected to be equipped to deal with snowstorms, but if they were to face a sudden sandstorm, they may be forgiven for taking reasonable but improvised, amateurish measures to tackle the situation. The same would be true of emergency services in Saudi Arabia facing a freak snowstorm. If, however, global warming reaches the point where sandstorms become commonplace in Sweden, amateurism will no longer be tolerated, and the police, fire-fighters and other emergency services will be expected to be trained and equipped to deal with them professionally. The same would be true if a new ice age sets in, and snowstorms become a regular feature of the Saudi Arabian climate.

[132] See *supra*, Ch 7, Section A.

of methods such as loud music, white noise, extreme heat and cold—and even 'stress positions' and sleep deprivation.

Thus the torture methods recommended by Dershowitz, 'a sterilized needle inserted under the fingernails to produce unbearable pain without any threat to health or life, or...a dental drill through an unanaesthetized tooth'[133] would require doctors, dentists, needles, sterilization equipment, dental drills (and possibly chair), x-ray equipment (to ensure the tooth drilled has not had root-canal treatment) and the kind of gear needed to keep the detainee's hands and fingers firmly in place, his mouth open and so on. More subtle, psychological means, such as (among) those used by the USA in its 'war on terror,' would require— indeed *has* required, a full 'Behavioral Science Consultation Team' (BSCT), including a psychiatrist and psychologist.[134] More generally, Arrigo's detailed discussion of the 'routine participation of medical personnel in state-sponsored torture interrogation' includes a reference to studies of survivors which:

...show medical participation in the range of 20% to 40% of torture cases, or even 'the majority'.[135]

On top of which, the suggestions by Dershowitz and others that judges decide whether or not to torture obviously mean that we would have 'torturing judges' in the moral (and legal) sense that our definition of torture provides for. This would also be true where courts permit torture *ex post facto*, as suggested by Sheleff (in urgent cases), Benvenisti, Israel's Supreme Court and O Gross, since such permission would constitute, as a minimum, 'consent' or 'acquiescence' under that definition. These models—and issues—will be discussed in Parts III and IV.

Is all this really necessary? Why not just use a good old twist of the arm, which any police officer can surely do without much training? The answer lies, again, in the 'ticking bomb scenario' itself— the state cannot be content, where the lives of so many innocent civilians are at stake, with rudimentary means of questionable effect. Unless it has prepared and put in place all the trained humanpower, equipment and institutions necessary for efficient torture, a government of a state facing terrorism authorized to use interrogational torture would be failing[136] in carrying out one of its prime duties—to protect its citizens from harm. Thus the CIA, rather than claiming that its interrogators are brilliant improvisers, has insisted that those involved in its 'High Value Terrorist Detainee Program' (which, as will be seen, has involved torture), were immensely experienced (their average age

---

[133] Dershowitz, *supra* n 58, 144.

[134] See MG Bloche and JH Marks, 'Doctors and Interrogators at Guantanamo Bay' 351 (No 1) *New England J Med* 6 (2005). See also eg RJ Lifton, 'Doctors and Torture' 351 *New England J Med* 415 (2004).

[135] Arrigo, *supra* n 4, 547. See fn 16 *ibid* for the studies cited. Arrigo discusses in detail the related issues of assistance of health professionals in torture interrogation (547–8) and biomedical research for torture interrogation (551–2).

[136] Assuming it is not hampered by budgetary or similar constraints.

being 43) and having completed 'more than 250 hours of specialized training' being allowed 'to come face-to-face with a terrorist'.[137]

Whatever one's views may be regarding the morality of a single, isolated act by a private individual—or even by agents of a state suddenly facing an unforeseen TBS, when it comes to acts and operations performed by a state facing terrorism, such ominous 'institutionalization' is inherent in the very notion of justifying torturous interrogations.

The result may well be, as Shue points out, not only institutionalization, but bureaucratization, where '[s]ome bureaus collect taxes, other bureaus conduct torture'.[138]

Statman points to further implications:

... members of organizations ... tend to justify in their own eyes and in the eyes of others the existence of their organization and their role within it. [...] when persons are trained for the purpose of violent interrogation, special facilities are prepared and jobs assigned, there is a danger that the Golem[139] would overcome its creator, would continue operating even when there is no longer real need for its services, and at any rate would work vigorously far beyond the real needs. The body charged with interrogations would find it difficult to admit that its services are no longer required, and would therefore try to convince the powers that be that violent interrogations are still necessary, even though in fact torture would go beyond the real needs.[140]

Having described how torture in Israel, which was initially authorized '[w]ith an eye to the "ticking bomb" scenario' later became routine, Steven Chapman similarly warns:

The problem is not with Israel but with human nature. To a man with a hammer, said Mark Twain, everything looks like a nail. Give police and security agents in any country a tool, and they'll want to use it, and even overuse it.[141]

One solution may be to have secret, special torture units, with their own professionals, isolated from the official system, and thus minimizing the damage to other branches of government. As Arrigo points out, however:

... like the Nazi Deaths Head SS, an elite torture interrogation corps would be isolated from the regular military and intelligence. Its commander would inevitably gain special powers, and *his* elite corps would have a destabilizing effect on the military and government.[142]

---

[137] Office of the Director of National Intelligence (DNI) Summary of the High Value Terrorist Detainee Program, nd (published in October 2006), <http://www.defenselink.mil/pdf/thehighvaluedetaineeprogram2.pdf>, accessed 6 October 2006, 2.

[138] Shue, *supra* n 75, 138.

[139] Roughly speaking, a Jewish version of Frankenstein's monster. (Footnote added.)

[140] Statman, *supra* n 68, 178.

[141] S Chapman, 'Should we use torture to stop terrorism?' *Chicago Tribune* (1 November 2001).

[142] Arrigo, *supra* n 4, 559. The issue of secret torture is discussed further in Ch 11.

The subject of institutionalization will be revisited in Chapter 20, following the discussion of models legalizing anti-terrorist interrogational torture.

(b) Legitimate weapons in the war against terrorism

The following is actually a 'slippery surface'[143] argument, that is, one claiming that no morally relevant distinction exists between a specific measure, in this case, torture in a TBS and other measures, therefore justifying one is impossible without justifying the others—other anti-terrorist measures, in this case. Rather than make a detailed argument, I will discuss, by way of example, additional anti-terrorist measures approved by two of the supporters of legalized torture in a TBS, Sheleff and Dershowitz, both of whom address the case of Israel and Palestinian terrorists.

Expressing his opposition to Israel's use of 'moderate physical pressure . . . during the interrogation of terrorists in *normal* conditions of routine interrogation', (emphasis added) Sheleff argues that '[Israeli] security forces have enough means of providing security requirements, all subject to the need to preserve humane and enlightened values'.[144] In a footnote, Sheleff lists as examples 'administrative detention and blowing up houses'. While stating his opposition to 'such punitive supervisory measures', Sheleff adds:

> However, as long as they are at the disposal of the security forces, there are certainly less reasons to use moderate physical force in their normal interrogations. At any rate, in the absence of emergency conditions, security forces' staff have time to try other ways of extracting the necessary information.[145]

Sheleff's position is not altogether clear to me, but what *is* clear is that he does not rule out the use of administrative detention and the blowing up of homes (of suspected terrorists) 'as long as they are at the disposal of the security forces', which they were at the time he wrote the article. For instance, according to B'Tselem, the Israeli Information Centre for Human Rights in the Occupied Territories, Israel had, between October 2001 and 21 January 2003 demolished 137 homes of suspected terrorists (and, of course, of their families) fully and demolished one partially as 'such punitive supervisory measure'. Between December 1987 and the end of 1997 (ie during the first *Intifadah*), Israel had demolished at least 449 homes fully and 62 partially. On 2 January 2003 there were, according to a B'Tselem press release (based on official Israeli data), 1,007 Palestinians in administrative detention (namely detention without charge or trial).[146] I doubt very much that Sheleff would have approved of this state of affairs, but if these measures were perceived as the only reasonable means of preventing terrorist

---

[143] See Part I, Ch 4.
[144] Sheleff, 'Maximising Good and Minimising Evil . . .' *supra* n 74, 197.
[145] *Ibid,* n 40.
[146] B'Tselem website <www.btselem.org>, accessed 21 January 2003.

attacks, he would not really have had a moral weapon in his armoury to oppose them with, beyond an unsubstantiated claim that they were ineffective.

Israeli officials often argued that demolishing houses in particular, and harming a suspected terrorist's family in general, is a crucial means of preventing devastating terrorist attacks. Thus Israel's Ministry of Foreign Affairs website carried the following story in August 2002:

Over the past two weeks, two terrorists who has [*sic*] expressed their desire to carry out suicide attacks and were recruited for this purpose by terrorist organizations, were arrested by the Israel security apparatus after having reconsidered their original intention due to their concern that that their families' houses would be demolished as a result.[147]

In defending a new policy of deporting ('assigning residence', according to the official description) members of suspected terrorists' families from the West Bank to the Gaza Strip before Israel's Supreme Court in 2002, a representative for the state reportedly declared:

We will show strong evidence that the move has borne fruit. This is crystal clear: terrorist attacks have been prevented—not just one, two or three. We have testimonies of terrorists who gave themselves in for fear that their families would be harmed. We also have statements from senior officials on the other [ie Palestinian] side that Israel has at long last found the way to act against the suicide terrorist attacks.[148]

Dershowitz, taking this logic even further, recommends a new 'policy' for Israel:

Israel's first step in implementing this policy would be to completely stop all retaliation against terrorist attacks for five days. It would then publicly declare precisely how it will respond in the event of another terrorist act, such as by destroying empty houses in a particular village that has been used as a base for terrorists, and naming that village in advance. The next time terrorists attack, the village's residents would be given twenty-four hours to leave, and then Israeli troops would bulldoze the houses.[149]

Dershowitz concedes that '[t]here is something seriously troubling, of course, about bulldozing an entire village, even if its residents have been evacuated.' He

---

[147] 'Two would-be suicide terrorists deterred by concern over family property' (Communicated by the Prime Minister's Media Adviser), Israel's Ministry of Foreign Affairs website <http://www. mfa.gov.il/MFA/Government/Communiques/2002/Two+would-be+suicide+terrorists+deterred +by+concer.htm>, accessed 19 October 2007. A similar story is told by Israeli soldiers about an Islamic Jihad activist, Ra'ed Harraz, who was 'on his way to carry out a suicide terrorist attack in the market of Natanya. Harraz was arrested following information provided by a relative, who feared that his house would be blown up in retaliation' A Beqer, 'An Enlightened Demolition' [Hebrew] *Haaretz Weekly* (26 December 2002).

[148] M Gorali, 'What is the Punishment for Someone who Prepared a Sandwich for the Terrorist?' [Hebrew] *Haaretz* (1 September 2002).

[149] Dershowitz, *supra* n 58, 177. Dershowitz adds that the 'point is to make the destruction the fault of the terrorists, who will have received plain advance warning of the specific consequences of their actions'. He further adds, in a manner I found chilling, that the 'Israeli soldiers would act automatically, carrying out a previously announced policy' (*ibid*). This rational of shifting responsibility fully onto the terrorists by means of issuing 'plain advance warning' would have applied equally had Dershowitz' suggested 'policy' involved Israeli forces destroying inhabited houses.

even admits that '[n]ot all those whose home will be destroyed are equally complicit in terrorism'.[150] Nevertheless he justifies such a step as 'directing proportionate, nonlethal deterrents against those who support and benefit from terrorism', though it is unclear to me how exactly it could be claimed, let alone proven, that the population of an entire village, including children, the elderly etc, 'support and benefit from terrorism'. It is similarly unclear how, on this view, torture in *punitive* rather than interrogational form can be ruled out as such 'proportionate, nonlethal deterrent'. It is not unreasonable to believe that were Israel to start punishing convicted terrorists by torture, its officials would soon be able to cite cases of would-be murderous terrorists who 'reconsidered their original intention' for fear of being tortured.

The inability of the 'lesser evil' moral view to distinguish the guilty (or suspect) from the innocent, especially in extreme emergencies (discussed in Part I[151]) may, and from that view *should*, manifest itself in states resorting, alongside torture, to drastic and massive, albeit 'nonlethal'[152] acts against those who are innocent morally, legally or both, as Sheleff and Dershowitz have illustrated.

(c) Deciding whom to torture—enemy POWs and dangerous criminals

This is, again, a 'slippery surface' argument, to wit, that if torturing a suspected terrorist is justified, the same must hold for the torture of prisoners of war and criminal suspects possessing information on military or criminal operations likely to cause death and injury on a large scale.

Kremnitzer poses the following (rhetorical) question, addressing the Landau Commission's 'lesser evil' rationale:

Would it not be justified, according to the Commission's logic, to employ physical pressure in the interrogation of a prisoner-of-war in order to extract from him information essential to the success of a military operation or to the rescue of our soldiers?[153]

The Petitioners in the *Israel Torture* case made this point to the Court, considering the possibility of an Israeli pilot being tortured and a 'lesser evil' defence invoked in justification:

How would Israel bring about an international outcry and raise a storm of protests if, heaven forbid, one of its pilots or soldiers were to be captured by an enemy state, and members of the security service of that state tortured him, claiming that they were protected by the defence of necessity?[154]

---

[150] *Ibid.*

[151] Chapter 5, Section B.

[152] Though in the absence, here too, of a utilitarian 'inherent limiting principle' (Dershowitz, *supra* n 58, 146) others may go beyond 'non-lethality', relying on the same view.

[153] Kremnitzer, *supra* n 72, 262.

[154] *Israel Torture* case, *supra* n 91, *Supplementary Statement by the Respondents*, 17 May 1998, para F(9). The passage quoted was written by me. The statement was submitted by Adv Allegra Pacheco and Leah Tzemel. On the defence of necessity as corresponding to the 'lesser evil' moral view see Part IV, Ch 19.

On this question, Statman begs to differ: considering a similar fictional scenario, he states that such torture would be wrong, even in pure theory, both on the basis of the 'just war' theory, which distinguishes combatants and non-combatants and 'prohibits harming the defenceless, be they civilians or soldiers who have laid down their arms', and the issue of the tortured person's guilt where, unlike the terrorist:

...commanders and soldiers do not bear responsibility for the war, and if they fight in accordance with the rules of 'just war,' they cannot be morally blamed...[155]

However, if the scenario shifts slightly, to where the prisoner-of-war has knowledge of planned, or ongoing, attacks which would be *illegitimate*, in breach of the rules of just war, for instance targeting (many) civilians, that distinction disappears, soldiers *do* carry moral blame and torture must, even according to Statman's reasoning, be allowed.[156]

Hussein Ibish, the communications director for the Arab-American Anti-Discrimination Committee, makes a similar point regarding dangerous criminals, during a television programme in the USA devoted to the question of whether torture should be used against terrorists in the wake of the terrorist attacks on 11 September 2001:

Believe me, if you justify it in this case, there will be another case involving drug dealers and major shipments of cocaine, there will be all kinds of cases involving the Mafia. Either we do it or we don't do it...[157]

Kremnitzer briefly mentions a similar example of persons 'dealing hard drugs to children'[158] which may be expanded: what if we caught a criminal who has just sold a huge amount of heroin and crack cocaine to a gang which routinely sells them on to children, often providing them with free samples as a means of getting them 'hooked'. Unless we know where the drugs are within the next few hours, they will be distributed to dealers and disappear unto the streets. We know the inevitable consequences for the victims: their health, dignity and wellbeing will deteriorate, they will turn to crime and prostitution, they will die young. In other words, torture is definitely the life-saving 'lesser evil' here.

In July 2003, three teenagers armed with 'rifles, handguns, knives, machetes and 2,000 rounds of ammunition', were arrested in the New Jersey town of Okalyn, before carrying out a plan to kill many, including classmates. According to a police

---

[155] Statman, *supra* n 68, 183–7. The quotations are from 184 and 186, respectively.

[156] Sheleff argues that 'ordinary soldiers' should also be briefed about torturing, as they may, eg, capture a terrorist when they know his comrades are on their way to attack 'a civilian settlement' but not which one. 'Maximising Good and Minimising Evil...' *supra* n 74, 209. I cannot see how the argument could logically be different if the would-be attackers of the 'civilian settlement' are uniformed soldiers rather than 'terrorists'.

[157] Joie Chen, host, CNN Talkback Live: Torture: Should It Be an Option When Dealing With Terrorists? Aired 7 November 2001 15:08 ET, CNN website <www.cnn.com/transcripts>, accessed 12 September 2002.

[158] Kremnitzer, *supra* n 72, 261.

officer, the three 'planned on not being taken alive'.[159] There is very little between this type of plan for mass murder and a terrorist plot for a suicide bombing attack.

Nor would it be very easy to rely on the 'lesser evil' rationale in defending the line between 'interrogational torture' and torture for other purposes, which is unanimously condemned by supporters of torture in a TBS.[160] For instance, if the police knows, but cannot prove, that a certain detainee is that 'serial killer-rapist', how could a society where torture in a TBS is justified prohibit the police from torturing him if this is the only way to extract a confession, reveal compelling evidence or the names of witnesses, when the alternative is releasing him and risking the lives, dignity and wellbeing of many more innocent civilians?[161]

(d) Us and Them

One of the 'slippery slope' dangers that Amnesty International warns of, namely that 'torture will almost inevitably be used... against an increasing proportion of the population'[162] may, indeed *has* in many cases been averted by phenomena often associated with torture, but themselves, unfortunately, no less dangerous: prejudice and discrimination against vulnerable groups—minorities, criminals, and any other perceived 'enemies' within or without, or merely because of their vulnerability. Rodley links this issue, 'dehumanization', to the institutionalization of torture:

For one person to treat another in the ways that have been described above [namely torture] may, in the isolated case, be psychopathic behaviour. But when such behaviour is part of an institutional practice then something else is at work: the victim is—must be—dehumanized, seen as an object. This is the traditional and inevitable means of considering 'the enemy', be it a class enemy, a race enemy, a religious enemy, or a foreign enemy. Whatever the group, its members must be stripped of their inherent dignity as human beings in order to mobilise the rest against them.[163]

As Michael Gross puts it, within the narrower ambit of 'security'-related torture,

---

[159] TJ Lueck with D Kocieniewski, 'Youths' Arrest Said to Foil Killing Spree' *New York Times* website (7 July 2003) <http://www.nytimes.com>, accessed 7 July 2003. On 20 April 1999, 15 persons were murdered at Columbine High School in Littleton, Colorado, USA, when a similar planned attack was not, unfortunately, thwarted.

[160] See eg RS Gerstein, 'Do Terrorists Have Rights?' in DC Rapoport and Y Alexander (eds) *The Morality of Terrorism* (New York: Pergamon Press, 1982) 290–307, 296; M Levin, 'Torture and Other Extreme Measures Taken for the General Good: Further Reflections on a Philosophical Problem' in P Suedfeld (ed) *Psychology and Torture* (New York: Hemisphere Publishing, 1990) 89–98, 90; MS Moore, *supra* n 53, 341; Paskins, *supra* n 70, 142; Twining and Paskins, *supra* n 70; Sheleff, 'Maximising Good and Minimising Evil...' *supra* n 74, 197; Shue, *supra* n 75, fn 11 at 134; Statman, *supra* n 68, 181.

[161] And, under this rationale, if legislation prohibiting reliance on evidence obtained through illegal means is what stands between convicting extremely dangerous persons and releasing them to continue raping and murdering, should such legislation not be scrapped?

[162] Amnesty International, *supra* n 62.

[163] NS Rodley, *The Treatment of Prisoners under International Law* (2nd edn, Oxford: OUP, 1999) 14–15.

...the effects of intermittent torture in the name of national security are blunted, iron-ically enough, when the victims belong to a clearly delineated and hostile outgroup that often resides beyond the territorial boundaries of the affected nation.[164]

Limiting torture to members of 'outgroups' has been, to use Dworkin's terms,[165] a 'defensible line' that states were able to 'draw and maintain' against its spread onto the wider population, but not, obviously, without other negative consequences.

During a worldwide campaign against torture, in 2000–2001, Amnesty International itself showed very convincingly how torture, prejudice and discrim-ination are, more often than not, inextricably interlinked, as the titles of some of the reports published during the campaign indicate: *Racism and the admin-istration of justice*;[166] *Hidden scandal, secret shame: Torture and ill-treatment of children*;[167] *Broken bodies, shattered minds: Torture and ill-treatment of women*;[168] *Crimes of hate, conspiracy of silence: Torture and ill-treatment based on sexual iden-tity*.[169] The attitudes which give rise to torture against such populations and groups shield those not belonging to any of them from torture.

These, of course, are not the types of targets that supporters of torture in a TBS have in mind. Nevertheless, the same dangers exist where torture is con-fined to terrorist suspects. Explaining the readiness of Israeli public opinion to ignore the torture of Palestinian suspects and give those practicing it a free hand, Kremnitzer and Segev argue the following:

It seems that the only possible explanation of the fact that permission to use force in GSS interrogations in order to expose information regarding terrorist organisations has been accepted with calm and understanding by the vast majority of the Israeli public, is the assumption by the Jewish public—which constitutes the majority of the Israeli public...—that there is no chance of these interrogation methods being used against them.[170]

Describing the 'essential atmosphere in which torture could become institution-alised within the French army in Algeria', Alistair Horne writes:

Noting the growing indifference to the 'enemy' as a human being, such a tough para commander as Colonel François Coulet himself admits that the army had come to regard a prisoner as 'no longer an Arab peasant' but simply 'a source of intelligence'.[171]

---

[164] Michael L Gross, 'Regulating Torture in a Democracy: Death and Indignity in Israel ' 36 (No 3) *Polity* 367 (2004) 377. Oren Gross similarly argues that 'Counterterrorism measures and emergency powers are often perceived as directed against a clear enemy of "others"' (*idem*, 'Chaos and Rules: Should Responses to Violent Crises Always be Constitutional?' 112 *Yale L J* 1011 (2003) 1082 and see his discussion of 'Us vs. Them' 1082–1089).

[165] See Dworkin, *supra* n 60 and accompanying text.

[166] AI Index: ACT 40/020/2001, 2001.

[167] AI Index: ACT 40/38/00, 2000.

[168] AI Index: ACT 40/001/2001, 2001.

[169] AI Index: ACT 40/016/2001, 2001.

[170] Kremnitzer and Segev, *supra* n 17, 680–1.

[171] A Horne, *A Savage War of Peace: Algeria 1954–1962* (London: Papermac, 1987) 198.

Williams, writing in the context of the USA's counter-terrorist policies follow-ing 9/11, makes the link between the absoluteness of what we need to know, and the selectivity regarding whom we choose to question (and torture) for that knowledge:

Torture is an investment in the right to be all-knowing, in the certitude of what appears 'obvious.' It is the essence of totalitarianism. Those who justify it with confident proc-lamations of 'I have nothing to hide, why should they?' overlap substantially with the class of those who have never been the persistent object of suspect profiling, never been harassed, never been stigmatized just for the way they look.[172]

Dershowitz acknowledges, whilst comparing the possibility of shooting down a highjacked American plane to avoid it colliding with a building with that of torturing a suspected terrorist, that such distinctions may come back as 'slippery slope' dangers *within* interrogations:

The suspected terrorist we may choose to torture is a 'they'—an enemy with whom we do not identify but with whose potential victims we do identify. The risk of making the wrong decision, or of overdoing the torture, is far greater, since we do not care as much what happens to 'them' as to 'us'.[173]

Thus torturing suspected terrorists may both be encouraged by prejudice and encourage such prejudice further.

(e) The effects of torture on a conflict

Immanuel Kant, setting out his 'preliminary articles of a perpetual peace between states'[174] provides that:

No state at war with another shall permit such acts of hostility as would make mutual confidence impossible during a future time of peace.[175]

While Kant's examples do not include torture, it does seem a mutual-confidence-busting act worthy of such prohibition, which he deems absolute. Kant explains, this time in practical terms, that:

... it must still remain possible, even in wartime, to have some sort of trust in the attitude of the enemy, otherwise peace could not be concluded and the hostilities would turn into a war of extermination ... [such a war,] in which both parties and right itself might all be simultaneously annihilated, would allow perpetual peace only on the vast graveyard of the human race.[176]

---

[172] Williams, *supra* n 97.
[173] Dershowitz, *supra* n 58, 155.
[174] Immanuel Kant, 'Perpetual Peace: A Philosophical Sketch' [1795] in *idem, Political Writings, supra* n 36, 93–130, 93.
[175] Article 6, *ibid*, 96.
[176] *Ibid.*

In our context Statman, having warned of torture leading to revenge attacks by victims and their comrades and decreasing the chances of peace, turns to the possible deterrent effect of torture and adds:

Torture creates such deep residues of anger and hatred among those tortured and their supporters, that those feelings overcome the feelings of fear from torture itself. Some indeed break down; but those who do not often emerge from torture stronger and more cohesive, both as individuals and as groups.[177]

Perry, the former GSS head, confirms that such warnings have actually materialized:

Unlike common beliefs, religion was not the suicide bombers' only motive. The *Intifadah* stirred in many young persons a desire to take revenge of the Israeli authorities for a long list of issues: prolonged detention in difficult conditions, the loss of a family member or a close friend in one of the clashes, humiliating conduct during a search and much more.[178]

In 2004, the then US Secretary of Defense, Donald H Rumsfeld, expressing regret for his failure to prevent or put a quick end to the 'abuse' at Abu Ghraib, spoke more generally of dangers which such 'abuse' may bring in its wake when testifying before a joint meeting of the US Senate and House Armed Services Committees:

Let me be clear. I failed to identify the catastrophic damage that the allegations of abuse could do to our operations in the theater, to the safety of our troops in the field, the cause to which we are committed.[179]

(f) Effectiveness and alternatives

> It is not a universal truth that those to whom evil is done do evil in return, but it is true often enough.
>
> Jonathan Glover[180]

It is difficult to assess the extent to which torture is effective in the wider context of anti-terrorist operations, and even more so in the yet-wider ones of relations within a society and between societies, and I will not attempt this here. In what follows I will confine myself to providing two examples, one of torture being of limited effectiveness as an anti-terrorist measure, the other of torture not being

---

[177] Statman, *supra* n 68, 181. For similar arguments see B Cohen, 'Democracy and the Mis-Rule of Law: The Israeli Legal System's Failure to Prevent Torture in the Occupied Territories' 12 *Ind Int'l & Comp L Rev* 75 (2001) 90; Kremnitzer, *supra* n 72, 263; WP Nagan and L Atkins, 'The International Law of Torture: From Universal Proscription to Effective Application and Enforcement' 14 *Harvard Human Rights J* 87 (2001) 90.

[178] Perry, *supra* n 125, 233.

[179] Testimony as Prepared by Secretary of Defense Donald H. Rumsfeld, Before The Senate and House Armed Services Committees, Friday, May 7, 2004, <http://www.defenselink.mil/speeches/2004/sp20040507-secdef1042.html>, accessed 11 August 2004.

[180] J Glover, *Humanity: a moral history of the twentieth century* (London: Pimlico, 2001) 407.

effective in achieving wider, long-term goals despite being, arguably, effective in combating terrorism in the short run.

Israel has used torture (alongside other anti-terrorist methods) and lesser means of ill-treatment during the interrogation of suspected terrorists and less violent (and even non-violent) Palestinians at least since its occupation of the West Bank and the Gaza Strip in June 1967.[181] Between 1987 and 1999, such practices were used extensively and legally, under the Landau Commission's guidelines. Even since the Supreme Court ruling in the *Israel Torture* case in 1999, torture has been legal, albeit limited—at least in law—to TBSs. Both these models will be discussed in Part III. The relevant point here is that to date, torturing tens of thousands up to 1999, and hundreds, if not more since,[182] has not worked.

Israel has consistently cited horrifying statistics of terror victims to justify its resort to torture.[183] This, however, is a two-edged sword, attesting as much to the failure of torture in the past as to the alleged need for its continued use in the present and future. Israel has also claimed that GSS interrogators have thwarted many terrorist attacks,[184] which may be construed as a claim that had torture not been allowed, the situation would have been even worse. To confirm or refute this claim (as a general rather than case-specific one), however, one would have to take into account a myriad of other factors, some discussed here, others to do with political, military and other aspects of the situation. At any rate, such a claim would be that torture is *relatively*, or *comparatively*, efficient only.

More specifically, in September 1994, following the first suicide terrorist attacks, the Israeli government allowed the GSS additional 'special permissions' to use what the press termed 'enhanced physical pressure,' presumably going beyond the 'moderate measure of physical pressure' which the Landau guidelines had originally allowed. These 'permissions', ostensibly granted for a limited period of time, were in fact routinely extended up until the 1999 ruling.[185] However, the

---

[181] According to the published part of the Landau Report, written in 1987, it described, in the secret part, '…the methods of interrogation of HTA [hostile terrorist activity] interrogees practiced by the Service [GSS] since 1967, and the permission given to interrogators to use, on occasion, methods of pressure, including physical pressure' (*Landau Report, supra* n 89, para 2.21). In the one case described by the Commission, such 'pressure' included slapping, beating, kicking, shaking, pulling by the hair, knocking to the ground, making the detainee stand for long hours, sleep deprivation, cold showers, threats and insults (*ibid,* para 2.1). GSS interrogators, having denied in court the use of any of these methods, later admitted to having used all but the first two, claiming that, in the Commission's words, 'in applying the pressure methods they had not gone beyond what they were permitted to do under Service instructions extant at that time' (*ibid,* para 2.5).

[182] See *infra,* Part III, Chs 12 and 14.

[183] See eg HCJ 4045/95 *The Association for Civil Rights in Israel v the Prime Minister et al.*), *Response by the Respondents,* 13 December 1995, para 41; HCJ 5100/94 (*Israel Torture* case), *supra* n 91, *Supplementary Statement by the Respondents,* 17 May 1998, para 10.

[184] See eg HCJ 4045/95, *Response, ibid,* para 42; Israel's report to the UN Committee against Torture, Consideration of Reports Submitted by States Parties under Article 19 of the Convention, *Special Report of Israel,* UN Doc CAT/C/33/Add.2/Rev.1, 18 February 1997, para 24.

[185] See eg Y Ginbar, *Legitimizing Torture* (Jerusalem: B'Tselem, 1997) 3; C Gilon, *Shin-Beth between the Schisms,* [Hebrew] R Tal ed, (Tel-Aviv: Miskal, 2000) 385–7.

beginning of 1996 saw a wave of suicide attacks in Israel's main cities, Jerusalem and Tel-Aviv, in which 65 Israelis were killed,[186] and which the GSS, even with 'enhanced' powers, obviously failed to prevent. Nor would GSS interrogators torturing under the individual shield of the 'defence of necessity' granted by Israel's Supreme Court to those torturing in a TBS succeed in thwarting an even worse wave of attacks during the second *Intifadah*, since September 2000, in which, according to B'Tselem, 757 civilians were killed up to the mid-August 2007.[187]

Avi Dichter, at the time the Head of the GSS, declared the following in December 2003:

We have to say honestly: we have not provided the nation with the security it deserves.[188]

Dichter's solution was:

We should construct the fence quickly. Fence now, enclaves later.[189]

By 'fence' Dichter was referring to the separation 'barrier', 'wall' or 'fence' which Israel started constructing in 2002 in the West Bank as a solution to the problem of terrorist attacks. Whatever else may be said about this barrier,[190] it clearly does not rely on, or even involve, the torturing of detainees. That barrier, then, is a monument to the failure of interrogational torture as an anti-terrorist weapon.

An earlier case is that of 'the battle of Algiers', in early 1957, when the French rulers of Algeria at the time, facing a wave of attacks, including terrorist ones (in the 'hard core of settled meaning' sense used here[191]), by the local *Front de Libération Nationale* (FLN), handed over police powers in Greater Algiers to General Jacques Massu, Commander of the Tenth Parachute Division.[192] The paratroopers used torture extensively[193] (alongside other extreme anti-terrorist methods) against

---

[186] See eg the Terror Victims Association website <http://www.terrorvictims.com/1996htm>, accessed 7 February 2003.

[187] See the organization's website <http://www.btselem.org> accessed 18 August 2007. According to B'Tselem, altogether 4,244 Palestinians and 1,024 Israelis, as well as 63 foreign nationals, died in the mutual bloodshed during that period. For earlier statistics see Amnesty International, *Israel, the Occupied Territories and the Palestinian Authority: Without distinction— attacks on civilians by Palestinian armed groups*, AI Index: MDE 02/002/2002, 2002, 4.

[188] Quoted in B Kaspit, 'A Fence Now' [Hebrew] *Maariv* (17 December 2003).

[189] *Ibid*. Both Kremnitzer and Dershowitz argue that total security can only be attained by relinquishing the democratic and liberal nature of a state. See Kremnitzer, *supra* n 72, fn 19 on 228–9; Dershowitz, *supra* n 58, 126–7.

[190] See eg *Legal Consequences of the Construction of a Wall in the Occupied Palestinian Territory*, Advisory Opinion, the International Court of Justice (9 July 2004).

[191] See Part I, Ch 1, Section B.

[192] For Massu's version of events see eg *idem, La Vraie Bataille d'Alger* (Paris: Plon, 1971); *Le Torrent et la Digue* (Paris: Plon, 1972). For the general strategic and tactical approach to anti-guerrilla warfare (including justification of torture and anti-guerrilla terrorism) used in Algiers see R Trinquier, *Modern Warfare: A French View of Counterinsurgency*, trans D Lee, (London: Pall Mall Press, 1964). Colonel Trinquier was in charge of the DPU (*Dispositif de Protection Urbaine*) created during the Battle of Algiers. See also Part I, Ch 4, Sec C(5).

[193] On torture during the French-Algerian war see eg Alleg, *supra* n 77; M Evans and R Morgan, *Preventing Torture* (Oxford: OUP, 1998) 27–32; Horne, *supra* n 171, *passim*, especially 195–207;

thousands of Algerians; many were tortured to death, many 'disappeared'. The paratroopers' torture techniques included fastening electrodes to various parts of the body, torture by water in various forms (some resembling the *question d'eau* of the eighteenth century, described above[194]), sexual torture, including rape, and more.

Unlike in the case of Israel, however, the 'Battle of Algiers' ended in victory for the French—all leading FLN activists were arrested, its military apparatus destroyed, and by March 1958 the city was safe enough for the paratroopers to go back to the countryside.

This is not, however, where the story ends.[195] France's attempt to hold on to Algeria, for which the 'Battle for Algiers' was fought, failed, and Algeria became independent in 1962, a year that saw the exodus of over a million Europeans from the country. The link between the methods used in crushing the FLN and that later withdrawal from Algeria was made by several commentators.

Discussing the shorter and longer-term effects of torture on the conflict and the French, Horne observes:

Outside the army, in Algeria the rifts created by torture led to a further, decisive step in eradicating any Muslim 'third force' of *interlocuteurs valables* with whom a compromise peace might have been negotiated; while in France the stunning, cumulative impact it had was materially to help persuade public opinion years later that France had to wash her hands of the *sale guerre*. As Paul Teitgen remarked: 'All right, Massu won the Battle of Algiers, but that meant losing the war.'[196]

Rita Maran, taking an even broader view, argues the following:

Terrorism was then and indeed now continues to be a barbaric destructive act, criminal in nature. Attempts by the French to halt terrorism were unsuccessful until the use of torture was institutionalised; at that point, terrorism was for the first time being halted.

R Maran, *Torture: the Role of Ideology in the French-Algerian War* (New York: Praeger, 1989); E Peters, *Torture* (Expanded edn, Pennsylvania: University of Pennsylvania Press, 1996) 32–40; P Vidal-Naquet, *Torture: Cancer of Democracy, France and Algeria, 1954–62*, trans B Richard (Baltimore: Penguin Books, 1963).

[194] See *supra* nn 118–119 and accompanying text; *cf* Alleg, *ibid*, 48–50.

[195] Nor is January 1956 where it begins—earlier brutality may have contributed to the attacks that occasioned the 'Battle of Algiers' in the first place. Thus Evans and Morgan argue that '... the massive deployment and repressive tactics of the French military forces in response to these [the first "largely ineffective" FLN] attacks...proved to be a most effective recruiting sergeant for the FLN...' (*idem, supra* n 193, 28). In a similar vain, Vidal-Naquet states the following: 'On 19 June [1956] the first guillotining of two members of the F.L.N. took place in the Barbarossa Prison courtyard. On 20 June, the F.L.N. replied by organizing the first random attacks against the European population' (*idem, supra* n 193, 48). These arguments and facts are not brought here to justify terrorism, which, it be clear by now, I believe is never justified. Rather, my purpose is to question the prudence, therefore effectiveness, of torture and other types of brutality.

[196] Horne, *supra* n 171, 206–7. Paul Teitgen served as secretary-general at the Algiers' prefecture, with special responsibilities for overseeing police, during part of the Battle of Algiers. He strongly opposed the use of torture and other oppressive measures, and feeling unable to halt them, he eventually resigned. For a real TBS involving Teitgen, see Annex. And see similarly Vidal-Naquet's view that '...the means of achieving that military victory inevitably involved political defeat' (Vidal-Naquet, *supra* n 193, 42). See similarly Evans and Morgan, *supra* n 193, 32.

However the French government's choice of an illegal modus operandi was short-sighted and in the end ineffective. The war went on. Algeria became independent. The psychological scars many French soldiers bear from having committed torture remain. The use of torture embittered many fence-straddling Muslims and drove them into the arms of the F.L.N. Terrorists claim that they resort to violent acts against random populations because their goals cannot be achieved through normal channels. When governments that construct law and rightly demand respect for law are themselves the violators, the prevailing law is that of the jungle.[197]

Dershowitz, discussing the effectiveness issue, argues that whatever the merits of such arguments, they would not hold for cases of 'mega-terrorism':

It is also sometimes argued that even when torture does produce accurate information that helps to foil a terrorist plot... there is no hard evidence that the *total amount* of terrorism is thereby reduced. The foiling of any one plot may simply result in the planning of another terrorist act, especially given the unlimited reservoir of potential terrorists. This argument may have some merit in regard to recurring acts of retail terrorism, such as the suicide bombings in Israel. Preventing one bombing may not significantly reduce the total number of civilian deaths, though it does, of course, make a difference to those who would have been killed in the thwarted explosion. But the argument is much weaker when it comes to acts of mega-terrorism, such as those prevented by the Philippine torture or the attacks perpetrated on September 11, 2001. It is the prospect of such mega-acts— and the possibility of preventing them—that raises the stakes in the torture debate.[198]

It should first be noted that the argument Dershowitz faces is stronger than that which he describes, namely that torture actually contributes to the *expansion* of the 'reservoir of potential terrorists'[199]—as argued here and above, torture may increase general hostility, encourage prejudice and shatter trust.[200] Secondly, Dershowitz' presentation of his views here is somewhat misleading, as he has consistently supported anti-terrorist torture in Israel since as early as 1989—years before the first suicide bomb exploded there,[201] let alone 'mega-terrorism'. The logic of Dershowitz' support for torture against 'retail terrorism' in cases such as Israel and Algiers (which Dershowitz does not mention) may therefore lead to 'mega-torture' to prevent 'mega-terrorism', a point which will be discussed further in the conclusion of this Part.

---

[197] Maran, *supra* n 193, 97–8.

[198] Dershowitz, *supra* n 58, 137–8.

[199] To my mind, Dershowitz' claim that this reservoir is 'unlimited', like his sweeping assumption, discussed above (Ch 9, Section D(2)(b)), that the population of entire Palestinian villages can be blamed (to one extent or another) for terrorist attacks, may be driven more by prejudice than observation.

[200] See *supra*, Ch 9, Sections D(2)(d) and D(2)(e).

[201] See A Dershowitz, 'Is It Necessary to Apply "Physical Pressure" to Terrorists – and to Lie about it?' 23 *Israel L Rev* 192 (1989). The first suicide bombing attack in Israel took place in April 1994. For Dershowitz' (similar) views on Israel later—but before 9/11—see eg *idem*, 'Israel: The Jew among Nations' in AE Kellermann *et al* (eds), *Israel among the Nations* (The Hague: Kluwer, 1998) 129–136.

(g) Resort to torture as victory for terrorism

According to Israel's Supreme Court, 'a democracy must often fight with one hand tied behind its back'.[202] To my mind, this metaphor is flawed, as by unleashing that other 'hand' a state would lose some of the very attributes of 'a democracy'. At any rate, it is quite widely agreed that 'fighting dirty' against terrorism is, to that extent, already losing the war.

Few, if any, would argue that the fight against terrorism is solely about security or saving lives. President George W Bush of the USA, addressing his nation on 11 September 2001, started with the following words:

Good evening. Today, our fellow citizens, *our way of life, our very freedom* came under attack in a series of deliberate and deadly terrorist acts.[203] [Emphasis added.]

Bush added:

America was targeted for attack because we're the brightest beacon for freedom and opportunity in the world. And no one will keep that light from shining.[204]

Nine days later, in an 'Address to a Joint Session of Congress and the American People', Bush reiterated that:

These terrorists kill not merely to end lives, but to disrupt and end a way of life.[205]

In outlining his national security strategy a year later, Bush stated that:

In the twenty-first century, only nations that share a commitment to protecting basic human rights and guaranteeing political and economic freedom will be able to unleash the potential of their people and assure their future prosperity.[206]

The British Prime Minister, Tony Blair, speaking in the House of Commons after the terrorist attacks on London in July 2005 told his nation:

Together, we will ensure that, though terrorists can kill, they will never destroy the way of life that we share and value, which we will defend with such strength of belief and conviction that it will be to us and not to the terrorists that victory will belong.[207]

---

[202] *Israel Torture* case, *supra* n 91, Judgment, para 39. The Court hastens to add (*ibid*) that a democracy 'nonetheless has the upper hand' as '[p]reserving the Rule of Law and recognition of an individual's liberty constitutes an important component in its understanding of security'.

[203] *Statement by the President in His Address to the Nation*, 11 September, 8:30 pm EDT, White House website <http://www.whitehouse.gov/>, accessed 11 November 2002.

[204] *Ibid*.

[205] *Address to a Joint Session of Congress and the American People*, see the website *supra* n 203.

[206] From a document entitled *The National Security Strategy of the United States*, signed by Bush on 17 September 2002. For full text see *ibid*; <http://www.whitehouse.gov/nsc/nss.pdf>, accessed 12 November 2007. See similarly the speech by the UK Prime Minister, Tony Blair, at the Labour Party conference, 2 October 2001, 'Full text: Tony Blair's speech' *The Guardian* website, <http://politics.guardian.co.uk/speeches/story/0,,590775,00.html>, accessed 12 November 2001.

[207] House of Commons *Hansard* debate for 11 July 2005, cols 565–7 <http://www.publications.parliament.uk/pa/cm200506/cmhansrd/cm050711/debtext/50711–06.htm>, accessed 15 July 2005.

Surely, had the sole aim, or duty of, say, the US government been to save lives, it would have found in *al-Qai'idah* an accommodating partner in negotiating a peace agreement involving the constitutional and other modifications needed to enable Usamah Bin Laden to become the American President (or *Khalifah*) and impose his version of Islam over it. In contrast, most states facing terrorism confront it over *how* people are to live rather than solely to ensure that they do. The question then becomes to what extent a state may in the interest of security compromise, curtail or abolish certain freedoms, norms or institutions without losing its very 'way of life'.

The argument that the struggle against terrorism is waged on the constitutional front as well was succinctly made by Harley Sorenson. Commenting on the 'USA PATRIOT Act'[208] enacted in October 2001, which provided the government with far-reaching 'anti-terrorist' powers—but not as far as to licence torture or any other form or brutality against terrorist suspects, Sorenson remarked:

Osama bin Laden, the alleged culprit behind the events of Sept. 11, must be chuckling in his beard. Three bombs and the feckless Americans are willing to chuck 225 years of freedom.[209]

As for torture, even those supporting its use in a TBS regard it, in Dershowitz' words, as 'so extraordinary a departure from our constitutional norms'.[210]

Kremnitzer, unlike Dershowitz, argues that compromising the freedom from torture is an *unacceptable* departure from such norms. His argument deserves a somewhat lengthy quotation:

The licence to employ physical pressure in interrogations constitutes a victory for terror, which has succeeded in causing the State to stoop to quasi-terrorist methods. The belief that the end justifies the means, the willingness to harm fundamental human values and innocent victims in order to attain a goal, action not in accordance with the law and even contrary to it—these are salient characteristics of terrorism. One of the objectives of terrorist organizations is just that: to cause the state to react in ways that lend it a ruthless, tyrannical image. An ever-present danger faced by a state confronting terrorism is that

---

[208] 'Uniting and Strengthening America by Providing Appropriate Tools Required to Intercept and Obstruct Terrorism (USA PATRIOT) Act of 2001' HR 3162, enacted by Congress and signed by the President on 26 October 2001.

[209] H Sorensen, 'As You Wave The Flag, Wave Goodbye To Our Freedoms', *San Francisco Chronicle* (12 November 2001) <http://www.sfgate.com/cgi-bin/article.cgi?file=/gate/archive/2001/11/12/hsorensen.DTL>, accessed 19 October 2007.

[210] Dershowitz, *supra* n 58, 159. This statement is somewhat surprising in view of Dershowitz' earlier claim that torturing in a TBS is not in violation of the Eighth Amendment to the US Constitution (prohibiting 'cruel and unusual punishment') (*ibid*, 134–6), and therefore 'The only constitutional barriers would be the "due process" clauses of the Fifth and Fourteenth Amendments, which are quite general and sufficiently flexible to permit an argument that the only process "due" a terrorist suspected of refusing to disclose information necessary to prevent a terrorist attack is the requirement of probable cause and some degree of judicial supervision' (*ibid*, 136). For a thorough criticism of Dershowitz' legal position see Kreimer, *supra* n 63.

in the course of combatting terror and ensuring the state's survival, its character as a law-abiding state will suffer.

[...] When a state employs forceful means which no ends can justify, such as torture, it reduces the moral distance between a governmental act and a criminal act. With the state's loss of its dignity and moral superiority as compared to other social elements which use force, the moral justification for the liberty-curtailing power accorded the state disappears, and the basis for the citizens' faith in the state is undermined. One may, without risking exaggeration, regard this process as the self-destruction of the state. The existence of a particular state is not merely physical; it lies also in the state's constitution, its ideological foundations, its credo. These lose their meaning when the moral basis for the power of the state is subverted.[211]

(h) *The effects of legalizing torture in TBSs on laws and their enforcement*

This section will not deal with questions of law, to be discussed in Parts III and IV, but only with the practical implications of changing it to allow the torture of terrorist suspects in a TBS.

Laws imposing a total prohibition are easier to explain, instil and enforce than those imposing an almost total one. Obversely, a breach of a total legal prohibition is easier to detect and prove than that of an almost total one. In one case the task of investigators, prosecutors, juries and judges is limited to determining whether or not an agent of the state has tortured a detainee; in the other they have, in addition, to determine whether a TBS did in fact exist (or whether the agent reasonably believed that it did), whether the detainee had the life-saving information (or whether the agent reasonably believed that he did), whether humane methods were tried and exhausted (if there was time for that—which they would also have to determine), whether torture was used strictly for the purpose of extracting life-saving information, and so on.

Establishing all the above is particularly problematic because, in the case of interrogational, anti-terrorist torture, the information relevant is often in the hands of one side only, and is often confidential. In Israel, where the legality of the use of violent interrogation methods[212] has been openly argued in the courts, the intelligence upon which the court allowed torture to proceed, and sometimes information on the methods used, were not available to counsel for the detainee. Kremnitzer and Segev explain the situation under the Landau system:

Ostensibly the GSS, like any other public institution, is subject to review by the HCJ [High Court of Justice], but in practice judicial review of security issues differs greatly from other matters, for a number of reasons: first, as a result of the general veil of secrecy cast over the operation of the GSS, it is impossible to obtain information regarding this operation from sources other than the GSS itself. Secondly, the routine granting of confidentiality orders prevents bilateral and realistic discussion of the facts, as lack

---

[211] Kremnitzer, *supra* n 72, 263–4.
[212] Not named or conceded as torture, but see *infra*, Part IV, Ch 18.

of knowledge precludes any possibility of real adversarial debate and any meaningful cross-examination of the interrogators. Thirdly, the judges have no real opportunity to challenge the statements of the security bodies regarding their assessment of the security situation, as they do not possess the full information, and obviously do not have on-hand intelligence assessments from other sources. Under these circumstances, the tendency to accept the GSS' explanations is understandable, but the result has been blind and almost total reliance on those facts which the GSS interrogators choose to bring before the Court.[213]

These could hardly be described as problems unique to the Israel, and are likely to plague any 'torture warrant' or 'ex post' system. This point will be discussed further in Part III.

When it comes to international law, the abovementioned difficulties are much exacerbated. Sheleff suggests the following:

... why not omit the addition in international law which prohibits torture even in times of emergency?[214]

This may not be as simple as it sounds. The following is a non-exhaustive list of international agreements will have to be amended for that 'addition' to be 'omitted' and for torture in a TBS to become legal. The list does not include a host of regional treaties and 'soft law' instruments:

- Universal Declaration of Human Rights;[215]
- International Covenant on Civil and Political Rights;[216]
- Convention against Torture and Other Cruel, Inhuman and Degrading Treatment or Punishment;[217]
- UN Convention on the Rights of the Child;[218]
- 1949 Geneva Convention I for the Amelioration of the Condition of the Wounded and Sick in Armed Forces in the Field;[219]
- 1949 Geneva Convention II for the Amelioration of the Condition of the Wounded, Sick and Shipwrecked Members of Armed Forces;
- 1949 Geneva Convention III relative to the Treatment of Prisoners of War;

---

[213] Kremnitzer and Segev, *supra* n 17, 678.

[214] Sheleff, 'Maximising Good and Minimising Evil...' *supra* n 74, 205–6.

[215] Universal Declaration of Human Rights, UNGA res. 217 A(III), adopted 10 December 1948. This is a declaration rather than an agreement, but I have included it as it is widely referred to as the foundation of all human rights treaties.

[216] International Covenant on Civil and Political Rights, UNGA res 2200 A (XXI), adopted 16 December 1966, entered into force 23 March 1976.

[217] Convention against Torture and Other Cruel, Inhuman and Degrading Treatment or Punishment, UNGA res 39/46 adopted 10 December 1984, entered into force 26 June 1987.

[218] Convention on the Rights of the Child, UNGA res 44/25 adopted 20 November 1989, entered into force 2 September 1990.

[219] Approved on 12 August 1949 by a diplomatic conference (as were the three other Conventions immediately below). For text of international humanitarian law treaties see eg A Roberts and R Guelff (eds), *Documents on the Laws of War* (3rd edn, Oxford: Clarendon Press, 2000) and the ICRC website, <http://www.icrc.org>.

- 1949 Geneva Convention IV relative to the Protection of Civilian Persons in Time of War;
- 1977 Geneva Protocol I Additional to the Geneva Conventions of 12 August 1949, and Relating to the Protection of Victims of International Armed Conflicts;[220]
- 1977 Geneva Protocol II Additional to the Geneva Conventions of 12 August 1949, and Relating to the Protection of Victims of Non-International Armed Conflicts;
- Rome Statute of the International Criminal Court.[221]

The inclusion of the agreements related to the wounded and sick may need an explanation: denying medical treatment could be a useful form of torturing detainees into disclosing life-saving information. The *Washington Post* gave a real-life example of such methods being used by the USA's Central Intelligence Agency (CIA):

Abu Zubaida, who is believed to be the most important al Qaeda member in detention, was shot in the groin during his apprehension in Pakistan in March. National security officials suggested that Zubaida's painkillers were used selectively in the beginning of his captivity. He is now said to be cooperating, and his information has led to the apprehension of other al Qaeda members.[222]

Dershowitz, discussing the possibility that the USA adopt his model and legalize torture, is aware of the considerable 'slippery slope' dangers that such legalization may entail globally, though he does not consider them prohibitive:

Were the United States ... to declare its intention to allow nonlethal torture in the ticking bomb case, that declaration would effectively change international law, since our actions help define the law. Accordingly, the stakes are far higher in the debate now taking place in this country.

[...] Experience has shown that if torture, which has been deemed illegitimate by the civilized world for more than a century, were now to be legitimated—even for limited use in one extraordinary type of situation—such legitimation would constitute an important symbolic setback in the worldwide campaign against human rights abuses. Inevitably, the legitimation of torture by the world's leading democracy would provide a welcome justification for its more widespread use in other parts of the world.[223]

---

[220] Adopted on 8 June 1977 by the Diplomatic Conference on the Reaffirmation and Development of International Humanitarian Law in Geneva (as was the other Protocol immediately below in the text).

[221] Rome Statute of the International Criminal Court, adopted on 17 July 1998 (A/CONF.183/9). For text see eg the Court's website <http://www.icc-cpi.int/about.html>.

[222] D Priest and B Gellman, 'U.S. Decries Abuse but Defends Interrogations: "Stress and Duress" Tactics Used on Terrorism Suspects Held in Secret Overseas Facilities' *Washington Post* (26 December 2002). The article quotes an unnamed official as stating 'in a deadpan voice' that 'pain control [in wounded patients] is a very subjective thing' (added comment is in the original) (*ibid*). All officials speaking on-the-record for the article denied any resort to torture by US personnel. *CF supra*, nn 112–14 and accompanying text.

[223] Dershowitz, *supra* n 58, 142, 145.

These words were written before the USA's own 'torture model', to be discussed in Parts III and IV, came into being, or rather out of the shadows. At any rate, if a course of straightforward amendment of international law were adopted, once this considerable—though obviously not impossible—task has been accomplished, international and regional monitoring bodies charged with ensuring that states respect rules set out in human rights and international humanitarian law treaties will have their work cut out. While international law as it now stands, deems all torture (as well as 'cruel, inhuman or degrading treatment or punishment') illegal, therefore evidence of officials brutalizing detainees is all that is needed to establish a violation of such law,[224] under the revised system, establishing that torture has taken place is not enough—it needs to be established that the torture has been *unjustified*.

To take the case of one such body, the International Committee of the Red Cross, consider its following description of its activities:

> ICRC visits to prisoners seek to obtain decent and humane conditions for all persons in custody. To this effect, its delegates and physicians do [*sic*] document torture in all contexts where they come across victims having suffered its many different forms, so as to intervene at the highest level possible to try to put a stop to torture. [...] It is undeniable that the ICRC, in the course of its visits, comes across the full spectrum of people in custody, and is in no case in a position to determine who has or hasn't done what—nor does it intend to.[225]

Once torture is legalized, the ICRC would no longer be able to complain about torture without first having determined 'who has or hasn't done what'—or rather, 'who has or hasn't known what'.

Implementing such and similar changes may not involve insurmountable difficulties, but it will involve at least very serious ones, all the more so because of the confidentiality aspect, described above. It is unclear to me how the international legal system would be able to respond to a submission from a state admitting that a certain person was tortured by its interrogators but adding that: (1) he was a terrorist; (2) it was a TBS; (3) a domestic court, having established the above two points, has ruled that the torture was legal; and (4) that regrettably, the information which formed the factual basis for that ruling cannot be revealed, for reasons of national security. For those supporting torture in TBSs, this may not be a problem in states where the domestic system has worked properly and in good faith, but how to distinguish between such states and those which use TBS as an excuse and a cover-up for 'illegitimate' torture?[226]

---

[224] The state would not be in violation of international law where the individual acted on his/her own, in breach of the law, and the state, acknowledging that, promptly took the necessary steps to investigate, prosecute, punish (if necessary) and compensate for the act, and to ensure that it is not repeated.

[225] 'The ICRC and the International Day in Support of Victims of Torture' ICRC website, <http://www.icrc.org> 26 June 2002, accessed 21 November 2002.

[226] These issues will be discussed further in Part IV.

In early 2002, the Legal Adviser at the US Department of State, aware of the attempts by Department of Justice lawyers to create for detained terrorist suspects what Diane Marie Amann calls 'law-free zones of detention',[227] *inter alia* by denying them protection under the Geneva Conventions, warned the White House Counsel:

A decision that the [Geneva] Conventions do not apply to the conflict in Afghanistan in which our armed forces are engaged deprives our troops there of any claim to the protection of the Convention in the event they are captured and weakens the protections afforded by the Conventions to our troops in future conflicts.[228]

The wider question is, of course, do we really believe that a world where torture is no longer taboo would be a safer one?

E. Abu Ghraib—the Quintessential 'Slippery Slope' Case

The most well-known torture-related 'slippery slope' case in recent history has been the torture of Iraqi detainees by US soldiers at the Abu Ghraib detention centre in Iraq, which may perhaps be described as part-sadistic, part-professional in nature. Photographs of the torture in Abu Ghraib were first broadcast on CBS' '60 Minutes' on 28 April 2004.[229] The photographs showed most of what a US army Major-General conducting an internal military criminal investigation

---

[227] DM Amann, 'Abu Ghraib,' 153 *U Pennsylvania L Rev* 2085, 2086. See further in Part III, Ch 15.

[228] Memorandum to Counsel to the President. Subject: Comments on your paper on the Geneva Conventions. From: William H Taft, IV, 2 February 2002.

[229] The first detailed written account was by SM Hersh, 'Torture at Abu Ghraib' *The New Yorker* (1 May 2004) <http://www.newyorker.com/fact/content/?040510fa_fact>, accessed 1 May 2004. The list of books and academic articles covering various aspects of the scandal has already become too long for a footnote, the following is therefore merely a sample of early discussions: Amann, *supra* n 227; R Arnold, 'The Abu Ghraib Misdeeds: Will There Be Justice in the Name of the Geneva Conventions?' 2 *J Int'l Crim Just* 999 (2005); M Benvenisti, M Danner and D Matlin, *Abu Ghraib: The Politics of Torture* (Berkley, Cal: North Atlantic Books, 2005); CH Brower II, 'The Lives of Animals, the Lives of Prisoners, and the Revelations of Abu Ghraib' 37 *Vanderbilt J Transnat'l L* 1353 (2004); M Danner, *Torture and Truth: America, Abu Ghraib and the war on terror* (New York: New York Review of Books, 2004); KJ Greenberg and JL Dratel, *The Torture Papers: The road to Abu Ghraib* (Cambridge, CUP, 2005); SM Hersh, *Chain of Command: The Road from 9/11 to Abu Ghraib* (New York: HarperCollins, 2004); J Karpinski, *One Woman's Army: The Commanding General of Abu Ghraib Tells Her Story* (New York: Miramax Books, 2005); HH Koh, 'A World Without Torture' 43 *Columbia J Transnat'l L* 641 (2005); Luban, *supra* n 72, *passim*; MJ Martin, *Iraqi Prisoner Abuse Scandal* (San Diego, Cal: Lucent Books, 2005); SL Schooner, 'Contractor Atrocities at Abu Ghraib: Compromised Accountability in a Streamlined, Outsourced Government' 16 *Stanford L & Policy Rev* 549 (2005); S Strasser (ed), *The Abu Ghraib Investigations: The Official Reports of the Independent Panel and Pentagon on the Shocking Prisoner Abuse in Iraq* (New York: Public Affairs, 2004). See also the sources cited in Part III, Ch 15.

(initiated and carried out well before the public outcry)[230] had already reported in his findings:

I find that the intentional abuse of detainees by military police personnel included the following acts:

a. (S) Punching, slapping, and kicking detainees; jumping on their naked feet;
b. (S) Videotaping and photographing naked male and female detainees;
c. (S) Forcibly arranging detainees in various sexually explicit positions for photographing;
d. (S) Forcing detainees to remove their clothing and keeping them naked for several days at a time;
e. (S) Forcing naked male detainees to wear women's underwear;
f. (S) Forcing groups of male detainees to masturbate themselves while being photographed and videotaped;
g. (S) Arranging naked male detainees in a pile and then jumping on them;
h. (S) Positioning a naked detainee on a MRE Box, with a sandbag on his head, and attaching wires to his fingers, toes, and penis to simulate electric torture;
i. (S) Writing 'I am a Rapest' (*sic*) on the leg of a detainee alleged to have forcibly raped a 15-year old fellow detainee, and then photographing him naked;
j. (S) Placing a dog chain or strap around a naked detainee's neck and having a female soldier pose for a picture;
k. (S) A male MP guard having sex with a female detainee;
l. (S) Using military working dogs (without muzzles) to intimidate and frighten detainees, and in at least one case biting and severely injuring a detainee;
m. (S) Taking photographs of dead Iraqi detainees.[231]

None, or at least virtually none of those thus tortured were being interrogated in a perceived TBS.[232] Nor were they considered by the US administration to be unprotected by international or US laws, in contrast to terrorist suspects detained in Afghanistan and Guantánamo or, secretly, elsewhere[233]—the USA maintained consistently that 'the Geneva Conventions have been fully applicable' to the conduct of its forces in Iraq, including its interrogations policies.[234] In other words, their torture was not permitted even under the US torture-legalizing model which, I will

[230] For a useful and regularly updated online 'timeline' of events concerning the Abu Ghraib torture scandal see 'Prison Abuse Investigation,' CBS News website, <http://www.cbsnews.com/elements/2004/05/07/iraq/timeline616248_0_main.shtml>, accessed 2 August 2005.

[231] Major-General Antonio M. Taguba, *Article 15–6 Investigation of the 800th Military Police Brigade*, March 2004 <http://www.msnbc.msn.com/id/4894001>, accessed 5 May 2004, 16–17.

[232] According to the Taguba report 'Currently, there are a large number of Iraqi criminals held at Abu Ghraib (BCCF). These are not believed to be international terrorists or members of Al Qaida, Anser Al Islam, Taliban, and other international terrorist organizations' (*ibid,* 8). However, a later report suggests there was at least one exception. See J White, 'Detainee in Photo With Dog Was "High-Value" Suspect,' *Washington Post* (13 March 2006).

[233] See the discussion in Part III, Ch 15.

[234] 'Military Official: Geneva Conventions Applied to Iraqi War Prisoners' 17 May 2004, <http://usinfo.state.gov/dhr/Archive/2004/May/19–396279.html>, accessed 25 May 2004. The official quoted was not named.

submit in Part III, existed at the time, but under which torture would be allowed only in the interrogation of certain 'high-value detainees'. And yet even official inquiries pointed to a link—surely of the 'slippery slope' type—between the interrogation of such 'high-value detainees' in the 'global war on terror' and the torture at Abu Ghraib. A report by an '[i]ndependent Panel' appointed by the US Secretary for Defense, Donald Rumsfeld, in May 2004 (the 'Schlesinger Report') stated:

During July and August 2003, the 519th Military Intelligence Company was sent to the Abu Ghraib detention facility to conduct interrogation operations. Absent any explicit policy or guidance, other than FM 34–52, the officer in charge prepared draft interrogation guidelines that were a near copy of the Operating Procedure created by SOF [Special Operation Forces]. It is important to note that techniques effective under carefully controlled conditions at Guantanamo became far more problematic when they migrated and were not adequately safeguarded.[235]

Similarly, an internal US army investigation found that:

[T]he JIDC [Joint Interrogation and Detention Centre, in Iraq] October 2003 SOP [Standing Operating Procedure]...created by CPT [Captain] Wood, was remarkably similar to the Bagram (Afghanistan) Collection Point SOP. Prior to deployment to Iraq, CPT Wood's unit (A/519 MI BN) allegedly conducted the abusive interrogation practices in Bagram resulting in a Criminal Investigation Command (CID) homicide investigation.[236]

Techniques designed to be used 'under carefully controlled conditions' in the interrogation of, to use Secretary Rumsfeld's words, 'only those we believe there is a prospect of gathering intelligence from that can save people's lives'[237] and therefore deemed by the USA to be legitimate, indeed legal, had been transformed, or 'migrated', into 'sadistic, blatant and wanton criminal abuse'[238] of ordinary 'security' detainees in occupied Iraq, resulting, in the words of the Schlesinger report, in:

...damage...to U.S. policy, to the image of the U.S. among populations whose support we need in the Global War on Terror and to the morale of our armed forces.[239]

In other words, torture has backfired, undermining the very cause which had purportedly justified its use. Those arguing that 'slippery slope' is unavoidable once interrogational torture is introduced in the real world may claim to rest their case.

---

[235] *Final Report of the Independent Panel To Review DoD Detention Operations*, August 2004 (the 'Schlesinger Report') <http://www.defense.gov/news/Aug2004/d20040824finalreport.pdf>, accessed 25 August 2004, 9.

[236] AR 15–6 Investigation of the Abu Ghraib Detention Facility and 205th Military Intelligence Brigade MG George R Fay, nd (published August 2004), <http://www.defenselink.mil/news/Aug2004/d20040825fay.pdf>, accessed 25 August 2004, 29.

[237] David Wastell, 'Rumsfeld: My plans for our British prisoners' *Daily Telegraph* (25 February 2002) 4–5.

[238] Major-General Tabuba's report, *supra* n 231 at 16.

[239] Schlesinger report, *supra* n 235, 18–19. And see Rumsfeld's similar statement, *supra*, text accmpanying n 179.

10

Part II—Conclusions

As early as the sixth century AD, in Rome, where torture was part and parcel of legal investigative procedures, the Roman jurist Ulpian explained why it should be treated with suspicion:

…*etenim res est fragilis, et periculosa, et quae veritatem fallat*—for indeed it is a delicate and risky affair and may be deceptive.[240]

Introducing torture into the interrogation rooms of a democratic state at the beginning of the twenty-first century entails drastic changes within those rooms and (at least arguably) without. Those supporting torture in TBSs intend it to be used only in the direst of emergencies, hopefully as a rare and short departure from routine, non-violent and humane interrogation procedures. I have listed here what I consider the main difficulties and dangers which states introducing torture, even with such limitations in mind, may face.

Once torture in a TBS is allowed, decisions on what happens in the interrogation rooms must include whom to torture, when to start torturing, how to torture, how much to torture and when to stop torturing. All are fraught with 'slippery slope' dangers. Uncertainties abound, as what we are seeking is something stored inside a person's mind. Or is not. In a state confronting terrorism, where torture is a legitimate option, erring on the side of caution, which for officials is most likely to be public security or saving lives, may mean deciding to torture even where those uncertainties are many and substantial, resulting in torture in situations which are less than TBS, or non-TBS, and the torture of the less knowledgeable, the less involved and even the totally innocent.

Outside the interrogation rooms, the introduction of torture may shake the very foundations of a democratic state. As a tool of the democratic state, torture must be applied by those properly authorized, trained and equipped to do so, under proper command structure, instructions, regulations, laws and supervision. To be efficient and save lives, torture must similarly be applied and supervised by professionals. This will involve and have repercussions for a myriad of professions, institutions and persons, including members of the various security

---

[240] Quoted in *The Digest of Justinian* (6th Century ad), Lib 48, title 18. For English text see A Watson (ed) *The Digest of Justinian* (Philadelphia: University of Pennsylvania Press, 1998). For the Latin text see eg <http://www.thelatinlibrary.com/justinian.html>, accessed 21 February 2003.

services, the army, police and prison system, doctors and other medical professionals, judges, legislators and government ministers—all will be affected, all
persons involved will become torturers, or complicit in torture, in the moral sense
of the term, and most in the legal sense as well.

Torture would thus become an institution, and as such may breed self-perpet-
uation; the same may be true of any conflict of which torture forms a (morally
illegitimate) part, once torture is introduced as a counter-terrorist weapon. Even
if not intended as an expression of hatred or a means of humiliating a person for
his or her membership of a certain ethnic group, religion or nationality, torture
would often be perceived as such, especially when (as is likely to be the case) those
tortured would invariably be such members—Palestinians, Iraqis, Muslims and
so on, in other words Them rather than Us—intensifying hostility between bel-
ligerent armies, groups and peoples. Wars, including (or as well as) the 'war on
terror', may thus become more vicious, bloody and protracted.

To the extent that terrorists actually want to change the world, it may reasonably be argued that they would have scored an important victory if the taboo on
torture were to be officially and legally lifted worldwide. The world would have,
by taking that step, endorsed in principle part of their ends-justify-all-means
philosophy, and in practice ensure the kind of no-holds-barred conflicts in which
terrorists thrive.

***

I submit that this last one may be the most serious of dangers. A decision, on
either state or international level, to allow torture in TBSs, would rely on the
same moral justification as would one taken on an individual level, discussed
in Part I, namely that such torture would prevent disastrous consequences, far
worse than those incurred by torturing. We have seen that theorists advocating
torture by government agencies in the real world justify it on the basis of general
considerations of morality rather than specifically 'public' ones. These combine
anti-absolutism with consequentialism, at least in extreme situations.

It does not follow that whether the question of justifying torture in a TBS is
posed in the public or the private arena is morally irrelevant. Unlike private individuals, states have a positive moral duty to protect their citizens—this is perhaps
the modern democratic state's *raison d'être*. On the other hand, a single individual act will rarely, if ever, have long-term, society-wide and possibly worldwide
repercussions, while a change of state policy would, or at least may. The stakes in
the latter case are therefore higher.

In view of this, anti-absolutists, namely consequentialists and deontologists
with a 'disastrous consequences' clause[241] would only allow a state to change its
policy on torture if the disastrous consequences are not only far worse than the

---

[241] See Part I, Ch 3.

pain and humiliation that the tortured person may suffer, but also far worse than any damage which the 'slippery slope' and other dangers detailed in this Part are calculated to produce.

Addressing situations in the real world, anti-absolutist theorists can be—and are—much more flexible than in a pure theoretical discussion. We saw, in Part I, that in such discussion, those holding anti-absolutist views cannot come up with a moral argument against, say, committing a genocide that would annihilate 90 per cent of the population of Lichtenstein if it is the only way to prevent some Lichtensteinians from committing a genocide that would wipe out 90 per cent of the population of India or China.[242] In other words, they cannot, theoretically, support an absolute ban on genocide. The minute we move unto the real world, however, the sheer implausibility of such scenarios and the dire implications of even entertaining the idea that genocide may ever be justifiable would suffice to convince, I dare say, *all* such thinkers to support the absolute prohibition on genocide adopted by the international community in the wake of World War II.

Sophisticated consequentialist theories similarly accommodate offsetting the 'quantitative' imbalance between any rights that one or few individuals may claim and those of the majority, or 'the common good', by declaring individual rights, to use Dworkin's term, as 'trumps',[243] namely as being placed outside policy considerations to the extent that those are based on a simple, act-consequentialist calculus. Indeed, we have even seen that some have gone as far as to argue, on *consequentialist* grounds, that certain individual rights, and freedom from torture in particular, must in the real world be absolute.[244]

In an interview, Dershowitz epitomizes the opposite view:

My whole life has been devoted to trying to prove to my civil libertarian absolutist friends that there is no such thing as absolute rights, at all, period.[245]

This is echoed by other advocates of anti-terrorist interrogational torture—thus Mirko Bagaric and Julie Clarke, whose argument for the use of interrogational torture involves an analysis of theories of right, conclude, *inter alia*, that 'an absolute right does not exist'.[246]

These statements represent archetypal anti-absolutism—at least on a small scale. It refuses, not in some fantastic philosophers' scenario but in the *real* world,

---

[242] See Part I, Ch 4, Section C(2).

[243] R Dworkin, 'Rights as Trumps' in J Waldron (ed), *Theories of Rights* (Oxford: OUP, 1984) 153–167. For a more detailed discussion of Dworkin's view of rights see *idem*, *Taking Rights Seriously* (London: Duckworth, 1978).

[244] See *supra*, Ch 9, Section B.

[245] Quoted in S Hansen, 'Why terrorism works,' <http://www.salon.com/books/int/2002/09/12/dershowitz/index.html> 12 September 2002, accessed 22 November 2002.

[246] M Bagaric and J Clarke, 'Not Enough Official Torture in the World? The Circumstances in which Torture is Morally Justifiable' 39 *U of San Francisco L Rev* 581 (2005) 603. The two attribute this conclusion to rights theorists as well. M Ignatieff's position that 'nothing trumps' is not essentially different. See *idem*, *supra* n 67, *passim* (quotation from p 9).

to accept that each and every woman has the right never to be raped, that all Africans have (and always had) the right never to be enslaved, or that all children have the right never to be molested. I have pointed to certain logical and internal conceptual inconsistencies in Dershowitz' theories. His statement just quoted, however, is not one. In fact, I submit that authorizing torture in TBSs is adopting and applying this very archetypal, small-scale anti-absolutist moral view—to wit, that in extreme circumstances, states are may do *absolutely anything* to (one or few) individuals subject to their power if a dire enough need arises.

Once this view is adopted and applied, in the shape of anti-terrorist interrogational torture, it is difficult to see how any limitations, constraints, safeguards or 'principled breaks'[247] would stand in its way. Would it not, under such view, be justified to torture a hundred persons when our information indicates that one—but not *which* one—of them knows about a bomb that would (or even may) kill a thousand people? Would an interrogator authorized and trained to use torture 'as a last resort' and applying an anti-absolutist calculation, risk having the blood of small children on his hands if he is told that there is only 25 per cent chance that the person he is interrogating knows about a deadly bomb? Would he wait for days until the need is likely to become 'immediate' and only then start torturing, if there is a small chance that by this time it would be too late?

Even the 'principled break' of innocence cannot work here: once placed on the rigid, anti-absolutist consequentialist scale which allows of 'no such thing as absolute rights' one innocent person's rights will always be outbalanced by those of a thousand other innocent ones.[248] In practice, there is in any case no time to find out whether the suspect is innocent or not. A detained suspect is squarely in the hands of the law and totally at its mercy, and the law in democratic states provides for a procedure which separates the innocent from the guilty—a trial. Pending such procedure, as in a TBS, the tortured terrorist suspect (like any suspect) *is* in fact innocent in the eyes of the state that is torturing him.

Consider the interrogator, the police, the judges, and indeed the public in a state facing terrorism. They have seen the blood of fellow innocent civilians being deliberately shed by evil men—an act which no cause can justify. If they use an anti-absolutist view and a simple consequentialist calculus to determine whether or not a person suspected of planning further such atrocities may be tortured, how often is the answer likely to be 'no'? The uncertainty regarding a particular situation, or a particular detainee, is likely to be offset and overwhelmed by the certainty of the general threat posed by terrorists, the scale of the possible—even if *faintly* possible—disaster, and the strength of feelings towards such a person, who very often is certainly one of 'Them' even when it is not certain that he is a terrorist.

---

[247] This term used by Dershowitz. See *supra* n 58 and accompanying text.
[248] See Part I, Ch 5, Section B.

But is it not the anti-torture absolutists who seem rigid and inflexible when it comes to the ultimate argument that theorists supporting torture in a TBS often come up with—a nuclear TBS,[249] where torturing a single person would save not just hundreds, but possibly hundreds of thousands of innocent lives?

Unfortunately, the suggestion that terrorists may acquire nuclear weapons cannot be described, at the beginning of the twenty-first century, as totally improbable. However, should the stakes be that high, they would be so for the terrorists as well, and fanatic suicide terrorists have been known to possess an ultimate weapon against torture. It is quite probable that when planning a nuclear attack, terrorist organizations will invest heavily in 'conventional' precautions, such as compartmentalizing cells; frequent changes in codes, means of communication, meeting and hiding places; torture-resistance training; and immediate changes in plans the minute a knowledgeable member is captured. However, it is not unlikely that those involved in the crucial stages of a project as pivotal as a nuclear terrorist attack would wear cyanide suicide capsules around their necks or have a similar means of disposing of themselves, and of any information they possess, in the event of capture.

This would not be without precedent—the Liberation Tigers of Tamil Eelam (LTTE, known also as the Tamil Tigers) in Sri Lanka have used this tactic for years[250] and are continuing to do so to this day. Thus in April 2007, AP quoted a Sri Lankan military spokesman as stating that a Tamil 'rebel', captured at a checkpoint, 'swallowed a cyanide capsule' once his interrogation began, and died shortly later.[251] Perhaps no less pertinently, the same was true of US General Paul Tibbets, who commanded the Enola Gay, the plane that dropped the atomic bomb on Hiroshima on 5 August 1945, and who had cyanide pills for his crew in case they fell into enemy hands.[252]

Because of the reasonable chances that nuclear terrorists will not be caught in the later, 'classic' TBS stages of their attack, and the possibility that they would take precautions not to stay alive if they are, the chances of a torture-one-or-millions-would-die dilemma are slim. The real, and much starker choice that would face—indeed would *now* face—states fearing nuclear terrorism should they adopt the anti-absolutist, torture-justifying view, is this: Should they or should they not counter what Dershowitz termed 'mega-terrorism'[253] with 'mega-torture'? By

---

[249] See eg Paskins, *supra* n 70, 141–2; Sheleff, eg *Ultimate Penalties...*, *supra* n 53, 310, 448; Shue, *supra* n 75, 141; Statman, *supra* n 68, 171.

[250] See eg P Goodspeed, 'Leader of Tamil Tigers known for ruthless warfare: Rebel group has fight-to-the-death determination' *The Toronto Star* (21 August 1994), reprinted on <http://www.tamiltigers.net/tamilcanadian/canada9405.html>, accessed 24 February 2003.

[251] Associated Press, 'Military says Tamil rebel captured by army kills himself by taking cyanide,' <http://news.aol.com/topnews/articles/_a/military-says-tamil-rebel-captured-by/n20070419042109990007>, 18 April 2007, accessed 20 April 2007.

[252] This fact was mentioned in several articles in August 2005, when the 60th anniversary of the event was commemorated. See eg D Smith, 'I don't blame them but I hope they mourn the dead' *The Observer* (24 July 2005).

[253] Dershowitz, see *supra* n 198 and accompanying text.

'mega-torture' I mean massive, often of necessity arbitrary torture, on a global scale, applied to anyone remotely suspected of being able to disclose, or lead to, information on nuclear (or other 'mega') terrorist attacks. This would be justified by comparing the, say, thousands tortured with the hundreds of thousands which a nuclear bomb could kill and maim. Consistent torture advocates have acknowledged, or at least implied, that 'mega-torture' may be unavoidable. Thus Richard A Posner states the following:

> If there is only a *small probability* that a terrorist is at large with a nuclear bomb or plague germs, the fact that, should the risk materialize, thousands or millions of people will die becomes a compelling argument for torture...[254] [Emphasis added.]

By reducing to a minimum the requirement of certainty, at least in cases of 'mega-terror', Posner, though not acknowledging it, is actually throwing wide open the gates to large-scale torture.

Major pre-emptive military operations, possibly involving large-scale killing and destruction, would also (under the 'slippery surface' rationale) be considered justifiable. Torture 'only' in a TBS (or even 'mega-torture' alone) would, under these circumstances and this view, amount to moral negligence of the worst kind.

The choices may not be that different for those states facing smaller-scale types of terrorism.

This means that the kind of solutions advocated by Levinson[255] and Oren Gross,[256] combining adherence to a general commitment ('precommitment', to use Levinson's term) to the prohibition on torture with some kind of practical flexibility allowing for its use in TBSs (such as 'ex-post facto ratification', to use Gross' term[257]), based heavily as they do on the presumption that torture would be needed only in rare cases against a few individuals, amount to a luxury that states in the real world cannot afford, at least if governments' own accounts of the threats they face are to be believed, and, based as they are on confidential material, we have no means of refuting them. Unless states find ways both of blocking a vast array of 'slippery slope' and other dangers described here and of limiting the extent (or perceived extent) of the threat posed by terrorists, the real choice would be between large-scale, professionalized, institutionalized, legalized, hatred-enhancing, prejudice-encouraging, conflict-perpetuating torture and an absolute prohibition. This point will be revisited and elaborated further in Part IV, following a discussion of models of legalized torture adopted by states facing terrorism.

---

[254] *Idem*, 'Torture, Terrorism and Interrogation' in Levinson (ed), *supra* n 80, 291–8, 294.

[255] S Levinson, ' "Precommitment" and "Post-Commitment": The Ban on Torture in the Wake of September 11' 81 *Texas L Rev* 2013 (2003).

[256] O Gross, 'The Prohibition on Torture and the Limits of the Law' in Levinson (ed), *supra* n 80, 229–253; *idem*, 'Chaos and Rules ...' *supra* n 164; *idem*, 'Are Torture warrants warranted? Pragmatic absolutism and official disobedience' 88 *Minn L Rev* 1481 (2004).

[257] See in detail *idem* and FN Aoláin, *Law in Times of Crisis: Emergency Powers in Theory and Practice* (Cambridge: CUP, 2006).

Dershowitz does not extend his anti-absolutism to measures which he considers would have significant, society-wide repercussions, even in the face of disastrous consequences. He writes the following:

The United States would be incapable of mounting an unlimited war against terrorism because we are constrained by our Constitution, our commitment to the rule of law, and our heritage of fairness, humaneness, and proportionality. Were we to face an imminent and near certain threat of nuclear, biological, or chemical destruction, we might well move in the direction of such an all-out war, but it would be too late. For a total, immoral approach to work most effectively, considerable lead time would be required. We are not about to goose-step down this road—and surrender our liberties and our heritage—on the basis of uncertain risks.[258]

I submit, however, that the only way for states to steer clearly away from such goose-stepping is to adopt and apply a minimal absolutist moral approach, prohibiting *any* violation of certain fundamental rights, or interests, of *any* individual, including freedom from torture—rather than confine absolutist prohibitions to genocide and other operations affecting large numbers, the majority, or a crude version of 'the common good'.

A modern democratic state needs minimal absolutism as part of its constitution—and Constitution—on both the principled and practical levels. On the principled level, minimal absolutism symbolizes the crucial difference between the rights of individuals and the 'rights' (or powers) of a modern democratic state, as Kremnitzer and Segev explain:

…while the default principle regarding an individual provides that every human being has the right to act as they please, the default principle regarding an authority provides that it is allowed to act only within the areas allocated for it and within the limits of the powers granted it.[259]

In other words, authorities may do nothing except that which they are specifically allowed, whilst individuals may do everything except that which they are specifically prohibited. The state is a means to individuals' wellbeing. Allowing states to torture is turning this relationship on its head—it empowers the state, in certain circumstances, to do *anything* to an individual, who then becomes nothing but a means to the state's wider interests. A minimal absolutist approach would halt the state's encroachment firmly and finally at the 'gates' of the person of each human being within its power, ensuring that the proper means-end relationship is, at least to that extent, maintained.

On the more practical level, a minimal absolutist approach would prohibit the state and its agents, even in extreme situations, from placing the most fundamental rights, or interests, of any individual on crude consequentialist scales which are bound to be tilted against him or her, not just by the sheer weight of numbers,

[258] Dershowitz, *supra* n 58, 126–7.
[259] Kremnitzer and Segev, *supra* n 17, 703.

but also by the enormity of the danger and the pressures of time, responsibility, allegiance, prejudice and fear that are unavoidable when the stakes are so high, time is so limited, responsibility so heavy, allegiances so sharply divided, preju- dice so prevalent and emotions so intense. Torture will simply be no more avail- able as an option to anti-terrorist units than would punishing the innocents as a deterrent be available to judges (or, for that matter, to anti-terrorist units), human guinea pigs to scientists desperately looking for a cure to HIV/AIDS, which has already killed millions, or incendiary weapons to armies on the brink of defeat. All would use only those means which society has deemed legitimate and placed at their disposal, none would have to calculate how many innocent lives they might save by committing small-scale atrocities. The state may thus not be able to guarantee us absolute safety from the terrorists, but no torturing state has been able to do that either, and at least we will all be absolutely safe, in this respect, from abuse by our own state.

This practical aspect of minimal absolutism on the public level may well be endorsed by some consequentialists, or deontologists with 'disastrous conse- quences' clauses. Others, however, may (and do) claim that placing proper con- straints, regulations and supervision would limit torture to a degree where its overall consequences would, despite all that has been said here, be preferable to allowing terrorists to carry out their attacks. Even if our state achieves this con- siderable feat, however, can we trust all *other* states to manage that, in a world were torture is no longer taboo? Can we trust our enemies to torture our captured soldiers (or civilians) 'only' in TBSs? Even if we are able to erect effective barriers against 'illicit' torture within our state, can the international community do so as well?

As noted, there are no ultimate answers to those questions, as it is impossible to agree as to how much 'collateral damage' is acceptable, and a theoretically unlim- ited number of models may be suggested to tackle the more practical problems. We can, however, look at specific models designed to allow torture in limited instances only, assess their potential or real success and draw at least limited con- clusions. This will be done in the next two Parts.

PART III

LEGALIZING TORTURE 1—FOUR MODELS

11

Part III—Introduction

A. The Problem Defined

Where states deem it justified, could a model of legalized torture be constructed so as to allow agents of democratic states facing terrorism to torture terrorist suspects in 'ticking bomb situations' (TBSs), while avoiding the 'slippery slope' and other dangers discussed in Part II? What models of this or similar type have so far been constructed, and even tried?

The relevant definitions used in Part II, particularly of a TBS; of torture, namely that included in the UN Convention Against Torture; and of 'a state facing terrorism', will be used here, unchanged.

'Model' is used here to denote the totality of a system established by law, encompassing legislation or other legal constructs providing for torture, instructions or directives regulating its application and their implementation in reality. 'Legalized' may, but not necessarily does entail adoption of statutory provisions for lawful torture: at a minimum it would mean that the legal system ensures that those who torture in a TBS need not fear legal sanction. One of the models discussed may or may not have reached even that level of legalization, and will be referred to as a model of 'quasi-legalized' torture.

Three models of legalized and one quasi-legalized anti-terrorist interrogational torture will be examined here, the examination naturally focusing, in the main, on the legal issues involved. However, as my project, in this Part and in the study as a whole, is to address both the theoretical and the practical, the examination will not be confined to the law: issuing a ruling, producing a memorandum or drafting a law allowing torture but restricting it to TBSs is relatively straightforward; ensuring that official practice is so restricted may not be. I will therefore, in this Part of the study, both examine each model in the narrower legal context[1] and try to assess whether it may, or has, achieved what it had set out to do which is, in all cases, to allow torture in limited circumstances only while avoiding the 'slippery slope' and other dangers discussed in Part II. This will include examining issues such as the institutional mechanisms which facilitate and supervise the functioning of each model, interrogation methods and the scope of their use.

---

[1] The Landau model being the exception, for reasons explained.

The first model to be examined (in Chapter 12) is the Landau model, recommended to the Israeli government by a Commission of Enquiry in 1987. The Commission's report established methods for interrogating suspected terrorists and set out the legal (and moral) framework within which they were practised in Israel in 1987–1999. I will then examine (in Chapter 13) the 'torture warrants' model, suggested by theorists and partly, I will argue, actually implemented in Israel under the Landau model. This will be followed (in Chapter 14) by an examination of a specimen of the 'defence of necessity' (DoN) model ('the HCJ model'), which succeeded the Landau model following a ruling by Israel's Supreme Court, sitting as the High Court of Justice (HCJ) and applied in that country between the date of the ruling, in September 1999, and the time at which this study was completed. Then (in Chapter 15) the USA's model of 'quasi-legalized torture' in the interrogation of detainees, applied mostly to 'high value detainees' (HVDs) in the 'war on terror' that it declared following the 11 September 2001 terrorist attacks, will be considered.

Certain legal and other issues arising from the theory and practice of these models will be explored in Part IV.

The rest of this introduction will be devoted to discussing briefly two additional models of state torture which, using secrecy, function without torture being or becoming legal, before setting them aside.

B. Secrecy Models

1. A 'total secrecy' model?

In Part I, I cited Lincoln Allison who, making the utilitarian case for torture in a TBS, namely that 'a single act [of torture] might have benefits which outweigh the dis-benefits', argues that the 'possibility is enhanced when we consider that the act might be kept secret'.[2]

I countered that such secrecy can only be achieved through additional drastic measures, unacceptable in democratic states, such as killing the tortured person and hiding his body, or holding him in total isolation from the outside world for the rest of his life.

While the possibility that anti-terrorist torture is being used in total and perpetual secrecy in an early twenty-first century democracy seems to me remote, it cannot be logically ruled out, of course. When David Bowen, a British forensic pathologist, was asked during a BBC interview: 'Is there a perfect crime?' he

---

[2] L Allison, 'The Utilitarian Ethics of Punishment and Torture' in *idem* (ed), *The Utilitarian Response: The Contemporary Viability of Utilitarian Political Philosophy* (London: Sage, 1990) 9–29, 24. See Part I, Ch 3, Section A. For further discussion of the practical aspect of such a model see JM Arrigo, 'A Utilitarian Argument Against Torture Interrogation of Terrorists' 10(3) *Science and Engineering Ethics* 543 (2004) 560–1.

replied, sensibly: 'Well, we don't know, do we?'[3] The same holds for a perfectly secret torture model. For that very reason, however, there is little one could say further on this subject.

2. A 'hypocrisy' model?

Several writers, especially outside the legal profession, appalled by the idea that torture may be legalized, but supporting its application in extreme cases, have nevertheless argued for *some* degree of secrecy, keeping torture 'off the books and below the radar screen'[4] without resorting to the drastic measures mentioned above. Some go as far as to advocate hypocrisy, but in doing so seem to undermine their own project. Thus in 2003 Mark Bowden argued the following:

The Bush Administration has adopted exactly the right posture on the matter. Candor and consistency are not always public virtues. Torture is a crime against humanity, but coercion is an issue that is rightly handled with a wink, or even a touch of hypocrisy; it should be banned but also quietly practised. Those who protest coercive methods will exaggerate their horrors, which is good: it generates a useful climate of fear. It is wise of the President to reiterate U.S. support for international agreements banning torture, and it is wise for American interrogators to employ whatever coercive methods work. It is also smart not to discuss the matter with anyone.[5]

These remarks come, however, at the end of a lengthy article, much of which is devoted to a detailed description of the USA's 'coercive' (and at the time secretive) interrogation techniques. The hypocrisy Bowden advocates is hardly effective when exposed.

Criticizing both Dershowitz' proposition that torture be legalized and debates, in the media and elsewhere, on the morality and legality of anti-terrorist torture, Slavoj Žižek similarly argues:

... we should ... paradoxically stick to the apparent 'hypocrisy': OK, we can well imagine that in a specific situation, confronted with the proverbial 'prisoner who knows' and whose words can save thousands, we would resort to torture—even (or, rather, precisely) in such a case, however, it is absolutely crucial that we do not elevate this desperate choice into a universal principle; following the unavoidable brutal urgency of the moment, we should simply do it. Only in this way, in the very inability or prohibition to elevate what

---

[3] 'Midweek', BBC Radio 4, 5 March 2003.

[4] AM Dershowitz, *Why Terrorism Works: understanding the threat, responding to the challenge* (New Haven: Yale University Press, 2002) 150 *et sec*, citing (disapprovingly) Floyd Abrams. Such policy is also advocated eg by J Alter, 'Time To Think About Torture' *Newsweek* (5 November 2001) reproduced on <http://www.sweetliberty.org/issues/war/safety/torture1.htm>, accessed 3 July 2003; M Bowden, 'The Dark Art of Interrogation' *The Atlantic Monthly*, October 2003, <http://www.theatlantic.com/issues/2003/10/bowden.htm>, accessed 19 October 2003; S Žižek, *Welcome to the Desert of the Real* (London: Verso, 2002) 102–5; See also the discussion of the HVD model *infra*, Ch 15, and some of the media debates cited there.

[5] Bowden, *ibid*. The validity of the coercive interrogations/torture distinction is discussed below, in Part IV, Ch 19.

we had to do into a universal principle, do we retain the sense of guilt, the awareness of the inadmissibility of what we have done. [. . .] such debates, such exhortations to 'keep an open mind' should be the sign for every authentic liberal that the terrorists are winning.[6]

However, Žižek follows this with his own contribution to the 'debate' of that very topic.[7]

I believe that the combination, in both cases, of advocating hypocrisy and actually practising it, by debating or exposing that which purportedly must remain secret or unspoken is not coincidental. It stems from the futility of the attempt to avoid the reality of modern democracies, summed up in a remark attributed to US President Abraham Lincoln: 'You can fool some of the people all of the time, and all of the people some of the time, but you cannot fool all of the people all of the time.' In our particular case, if a democracy at the beginning of the twenty-first century practises torture, and does not accompany this with measures such as ensuring that no tortured person is ever able to communicate with the outside world again, or imposing strict, long-term censorship, the facts will sooner or later become common knowledge. Whatever their principled position, journalists like Bowden will not resist a good story, any more than writers like Žižek will resist entering a crucially important moral debate. And if they do resist, others will take up the topic.

The 'hypocrisy' option is thus of very limited value. Democratic states practising torture should do so in the knowledge that their practices will be exposed, and take into account the repercussions. To the extent that the USA attempted to integrate hypocrisy within its own model, that attempt unravelled disastrously in April and May of 2004. In the summer of 2006, even alleged top terrorist leaders kept in secret locations for years, resurfaced in Guantánamo, the methods used in interrogating them having been leaked to the media years earlier. Nevertheless, a certain degree of secrecy and, one could argue, hypocrisy, remains in all the models.

---

[6] Žižek, *supra* n 4, 103. And see the comment by S Levinson, ' "Precommitment" ' and "Post-Commitment": The Ban on Torture in the Wake of September 11' 81 *Texas L Rev* 2013 (2003) 2043.

[7] Žižek, *ibid,* 104–6, drawing mainly on 'slippery slope' arguments.

12

The Landau Model in Israel

A. Introduction

The Landau model operated in Israel between 1987 and 1999. It got underway when the Israeli government adopted the recommendations of a commission it had appointed, 'Commission of Inquiry in the matter of Interrogation Methods of the General Security Service regarding Hostile Terrorist Activity'[8] which was headed by retired President of the Supreme Court, Moshe Landau.[9] It is the first model of legalized torture to have actually been applied, at any length,[10] in a modern democracy, and extensive documentation has afforded opportunities for in-depth analysis and description.

However, while, the Landau model was the subject of numerous academic studies,[11] reports by human rights NGOs,[12] reports by UN human rights

---

[8] *Report of the Commission of Inquiry in the matter of Interrogation Methods of the General Security Service regarding Hostile Terrorist Activity*, First Part [Hebrew] (Jerusalem: October, 1987) (henceforth: Landau report). For extensive excerpts of the Government Press Office translation of the report, consulted but not used here (for reasons explained *infra* n 30) see 23 *Israel L Rev* 146 (1989).

[9] I use, in addition to 'the Landau model', loose terms such as 'the Landau system', and 'the Landau years'. Landau CJ (ret) remained unrepentant as late as 2000, when he said the following, in an interview: 'I do not retract my words. I do not regret a single word that Yitzhaq Hofi, Yaacov Meltz [the other members of the commission] and myself wrote in that report.' Landau nevertheless describes the ruling that abolished his system as 'possibly correct', calling for legislation which would allow the use of 'physical pressure' in GSS interrogations. See Ari Shavit, 'A State on Board the Titanic' [Hebrew] *Haaretz Weekly* (5 October 2000).

[10] The 'five techniques' applied by British forces to suspected IRA terrorists in 1971 may be another candidate. However, their use was too sparse and brief to warrant the title 'model'. See a brief discussion below, in Part IV, Ch 18, Section F.

[11] Many of the sources listed here have been cited within the discussion of the moral issues, in Parts I and II, the authors considering the two inseparable—like the Landau Commission itself, which stated its case for legalized 'pressure' in a chapter (3) entitled 'Legal and Moral Aspects'. In 1989, a whole volume (23) of *Israel Law Review* was devoted to the Landau Commission's report and featured a large number of articles, including by Dershowitz, Kremnitzer and MS Moore, that have been cited here.

See also eg E Benvenisti, 'The Role of National Courts in Preventing Torture of Suspected Terrorists' 8 *EJIL* 596 (1997); AM Dershowitz, *Why Terrorism Works, supra* n 4, 149–163 *et sec*; M Evans and R Morgan, *Preventing Torture* (Oxford: OUP, 1998) 42–51, 101; Y Dotan, 'General Petition and Judicial Policy in the High Court of Justice' [Hebrew] 20(1) *Iyunei Mishpat* 193 (1996); Y Ginbar, *The Face and the Mirror: Israel's View of its Interrogation Techniques Examined*, LLM Dissertation, University of Essex, 1996; 'O Giv'on, 'The Use of Violence in GSS Interrogations or the Element of Immediacy in the 'Necessity' Defence' [Hebrew] 10 *Mishpat ve-Tzava* 93 (1989–90); N Gordon and R Marton (eds), *Torture: Human Rights, Medical Ethics and the Case of Israel* (London: Zed Books, 1995), especially Parts I–III; M Kremnitzer and R Segev, 'The Application of Force in the Course of GSS Interrogations—A Lesser Evil?' [Hebrew] 4

monitoring mechanisms[13] and more, this model is now defunct. There was very little support even initially for a component of the legal basis for this model which was crucial for its implementation, namely the claim that the 'defence of necessity' could form the legal basis not only for the use of force and psychological

Mishpat u-Mimshal 667 (1998); R Morgan, 'The utilitarian justification of torture: Denial, desert and disinformation' 2(2) *Punishment and Society* 181 (1999) 184–6; *Proceedings of a seminar on Israel and international human rights law: the issue of torture*, 9 June 1995 (Jerusalem: Center for Human Rights, the Hebrew University of Jerusalem, 1995); J Quigley, 'International Limits on Use of Force to Elicit Confessions: A Critique of Israel's Policy on Interrogation' 14 *Brook J of Int'l L* 485 (1988); NS Rodley, *The Treatment of Prisoners under International Law* (2nd edn, Oxford: Clarendon, 1999) 83–84, 94–95; L Sheleff, 'Maximising Good and Minimising Evil—On the Landau Commission's Report, Terrorism and Torture' [Hebrew] 1 *Plilim* 185 (1990); *idem*, 'The Need to Defend the Honest Truth: Legal Agonies on the Subject of the Use of Torture' [Hebrew] 17 *Mehqarei Mishpat* 459 (2002); D Statman, 'The Absoluteness of the Prohibition Against Torture' [Hebrew] 4 *Mishpat u-Mimshal* 161 (1997). In addition, most studies of the 1999 HCJ ruling also, naturally, discuss the Landau system. These will be listed in Ch 14.

¹² B'Tselem, the Israeli Information Center for Human Rights in the Occupied Territories, provided the first systematic description and analysis of GSS interrogations under the system period in 1991, and thereafter a constant stream of reports, closely following legal and 'practical' developments within the Landau model. See D Golan and S Cohen, *The Interrogation of Palestinians during the Intifada: Ill-Treatment, 'Moderate Physical Pressure' or Torture?* (Jerusalem: B'Tselem, March 1991); *idem*, *The Interrogation of Palestinians during the Intifada: Follow-up to B'Tselem Report of March 1991* (Jerusalem: B'Tselem, March 1992); T Bash and Y Ginbar, *The Death of Mustafa Barakat in the Interrogation Wing of the Tulkarm Prison* (Jerusalem: B'Tselem, September 1992); Y Ginbar, *The 'New Procedure' in GSS Interrogation: The Case of 'Abd a-Nasser 'Ubeid* (Jerusalem: B'Tselem, November 1993); Y Ginbar and Y Stein, *Torture during Interrogations: Testimony of Palestinian Detainees, Testimony of Interrogators* (Jerusalem: B'Tselem, November 1994); Y Ginbar, *Detention and Interrogation of Salem and Hanan 'Ali, Husband and Wife, Residents of Bani Na'im Village* (Jerusalem: B'Tselem, June 1995); *idem*, *Legitimizing Torture: The Israeli High Court of Justice Rulings in the Bilbeisi, Hamdan, and Mubarak Cases* (Jerusalem: B'Tselem, January 1997); *idem*, *Routine Torture* (Jerusalem: B'Tselem, May 1998).

For reports by other human rights NGOs see eg Al-Haq, *Palestinian Victims of Torture Speak Out* (Ramallah: Al-Haq, 1993); Al-Haq, *Torture for Security: The Systematic Torture and Ill-Treatment of Palestinians by Israel* (Ramallah: Al-Haq, 1995); Amnesty International, *Israel and the Occupied Territories: The Military Justice System in the Occupied Territories; Detention, Interrogation and Trial Procedures* (London: AI, 1991); Amnesty International, *Under constant medical supervision: Torture, ill-treatment and the health professions in Israel and the Occupied Territories*, AI Index: MDE 15/037/1996, August 1996 (and see also the organization's annual reports during the period); Human Rights Watch, *Torture and Ill-Treatment: Israel's Interrogation of Palestinians from the Occupied Territories* (New York: HRW, 1994) (and see also the organization's annual reports during the period); The Public Committee Against Torture in Israel and IMUT—Mental Health Workers for the Advancement of Peace, *Dilemmas of Professional Ethics as a Result of the Involvement of Doctors and Psychologists in Interrogations and Torture: A Symposium* (Jerusalem: PCATI and IMUT, 1993); A Pacheco, *Torture by the Israeli Security Services: The Case of Abdel Rahman Ahmar*, (Jerusalem: PCATI, 1996; *idem* (ed and trans.), *The Case Against Torture in Israel: A Compilation of Petitions, Briefs and Other Documents Submitted to the Israeli High Court of Justice* (Jerusalem: PCATI, 1999).

¹³ See eg the conclusions and observations of the UN Committee Against Torture (henceforth: CAT) on Israel's reports in 1994, UN Doc A/49/44, paras 159–171; in 1997, UN Doc A/52/44, paras 253–260, and in 1998, UN Doc A/53/44, paras 232–242; the concluding observations of the Human Rights Committee on Israel's report, UN Doc CCPR/C/79/Add.93, 18 August 1998, para 19; and the reports of the UN Special Rapporteur on torture, UN Doc RE/CN.4/1996/35, 9 January 1996, para 90; UN Doc E/CN.4/1997/7, 10 January 1997, paras 119–121; UN Doc E/CN.4/1998/38, 24 December 1997, paras 119, 121. I am referring to general discussions of the Landau system in the Special Rapporteur's reports. Earlier reports contained only descriptions of interrogation methods and of individual cases.

pressure in the interrogation of suspected terrorists, but also for otherwise illegal interrogation methods to be 'defined and limited *in advance*, by way of binding instructions'[14] (emphasis added).

This latter claim was rejected by the vast majority of legal experts, both Israeli and non-Israeli,[15] as well as all relevant UN bodies and even by some of those supporting torture in a TBS.[16] The Supreme Court of Israel, which initially expressed support for the model[17] and allowed it, through dozens of decisions, to operate for twelve years, as shown below, made a complete turnabout in its ruling of 1999 (see Chapter 14), rejecting the Landau system and declaring it unlawful.

Because the model is no longer functioning and there is little, if any, support for its reintroduction, I will confine myself in this chapter to a short description. The three aspects of the model which still have, or may have, relevance to early twenty-firstcentury anti-terrorist interrogations will be examined in subsequent chapters. The first of these, in the next chapter, is the Landau model's function as a 'torture warrant' model.

The second aspect, which is crucial and by no means defunct, is the Landau Commission's *fundamental* legal position, namely that the torture of detainees in TBSs may be justified and legalized under the 'defence of necessity' provision in the Penal Law. The Commission explicitly based its legal position on a moral one: '[e]verything depends on weighing the evils against each other'[18] which, as we have seen, is the prime, indeed the only moral justification put forward for torture in a TBS. This moral-cum-legal position was upheld by the Supreme Court in the 1999 ruling—albeit in an individual and *post facto* form—and also features in the US model, to be discussed in Chapters 14 and 15, respectively. Its application elsewhere has been suggested. Because of its prevailing importance I have chosen to discuss it in a wider context than just Israeli law or even domestic law, in Part IV.

The third aspect is the lawfulness or otherwise, under international law, of interrogation methods used under the Landau model and whether or not they constitute torture. This aspect will be considered in relation to the type of interrogation methods used in all current torture-legalizing models, also in Part IV.

---

[14] *Landau Report, supra* n 8, para 3.16.

[15] MS Moore is the notable exception among the sources cited *supra* n 11.

[16] See eg A Dershowitz, 'Is It Necessary to Apply "Physical Pressure" to Terrorists—and to Lie about it?' 23 *Israel L Rev* 192 (1989); Sheleff, 'The Need to Defend the Honest Truth...' *supra* n 11.

[17] In *Anonymous Persons, supra* n 40 Justice (as was his title then) Aharon Barak stated that the 'solution' offered by the Landau Commission for the problem of GSS interrogations 'is an appropriate one'. See also HCJ 2581/91 *Murad 'Adnan Salahat et al v the Government of Israel,* 47(4) PD 837, in which the Court rejected a principled petition against the adoption of the Landau Commission's recommendations on grounds of generality, the Court (then) seeing its duty as limited to addressing specific cases only (para 4). The Court stated, at the same time, that 'when the question of the legality of such acts [ie interrogation methods] arises in the future, within a concrete procedure, I reserve my right to accept or reject any part of the Landau Commission's recommendations...' (para 8, per Levin J). For a criticism of the latter ruling see Dotan, *supra* n 11, 109*ff*.

[18] *Landau Report, supra* n 8, para 3.16.

B. Model Outline

1. The Landau Commission—establishment, findings

The Israeli government established the Landau Commission[19] to look into, and make recommendations regarding 'the interrogation methods and procedures of the GSS on HTA [hostile terrorist activity] and the giving of testimony in court related to such interrogations'.[20]

Regarding the past, the Commission found that 'occasionally' force had been used to pressure terrorist suspects during interrogation,[21] and that there had been 'a norm of false testimonies' within the GSS whose agents, according to the Commission, had for 16 years (since 1971) routinely lied to courts, denying having used force when interrogating Palestinian detainees.[22]

In the one actual case described by the Commission, interrogational 'pressure' had included slapping, beating, kicking, shaking, pulling by the hair, knocking to the ground, making the detainee stand for long hours, sleep deprivation, cold showers, threats and insults.[23] GSS interrogators, having denied in court, under oath, the use of any of these methods in this case, later admitted to having used all but the first two. They claimed that, in the Commission's words, 'in applying the pressure methods they had not gone beyond what they were permitted to do under Service instructions extant at that time'.[24] More significantly, the Commission itself argued that the interrogation methods used by the GSS up to that time 'are largely to be defended, both morally and legally'.[25]

In stark contrast, the Commission vehemently rejected any legal or moral justification for giving false testimonies:

Here the interrogator cannot rely on the defence of necessity...or of obeying superior orders...as giving false testimony is a serious criminal offence and a manifestly illegal act, above which flies that black flag saying: 'prohibited.'[26]

---

[19] In accordance with sec 1 of the Commissions of Inquiry Law (1968).

[20] The Israeli government decision on 31 May 1987, quoted in the *Landau Report, supra* n 8, para 1.1.

[21] *Ibid,* para 2.21, where it is added that details were provided in a secret annex.

[22] *Ibid,* paras 2.27–2.53, the phrase quoted is used eg in paras 2.33, 2.49. Perjury was at the time (and still is) an offence under sec 237 of Israel's Penal Law (1977).

[23] Landau Report, *ibid,* para 2.1.

[24] *Ibid,* para 2.5.

[25] *Ibid,* para 1.8. It is little wonder, then, that once the Landau methods began to emerge, in reports of human rights NGOs and later in official documents, they turned out to resemble, to a large extent, the methods described by the Commission in this case.

[26] *Ibid,* para 4.22. The Commission was quoting from a ruling, famous in Israel, by a military court in a case concerning the killing of 47 Israeli civilians by an army unit charges with imposing a curfew on the village of Kaffar Qassem at the beginning of the Suez affair in October 1956. The victims, including 15 women and 11 children, were returning from the fields, unaware that a curfew had been imposed. The soldiers were following explicit orders. The words of the Court regarding a 'manifestly illegal order' which the Commission echoed, are worth quoting: 'The distinguishing

In the terms discussed in Part I, the Landau Commission provided an interesting combination of a clearly utilitarian, lesser evil, anti-absolutist view on torturing in a TBS,[27] and full-fledged absolutism on the issue of perjury.[28]

2. The Landau Commission—recommendations

The Commission recommended that when interrogating suspected terrorists, the GSS use, where necessary, methods combining 'non-violent psychological pressure of an intense and prolonged interrogation...with a moderate measure of physical pressure',[29] all detailed in a secret annex ('the second part') of its report. By that Commission's own definition, such pressure '...must not reach physical torture, ill-treatment of the interrogee or severe harm to his honour which would deprive him of his human dignity'.[30] It should be noted that, as a possible qualification of the above, the Landau Commission cites earlier an imagined TBS, then goes on to describe it as 'an extreme example of *real torture*, the use of which

mark of a manifestly illegal order is that above such an order should fly, like a black flag, a warning saying: "Prohibited!" Not a formal, hidden or half-hidden illegality, not the sort of illegality known only to those versed in the law is important here. Rather, it is an open and clear breach of the law, a certain and necessary illegality, which appears on the face of the order itself, a definite criminality of the order or of the action the carrying out of which it commands, illegality which shocks the eye and enrages the heart, if the eye is not blind and the heart is not callous or corrupt—this is the extent of "manifest" illegality needed to invalidate the soldier's duty to obey, and impose upon him criminal liability for his actions' (Mil Ct Mr[Central Command]/57/3 *Military Prosecutor v Major Melinski*, P.M. 17 90, 213).

[27] See the discussion in Part I, Ch 3.

[28] Understandably, the Commission (headed, it will be recalled, by a judge) was concerned that the rule of law would be undermined by any legitimization of perjury, even in rare occasions. This may validate its absolutist stance, but does not explain why the 'weighing the evils against each other' yardstick was used in one case and not (at least not explicitly) in the other.

[29] *Landau Report, supra* n 8, para 4.7.

[30] *Ibid,* para 3.16. The official English translation (see *Israel L Rev* 146, 175) reads: '...the pressure must never reach the level of physical torture or the maltreatment of the suspect...' However, there is no trace, in the Hebrew original, of the word 'never' (the Hebrew equivalents being *le-'olam, ey pa'am, af pa'am*)—only the word *asur*, meaning 'must not' or 'prohibited', is used. Elsewhere, when the Commission cites GSS agents as declaring before it that they would ensure that (coerced) confessions brought before courts would be truthful, its report goes on to state (my translation, para 2.41) 'We were satisfied that this indeed was always [*tamid* in Hebrew] the purpose of interrogations by GSS interrogators.' However, in the official English version the word 'always' disappeared. Kremnitzer points this out, *idem,* 'The Landau Commission Report—Was the Security Service Subordinated to the Law, or the Law to the "Needs" of the Security Service?' 23 *Israel L Rev* 216 (1989) 224. These two more-than-incidental variations have led me to refrain from relying on that translation.

In this context it may be worth adding that on one occasion, the official translation got the Commission into *unwarranted* trouble. Morgan, quoting the Commission's warning (in the official translation) that 'unbridled, arbitrary use of coercion against a suspect' would harm 'the image of the State as a law-abiding polity...' (para 3.16), comments: '...note the *image*, not the *reality* of the state' (*supra* n 11, 186). However, the Hebrew word that the Commission uses, *dmut(ah)*, has a reflective nuance, and is closer to 'identity' or 'character', as it lacks the 'how-do-I-look?' air of 'image' (to which the Hebrew *tadmit* is a closer equivalent).

would perhaps be justified in order to uncover a bomb about to explode in a building full of people'[31] (emphases added).

The Landau model allowed the use of 'pressure' methods far beyond TBSs. The Commission states (rightly, to my mind[32]) that:

... information which the interrogator may obtain from the interrogee regarding caches of explosives...conspiracies for terrorist activities which may be carried out soon, the terrorist cell of which he is member, headquarters of terrorist organisations locally and abroad and training camps for terrorists—any such information may thwart acts of mass killing and individual terrorist acts about to take place.[33]

It was therefore the Commission's position that it was permissible to use 'pressure' to get any such information.[34]

As noted, the Commission, while acknowledging that it was in effect allowing civil servants to violate explicit provisions of the Penal Law,[35] nevertheless contended that GSS interrogators, just like any other person in extreme circumstances, could break the letter of the law but not be criminally liable for his[36] actions on the basis of the 'defence of necessity'.[37] In contrast, false testimonies in the courts must be abolished absolutely.

---

[31] *Landau Report, supra* n 8, para 3.15. See also Part I, text accompanying n 51.

[32] See Part II, Ch 9, Section D(1)(b).

[33] *Landau Report, supra* n 8, para 3.13.

[34] Under the 'defence of necessity'(*ibid*).

[35] For instance, Section 277(1) of the Israeli Penal Law (1977) provides: 'A public servant who commits one of the following is liable to imprisonment for three years: (1) Uses or orders the use of force or violence against a person for the purpose of extorting from him or from anyone in whom he has interest a confession of an offence or information relating to an offence'. Section (2) also criminalizes threatening any person for the same purposes. There are also provisions for malicious bodily harm (sec 329); grievous bodily harm (sec 333); assaulting a minor or defenceless person (sec 368b); assault (sec 380); assault in aggravating circumstances (sec 382).
All (and more) were cited in Mission Permanente d'Israël auprès de l'Office des Nations Unies et des Organisations internationales à Genève, *Statement by Ms. Nili ARAD...and Mr. Shai NITZAN*, 18th Session of the Committee Against Torture (CAT), Geneva, 7 May 1997, para 13, as proof of the absolute prohibition on torture and other ill-treatment under Israeli law.

[36] As far as I am aware, all GSS interrogators, and almost all of those being interrogated by them, were male.

[37] When the Landau Commission wrote its report, the 'defence of necessity' was provided for in sec 22 of the Penal Law (1977): 'A person may be exempted from criminal responsibility for an act or omission if he can show that it was done only in order to avoid consequences which could not otherwise be avoided, and which would have inflicted grievous harm or injury to his person, honour or property or to the person or honour of others whom he was bound to protect or to property placed in his charge, provided that he did no more than was reasonably necessary for that purpose and that the harm caused by him was not disproportionate to the harm avoided.'
At the end of the Landau period (and at the time this book was completed, in mid-2007, the relevant section of the Penal Law (sec 34(11)) provided: '*Necessity* A person shall not bear criminal liability for an act which was immediately necessary in order to save the life, freedom, person or property, be it his own or that of another, from a concrete danger of serious harm stemming from the conditions existing at the time of the act, and having no other way but to commit it.'
Subsequent provisions place limitations or conditions on this defence, notably that of reasonability, in sec 34(16).

The legal debate over the Landau model raged for almost twelve years. It reached its apex at the beginning of 1998, when the Supreme Court, sitting as High Court of Justice (henceforth, in this chapter: HCJ),[38] decided to join together several petitions of principle, spanning a variety of legal issues and interrogation techniques, possibly in an attempt to create 'the torture case to end all torture cases'. These petitions, in what I will call, in this Part, 'the *Israel Torture* case',[39] were eventually upheld, to a large extent—but not totally, an issue which will be discussed in Chapter 14.

3. Incommunicado detention; seclusion of GSS facilities; in-house investigations of complaints

Under the Landau model, detainees under interrogation were often held incommunicado; GSS interrogation facilities were secluded from the outside world; in-house investigations were conducted into allegations of ill-treatment which assured that, in all but one case,[40] no GSS interrogator would face criminal charges.

These elements of the model were not abolished by the Supreme Court ruling in the *Israel Torture* case. While they have undergone some minor changes over

[38] A Reichman explains this function of Israel's Supreme Court, set out in Basic Law: Judicature (1984), sections 15(c) and 15(d), succinctly and clearly: 'The High Court of Justice, a remnant of British rule, is a procedural design under which a panel of Supreme Court Justices hear, as a court of first instance, applications for judicial review of state actions. The Court is empowered to issue a set of orders against the state and its agencies, including injunction and mandamus. Since the Court is sitting as that of first instance, it accepts affidavits on matters of facts; however, the procedures governing adjudication in the High Court of Justice do not include robust discovery. Therefore, cases involving acute factual disputes would likely be referred to a lower court. The Court has developed relatively lax standing requirements. As a result, the Supreme Court sitting as a High Court of Justice is the main avenue through which applicants challenge the legality of state actions in Israel' (*idem*, 'When We sit to Judge We Are Being Judged: The Israeli GSS Case, Ex Parte Pinochet and Domestic/Global Deliberation' 9 *Cardozo J Int'l & Comp Law* 41 (2001) 42, fn 3).

[39] HCJ 5100/94 *The Public Committee against Torture in Israel v Government of Israel et al*, PD 53(4) 817. The title refers only to the first (chronologically) among seven petitions consolidated by the Supreme Court, most of them at the beginning of 1998, to one case. The other six are (in chronological order): HCJ 4054/95 *The Association for Civil Rights in Israel v Prime Minister et al*; HCJ 5188/96 *Wa'el al-Ka'ka' and HaMoked v the GSS et al*; HCJ 6536/96 *Hatem Yusuf Abu Zaida v the GSS*; HCJ 7563/97 *'Abd al-Rahman Ghaneimat and PCATI v Minister of Defence et al*; HCJ 7628/97 *Fu'ad 'Awad Qur'an and PCATI v Minister of Defence et al*; HCJ 1043/99 *'Issa 'Ali Batat and PCATI v the GSS*. The last case was only added to the previous six by a decision of 25 February 1999. Henceforth, for documents relating to the case generally I will use: HCJ 5100/94 (*Israel Torture* case). Note that some of the proceedings in individual cases referred to here took part before they were joined. Note that from this footnote onwards 'the Public Committee Against Torture' and 'General Security Service' are replaced by the acronyms 'PCATI' and 'GSS' respectively in case-references, and HaMoked: Center for the Defence of the Individual by 'HaMoked'. The full references are provided in the Table of Cases.

[40] In December 1989, GSS interrogators beat a Palestinian detainee, Khaled Sheikh 'Ali, to death in Gaza prison. Two interrogators were convicted of homicide through 'criminal negligence' and sentenced to six months' imprisonment each. The Supreme Court upheld the convictions and sentences. See Crim App 532/91, *Anonymous Persons v the State of Israel*.

the years, the changes were not substantial enough to justify describing these elements in detail twice. As with other elements of the Landau model still extant under the present one, I will go into some detail below, in Chapter 14, where the latter model is examined.

4. Interrogation methods

It should first be noted that incommunicado detention was, in effect, an interrogation technique. The very military order on the basis of which GSS personnel (namely the 'person in charge of the interrogation') could issue an order prohibiting an interrogee from seeing his lawyer stipulates that this be done 'where it is required for reasons of the security of the area *or in the interest of the interrogation*'[41] (emphasis added). It is little wonder, then, that 'the interest of the interrogation' was routinely used both by the State defending such orders in front of the Supreme Court[42] and by the Court itself in rejecting petitions against such orders,[43] which it invariably did.[44]

To use an expression from the US model, this element at the very least helped interrogators 'setting the conditions for successful exploitation of the internees'.[45] The same could be said of the poor hygiene and other conditions in which interrogees were held.[46]

As will be seen below, under international standards, incommunicado detention for a long period may in itself constitute ill-treatment.[47] A description of the Landau methods of interrogation[48] and its effects from the point of view of a

---

[41] Section 78(c) (c) (1) of the (military) Order Concerning Security Provisions, No 378 (1970).

[42] See eg HCJ 1795/98 *Ahmad Balbul et al v the Minister of Defence et al, Statement by the State Attorneys Office*, 19 March 1998, para 1; HCJ 6951/98 *Ayman Abu 'Id et al v the GSS, Response by the Respondent*, 8 November 1998, para 4.

[43] See eg HCJ 5231/97 *Raji Mahmud Saba' et al v the GSS*, ruling of 4 September 1997; HCJ 1622/96 *'Abd al-Rahman al-Ahmar and HaMoked v the GSS*, ruling of 3 March 1996, para 2; HCJ 2193/96 *Yunis Ahmad 'Abd al-Fattah 'Awad et al v the GSS*, ruling of 24 March 1996, para 2.

[44] In many cases petitions were withdrawn once the order expired, but the Court never once ruled that such an order be rescinded or the period of access denial it stipulated be shortened. The same has held true, without significant changes, under the HCJ model. See *infra*, Ch 14, Section B(2)(b).

[45] According to the Taguba report on Abu Ghraib, a team headed by a Major-General who commanded the detention centre at Guantánamo Bay, Cuba, recommended that in Iraq too '... it is essential that the guard force be actively engaged in setting the conditions for successful exploitation of the internees' (quoted in AM Taguba, *Article 15–6 Investigation of the 800th Military Police Brigade*, March 2004, <http://www.msnbc.msn.com/id/4894001> (henceforth: Taguba report), accessed 5 May 2004, 8.

[46] Thus a GSS interrogator testified in a military court that as a rule, interrogees 'shower... to the best of my knowledge once a week' (File 10304/93 (Hebron Military Court), *The Military Prosecutor v Jalal Ra'i*, 25 May 1994. Jerusalem District Court judge, Ruth Or, described the cells provided for interrogees in one GSS facility as follows: '... the detention cells at the disposal of the GSS... are small, crowded, and lack minimal living conditions' (App 13/96 (Jerusalem Dist Ct), *Al-Natshah v Israel Prison Service*, decision of 12 March 1996, para 3.

[47] Part IV, Ch 18, Section F.

[48] The actual instructions within the Landau Commission's report being confidential, the description here is limited to methods as actually applied.

detainee is provided in Part I.[49] The description here will mainly rely on official sources.[50]

(a) 'Shaking' (Tiltul)[51]

Shaking 'in the manner established by the regulations' was carried out, according to a statement on behalf of the Attorney General, while 'holding the front part of his [the interrogee's] garment'.[52] On 25 April 1995, a Palestinian detainee, 'Abd a-Samad Harizat, died as a direct result of this method, although it was claimed that one of the interrogators had held Harizat by the shoulders rather than by the collar.[53] The State nevertheless acknowledged that Harizat may have died as a result of 'shaking' in the 'regulated' way. Nor did it exclude the possibility of further deaths as a result of 'shaking'. In response to a petition in principle against the use of this method,[54] the State argued, rather, that this method does not constitute torture, as 'the risk expected to the life of a GSS interrogee as a result of shaking is a *rare* risk'.[55] The HCJ refused to issue an interim injunction prohibiting the use of this method pending its decision in the *Israel Torture* case, which came four years after the request for such injunction was filed.

(b) The 'Shabeh' combination

'Shabeh'[56] was a combination of methods, used mostly between sessions of questioning for periods of days and, intermittently, weeks. It combined sensory isolation, sleep deprivation, and the infliction of physical pain. Regular *'shabeh'* entailed shackling the interrogee's hands and legs to a small chair, angled to slant forward so that the interrogee cannot sit in a stable position. The interrogee's head was covered with an often filthy sack and loud music was played continuously through loudspeakers. Detainees in *'shabeh'* were not allowed to sleep. Sleep deprivation was achieved mainly by using the aforementioned methods and also by having the guard on-duty wake up any detainee who nevertheless managed to doze off.

Some writers attribute great legal and even moral significance to the distinction between 'physical' and 'psychological' methods. For instance, Michael Ignatieff

---

[49] Part I, Ch 5, Section B.

[50] Principally, but not solely, as cited in Ginbar, *Legitimizing Torture* and *Routine Torture, supra* n 12 and *The Face and the Mirror, supra* n 11.

[51] For a detailed description and analysis see Ginbar, *The Face and the Mirror, ibid,* Ch 4.

[52] HCJ 5380/95 *PCATI et al v the Attorney General et al, Statement on behalf of the Attorney General,* 28 September 1995, paras 12, 10, respectively.

[53] For a detailed analysis of this case see Amnesty International, *Death by Shaking: the Case of 'Abd al-Samad Harizat,* London, October 1995, AI Index: MDE 15/23/95.

[54] *Association for Civil Rights* case, *supra* n 39, later merged into the *Israel Torture* case.

[55] *Ibid, Response by the Respondents,* 13 December 1995, para 27. Emphasis in the original. See also para 21. The argument is repeated in paras 28, 34, 35.

[56] Spelled 'Shabach' in the English version of the HCJ judgment in the *Israel Torture* case. I have preferred a spelling closer to the Arabic origin. The word means 'ghost'. In GSS documents the period during which *Shabeh* was inflicted is referred to as 'waiting' or 'waiting for interrogation'.

seems to believe that the line between 'coercion' (which he deems lawful and morally acceptable) and torture (which he deems unacceptable) lies between 'sleep deprivation, permanent light or permanent darkness, disorientating noise…isolation…[and] disinformation that causes stress' on the one hand and 'physical duress or cruelty' on the other.[57]

The fact that sleep deprivation, requires—here, in the other models described in this Part and elsewhere—the use of stress positions and other *physical* means belies that assumed distinction.

(c) Other methods

These included variations on the '*shabeh*' position, such as forcing the interrogee to stand rather than sit;[58] stretch positions, such as one described by a GSS document as 'sitting on a small chair with his arms raised backwards';[59] forced crouching (*Qambaz*, or 'frog position');[60] slaps,[61] kicks and beatings (the latter two not acknowledged officially during the Landau years).

Another method was described by a GSS document as 'tightening shackles':[62] A GSS interrogator described this as 'closing the handcuff to the last notch allowed by the diameter of the interrogee's wrist, for a certain period of time'.[63]

Threats,[64] curses[65] and humiliations were routinely mentioned by detainees, but very seldom acknowledged officially.

In addition, interrogees were exposed to extreme heat or cold, mostly through streaming cold (and sometimes hot) air into the cell or the interrogation room

---

[57] M Ignatieff, *The Lesser Evil: Political Ethics in an Age of Terror* (Edinburgh: Edinburgh University Press, 2005) 138, 141 and 138, respectively.

[58] See eg File 2332/92 (Hebron Military Court) *Military Prosecutor v Muhammad 'Adawi'*, testimony by GSS agent 'Mussa'.

[59] Details from the Interrogation of Sa'id Zu'rub id. 908533243, provided to Zu'rub's lawyer, Leah Tzemel, on 28 October 1998.

[60] 'Crouching' is indeed the official term for this position. See eg *ibid*.

[61] This was acknowledged, as far as I am aware, only in late 2006, in an *in camera* testimony given by GSS agents in a US case in which the reliability of one defendant's confession to the GSS in 1993 was a crucial issue. See *US v Marzouq et al*, Dist Ct Northern Dist Ill Eastern Div, No 03 CR 978. In a summary of the testimonies, entitled '*United States v Salah, Substitutions*' presented to defence lawyers for Muhammad Salah, the document lists 'slapping a detainee' among the 'interrogation methods…authorized to be used by the…General Security Service.' A copy of the document is with me.

[62] See Details from the Interrogation of Sa'id Zu'rub, *supra* n 59. This is the only document where the GSS admitted to using this method, but detainees frequently complained of shackles being painfully tight. For a case where this has led to permanent damage see Ginbar, *Routine Torture, supra* n 12, sec 2.

[63] F 124/97 (Gaza Military Court), *Military Prosecutor v Sa'id Salem Ibrahim Zu'rub*, Hearing of 20 October 1998, *Proceedings*, 34.

[64] 'Threatening to harm a detainee or threatening to arrest family members of the detainees' was also listed among the interrogation methods in *United States v Salah, Substitutions, supra* n 61.

[65] In response to a civil claim in Tel Aviv Magistrate Court, Civ Cl 78615/96 *Jamal Amin Mustafa Hindi v alias 'Tzadoq' et al, Defence*, 27 January 1998, para 8(h), the Attorney General's representative, as counsel for defendants, wrote to 'deny all of the all Plaintiff's claims' in a certain section of the Statement of Claim (entitled 'Threats and Humiliations'), but 'with the exception of uttering curses at the interrogee'.

using an air conditioner. The State has not acknowledged using this method, but it should be noted that there was (and is) no flow of natural air into the interrogation rooms or cells in GSS interrogation wings, so all air is provided by air conditioners. This method is therefore as easy to apply as it is difficult to prove.

5. Executive, legislative and judicial supervision

During the Landau years, GSS interrogation facilities (and interrogation techniques) were overseen by a Ministerial committee, a Knesset sub-committee, an internal comptroller as well as the State Comptroller.[66] Reporting to CAT, Israel openly acknowledged that a Ministerial Committee determined the interrogation methods to be used, and agents of an official intelligence force, the GSS, applied these methods.[67] However, all these bodies' activities regarding GSS interrogation were shrouded in total secrecy—the sole exception being a State Comptroller's report, which covered the years 1988–1992, a summary of which was published in 2000, five years after being presented to a Knesset sub-committee, and only because of the 'changed circumstances' following the HCJ ruling.[68]

C. Evaluation

During the Landau years (1987–1999), tens of thousands of Palestinians were interrogated by the GSS,[69] the annual numbers fluctuating with the situation. The interrogation methods described above were routinely applied on a massive scale. Thus the potentially lethal method of 'shaking' the interrogee was used, according to both the Prime Minister and the Head of the GSS of the time, against 8,000 Palestinians up to the mid-1990s.[70] In May 1998 (a relatively quiet time as far as terrorist attacks were concerned), B'Tselem estimated:

...based on official sources, human rights organizations, and attorneys, that the GSS annually interrogates between 1,000–1,500 Palestinians. Some eighty-five percent of them—at least 850 persons a year—are tortured during interrogation.[71]

---

[66] See eg Israel's reports to CAT, UN Doc CAT/C/33/Add.2/Rev.1, 18 February 1997, paras 11–12, 15; UN Doc CAT/C/33/Add.3, March 1998, paras 18, 33, 34.

[67] eg Israel's latter report *ibid,* paras 35–6.

[68] The State Comptroller, Summary of the Audit Report on the Interrogation System in the General Security Service (GSS) for the years 1988–1992, Report No 1/year 2000 (Jerusalem, 2000) 6. The full report has not been published.

[69] Michael Ben-Yair, the Attorney General at the time, stated at the beginning of 1995 that between 1987 and then, some 23,000 Palestinians had been interrogated by the GSS. Quoted in *Haaretz* (15 January 1995).

[70] PM Yitzhaq Rabin, interviewed in 'Weekly Diary', *Kol Yisrael* (Israel's state-owned radio station), 29 July 1995, quoted in both *Haaretz* and *Davar* daily newspapers (30 July 1995); K Gilon, *Shin-Beth Between the Schisms,* [Hebrew] (Tel-Aviv: La-Miskal, 2000) 392.

[71] Ginbar, *Routine Torture, supra* n 12, 8. During a conversation with the head of the delegation of a well-placed international humanitarian organization later that year, I was advised that the estimated ratio was too conservative.

In view of this use, on an industrial scale, of methods which, as will be seen below, have been pronounced by UN bodies to amount to torture, the Landau model, and the GSS, are hardly worth the praise heaped on them by Eric A Posner and Adrian Vermeule, who cite 'the Israeli experience' as their prime example of how 'coercive interrogation can be done well' as long as it is 'under elaborate guidelines' and 'constant supervision of superiors'.[72] Rather, it may be safely concluded that the Landau model did not succeed as a legalized torture model which limits torture to TBSs. It must be repeated, however, the Landau Commission did not seek such limitation. This makes assessing the effectiveness of the governmental, parliamentary and other official review mechanisms difficult. However, the huge number of those tortured, far outweighing those convicted or even charged of 'security' offences, let alone of involvement in TBSs, and the fact that only in a single case were GSS agents charged (and convicted) of 'excessive' use of force, point to rather limited effectiveness. As for the courts—the Supreme Court played an important role not only in allowing the system to operate for 12 years, but in approving torture (not so named) in specific cases. In this role, Israel's Supreme Court provided a case study for a 'torture warrant' model, which will now be examined.

---

[72] EA Posner and A Vermeule, 'Should Coercive Interrogation Be Legal?' *U of Chicago Public Law Working Paper No 84*, March 2005, 13. See also *ibid*, 18. Their study suffers, on this count, from insufficient research. A quick glance, for instance, at the summary of the State Comptroller's report (*supra* n 68) which, while expressing strong support for the Landau system, found 'a web of failures which demonstrates that those responsible for the organization [the GSS] failed miserably in their duty to maintain GSS operations within the law' (at 3), would have sufficed to render their assessment more cautious.

13

The 'Torture Warrants' Model

A. Model Outline

The term 'torture warrants' was coined by Dershowitz,[73] but the model suggested by Leon Sheleff[74] is very similar. Sanford Levinson later wrote in support of Dershowitz' model, adding some suggestions of his own regarding its implementation.[75] Posner and Vermeule also provide for 'torture warrants' as part or their model of legalized torture.[76] In addition, the 'Torture by public committee' system suggested by Michael L Gross may be viewed as a form of a 'torture warrants' model.[77]

The idea is simple: just as in many countries, police believing there to be 'probable cause' for searching a person's home or other property or tapping onto his or her communications must first—in many cases—obtain a

---

[73] Dershowitz, *Why Terrorism Works, supra* n 4, Ch 4, *passim*. See also eg *idem*, 'Commentary' *Los Angeles Times* (8 November 2001); *idem*, 'Tortured Reasoning' in S Levinson (ed), *Torture: A Collection* (Oxford, OUP, 2004) 257–280, especially 270–2. For critical views of his proposal see eg SF Kreimer, 'Too Close to the Rack and the Screw: Constitutional constraints on torture' 6 *Univ of Penn J of Const L* 278 (2003), especially 318–324; E Scarry, 'Five Errors in the Reasoning of Alan Dershowitz' in Levinson (ed), *ibid*, 281–290, especially 286–8.

[74] LS Sheleff, *Ultimate Penalties: Capital Punishment, Life Imprisonment, Physical Torture* (Columbus: Ohio State University Press, 1987) Ch 11; 'Maximising Good and Minimising Evil...' *supra* n 11; 'The Need to Defend the Honest Truth...' (*ibid*).

[75] Levinson, *supra* n 6.

[76] Posner and Vermeule, *supra* n 72. Curiously, the role they assign to 'warrants' undermines their own first principle (torture to be used only to 'prevent an imminent crime that will kill at least *n* people' 28): they suggest that 'warrants' be sought 'when the harm is *not* imminent' (principle 4, 29, emphasis added). This illustrates again how supporters of torture in a TBS may slide down 'slippery slopes' which Posner and Vermeule tend to dismiss (see *ibid*, 16–18), even at a very theoretical stage. While Posner and Vermeule use the term 'coercive interrogation' rather than torture, they have no qualms about the former amounting to the latter, see *ibid*, 1–2.

[77] ML Gross, 'Regulating Torture in a Democracy: Death and Indignity in Israel' 36 (no 3) *Polity* 367 (2004). Gross, writing specifically in the context of Israel, suggests a combination of torture-specific legislation; applying the existing 'defence of necessity'; and that a 'committee of lay and professional members acts in the court's stead to decide each case on its merits' (*ibid*, 386). How Gross proposes the three to combine is not quite clear to me, and my discussion of his model will therefore be confined to the issue of a public committee.

warrant from a judge, so would state agents believing they are facing a TBS need to approach a judge and secure a 'torture warrant' before torture may commence.

Sheleff outlines the model in the following way:

> No use of exceptional force, including torture in emergency circumstances, will be carried out without permission from an authorised body, preferably the court. Such permission should be granted in advance, and *ex post facto* where the urgency of the situation rules out prior recourse. This supervision would be of the kind applied to other violations of fundamental human rights, necessary for defending the public and maintaining social control, such as the deprivation of liberty during arrest, the infringement of privacy during surveillance or wiretapping in times of danger. [...] It is precisely the permission of such a serious phenomenon that necessitates very strict supervision. It seems that the court is the most appropriate body for this.[78]

Dershowitz similarly suggests a 'formal requirement of a judicial warrant as a prerequisite to nonlethal torture',[79] the procedure envisaged as follows:

> [The suspect would be] granted immunity, told he was now compelled to testify, threatened with imprisonment if he refused to do so, and given the option of providing the requested information. Only if he refused to do what he was legally compelled to do—provide necessary information, which could not incriminate him because of the immunity—would he be threatened with torture. Knowing that such threat was authorized by the law, he might well provide the information. If he still refused to, he would be subjected to judicially monitored physical measures designed to cause excruciating pain without leaving any lasting damage.[80]

There is little point in detailing the kind of legislative measures that would be needed to make this model viable. Instead I propose to discuss briefly, by way of example, the legal principles underlining the issue of search warrants.[81] Taking, for the most part, the laws of the two states concerned (the USA and Israel) as cases in point, I will attempt to determine whether a similar model of 'torture warrants' would strike a proper balance, as its advocates claim, between the requirements of national security and of individual human rights—obviously in the non-absolute version being proposed. Torture warrant-type decisions by Israel's Supreme Court during the Landau period will then be examined.

---

[78] Sheleff, 'Maximising Good and Minimising Evil...' *supra* n 11, 217. *Cf* eg *idem, Ultimate Penalties, supra* n 74, 310; 'The Need to Defend the Honest Truth...' *supra* n 11, 469.

[79] Dershowitz, *Why Terrorism Works, supra* n 4, 158.

[80] *Ibid,* 159. The issues of 'nonlethal' torture and one which would not leave 'any lasting damage' are discussed below, Ch 13, Section C(5).

[81] This is a somewhat arbitrary choice: surveillance, wiretapping and body searches would have done just as well.

B. Search Warrants—General Principles

The institution of search warrants itself is designed to strike a not dissimilar balance—in this case between society's need to enable police officers to arrest suspects or obtain evidence of crimes by searching premises and seizing potential evidence material on the one hand; and individuals' right to privacy on the other. It should be noted at the outset that not in all cases—perhaps not in most of them—is a warrant required for a search to take place. This issue will be largely ignored here, and I will limit the discussion to cases where warrants are required, as I assume, following Dershowitz and Sheleff, that in the suggested model judicial 'monitoring' is mandatory, and so 'torture warrants' must always be sought, the sole exception being 'where the urgency of the situation rules out prior recourse', in which case judicial authorization would be sought *ex post facto*.[82]

The foundations of the institution of search warrants in both countries were laid down, historically, in English law, along the following lines, as described by Daniel C Préfontaine:

[Firstly] state agents have been required to have legal authority for undertaking searches and seizures. Secondly, it is clear that the preference by the courts has been established requiring warrants that must be issued by an independent authority, usually a judicially constituted body such as a judge or magistrate. And thirdly, reasonable grounds on the part of the police for searching and seizure must have been demonstrated.[83]

It should be noted that whereas in the classic seventeenth century English case, *Entick v Carrington*,[84] individuals' rights to freedom from unwarranted search of their homes was couched in terms of property ownership,[85] the US Supreme

---

[82] See Sheleff, *supra* n 78 and accompanying text.

[83] DC Préfontaine, 'Implementing International Standards in Search and Seizure: Striking the Balance between Enforcing the Law and Respecting the Rights of the Individual', paper presented at the *Sino Canadian International Conference on the Ratification and Implementation of Human Rights*: Beijing, China, October 2001 <http://www.icclr.law.ubc.ca/Publications/Reports/International_Standards.pdf>, accessed 11 March 2003. For a discussion of current UK law see eg SH Bailey, J Ching, MJ Gunn and D Ormerod, *Smith, Bailey and Gunn on the Modern English Legal System* (4th edn, London: Sweet & Maxwell, 2002) 801–13; LA Mulcahy, *Human Rights and Civil Practice* (London: Sweet & Maxwell, 2001) 189–191, 527–8 (discussed in the context of Art 8 of the European Convention on Human Rights); R Stone, *Entry, Search and Seizure: A Guide to Civil and Criminal Powers of Entry* (London: Sweet & Maxwell, 1997).

[84] [1765] 19 Howell's State Trials 1029.

[85] The Court stated, *inter alia*: 'The great end, for which men entered into society, was to secure their property. That right is preserved sacred and incommunicable in all instances, where it has not been taken away or abridged by some public law for the good of the whole. [...] By the laws of England, every invasion of private property, be it ever so minute, is a trespass. No man can set foot upon my ground without my license but he is liable to an action though the damage be nothing' (*ibid*, 1035).

Court, elaborating on the requirement for limitations on government agents' right to enter private premises, search, and seize, as enshrined in the Fourth Amendment to the Constitution,[86] abandoned this line for a reliance on the right to privacy:

The premise that property interests control the right of the Government to search and seize has been discredited... We have recognized that the principal object of the Fourth Amendment is the protection of privacy rather than property...[87]

Israel has no written constitution, but the issue, regulated by an Ordinance originally dating back to pre-independence British Mandatory law,[88] is nevertheless subject to the provisions of the quasi-constitutional Basic Law: Human Dignity and Freedom (1992), which provides, *inter alia*, for the right to privacy:

(b) There shall be no entry into the private premises of a person who has not consented thereto.

(c) No search shall be conducted on the private premises of a person, nor in the body or personal effects.[89]

This right, like all other rights guaranteed by the Basic Law,[90] is, according to its 'limitation clause', subject only to infringements:

...by a law befitting the values of the State of Israel, enacted for a proper purpose, and to an extent no greater than is required, or by regulation enacted by virtue of express authorization in such Law.[91]

---

[86] Which reads: 'The right of the people to be secure in their persons, houses, papers, and effects, against unreasonable searches and seizures, shall not be violated, and no Warrants shall issue, but upon probable cause, supported by Oath or affirmation, and particularly describing the place to be searched, and the persons or things to be seized.' For a discussion see eg 'US Constitution: Fourth Amendment: Annotations.' FindLaw <http://caselaw.lp.findlaw.com/data/constitution/ amendment04>, accessed 11 March 2003; AR Amar, 'Fourth Amendment First Principles' 107 *Harv L Rev* 757 (1994); *idem, The Constitution and Criminal Procedure: First Principles* (New Haven, Connecticut: Yale University Press, 1997) Ch 1; W Cohen and DJ Danelski, *Cohen and Danelski's Constitutional Law Civil Liberty and Individual Rights* (5th edn, Westbury, NY: Foundation Press, 2002) Ch 20; K Gormley, 'One Hundred Years of Privacy' 1992 *Wis L Rev* 1335 (1992); DP Kommers and JE Finn, *American Constitutional Law: Essays, Cases and Comparative Notes* (Belmont, CA: West/Wadsworth, 1998), Ch 10; WR LaFave, *Search and Seizure: A Treatise on the Forth Amendment* (3rd edn, St Paul, Minn: West Publishing Company, 1995).

[87] *Warden v Hayden*, 387 US 294, 304 (1967).

[88] Criminal Procedure Ordinance (Search and Seizure) [New Version] (1969). For a discussion of search and seizures in Israeli law see, eg, S Gez and M Ronen, *Criminal Law: A Guide to Criminal Law in Israel* [Hebrew] (Tel-Aviv: Hemed, 2001) Ch 3; Y Kedmi, *On Criminal Procedure* [Hebrew] (Part 1, Tel-Aviv: Dyunon, 1997) Ch 15; M Shalgi and Z Cohen, *Criminal Procedure* [Hebrew] (2nd edn, Jerusalem: Din, 2000) 59–71. For a brief discussion in English see K Mann, 'Criminal Procedure' in A Shapira and KC DeWitt-Arar (eds), *Introduction to the Law of Israel* (The Hague: Klower Law International, 1995) 267–294, 274–5.

[89] Section 7 (Privacy and Confidentiality of Individuals' Lives). I have generally followed the official English translation (see eg on the Knesset (Israel Parliament) website <http://www.knesset. gov.il/>), with one notable departure, regarding sec 8, (see below) where I translated the Hebrew *pgi'ah* as 'infringement' rather than 'violation'.

[90] Including the prohibition of any 'violation of the life, body or dignity of any person as such' in sec 2 of the Basic Law.

[91] Section 8 (Infringement of Rights). The term 'limitation clause' was used by the President of Israel's Supreme Court, Aharon Barak, in *idem*, 'The Constitutionalization of the Israeli Legal

Significantly, however, further infringement may be allowed through 'emergency regulations':

> ...when a state of emergency exists, by virtue of a declaration under section 9 of the Law and Administration Ordinance, 5708–1948... provided the denial or restriction [of rights under the Basic Law] shall be for a proper purpose and for a period and to an extent no greater than required.[92]

The importance of the right to privacy was underlined by a Supreme Court ruling in a case where a man, Yaacov Afanjar, assaulted two plain-clothed policemen who, having obtained a warrant to search a home in which Afanjar was a guest, broke into it without asking permission first. The Court acquitted Afanjar, determining that he had acted instinctively, in defence of his hosts from intruders, despite the fact the he had identified them as policemen.[93]

Among the general legal principles governing the issuance of search warrants are the following relevant[94] ones:

1. Issuance by an independent authority

A US Supreme Court Judge outlined the rationale behind the Fourth Amendment's requirement that judges, rather than police or similar officials, be authorized to issue search warrants in terms that seem indeed to address 'slippery slope' dangers comparable to those of torturing in a TBS, discussed in Part II:

> The point of the Fourth Amendment, which often is not grasped by zealous officers, is not that it denies law enforcement the support of the usual inferences which reasonable men draw from evidence. Its protection consists in requiring that those inferences be drawn by a neutral and detached magistrate instead of being judged by the officer engaged in the often competitive enterprise of ferreting out crime. Any assumption that evidence sufficient to support a magistrate's disinterested determination to issue a search warrant will justify the officers in making a search without a warrant would reduce the Amendment to a nullity and leave the people's homes secure only in the discretion of police officers.[95]

2. Specific—rather than general—authorization

A search warrant must point to specific premises and (concerning seizure) often to specific items. The US Supreme Court explained the constitutional rejection of

---

System as a Result of the Basic Laws and its Effect on Procedural and Substantive Criminal Law' 31 *Israel L Rev* 3 (1997), *passim*.

[92] Section 12 (Stability).

[93] Crim App 89/78 *Yaacov Afanjar v State of Israel*, PD 33 (3) 141.

[94] This must not be seen as an attempt at a comprehensive discussion of the principles guiding search warrants *per se*.

[95] *Johnson v United States*, 333 US 10, 13–14 (1948), per Jackson J.

searching an individual's home on the strength of a *general* warrant in historical terms:

The [Fourth] Amendment was in large part a reaction to the general warrants and warrantless searches that had so alienated the colonists and had helped speed the movement for independence. In the scheme of the Amendment, therefore, the requirement that 'no Warrants shall issue, but upon probable cause,' plays a crucial part.[96]

Justice Kedmi emphasizes similarly that under Israeli law:

The warrant is directed at specific premises the details of which are noted in the warrant, it therefore appears impossible to issue a general warrant for searching any premises where a suspected item 'may' be found.[97]

3. Reasonableness

The 4th Amendment prohibits 'unreasonable searches' and provides for 'probable cause' for a warrant to be issued, both underlining the need for there to be ample reason for intruding a person's privacy. The latter provision was explained in terms of the former by the Supreme Court:

In determining what is probable cause...we are concerned only with the question whether the affiant had reasonable grounds at the time of his affidavit...for the belief that the law was being violated on the premises to be searched; and if the apparent facts set out in the affidavit are such that a reasonably discreet and prudent man would be led to believe that there was a commission of the offense charged, there is probable cause justifying the issuance of a warrant.[98]

There is a related requirement of proportionality couched not in utilitarian, 'lesser evil' terms, but in the need for places searched and materials seized to be limited and specified in the warrant:

As to what is to be taken, nothing is left to the discretion of the officer executing the warrant.[99]

---

[96] *Chimel v California*, 395 US 752, 761 (1969). See similarly Gormley, *supra* n 86, 1358–9. American courts challenged the right of the (British) government to search premises on the basis of general warrants even before independence. See eg L Fisher, *Constitutional Structures: Separated Powers and Federalism* (vol 1, New York: McGraw-Hill, 1995) 45.

[97] Kedmi, *supra* n 88, 443. See also Jerusalem District Court, Req 1153/02 *State of Israel v Mikhael Abarjil*, Decision of 9 June 2002, para 78 (per Justice Moshe Drori) 'The search warrant must describe in a clear and precise way the place where a search may be conducted.'

[98] *Dumbra v United States*, 268 US 435, 439, 441 (1925). In a leading case concerning wiretapping, the Court tied the requirement of privacy with that of reasonableness, stating that under the Fourth Amendment, 'a person has a constitutionally protected reasonable expectation of privacy' (*Katz v United States*, 389 US 347, 360 (1967) (per Justice Harlan, concurring)).

[99] *Marron v United States*, 275 US 192, 196 (1927). As FindLaw's Annotations explain, however, police who are lawfully on the premises pursuant to a warrant may seize evidence of crime in 'plain view' even if that evidence is not described in the warrant. See *supra* n 86, at fn 111, citing *Coolidge v New Hampshire*, 403 US 443, 464–71 (1971).

Chief Justice (as he was then) Barak, discussing legislation under Israel's Basic Laws, similarly states that 'the law authorizing searches and seizures must fulfil the requirements set out in the limitation clause'. He too stresses, in this context, the requirements of proportionality and reasonableness:

Within the framework of the limitation clause, I believe the main hurdle will be in the requirement of proportionality. [. . .] The test consists of a three-tier rationality: the least harmful means, and reasonableness of the means in view of the ends.[100]

It may be worth mentioning here that in European human rights law, the requirement for reasonableness is explicitly provided in terms of necessity as well as proportionality. Under the European Convention for the Protection of Human Rights and Fundamental Freedoms,[101] any 'interference' with the right to privacy, including by searching, is explicitly limited by that which is 'necessary'[102] and the European Court of Human Rights has on several occasions added the related—and equally relevant—requirement of proportionality.[103]

C. Applying Search Warrants Principles to 'Torture Warrants' Procedures

It seems that there will be few procedural problems in applying the legal principles governing search warrants to 'torture warrants'. In addition, enforcing the principles of issuance by an independent authority, specificity and reasonableness may indeed deter some 'zealous officers' from torturing and alleviate other 'slippery slope' dangers. However, whether by authorizing judges to issue

---

[100] Barak, *supra* n 91, 10. I find the mathematics of this statement somewhat elusive.

[101] Adopted 4 November 1950, entered into force 3 September 1953. Henceforth: European Convention on Human Rights. Texts of Council of Europe human rights treaties are available eg at the European Court of Human Rights Court's website <http://www.echr.coe.int>. For the texts of human rights treaties generally see eg Office of the High Commissioner for Human Rights, *Human Rights: A Compilation of International Instruments* (2 volumes, New York and Geneva: UN 1997) and that Office's website, <http://www.ohchr.org>.

[102] The relevant Article, Art 8, reads:

'1. Everyone has the right to respect for his private and family life, his home and his correspondence.

2. There shall be no interference by a public authority with the exercise of this right except such as is in accordance with the law and is necessary in a democratic society in the interests of national security, public safety or the economic well-being of the country, for the prevention of disorder or crime, for the protection of health or morals, or for the protection of the rights and freedoms of others.'

For a discussion of this article see eg DJ Harris, M O'Boyle and C Warbick, *The Law of the European Convention of Human Rights* (2nd edn, London: Butterworths, 2001) Chs 8–9.

[103] Stating that such interferences—in these cases searches—must be 'strictly proportionate to the legitimate aim pursued'. See *Funke v France*, Series A No 256-A, Judgment of 25 February 1993, para 57; *Miailhe v France*, Series A No 256-C, Judgment of 25 February 1993, para 38; *Cremieux v France*, Series A No 256-B, Judgment of 25 February 1993, para 40.

'torture warrants', states facing terrorism would be able to 'draw and maintain a defensible line'[104] between 'justifiable' torture in TBS cases and 'unjustified' ones, rather than 'lowering this barrier' that would 'sweep away the dam'[105] is, to my mind, questionable.

In Part II, the conceptual and practical difficulties that a judge—or any other official— would face when deciding whether or not torture is justified in a specific case (once the theoretical—to which in this case must be added the legal— premise that is could be has been adopted) was discussed at some length. Bearing these in mind, the 'torture warrant' model would also, I submit, suffer from the following, law-related weaknesses:

1. The limited value of a judge's decision

When advocating the use of torture in limited cases, Jeremy Bentham demanded safeguards tantamount, in effect, to a full trial before torture may commence:

> If Torture then should be fit to be employed in any case it cannot be till after at least as effectual precautions have been taken to prevent its falling upon the innocent, as to prevent punishment from falling upon the innocent.[106]

A judge's decision to issue a search warrant, however, is nowhere near affording that level of protection from abuse. As the Israeli Supreme Court has pointed out, it is basically an administrative decision rather than a 'purely judicial' one:

> Essentially the [judge's] task is administrative; although ... the judge is the one making the decision on the basis of his own reasoning and of the *prima facie* evidence brought in front of him that conditions for conducting the search have been fulfilled. [...] Nevertheless, the issuance of such a warrant does not constitute a purely judicial act by a court. It may take place before a trial, and even before anyone has been charged, and there is no procedure for the participation of the persons concerned, or of those who may be harmed by the warrant, in the hearing before the judge. [...] Whoever is harmed by [a warrant] has no means of challenging its legality or appropriateness in front of another court, with the exception of the High Court of Justice ...[107]

In the US, search warrants are usually issued by magistrates, whose position is quasi-judicial, rather than by a full-fledged judge.[108]

---

[104] R Dworkin, *Life's Dominion: An Argument about Abortion and Euthanasia* (London: HarperCollins, 1993) 198. See Part II, Ch 9, text accompanying n 60.

[105] Kremnitzer, *supra* n 30, 254. See Part II, Ch 9, text accompanying n 211.

[106] Jeremy Bentham, 'Of Torture' *Bentham Manuscripts, University College London* 46/63–70, reprinted in WL. Twining and E Twining, 'Bentham on Torture' 24(3) *Northern Ireland Legal Quarterly* 305 (1973) 308–320, 312.

[107] HCJ 49/62 *Kluger v the General Director of Israel Police et al* PD 16 1267, 1273. Such a challenge would have to be mounted *ex post facto*.

[108] See eg Amar, 'Fourth Amendment First Principles' *supra* n 86, 780.

2. The tendency of judges to grant requests for warrants unquestioningly

Gez and Ronen argue that judges in Israel considering requests for search warrants *ex parte*[109] simply lack the tools to challenge the information brought in front of them by the police. The result has been that, according to studies they cite, in 1982 Tel Aviv magistrates granted 100 per cent of police requests for search warrants (in a sample); between 1 January and 1992 and 1 December 1994 they granted 99.87 per cent of such requests (11,488 out of 11,505 requests), and during the whole of 1996, 99.95 per cent of requests were granted (3,873 out of 3,875 requests).[110]

Regarding the US, Amar similarly speaks of 'the current system of practically unreviewable rubberstamp magistrates acting ex parte'.[111] Seth F Kreimer argues that similarly,

... a 'torture warrant' court may not be the most skeptical bench, and they, like executive officials, would be subject to public pressure to do everything possible to prevent a recurrence of September 11.[112]

Scarry provides a very relevant statistic:

The court set up to issue warrants under the Foreign Intelligence Surveillance Act (FISA) has declined only one requested warrant in twenty-five years; the estimated number or warrant requests is twenty-five thousands.[113]

All of which hardly indicate that a 'torture warrant' system would provide an effective barrier against abuse.

3. Searches versus torture—the difference in scale of harm caused

One explanation as to why search warrants are issued routinely, despite being an infringement of a basic right, is that while a search and seizure raid on a home may be an unpleasant experience, the harm which it causes is by and large limited, temporary and, in the case of seizures, fully reparable.

Dershowitz, and to a lesser extent Sheleff, argue that torture may similarly be of limited effect. As noted, Dershowitz proposes limiting torture to methods which are 'nonlethal' and do not leave 'any lasting damage'.[114] Sheleff

---

[109] Obviously, informing the occupants of a premises of an impending police raid may defeat its purpose.
[110] Gez and Ronen, *supra* n 88, 42–3.
[111] Amar, 'Fourth Amendment First Principles', *supra* n 86, at 817.
[112] Kreimer, *supra* n 73, 320.
[113] Scarry, *supra* n 73, 286.
[114] *Supra*, text accompanying n 80.

speaks of torture as causing 'temporary harm to a person's dignity'.[115] Three brief comments will now be made regarding this point. First, limiting torture methods to 'nonlethal' ones should be seen as an (obvious) practical requirement of the interrogation, rather than a moral constraint which, as seen, cannot be consistent with the 'cost-benefit analysis' moral view of both Dershowitz and Sheleff.[116] As also noted,[117] Dershowitz suggests, by way of example, the use of 'a sterilized needle inserted under the fingernails to produce unbearable pain without any threat to health or life, or...a dental drill through an unanaesthetized tooth'.[118] I submit, secondly, that the extent to which the physical damage caused by such methods is guaranteed to be 'merely' temporary is debatable. Thirdly, I submit that by arguing this lack of 'lasting damage' or 'threat to health or life', and 'temporariness', Dershowitz and Sheleff clearly do not have in mind the *mental* effects of torture, which are hardly foreseeable even by mental health professionals, let alone by a judge considering *ex parte* an urgent appeal for a 'torture warrant'. Such effects are often long-term or permanent,[119] and sometimes include death (by suicide).[120]

It may therefore be doubted whether a procedure for authorizing official action that causes relatively little harm, which may account for the limited safeguards it provides against error, is suitable for actions which by definition cause 'severe pain or suffering', and may also result in serious and long-term harm, and even death.

---

[115] Sheleff, 'The Need to Defend the Honest Truth...', *supra* n 11, 477. Note, however that Sheleff's model provides for the court acting as 'a whip [against undue torture]...if a victim of unjustified torture should die of his wounds' (*idem*, 'Maximising Good and Minimising Evil...' *supra* n 11, 217). This seems to imply including means of torture that have more than temporary effect. See the discussion in Part I, Ch 5, Section B.

[116] See Part I, especially Ch 5. The term quoted is used by Dershowitz, *Why Terrorism Works*, *supra* n 4, eg on 143, 148. Dershowitz does not provide a specific moral argument for limiting torture to 'nonlethal' methods.

[117] Part II, Ch 9, Section D(2)(b).

[118] Dershowitz, *Why Terrorism Works*, *supra* n 4, 143.

[119] For a review of studies on this subject see eg M Başoğlu, M Livanou and C Crnobarić, 'Torture vs Other Cruel, Inhuman, and Degrading Treatment: Is the Distinction Real or Apparent?' 64 *Arch Gen Psychiatry* 277 (2007); M Basoglu, JM. Jaranson, R Mollica and M Kastrup, 'Torture and Mental Health: A Research Overview' in E Gerrity, TM. Keane and F Tuma (eds), *The Mental Health Consequences of Torture* (New York: Kluwer Academic / Plenum Publishers, 2001) 35–62. All studies reviewed in the latter work show considerably higher levels of Post-Traumatic Stress Disorder (PTSD) and depression among torture survivors than among un-tortured control groups. These effects are often of long-term, or 'lifetime' duration.

[120] Cases of suicide and attempted suicide by victims of torture are abundant. See eg Report of the UN Special Rapporteur on torture on his visit to Brazil, UN Doc E/CN.4/2001/66/Add.2, 30 March 2001. The report included three cases of attempted suicide by detainees following (obviously 'nonlethal') torture—Sandro Perreira, para 28, Sheila Barbosa, para 111, and Wilton Oliveira Santos, para 281. The 2002 report of the same Rapporteur (Addendum: Summary of cases transmitted to Governments and replies received, UN Doc E/CN.4/2002/76/Add.1, 14 March 2002) details seven cases of torture-related suicide and suicide attempts by detainees or prisoners, from six states. For another case of suicide by a torture victim, described by Henry Alleg, see Part II, Ch 9, n 123.

4. Assured immunity and impunity for torturers

In one sense, the issuance of search warrants is more protective of government officials than of individuals' rights: once a warrant has been issued (assuming the police have acted properly and in good faith in applying for it) a wall of immunity is erected around all officials involved, guarding them from criminal prosecution, and often from civil suits as well.[121]

Amar argues that for this reason, search warrants 'should be allowed only for items akin to contraband and stolen goods' as, he contends, was the Framers' intention.[122] Most searches should be warrantless, with the question of whether the constitutional requirement of reasonableness was fulfilled being determined, where necessary, by a jury.[123]

In a 'torture warrants' model drawn along the lines of search warrants, torturers would only face criminal prosecution in cases where warrant procedures were not followed in good faith. All officials involved in cases where innocent persons were tortured as a result of a reasonable mistake, would be immune from prosecution.

5. Torture by public committee?

Writing in the specific context of Israel, M Gross attempts to avoid the weaknesses of judicial torture warrants by replacing judges with a 'committee of lay and professional members' fashioned on 'hospital ethics committees [in Israel] that convene with judicial authority to consider patients' request to end life sustaining treatment as well as physicians' requests to treat critically ill patients against their will.' Gross explains that '[i]n each case, be it torture or medical care, one makes a stark choice between death and indignity.'[124] However, since Gross proposes, by way of justifying torture in a TBS (and beyond),[125] that this committee be authorized to 'strip a suspect of his moral status as a human being',[126] a power that no public committee (or, for that matter, court) in Israel holds (or has ever held), his proposal is not altogether clear to me.

---

[121] This would apply to the torturers, but also to the judges warranting torture. See eg the following by the USA Supreme Court: 'A judge will not be deprived of immunity because the action he took was in error, was done maliciously, or was in excess of his authority; rather, he will be subject to liability only when he has acted in the "clear absence of all jurisdiction."' (*Stump v Sparkman*, 435 US 349, 356–7 (1978), citing (and quoting) *Bradley v Fisher*, 13 Wall 335, 351 (1872)).

[122] Amar, 'Fourth Amendment First Principles' *supra* n 86, 779. The parallel torture-legalizing model to what Amar proposes regarding searches would be the HCJ model, discussed *infra*, Ch 14.

[123] This is Amar's main thesis on this issue in both studies cited here, *supra* n 86.

[124] M Gross, *supra* n 77, 386.

[125] See *ibid*, 383: '[terrorists] may be tortured under weaker conditions than ticking bombs strictly entail'.

[126] *Ibid*, 384.

In addition, Gross himself wonders: 'Can the public regulate torture? Do they have the stomach for it?'[127] Earlier, Gross offers some indications as to what the answers may be, which do not seem promising:

> ...the best efforts to convince...Israelis that torture is a malignant cancer growing in their society will fail. On the contrary, democracy is, in their view, under siege, and torture is a necessary evil to save it. They are not moved when confronted with increasingly severe interrogation techniques even when they occasionally infringe on the rights of national minorities. Nor have Israelis seen their nation's international standing fallen as they fight the scourge of terror. It is unlikely, then, that long term consequences of torture would persuade many citizens of democratic nations to curtail torture.[128]

Nor could one hope that such 'curtailment' be endorsed by Israeli physicians (who may sit on the proposed committee) as, in Gross' view:

> The attitude of many prominent Israeli physicians...is...: when life is at stake, respect for dignity runs a poor second.[129]

D. 'Torture Warrants' in Israel Under the Landau Model

I submit that a system of 'torture warrants' in effect operated in Israel during the Landau period; this aspect of the model therefore deserves some discussion. During that period, human rights NGOs and lawyers acting on behalf of detainees under GSS interrogation would petition the Supreme Court for, *inter alia*, an interim injunction ordering that the GSS halt the use of torturous interrogation methods against a particular detainee.[130] This happened in dozens of cases. Deliberating these cases, the Court was not following explicit legal (let alone constitutional) provisions and procedures for issuing torture warrants, and the term 'torture' itself was used only by petitioners (or by the Court citing them). However, beyond these superficial differences, the following should be considered: (1) the issue before the Court in those petitions was whether or not to allow the GSS to use interrogation methods found by international monitoring bodies to amount to torture;[131] (2) these methods were to be used, if the Court so allowed, *in the future*; (3) the cases revolved around the torture of a specific individual, and at

---

[127]   *Ibid,* 388.
[128]   *Ibid,* 380.
[129]   *Ibid,* 386.
[130]   In some cases up to four detainees were petitioners in a single petition.
[131]   See below, Part IV, Ch 18, Section E(1). It should be noted that the 1997 conclusions of the UN Committee Against Torture (for which see that section) finding Israel's interrogation methods to constitute torture were cited, and even quoted in full, in subsequent petitions to the Supreme Court. See eg HCJ 3359/97 *Ahmad Siyam Suleiman Abu Ahmad and HaMoked v the GSS,* Petition for Order Nisi and Interim Injunction, 30 May 1997, para 4; HCJ 3715/97 *Bassam 'Ali Mahmud Diriyyah and HaMoked v the GSS,* Petition for Order Nisi and Interim Injunction, 17 June 1997, para 5; HCJ 4869/97 Gheith *'Abd al-Hafez Gheith and LAW—Palestinian Society for the Protection*

times around specific methods; and (4) the Supreme Court, acting in its capacity as administrative court (High Court of Justice), obviously had to determine whether the State was acting—or proposed to act—reasonably.[132] Thus the Supreme Court's handling of these petitions constituted, in substance if not in form, a 'torture warrant' system; both the process and the principles governing it were similar to those applicable to cases where a judge decides whether or not to grant the police a search warrant. This system will now be examined briefly.

The petitions were often presented during a period where the detainees concerned were prohibited, by a GSS or police order, from meeting their attorneys,[133] therefore petitioners based their requests for injunctions halting torture based on GSS 'general practice' rather than on any known facts in the specific case. In several cases, the Court allowed the petitions and granted the requested injunction;[134] in others the petitions were turned down.[135] Considering such cases, the Court would often talk to GSS representatives *in camera*, or consult confidential GSS documents,[136] and therefore it is quite difficult to assess the factual basis of those decisions.

However, there is enough evidence to show that the picture was not one of a balanced practice of judicial review. Three observations may shed more light on this aspect of the Landau model. Firstly, in the vast majority of cases where the Court issued interim injunctions to halt the torture, the State did not object. This was because torture was used routinely rather than limited to cases where it was deemed absolutely vital;[137] and, at any rate, by the time the case was considered, the GSS would have had ample time—in some cases weeks—to interrogate

---

of Human Rights and the Environment v. the Minister of Defence et al, Petition for Order Nisi and Interim Injunction, 10 August 1997, para 11. The Court never commented on this issue.

[132] Beyond the general requirement of reasonableness, sec 34(16) of Israel's Penal Law specifically provides that the 'defence of necessity' be available only where the act is 'reasonable in the circumstances to prevent the harm'. In fact, the regulated use of the Landau methods was eventually deemed unlawful by the Supreme Court precisely because they did no constitute practices of 'reasonable investigation'. See *infra*, Ch 14.

[133] This point is elaborated in Ch 14, Section B(2)(b). The system has not essentially changed, in this respect, between the Landau and HCJ models.

[134] See eg HCJ 4774/95 *Ahmad Khalil Rashid v the GSS et al*, decision of 28 July 1995; HCJ 1494/97 *'Issam Sami Sirhan Nahhal and HaMoked v the GSS*, decision of 6 March 1997; HCJ 4869/97 *Jeit 'Abd al-Hafez Jeit v Minister of Defence et al*, decision of 10 August 1997; HCJ 3195/99 *Muhammad Khalaf and PCATI v the GSS*, ruling and injunction of 13 May 1999.

[135] See eg HCJ 3124/96 *Khader Mubarak and PCATI v the GSS*, decision of 17 November 1996; HCJ 2317/97, HCJ 2449/97 and HCJ 2673/97 *Ayman Muhammad Hassan Kafishah and HaMoked v the GSS*, decisions of 16 April 1997, 1 May 1997 and 4 May 1997, respectively (three petitions to halt the torture of the same person rejected); *'Abd al-Rahman Ghaneimat* case, *supra* n 39, decision of 8 January 1998; HCJ 6296/98 *'Abd Hasib et al v the GSS*, ruling of 9 October 1998; HCJ 6976/98 *Munir Samarin, Samir Samarin and PCATI v the GSS*, decision of 5 November 1998.

[136] The Court would do either only with the consent of Counsel for the petitioner. However, in *'Abd Hasib* (see *ibid*), where the latter refused to consent to the Court 'seeing confidential material', the Court cited this as a reason for not issuing the requested interim injunction. See para 3 of the ruling.

[137] See *supra*, Ch 12, Section B(2).

the detainee to its satisfaction.[138] In many other cases, petitions were withdrawn after the State announced that the GSS no longer intended to use the methods in question.[139]

Secondly, consider the cases of *Bilbeisi* and *Hamdan*, the only two cases I am aware of where an interim injunction was issued, with the State's consent,[140] but where later it appealed, citing new developments, and requesting that the injunction be rescinded. The State even explicitly requested that the Court allow the GSS to use 'physical force' when interrogating the specific detainees. In both these cases the Court granted these requests.[141]

Thirdly, the Court held a rather expansive view of at least the time-frame within which torture may be justifiable. Two of the cases where petitions seeking interim injunctions were rejected, *Mubarak* and *Ghaneimat*, may illustrate this point.

Within proceedings in the *Mubarak* case, the State admitted that during Mubarak's interrogation, he had been subjected to prolonged sleep deprivation,[142] shackling (on a small and slanted chair) for long periods,[143] hooding,[144] and loud music[145]—the four methods invariably being used in combination. By the time the case reached the Supreme Court, these methods had been used, intermittently, for almost a month.[146] The petition was nevertheless rejected.

During proceedings in the *Ghaneimat* case, the State similarly admitted that in the process of his interrogation, he was subjected to prolonged sleep deprivation,[147]

---

[138] For instance, in the cases cited *supra* n 134, the Supreme Court's injunction in *Rashid* was issued four days after his arrest; 28 days in *Nahhal*, 28 days in *Jeit*, and 32 days in *Khalaf.*

[139] See eg HCJ 7246/95 *Jihad 'Abd Ghani Anis al-Hasan et al v the GSS*, decision of 22 November 1995; HCJ 3283/97 *'Omar' Abd al-Rahman Ghaneimat v the Minister of Defence et al*, ruling of 29 May 1997 [a different petitioner from HCJ 7563/97]; HCJ 6114/97 *Jamal Musa Abu al-Jada'il v the GSS*, ruling of 15 October 1997; HCJ 6978/98-B *'Abd Mu'tan, Zaher Jabarin and PCATI v the GSS*, decision of 10 November 1998.

[140] In *Bilbeisi*, the GSS initially accepted the injunction and stated that it would not use 'physical force' in his interrogation. See HCJ 7964 *'Abd al-Halim Bilbeisi v the GSS, Response—Affidavit by Respondent* (affidavit by 'alias 'Abu Id''' of the GSS, 31 December 1995). In *Muhammad Hamdan*, the Court's decision itself is 'based on the Respondent's consent . . . to the issuance of an interim injunction'. See HCJ 8049/96 *Muhammad 'Abd al-'Aziz Hamdan v the GSS, Order Nisi and Interim Injunction*, 13 November 1996.

[141] *Bilbeisi, ibid*, decision of 11 January 1996; *Muhammad Hamdan, ibid*, decision of 14 November 1996.

[142] *Mubarak, supra* n 135, *Statement by the State Prosecutor's Office*, 17 November 1996, para 4.

[143] *Ibid*, para 10.

[144] *Ibid*, para 6.

[145] *Ibid*, para 7.

[146] Mubarak was arrested on 21 October 1996 and his interrogation commenced on the same day. See a GSS document detailing the periods of 'interrogation', 'waiting' (see *supra* n 56) and 'rest' during Ghaneimat's interrogation. The document, entitled 'Details of the Process of Interrogation and Detention of Mubarak' was attached, in his case (*supra* n 135), to a *Statement by the State Prosecutor's Office*, 17 November 1996. The case was decided on that same day.

[147] *'Abd al-Rahman Ghaneimat* case, *supra* n 39, *Statement by the State Prosecutor's Office*, 31 December 1997, para 8.

shackling (on a small and slanted chair) for long periods,[148] hooding,[149] and loud music[150]—the four methods invariably being used in combination. By the time the case reached the Supreme Court, these methods had been used, intermittently, for almost two months.[151]

To illustrate the point further, according to a GSS document,[152] Ghaneimat was allowed only four hours of 'rest', namely sleep and respite from the above-mentioned measures, between 2.25pm on 21 December 1997 and 4.40pm on 25 December.[153] This means that Ghaneimat was allowed an average of one hour's sleep and respite in every 24 hours during four days. During that whole period, Ghaneimat was actually interrogated for a total of four hours and 50 minutes, the rest of the time he spent hooded, shackled to a small chair and exposed to loud music. The Supreme Court rejected the petitioners' request for an interim injunction prohibiting the continued use of these methods,[154] thus accepting (albeit in a 5:4 majority) the State's claim that, even after more than two months, the 'intensive interrogation' to which Ghaneimat was subjected was necessary for 'the immediate procurement' of information on which 'human life' depended.[155]

All of which indicates the Court's expansive view of the circumstances in which a 'torture warrant' may be granted.

E. Evaluation

Sheleff actually acknowledges the torture warrant-issuing role of Israel's Supreme Court under the Landau system. He nevertheless criticizes it strongly:

...within Israel's struggle against terrorist attacks, unacceptable acts were performed under a conspiracy of silence which covered so many, including the HCJ itself, which in previous cases had chosen not to intervene, either by ignoring...by evading...or by explicit *licence*...[156] [Emphasis added.]

---

[148] *Ibid*, para 6.

[149] *Ibid*, para 9.

[150] *Ibid*, para 7.

[151] Ghaneimat was arrested on 13 November 1997, and his interrogation commenced on that same day. See p 1 of a GSS document entitled 'Interrogation Log (detailed)' presented by the State Prosecutor's Office to the Supreme Court and to Ghaneimat's attorneys, Allegra Pacheco and Leah Tzemel, on 7 January 1998.

[152] *Ibid*, document entitled 'Interrogation Log (detailed)'.

[153] *Ibid*, 6–7.

[154] *'Abd al-Rahman Ghaneimat* case, *supra* n 39, decision of 8 January 1998, para 2.

[155] All quotations are from *ibid, Statement by the State Prosecutor's Office*, 31 December 1997, para 4. On other aspects of this case, which was part of the *Israel Torture* case, see *infra*, Ch 14.

[156] Sheleff, 'The Need to Defend the Honest Truth...' *supra* n 11, 460–1. He charges similarly, at 459, that 'hundreds of Palestinians were exposed to physical agonies and psychological humiliations'.

Sheleff's position is curious, for two reasons. Firstly, at least two of the three cases he cites as examples of the Supreme Court's complicity in 'unacceptable acts' were, according to the State, either a TBS or something close to one,[157] namely the very situations where, in Sheleff's opinion, courts *should* facilitate torture. Sheleff provides no factual arguments to contradict the State's claims in these cases, and the basis for his criticism is therefore unclear. Secondly, Sheleff provides only the following reason why, despite the Court's failures, a 'torture warrants' model should be put in place:

> ...it is true that in the past both the Attorney General's Office and the courts failed in effecting real and efficient control, but it is reasonable to trust the judicial system to remedy the situation more than the security system...[158]

Sheleff does not offer any suggestions as to how the repetition of similar failures could be avoided. Dershowitz discusses the Landau system,[159] but not this aspect of it. Like Sheleff, his argument for a 'torture warrant' model is essentially that 'a double check is always more protective than a single one',[160] which is reasonable enough, but falls short of allaying the fears that the examination of both the search and seizure warrant system and the 'torture warrants' system under Landau will have raised. Levinson acknowledges that 'we can wonder if there really are a sufficient number of detached magistrates to withstand the blandishments of the state' but offers 'ways at least to partially correct for deficiencies on this score'.[161] He suggests the following:

> First...all torture warrants should be public, with written opinions that can be subjected to analysis even if, as may necessarily be the case, the opinion cannot specify all of the evidence that persuaded the judge that this is one of the rare cases justifying issuance of the warrant. Secondly, the person whom the state proposes to torture should be in the presence of the judge, so that the judge can take no refuge in abstraction. In effect, the judge should personally become fully aware of his or her complicity in the act of torture.[162]

---

[157] Sheleff cites the following cases:
–*'Omar Ghaneimat* case, *supra* n 139, ruling of 29 May 1997, where a representative of the State told the Court that 'the petitioner is [a member of] an active faction of Hamas'. See *Protocol*, hearing of 29 May 1997.
–*Muhammad Hamdan*, *supra* n 140, ruling of 14 November 1996, where the Court stated, at para 6, that the GSS has information supporting a '...substantiated suspicion that the Petitioner possesses extremely vital information, the immediate procurement of which would prevent an awful disaster, would save human lives, and would prevent very serious terrorist attacks.'
–*Salahat*, *supra* n 17, was a principled petition against the Landau rules, and the suspected activities of Salahat or information he may have possessed were discussed neither by the two sides nor by the Court.

[158] *Ibid*, 469.

[159] Dershowitz, *Why Terrorism Works, supra* n 4, Ch 4, *passim*; 'Is It Necessary to Apply "Physical Pressure" to Terrorists—and to Lie about it?' 23 *Israel L Rev* 192 (1989).

[160] Dershowitz, *Why Terrorism Works, ibid*, 158.

[161] Levinson, *supra* n 6, 2048.

[162] *Ibid*.

All Israeli Supreme Court cases cited above were heard in public.[163] The effect of judges actually seeing the would-be tortured person is hard to assess, but it would have to be quite dramatic to offset the general picture portrayed here.[164]

To recapitulate, under the 'torture warrants' model, interrogators believing they are facing a TBS would apply to judges, who would decide whether this is in fact the case, and accordingly whether torture may be applied. Fashioned on legal provisions and practices governing search warrants, such a model would be based on principles of issuance by an independent authority; specific (rather than general) authorization; and reasonableness. However, procedures for issuing search warrants are administrative, or quasi-judicial, and *ex parte*, affording few of the safeguards that courts can offer. In practice, search warrants tend to be issued unquestioningly in the overwhelming majority of cases in the two states examined here. This is perhaps because of the limited, temporary nature of the damage searches may cause, unlike the severe, often long-lasting harm that tortured persons suffer. A properly-issued warrant grants the officials concerned immunity from prosecution, which would mean that officials may torture even innocent persons (in good faith) with impunity.

Israel's Supreme Court in effect issued 'torture warrants' during the Landau years. However, despite being the highest court in the land, that Court's record is not much better than those of lowly Israeli and US magistrates considering search warrant applications: petitions against torture were granted only with the State representatives' acquiescence. Otherwise the Court consistently allowed the continuation of torture whenever the State insisted that there was need for it, even weeks after it had begun. Sheleff himself disapproves of the performance of that particular 'torture warrant' system, but neither he nor Dershowitz offers remedies for the weaknesses of their suggested model. M Gross' proposal that a 'public committee', rather than a court, issue the 'torture warrants' is defeated by his own reasoning and assessments of the (Israeli) public's strong support for torture. One of the two remedies suggested by Levinson has proved ineffective, at least in the case of Israel, and we are left with his proposal that judges face the persons about to be tortured as the only possibly effective means of redressing this model's weaknesses.

---

[163] Occasionally with *in camera* sessions, as explained *supra* n 135 and accompanying text.

[164] A case in which a detainee stood before that Court with the effects of torture visible on his body, *'Omar Ghaneimat, supra* n 139, is described in Ginbar, *Routine Torture, supra* n 12. The Court ordered an investigation, which, despite Ghaneimat having suffered permanent nerve damage, found that the interrogators had acted properly. The Court later refused to revisit the case.

14

Israel's High Court of Justice Model

A. Introduction

The 'defence of necessity' (DoN) model refrains from specific legislation, regulation or other ways of authorizing officials to torture *in advance*, choosing instead to leave the questions of whether, how and how much to torture at the discretion of the individual interrogator. Under this model, however, the law, while regarding torture as a serious crime, nevertheless considers its infliction justified in a TBS under the 'defence of necessity' or similar criminal law defences, thus exempting the torturer from criminal liability. Where torture takes place, prosecutors and/or courts[165] would determine, *ex post facto*, whether the situation was a (real or reasonably perceived) TBS, namely whether torture was the only reasonable means of obtaining urgently-needed information crucial for the thwarting of planned terrorist attacks which, if carried out, were likely to kill many innocent civilians.[166] On this basis, the prosecutor would decide whether the torturer should face trial. If the prosecutor decides to prosecute, the courts may still rule that the defence applies and acquit the torturer.

A DoN model had been in full operation in Israel for almost eight years at the time this study was prepared for publication, in mid-2007, since Israel's Supreme Court, sitting as High Court of Justice (henceforth: Court, HCJ) ruled, on 9 September 1999, in the case I call here the *Israel Torture* case.[167] The model will be described and analysed first, in this chapter. It is, to my knowledge, the only model of court-sanctioned interrogational torture in force anywhere in the world at this time. The 'defence of necessity' at its heart played a crucial role in the Landau model, forms a (albeit, so far, latent) part of the USA's HVD model, and its adoption by other states facing terrorism has been recommended by academics. For example, the 'ex-post facto ratification' model suggested by Oren Gross (and

---

[165] But see JT Parry and WS White, 'Interrogating Suspected Terrorists: Should Torture Be An Option?' 63 *University of Pittsburgh L Rev* 743 (2002), who argue (at 765), in supporting a DoN model, that prosecution in these cases should be mandatory. Curiously, they express this view in the form of a recommendation to the Department of Justice (to declare prosecutions mandatory), thereby leaving the issue to the discretion of the Executive branch.

[166] This definition is taken from Part II, Ch 7, Section A.

[167] HCJ 5100/94 *The Public Committee against Torture in Israel v Government of Israel et al*, PD 53(4) 817, ruling of 9 September 1999. Henceforth, in the text: 'HCJ ruling' or 'ruling', with relevant paragraph/s added between brackets.

Fionnuala Ní Aoláin) is not essentially different, at least as far as its legal implications are concerned, from the DoN model. Gross proposes that:

…legal models of ratification may include exercising prosecutorial discretion not to bring criminal charges against persons accused of using torture, jury nullification where criminal charges are brought, executive pardoning or clemency where criminal proceedings result in conviction…[168]

Moreover, Gross and Aoláin actually cite the ruling in the *Israel Torture* case as such a 'legal model'.[169]

The HCJ model provides both for prosecutorial and court 'discretion', although in practice the across-the-board use of the first has rendered resort to the second unnecessary. The one important difference, the view of Gross and Aoláin (and others) that torturers would enjoy an excusatory rather than a justificatory defence, is discussed in Part IV.[170]

The DoN model is also, historically, the only model which has ever attempted to limit torture to TBSs, hence its importance for the purposes of this study.

As already noted, some aspects of the HCJ model deserve discussion beyond the immediate Israeli context; they will be addressed in Part IV.

While the HCJ ruling has been the subject of several studies,[171] most of them have addressed the abstract legal issues it aroused. However, at the time this is

---

[168] O Gross, 'The Prohibition on Torture and the Limits of the Law' in Levinson (ed), *supra* n 73, 229–253, 241. See almost the exact same wording in O Gross and FN Aoláin, *Law in Times of Crisis: Emergency Powers in Theory and Practice* (Cambridge: CUP, 2006) 137–8. For O Gross' views see also *idem*, 'Chaos and Rules: Should Responses to Violent Crises Always be Constitutional?' 112 *Yale L J* 1011 (2003); 'Are Torture warrants warranted? Pragmatic absolutism and official disobedience' 88 *Minn L Rev* 1481 (2004). For a criticism of this approach, which they call 'outlaw and forgive', see Posner and Vermeule, *supra* n 72, 21–4.

[169] Gross and Aoláin, *ibid*, fn 103, p 137.

[170] In Ch 19, Section A(3). It should be noted that Gross and Aoláin consistently call for a public '*justificatory* exercise' by officials acting illegally. See eg *ibid*, 140, 154 (emphasis added). No attempt is made to reconcile the contradiction, or at least tension, between justification in the public sphere and excuse in the legal one.

[171] See eg MG St Amand, 'Public Committee Against Torture in Israel v the State of Israel et al: Landmark Human Rights Decision by the Israeli High Court of Justice or Status Quo Maintained?' 25 *North Carolina J of Int'l L and Commercial Regulation* 655 (2000); A Biletzki, 'The Judicial Rhetoric of Morality: Israel's High Court of Justice on the Legality of Torture' January 2001, Paper no 9, *Occasional Papers of the School of Social Science*, Princeton, NJ <http://www.sss.ias.edu/publications/papers/papernine.pdf>, accessed 19 October 2007; RA Burt, 'Judicial Supremacy, Judicial Impotence and the Rule of Law in Times of Crisis' unpublished manuscript, June 2000 <http://islandia.law.yale.edu/sela/eburt.pdf>, accessed 25 October 2007; B Cohen, 'Democracy and the Mis-Rule of Law: The Israeli Legal System's Failure to Prevent Torture in the Occupied Territories' 12 *Ind Int'l & Comp L Rev* 75 (2001); ML Clark, 'Israel's High Court of Justice Ruling on the General Security Service Use of "Moderate Physical Pressure": An End to the Sanctioned Use of Torture?' 11 *Indiana Int'l and Comp L Rev* 145 (2000); M Gross, *supra* n 77; O Gross, *supra* n 168; CM Grosso, 'International Law in the Domestic Arena: The Case of Torture in Israel' 86 *Iowa L Rev* 305 (2000); M Gur-Arye, 'Legitimating Official Brutality: Can the War against Terror Justify Torture?' *Center for the Study of Law and Society Faculty Working Papers* (University of California, Berkeley), Year 2003, Paper 11 <http://repositories.cdlib.org/cgi/viewcontent.cgi?article=1010&context=csls>, accessed 13 August 2003; *Idem*, 'Can the War against

being written there is already enough information to consider the 'HCJ model' as a working model in the full sense used in this Part. I believe that the reality of this model will offer us some feedback into the arguments of the purely theoretical commentators. Therefore, the HCJ ruling will be outlined immediately below, but full conclusions, theoretical and practical, to be drawn from this model will be arrived at only at the end of the next Part, once both the 'on-the-ground' consequences of that ruling and the its broader legal aspects have been examined.

B. Model Outline

1. The ruling of Israel's Supreme Court

In its ruling, the HCJ invalidated the Landau model and replaced it with its own. Writing for the Court, its (then) President, Aharon Barak, raised at the outset two questions: whether GSS agents were authorized to interrogate suspects; and whether the sanctioning of interrogation methods such as 'shaking' and the '*Shabach*' position, applied under directives, and permitted on the basis of being 'deemed immediately necessary for saving human lives', was lawful (ruling, at the introduction). However, the ruling was not confined to these two questions.

One other issue, which provides an example of the limited value of purely theoretical discussions of this ruling, and which will now be considered briefly, was possible future legislation. The Court noted that authorizing interrogators to use force and thereby harming the 'dignity and liberty' of suspects would raise:

… basic questions of law and society, of ethics and policy, and of the Rule of Law and security. These questions and the corresponding answers must be determined by the Legislative branch. (para 37)

Terror Justify the Use of Force in Interrogations? Reflections in Light of the Israeli Experience' in Levinson (ed), *supra* n 73, 183–198; A Imseis, ' "Moderate" ' Torture On Trial: Critical Reflections on the Israeli Supreme Court Judgment Concerning the Legality of General Security Service Interrogation Methods' 19 *Berk J Int'l Law* 328 (2001); E Inbar, *Constitutional Law as Reflected in Judicial Rulings* [Hebrew] (Tel-Aviv: Karmel, 2001) 177–180; M Kremnitzer and R Segev, 'The Legality of Interrogational Torture: A Question of Proper Authorization or a Substantive Moral Issue?' 34 *Israel L Rev* 509 (2000); Parry and White, *supra* n 165; JT Parry, 'Judicial Restraints on Illegal State Violence: Israel and the United States' 35 *Vanderbilt J of Transnational L* 73 (2002); *idem*, 'What is Torture, Are We Doing It, and What if We Are?' 64 *University of Pittsburgh L Rev* 237 (2003); Reichman, *supra* n 38; A Reichman and T Kahana, 'Israel and the Recognition of Torture: Domestic and International Aspects' in C Scott (ed), *Torture as Tort: Comparative Perspectives on the Development of Transnational Human Rights Litigation* (Oxford: Hart Publishing, 2001) 631–659; Sheleff, 'The Need to Defend the Honest Truth…' *supra* n 11, *passim*, especially 464–9; AJ Weisbard, 'Comments on A Biletzki, "The Judicial Rhetoric of Morality: Israel's High Court of Justice on the Legality of Torture" ' January 2001, Paper no 9, *Occasional Papers of the School of Social Science,* Princeton, NJ <http://www.sss.ias.edu/publications/papers/papernine.pdf>, accessed 19 October 2007.

The Court, however, emphasized that should the Knesset choose to legislate, any resulting laws would be subject to judicial review, under sec 8 of the Basic Law: Human Dignity and Liberty (para 39).

The shape and fate of possible future legislation has (naturally) aroused much debate among legal scholars.[172] Some saw the opening, however narrow, that the Court left for future legislation as a serious fault of the ruling,[173] while for others it was a 'simple description[s] of Israel's political structure',[174] which may not necessarily leave realistic scope for legislation.[175] At any rate, the fact is that, almost eight years later, and with Israel facing sustained terrorist attacks through much of that period, the law on interrogations has not been changed. The issue of future legislation may therefore be set aside. I will argue below that the HCJ ruling laid down sufficient grounds for legalized torture on a large scale to render such legislation redundant.

Much more relevant here is the issue of the legality of torture (the Court used terms such as 'physical means' instead) in general, and in a TBS in particular, under existing law. I would suggest examining the Court's ruling in this respect on two levels, roughly corresponding to what Kremnitzer and Segev[176] termed 'administrative' and 'criminal'.

(a) Level 1—authority, legality and the DoN in 'regular' interrogation

Having determined that GSS agents were authorized to conduct interrogations,[177] which need not concern us here,[178] the Court went on to consider the scope of this authority. It ruled:

> The power to interrogate given to the GSS investigator by law is the same interrogation powers the law bestows upon the ordinary police force investigator (para 32).

GSS agents are therefore only authorized to conduct 'ordinary', 'reasonable', or 'regular' interrogation (eg paras 21–3, 32), which the Court defined as:

> …the asking of questions which seek to elicit a truthful answer (subject to the limitations respecting the privilege against self-incrimination…) (para 18).

---

[172] For a thorough examination of this issue see especially Reichman and Kahana, *ibid*; Reichman, *supra* n 38, 50 *et seq*.

[173] See eg Amand, *supra* n 171, 677–680; Biletzki, *supra* n 171, 12; Grosso, *supra* n 171, 336; Imseis, *supra* n 171, 346–9.

[174] Parry, 'Judicial Restraints…' *supra* n 171, 140.

[175] This is the view of co-author Kahana in Reichman and Kahana, *supra* n 171, 633–8.

[176] Kremnitzer and Segev, *supra* n 171, *passim*.

[177] The Court determined, at para 20, that while the GSS as a body was not recognized in law as authorized to interrogate suspects, individual agents who were issued authorization by the Minister of Justice under sec 2(1) of the Criminal Procedure (Testimony) Ordinance (1944) were thus legally authorized.

[178] At any rate, this point is no longer actual, as the Knesset has since enacted the General Security Service Law (2002), which explicitly includes the interrogation of suspects among GSS powers—see especially sec 8(a)(3). The law grants GSS interrogators powers of police for this task, in sec 8(b), and includes no authorization for the use of extraordinary methods of interrogation.

Such interrogation:

...is necessarily one free of torture, free of cruel, inhuman treatment of the subject and free of any degrading handling whatsoever. There is a prohibition on the use of 'brutal or inhuman means' in the course of an investigation. [...] This conclusion is in perfect accord with (various) International Law treaties—to which Israel is a signatory—which prohibit the use of torture, 'cruel, inhuman treatment' and 'degrading treatment'...(para 23)

Applying these criteria to specific methods or interrogation used by the GSS under the Landau system, and challenged by the Petitioners, the Court examined each of the methods[179]— 'shaking' (para 24); 'crouching on the tips of his toes' (para 25, termed '*Qambaz*' here); 'the "Shabach" method' (paras 26–30); 'sleep deprivation...for the purpose of tiring him out or "breaking" him [the interrogee]' (para 31). In each case the Court determined that 'the general power to conduct interrogations' (para 27) does not include the use of the method, for a combination of strictly administrative reasons, such as there being 'no essential link' between the method and its declared goal,[180] and more substantive ones, with a hint of the constitutional,[181] such as that the method 'harms the suspect's body. It violates his dignity' (concerning shaking—para 24), or 'gives rise to particular pain and suffering' (concerning the '*Shabach*' combination—para 30).[182] It should be noted that the Court qualified its denial of authority regarding sleep deprivation and shackling—this point will be discussed below.

Nor would the DoN be of any relevance here. The State had argued (following the Landau Commission) that authority to use such methods, through detailed directives (obviously laid down in advance), exists under the provisions of the DoN.[183] The Court rejected this position, ruling that:

This defence deals with deciding those cases involving an individual reacting to a given set of facts; It is an ad hoc endeavour, in reaction to an event. It is the result of an improvisation given the unpredictable character of the events...Thus, the very nature of the defence does not allow it to serve as the source of a general administrative power. The administrative power is based on establishing general, forward looking criteria...In other words, general directives governing the use of physical means during interrogations must be rooted in an authorization prescribed by law and not from defences to criminal liability. The principle of 'necessity' cannot serve as a basis of authority. (paras 36–7)

With this, the demolition of the Landau model was complete. There was, in Israeli law, no authorization to use 'physical means' such as the ones the Court considered, during 'regular', or 'reasonable' interrogation, nor could the DoN provide

---

[179] For descriptions see *supra*, Ch 12, Section B(2).

[180] This term used in para 28 regarding the use of a hood to prevent contact among interrogees.

[181] See *supra* n 90.

[182] Note the closeness to 'severe pain and suffering' in the definition of torture in the UN Convention Against Torture.

[183] See eg HCJ 5100/94 (*Israel Torture* case), *Principal Arguments by the Respondents*, 17 May 1998, paras 7–13; *Additional Arguments by the Respondents*, 8 June 1999, paras 1–25.

the legal basis for issuing—and following—directives regulating the application of such methods.

(b) Level 2—the TBS and the DoN

When considering ' "ticking time bomb" circumstances' (para 14)[184] (what is here called a TBS), and the question of whether the DoN applies to GSS interrogators using 'physical interrogation methods' under it, the picture shifts dramatically. In a crucial paragraph, the Court ruled as follows:

> We are prepared to assume that—although this matter is open to debate . . . the 'necessity' defence is open to all, particularly an investigator, acting in an organizational capacity of the State in interrogations of that nature. Likewise, we are prepared to accept—although this matter is equally contentious . . . that the 'necessity' exception is likely to arise in instances of "ticking time bombs", and that the immediate need ("necessary in an immediate manner"[185] for the preservation of human life) refers to the imminent nature of the act rather than that of the danger. Hence, the imminence criteria is satisfied even if the bomb is set to explode in a few days, or perhaps even after a few weeks, provided the danger is certain to materialize and there is no alternative means of preventing its materialization. In other words, there exists a concrete level of imminent danger of the explosion's occurrence . . .
>
> Consequently we are prepared to presume, as was held by the *Inquiry Commission's Report*, that if a GSS investigator—who applied physical interrogation methods for the purpose of saving human life—is criminally indicted, the 'necessity' defence is likely to be open to him in the appropriate circumstances. [. . .] A long list of arguments, from both the fields of Ethics and Political Science, may be raised for and against the use of the "necessity" defence [. . .] This matter, however, has already been decided under Israeli law. Israel's Penal Law recognizes the 'necessity' defence. (para 34)[186]

This is the moral and legal cornerstone of the HCJ model of legalized torture. Morally, as Kremnitzer and Segev state:

> The premise underlying this assumption must be that the use of these measures might be justified from a moral and therefore a legal point of view.[187]

Having cited a string of sources[188] who argue either for or against the 'Ethics' of torturing in a TBS, the Court ruled that Israeli law had 'already' opted, by way of recognising the DoN, *for* a torture-justifying 'lesser evil' moral view.[189] Any

---

[184] The Court describes a TBS, similar to its description in this study, in para 14, and again in para 33. See Annex.

[185] The Court is quoting from the provision for the 'necessity' defence in sec 34 of Israel's Penal Law. (Footnote added.)

[186] This passage was interspersed with references, omitted here. See also the discussion on the 'immediacy' aspect addressed in this passage in Part II, Ch 13, Section D(1)(b).

[187] Kremnitzer and Segev, *supra* n 171, 557.

[188] The vast majority of them referred to previously in this study.

[189] The Court uses the term 'lesser evil' later when citing, in this case approvingly, the Landau Commission, in para 36. It should be recalled that the Commission discussed the DoN (as a 'lesser evil' defence) in a chapter (3) entitled 'Legal and Moral Aspects'.

other view of the DoN would have lead the Court to rule that this defence was *not* 'open' to torturers, at least not as justification. Note also that at the end of the paragraph, the Court abandons the less-than-fully-committed 'we are ready to accept' tone of its opening words in favour of an unambiguous 'this matter . . . has already been decided under Israeli law'.

It has been suggested to me that the Supreme Court is merely reiterating a legal situation already created by the Legislature, therefore immutable. The text, however, indicates otherwise. The Court concludes that 'Israel's Penal Law recognizes the "necessity" defence'—but out of context this is a redundant statement of an undisputed statutory fact. What *was* disputed was the availability of this defence to torturers in a TBS. Therefore the Court's declaration of the 'matter' as already 'decided', can only be understood as siding with the 'ayes', a determination that the defence *would* apply to such torturers, once its conditions are met. I use 'determination' rather than 'statement' because the Penal Law, while providing for the DoN, did *not* categorize it as having an unlimited scope.[190] In fact, as noted, the Landau Commission had no qualms about 'capping' the DoN, by declaring that interrogators charged with perjury 'cannot rely on the defence of necessity', as perjury is 'a manifestly illegal act, above which flies that black flag saying: "prohibited." '[191] There was nothing to stop the Supreme Court, having cited the absolute prohibition on all acts of torture and ill-treatment in treaties to which Israel was party (see below), from declaring that the same 'black flag' flies above these acts.[192] Instead, the Court *chose* to interpret the DoN as providing torturers in a TBS with an escape route.

With the Court's subsequent instruction that where a GSS interrogator has tortured (not the term used), '[h]is potential criminal liability shall be examined in the context of the "necessity" defence' (para 38) and its suggestion that the Attorney General 'instruct himself' as to when the DoN would be used to prevent GSS interrogators from prosecution altogether (discussed below), the picture becomes even clearer: the Court is creating a new model of legalized torture.

To complete the picture, one significant omission in the ruling is worth mentioning. The Court describes the international legal prohibition of torture and other ill-treatment accurately and succinctly:

These prohibitions are 'absolute'. There are no exceptions to them and there is no room for balancing. (para 23)

However, when discussing the TBS, international law simply vanishes:[193] the Court does not refer to it at all, and most significantly fails to address, let alone attempt to reconcile, the apparent contradiction between that absolute prohibition

---

[190] Or more precisely as an uncapped 'lesser evil' justificatory defence. See Part IV, Ch 19.

[191] See *supra*, text accompanying n 26.

[192] The Knesset could then, if it disagreed, attempt to impose a different interpretation through legislation.

[193] For similar criticism see Grosso, *supra* n 171, 336.

and its own facilitation of violent interrogation. The Court's view, presumably, is that *necessitas non habet legem universalem* (necessity has no international law).[194] Whether this position is acceptable from the angle of international law itself will be examined below, in Part IV.

2. The model in practice

My description will cover three aspects: the 'building blocks', of the HCJ model, combining the rudimentary outline by the HCJ in its ruling and elements external to the ruling, mostly inherited from the Landau years; interrogation methods; and an attempt to quantify the scope of their use.

(a) 'Building blocks'(1): elements of the model set out within the HCJ ruling

Two elements of the model are already clear from the discussion above: the DoN as the torture-facilitating legal provision; and its extension to a wider temporal definition of a TBS, spanning up to 'perhaps...a few weeks' (para 34), the Court (rightly, to my mind[195]) tying the immediacy dimension of the defence to the need for information and to a lack of alternatives rather than to the imminence of the danger.[196]

Two other essential elements were included in another passage within the ruling:

The Attorney General may instruct himself as to the circumstances in which interrogators, who allegedly acted in a single case from a sense of "necessity," would not stand trial. (para 38—my translation)[197]

The last four words are worth emphasising in view of Ignatieff's claim that in its ruling, the HCJ 'was prepared to accept necessity as a plea in mitigation, not as a justification or an excuse'. Ignatieff builds a whole argument that the Court rejected torture around this claim, but has obviously missed this point—for the

---

[194] I am grateful to Ms Nancy Llewellyn, President of SALVI, the North American Institute for Living Latin Studies (<http://www.latin.org>), for providing the Latin rendition, for which she alone is responsible.

[195] See Part II, Ch 9, Section D(1)(b).

[196] *Cf* eg Rose LJ of the English Court of Appeal 'But the execution of the threat need not be immediately in prospect...' (*R v Abdul-Hussain; R v Aboud; R v Hasan; R v Naji; R v Muhssin; R v Hosham* [1999] Crim LR 570, para 5). See also Paul H Robinson's comment on the Landau report 'The Commission is right, I believe, to conclude that imminent threat need not be required. [...] Rather than requiring that the *threat* be imminent, I believe it is appropriate to require only that the responsive *action* be "immediately necessary" ' (*idem*, 'Letter to the Editor' 23 *Israel L Rev* 189 (1989) 189). Kremnitzer and Segev's remark that this would apply only 'in extremely rare occasions', *supra* n 171, 524, is not a principled objection to this reasoning.

[197] The official translation omits 'in a single case' (in the original Hebrew: *be-miqreh boded*); personalizes the allegation of 'necessity', which was person-neutral in the Hebrew (*lefi ha-ta'anah*), and translates the Hebrew *tehushah* into the more emotive 'feeling'.

Court the DoN is a plea for *exemption from criminal liability* and only as such may, unlike mitigation, vitiate the very need to prosecute.[198]

The Court, then, elaborated the mechanism that will trigger into action once an interrogator is found to have tortured in what he perceived as a TBS, and suggested that the Attorney General detail it further. This the Attorney General of the time, Elyakim Rubinstein, proceeded swiftly to do.[199]

The Attorney General's 'self-instruction' is of some theoretical significance. As Kremnitzer and Segev assert, the document constitutes, by and large:

... not much more than a general restatement of the statutory conditions of the necessity defense.[200]

There are, however, some exceptions. Among them is Rubinstein's expansion of the DoN to 'the prevention of substantial danger of serious harm to the *security of the State*'[201] (emphasis added), a notion not only absent from the provision for the DoN in Israeli law, but one actually proposed and *rejected* during the drafting of that provision.[202] On the other hand, the document states unequivocally that the DoN would not apply to any 'measure of interrogation the use of which constitutes "torture" within the meaning of the Convention Against Torture'.[203] This is at variance with the HCJ ruling, which includes no such qualification. However, as will be seen below, it was of little, if any, significance in practice—and by this is also meant this Attorney General's *own* practice.[204] Of much more practical significance was Rubinstein's inclusion, among his considerations for determining that the DoN applies and foregoing prosecution, of:

... the command-levels which authorised the act, their involvement in the decision and their reasoning during the act...[205]

Unlike the abovementioned declaratory elements, this one has been fully implemented. Thus in November 2006 the GSS 'clarified' that 'permission to use

---

[198] See Ignatieff, *supra* n 57, 140–1 (the quotation is from 140).

[199] E Rubinstein, 'GSS Interrogations and the Defence of Necessity—a Framework for the Attorney General's Considerations (following the HCJ ruling)' [Hebrew] 28 October 1999 press release, later published, under the same title, in 44 *Ha-Praklit* 409 (1999). For a brief discussion see Kremnitzer and Segev, *supra* n 171, 541–2.

[200] Kremnitzer and Segev, *ibid*, 542.

[201] Rubinstein, *supra* n 199, para G(1).

[202] See eg A Enker and R Kanai, 'Self-Defence and Necessity following Amendment no. 37 to the Penal Law' [Hebrew] 3 *Plilim* 5 (1992) 29. See also Annexes 6 and 7 to that article, for the proposed drafts of SZ Feller and M Kremnitzer which included a similar notion ('a security interest of the State').

[203] Rubinstein, *supra* n 199, para G(1). Rubinstein remains silent on the issue of 'cruel, inhuman and degrading treatment or punishment'.

[204] Of similar rhetorical value, and—as his practice has proven—little else, was Rubinstein's statement that the 'defence of necessity is... intended to apply in very exceptional circumstances and cannot be included within the routine of interrogation work' (*ibid*, para G(2)(b)(5)). See also para G(2)(b)(2).

[205] *Ibid*, para G(1).

special measures during interrogations may only be granted by the Head of the GSS'.[206] The result, however, is a system where the use of 'physical means' is authorized *in advance*—exactly what the HCJ set out to abolish.

The ruling also included a qualification as to the prohibition of two methods, sleep deprivation and shackling. The ruling prohibited their use as methods of interrogation, but nevertheless determined that they do fall within the GSS' 'general power to investigate' (para 26). Thus sleep deprivation is allowed, so long as it only occurs as a 'side effect' to a 'lengthy' interrogation (para 31), but not 'for a prolonged period' (para 23); 'cuffing' is allowed only 'for the purpose of preserving the investigators' safety' and must not involve 'causing pain' (para 26).

These distinctions, however significant in theory, were not accompanied by any instructions as to how they should be applied in practice, with results which the Court should have foreseen. As PCATI remarked:

...given the poor record of the GSS in all that involves turning 'security measures' into methods of torture, the HCJ ruling is wanting in that it fails to place clear and firm limitations on the use of these measures. What is the meaning of a 'prolonged' period...—10 hours? 20 hours? Two days? Who determines when 'handcuffing' becomes 'painful handcuffing'—the detainee? The interrogator? Or perhaps a medic or a physician?[207]

(b) 'Building blocks' (2): elements of the model outside the HCJ ruling

Other important elements of the HCJ model, combining the legal and the practical, add up to what may be termed a three-dimensional isolation of GSS interrogation procedures, which include incommunicado detention of interrogees, the seclusion of GSS interrogation facilities from the outside world, and in-house investigations of allegations of ill-treatment. While they have undergone some minor changes over the years, these elements have essentially remained as they had been under the Landau system.

(i) Incommunicado detention of interrogees

A Palestinian detainee from the West Bank or Gaza (until the July 2005 withdrawal) suspected of 'hostile terrorist activity' may be held for as long as eight days before being brought in front of a (military) judge,[208] and for up to

---

[206] 'Clarification' *Haaretz* (12 November 2006). An earlier article in *Haaretz* had claimed that such authorization might be granted by lower-ranking personnel.

[207] Y Ginbar, *Flawed Defense: Torture and Ill-Treatment in GSS Interrogations Following the Supreme Court Ruling, 6 September 1999–6 September 2001*, trans Jessica Bonn (Jerusalem: PCATI, September 2001) 17. The UN Committee Against Torture later made a similar comment (regarding sleep deprivation); see Conclusion and Recommendations of the Committee against Torture: Israel. UN Doc CAT/C/XVII/Concl.5, 23 November 2001, para 6(a)(ii).

[208] Under sec 78 of the (military) Order Concerning Security Provisions, No 378 (1970), any soldier or policeman may detain a Palestinian in the Occupied Territories for up to 96 hours, and a police officer may extend the detention for up to eight days. It should be noted that the military orders follow the Palestinian from the West Bank into Israel. Thus a Palestinian could be arrested inside Israel, and remanded in custody within Israel by a military court for an area within the West

90 days before meeting his attorney, according to Israeli military orders governing the Territories.[209] Under Israeli law (now applicable also to Palestinians from Gaza), such suspects may be held for up to four days (96 hours) before being brought in front of a judge,[210] and denied access to counsel for up to 16 days.[211]

Over the years, the length of incommunicado detention has undergone fluctuations, the most radical ones being a military order, issued in April 2002,[212] which provided for the detention of Palestinians from the West Bank for up to 18 days without access to either lawyers or courts. Following that period, access to lawyers could be further denied under the 'normal' procedures cited above. Subsequent orders reduced the periods gradually,[213] and a Supreme Court ruling declared the period without recourse to courts (but *not* the period without recourse to lawyers) 'excessive.'[214] A subsequent order restored the original eight-day period.[215]

In an *obiter dictum* in that ruling, the HCJ tried to counter accusations that Palestinian detainees are held incommunicado. While the Court referred to detention under the specific orders at issue, its arguments apply equally to any Palestinian detainee being denied access to counsel and family (or any other) visits:

Even if meetings with counsel are denied, this does not justify the claim that the detainee is cut off from the outside world. Suffice for us to mention that upon being transferred to

---

Bank and applying the military law extant there, but sitting within Israel. This according to the HCJ's interpretation of Regulation 6(b) of the Annex to the Law Concerning the Extension of the Emergency Regulations (Judea, Samaria and the Gaza District—Adjudication and Judicial Assistance) (1977). See eg HCJ 253/88 *Sajadia v Minister of Defence*, P.D. 42(3) 801 (1988); HCJ 6504/95b *Wajih Muhammad 'Abd al-Karim et al v State of Israel*, decision of 1 November 1995.

[209] Under sections 78 b-d of the same Order, the 'official in charge of the interrogation' may, in a written decision giving reasons, preclude detainees from meeting their attorney for up to 15 days. A police officer of a rank of Chief Superintendent and above may extend the period for an additional fifteen days. A military judge may extend the period of preclusion for thirty days more, and the chief military judge or the on-duty chief judge may extend it for an additional thirty days.

[210] Criminal Procedure (Detainee Suspected of Security Offence) (Temporary Provision) Law, 2006, sec 3.

[211] The 'official in charge' may prohibit meeting with counsel for up to six days, and a police officer with a rank of commander and above, or the head of the Interrogations Division of the GSS may extend the period for up to ten more days, see sec 2(a-b) of the Criminal Procedure Regulations [delaying meeting of a detainee suspected of security offences with attorney] (1997).

[212] Order Concerning Detention During Combat Operations (Temporary Provision) (Judea and Samaria) (No 1500) (2002), issued on 5 April 2002 by General Yizhak Eitan, the 'Commander of IDF Forces in the Judea and Samaria Area'.

[213] Order No 1505 reduced the period before being brought before a judge to twelve days and the period without access to counsel to four days, Order No 1518 reduced the latter period to two days.

[214] HCJ 3239/02 *Iyyad Ishaq Mahmud Mar'ab et al v Commander of IDF Forces in the Judea and Samaria Area et al*, ruling of 5 February 2003. The term 'excessive' is used in para 47.

[215] Order Concerning Security Regulations (Amendment no 87) (Judea and Samaria) (No 1531) (2003).

the detention centre—which takes place within 48 hours of their arrest during combat operations—detainees are entitled to visits by the Red Cross; notice of where they are being detained is served on family members; it is possible at any time to submit a petition to the High Court of Justice against the arrest (section 15(d)(1) of Basic Law: Judgement). Such submission could be made not only by the detainee himself, but also by a family member. In addition, and in accordance with our approach to the issue of legal standing, so can any person or association interested in the wellbeing of the detainee . . . [. . .] Under these circumstances it is impossible to claim that those detained . . . are held incommunicado.[216]

There is a serious factual error, or misrepresentation, here concerning visits by the ICRC: Israel officially described its long-standing agreement with the ICRC as providing that:

[d]elegates from the ICRC are permitted to meet with detainees in private within 14 days of the arrest.[217]

This has meant that up to two weeks may elapse before a detainee is visited by an ICRC representative, rather than forty-eight hours.

As for the 'detainee himself' submitting a petition to the Supreme Court—such 'possibility' is purely theoretical, has not been exercised in a single case, and the Court is probably referring, rather, to attorneys appointed by the family, PCATI or other human rights NGOs submitting a petition on the detainee's behalf.[218] This, and the rest of the Court's points, involve communications to which the detainee is not party and of which he may not be aware, so their relevance to 'incommunicado detention' is unclear.

The HCJ, it should be noted, is defending *its own* record. It is a 100 per cent record—between its ruling and the end of 2006, the Court did not uphold *even one* of over 340 petitions submitted by PCATI against prohibiting detainees under interrogation from meeting their attorneys.[219] The same had been true for hundreds of petitions submitted during the Landau years. Here are a few examples (from the HCJ model). In *al-Matur*, the Court decided to deny a detained 17-year-old Palestinian child access to counsel for three weeks.[220] In *Natshe*, the Court refused to instruct the GSS to inform a Palestinian detainee that an order had been issued preventing him from meeting with his attorney—citing

---

[216] *Ibid*, para 46.

[217] Israel's 1997 (special) report to CAT, *supra* n 66, para 13.

[218] Barak CJ is therefore similarly imprecise when he claims elsewhere that 'Petitions from suspected terrorists reach the Supreme Court—which has exclusive jurisdiction over such matters—in real time' (A Barak, 'A Judge On Judging: the Role of a Supreme Court in a Democracy' 116 *Harv L Rev* 16 (2002) 157).

[219] Between September 2000 and May 2003, the number stood at 124. See Yuval Ginbar, *Back to a Routine of Torture: Torture and Ill-treatment of Palestinian Detainees during Arrest, Detention and Interrogation, September 2002–April 2003*, trans Jessica Bonn, Jerusalem, PCATI, 2003, 83. The updated number was provided to me by PCATI.

[220] HCJ 5242 *Muhammad Ibrahim Muhammad al-Matur and PCATI v Erez Military Court*, decision of 15 February 2000.

'reasons of State security'.[221] In *Harraz*, the Court rejected Counsel's request for the Petitioner, who was held incommunicado, to be present at a (Supreme Court) hearing of his case, again for reasons of 'State security and the interest of the interrogation'.[222] As in the Landau model, incommunicado detention was thus openly justified as serving the interest of, and in effect constituting a method of, interrogation.

While certainly not victims of enforced disappearances, Palestinian interrogees who are denied any visits are clearly being held in 'incommunicado detention', as found consistently by UN human rights monitoring bodies.[223]

(ii) Seclusion of GSS interrogation facilities from the outside world

The GSS' four official interrogation wings are located in facilities ostensibly under police jurisdiction (in the city of Petah Tikvah and the Russian Compound in Jerusalem) or that of the Israel Prisons Service (Shikmah prison in the city of Ashkelon and Kishon, near the city of Haifa), as the GSS, even under the 2002 law, is not authorized to run detention facilities. However, in practice the interrogation wings are completely separate and independent kingdoms. Police or IPS personnel working in those wings follow orders by GSS interrogators. No visitors are allowed, and lawyers, ICRC representatives and even police or IPS doctors see interrogees outside the interrogation wing.

The only on-the-spot documentation of interrogations is internal GSS memos. In 2002, the Knesset passed a law that would require 'visual recording' (video and audio) of police interrogations concerning serious crimes.[224] However, the law applies to police interrogations only, and while the Minister for Home Security is authorized to extend its provisions to 'other agencies lawfully authorized to conduct interrogations',[225] of which the GSS is one, no such extension has so far taken place.

As for official 'visitors' from the outside, in 2002 the Knesset enshrined in law a situation which had already existed in practice following the Landau recommendations: a Ministerial committee, a Knesset sub-committee, an internal comptroller[226] and the State Comptroller[227] all have access to and perform respective supervisory and auditory functions over the GSS interrogation

---

[221] HCJ 801/00 *Bassam Natshe and PCATI v the GSS*, decision of 1 February 2000, 2.

[222] HCJ 8353/99 *Radwan Sadeq Sa'id Harraz and PCATI v the GSS*, decision of 20 July 2000.

[223] See eg Report of the UN Special Rapporteur on torture, UN Doc E/CN.4/2001/66, 25 January 2001, para 665 (see also previously, eg UN Doc E/CN.4/1999/61, 12 January 1999, para 374); Conclusion and Recommendations of the Committee against Torture: Israel. UN Doc CAT/C/XVII/Concl.5, 23 November 2001, para 6(f); the UN Human Rights Committee refers to 'the use of prolonged detention without any access to a lawyer or other persons of the outside world' (Concluding observations of the Human Rights Committee: Israel. UN Doc CCPR/CO/78/ISR, 5 August 2003, para 13).

[224] Criminal Procedure Law (Interrogation of Suspects) (2002).

[225] Ibid, sec 16(c).

[226] See secs 5, 6 and 13 of General Security Service Law (2002), respectively.

[227] By virtue of sec 9 of State Comptroller Law [Consolidated Version] (1958).

system. However, all these bodies' activities regarding GSS interrogation are still shrouded in secrecy.

No less importantly, these mechanisms have all acted *within* the Landau/HCJ torture-justifying paradigm,[228] the result being that the premises upon which the torture models worked are unlikely to have been challenged.[229]

(iii) In-house investigations of allegations of ill-treatment

In 1992, investigations of detainees' complaints against their GSS interrogators were ostensibly transferred from an internal investigation mechanism to the newly-established Department for the Investigation of Police within the Ministry of Justice.[230] Following the HCJ ruling, this responsibility was shifted, for reasons not explained officially, to the State Prosecutor's Office. Detainees' complaints, mostly channelled through PCATI, have since been sent to that Office. What has not changed since 1992 is that the complaint is then forwarded for investigation to an official whose title is 'Comptroller for Interrogees' Complaints'. That official is a GSS agent. In 2003, Adv Talia Sasson of the State Prosecutor's Office described the official to a Knesset committee as 'a senior investigator of the General Security Service and . . . professionally instructed by me'.[231] Such instruction notwithstanding, the reality this situation creates is that investigations of the facts as to complaints of ill-treatment are conducted internally.

From the description in the previous section it is clear that there are no neutral witnesses to what happens inside the GSS interrogation rooms—it is the detainee's word against that of the GSS interrogators. As it happens, the material that the State Prosecutor's Office, and subsequently the Attorney General, examine in determining the facts, and then deciding if the DoN applies to the case, consists of the detainee's version and that of the GSS interrogators, both as presented by a senior GSS investigator.

As an (unsurprising) consequence, the State Prosecutor's Office, in dealing with interrogees' complains, has *invariably* preferred the version of events presented by the GSS to that of the complainant. Perhaps more significant is yet another 100 per cent record: in each and every case where the use of violence

---

[228] See TS Kuhn, *The Structure of Scientific Revolutions* (rev 3rd edn, Chicago: University of Chicago Press, 1996) especially Ch V.

[229] In her 1995 report, State Comptroller Justice Miriam Ben Porat even indicated quite clearly that in her view, GSS interrogators should be permitted to use *more* 'pressure'. See *supra* n 68, 6, 8.

[230] The Department was set up to deal with complaints against police officers as well. See eg Israel's Initial Report to the UN Human Rights Committee, UN Doc CCPR/C/81/Add.13, 9 April 1998, para 144. Its powers are defined in a 1994 amendment to the Police Ordinance (1971), now in sec 49 of the Ordinance.

[231] 16th Knesset, First Session, 'Minutes [number missing] of Meeting of the Constitution, Law and Justice Committee, 8 June 2003' minutes/Constitution Committee/6610, 13. Available (in Hebrew) on the internet at <http://www.knesset.gov.il/protocols/data/html/huka/2003-06-08.html>, accessed 29 June 2003. See similarly Comments by the Government of Israel on the concluding observations of the Human Rights Committee, UN Doc CCPR/CO/78/ISR/Add.1, 24 January 2007, sec IV, paras 4.1–4.3.

has been acknowledged, explicitly or implicitly (see below), the Attorney General has determined that such use had been justified by circumstances, invoking (in most cases implicitly) the 'defence of necessity'. Not one criminal prosecution has been made against a GSS interrogator since the HCJ ruling.[232] As PCATI commented, the 'idea that . . . GSS interrogators are all as pure as the driven snow and completely infallible, is unconvincing'.[233]

To recapitulate, a three-dimensional isolation engulfs GSS interrogation procedures: the interrogee is held incommunicado during the crucial period of interrogation, which often lasts weeks, and in law could last months; no body or mechanism that is outside Israel's torture-justifying officialdom is allowed to monitor interrogations; and factual investigations of complaints are carried out internally. The result has been a complete, hermetic, impenetrable and unconditional protection that envelops the system of GSS interrogation and enables torture to continue undisturbed, with no external, or extra-paradigmatic, supervision or scrutiny to speak of. There is one exception—the visits by ICRC representatives, but these are allowed only up to fourteen days following arrest, and ICRC reports are confidential.

(c) Interrogation methods

Curiously, PCATI was the only NGO to publish (two) detailed reports on GSS interrogations in the first seven and a half years after the HCJ ruling, before being joined, in May 2007, by a joint B'Tselem and HaMoked report,[234] when a third PCATI report was also published.[235] The following will summarize the factual findings of these reports, with some added information from affidavits and other sources.

(i) Data

The reports describe mainly the use of the following interrogation methods, some of them used previously under the Landau model (and described above):

1. Violence: The most prevalent forms of violent interrogation methods are:

- *Beating, slapping, kicking, stepping on shackles.*
- *Forced squatting in the 'frog position' ('qambaz').*

---

[232] Thus the Ministry of Justice told B'Tselem that over 500 complaints of ill-treatment by GSS interrogators were filed between January 2001 and October 2006, none resulting in prosecution Letter to B'Tselem from Attorney Boaz Oren, head of the International Agreements Unit, Ministry of Justice, 26 June 2006, cited in Y Lein, *Absolute Prohibition: The Torture and Ill-treatment of Palestinian Detainees*, trans. Shaul Vardi and Zvi Shulman (Jerusalem: B'Tselem and Hamoked, May 2007), <http://www.btselem.org/Download/200705_Utterly_Forbidden_eng.doc>, accessed 23 June 2007, 75. See also Comments by the Government of Israel, *ibid*, sec IV, para 4.7. The last criminal prosecution against a GSS interrogator took place in 1990. See *supra*, n 40 and accompanying text.

[233] Ginbar, *Back to a Routine of Torture, supra* n 219, 83–4.

[234] *Supra* n 232.

[235] N Hoffstater *'Ticking Bombs': Testimonies of Torture Victims in Israel*, trans Jessica Bonn (Jerusalem: PCATI May 2007) <http://www.stoptorture.org.il//eng/images/uploaded/publications/140.pdf>, accessed 23 June 2007.

- *Bending the interrogee and placing him in other painful positions.* The 'bending' or 'tilting' method is usually carried out by forcing the interrogee, who is tied to a chair with no backrest (or placed so that the backrest is not behind him), leaning him backward at an angle of 45 degrees or more, for half an hour or more each time. Interrogators often do this by applying pressure to the chin or chest of the interrogee, in combination with slapping, beating, stepping on shackles, etc. Other forms of placing in painful positions often used are forward bending, forcing the interrogee to stand, to lift his arms, or remain in a position that is somewhere between standing and squatting for long periods.

- *Intentional tightening of handcuffs*, at times to the point of bleeding.

- *Violent shaking, jolting.* Whereas PCATI listed violent shaking among the GSS interrogation methods, B'Tselem and Hamoked did not. However, the latter did include the not-dissimilar method of 'sudden pulling of the body' as well as 'sudden tilting of the head'.[236]

2. Sleep deprivation Under the HCJ model, sleep deprivation is enforced through what is called a 'lengthy interrogation',[237] which for the most part involves keeping the interrogee in the interrogations room, whether or not he is being interrogated. Different forms of violence (see above) and/or additional methods described here are often used, including shackling to a chair—usually standard-sized but unpadded—in a variety of uncomfortable positions (that in time become painful), and still termed '*shabeh*' by detainees; questioning replete with shouting, curses etc; transferring the detainee to the cell and back, and using the air conditioning system to stream cold air into the interrogation room or the cell. Interrogees are often deprived of sleep for periods of three or more consecutive days. In other cases, their sleep is limited to two or three hours in twenty-four, over the course of many days.

3. Additional interrogation methods

- *Prolonged shackling.* In most cases hands are tied behind the back, to the chair, and so are the legs, throughout the interrogation sessions, which often last many hours. In some of the cases, only the hands are tied.

- *Curses, threats, humiliations.* These usually include curses of a sexual nature; threats to use methods indeed taken by the IDF, such as demolition of the detainee's home, arrest or even assassination of family members; and spitting at him. Strip searches are often conducted in a deliberately humiliating manner. In addition, PCATI has also documented a case of physical sexual abuse while B'Tselem and HaMoked mention spitting at interrogees and yelling in their ears;

---

[236] B'Tselem and HaMoked, *supra* n 232, 50–1.
[237] HCJ ruling, para 31. See also HCJ 970/01 *Aminah Muna v The State of Israel—the GSS*, ruling of 15 February 2001, in which the Supreme Court rejected a petition against such lengthy interrogation.

- *Deprivation of essential needs.* During a 'lengthy interrogation' the interrogee is deprived, sometimes, of food, water, use of the bathroom and medical care.

4. Secondary methods:

- *Isolation and secrecy* (see above);

- *Imprisonment under inhuman conditions.* Palestinian interrogees are held mainly in filthy cells, are not permitted to shower, sometimes for two weeks or more,[238] receive food in a poor state, described by one detainee as 'not suitable even for animals',[239] and do not receive a change of clothes. As there are no objective reasons for maintaining such conditions, they too are means of degrading interrogees and thereby pressuring them.

To all of the above should be added a range of other methods reported in specific cases, including tying a detainee, naked, to a pipe,[240] choking,[241] arresting an interrogee's wife,[242] pressing a leg hard against a detainee's testicles[243] and more.

(ii) Official acknowledgement

Unlike during the Landau years, official acknowledgements of specific methods are few and far between. This may easily be explained by the fact that under the HCJ ruling, what an interrogator uses in a TBS would not—indeed must not—be interrogation *methods*, namely, acts that are the result of planning, preparation, regulation and authorization. Those would be in contravention of the ruling. Only acts of 'improvisation given the unpredictable character of the events...in a single case' (ruling, paras 36, 38) would enjoy the shield of the DoN. Nevertheless, the use of certain methods has been explicitly acknowledged by officials on several occasions.

1. Beating, 'shaking' As noted in Part II, 'P', a GSS interrogator, asked in 2002 about torturing in a TBS, replied, *inter alia*:

Here you use all possible manipulations up to shaking and beating, and you will beat the hell out of him.[244]

---

[238] In sad contrast, Khalil Marwan al-Khalili testified as follows: '...they forced me to shower four times in one night, since during my time in the *shabeh* I would wet myself, and that happened twice, as a result of the force of the torture and the beating and from lack of sleep' (Ginbar, *Back to a Routine of Torture, supra* n 219, 54).

[239] Testimony of Usamah Natshe, *ibid*, 50.

[240] Testimony of Kamel 'Obeid, Ginbar, *Flawed Defense, supra* n 207, 32.

[241] Testimony of Nasser 'Ayyad, *ibid*, 38; of MG, B'Tselem and HaMoked report, *supra* n 232 48; of 'Abd al-Halim 'Izz a-Din and Mustafa Abu Mu'ammar, PCATI report, *supra* n 235, chs 7 and 11, respectively.

[242] Da'ud Dar'awi, Ginbar, *Back to a Routine of Torture, supra* n 219, 53.

[243] Testimony of Suheib Daraghmeh, *ibid*, 62.

[244] A Navon, 'Stories from the Interrogation Rooms' [Hebrew] *Maariv Weekend Supplement*, 5 July 2002. The first quotation is from the question.

2. 'Bending' and beating In a testimony during 'mini-trial' at the Jerusalem Central Court,[245] a detainee, Medhat Tareq Muhammad, described in detail the interrogation methods used against him.[246] Cross-examining Muhammad for the State, Adv Geulah Cohen did not deny the use of any of those methods.[247] She did, however, argue about timing and 'quantities' of two specific (and combined) methods. Relying on GSS documents, she told Muhammad:

I put it to you that... your interrogation by the GSS...started on the 28th at 09:20, namely after the time when, according to the State, they stopped beating you...[248]

[...] I put it to you that you were taken to the doctor a whole night before making your statement to the police...You had already received a drip and afterwards you slept all night and only on next morning did you go to the police investigator.[249]

[...] I put it to you that you were beaten only within a period of about 10 hours, during which you sat on the chair [in the 'bending' position[250]] one hour, twice, for half an hour each time, and you received only 5 slaps.[251]

A Supreme Court decision in Muhammad's case revealed that:

...the Attorney General and State Prosecutor decided that the forms of interrogation which were applied fall under the 'defence of necessity,' and therefore the interrogators bear no criminal liability in this case for the forms of interrogation applied by them...[252]

In another case, that of Husam 'Ataf 'Ali Badran, a GSS document[253] was attached to a letter sent to his lawyer, Adv Labib Habib.[254] The document's

---

[245] *PH 004071 State of Israel v Medhat (bin Tareq) Muhammad*, Jerusalem District Court, hearing of 14 November 2002, *Minutes*, 28–34. Muhammad is an East-Jerusalemite, hence the civilian rather than military court.

[246] Including the following: 'The chair's backrest was to my left. My hands were cuffed, the chair was attached to the floor by means of a lock, the hands tied backwards. Adam [a GSS interrogator's alias] placed his hand on my chest and pushed me towards the floor keeping me at an angle of about 45 degrees. With his other hand Adam slapped me on the face. At one point when I could no longer bear it I went all the way back so that my head was on the floor. My head reached the floor. Adam would sit behind me and slap my face to make me rise again and told me to get up. When I attempted to, Adam stopped me and kept me at an angle of 45 degrees. I couldn't bear it and went back down. I was like a doormat to them, I couldn't get back, I felt that my back would break from the downward pressure on my head' (*ibid*, 29). See also Ginbar, *Back to a Routine of Torture, supra* n 219, 65–8.

[247] Adv Cohen did not refer directly to other methods which Muhammad mentioned, such as sleep deprivation, threats and curses and cold air, though the use of the first method is hinted at in the quotation below.

[248] *Ibid*, 43.

[249] *Ibid*, 45.

[250] This is obvious from the preceding debate, see eg *ibid*, 28–9; 31; 43–4. Thus following the passage quoted here, Adv Cohen says, 46: 'I put it to you that during two days you were on the chair only for one hour'—clearly not denoting a normal sitting position. (Footnote added.)

[251] *Ibid*, 46.

[252] Crim App 4705/02 *Anon v State of Israel*, decision of 30 December 2002, para 1. Note, again, the use of the plural.

[253] To: interrogation file, re: Husam 'Ataf 'Ali Badran, signed 'alias "Oz" ', Head of Interrogations Department, Samaria, no date.

[254] Letter no 6585 from Major Nitzan Sultani, Deputy Attorney for Judea and Samaria and the Gaza Area to Adv Labib Habib, 1 August 2004.

author ('alias "Oz"'), Head of Interrogations Department, Samaria, wrote for the benefit of the 'interrogation file'. Citing 'the urgency of obtaining information for the purposes of thwarting a mass terrorist attack, which according to the intelligence in our possession was due to take place in the immediate future', he reported that:

...on 6 May 02 between 10:45 and 18:45 the following actions were carried out in his interrogation:

1. 3 Slaps
2. 3 tiltings of the torso[255] (the first for 10 minutes, the second for 30 minutes, the third for 22 minutes).

3. Sleep deprivation The use of this method—as an interrogation method rather than as a 'side effect' to a 'lengthy' interrogation, was acknowledged on one occasion, albeit circuitously, in a letter from Adv Sasson to PCATI regarding Usamah Muslim 'Ali Shreitah,[256] clarifying that during an HCJ hearing of his case, her Office's 'response regarding reasonable hours of sleep referred to the time at which the submission to the HCJ was made and not as a response regarding an earlier period'.[257]

4. Prolonged shackling behind the back As the HCJ allowed 'cuffing', albeit not as an interrogation method,[258] the problem here is less one of acknowledgment than of interpretation. The following exchange, which took place during a court hearing on the extension of the detention of a GSS detainee, Gerard (Jihad) Shuman, will illustrate this point:

q:[259] Could you explain to me why he [Shuman] has to be shackled throughout the interrogation, with his hands shackled behind his back.

a:[260] For the security of the interrogators.

q: There is a danger that unless he is shackled he would attack the interrogators.

a: Yes.

q: And you think the safety of the interrogator cannot be guaranteed if his hands are shackled in front.

a: This is a matter at the discretion of the interrogators.[261]

---

[255] In Hebrew: *hatayot gev*.

[256] Letter no 2003-0087-2608 from Adv Talia Sasson, Head of the Special Tasks Division at the State Prosecutor's Office, to Hannah Friedman, PCATI Executive Director, 11 January 2004. Henceforth a shorter form of reference will be used.

[257] *Ibid*, para 7. Note the legal situation, implied here, that the DoN, which requires reasonability, would be available (in a TBS) to an interrogator who denied a detainee 'reasonable hours of sleep'.

[258] See *supra*, Ch 14, Section B(2)(a).

[259] Adv Leah Tzemel, Shuman's attorney.

[260] Chief Warrant Officer Avi Sasson of the Israel Police.

[261] Jerusalem Magistrate's Court, *M 007453/01 Israel Police v Shuman Jihad*, 2 February 2001, *Minutes*, 7.

As it turned out, Magistrates' Court Justice Haim Lahovitzki was not impressed by this explanation. At the end of his decision regarding extending the detention of Shuman he made the following comment:

As an aside, let the following be said: The Respondent [Shuman] claims, through his attorney, that even today, during his interrogations, his interrogators regularly shackle him with his hands behind his back. When Advocate Tzemel posed a question to the police representative on this matter, the latter responded that it was done for reasons of his [Shuman's] interrogators' security. *I tend to doubt this argument* and yet, if there is indeed a danger to the well-being of the interrogators—and I leave that solely to their discretion—it appears to me that it is possible to assure their security in another manner. On the other hand, if the shackling is performed in this manner as a means of pressuring the respondent, it seems to me that there is no point to it and I do not believe that such a means will further in any way the goal of the interrogation. I say these things based on what I saw and what has been presented to me up to now.[262] [Emphasis added.]

It may be concluded that while the State Procsecutor's Office often denies the use of certain interrogation methods in specific cases, and while there is disagreement as to how long certain methods are applied for (and also, as will be seen below, on how often they have been applied), official sources have acknowledged, in one way or another, the use of most methods alleged by detainees.

C. Evaluation

1. Numbers of interrogees

Tens of thousands of Palestinians have been arrested by Israel's security forces since the HCJ ruling.[263] Thousands of those were interrogated by the GSS. Official data on detainees under GSS interrogations is not published regularly, but various officials occasionally supply information to bodies such as Knesset committees and plenary or the media.

Eliezer Rosenblum, Deputy Director at the Ministry of Internal Security, told the Knesset Constitution, Law and Justice Committee in May 2003 that 'as for the GSS, there are always about 214 interrogees in its facilities'.[264] To this should be added GSS interrogations carried out outside it facilities, as well as the units of Palestinian collaborators in various prison facilities who work for the GSS trying

---

[262] *Jihad* case, *ibid,* decision of 2 February 2001, at 9 (per Justice Haim Lahovitzki).

[263] See eg Addameer, press release, 17 April 2003. See also <http://www.addameer.org>.

[264] 16th Knesset, First Session, 'Minutes no. 12 of Meeting of the Constitution, Law and Justice Committee, 19 May 2003' minutes/Constitution Committee/6485, 17, <http://www.knesset.gov.il/protocols/data/html/huka/2003–05-19.html>, accessed 29 October 2003. This accords, for instance, with IPS data provided to B'Tselem on 3 April 2003, that at that time, 52 Palestinians were held for interrogation in the GSS interrogation facility at the Shikmah Prison (one of the four GSS facilities). This statistic does not appear on the B'Tselem website, and is on file with me.

to induce detainees to talk.[265] As seen in the cases above, an interrogation may last weeks and sometimes months, but cases of interrogations lasting a few days have also been documented.[266] It could therefore be safely estimated that the number of Palestinian detainees interrogated each month by the GSS is in the dozens, and in extreme situations rose to hundreds.

2. Extent of use of torturous methods—NGO estimates

How frequently are the various interrogation methods used? This question is important in assessing the success of the HCJ model in limiting torture to TBSs. PCATI have published a sample quantitative assessment, in early 2003,[267] and B'Tselem and HaMoked in 2005.[268] Under the circumstances, neither can—or has—claimed to conform to scientific standards of statistical research, and different categorizations have been used.

Both researches have found that incommunicado detention, prolonged shackling, threats, curses and humiliations have been used against practically every interrogee.[269]

As to harsher methods, PCATI found that direct violence was used in 58 per cent of the cases, and sleep deprivation in 52 per cent. B'Tselem and HaMoked found that over a third have been exposed to violence and/or sleep deprivation.

There is agreement that:

1. Virtually no Palestinian under GSS interrogation has escaped at least one, and usually more, forms of ill-treatment, which should have been banned for non-TBS interrogations under the HCJ ruling;

2. Sleep deprivation and directly violent interrogation methods have been used at least against a large minority of interrogees—38 per cent of them according to the lowest estimate[270]—often in combination, and to an extent that the three organizations agree amounts to torture.

In 2003, PCATI concluded that under the HCJ model torture in Israel gradually became routine once more. B'Tselem and Hamoked, whose research in 2005

---

[265] In official Hebrew: *Medovevim* ('encouragers to talk'); in detainees' parlance: *'Asafir'* (birds).

[266] Thus Walid Abu Khdeir was released after five days of interrogation in February 2001 (affidavit taken by Adv Hanan Khatib of PCATI on 30 May 2001); Azzam Yusuf was interrogated for three days in January 2002 (affidavit taken by Adv Muhammad Darawshah for PCATI on 13 January 2002); and Khalil Abu Dush was interrogated for seven days in January 2003 (affidavit taken by Adv Fida Qa'war on 9 April 2003). All affidavits are on file with PCATI and with me.

[267] See Ginbar, *Back to a Routine of Torture*, *supra* n 219, especially 18–22, including 48 cases.

[268] See B'Tselem and HaMoked, *supra* n 232 especially Chs 3 and 4, including 73 cases.

[269] For instance, PCATI found that 90 per cent of interrogees were exposed to prolonged shackling, and 79 per cent to curses, threats, and other humiliations. In the B'Tselem and HaMoked report, the figures were 96 per cent and 73 per cent, respectively.

[270] B'Tselem and HaMoked report, *supra* n 232, table on p 70.

covered a much quieter period,[271] talk, more cautiously, of 'routine ill-treatment' but since, in addition to the 38 per cent mentioned above, those organizations argue that the 'routine' methods may also, 'in certain circumstances... fall under the definition of torture',[272] the picture that the two reports portray is not essentially different.

3. The frequency of TBSs necessitating torture—official data

According to official figures provided to the press, ninety Palestinians, defined as 'ticking bombs', were interrogated, using 'exceptional means of interrogation' between September 1999 and July 2002.[273]

In June 2003, Adv Sasson, asked about the number of 'permissions' (for the use of 'exceptional' means) given, told the Knesset Law, Constitution and Justice Committee: 'We are not talking hundreds.'[274]

Taking into account that suicide attacks started a few months into the second Intifada, in late 2000, this means that the ninety official TBSs (or at least the vast majority of them) actually took place within less than two years.

As seen above, there is every reason to believe that torturous interrogation methods have in practice been used much more frequently than is officially acknowledged. For obvious reasons, neither an academic researcher nor a human rights NGO can determine whether the situation in each, or any, of the cases amounted to a TBS. The crucial fact here is, that according to official data, based on confidential (therefore irrefutable) information, TBSs necessitating torture may occur—and *did* occur—dozens of times during a single year.

The practical-cum-legal repercussions of this will be discussed in the conclusion of Part IV, within the wider context of the 'war on terror'.

***

To recapitulate—the HCJ ruling in the *Israel Torture* case prohibits authorizing officials to torture, therefore no regulations may be issued, no methods may be developed and no prior authorization is permitted for interrogations involving torture or other internationally prohibited ill-treatment. However, if an interrogator tortures a terrorist in a TBS (inevitably, in view of the above, by 'improvisation'), 'the "necessity" defence is likely to be open to him' in prosecutorial or judicial proceedings after the fact. The Court instructed the Attorney General to elaborate further on this availability, which he duly did, and a new model emerged.

---

[271] A partial ceasefire ('*tahdi'ah'*) was in force during 2005, possibly affecting the perceived frequency of (real or perceived) TBSs.

[272] B'Tselem and HaMoked report, *supra* n 232, 59.

[273] A Harel, 'GSS Has Used "Exceptional Interrogation Means" 90 Times Since 1999 HCJ Ruling' *Haaretz* (25 July 2002).

[274] See *supra* n 231, 15.

This model combined certain 'building blocks' inherited from the Landau model, such as routine, Supreme Court-approved incommunicado detention, intra-paradigmatic government and parliamentary supervision and in-house investigation of detainees' complaints, with new ones, particularly the *ex post facto* approval, through the application of the DoN, of the use of interrogation methods, by the Attorney General. Just as the Supreme Court has invariably approved incommunicado detentions and the GSS investigator has always either rejected detainees' complaints of ill-treatment or else claimed the use of violent methods had been justified, so has the Attorney General invariably determined that where violent interrogation methods were used, they were justified and the DoN exempted the interrogators from incurring any criminal liability.

As far as interrogation methods are concerned, there have been certain changes since the Landau period, some of them necessitated by the HCJ ruling, but the 'spirit' of the earlier model's methods has been preserved: methods the impact of which is likely to be gradual, such as incommunicado detention, sleep deprivation, painful shackling and humiliation are combined with violent methods the effect of which is instant, such as beating and 'bending'.

Unfortunately (for this study—and more so for many detainees), the GSS, the Israeli government and, indeed, the HCJ itself have not in practice made a full-hearted effort to restrict the application of such methods to TBSs; instead GSS interrogators have been granted unquestioning support and total impunity. So while I believe it is safe to say, following PCATI, B'Tselem and HaMoked, that torture has not been limited to TBSs, at least some of this failure may be attributed to the absence of proper safeguards against 'abuse' within the model. This makes the HCJ model weaker than it could have been as a case in point for a general argument that any relaxation of the absolute prohibition on torture would lead to its widespread use—a 'slippery slope' argument discussed in Part II. A different 'slippery slope' argument could nevertheless be made—that once a state grants its torturing interrogators any exemptions from criminal liability in TBSs, it is likely to develop mechanisms and practices which would trigger these exemption and defend the interrogators beyond the strict limits of such situations.

15

The USA's 'High Value Detainees' Model

A. Introduction

> We knew that Zubaydah had more information that could save innocent
> lives, but he stopped talking. As his questioning proceeded, it became clear
> that he had received training on how to resist interrogation. And so the CIA
> used an alternative set of procedures.[275]

This model has developed in the USA's 'war on terror', declared following the
terrorist attacks on its territory on 11 September 2001.

In the wake of the attacks, there was considerable media discussion in the
USA, and to a lesser extent elsewhere, about the morality, and to a lesser extent
the legality, of torturing terrorists in extreme situations to save lives.[276] The

---

[275] George W Bush, quoted in 'President Discusses Creation of Military Commissions to Try Suspected
Terrorists' 6 September 2006 <http://www.whitehouse.gov/news/releases/2006/09/20060906–3.html>,
accessed 10 October 2006.

[276] Some of them have been mentioned in previous Parts, *passim*. See also eg L Adams,
'Terrorism and the English Language: This year's crop of terrorism books offers thrills over insight'
The Washington Monthly (September 2002); Alter, *supra* n 4; S Chapman, 'Should we use torture to stop terrorism?' *Chicago Tribune* (1 November 2001); Joie Chen, host, 'CNN Talkback
Live: Torture: Should It Be an Option When Dealing With Terrorists?' aired 7 November 2001,
15:08 ET <www.cnn.com/transcripts>, accessed 12 September 2002; R Cohen, 'Using Torture to
fight Terrorism' *Washington Post*, 6 March 2003; 'Defending an Open Society' John F Kennedy
Library and Foundation: Responding to Terrorism, 14 November 2001, John F Kennedy Library
and Museum website, <http://www.jfklibrary.org/forum_totenberg.html>, accessed 10 February
2003; 'Ends, Means and Barbarity' *The Economist,* 9 January 2003; 'Is Torture Ever Justified?' *ibid.*;
B Hoffman, 'A nasty business' 289 (issue 1) *The Atlantic Monthly* (January 2002) 49–52; J Jacoby,
'How Not to Win the War' *The Boston Globe* (26 January 2003) at H11; S Johnson, 'Unravelling
the psyche of al-Qaida: Experts say painful torture is wrong method for questioning Mohammed'
MSNBC news website, <http://www.msnbc.com/news/881132.asp>, 5 March 2003, accessed
21 May 2003; D Lithwick, 'Tortured Justice' *MSN Slate Magazine*, 24 October 2001, <http://slate.
msn.com>, accessed 2 March 2003; 'Legal Torture?' *60 Minutes*, CBS News, 20 September 2002.
For the full transcript see <http://www.midnightspecial.net/FBItorturearticle.htm>, accessed
3 July 2003; P Maass, 'If a Terror Suspect Won't Talk, Should He Be Made To?' *New York Times
Week in Review* (9 March 2002); RA Posner, 'The Best Offense' *The New Republic* (2 September
2002); E Press, 'In Torture We Trust?' *The Nation Magazine* (31 November 2003); J Raskin, 'The
Flawed Calculus of Torture' *Toronto Globe & Mail* (11 April 2002); Jim Rutenberg, 'Media Stoke
Debate on Torture as US Option' *New York Times* (6 November 2001); HA Silverglate, 'Torture
Warrants?' *The Boston Phoenix* (6–13 December 2001); A Solomon, 'A New US Threat to Human
Rights: The Case Against Torture' *The Village Voice*, Week of November 28—December 4, 2001;

issue, however, has been far from merely theoretical. The war in Afghanistan, as of October 2001, and the steady stream of extraditions and 'renditions' it has engendered, from countries such as Pakistan,[277] then the occupation of Iraq, as of March 2003 (and its aftermath), which was challenged by a wave of attacks, many of them terrorist in nature, have all resulted in the USA detaining tens of thousands person who are, at least in its terms, suspected terrorists.[278] Importantly for our topic, in early 2002 the US Secretary of Defense described the criteria for detaining such suspects as follows:

> My goal is to have as few [detainees] as humanly possible. We are taking only those we believe there is a prospect of gathering intelligence from that can save people's lives and we have been successful.[279]

In several official documents such detainees have been labelled 'high-value detainees.'[280] A 'Joint Doctrine for Detainee Operations' issued by the US Joint Chiefs of Staff in March 2005 included the following definition:

> High Value Detainee (HVD). A detainee who possesses extensive and/or high level information of value to operational commanders, strategic intelligence or law enforcement agencies and organizations.[281]

H Sorensen, 'As You Wave The Flag, Wave Goodbye To Our Freedoms' *San Francisco Chronicle* (12 November 2001) <http://www.commondreams.org/views01/1113–04.htm>, accessed 25 October 2007; PJ Williams, 'Any Means Necessary' *The Nation Magazine* (26 November 2001).

[277] See eg U Schmetzer, 'Pakistan's scientists under scrutiny' *Chicago Tribune* (1 November 2001); '20 al-Qaeda men handed over to US' *Dawn/The News International, Karachi* (1 April 2002) <http://www.karachipage.com/news/Apr_02/040102.html>, accessed 10 July 2003; 'Binalshibh to go to third country for questioning' *CNN website* (16 September 2002) <http://www.cnn.com>, accessed 10 July 2003; '3 in Al-Qaeda missile plot extradited to US: report' *Philippine Daily Enquirer* (6 March 2003) <http://www.inq7.net/brk/2003/mar/06/brkafp_11–1.htm>, citing Agence France-Presse, accessed 30 July 2003; 'Pakistan Illegally hands over 440 to US' <http://www.khilafah.com/home/category.php?DocumentID=6445&TagID=6>, 10 March 2003, citing ANI (Asian News International), accessed 30 July 2003.

[278] In May 2005, the cumulative number stood at 'more than 70,000'. See Deputy Inspector General for Intelligence, Review of DoD-Directed Investigations of Detainee Abuse, Report No. 06-INTEL-10, 25 August 2006, <http://www.fas.org/irp/agency/dod/abuse.pdf>, accessed 30 May 2007, Executive Summary, 1. There was 'a peak population of 11,000 in the month of March 2004'. See *Final Report of the Independent Panel To Review DoD Detention Operations*, August 2004, 11, <http://www.defense.gov/news/Aug2004/d20040824finalreport.pdf>, accessed 25 August 2004. 'DoD' stands for Department of Defense. This report is often (and here too, henceforth) referred to as the 'Schlesinger report' after the Panel's Chairman, James R Schlesinger. The Panel had been appointed by Secretary of Defence Donald Rumsfeld in May of that year, following the exposure of the Abu Ghraib scandal, 'to review Department of Defense (DoD) Detention Operation' (*ibid*, 21).

[279] David Wastell, 'Rumsfeld: My plans for our British prisoners' *Daily Telegraph* (25 February 2002) 4–5.

[280] See eg AR 15–6 Investigation of the Abu Ghraib Prison and 205th Military Intelligence Brigade LTG Anthony R Jones; AR 15–6 Investigation of the Abu Ghraib Detention Facility and 205th Military Intelligence Brigade MG George R Fay, nd (published August 2004), <http://www.defenselink.mil/news/Aug2004/d20040825fay.pdf>, accessed 25 August 2004, 86; Taguba report, *supra* n 45, 7, 10, 13, 22, 37; the slightly different wording in Office of the Director of National Intelligence (DNI) *Summary of the High Value Terrorist Detainee Program*, nd (published in October 2006) <http://www.defenselink.mil/pdf/thehighvaluedetaineeprogram2.pdf>, accessed 6 October 2006; and the document cited immediately below.

[281] Joint Chiefs of Staff, 'Joint Doctrine for Detainee Operations: Joint Publication 3–63'(JP 3–63), 23 March 2005 <www.dtic.mil/doctrine/jel/pd/3_63pd.pdf>, accessed 10 April 2005, at I-13.

The Schlesinger report explicitly makes the TBS connection: '[f]or the US, most cases for permitting harsh treatment of detainees on moral grounds begin with variants of the "ticking time bomb" scenario'.[282]

The term HVD thus seems to also cover circumstances beyond a TBS, but preserves its essential features—the urgent need for life-saving information. TBSs have often been invoked elsewhere, including by officials, to justify the torture of HVDs. For instance the August 2002 Department of Justice (DoJ) memorandum which formed the cornerstone of the HVD model argued that,

Standard criminal law defenses of necessity and self-defense could justify interrogation methods needed to elicit information to prevent a direct and imminent threat to the United States and its citizens.[283]

A final 'definitional' note—the use of the term HVD here will not necessarily mean that I have established that the person or persons concerned were so classified by the US authorities.

While, as will be seen, US officials have indeed tortured suspected terrorists since 9/11, at times to death, there are good reasons to argue that this was not done within a real, or a full, model of legalized torture. No laws have so far been promulgated explicitly allowing the brutalization of terrorist suspects, nor have any courts explicitly interpreted existing US legislation as so allowing. Nor yet have courts directly approved any such interpretation of the law by the government, or for that matter any acts of torture in the interrogation of terrorist suspects.

On the other hand, four facts militate strongly for treating the HVD system as a model of legalized torture. Firstly, high-ranking US government lawyers wrote memoranda which became official (albeit confidential) policy, detailing

---

[282] See Schlesinger report, *supra* n 278, Appendix H, 2. In the case of Iraq, 'HVD' appears to have acquired a different, or additional, meaning—high-ranking members of the ousted regime, possibly regardless of whether or not they possess intelligence information. The Taguba report, *supra* n 45, mentions a 'High Value Detainee (HVD)' detention camp in Baghdad airport, 7, as does the ICRC, see Report of the International Committee of the Red Cross (ICRC) on the Treatment by Coalition Forces of Prisoners of War and Other Protected Persons by the Geneva Conventions in Iraq During Arrest, Internment, and Interrogation, February 2004, para 34. The report, which was not published officially by the ICRC is available eg at <www.stopwar.org.uk/Resources/icrc.pdf>, accessed 11 August 2004. See also eg B Gertz, 'Most prisoners in Iraq jails called 'threat to security', *Washington Times*, 4 May 2004.

[283] Memorandum for Alberto R Gonzales, Counsel to the President, from Jay S Bybee, Assistant Attorney General, US Department of Justice, Office of the Legal Counsel, *Re: Standards of Conduct for Interrogation under 18 USC. §§ 2340-2340A*, August 1, 2002 (henceforth: the August 2002 DOJ memo), 39, posted eg at the *Washington Post* website, <http://www.washingtonpost.com/wp-srv/nation/documents/dojinterrogationmemo20020801.pdf>, on 13 June 2004, accessed 14 June 2004. Most official memoranda and reports cited here may be found in KJ Greenberg and JL Dratel, *The Torture Papers: The road to Abu Ghraib* (Cambridge: CUP, 2005). The book contains material released up to October 2004, with an afterward containing material released later that year. See also M Danner, *Torture and Truth: America, Abu Ghraib and the war on terror* (New York: New York Review of Books, 2004), appendices.

arguments that torture—so named—could be ordered and used legally within the 'war on terror', an argument based on provisions for the President's authority in the US Constitution, as Commander-in-Chief of the armed forces during war. Secondly, interrogation methods have been approved by the US Secretary of Defence, some of which have been described as torture by international human rights monitoring mechanisms, the ICRC and international experts, at least with the accumulation of time and methods.[284] Other security forces, especially the CIA, have been allowed to hold suspected terrorists for years in secret prisons as well as to use a variety of interrogation methods, reportedly harsher than those of the army.

The DoJ's radical interpretation of the Constitution has neither been explicitly withdrawn by the administration, nor explicitly rejected by the courts. Nor have, to my knowledge, US officials, especially CIA and similar agents (as opposed to the military), that used officially-sanctioned methods to torture HVDs, probably on the basis of such interpretation, been prosecuted.

Moreover, the third fact is that the US Congress enacted, in 2005 and 2006, retroactive legislation in effect exempting past torturers (not so named) from criminal liability, thus adding a total-immunity dimension not unlike that of the HCJ model.

Fourthly, US the administration has consistently interpreted this legislation, and relevant international legal provisions, as allowing the use of methods which, I will submit in the next Part, may amount to torture—and have done so.

All this may not necessarily constitute a full-proof basis for arguing the existence of 'legalized torture'. Hence my use of the qualifying prefix, 'quasi' in characterising this model.

The HVD system is far less 'neat and tidy' than the two Israeli models, thus lending itself much less easily to legal analysis: it does not rely on one single document which lays down the law; it lacks stability—there has been much to'ing and fro'ing, both regarding the legal grounds justifying torture and actual interrogation methods and in practice. Rather than involving one agency (the GSS) working mostly in four detention centres within a small country, a myriad of forces and agencies are at work here, in acknowledged detention centres as well, unacknowledged ones, practically all around the globe. All of which has created a far-from-uniform picture. To complicate matters further, in mid-2007, when this study was prepared for publication, the situation was still very much evolving, with some documents declassified (while others remained secret), legislation enacted and challenged, investigations ongoing and cases pending.

In an effort to introduce some order, I propose to describe and analyse the HVD model in two stages. Firstly, in its original form, namely as it evolved between 9/11 and the spring of 2004.[285] Later developments, following the exposure of

---

[284] See the discussion below, in Part IV, Ch 18.
[285] These temporal boundaries will not always be strictly respected here.

ure of much (although not all) of the system since that point in time, including the withdrawal, and subsequent replacement, of the aforementioned memoranda as well as relevant court decisions and legislation, will then be discussed. The questions of whether or not the HVD system was initially a model of legalized torture, and how an answer to that question would be effected by those later developments, will also be addressed.

As the subject of this Part is 'legalizing torture', the inquiry here will be confined to approved torturous (or putatively torturous) methods of interrogation used against suspected terrorists[286] since the 9/11 attacks. This means that where the state has treated acts of ill-treatment of detainees as illegal, namely investigated complaints, prosecuted and punished perpetrators and denied them any justificatory defences or other means of escaping justice, such ill-treatment cannot be seen as forming part of the model. This means setting aside, to that extent, the torture and ill-treatment of Iraqi detainees at the prison Abu Ghraib by the US military, the exposure of which, in the spring of 2004, created a huge, global scandal which was largely responsible for the wealth of information we now have about this model. The US authorities had investigated those acts even before they came to light, and prosecuted, convicted and punished those held responsible (at least directly); the military courts neither heard nor themselves voiced arguments that the acts had been justified. All these procedures may have been partial and flawed, but the relevant point here is that they foreclose describing the USA's attitude to these acts as justification. The link between the official positions and policies described below and the torture at Abu Ghraib is therefore largely one of the 'slippery slope' variety and was examined briefly in Part II above.

B. Original Outline of Model

1. The legal argument[287]

This model initially legalized, or sought to legalise, interrogational torture of certain terrorist suspects through four main legal arguments. The relations between

---

[286] Some individuals interrogated, for instance in Iraq since the US-led offensive in early 2003, may have been suspected solely of targeting US (or allied) troops rather than civilians. However, as far as I am aware, all armed groups fighting US forces in Iraq and Afghanistan have also resorted extensively to terrorism, as defined in this study; therefore the term 'suspected terrorists' will be used here, with this caveat in mind.

[287] Earlier versions of the analysis presented here may be found in Amnesty International, *The United States of America—Human dignity denied: Torture and accountability in the 'war on terror'* AI Index: AMR 51/145/2004, 27 October 2004, point 5.1, 134–9; Amnesty International's submission to the House of Lords in *A and others v the Secretary of State for the Home Department*, Part 8, available at <http://web.amnesty.org/library/print/ENGEUR450272004>, accessed 21 November 2004. In both cases mine were small contributions to larger projects, and were significantly improved by comments and advice from my colleagues. For early academic commentaries on the USA's conduct of its 'war on terror' see eg MO Chibundu, 'For God, for Country, for Universalism: Sovereignty as Solidarity in Our Age of Terror' 56 *Fla L Rev* 883 (2004); D Luban,

the four have not been explicitly elaborated, and appear to fluctuate between the mutually overlapping, the complementary, the alternate and the overarching:

1. The *sui generis* argument: terrorist suspects are not protected by any laws, either national or international.
2. The limited scope of 'torture': to include only 'extreme acts'.
3. The applicability of criminal law defences (necessity, self-defence and superior orders) to officials who torture in certain circumstances.
4. The unlimited authority of the President at war: there can be no legal challenge to a President's order to torture.

(a) *The* sui generis *argument*

Any person detained by a state anywhere in the world, is, or should be, protected by three layers of law:

1. *Domestic law*: With the exception cited immediately below, US Constitution and laws do not refer explicitly to torture, but have consistently been interpreted as prohibiting torture.[288] 18 USC § 2340 (1994), entitled 'Torture', provides for penalties including up to twenty years' imprisonment (or death, if the torture victim dies) for acts of torture by US or any other officials, albeit only when committed outside the USA.
2. *International treaties*: In the case of the USA, these treaties include the International Covenant on Civil and Political Rights, the UN Convention Against Torture and Other Cruel, Inhuman Or Degrading Treatment Or Punishment and the four Geneva Conventions. As elaborated below, all of these prohibit torture absolutely.[289]
3. *Relevant rules of customary international law*: As elaborated below, it is universally agreed that the prohibition on torture is indeed customary, and a peremptory rule of international law.[290]

However, under the HVD model the US administration, or at least parts thereof, have sought to strip terrorist suspects detained by its forces abroad of every single one of these protections, and place detainees in effect beyond the reach, or protection, of *any* law, with the exception of military law which the President, under this view, may also ignore. If no laws apply, obviously laws prohibiting torture would be void, and interrogational torture may 'legally' proceed.

'Liberalism, Torture, and the Ticking Bomb' 91 *Virginia L Rev* 1425 (2005); A Roberts, 'Righting Wrongs Or Wronging Rights? The United States and Human Rights Post-September 11' 15 *Eur J Int'l L* 721 (2004); KF Ryan, 'LEX ET RATIO ... State of the Union' 30 *Vermont Bar J* 7 (2004); W Bradley Wendel, 'Professionalism as Interpretation' 3 *Northwestern U L Rev* 99 (2005).

[288] See eg the wealth of cases provided by Kreimer, *supra* n 73.
[289] See *infra*, Part IV, Ch 19, Section B(1).
[290] See *ibid*.

(a) Domestic law

A Presidential military order issued in November 2001,[291] provided for placing 'Al Qaida' detainees (who are not US citizens) named in accordance with the order, under the 'exclusive jurisdiction' of military tribunals, denying them 'the privilege to seek any remedy' from '(i) any court of the United States, or any State thereof, (ii) any court of any foreign nation, or (iii) any international tribunal.'[292]

Similarly, a Pentagon Working Group report of April 2003,[293] relying on the August 2002 DOJ memo, makes the administration's position clear that:

> ...the United States Constitution does not protect those individuals who are not United States citizens and who are outside the sovereign territory of the United States.[294]

In a *habeas corpus* case concerning a Libyan national held at the US naval base in Guantánamo Bay, Cuba, Faren Gherebi, a US Court described the government's position, and commented on it, thus:

> Even in times of national emergency—indeed, particularly in such times—it is the obligation of the Judicial Branch...to prevent the Executive Branch from running roughshod over the rights of citizens and aliens alike. [...] Under the government's theory, it is free to imprison Gherebi indefinitely along with hundreds of other citizens of foreign countries, friendly nations among them, and to do with Gherebi and these detainees as it will, when it pleases, without any compliance with any rule of law of any kind, without permitting him to consult counsel, and without acknowledging any judicial forum in which its actions may be challenged. Indeed, at oral argument, the government advised us that its position would be the same even if the claims were that it was engaging in acts of torture or it was summarily executing the detainees. To our knowledge, prior to the current detention at Guantanamo, the US government has never before asserted such a grave and startling proposition.[295]

Keeping foreign detainees held abroad outside the protection of the US judiciary has been a central tenet of the administration's 'war on terror' policy. This policy received its first serious blow on 28 June 2004 when the US Supreme Court ruled in *Rasul v Bush* that the US courts did have jurisdiction, under the federal habeas corpus statute,[296] over the Guantánamo Bay detainees, to be discussed below. However, the administration responded with a litigation strategy designed to

---

[291] *Detention, Treatment, and Trial of Certain Non-Citizens in the War Against Terrorism, Part IV*, 66 *FR* 57833, 13 November 2001.

[292] *Ibid*, secs 7(1) and 7(2), respectively.

[293] See also *infra*, Ch 9, Section D.

[294] *Working Group Report on Detainee Interrogations in the Global War on Terrorism: Assessment of Legal, Historical, Policy, and Operational Considerations*, 4 April 2003 (henceforth: Pentagon Working Group report) <http://www.defenselink.mil/news/Jun2004/d20040622doc8.pdf>, accessed 14 June 2004, 67; August 2002 DOJ memo, *supra* n 283, 2, 31–9.

[295] *Gherebi v Bush* (9th Cir), opinion filed 18 December 2003, amended 8 July 2004, per Reinhardt J, 46.

[296] USC 2241–3.

minimize the impact of the ruling, and eventually nullify it through legislation (see below).

(b) International treaty law

In a memorandum sent to the Vice President, the Secretary of State, the Secretary of Defense and others in February 2002,[297] President George W Bush set out his country's view of the status of 'Taliban and al Qaeda' detainees. The President determined, *inter alia*, the following:

1. That 'none of the provisions of Geneva apply to our conflict with al Qaeda in Afghanistan or elsewhere throughout the world' [para 2(a)];

2. That, specifically, 'common Article 3 of Geneva does not apply to either al Qaeda or Taliban detainees' [para 2(b)];

3. That, specifically, 'because Geneva does not apply to our conflict with al Qaeda, al Qaeda detainees also do not qualify as prisoners of war' [para 2(d)].

To this may be added the administration's consistent position that human rights treaties are not self-executing and that they do not apply to detainees outside US territory—that is, in Guantánamo Bay, Afghanistan, Iraq, and so on. For instance, as the administration claimed in a court case, 'by its own terms, the ICCPR is inapplicable to conduct by the United States *outside* its sovereign territory'.[298]

One exception was the Pentagon Working Group's conclusion that the UN Convention Against Torture does apply to the 'interrogation of unlawful combatant detainees', but only under US understandings, which greatly limit its scope in practice (see below).[299] In addition, the President's determination that certain detainees are not legally entitled to humane treatment (discussed immediately below) may have had the effect of placing these detainees wholly beyond the scope of this Convention as well.

---

[297] Memorandum for the Vice President *et al. Subject: Humane treatment of al Qaeda and Taliban detainees*, The White House, 7 February 2002, available eg in Greenberg and Dratel, *supra* n 283, 134–5.
See similarly the Pentagon Working Group Report, supra n 294, 6.

[298] *Rasul et al v Bush*, Brief for the Respondents, March 2004, 49 (emphasis in original). See similarly Pentagon Working Group Report, *ibid*, 6: 'The United States has maintained consistently that the Covenant does not apply outside the United States or special maritime and territorial jurisdiction and that it does not apply to operations of the military during an international armed conflict.' Note that the President's Memorandum, *ibid*, determined that the Geneva Conventions did not apply to 'al Qaeda' detainees because the conflict against that organization was *not* an international one. The USA's report to the Human Rights Committee in 2005 contained an Annex defending the position that this Covenant does not apply extraterritorially. See Combined Second and Third Periodic reports of the United States of America to the Human Rights Committee, UN Doc CCPR/C/USA/3, 28 November 2005, Annex I.

[299] Pentagon Working Group Report, *supra* n 294, 4–6.

To this may also be added the US courts' position that the language in the Geneva Conventions is not 'self-executing' and does not 'create private rights of action in the domestic courts of the signatory countries'.[300]

(d) Customary international law

A Department of Justice memorandum, submitted to the White House in preparation for the President's February 2002 memorandum, and which the latter seemed to accept in its entirety, concluded, *inter alia*, that:

...customary international law has no binding legal effect on either the President or the military.[301]

All of which has left suspected terrorist detainees, in the words of a UK court, 'arbitrarily detained in a "legal black-hole." '[302]

With both national and international legal protections being largely tossed aside, would terrorist suspects enjoy, in the US administration's view at the time, *any* legal protection, international or otherwise? In this regard, the President's memorandum of February 2002 includes the following statement:

Of course, our values as a Nation, values that we share with many nations in the world, call for us to treat detainees humanely, including those who are not legally entitled to such treatment. Our Nation has been and will continue to be a strong supporter of Geneva and its principles. As a matter of policy, the United States Armed Forces shall continue to treat detainees humanely and, to the extent appropriate and consistent with military necessity, in a manner consistent with the principles of Geneva.[303]

By this the President established the following:

• That there are detainees, and presumably 'al Qaeda' detainees are among them, who in the US administration's view 'are not legally entitled' to be treated

---

[300] See *Hamdi v Rumsfeld*, 316 F.3d 450 (4th Cir 2003), at III(B), citing *Huynh Thi Anh v Levi*, 586 F.2d 625, 629 (6th Cir 1978). Curiously, the Court added that Hamdi 'is being held as an enemy combatant pursuant to the well-established laws and customs of war' (*ibid*, at V(B)(2)).

[301] Memorandum for Alberto R Gonzales, Counsel to the President, and William J. Haynes II, General Counsel of the Department of Defense. *Re: Application of treaties and laws to al Qaeda and Taliban detainees*. From Jay S. Bybee, Assistant Attorney General, Office of Legal Counsel, US Department of Justice, 22 January 2002. See similarly Pentagon Working Group Report, *supra* n 294, 6. This is a sharp turn away from the USA's long tradition of jurisprudence confirming that international law is part of the law of the USA. See eg *The Paquete Habana* 175 US 677 (1900).

[302] *Abbassi & Anor v Secretary of State* [2002] EWCA Civ 1598, para 64. The case concerned a claim by a UK citizen detained at Guantánamo Bay that the Court compel the Foreign Office to intervene with the US government on his behalf. The Court accepted the legality of detaining foreign nationals as alleged enemy combatants (*ibid*, para 65), but added: 'What appears to us to be objectionable is that Mr Abbassi should be subject to indefinite detention in territory over which the United States has exclusive control with no opportunity to challenge the legitimacy of his detention before any court or tribunal' (*ibid*, para 66).

[303] Memorandum for the Vice President *et al*, *supra* n 301, para 3.

humanely. This is a sweeping and innovative position, for which I could find no support in international legal materials.

• That the USA would nevertheless treat those detainees 'humanely'.

However, three crucial problems arise here.

Firstly, this *ex gratia* 'humane' treatment would be pursued 'as a matter of policy' rather than as a matter of the state's international legal obligations. This position was officially reiterated by the USA, for instance in a letter sent to the UN Commission on Human Rights in April 2003.[304]

Secondly, the USA may treat those detainees 'in a manner consistent with the principles of Geneva', but would only do so 'to the extent appropriate and consistent with military necessity'. While the Geneva Conventions in particular and international humanitarian law in general permit military necessity to play a role in deciding whether certain acts (such as destruction or appropriation of property) are lawful,[305] they prohibit other acts, such as targeting civilians and ill-treating detainees and prisoners, in all circumstances, regardless of whether or not these acts could be, or are perceived as being, militarily beneficial.[306] The USA thus downgraded the prohibition on torture and ill-treatment from a fundamental legal obligation applicable at all times to a policy option subjugated to considerations of military advantage.

Thirdly, the Geneva Conventions certainly does contain a 'principle' of humane treatment,[307] but since the President ordered that this 'principle', like the rest of

---

[304] Letter dated 2 April 2003 from the Permanent Mission of the United States of America to the United Nations Office at Geneva addressed to the secretariat of the Commission on Human Rights, UN Doc E/CN.4/2003/G/73, 7 April 2003, 4. See also the Secretary of Defense's *Memo for Commander, SOUTHCOM: Counter Resistance Technique in the War on Terrorism*, dated 16 April 2003 <http://www.defenselink.mil/news/Jun2004/d20040622doc9.pdf>, accessed 23 June 2004.

[305] See eg Convention (IV) respecting the Laws and Customs of War on Land and its annex: Regulations concerning the Laws and Customs of War on Land. The Hague, 18 October 1907, Arts 15, 23(g), 54. 1949 Geneva Convention III relative to the Treatment of Prisoners of War, Adopted on 12 August 1949, entered into force 21 October 1950, Art 126; 1949 Geneva Convention IV relative to the Protection of Civilian Persons in Time of War, Arts 56, 108, 143, 147; 1977 Geneva Protocol I Additional to the Geneva Conventions of 12 August 1949, and Relating to the Protection of Victims of International Armed Conflicts, adopted on 8 June 1977, entered into force 7 December 1978, Arts 54(2,5), 62(1), 67(4), 71(3).

For text of international humanitarian law treaties see eg A Roberts and R Guelff (eds), *Documents on the Laws of War* (3rd edn, Oxford: Clarendon, 2000), and the ICRC website <http://www.icrc.org>.

[306] See the discussion in Part IV, Ch 18 below. Military necessity may justify limiting visits to prisoners of war and internees, but 'only as an exceptional and temporary measure.' See Geneva Convention III, Art 126 and Geneva Convention IV, Art 143, respectively. Under Art 108 of the latter Convention, military necessity may also justify limiting the shipment of parcels to internees. This is the full extent to which international humanitarian law allows 'military necessity' to affect the treatment of detainees. There is one category of detainees, consisting mainly of spies and saboteurs, who are 'regarded as having forfeited rights of communication'. However, such detainees 'shall nevertheless be treated with humanity' and their communication rights must be restored 'at the earliest date consistent with the security of the State or Occupying Power, as the case may be'. See Geneva Convention IV, Art 5.

[307] See *infra*, Part IV, Ch 18.

the 'Geneva principles' would not apply where 'military necessity' dictates otherwise, the USA's policy would include instead the provision of what must, logically, be its own version of 'humane treatment'. Examples of that version will be shown below. The USA thus replaced a well-defined, internationally binding legal rule[308] with a non-legal notion to be defined by its own military commanders and politicians.[309]

This position did not remain on the level of theoretical statements. It was followed by an official policy combining a declaratory commitment to 'humane treatment' with actual detention and interrogation methods which were patently inhumane. Thus in his memorandum of January 2003, Secretary of Defense Donald Rumsfeld ordered that:

In all interrogations, you should *continue* the humane treatment of detainees, regardless of the type of interrogation technique employed.[310] [Emphasis added.]

Among such 'humane' techniques, which had been approved by Secretary Rumsfeld previously for use in Guantánamo, and under the later memorandum could still be used, albeit 'only' with Secretary Rumsfeld's prior approval, were:[311]

* 'The use of stress positions (like standing) for a maximum of four hours'.[312]
  'Use of the isolation facility for up to 30 days'.

* 'Deprivation of light and auditory stimuli'.

* Use of 'a hood placed over his head during transportation and questioning'.

---

[308] See *ibid.*

[309] In the eyes of at least one US commander, the issue of 'humane treatment' seems to be separate from that of interrogation methods. At a meeting with ICRC representatives in October 2003, Major-General Geoffrey D Miller, then Commander of the task force that runs the detention centre at Guantánamo Bay, responding to complaints on interrogation methods used at the centre (including the manipulation of the basic needs of detainees), stated that the detainees concerned '…are enemy combatants picked up on the field of battle in Afghanistan. There is no issue with interrogation methods. The focus of ICRC should be the level of humane detention being upheld not the interrogation methods. JTF GTMO [Joint Task Force Guantánamo] treats all detainees humanely' (Department of Defense Memorandum for Record, ICRC Meeting with MG Miller on 9 October 2003, <http://www.washingtonpost.com/wp-srv/nation/documents/GitmoMemo10–09-03.pdf>, accessed 4 September 2004).

[310] *Secretary of Defense Memorandum for the Department of Defense General Counsel Ref: Detainee interrogations* dated 15 January 2003, available eg at <http://www.defenselink.mil/news/Jun2004/d20040622doc7.pdf>, accessed 23 June 2004.

[311] As detailed in *Memorandum by Major General Michael E. Dunlover, Commander of Joint Task Force 170, Guantanamo Bay, Cuba, for Commander, United States Southern Command, SUBJ: Legal Review of aggressive interrogation techniques* dated 11 October 2002, available eg at <http://www.defenselink.mil/news/Jun2004/d20040622doc3.pdf>, accessed 23 June 2004.

[312] In approving this technique initially, Rumsfeld added the following, in handwriting: 'However, I stand for 8–10 hours a day. Why is standing limited to 4 hours? D.R.' *Action memo, For Secretary of Defense, from William J Haynes, General Counsel. Counter-Resistance Techniques.* 27 November 2002. Approved 2 December 2002, available eg at <http://www.defenselink.mil/news/Jun2004/d20040622doc5.pdf>, accessed 23 June 2004. It is not clear whether this remark had the effect of doubling, or otherwise increasing, at least for the time, the duration of that technique.

- 'Removal of clothing'.
- 20-hour interrogations.
- 'Using detainees individual phobias (such as fear of dogs) to induce stress'.
- 'Use of mild, non-injurious physical contact such as grabbing, poking in the chest with a finger and light pushing'.

There was no explicit limitation on combining some or all of these (and other listed) methods.

(b) The limited scope of 'torture'

According to the August 2002 DOJ memo:

Physical pain amounting to torture must be equivalent in intensity to the pain accompanying serious physical injury, such as organ failure, impairment of bodily function, or even death.[313]

This is stated in regard to US rather than international law. The legislation discussed (mainly, as seen, below, 18 US C § 2340) was enacted 'to implement'[314] the UN Convention against Torture, and contains some of the language of that Convention's definition. However, upon ratification of the Convention, the USA entered a series of reservations and understandings, concerning, *inter alia*, its interpretation of that definition,[315] and it is upon the revised definition emerging from those that the memorandum based the position quoted above.

For that reason, we need not go into the memorandum's definitional reasoning. Obviously, states can in practice define torture within their *domestic* legal system in whatever terms they choose, including in ways that have the effect of excluding interrogation techniques they intend to use from that definition. The question of whether torture was (or has been) nevertheless practised under this model in the terms used in this study, namely those of an *internationally* recognized legal definition, will be discussed in Part IV.

(c) The applicability of criminal law defences to officials
who torture in certain circumstances

Both the August 2002 DOJ memo and the Pentagon Working Group report suggested that officials who had tortured (according to the definition they

---

[313] August 2002 DOJ memo, *supra* n 283, 1. This argument is elaborated in 5–6.

[314] *Ibid*, 14. One paragraph is dedicated to the Convention's drafting process in this regard (*ibid*, 20–21) in support of the memorandum's understanding of the definition, but no mention is made in it of 'organ failure, impairment of bodily function, or even death' being essential for the threshold of torture to be crossed.

[315] US reservations, declarations, and understandings, Convention Against Torture and Other Cruel, Inhuman or Degrading Treatment or Punishment, Cong Rec S17486–01 (daily ed., Oct 27, 1990). For text see eg <http://www1.umn.edu/humanrts/usdocs/tortres.html>, accessed 14 February 2005.

propose) could be exempt from criminal liability under criminal law defences, the 'defence of necessity' and 'self-defence'.[316] The question of whether the former defence in its existing forms could provide legal grounds for torturing in a TBS will be discussed below, in Part IV, where US law is examined as a case in point, and where the applicability of the defence of 'self-defence' is also discussed, briefly. As of mid-2007, these defences have not been pleaded by torturers (although it must be noted that no one has as yet been charged with 'torture' as such) in front of US courts, let alone endorsed by them, in the context of the 'war on terror'. Later retroactive legislation providing for a blanket 'good faith' defence will be discussed below.

(d) The unlimited authority of the President at war

At the heart of the initial model, and serving as its ultimate fallback position, where torture under *any* definition would be justified and legal, lies the notion, explained and defended in detail by the August 2002 DOJ memo and the report of the Pentagon Working Group that:

> In order to respect the President's inherent constitutional authority to manage a military campaign, 18 USC. 2340A (the prohibition against torture) as well as any other potentially applicable statute must be construed as inapplicable to interrogations undertaken pursuant to his Commander-in-Chief authority. Congress lacks authority under Article 1 [of the US Constitution] to set the terms and conditions under which the President may exercise his authority as Commander-in-Chief to control the conduct of operations during a war. The President's power to detain and interrogate enemy combatants arises out of his constitutional authority as Commander in-Chief. A construction of Section 2340A that applied the provision to regulate the President's authority as Commander-in-Chief to determine the interrogation and treatment of enemy combatants would raise serious constitutional questions. Congress may no more regulate the President's ability to detain and interrogate enemy combatants than it may regulate his ability to direct troop movements in the battlefield. Accordingly, we would construe Section 2340A to avoid this constitutional difficulty, and conclude that it does not apply to the President's detention and interrogation of enemy combatants pursuant to his Commander-in-Chief authority.[317]

While arguing, for page after page, that torture is limited to acts that would cause pain 'associated with . . . death, organ failure, or serious impairment of body function'; that for death threats to be torturous the threat must be of 'imminent death';[318] that cruel, inhuman or degrading treatment or punishment are 'a category of acts that are not to be committed and that states must endeavour

---

[316] See August 2002 DOJ memo, *supra* n 283, 39–46; Pentagon Working Group report, *supra* n 294, 25–31. Both cite the definition of the 'defence of necessity' under the Model Penal Code, to be discussed *infra*, Part IV, Ch 19, Sections A(2)(a) and A(4).

[317] Pentagon Working Group report, *ibid*, 21. See similarly, August 2002 DOJ memo, *supra* n 283, 31–9.

[318] Pentagon Working Group report, *ibid*, 18.

to prevent, but... need not criminalize';[319] and that certain (in effect all) human rights and humanitarian law treaties do not apply to the 'war on terror' generally and to detained terrorist suspects in particular, the August 2002 DOJ memo and the Pentagon Working Group report claim here, in effect, that none of this matters: the President is authorized by the US Constitution to order *absolutely anything he wishes* in his capacity as Commander-in-Chief of US forces during war,[320] as no laws, either international or national, can touch him. More specifically, the President is constitutionally authorized to order the torture of detained terrorist suspects.

This caused problems for the FBI, an email from whose 'on scene commander— Baghdad' in May 2004, refers to an instruction to FBI personnel in Iraq, 'not to participate in interrogations by military personnel which might include techniques authorized by Executive Order but beyond the bounds of standard FBI practice'.[321] The email seeks clarifications regarding another instruction, from FBI's Office of General Counsel (OGC), requiring FBI personnel to report any 'abuse' that they may witness, and poses an interesting dilemma:

This instruction begs the question of what constitutes 'abuse'. We assume this does not include lawful interrogation techniques authorized by Executive Order. We are aware that prior to a revision in policy last week, an Executive Order signed by President Bush authorized the following interrogation techniques among others: sleep 'management', use of MWDs (military working dogs), 'stress positions' such as half squats, 'environmental manipulation' such as use of loud music, sensory deprivation through the use of hoods, etc. We assume the OGC instruction does not include the reporting of these authorized interrogation techniques, and that the use of these techniques does not constitute 'abuse'.[322]

---

[319] August 2002 DOJ memo, *supra* n 283, 15. In January 2005, during Senate deliberations of his nomination for Attorney General, Alberto R Gonzales gave a slightly different version: 'As you know, when the Senate ratified the Convention Against Torture, it took a reservation and said that our requirements under Article 16 were equal to our requirements under the Fifth, Eighth and 14th Amendment. As you also know, it has been a long-time position of the executive branch, and a position that's been recognized and reaffirmed by the Supreme Court of the United States, that aliens interrogated by the US outside the United States enjoy no substantive rights under the Fifth, Eighth and 14th Amendment. So as a legal matter, we are in compliance' (*Transcript of the Senate Judiciary Committee's hearings on the nomination of Alberto R. Gonzales to be attorney general as transcribed by Federal News Service*, 6 January 2005, <http://www.nytimes. com/2005/01/06/politics/06TEXT-GONZALES.html?oref=login&pagewanted=print& position=>, accessed 7 January 2005).

[320] By a joint resolution adopted on 21 September 2001 and entitled Authorization for Use of Military Force (Enrolled Bill), S.J.Res.23, the US Congress authorized the President 'to use all necessary and appropriate force against those nations, organizations, or persons' which he determines were involved in the 9/11 attacks.

[321] Email from REDACTED to MC Briese, Gary Bald, TJ Harrington, Frankie Battle and other redacted parties Re Request for Guidance regarding OGC EC, dated 19 May 2004, signed [REDACTED], 'On scene Commander—Baghdad' <http://www.aclu.org/torturefoia/released/ FBI.121504.4940_4941.pdf>, accessed 22 December 2004.

[322] *Ibid.*

The Secretary of Defense's instructions regarding 'interrogation techniques' are another, officially acknowledged example, which goes beyond the listing of authorized techniques. While later memoranda have limited the scope of 'techniques' which military interrogators may use routinely, the Secretary of Defense has left an opening for unspecified—and potentially unlimited—'additional interrogation techniques':

> If, in your [ie Commander of US Southern Command's] view, you require additional interrogation techniques for a particular detainee, you should provide me, via the Chairman of the Joint Chiefs of Staff, a written request describing the proposed technique, recommended safeguards, and the rationale for applying it with an identified detainee.[323]

This 'blue-sky thinking' approach to interrogation methods may still be in force as this book is finalized, in mid-2007.

As an attempt, in summing up the HVD model's initial legal position, to run a narrative thread through the various arguments, I would suggest that it proceeds as follows:

1. International laws prohibiting torture and ill-treatment do not apply to terrorists, except for the prohibition on torture in the UN Convention Against Torture, *but…*

2. this prohibition covers only the most severe acts of brutality, while other prohibitions (on cruel, inhuman and degrading treatment) are weak, vague and may be neglected, so that interrogation methods which fall within the administration's concept of 'humane treatment' are lawful, *and at any rate…*

3. torturers may be exempted from criminal liability through the pleas of 'defence of necessity' and 'self-defence', *and ultimately…*

4. during war, the President is authorized under the Constitution to issue orders to torture.

2. Interrogation methods I: Incommunicado detention, 'ghost detainees', 'black sites'[324]

As in the Israeli models, US interrogations have invariably been carried out away from the prying eyes of the outside world, but the USA has used this method far more intensively.

---

[323] Secretary of Defense' *Memo for Commander, SOUTHCOM* 16 April 2003, *supra* n 304.

[324] See generally eg Amnesty International, *Human Dignity Denied, supra* n 287, point 3.1, 100–106; Human Rights Watch, *The United States' "Disappeared": The CIA's Long-Term "Ghost Detainees"* (Briefing paper, October 2004 <http://www.hrw.org/backgrounder/usa/us1004/us1004.pdf>, accessed 14 April 2005). For a summary of media and (other) human rights NGO reports on the subject of 'ghost detainees' see letter from Barbara Olshansky *et al* of the Center for Constitutional Rights re: Request submitted under the Freedom of Information Act to Scott A Kotch, Information and Privacy Coordinator, Central Intelligence Agency, 21 December 2004, available on the organization's website <http://www.ccr-ny.org>, accessed 30 December 2004. The

According to the Schlesinger report, the USA had up to that time operated approximately 25 detention facilities in Afghanistan, and another 17 in Iraq.[325] In addition, it held people in Guantánamo Bay and elsewhere. Lawyers and relatives were systematically denied access to detainees. While the ICRC (eventually) had access to most detainees, this was often facilitated only after a considerable delay. For example, the ICRC had access to detainees held in the US air base in Bagram in Afghanistan, but not immediately following their arrest. In addition, more remote 'CPs' (collection posts) at 'point of capture' in both Afghanistan and Iraq, seemed to be less—or not—accessible to ICRC visits, and for the first two years detainees were held at such facilities for as long as 30 days, instead of the 12 hours allowed under US army doctrine.[326] This period appears to have been subsequently reduced, but not to below two weeks.[327]

In addition, specific detainees, held under the CIA's 'High-Value Terrorist Detainee Program',[328] were held in total secrecy for months and years. Some were held, during the initial period of the 'war on terror', within recognized detention facilities such as Guantánamo Bay, Camp Cropper (the HVD facility in Baghdad airport) and Bagram airbase and deliberately kept away from ICRC delegates. Others were held in undisclosed places of detention all over the world.[329] In September 2004, General Paul Kern, who had overseen the Fay investigation, stated that the number of 'ghost detainees' was 'in the dozens, to perhaps up to 100'.[330]

CCR submitted similar requests (to receive all relevant material) to the Departments of Defense, Justice and State.

For a detailed study of secret CIA prisons in Europe see Committee on Legal Affairs and Human Rights, Parliamentary Assembly, Council of Europe, *Secret detentions and illegal transfers of detainees involving Council of Europe member states: second report*, 11 June 2007, <http://assembly.coe.int/Documents/WorkingDocs/Doc07/edoc11302.pdf>, accessed 25 October 2007.

[325] Schlesinger report, *supra* n 278, 11.

[326] Department of the Army, the Inspector General, *Detainee Operations Inspection*, 21 July 2004, available eg on <http://www.globalsecurity.org/military/library/report/2004/daig_detainee-ops_21jul2004.pdf>, accessed 30 December 2004, 28.

[327] This is according to information I have received in my Amnesty International capacity. See more generally the statement of the ICRC: 'The ICRC has had regular access to the persons detained at Bagram, but not immediately after their arrest' (ICRC Operational update, 'US detention related to the events of 11 September 2001 and its aftermath—the role of the ICRC' <http://www.icrc.org/Web/Eng/siteeng0.nsf/html/66FGEL?OpenDocument>, 29 March 2005, accessed 13 April 2005).

[328] See *supra* n 280.

[329] According to *The Guardian*, the USA used 'dozens of facilities in Pakistan, Uzbekistan, Jordan, Egypt, Thailand, Malaysia, Indonesia and the British island of Diego Garcia in the southern Indian Ocean' (A Levy and C Scott-Clark, 'One huge US jail' *The Guardian* (19 March 2005). The study for the European Parliament found that 'secret detention operations' were carried out in Poland and Rumania. See *supra* n 324, parts III and IV, respectively.

[330] Oral testimony before the Senate Armed Services Committee, 9 September 2004, quoted in D Priest, 'Memo Lets CIA Take Detainees Out of Iraq Practice Is Called Serious Breach of Geneva Conventions' *Washington Post* (24 October 2004).

In September 2006, US President Bush revealed that 14 HVDs had been transferred to Guantánamo Bay, thus officially acknowledging the secret detention programme. President Bush declared that '[t]he current transfers mean that there are now no terrorists in the CIA program' but made it clear that the 'program' is ongoing.[331]

3. Interrogation methods II: more direct methods

Two facts should be borne in mind when considering the US's other interrogation methods. Firstly, all methods listed in the various official documents released so far have referred to the US military. The other main arm of the US government which has been interrogating terrorist suspects in the 'war on terror', the CIA,[332] has remained to a large extent in the shadows, its interrogation methods remain classified at the highest level of secrecy, and information regarding them comes almost entirely from unofficial sources such as the media and human rights NGO reports. This, and the much slower pace of investigations into abuse by CIA agents,[333] and the fact that none of them has been prosecuted, make it difficult to provide a credible, let alone exhaustive, list of approved direct techniques.

Secondly, as noted, even the military's list of interrogation methods was (and arguably is) ultimately open-ended, and the Secretary of Defense consistently left himself the option of approving undefined, therefore, at least in theory unlimited 'additional interrogation techniques' in individual cases where the need for them is perceived as arising.[334]

(a) Official acknowledgement (1)—military techniques

Various lists of Pentagon-approved interrogation methods for use by the US military at Guantánamo were approved, rescinded and modified between October 2002 and April 2003. The former date was when, according to a Department of Defense report, 'the initial push for interrogation techniques beyond those

---

[331] 'President Discusses Creation of Military Commissions ...' *supra* n 275, And see below, at the conclusion of this Chapter.

[332] Both these services appear to have also sub-contracted some interrogation operations to private contractors. There is little sense in addressing these operations, or operators, separately in the present study, as neither legal nor moral responsibilities may be sub-contracted in this fashion.

[333] As of mid-2007, only one civilian—a sub-contractor of the CIA rather than an agent— has faced criminal charges for ill-treating detainees. According to the *New York Times*, the CIA's Inspector General reviewed 'at least a half-dozen other cases, and perhaps many more.' D Jehl and D Johnston, 'Within CIA, Growing Worry of Prosecution for Conduct', *New York Times* (27 February 2005). In comparison, around that time the *Washington Post* cited Department of Defense figures to the effect that 33 'military workers' had faced courts-martial and another 55 reprimanded for 'mishandling' detainees. D Priest, 'CIA Avoids Scrutiny of Detainee Treatment' *Washington Post* (3 March 2005). See further data below, Ch 15, Section D(2)(a).

[334] See *supra*, n 323 and accompanying text.

found in FM 34–52[335] came' as the latter 'have at times proven inadequate in the Global War on Terror'.[336] The initiative, originating from Major General Michael E Dunlavey, Commander of Joint Task Force 170, Guantánamo Bay, Cuba,[337] contains a list of interrogation methods which was then proposed to Secretary of Defense Rumsfeld. The latter date was when Secretary Rumsfeld approved a list of methods for Guantánamo Bay.

As noted, in December 2002 Secretary Rumsfeld allowed the use of a list comprising of most of the methods proposed in that memorandum.[338] In January 2003, Secretary Rumsfeld established a working group 'to assess the legal, policy and operational issues relating to the interrogation of detainees held by the US Armed Forces in the war on terrorism'.[339] Concurrently Secretary Rumsfeld rescinded his approval of the aforementioned methods, ordering that they can only be used in individual cases following authorization from him. [340]

The Working Group recommended the use of 35 techniques (listed in an annex to its report), but Secretary Rumsfeld rejected the most severe ones (including 20-hour interrogations, prolonged standing, sleep deprivation, slapping and the 'simple presence of dogs'), approving 24 techniques out of the Working Group list for use at Guantánamo Bay.[341] Attached to this list were 'general safeguards', which include ensuring that 'the detainee is medically and operationally evaluated as suitable (considering all techniques to be used in combination)', that proper authorization and supervision are in place, that an 'interrogation plan' stipulating, *inter alia*, limits on duration, intervals between applications and 'termination criteria' is set out. Methods are to be 'always applied in a humane and lawful manner'.[342] However, the 'general safeguards' also state the following:

It is important that interrogators be provided reasonable latitude to vary techniques depending on the detainee's culture, strengths, weaknesses, environment, extent of

---

[335] The US Army field manual for interrogations, issued originally in 1987: Headquarters, Department of the Army, *FM 34–52 Intelligence Interrogation*, Washington, DC, 8 May 1987, <http://www.globalsecurity.org/intell/library/policy/army/fm/fm34–52/>, accessed 6 March 2005. A revised version was issued in 1992—Headquarters, Department of the Army, *FM 34–52 Intelligence Interrogation*, Washington, DC, 28 September 1992 <http://www.fas.org/irp/doddir/army/fm34–52.pdf>, accessed 8 April 2005. However, the latter version seems to have been largely ignored. Discussing 'Interrogation Historical Review' the Pentagon Working Group report speaks of 'the issuance of current doctrine in 1987 (FM 34–52)' without mentioning the 1992 update. See *supra* n 294, 51. Footnote added. The 2006 field manual will be discussed *infra*, Ch 15, Section D(3).

[336] Vice Admiral Albert T Church III, [US] Department of Defense, Review of Detention Operations and Interrogation Techniques – Executive Summary, <http://www.dod.mil/cgi-bin/dlprint.cgi?http://www.dod.mil/transcripts/2005/tr20050310–2262.html>, accessed 16 March 2005, 5, 1, respectively.

[337] *Memo for Commander, United States Southern Command*, 11 October 2002, *supra* n 311.

[338] See *supra* n 311 and accompanying text.

[339] *Secretary of Defense Memorandum*, *supra* n 310.

[340] *Ibid*.

[341] Secretary of Defense's *Memo for Commander, SOUTHCOM*; 16 April 2003, *supra* n 304, TAB A.

[342] *Ibid*, TAB B.

training in resistance techniques as well as the urgency of obtaining information that the detainee is known to have.[343]

In addition, there is a hint in the 'general safeguards' that other 'policies' may be used as pressure techniques:

The policies established by the detaining units that pertain to searching, silencing, and segregating also play a role in the interrogation of a detainee.[344]

In other words, interrogators may, as in the Landau model, resort to out-of-the-interrogations-room methods—searches, including stripping (see the example below), 'silencing' (possibly involving some type of gagging device) and 'segregating' (possibly hooding or isolation methods different from technique X above).

Most crucially for our purposes, Secretary Rumsfeld added, as noted, a 'blue skies' clause opening the possibility of using unnamed and potentially unlimited, 'additional interrogation techniques for a particular detainee'.[345] An example of such procedures may be found in a 'request for exception' to interrogation policies followed in Abu Ghraib detention centre, Iraq, submitted in November 2003, which involved *inter alia* threats, 'sleep adjustment', use of dogs, loud music and stress positions.[346]

(b) Official acknowledgement (2)—CIA techniques

Unlike the techniques used by the military, no lists have been provided by CIA officials or their politician superiors, and the official investigations—at least the published ones—have largely ignored CIA interrogations, although, as seen, their apparent authority to hold detainees in total secrecy was noted.[347] Thus regarding CIA interrogations in Iraq, the Schlesinger report noted that:

No memorandum of understanding existed on interrogations operations between the CIA and CJTF-7, and the CIA was allowed to operate under different rules.[348]

A glimpse of these 'different rules' was offered in March 2005 by the CIA director, Porter J Goss. During his testimony before the Senate Armed Services Committee, the following exchange took place:

---

[343] *Ibid.*
[344] *Ibid.*
[345] See *supra*, text accompanying n 323.
[346] Thomas M Pappas, COL, MI, Memorandum for Commander, CJTF-7, LTG Sanchez, Subject: Request for Exception to CJTF- 7 Interrogation and Counter Resistance Policy, 30 November 2003, <http://www.publicintegrity.org/docs/AbuGhraib/Abu7.pdf>, accessed 28 March 2005. Col Pappas commanded The 'Joint Interrogation and Debriefing Center, Abu Ghraib' and Lieutenant-General Ricardo Sanchez headed US forces in Iraq. The memorandum was annexed (annex no unclear) to the Taguba report, *supra* n 45.
[347] See *supra*, Ch 15, Section B(2).
[348] Schlesinger report, *supra* n 278, 70.

SEN. MCCAIN: Well, some of those policies at one time were to make one have the prisoner feel that they were drowning.

MR. GOSS: You're getting into, again, an area of what I will call professional interrogation techniques...[349]

Nevertheless, instructions, and possibly lists of approved interrogation techniques applicable to HVDs, have in all likelihood been issued. A Human Rights First statement lists, among documents which, the organization demands, should be released to the Senate Judiciary Committee, a 'DOJ memorandum to Alberto Gonzales specifying interrogation methods that the CIA may use against Al Qaeda leaders'.[350] According to a CIA agent, a DoJ memorandum dated 1 August 2002, advised the CIA on the legality of 'alternative interrogation methods by which the CIA seeks to collect critical foreign intelligence to disrupt terrorist attacks'.[351] As of mid-2007, no such documents have been released.

(c) Interrogation techniques used according to other sources

As CIA agents worked alongside the military in Afghanistan, Guantánamo Bay and Iraq, and detainees and other unofficial sources are often not aware of the exact identity of the interrogators, I will not attempt to separate the two in this section, though some of the reports cited do point to one or the other.[352] Nor will I, in view of the impossibility of exhaustively covering the huge volume of evidence, which was still surfacing in mid-2007,[353] attempt to offer more than a handful of illustrations.

---

[349] Hearing of the Senate Armed Services Committee. Subject: Threats to US National Security. 17 March 2005. The Transcript is available at <http://www.humanrightsfirst.org/us_law/etn/docs/fedwires125g.htm>, accessed 9 April 2005.

[350] See <http://www.humanrightsfirst.org/us_law/etn/gonzales/statements/release-docs-gonzlaels-012105.pdf>, accessed 21 January 2005.

[351] See *ACLU et al v Department of Defense et al*, Sixth Declaration of Marilyn A Dorn, Information Review Officer, Central Intelligence Agency, in the US District Court, Southern District of New York, 5 January 2007.

[352] See particularly the detailed description and in-depth analysis of 10 CIA techniques in Physicians for Human Rights and Human Rights First, *Leave No Marks: Enhanced Interrogation Techniques and the Risk of Criminality*, August 2007 <http://physiciansforhumanrights.org/library/documents/reports/leave-no-marks.pdf>, accessed 14 August 2007.

[353] A primary source of such information has been official documents, revealed following lawsuits led by the American Civil Liberties Union (ACLU) under the US Freedom of Information Act, 5 USC § 552, following a series of orders by a New York District Court. See eg *ACLU et al v Department of the Army et al*, Opinion and Order of September 15, 2004, 339 F Supp 2d 501 (SDNY 2004). They are available at the ACLU website, <http://www.aclu.org.>. See also Amnesty International, *Human Dignity Denied*, supra n 287, *passim*; Amnesty International, *United States of America: Guantánamo and beyond: The continuing pursuit of unchecked executive power*, AI Index: AMR 51/063/2005, 13 May 2005, Chapters 12, 13 and Appendix 3; Human Rights Watch, *The Road to Abu Ghraib*, June 2004, esp Ch. IV; Physicians for Human Rights, *Break them down: systematic use of psychological torture by US forces* (Cambridge, Mass: Physicians for Human Rights 2005) especially Ch III.

The first detailed description of US interrogation techniques was published in December 2002 in a *Washington Post* article.[354] The article claims that much of the interrogation of key *al-Qa'idah* suspects took place 'at the US-occupied Bagram air base in Afghanistan...' in 'a cluster of metal shipping containers protected by a triple layer of concertina wire' or within other 'interrogation facilities' which 'are off-limits to outsiders, and often even to other government agencies'. When first arrested:

...captives are often 'softened up' by MPs and US Army Special Forces troops who beat them up and confine them in tiny rooms. The alleged terrorists are commonly blindfolded and thrown into walls, bound in painful positions, subjected to loud noises and deprived of sleep. The tone of intimidation and fear is the beginning, they said, of a process of piercing a prisoner's resistance.

The take-down teams often 'package' prisoners for transport, fitting them with hoods and gags, and binding them to stretchers with duct tape.[355]

Detainees still refusing to cooperate with their interrogators:

...are sometimes kept standing or kneeling for hours, in black hoods or spray-painted goggles, according to intelligence specialists familiar with CIA interrogation methods. At times they are held in awkward, painful positions and deprived of sleep with a 24-hour bombardment of lights—subject to what are known as 'stress and duress' techniques.[356]

Alternately, they are:

...turned over...to foreign intelligence services whose practice of torture has been documented by the US government and human rights organizations.[357]

As mentioned, the report states that in the particular case of Abu Zubaida, who had been shot during his arrest, painkillers were used sparingly as an additional

---

[354] D Priest and B Gellman, 'US Decries Abuse but Defends Interrogations: "Stress and Duress" Tactics Used on Terrorism Suspects Held in Secret Overseas Facilities' *Washington Post* (26 December 2002) at A01. For an earlier media report see eg M Elliott, 'The Next Wave' *Time Magazine* (17 June 2002) which describes the interrogation of a suspected *al-Qa'idah* leader as follows: 'Abu Zubaydah, say CIA and other US government sources, is not being tortured, but a variety of methods are being used to encourage him to talk. Typical military interrogation tactics would include depriving him of sleep, changing the temperature of his cell and "modulating caloric intakes"—spookspeak for withholding food and then providing it as a reward.' For later (but pre-Abu Ghraib scandal) reports see eg P Harris and B Wazir, 'Briton tells of ordeal in Bush's torture jail' *The Observer* (29 December 2002), <http://observer.guardian.co.uk>, accessed 30 December 2002; S Johnson, 'Unraveling the psyche of al-Qaida: Experts say painful torture is wrong method for questioning Mohammed' MSNBC News website <http://www.msnbc.com/news/881132. asp>, 5 March 2003, accessed 21 May 2003; O Craig, '"They will do what is needed to get the information—and fast"' *The Daily Telegraph* (9 March 2003); M Orecklin, 'Why They Crack' *Time Magazine* (24 June 2003); Bowden, *supra* n 4; J Risen, D Johnston and NA Lweis, 'Harsh CIA Methods Cited in Top Qaeda Interrogations' *New York Times* (13 May 2004).

[355] Priest and Gellman, *ibid*.

[356] *Ibid.*

[357] *Ibid.* The issue of transferring detainees to be tortured by other states ('renditions' or 'extra-ordinary renditions'), clearly unlawful under both treaty and customary international law, will not be discussed here.

method of interrogation.[358] Regarding Khalid Sheikh Muhammad, another alleged high-ranking *al-Qa'idah* leader, a newspaper report claimed that:

...interrogators used graduated levels of force, including a technique known as 'water boarding,' in which a prisoner is strapped down, forcibly pushed under water and made to believe he might drown.[359]

According to official documents seen by the Associated Press in early 2005,[360] Manadel al-Jamadi, an Iraqi whose corpse was photographed among smiling US soldiers at Abu Ghraib in November 2003, had died under CIA interrogation while suspended by his wrists, which had been handcuffed behind his back, a method known as 'Palestinian hanging'.[361] Like 'water boarding', this method is not to be found in any disclosed list of approved methods but since, as the European Court of Human Rights observed, 'this treatment could only have been deliberately inflicted; indeed, a certain amount of preparation and exertion would have been required to carry it out',[362] it too may have nevertheless been approved for CIA use as a 'professional interrogation technique'.

According to a February 2004 report by the ICRC, interrogation methods which 'appeared to be part of the standard operating procedures by military intelligence personnel'[363] in Iraq, and used 'in a systematic way to gain confessions and extract information or other forms of co-operation'.[364] The report listed some of the methods of sexual humiliation, beating and the use of dogs described by General Taguba,[365] but also methods of the 'stress and duress' type, including hooding (for 'up to 2 to 4 consecutive days'); solitary confinement, naked in dark cells; threats (including towards family members); 'sleep, food or water deprivation'; prolonged shackling; exposure to loud noise or music; exposure to the sun for hours ('including the hottest time of the day when temperatures could reach 50 degrees Celsius'); and being forced into 'stress positions such as squatting or standing with or without the arms lifted'.[366]

An FBI agent described scenes s/he had been witness to in Guantánamo Bay:

On a couple of occasions, I entered interview rooms to find a detainee chained hand and foot in a fetal position to the floor, with no chair, food or water. Most times they had

---

[358] Priest and Gellman, *ibid*, and see Part II, Ch 9, Section D(2)(h), fn 220 and accompanying text.

[359] Risen, Johnston and Neil, *supra* n 354.

[360] 'AP: Abu Ghraib Inmate Died in '"Palestinian Hanging"'', Foxnews website, <http://www.foxnews.com/story/0,2933,147957,00.html>, 17 February 2005, accessed 17 February 2005.

[361] For a description of this method see eg *Aksoy v Turkey*, ECHR *Reports* 1996-VI, Judgment of 18 December 1996, paras 14, 23, 60 and 64 (where the Court rules that this method amounts to torture).

[362] *Ibid*, para 64.

[363] ICRC report, *supra* n 282, para 24.

[364] *Ibid*, para 26. The report cites detainees' complaints, but states that US military personnel and its own medical staff have confirmed the veracity of these claims, see *ibid*, paras 24, 27 (the latter detailing an incident where ICRC delegates actually witnessed 'a variety of methods' being used at Abu Ghraib).

[365] See Part II, Ch 9, Section E.

[366] ICRC report, *supra* n 282, para 25.

urinated or defecated on themselves and had been left there for 18, 24 hours or more. On one occasion, the air conditioning had been turned down so far and the temperature was so cold in the room, that the barefooted detainee was shaking with cold. When I asked the MPs what was going on, I was told that interrogators from the day prior had ordered this treatment, and the detainee was not to be moved. On another occasion, the A/C had been turned off, making the temperature in the unventilated room probably well over 100 degrees. The detainee was almost unconscious on the floor with a pile of hair next to him. He had apparently been literally pulling his own hair out throughout the night. On another occasion, not only was the temperature unbearably hot, but extremely loud rap music was being played in the room, and had been since the day before, with the detainee chained hand and foot in the fetal position on the tile floor.[367]

According to Human Rights First and Physicians for Human Rights, the CIA's 'enhanced interrogation techniques' included ten methods: stress positions; beating; temperature manipulation; waterboarding; threats of harm to person, family or friends; sleep deprivation; sensory bombardment (noise and light); violent shaking; sexual humiliation; prolonged isolation and sensory deprivation.[368]

The Council of Europe's Parliamentary Assembly investigation found, *inter alia*, that detainees in CIA secret prisons were exposed, in addition to secret, incommunicado detention for months and years, to 'months of *solitary confinement and extreme sensory deprivation* in cramped cells, shackled and handcuffed at all times',[369] including where for a period (or more) of 'over 120 days, absolutely no human contact was granted with anyone but masked, silent guards';[370] to extreme cold or heat;[371] to being 'regularly forced into *contorted shapes* and chained to [a] ring [in the wall] for long, painful periods';[372] and to 'a constant, low-level hum of white noise' loud music or other disturbing noises from loudspeakers.[373]

C. Evaluation 1—the HVD Model Before the Abu Ghraib Scandal

A quantitative evaluation of this system is much more difficult than of the previous ones. As noted, the USA has detained tens of thousands of persons during the first few years of its 'war on terror'.[374] Only a relatively small number of people have 'officially' been detained as HVDs.[375]

---

[367] E-mail from REDACTED to REDACTED, <http://www.aclu.org/torturefoia/released/FBI.121504.5053.pdf>, accessed 30 December 2004.

[368] See *Leave No Marks*, *supra* n 352. The techniques are described in detail, as are their physical and psychological effects, and their resultant status in (US) law.

[369] See *supra* n 324, para 247.

[370] *Ibid*, para 252.

[371] *Ibid*, para 254.

[372] *Ibid*, para 266.

[373] *Ibid*, para 268.

[374] See *supra* n 278.

[375] 'Fewer than 100' have been 'placed in the [CIA] program' according to CIA Director, General Michael V Hayden. See 'Director's Statement on Executive Order on Detentions,

It is virtually impossible to assess how many been subjected to the interrogation techniques described above, and even more difficult to assess in how many of the latter cases such techniques were used because the situation was considered to be a TBS, or the detainee classified an HVD.[376] What is nevertheless known, is that a few dozens have died in US custody, many of them in interrogation-related incidents;[377] that a variety of interrogation techniques have been used widely and even, according to the ICRC, 'in a systematic way'; and that at least some of them, according to that same organization, 'might amount to torture'.[378] Dozens have also been held and interrogated, including by the CIA, beyond the reach of the ICRC, where a range of no less harsh interrogation techniques have been reported.

Likewise, a legal assessment of this model, even at that initial stage, is far more difficult than of its Israeli predecessors. The HVD model at that stage involved no legislation or court decisions explicitly legalizing brutality in interrogations or exempting individual torturers from legal sanction. However, (lower) federal courts supported the government's view that non-citizens being held by US forces outside its territory could not resort to US courts in any event. In 2003, the DC Circuit Court, ruling in three similar cases it had consolidated, summed this position in no uncertain terms:

They [Guantánamo Bay detainees] cannot seek release based on violations of the Constitution or treaties or federal law; the courts are not open to them. Whatever other relief the detainees seek, their claims necessarily rest on alleged violations of the same category of laws listed in the habeas corpus statute, and are therefore beyond the jurisdiction of the federal courts.[379]

Interrogations', 20 July 2007, <https://www.cia.gov/news-information/press-releases-statements/statement-on-executive-order.html>, accessed 13 August 2007.

[376] 'Well under' 50, according to the CIA Director, *ibid*. It is unclear, however, what Gen Hayden considers as 'enhanced interrogation measures'—certainly not being 'placed in the program', that is, being forcibly disappeared for months or years and held in extreme isolation.

[377] In May 2005, a newspaper report included the following: 'A recent Army report counted 27 detainees who died under military supervision in those two countries [Afghanistan and Iraq] as a result of homicide or suspected homicide, and new anecdotal evidence suggests others may have died during CIA interrogations' (D Westphal, 'The spread of terrorism muddies torture debate' *The Star Tribune* (8 May 2005)<http://www.startribune.com/stories/484/5391312.html>, accessed 9 May 2005). See also eg Hina Shamsi, *Command's Responsibility: Detainee Deaths in U.S. Custody in Iraq and Afghanistan* (Deborah Pearlstein ed. New York: Human Rights First, February 2006) <http://www.humanrightsfirst.info/pdf/06221-etn-hrf-dic-rep-web.pdf>, accessed 14 April 2006.

[378] Report of the International Committee of the Red Cross, *supra* n 279, para 24. See discussion *infra*, Part IV, Ch 18.

[379] *Al Odah Khaled AF et al v United States et al*, No 02–5251, US DC Cir (2003), at III. In addition to *Al Odah*, a case brought by relatives of Kuwaiti detainees in Guantánamo Bay claiming mainly denial of due process guarantees under the US constitution and international law, the Court considered two petitions for writs of *habeas corpus* by Guantánamo Bay detainees dismissed by the DC District Court, *Rasul v Bush*, 215 F Supp 2d 55 (US District Ct for DC 2002); and *Habib v Bush* (No 02–5284). The Court relied heavily on *Johnson v Eisentrager*, 339 US 763 (1950), a petition for writs of *habeas corpus* by German civilians tried and imprisoned by the US army, having worked for the Japanese forces at the end of World War II, after Nazi Germany had capitulated, which the

It may reasonably be argued that at that point in time (11 March 2003), between, on the one hand, the administration's orders and legal memoranda determining, *inter alia*, that (a) the President may order the torture of certain detainees and (b) US courts have no jurisdiction over certain detainees; and, on the other, the *Al Odah* decision accepting the latter determination, thus by definition ruling out judicial intervention concerning any such Presidential order, a legal system, or model, was (at least briefly) in operation in the USA where torture was fully legalized, albeit not acknowledged.

However, this model has undergone several changes since, including significant ones, the attempts, as it were, to operate it as a 'secrecy model', having failed spectacularly with the exposure of the Abu Ghraib photos in the US media in April 2004. To these changes we now turn.

D. Later Developments, 2004 to 2007

1. December 2004 Department of Justice memorandum

In December 2004, the Department of Justice issued—and immediately published—a memorandum which, in its own words, 'supersedes the August 2002 Memorandum in its entirety'. It starts with the declaration that '[t]orture is abhorrent both to American law and values and to international norms'.[380] In terms of the legal analysis of the HVD model offered above, the memorandum deals a blow to the second legal argument, and to point 2 of the narrative offered at the end of that analysis.[381] However, the latter memo's anti-torture rhetoric notwithstanding, the other elements remained intact.[382]

The memo rejects its predecessor's position that to amount to torture—under US law—acts must result in 'serious physical injury, such as organ failure, impairment of bodily function, or even death'[383]: as the December 2004 memo states, 'we disagree' with such 'statements'.[384] It also rejects the August 2002 memo's

---

Supreme Court rejected. The later twists and turns in these and other cases are discussed below, in Ch 15, Section D(2).

[380] Daniel Levin, Acting Assistant Attorney General, *Memorandum for James B. Comey, Deputy Attorney General, Regarding Legal Standards Applicable Under 18 USC. §§ 2340–2340A,* 30 December 2004. For text see eg Greenberg and Dratel, *supra* n 283, 361–76. [henceforth: December 2004 memo], 1. The memorandum was annexed to the Second Periodic Report of the USA to CAT, *supra* n 369. For an analysis see eg Karen J Greenberg (ed), *The Torture Debate in America* (New York: New York University Press 2006) 361–376; Luban, *supra* n 287, 1456–8; HH Koh, 'Can the President Be Torturer in Chief?' 81 *Indiana L J* 1145 (2006), *passim*; WB Wendel, 'Legal Ethics and the Separation of Law and Morals' 91 *Cornell L Rev* 67 (2005), *passim*.

[381] Chapter 13, Section B(1).

[382] Issues such as the applicability of international treaties to terrorist suspects were not covered by this memo.

[383] See *supra* n 310 and accompanying text.

[384] December 2004 memo, *supra* n 380, 2.

position that to amount to torture, acts must be 'specifically intended' to cause severe pain or suffering,[385] therefore, even if an interrogator knew that his or her acts would result in such pain or suffering but did not intend this result, or acted 'with a good faith belief' that the acts would not have such a result, the acts would not constitute torture:[386] the December 2004 memo states that 'the term "specific intent" is ambiguous and...the [US] courts do not use it consistently.'[387] It then goes on to distinguish between clear cases where severe pain of suffering is 'consciously desired' and the act would constitute torture, and acts which resulted in such pain or suffering despite the perpetrator's 'reasonable investigations' and good faith, where it would not. Significantly, the memo adds that:

...specific intent must be distinguished from motive. There is no exception under the statute permitting torture to be used for a 'good reason'.[388]

On the issues of the President's unlimited authority and the availability of defences, the December 2004 memo states the following:

Because the discussion in that memorandum concerning the President's Commander-in-Chief power and the potential defenses to liability was—and remains—unnecessary, it has been eliminated from the analysis that follows. Consideration of the bounds of any such authority would be inconsistent with the President's unequivocal directive that United States personnel not engage in torture.[389]

This, however, leaves both avenues open at least as options. On the first issue, reference is made, in a footnote, to the US President's statement on the United Nations International Day in Support of Victims of Torture in June 2004 condemning torture as 'always wrong' and pledging to 'investigate and prosecute all acts of torture'.[390] There are two crucial problems with this approach. Firstly, it relies solely on the incumbent President's own words—this appears more like a claim that the President can be trusted not to exercise his authority to order torture than that he lacks such authority. In this sense it actually reinforces the position of the August 2002 DOJ memo, that ultimately decisions on these matters rest entirely with the President. Secondly, the US President had issued a very similar statement on United Nations International Day in Support of Victims of Torture in June 2003. This was at a time when, in (legal) principle, the August 2002 memo was 'in force', reflecting the US administration's legal

---

[385] The term 'specifically intended' is used in the definition of torture in *18 USC § 2340(1)*, which relies on the US's declared 'understanding' of the Article 1(1) definition of torture in the UN Convention Against Torture, see *supra* n 315, sec II(1)(a).

[386] See August 2002 DOJ memo, *supra* n 283, 3–5. The quotation is from p 4. This section is copied in its entirety into the Pentagon Working Group report, *supra* n 294, 8–10.

[387] December 2004 memo, *supra* n 380, 16.

[388] *Ibid*, 17.

[389] *Ibid*, 2.

[390] *Ibid*, p 2, fn 7. See the White House, Statement on United Nations International Day in Support of Victims of Torture, 40 Weekly Comp Pres Doc 1167–68 (July 5, 2004), <http://www.findarticles.com/p/articles/mi_m2889/is_27_40/ai_n6148650>, accessed 3 January 2005.

position that the US Constitution granted the President the authority to waive all international treaty obligations and US laws and order torture; in terms of policy, specific torturous interrogation methods were officially sanctioned at the highest (ministerial) level; and, in practice, torture and ill-treatment were being committed (as acknowledged later) in Abu Ghraib and elsewhere. On that occasion, the President had declared *inter alia* that:

Torture anywhere is an affront to human dignity everywhere...The United States is committed to the world-wide elimination of torture and we are leading this fight by example.[391]

In other words, the US administration did not seem to see any contradiction between the President issuing such declarations and him (at least potentially) issuing orders to torture. In comparison, a torture-legalizing-model busting position, consistent with the absolute prohibition in international law on torture and ill-treatment and their status (for the most part, in the latter case) as international crimes, regardless of the rank or position of the perpetrator,[392] would have been for the Department of Justice to state unequivocally that no one, the President included, has the right or the authority to torture or ill-treat detainees or to order their torture or ill-treatment and anyone, the President included, who does so will have committed a crime.

No less significantly, on the more practical level, the December 2004 was totally silent on cruel, inhuman or degrading treatment or punishment, which its predecessor had described as:

...a category of acts that are not to be committed and that states must endeavour to prevent, but that states need not criminalize, leaving those acts without the stigma of criminal penalties.[393]

As will be seen below, the administration seems to have tenaciously stuck to this position—as to the *ad hoc*, *pro tempora* and, indeed, *ad personam* grounds for rejecting torture, and to a similar 'closed-but-not-locked' approach vis-à-vis the 'defence of necessity'.

2. Litigation in US courts

Dozens (if not more) of cases concerning 'war on terror' detainees have been submitted to US civilian and military courts; some of them are ongoing. Below is a very thin outline of the cases most relevant to this study.[394]

---

[391] The White House, 'Statement by the President: United Nations International Day in Support of Victims of Torture', 26 June 2003, <http://www.whitehouse.gov/news/releases/2003/06/20030626–3.html>, accessed 29 July 2003.

[392] See *infra*, Part IV, Ch 18.

[393] August 2002 DOJ memo, *supra* n 283, 15. And see the supporting remarks of Alberto Gonzales, *supra* n 316. Note that the latter remarks were made in the wake of the December 2004 memo.

[394] The reader will note that it is even thinner going into 2006 and 2007. I have not discussed here the issue of the admissibility of coerced statements as evidence, as its relevance is limited. For

(a) Cases directly involving torture

The USA has launched investigations into allegations of ill-treatment of detainees in all the principal fronts of its 'war on terror'. These have resulted in administrative measures taken against those found responsible, and in dozens of cases in courts martial, with punishments of up to ten years' imprisonment being meted out.[395] However, while some of the accused have argued that they were following orders, none have pleaded justificatory defences or otherwise attempted to justify their actions on the basis of the need to extract vital information. It should be noted that in none of these cases were international legal terms such as 'torture', 'cruel, inhuman or degrading treatment or punishment', or 'outrages upon personal dignity' invoked. Nor were any persons charged with grave breaches of the Geneva Conventions or war crimes. Rather, those who faced court-martials were charged with offences under the Uniform Code of Military Justice such as 'assault', 'maltreatment', and 'indecent acts'.

A case was also brought against a civilian (CIA) contractor working with 'military' interrogators, who was charged with assault in the case of a detainee who died in US custody in Afghanistan in June 2003.[396]

In March 2005, a case which had the potential of becoming directly relevant to the issues raised in this study was put forward in a civil suit brought by ACLU and Human Rights First on behalf of eight persons who, according to the complaint, were subjected to 'torture or other cruel, inhuman or degrading treatment or punishment' in Iraq and Afghanistan, against Rumsfeld, Secretary of Defense at the time, 'whose policies, patterns, practices, derelictions of duty and command failures caused Plaintiffs' abuse' and other officials.[397] However, in 2007 the DC District Court granted the motions of Rumsfeld, and the other defendants to dismiss the case, on grounds of subject matter jurisdiction and immunity. The merits of what the Court called 'horrific torture allegations' were

a comprehensive list of 'homeland security' cases see eg the website of the University of Maryland Center for Health and Homeland Security <http://www.umaryland.edu/healthsecurity/other/cases.html>, first accessed 19 June 2005.

[395] These are detailed in the USA's Second Periodic to CAT, UN Doc CAT/C/48/Add.3, 6 May 2005, Annex I, Part 1, III(B)(2) (regarding Guantánamo Bay); Annex I, Part 1, III(B)(3) (regarding Afghanistan); and Annex I, Part II, III(B)(3) (regarding Iraq).

[396] *United States v Passaro*, No: 5:04-CR-211–1, (US District Ct. for Eastern District NC West Div), Indictment, 17 June 2004 <http://news.findlaw.com/cnn/docs/torture/uspassaro61704ind2.html>, accessed 28 June 2005.

[397] *Ali et al v Rumsfeld*, Complaint for Declaratory Relief and damages, filed in US District Ct, Northern District of Illinois, 1 March 2005 <http://www.humanrightsfirst.org/us_law/etn/lawsuit/PDF/rums-complaint-022805.pdf>, accessed 25 March 2005, paras 1 and 3, respectively. Complaints were concurrently lodged against three high-ranking commanders in Iraq at the time, under whose control the plaintiffs claimed they had been when tortured or otherwise ill-treated, *Ali et al v Janis Karpinski*, Complaint, US District Ct for the Northern District of Illinois (1 March 2005); *Ali et al v Ricardo Sanchez*, Complaint, US District Ct for the Northern District of Illinois (1 March 2005); *Ali et al v Thomas Pappas*, Complaint, US District Ct for the Northern District of Illinois (1 March 2005).

therefore not discussed. Under the ruling, the international legal aspects of the case may arise again with the US government as defendant.[398]

Further cases will be referred to in the conclusion of this chapter.

(b) Legal status of detained terrorist suspects

Much of the legal wrangling in US courts over detained terrorist suspects has revolved around this issue. As noted, the legal status of 'certain' (thus, potentially, any) of these detainees was initially determined by a US presidential order in November 2001, which (at leased potentially) placed them under the 'exclusive jurisdiction' of military tribunals.[399] Hundreds of suspected terrorist detainees[400] were held outside US territory, mainly at Guantánamo Bay, later to be far outnumbered by those held in Afghanistan and Iraq.

The *Al Odah* decision quoted above was not the US courts' final word on the subject. In June 2004, the US Supreme Court reversed and remanded that decision, ruling that US federal courts,

…have jurisdiction to consider challenges to the legality of the detentions of foreign nationals captured abroad in connection with hostilities and incarcerated at Guantánamo Bay.[401]

The wrangling continued in the federal courts,[402] before Congress intervened.

In a case involving the status of a US citizen designated an 'enemy combatant', decided on the same day as *Rasul*, the issue of torture came up in a dissenting opinion. Stevens J wrote:

Executive detention of subversive citizens, like detention of enemy soldiers to keep them off the battlefield, may sometimes be justified to prevent persons from launching

---

[398] *Ali et al v Rumsfeld et al*, Misc No 06–0145 (TFH), US DC Dist Ct, *Memorandum Opinion*, 27 March 2007, consolidating the cases *ibid*.

[399] See *supra*, Ch 15, Section B(1)(a).

[400] There have, in addition, been hundreds of arrests, in connection to the 'war on terror', of non-citizens on immigration charges, on criminal charges or as material witnesses, and a handful of US citizens deemed 'enemy combatants'. See eg Human Rights Watch, *World Report 2003*, New York, Human Rights Watch, 2003, 499–503; Human Rights Watch and the American Civil Liberties Union, *Witness to Abuse: Human Rights Abuses under the Material Witness Law since September 11* (New York: HRW and ACLU, June 2005).

[401] *Rasul v Bush* 542 US 466 (2004), ruling of 28 June 2004. The Court distinguished *Eisentrager* (*supra* n 379) mainly on the grounds that petitioners in that case had served the enemy and been tried and convicted whereas the *Rasul* petitioners had been detained without trial and denied serving the enemy, see *ibid*, 6–11, per Stevens, J.

On the same day, the Supreme Court granted the right of *habeas corpus* to a US citizen held as 'enemy combatant' inside the USA (*Hamdi v Rumsfeld*, 542 US 507 (2004), decided 28 June 2004).

[402] See eg the contrasting opinions issued in January 2005 by judges in the same court. In *Khalid v Bush*, Civ No 1:04–1142 (RJL), *Memorandum Opinion*, (US District Ct for DC, 19 January 2005), Leon J ruled that there was 'no viable legal theory' by which he could issue writs of *habeas corpus* to foreign detainees held at the Guantánamo naval base. In *In Re: Guantanamo Detainee Cases*, Civ No 02-CV-0299 (CKK), *Memorandum Opinion*, (US District Ct for DC 31 January 2005), Green J ruled that 'the procedures implemented by the government to confirm that the petitioners are "enemy combatants" subject to indefinite detention violates the petitioners' rights to due process of law.'

or becoming missiles of destruction. It may not, however, be justified by the naked interest in using unlawful procedures to extract information. Incommunicado detention for months on end is such a procedure. Whether the information so procured is more or less reliable than that acquired by more extreme forms of torture is of no consequence. For if this Nation is to remain true to the ideals symbolized by its flag, it must not wield the tools of tyrants even to resist an assault by the forces of tyranny.[403]

(c) The military commissions

This issue, overlapping that of detainees' legal status, centred on the lawfulness of the military commissions established under a November 2001 Presidential order.[404] It was eventually decided by the Supreme Court, hearing the case of Salim Hamdan, a Guantánamo Bay detainee charged and about to be tried by such a commission.[405] The Court declared the military commissions, as established, unlawful, thus overturning the President's order. It also declared, again overturning the President's position,[406] that Art 3 common to the four Geneva Conventions applied to 'war on terror' detainees.[407] This has meant, or could have meant, the collapse of what I called the administration's *sui generis* argument—the first pillar of the original model's legal structure.[408] In our narrower context it has meant that, in addition to Common Art 3's provision for 'judicial guarantees' (which was at the base of the Court's decision against the military commissions), its provisions for detainees to 'in all circumstances be treated humanely',[409] was now deemed applicable to the treatment of these detainees.

3. Legislation, regulations

Four documents will be discussed here. Two Acts passed by Congress in 2005 and 2006 relate directly to the issues of torture and ill-treatment during interrogations and the legal consequences for perpetrators of either, the second Act slightly modifying the first. Thirdly, a DoD field manual for interrogations, issued in 2006, will be briefly examined. Fourthly, the President's Executive Order applying (his understanding of) Common Art 3 to the CIA 'program of detention and interrogation' will be briefly reviewed.

---

[403]   *Rumsfeld v Padilla*, 542 US 426 (2004), Stevens J dissenting. The dissent (by four of the nine judges) essentially revolved around the jurisdiction of the New York courts over Padilla's *habeas corpus* petition.

[404]   See *supra* n 291 and accompanying text.

[405]   *Hamdan v Rumsfeld*, 548 US (2006) (also 126 S Ct 2749), decision of 29 June 2006.

[406]   See *supra*, Ch 15, Section B(1)(a).

[407]   *Hamdan*, *supra* n 405, 65–8.

[408]   See *supra*, Ch 15, Section B(1)(a).

[409]   See further discussions of the Article's provisions *infra*, Part IV, Chs 18 and 19.

(a) Detainee Treatment Act of 2005 (DTA)[410]

This Act provides *inter alia* that:

No individual in the custody or under the physical control of the United States Government, regardless of nationality or physical location, shall be subject to cruel, inhuman, or degrading treatment or punishment.[411]

Such ill-treatment is then defined as:

...the cruel, unusual, and inhumane treatment or punishment prohibited by the Fifth, Eighth, and Fourteenth Amendments to the Constitution of the United States, as defined in the United States Reservations, Declarations and Understandings to the United Nations Convention Against Torture.[412]

The Act goes on to provide a 'good faith' defence to officials who were involved in the:

...detention and interrogation of aliens who the President or his designees have determined are believed to be engaged in or associated with international terrorist activity that poses a serious, continuing threat to the United States, its interests, or its allies, and that were officially authorized and determined to be lawful at the time that they were conducted.[413]

For such officials:

...it shall be a defense that [they] did not know that the practices were unlawful and a person of ordinary sense and understanding would not know the practices were unlawful. Good faith reliance on advice of counsel should be an important factor, among others, to consider in assessing whether a person of ordinary sense and understanding would have known the practices to be unlawful. Nothing in this section shall be construed to limit or extinguish any defense or protection otherwise available to any person or entity from suit, civil or criminal liability, or damages, or to provide immunity from prosecution for any criminal offense by the proper authorities.[414]

Among other provisions, the DTA stipulates that no *habeas corpus* motions may be filed in US courts, nor:

...any other action against the United States or its agents relating to any aspect of the detention by the Department of Defense of an alien at Guantanamo Bay, Cuba...[415]

---

[410] Detainee Treatment Act of 2005 (DTA), included (as Title X) in the Department of Defense Appropriations Act, 2006 and signed into law on 30 December 2005.

[411] *Ibid*, sec 1003(a). Section 1002(a) limits treatment or interrogation methods used with DoD detainees to those 'authorized by and listed in the United States Army Field Manual on Intelligence Interrogation'.

[412] *Ibid*, sec 1003(d).

[413] *Ibid*, sec 1004(a).

[414] *Ibid*.

[415] *Ibid*, sec 1005(e)(1). Under sec (e)(2) the DC Cir Court has limited procedural overview powers.

(b) Military Commissions Act of 2006 (MCA)[416]

This Act was a direct response to the ruling in *Hamdan* and aimed at facilitating the revival of military commissions to try Guantánamo Bay detainees.[417] However, it also had other aims, closer to the focus of this study.

The text performs a delicate dance, choreographed so as to define crimes in a way that would facilitate the prosecution of suspected terrorists for violations of Common Art 3, in light of the *Hamdan* ruling, without thereby criminalizing acts of US officials, including interrogators, as well. Thus the MCA modifies the war crimes provisions in the Federal Criminal Code[418] and details what hitherto had been a general provision criminalising any 'violation of common Article 3'.[419] Significantly, the term 'violation' itself is replaced by 'a grave breach' of the Article.[420] The reason for this is clear: the Common Art 3-related offences listed in the Act include most, but not all of those listed in the Article itself.[421] Notable in its absence is the prohibition of 'outrages upon personal dignity, in particular, humiliating and degrading treatment'.[422] Very conscious of this elaborate omission, the Act explains that:

The definitions in this subsection are intended only to define the grave breaches of common Article 3 and not the full scope of United States obligations under that Article.[423]

However, this should be read together with another clarification that the Act makes:

The provisions of section 2441 of title 18, United States Code, as amended by this section, fully satisfy the obligation under Article 129 of the Third Geneva Convention for the United States to provide effective penal sanctions for grave breaches which are encompassed in common Article 3 in the context of an armed conflict not of an international character.[424]

In other words, whatever international obligations the USA has regarding 'outrages upon personal dignity', these are not seen as involving 'effective penal sanctions'. Instead, the Act provides for the President to:

...interpret the meaning and application of the Geneva Conventions and to promulgate higher standards and administrative regulations for violations of treaty obligations which are not grave breaches of the Geneva Conventions.[425]

---

[416] Signed into law on 30 September of that year.

[417] See *supra*, Ch 15, Section D(2)(c).

[418] 18 USC § 2441. War crimes.

[419] *Ibid*, sec 2441(c)(3).

[420] MCA, *supra* n 416 and accompanying text, sec 6(b)(1)(A). The Geneva Conventions themselves do not directly designate violations of Common Art 3 as 'grave breaches'.

[421] Other offences not explicitly provided in Common Art 3 have been added, including 'performing biological experiments', 'rape', and 'sexual assault or abuse'. See *ibid*, sec 6(b)(1)(B).

[422] Geneva Conventions, Common Art 3(1)(c). The MCA does provide for an offence of 'cruel or inhuman treatment' but with a 'threshold severity' identical to that of torture. See *supra* n 416 and accompanying text, sections 6(b)(4)"(d) "(1)"(B); 6(b)(4)"(d)"(2)"(D); and 6(b)(4)"(d)"(2)"(E).

[423] Section 6(b)(1)(B)"(d) "(5).

[424] Section 6(a)(2).

[425] Section 6(a)(3)(A). The President's interpretations, to be issued in the shape of an 'Executive Order', is to '... be authoritative (except as to grave breaches of common Article 3) as a matter of

Significantly, acts constituting 'cruel, inhuman or degrading treatment or punishment' are treated in the same way. The MCA repeats *verbatim* the prohibition of such acts, and the US understanding of such prohibition, already provided in the DTA.[426] However, ensuring compliance with this provision too was left to the President.[427]

Thus both the human rights violation of 'cruel, inhuman or degrading treatment or punishment' and its perceived international humanitarian law equivalent, 'outrages upon personal dignity', while prohibited, are rendered outside the realm of penal sanctions, and within that of Executive discretion.[428]

As to those who have tortured or ill-treated in the past, the MCA modifies the DTA, mainly by placing its provision for a 'good faith' defence[429] within a timeframe, namely 'actions occurring between September 11, 2001, and December 30, 2005'.[430]

A final element worth noting is that the MCA bars US courts from considering external legal sources in applying the Act:

No foreign or international source of law shall supply a basis for a rule of decision in the courts of the United States in interpreting the prohibitions enumerated [here] ... [431]

correspondingly, the MCA provides that:

No alien unlawful enemy combatant subject to trial by military commission under this chapter may invoke the Geneva Conventions as a source of rights.[432]

(c) New Field Manual for military interrogations

In September 2006, the US Department of the Army published a new Field Manual for 'intelligence collector operations', which includes interrogations.[433] The Manual states repeatedly that torture of 'all captured or detained personnel' is prohibited, as is cruel, inhuman or degrading treatment or punishment (albeit in its DTA form), and that all detainees must be treated humanely.[434] Some interrogation methods, including sexual humiliation, hooding and 'waterboarding' are explicitly prohibited.[435] One method allowed in previous manuals—'fear up

United States law, in the same manner as other administrative regulations' (*ibid*, secs 6(a)(3)(B) and 6(a)(3)(C)).

[426] MCA, *supra* n 416 and accompanying text, sec 6(c). For the provision in the DTA (*supra* n 410) see sec 1003(d).

[427] MCA, sec 6(c)(3).

[428] See below, at the conclusion of this Chapter.

[429] See *supra* nn 413–414 and accompanying text.

[430] MCA, *supra* n 416 and accompanying text, sec 8(b)(3).

[431] *Ibid*, sec 6(a)(2).

[432] MCA, *ibid*, sec 3, sec 948b(g), added to Title 10 USC.

[433] Headquarters, Department of the [US] Army, *FM 2–22.3 (FM 34–52) Human Intelligence Collector Operations*, Washington DC, 6 September 2006.

[434] *Ibid*, eg Preface, at VII; secs 4–41; 5–74. Quotation is from the second source.

[435] *Ibid*, sec 5–75. The Manual emphasizes that the list is not exhaustive. The prohibition on 'inducing hypothermia or heat injury' may be interpreted as allowing more limited exposure to temperature extremes.

(harsh)'[436]—was also abolished, while precautions and safeguards were added to others.[437]

However, Appendix M of this manual (limited to 'unlawful combatants') provides for an interrogation method described as 'physical separation' (that is, solitary confinement), initially for 30 days,[438] but with provisions for extension, and no limits on the number of extensions allowed.[439] In the field the Appendix allows for 'field expedient separation' which translates into the following:

As a last resort, when physical separation of detainees is not feasible, goggles or blindfolds and earmuffs may be utilized as a field expedient method to generate a perception of separation.[440]

This method could be applied initially for 12 hours[441] but is, again, extendible with no clear limitations.[442]

One of the (many) safeguards accompanying the provisions for these methods may actually be described as a two-edged sword:

Use of separation must not preclude the detainee getting four hours of continuous sleep every 24 hours.[443]

Here too, no limitations are placed as to how long a detainee's sleep may be so limited. This hardly guarantees sufficient sleep, especially when used over a period of 30 days, extendable indefinitely. A combination of prolonged 'physical separation' and limited sleep is clearly a breach of international norms—an issue which will be discussed in the next Chapter—but the tension between the no-ill-treatment declaratory stance and this particular method is not addressed.

(d) Executive Order applying Common Article 3 to the CIA program

The Executive Order signed by President Bush in July 2007, applying Common Art 3, as understood by his administration, to the CIA's 'detention and interrogation' program,[444] has assured that this program will go well into the future. Besides determining that Common Art 3 (as interpreted by the USA) applies to the program, and repeating the definitions in the DTA and MCA of torture, cruel,

---

[436] See eg Headquarters, Department of the Army, *FM 34–52 Intelligence Interrogation*, Washington, DC, 8 May 1987 <http://www.globalsecurity.org/intell/library/policy/army/fm/fm34–52/>, accessed 6 March 2005, Appendix H: Approaches. A revised version of the Field Manual which included these methods was issued in 1992, but US officials have referred to the 1987 version more often.

[437] See eg *FM 2–22.3, supra* n 433 secs 8–35; 8–48.

[438] *Ibid*, sec M-29.

[439] *Ibid*, sec M-30

[440] *Ibid*, sec M-27.

[441] *Ibid*, sec M-29.

[442] *Ibid*, sec M-30.

[443] *Ibid*, sec M-30.

[444] Executive Order: Interpretation of the Geneva Conventions Common Article 3 as Applied to a Program of Detention and Interrogation Operated by the Central Intelligence Agency (20 July 2007) <http://www.whitehouse.gov/news/releases/2007/07/20070720–4.html>, accessed 21 July 2007.

inhuman or degrading treatment or punishment, and (from the latter Act) acts specifically prohibited by Common Art 3,[445] the Order, *inter alia*, prohibits 'wilful and outrageous acts' (presumably corresponding to 'outrages upon personal dignity' in that Article) 'that any reasonable person, considering the circumstances, would deem the acts to be beyond the bounds of human decency',[446] as well as providing that 'detainees in the program receive the basic necessities of life'.[447]

Most of the problems lie less in what is included in the Order, more in what is missing—or omitted therefrom. Notably, the Order fails to repeat, or echo, Common Art 3's fundamental provision for humane treatment—even given the administration's expansive view of that provision (see below). There is no provision for ICRC visits to CIA's detainees, nor a prohibition on secret, incommunicado detention, nor yet on methods such as waterboarding. When asked, a person described officially as 'Senior Administration Official One' did not rule out the future use of this method. Asked about another absent prohibition—on sleep deprivation—'Official One' stated that:

…as to sleep, that's not something that is traditionally enumerated in the Geneva Convention provisions. And beyond that I'm not in a position to comment….[448]

E. Evaluation 2—the HVD Model as of Mid-2007

As this Chapter is being updated and finalized, in mid-2007, the USA has laws that explicitly prohibit cruel, inhuman or degrading treatment or punishment of any 'individual' in US control—obviously including HVDs. It also has laws explicitly criminalizing torture, 'cruel and inhuman treatment' and similar acts, and has applied Common Art 3 to CIA interrogations. Are there still any grounds for claiming that the USA is operating a torture-legalizing model in its 'war on terror'? I submit that at least a qualified positive answer ('quasi-legalized') is still the right one.

By way of substantiating this claim, I will briefly examine what has happened to the four main legal arguments of the original model,[449] and then provide a few illustrations.

1. *The* sui generis *argument.* There is now recognition that terrorist suspects are subject to certain US laws (notably the DTA and the MCA), as well as being protected by an international legal provision—Common Art 3. However, in a process which may be described as cooptation, this and other provisions

---

[445] See 'definitions' in sec 2 of the Order and references to other prohibited acts, including torture, in sec 3.

[446] *Ibid*, sec 3(E). Section 3(f) prohibits acts 'intended to denigrate' a detainee's religion.

[447] *Ibid*, sec 3(b)(iv).

[448] Transcript of Conference Call With Senior Administration Officials on the Executive Order Interpreting Common Article Three, Washington (20 July 2007), see eg <http://www.prnewswire.com/cgi-bin/stories.pl?ACCT=104&STORY=/www/story/07–20-2007/0004629772&EDATE=>, accessed 23 July 2007.

[449] See supra, Ch 15, Section B(1).

of international law have been constructed—and constricted—within the confines of the USA's own version of them, limiting that protection, and barring courts from directly applying international treaties or jurisprudence.

2. *The limited scope of 'torture'.* The December 2004 memo has modified the administration's concept of torture, but subsequent legislation maintained the USA's traditional (and restrictive) 'understanding' of the term. Beyond this, the administration has maintained an extremely expansive view as to what acts do *not* constitute torture—nor any other unlawful treatment, and qualify, instead, as 'humane treatment' (as illustrated below).

3. *The applicability of criminal law defences to officials who torture in certain circumstances.* This as a general statement of law has not been modified since stated by the August 2002 DoJ memo, but nor has it been tested in the courts. The DTA and MCA provided a defence likely to exempt all of those who tortured during interrogations between 9/11 and the end of 2005 from criminal or civil liability, while emphasising that other defences also remain available. As of mid-2007, no cases have arisen concerning persons who have tortured or ill-treated *after* the latter date. A precedent has been set, however, and it is not inconceivable, that should an extreme situation arise, the legislature, the prosecution or the judiciary will find a way to exempt torturers from liability again. One such option—the defence of necessity—will be discussed in the next Part.

4. *The unlimited authority of the President at war.* This point has also remained unchallenged, but moot. The President has repeatedly insisted that 'the United States does not torture. It's against our laws and it's against our values.'[450] However, this statement continued: 'I have not authorized it—and I will not authorize it' and does not clarify whether or not, in his view, he is 'authorized to authorize it'. The legislation covering cruel, inhuman or degrading treatment or punishment or outrages upon personal dignity actually did authorize the President to exercise discretion in 'regulating' these violations of international, law while placing no penal sanctions on violators, in line with the August 2002 DoJ memo.

Some official statements will now be discussed, to illustrate further the limited effect that developments since May 2004 have had on the legal situation—or at least on the administration's perception thereof.

In June 2006 (six months after the DTA had been enacted) the Department of Defense issued a statement concerning a case which involved the interrogation of Muhammad al-Qahtani in Guantánamo Bay in late 2002 and early 2003, under a special 'interrogation plan'. Interrogation methods included sleep deprivation; using a dog to growl, bark, and show his teeth to frighten al-Qahtani; 'strip-searching' in front of women; other sexual (and other) humiliations, exposure to extreme cold, playing loud music, repeatedly pouring

---

[450] 'President Discusses Creation of Military Commissions …' *supra* n 275.

water over his head and isolation for 160 days.[451] The statement included the following:

The Department of Defense remains committed to the unequivocal standard of humane treatment for all detainees, and Kahtani's interrogation plan was guided by that strict standard.[452]

If this is 'humane treatment' as required by Common Art 3, there is hardly any reason—certainly any legal reason—not to apply it in the future, especially in extreme circumstances. This point was illustrated further in the President's statement, when announcing the transfer of fourteen HVDs from secret prisons to Guantánamo Bay, that 'they will *continue to be treated with the humanity* that they denied others'[453] (emphasis added). The now officially acknowledged long years of incommunicado detention, the other CIA methods some of which have become an open secret, including extreme isolation, sleep and sensory deprivation and waterboarding—all fall under 'treating with humanity'—therefore are certainly not torturous, in the eyes of the US administration. Nothing has changed, in this respect, since the then Secretary for Defence made a similar statement in January 2003.[454]

This is not merely a reflection on the past. The MCA and the President's Executive Order have ensured that the CIA program remains active. Official statements announcing the transfer of persons to Guantánamo, but providing no information as to when or where they had been arrested (or subsequently detained) have borne this out.[455]

To the extent that there is a 'bottom line', it is this: HVDs are still, in all likelihood, being shipped to secret prisons where they are held totally

---

[451] See 'Interrogation Log, Detainee 063'. The log was obtained by Time magazine, <http://www.time.com/time/2006/log/log.pdf>, accessed 22 June 2006; Army Regulation 15–6: Final Report: Investigation into FBI Allegations of Detainee Abuse at Guantanamo Bay, Cuba Detention Facility, 1 April 2005 (amended 9 June 2005) (written by Lieutenant General Randall M Schmidt and Brigadier General John T Furlow) <http://www.defenselink.mil/news/Jul2005/d20050714report.pdf>, accessed 23 June 2006. For a more detailed description see Amnesty International, *United States of America: Memorandum to the US Government on the report of the UN Committee Against Torture and the question of closing Guantánamo*, AI Index: AMR 51/093/2006, 23 June 2006.

[452] US Department of Defense News Release, 'Guantanamo Provides Valuable Intelligence Information' <http://www.defenselink.mil/releases/2005/nr20050612–3661.html>, accessed 23 June 2006.

[453] *Supra* n 275.

[454] See *supra* n 310 and accompanying text.

[455] See eg American Forces Press Service, 'Defense Department Takes Custody of al Qaeda Leader' (27 April 2007) <http://www.defenselink.mil/news/newsarticle.aspx?id=32969>, accessed 28 April 2007.

The BBC was told by an anonymous 'US intelligence official' that al-Iraqi had been captured in late 2006. BBC Website, 'Profile: Abd al-Hadi al-Iraqi' <http://news.bbc.co.uk/1/hi/world/middle_east/6601087.stm>, accessed 28 April 2007. By mid-2007, the Department of Defense has announced a total of four such transfers. See similar statements on the same website (<http://www.defenselink.mil/news>) on 26 March, 6 June and 22 June 2007.

incommunicado for months on end (though perhaps no longer for years), and subjected to a raft of additional interrogation techniques, all deemed lawful by the administration. The DTA, the MCA and the President's Executive Order, ostensibly forming the domestic codification of an absolute international legal (and moral) principle—that detainees 'shall in all circumstances be treated humanely'—have become, in the hands of the US administration, an exercise in interpretational phraseology serving a single 'principle': the legal prohibition on torture and other ill-treatment must end where the USA's authorized interrogation techniques begin.

Where have the US courts been in all this? US-based human rights organizations have argued, my analysis above notwithstanding, that 'the MCA...under a reasonable interpretation currently prohibits the use of the "enhanced" techniques'.[456] But would the US courts be able—or willing—to reach a similar conclusion? As seen, these courts, while quite active in various other aspects of the treatment of 'war on terror' detainees,[457] have been reluctant to tackle head on issues such as interrogation methods, torture and ill-treatment. Moreover, it appears that, at least in the view of the lower federal courts, suspected terrorists under interrogation relying on the Constitutional Amendments referred to in the DTA[458] (and by analogy in the MCA) will find that they provided little if any protection, even from torture. Thus in February 2006, namely with the DTA already in force, the District Court for East New York District, addressing these Amendments' applicability in our context, stated the following in respect to for the Fifth Amendment (due process):

While one cannot ignore the 'shocks the conscience' test established in *Rochin v. California*..., that case involved the question whether torture could be used to extract evidence for the purpose of prosecuting criminal conduct, a very different question from the one ultimately presented here, to wit, whether substantive due process would erect a per se bar to coercive investigations, including torture, for the purpose of preventing a terrorist attack....whether torture always violates the Fifth Amendment under

---

[456] *Leave No Marks, supra* n 352, 35. Unfortunately, and inexplicably, this report did not treat as an interrogation technique prolonged incommunicado detention in secret locations, an inseparable part of the President's 'set of procedures' designed to elicit information through causing pain and suffering, just like the techniques that are listed. However, even without this component they reach the following conclusion:

This report demonstrates that 'enhanced' techniques of interrogation, whether practiced alone or in combination, may cause severe physical and mental pain. In fact, the use of multiple or 'enhanced' interrogation virtually assures the infliction of severe physical and mental pain upon detainees (*ibid*).

[457] In June 2006, the Supreme Court even left open the possibility of federal courts ruling that the MCA did not validly strip federal court jurisdiction over *habeas corpus* petitions from Guantánamo Bay detainees. Vacating its own decision in the same case in April and of lower courts, the Supreme Court ordered a 'rehearing' of two (consolidated) petitions on this issue, previously denied relying on the MCA. See *Boumediene v Bush* (Cert granted), 127 S Ct 1478 (2007).

[458] The Fourteenth Amendment will be set aside here, as it applies to US citizens only.

established Supreme Court case law prohibiting government action that 'shocks the conscience'... remains unresolved from a doctrinal standpoint.[459]

As for the Eighth Amendment, the Court applied the same logic:

In *Filartiga v. Pena-Irala*... this circuit... [indicated] that torture might be prohibited under the Eighth Amendment to the US Constitution, which bars 'cruel and unusual punishments'. See id. at 884, n. 13. But, this dictum does not address the constitutionality of torture to prevent a terrorist attack.[460]

In other words, the Court is suggesting a possibility that US courts would follow the Israeli Supreme Court in allowing torture in a TBS or comparable situation. Another court, the DC District Court, rejected that the Amendment's applicability to the interrogation of detainees on different grounds, stating that 'the Eighth Amendment applies only to convicted criminals'.[461]

My final point, and this is admittedly speculative in part, is that the US courts are unlikely to face up to the government in the full sense that international law demands, namely (as explained in the next Part) to determine that all acts of torture and (at the very least deliberate) cruelty in all their forms are prohibited and all perpetrators, including those in power who order or allow such acts, are criminals. Conceivably, they would consider such a determination as being beyond their powers, in concurrence with the administration's view. If this proves to be the case, either directly through court decisions or, I would submit, through consistent judicial inaction and avoidance of the issue, the claim that the HVD model is still one of 'legalized torture' would be even more persuasive.

---

[459] *Arar v Ashcroft*, Civil Action No CV-04–0249 (DGT)(VVP), US Dist Ct East NY, *Memorandum and Order*, 16 February 2006, sec 4(b), 56. The (civil) case concerned a Canadian citizen arrested in 2002 while in transit in the USA, 'rendited' to Syria and tortured there, before being released without charge. The District Court in DC had similarly stated (in a footnote): 'No federal court has ever examined the nature of the substantive due process rights of a prisoner in a military interrogation or prisoner of war context' (*OK v Bush*, Civil Action No 04–1136 (JDB), US Dist Court for DC, *Memorandum Opinion*, 12 July 2005, per Bates J, 18).

[460] *Ibid* (in a footnote).

[461] *Ali et al v Rumsfeld et al, supra* n 398, 27.

16

Part III—Conclusions

In this Part, I have examined three models of legalized torture and one of 'quasi-legalized' torture. I have tried to combine the legal with the practical and realistic, a crucial issue for those models, which seek to limit torture to cases of 'necessity' in the Landau case, and more narrowly to TBSs and other extreme circumstances only, in the other three.

The 'torture warrants' model proposes the legalization of torture while seeking to limit it to TBSs by granting judges the power to issue warrants, without which torture cannot be carried out. Modelling itself on existing provisions for search warrants, the proposed system would, it may be argued, be based on pertinent guiding principles, namely issuance by an independent authority, specific—rather than general—authorization, and reasonableness. However, as judges' decisions regarding search warrants, at least in the two states examined (the USA and Israel) have limited value, and warrants are granted almost invariably and without any meaningful scrutiny, it was difficult to see how a 'torture warrant' system would not become similarly automatic. Moreover, the Supreme Court of Israel, which during the Landau years in effect (though this was not legally couched in such terms) issued 'torture warrants', was exceptionally accommodating of the state's positions, granting injunctions prohibiting torture only when the state had no objections, lifting them whenever the state (subsequently) changed its mind, and adopting a very expansive temporal view (up to weeks) of the period during which the need for the 'the immediate procurement' of vital information justified the continued use of tortuous interrogation methods.

The proponents of the 'torture warrants' model have not come up with meaningful solutions for these problems, and some have actually joined the criticism of the Israeli Supreme Court for certain 'torture warrant' decisions.

The three other models are fully 'real life' ones. The first, the Landau model, which operated in Israel between 1987 and 1999, relied on explicit authorization and detailed instructions for the application of intense psychological and 'moderate physical' pressure on terrorist suspects (though not limited to TBSs). The model, launched by a Commission of Inquiry whose recommendations the Israeli government adopted in 1987, relied on the 'defence of necessity' (DoN), and considered it a legitimate source for issuing such instructions. The 'pressure' methods, applied against many thousands of Palestinians during the Landau years, combined sleep and sensory deprivation, painful positions, humiliations, all applied for days on end, as well as more direct violence, such as 'shaking'.

Secondly a current DoN model was examined. While adopting the same defence as the Landau model, and the same ('lesser evil') moral view as its legal basis, this 'prototype' of the DoN model, launched by a Supreme Court ruling in 1999, rejected any *ab initio* authorization, let alone regulation, of the use of any coercive interrogation methods. It limited the availability of the DoN to individuals and applied it *ex post facto* only. Moreover, the applicability of the DoN was restricted explicitly to a TBS only. However, with the advent of the second *Intifadah* in the summer of 2000, and a wave of vicious terrorist attacks in which many hundreds of Israelis died, the model succumbed to the increasing pressure. A combination of routine, court-approved incommunicado detentions; the total isolation of the GSS interrogation system; the lack of any meaningful scrutiny (with interrogees' complaints investigated by a GSS agent); the impunity granted by the Attorney General, through determining that the DoN applied, in every single case where GSS agents have admitted to using violence during interrogation—all made that defence yet again into a means of legalizing torture systemically. Many of the old 'moderate physical pressure' methods returned, albeit at times in slightly different forms. Sleep deprivation, humiliations, painful positions, kicking, slapping and tightening of shackles are once again used, as are, though less frequently, 'shaking' (with new 'jolting' variations) and 'the frog position' (*qambaz*). The 'bending' method, involving forcing the detainee into a backward-slanting position, often accompanied by beatings, is used as a means of applying instant, and excruciating, pain. According to PCATI, up to dozens of Palestinians suffered torture every month at the height of the *Intifadah*, and even the GSS has admitted to using 'exceptional means of interrogation' in what amounts to dozens of cases annually. In later years, and with the relative calm brought mainly by the wall/fence and political developments, the use of torture has dropped, but is still being practiced regularly, and nothing has been done to curb the model's propensity for expansion.

The third and final 'working' model examined was the legally less clear, conceptually less coherent, and practically less consistent model for the interrogation of 'war on terror' suspects detained by the USA since the terrorist attacks on its territory in 2001, particularly those believed to possess life-saving information, termed, originally loosely, 'high-value detainees' (HVDs). Initially the model's legal basis consisted of arguments by the Executive's legal advisers and Executive orders, which essentially combined classifying certain 'war on terror' detainees as having no legal rights, either under US or international law—not even to humane treatment (let alone freedom from torture), with a view that the President's constitutionally granted powers as Commander-in-Chief of the US armed forces in times of war are unlimited—including the power to order the torture of detainees. It also included a very narrow definition of torture, an argument that lesser ill-treatment of foreign terrorists abroad is not unlawful, and a claim that criminal law defences, 'necessity' and 'self-defence', are available to interrogators who torture terrorists. Between the interrogation of actual or perceived HVDs, instructions allowing the use of physical and mental pressure in the interrogation of much wider categories of detainees, the 'migration'[462] of interrogation techniques and a general 'gloves off'[463] mentality, 'slippery-slope' style, far beyond even what these instructions allowed, to reach rank-and-file detainees supposedly protected by the Geneva Conventions, hundreds of persons detained by US forces have been tortured, otherwise ill-treated, 'disappeared', detained indefinitely—or any combination of the above. Dozens have died, some of them as a result of torture. Interrogation techniques used included secret, incommunicado detention for months and years, sleep deprivation, painful positions, 'waterboarding', stripping, sexual and other humiliation, the use of dogs to induce fear, exposure to noise, exposure to hot or cold temperatures (to the point of death, in one case) and a wide array of violence—also, in some cases, to the point of death. Some of the techniques used were written in lists approved by the Secretary of Defense, others were, possibly, approved for CIA use, and yet others were used without authority, or in excess of what was authorized. The Abu Ghraib scandal caused much rethinking. The Supreme Court determined that certain aspects of international law (Common Art 3) and national law (*habeas corpus*) do protect 'war on terror' detainees. Legislation has been enacted explicitly prohibiting 'torture' and 'cruel, inhuman or degrading treatment or punishment' and applying Common Art 3 to 'war on terror' detainees, albeit while attempting to deny them *habeas corpus* rights and granting (past) torturers immunity. However, The US administration has doggedly maintained that it is ultimately for the President to determine which interrogation methods are appropriate—at least as regards the now narrowly defined HVDs. This includes secret, incommunicado detention and most of the CIA's other interrogation techniques. The administration has successfully negotiated legislative formulae that allow this CIA program to continue—at least until the courts determine otherwise, or legislation is tightened. In mid-2007, when this study was concluded, I would submit that a model of (at least) quasi-legalized torture is still in existence in the USA's 'war on terror.'

***

Neither Israel nor the USA have succeeded in limiting torture to TBSs (or to HVDs), although both states have refined their models in an effort to do so. Both states claim, probably rightly in some specific cases, that torturing (not so named)

---

[462] See Part II, Ch 9, Section E.

[463] At a joint hearing of the US House and Senate intelligence committees on 26 September 2002, Cofer Black, then head of the CIA's Counterterrorist Center, speaking about new 'operational flexibility' regarding the treatment of suspected terrorists stated: 'This is a very highly classified area, but I have to say that all you need to know: There was a before 9/11, and there was an after 9/11. After 9/11 the gloves come off' (see Priest and Gellman, *supra* n 354).

has thwarted terrorist attacks and saved lives. Neither, however, has claimed to have thereby put an end to such attacks, and the claim that torture has done more harm than good, including in terms of human lives, cannot easily be refuted.

Further conclusions regarding these models will be drawn once the salient legal issues to which they give rise have been analysed, in the next Part.

PART IV

LEGALIZING TORTURE
2—THREE ISSUES

17

Part IV—Introduction

In this Part, I will address three issues raised by the discussion of the models in the previous Part. Firstly, both Israel and the USA have denied that the methods of interrogation used under their respective models constitute torture, or are even unlawful at all under international law, for instance as 'cruel, inhuman or degrading treatment'. In claiming this, they have been supported by some academic and other writers. These 'definitional' aspects of the models will be dealt with in Chapter 18.

Secondly, the criminal law 'defence of necessity' provides the legal basis for the two (Israeli) models which fully legalized torture (not so named), as well as featuring in the US HVD model. Pending an HCJ-like judicial determination in the USA, in mid-2007 it is the only legal provision through which practices of interrogational torture have been allowed in law anywhere in the modern world. Its adoption as a torture-facilitating mechanism beyond Israel has been suggested both by academics and, in the case of the USA, accepted by officials, although not as yet applied (to my knowledge). Moreover, it is based, often explicitly, on the 'lesser evil' moral approach which, applied unreservedly in extreme situations, would, as we have seen in Part I, justify acts such as torture in a TBS. For these reasons, an extensive discussion of the applicability of this defence to such torture is undertaken in Chapter 19, covering both national and international legal systems.

Thirdly, in concluding this Part, I will examine the applicability of that defence, as well other 'private' criminal law defences and similar mechanisms, to the reality of states facing terrorism in the early twenty-first century.

18

Is it (Internationally) Legal? Is it Torture?

A. Introduction

How does international law view interrogation methods used in the Israeli and US models? This question will be addressed by discussing three narrower questions. Firstly, whether 'coercive interrogation' may be used involving methods which would not even constitute 'cruel, inhuman or degrading treatment' (henceforth also: ill-treatment), and therefore be by all accounts lawful under international law; secondly, whether methods not amounting to torture but 'only' to cruel, inhuman or degrading treatment may, at least in extreme circumstances, be lawfully used; thirdly, whether torture itself could ever be lawful; and fourthly whether or not the Israeli and US methods do, or may, amount to torture, as defined by the UN Convention Against Torture—the definition used in this study.[1]

Throughout this chapter, the 'law' in 'lawful' means international law; thus international treaties and custom, jurisprudence and other sources of law rather than the views of individual states, governments or domestic courts comprise the yardstick for 'lawfulness' used here.

B. Can 'Coercive Interrogation' be Less than 'Cruel, Inhuman or Degrading'?

Some officials, institutions and writers have suggested that interrogation methods may be used that are at once coercive and lawful, namely without

---

[1] This definition has been used far beyond the UN human rights treaty monitoring system, and some cases where it is are cited below. According to many sources, including the International Criminal Tribunal for the Former Yugoslavia (ICTY), it is 'representative of customary international law'. *Prosecutor v Zejnil Delalic et al*, Case No IT-96–21, ICTY Trial Chamber II, Judgment of 16 November 1998, para 259. However, in another case the same Court may have qualified this determination in respect of 'international criminal law relating to armed conflicts' where it found it 'appropriate to identify or spell out some specific elements that pertain to torture as considered from ... [this] specific viewpoint' (*Prosecutor v Anto Furundzija*, Case No IT-95–17/1-T, ICTY Trial Chamber II, Judgment of 10 December 1998, para 162). Subsequent ICTY decisions point in the same direction, see Malcolm D Evans, 'Getting to Grips with Torture' 51 *ICLQ* 365 (2002) 376–7, especially fn 48. Nevertheless, the added elements (or detracted ones, as in the case of official involvement) are not of a nature to have an effect on the substantive discussion here.

constituting even cruel, inhuman or degrading treatment, let alone torture. Thus Israeli officials consistently denied that the methods used by the GSS amounted to torture or any other ill-treatment—talking to the UN Committee Against Torture (CAT) in 2001, after the Landau model had been replaced by the HCJ one, they stated that:

…interrogation methods used by its General Security Service did not and never had amounted to violations of the Convention…[2]

The Harvard University and Kennedy School of Government 'Long-Term Legal Strategy Project for Preserving Security and Democratic Freedoms in the War on Terrorism'[3] speaks of:

…highly coercive interrogation, not forbidden by the UN Convention Against Torture or the Geneva Conventions….[4]

Benvenisti makes a more detailed argument. He claims that what he terms 'the conceptual approach' which 'appears in the texts of various international instruments: humanitarian law conventions… [and] human rights conventions… rejects the ban on any forceful measures during interrogations.'[5] On that basis Benvenisti proposes a way to:

…enable decision-makers, including national courts, to recognize circumstances which justify the use of force in interrogations of suspected terrorists….[6]

The only legal peg on which Benvenisti can possibly hang the rather surprising argument that there are circumstances in which international law may allow the 'use of force' during interrogations, rather than impose a total ban on such use, is the brief episode of confusion on this issue, created in 1969 when the now-defunct European Commission of Human Rights defined 'inhuman treatment' as:

…at least such treatment as deliberately causes severe suffering, mental or physical, which, in the particular situation, is unjustifiable.[7]

---

[2] UN Press Release: Panel Continues Review of Report of Israel, CAT 27th session, 21 November 2001, Afternoon <http://www.unhchr.ch/huricane/huricane.nsf/NewsRoom?OpenFrameSet>, accessed 30 November 2002.

[3] PB Heymann and JN Kayyem, *Long-Term Legal Strategy Project for Preserving Security and Democratic Freedoms in the War on Terrorism*, Harvard University and the Kennedy School of Government and Law, November 2004 <http://www.mipt.org/pdf/Long-Term-Legal-Strategy.pdf>, accessed 16 February 2005.

[4] *Ibid*, 23. 'Highly coercive interrogation methods' are defined as '… all those techniques that fall in the category between those forbidden as torture by treaty or statute and those traditionally allowed in seeking a voluntary confession under the due process clauses of the U.S. Constitution' (*ibid*, 24).

[5] E Benvenisti, 'The Role of National Courts in Preventing Torture of Suspected Terrorists' 8 *EJIL* 596 (1997) 604.

[6] *Ibid*, 602.

[7] *Denmark et al v Greece* (the Greek case), 12 *Yearbook* (1969) 186.

However, in a later case the Commission clarified that:

...it did not have in mind the possibility that there could be any justification for any treatment in breach of Art. 3.[8]

While the issue of justification raised by the Commission in the *Greek case* has attracted extensive academic attention, it has since been, to quote Rodley, 'abandoned by the European Court of Human Rights and rejected elsewhere'.[9]

I propose to examine the related issues of justifiability and 'below the threshold use of force/coercions' in interrogations further by looking at some examples from the work of the European Committee for the Prevention of Torture and Inhuman and Degrading Treatment or Punishment (CPT). The CPT works under the European Convention for the Prevention of Torture and Inhuman and Degrading Treatment or Punishment (1987).[10] According to the Directorate of Human Rights, the CPT 'should not seek to interfere in the interpretation and application of Article 3'[11] as its 'activities are aimed at future prevention rather than the application of legal requirements to existing circumstances'.[12] The CPT has nevertheless (and understandably) adopted an approach which is not exclusively future-oriented. Its country reports do provide extensive observations on practices of states.

Describing its own task, the CPT has stated that:

...to accomplish its preventive function effectively, it must aim at a degree of protection that is greater than that upheld by the European Commission and European Court of Human Rights when adjudging cases concerning the ill-treatment of persons deprived of their liberty and their conditions of detention.[13]

---

[8] *Ireland v UK*, 512 *Yearbook* (1976) at 750. It should be stressed, in addition, that even in the *Greek* Case, the Commission only mentions justifiability as relevant to 'inhuman treatment', not to torture or even to 'degrading treatment'.

[9] NS Rodley, 'The Definition(s) of Torture in International Law', 55 *Current Legal Problems* 465 (2002) 471. Manfred Nowak (re)introduces the concept of justifiability into his analysis of what constitutes torture and other ill-treatment. See *idem*, 'What Practices Constitute Torture?: US and UN Standards' 28(4) *Human Rights Quarterly* 809 (2006) eg at 821. However, he unequivocally rejects extending it to interrogations. See *ibid*, 836–9.

[10] ETS 126, adopted at Strasbourg on 26 November 1987, entered into force 1 February 1989. Texts of Council of Europe human rights treaties are available eg at the European Court of Human Rights Court's website <http://www.echr.coe.int>. For human rights treaties generally see eg Office of the High Commissioner for Human Rights, *Human Rights: A Compilation of International Instruments* (2 volumes, New York and Geneva: UN 1997) and that Office's website <http://www.ohchr.org>. On the work of the CPT generally see eg M Evans and R Morgan, 'The European Convention for the Prevention of Torture: Operational Practice' 41 *ICLQ* 590 (1992); *idem*, 'The European Convention for the Prevention of Torture: 1992–1997' 46 *ICLQ* 663 (1997); *idem*, *Preventing Torture* (Oxford: OUP, 1998) Chs 5–9; *idem*, *Combating Torture in Europe* (Strasbourg: Council of Europe Publishing, 2001); NS Rodley, *The Treatment of Prisoners under International Law* (2nd edn, Oxford: Clarendon, 1999) 161–166.

[11] Directorate of Human Rights, *Explanatory report on the European Convention for the Prevention of Torture and Inhuman and Degrading Treatment or Punishment,* (Strasbourg: Council of Europe, 1989) 10.

[12] *Ibid.*

[13] CPT, *1st General Report on the CPT's Activities Covering the Period November 1989 to December 1990*, CPT/Inf (91) 3, para 51.

While obviously not having official legal clout—certainly regarding states like Israel and the USA, the CPT has nevertheless been in a unique position where it could, and has, explored what may be described as the lower reaches of the prohibition on torture and other ill-treatment, where one would presumably find justification, or at least legal legitimacy, for what Benvenisti terms 'lawful use of force'[14] when interrogations are conducted in a 'ticking bomb situation' (TBS).[15]

The CPT, however, has regularly and consistently described (and invariably criticized) treatment such as slaps, punches, kicks, and beatings as 'ill-treatment' or 'physical ill-treatment',[16] that is, as unlawful. For instance, in the case of Slovenia, the CPT cites the following as 'allegations of physical ill-treatment' in the context of interrogation:

> ...blows (slaps and punches) inflicted by criminal investigation officers in the course of questioning.[17]

Nowhere in any of its reports does the CPT state that such blows, kicks, and so on, should be severe or excessive in order to qualify as ill-treatment or to be 'unjustified'. Only in the context of force used in apprehending suspects does the CPT refer to 'injuries' which 'could have resulted from the *excessive* use of force by the police',[18] (emphasis added) implying that 'non-excessive' force would have been justified.

This distinction is clearly explained, for instance, in a CPT report to Bulgaria:

> The CPT fully recognises that the apprehension of a suspect may often be hazardous, particularly if the individual concerned resists and/or the police have reason to believe that the person might be armed and dangerous. The circumstances may be such that the apprehended person, and possibly also the police, suffer injuries, without this being the result of an intention to inflict ill-treatment. However, no more force than is reasonably necessary must be used. Furthermore, *once apprehended persons have been brought under control, there can never be any justification for their being struck by police officers.*[19] [Emphasis added.]

---

[14] Benvenisti, *supra* n 5, 604.

[15] Benvenisti uses this term throughout.

[16] See eg *Report to the Maltese Government on the visit to Malta carried out by the CPT from 1 to 9 July 1990*, CPT/Inf (93) 13, para 29 [henceforth a shortened reference will be used:]; *CPT—Germany*, 1991, CPT/Inf (93) 13, para 64; *CPT—Greece*, 1993, CPT/Inf (94) 20, para 20, *CPT—Portugal*, 1996, CPT/Inf (98) 1, para 8; *CPT—Azerbaijan*, 2002, CPT/Inf (2004) 36, para 20; *CPT—Latvia*, 2002, CPT/Inf (2005) 8, para 10; *CPT—Bosnia and Herzegovina*, 2003, CPT/Inf (2004) 40, paras 18–19; *CPT—Georgia*, 2003, 2004, CPT/Inf (2005) 12, paras 17, 18, 143; *CPT—Austria*, 2004, CPT/Inf (2005) 13, para 13.

[17] *CPT—Slovenia*, 1995, CPT/Inf (96) 18, para 12.

[18] *Ibid.*

[19] *CPT—Bulgaria*, 1995, CPT/Inf (97) 1, para 31. Near-identical language is used elsewhere, eg in *CPT—Norway*, 1999, CPT/Inf (2000) 15, para 11; *CPT—UK*, 2003, CPT/Inf (2005) 1, para 148. A similar point is made by the CPT regarding the use of force in effecting the expulsion of aliens, see *CPT—Spain*, 1997, CPT/Inf (98) 9, para 11.

This line is strictly maintained in the CPT's work vis-à-vis state parties facing terrorism, the three obvious examples in the 1990s being Spain, Turkey and the United Kingdom.

In all three cases the CPT, using virtually identical language, emphasized that it 'abhors' terrorism, which justifies a 'strong response from state institutions'.[20] Nevertheless, it immediately adds, in all cases, and again using almost the same words:

> However, the Committee has also emphasised that the response to terrorism must never be allowed to degenerate into acts of torture or other forms of ill-treatment by law enforcement officials.[21]

Nor have the events of 11 September 2001 changed the CPT's approach. In a public statement concerning the Chechen Republic of the Russian Federation in 2003, the CPT stated:

> The CPT has witnessed for itself the extreme difficulties confronting the federal and republican authorities in their efforts to restore the rule of law and achieve a lasting reconciliation in this part of the Russian Federation. Acts causing great loss of life and human suffering have been, and continue to be, committed by combatants opposing federal power structures. The CPT condemns these acts and fully understands the need for a strong response from State institutions. However, that response must never degenerate into acts of torture or other forms of ill-treatment; a State must avoid the trap of abandoning civilised values.[22]

How low the threshold level at which 'acts' become such 'ill-treatment' may be gleaned from the CPT's comments on the UK's treatment of its detained terrorist suspects:

> The Committee also trusts that police and prison officers dealing with persons detained pursuant to the Anti-Terrorism, Crime and Security Act 2001 will bear in mind that all forms of ill-treatment, including verbal abuse, are not acceptable.[23]

Now there is, of course, independently of the issue of justifiability, a level below which Art 3 (and, by analogy, Art 7 of the ICCPR and Art 16 of the UN Convention Against Torture) does not apply. In a *dictum* in the *Ireland v UK* case, cited numerous times since, the European Court said:

> ... ill-treatment must attain a minimum level of severity if it is to fall within the scope of Article 3. The assessment of this minimum is, in the nature of things, relative; it depends

---

[20] *CPT—Spain*, 1994, CPT/Inf (96) 9, para 6; *CPT—Public Statement on Turkey*, 21 December 1992, 15 EHRR 309, para 28; *CPT—Public Statement on Turkey*, 6 December 1996 CPT/Inf (96) 34, para 11; *CPT—UK (Northern Ireland)*, 1993, CPT/Inf (94) 17, para 10.

[21] See the same respective paragraphs in all sources cited *ibid*.

[22] *CPT, Public statement concerning the Chechen Republic of the Russian Federation* (made on 10 July 2003), CPT/Inf (2003) 33, para 1.

[23] *CPT—UK*, 2002, CPT/Inf (2003) 18, para 12.

on all the circumstances of the case, such as the duration of the treatment, its physical or mental effects and, in some cases, the sex, age and state of health of the victim, etc.[24]

The jurisprudence of the Court points to that 'level of minimum severity' being somewhere between a boy being 'slippered three times on his buttocks through his shorts with a rubber-soled gym shoe by the headmaster in private'[25] leaving no marks, where no violation of Art 3 was found, and 'three strokes of the birch' on another (older) boy's bare posterior, administered by a policeman and which 'raised, but did not cut, the applicant's skin and he was sore for about a week and a half afterwards';[26] or 'the use of a garden cane, applied with considerable force, on more than one occasion'[27] on a third boy, in both of which cases the applicant was found to have been 'subjected to treatment of sufficient severity to fall within the scope of Article 3'.[28]

This raises a related question: if interrogators use 'sub-threshold' techniques, how effective would those actually be in 'coercing' hardened terrorists to talk?

This problem is acutely illustrated by a real-life example which Benvenisti provides for what he calls the 'ticking bomb paradigm', where the 'use of force' in interrogations would be 'lawful'. Benvenisti cites the case of Nachshon Wachsman, an Israeli soldier kidnapped in October 1994 by HAMAS terrorists, who then issued an ultimatum for the release of some of their leaders in exchange for him.[29] An aide to the kidnappers was captured and his interrogation,

---

[24] *Ireland v The UK*, Series A No 25 (1978), para 162. This *dictum* has gone beyond Europe. In *Voulanne*, the Human Rights Committee shamelessly 'observes' the following: 'The Committee... observes that the assessment of what constitute inhuman or degrading treatment falling within the meaning of article 7 depends on all the circumstances of the case, such as the duration and manner or the treatment, its physical and mental effects as well as the sex, age and state of health of the victim' (Human Rights Committee, *Antti Voulanne v Finland*, Communication No 265/1987 (7 April 1989), UN GAOR Sup No 40 (A/44/40), 1989, 249–258, para 9.2). The statement is obviously a *verbatim* quotation (with two very minor changes) from the above, but this fact is ignored. The issue of the relative importance of 'severity' vis-à-vis other elements will be discussed below in the context of the ill-treatment/torture threshold, in Ch 18, Section E.

[25] *Costello-Roberts v UK*, Series A No 247-C (1993), para 31.

[26] *Tyrer v UK*, Series A No 26 (1978), paras 9–10.

[27] *Case of A v UK* (100/1997/884/1096), Judgment of 23 September 1998, para 21.

[28] *Ibid*, para 23. In *Tyrer* the Court found, more specifically, that the applicant was subjected to 'degrading punishment'. See *supra* n 26, para 35.

[29] On 17 November 1995, *Haaretz* quoted Wachsman's mother, Esther, as saying: 'We have released 1500 terrorists for Hezi Shai [an Israeli soldier captured by Palestinians in Lebanon], we have released terrorists for half of an identity disk of a missing soldier, and it's impossible to release an old man for a 20-year-old boy?' (Sholomo Dror, 'Nachshon Wachsman's mother: "Rabin said he bears responsibility; I want to know what this means"', *Haaretz* (17 November 1995)). Mrs Wachsman was referring to the HAMAS leader, Sheikh Ahmad Yassin, at the time imprisoned in Israel. Sheikh Yassin was indeed released three years later, in exchange for the release of two Mossad agents by Jordan. Wachsman, another Israeli soldier and the three kidnappers were killed during the attempted rescue operation. All of which point to a more complex situation—and moral dilemmas—than the simple 'forceful-interrogation-or-loss-of-lives' equation described by Benvenisti. In 2004 Sheikh Yassin was assassinated by the Israeli air-force.

according to Benvenisti, 'provided accurate information as to the house, including its layout, where Wachsman was held'.[30]

Regarding that interrogation, Benvenisti states the following:

Although details of the interrogation methods were not disclosed, we cannot assume that the aide divulged the information upon his own free will.[31]

The assertion of absence of information is not altogether correct. On the 19th of the same month, the late Yitzhak Rabin, then Prime Minister and Minister of Defence, declared the following, at a press conference:

If the security services had acted according to the Landau guidelines in interrogating Hamas members, they wouldn't have reached the place where the kidnappers of Nachshon Wachsman were found, in Bir Naballah.[32]

Finding that place required, therefore, methods beyond the Landau guidelines, namely even more severe than those condemned by international bodies and experts as torture (see below). *A fortiori* those methods constitute torture, and must then come under what Benvenisti himself terms 'particularly brutal methods, methods so harsh that no exceptional circumstances could condone'.[33]

Turning back to the law, international humanitarian law provides a direct rebuttal of the notion that 'coercive interrogation' may be lawful. Treaties now ratified by every single state in the world use that very word (coercion), in that very context (interrogation) to denote unlawful acts. According to the Third Geneva Convention:

No physical or mental torture, nor any other form of coercion, may be inflicted on prisoners of war to secure from them information of any kind whatever. Prisoners of war who refuse to answer may not be threatened, insulted, or exposed to unpleasant or disadvantageous treatment of any kind.[34]

---

[30] Benvenisti, *supra* n 5, 600. This incident is described at length by the then GSS head, K Gilon, *Shin-Beth Between the Schisms* [Hebrew] (Tel-Aviv: La-Miskal, 2000) Ch 14.

[31] Benvenisti, *ibid*.

[32] Quoted in *Haaretz* (20 October 1994). According to Gilon, he requested, and received, approval from the then State Attorney (and later Supreme Court judge and President) Dorit Beinish, for interrogating detainees suspected of being involved in the kidnapping 'under special permissions' (*supra* n 30, 219–220).

[33] Benvenisti, *supra* n 5, 611.

[34] 1949 Geneva Convention III relative to the Treatment of Prisoners of War, Adopted on 12 August 1949, entered into force 21 October 1950, Art 17. See also 1977 Geneva Protocol I Additional to the Geneva Conventions of 12 August 1949, and Relating to the Protection of Victims of International Armed Conflicts, adopted on 8 June 1977, entered into force 7 December 1978, Arts 75(2)(a)(ii); 75(2)(b); 75(2)(e).

For text of international humanitarian law treaties see eg A Roberts and R Guelff (eds), *Documents on the Laws of War* (3rd edn, Oxford: Clarendon, 2000), and the ICRC website <http://www.icrc.org>.

The Fourth Geneva Convention, which regulates the treatment of civilians under occupation or otherwise under the power of a party to a conflict similarly provides that:

No physical or moral coercion shall be exercised against protected persons, in particular to obtain information from them or from third parties.[35]

If there is no *a fortiori* relationship between such provisions of international humanitarian law and those of international human rights law, theirs must at least be a *mutatis mutandis* one. Put differently, since international humanitarian law provides the applicable law for what in international human rights law is a state of emergency *par excellence*, surely it blocks the possibility of states resorting to less humane treatment under the latter law. International humanitarian law thus gives external content to what is 'cruel, inhuman or degrading treatment or punishment', and force to the interpretation thereof by the UN General Assembly, to wit:

The term 'cruel, inhuman or degrading treatment or punishment' should be interpreted so as to extend the widest possible protection against abuses.[36]

In sum, 'coercion' in interrogation would amount, at least, to 'cruel, inhuman or degrading treatment' and be clearly, and absolutely, unlawful under both international humanitarian law and international human rights law.

The conclusion is that while ill-treatment must, *inter alia*, reach a certain threshold of severity to become unlawful, international law does not recognize 'coercive interrogation' that is lawful or justifiable. The level of ill-treatment below the reach of international provisions is low to the extent that proponents of 'coercive interrogation' are left with techniques that are either, in practice, unlikely to be effective as means of coercing a terrorist to provide information, or, in law, constitute violations, crimes, or both. International law does not envisage detainees being legitimately coerced into providing information, and has therefore made no allowance for an effective means of doing so.

---

[35] 1949 Geneva Convention IV relative to the Protection of Civilian Persons in Time of War, adopted on 12 August 1949, entered into force 21 October 1950, Art 31. See also Arts 5, 27, 32, 37. The Rome Statute of the International Criminal Court uses similar language when providing, in Art 55(b), for the '[r]ights of persons during an investigation': '(b) [such a person] [s]hall not be subjected to any form of coercion, duress or threat, to torture or to any other form of cruel, inhuman or degrading treatment or punishment' (Rome Statue of the International Criminal Court, adopted on 17 July 1998 (A/CONF.183/9), entered into force 1 July 2002. For text see eg the Court's website <http://www.icc-cpi.int.>. (Henceforth: ICC Statute).

[36] UN Body of Principles for the Protection of All Persons under Any Form of Detention or Imprisonment, adopted by General Assembly resolution 43/173 of 9 December 1988, Principle 7. For this 'fusion' see eg the International Committee of the Red Cross (Jean-Marie Henckaerts and Louise Doswald-Beck, eds), *Customary International Humanitarian Law*, Vol 1: Rules (Cambridge: CUP 2005), where, in explaining rules of customary international humanitarian law, and specifically the definitions of 'humane treatment', 'torture', and 'inhuman treatment' therein, the ICRC relies upon sources from both international humanitarian law and international human rights law, see 307–8; 317–18; and 318–19, respectively.

C. Can 'Cruel, Inhuman or Degrading' Interrogation be Lawful?

For several officials, institutions; and writers, the international legal prohibition of cruel, inhuman or degrading treatment does not seem as restrictive as that of torture—it is not absolute, and may withdraw in the face of extreme situations, such as a TBS. As noted in the previous Part, the US administration memoranda claimed that acts of ill-treatment should be prevented but 'states need not criminalize' them,[37] and its interpretation of subsequent legislation seems to subtly follow this line. In 2001, Israeli delegates at a CAT session more than hinted that the use of ill-treatment, though not of torture, was sometimes justified:

The use of cruel, inhuman, or degrading procedures was prohibited in Israel, and perpetrators were subject to prosecution, the delegation said. In extreme and appropriate circumstances, where it was judged necessary to save lives, force could be used in interrogations, but it was not such force as to amount to torture.[38]

Mark Bowden distinguishes, relying on the KUBARK manual[39] and Israeli interrogation methods, between on the one hand 'methods that, some people argue, fall short of torture' which as noted he believes 'should be banned but also quietly practiced' and on the other 'outright torture' which he believes should always remain a crime.[40]

Levinson makes the same argument along legal lines:

The U.N. convention [Against Torture] also states that 'no exceptional circumstances *whatsoever*, whether a state of war or a threat of war, internal political instability or any other public emergency, may be invoked as a justification of torture' (emphasis added). This is as powerful a condemnation of torture as can be imagined. By the same token, though, it leaves open the argument that anything less than torture may be permissible during dire times.[41]

---

[37] See Part III, Ch 15, Section D(1).

[38] UN Press Release: Panel Continues Review of Report of Israel, CAT 27th session, 21 November 2001, afternoon <http://www.unhchr.ch/huricane/huricane.nsf/NewsRoom?OpenFrameSet>, accessed 30 November 2002.

[39] A CIA document entitled 'KUBARK Counterintelligence Interrogation' July 1963. For text see eg <http://www.gwu.edu/~nsarchiv/NSAEBB/NSAEBB27/01–01.htm>, accessed 12 November 2007.

[40] M Bowden, 'The Dark Art of Interrogation' *The Atlantic Monthly*, October 2003, <http://www.theatlantic.com/issues/2003/10/bowden.htm>, accessed 19 October 2003.

[41] S Levinson, 'Brutal Logic', *Village Voice* (11 May 2004). See similarly JT Parry, 'What is Torture, Are We Doing It, and What if We Are?' 64 *University of Pittsburgh L Rev* 237 (2003) 243; A Reichman 'When We Sit to Judge, Are We Being Judged? The Israeli GSS Case, Ex Parte Pinochet and Domestic/Global Deliberation' *Cardozo J. Int'l & Comp L* 41 (2001); A Reichman and T Kahana, 'Israel and the Recognition of Torture: Domestic and International Aspects' in C Scott (ed), *Torture as Tort: Comparative Perspectives on the Development of Transnational Human*

The study attached to the Harvard University and Kennedy School of Government Strategy Project similarly argues that under the UN Convention Against Torture:

> ... states may arguably engage in cruel, inhuman or degrading conduct and still fulfill their obligations under the Convention Against Torture so long as exceptional circumstances justify such conduct.[42]

Is the UN Convention Against Torture 'soft' on cruel, inhuman or degrading treatment? Perhaps, and this question would doubtless have warranted some discussion here had Art 16 of that Convention been the sole provision binding the states concerned. However, as the second paragraph of the same Article points out, 'other international instrument[s] ... prohibit cruel, inhuman or degrading treatment or punishment' and the Article stipulates that '[t]he provisions of this Convention are without prejudice' to these. The other instruments[43] concerned prohibit such ill-treatment absolutely, in exactly the same way that they prohibit torture. The two salient instances are the International Covenant on Civil and Political Rights, which prohibits torture and ill-treatment—without distinction—even 'in time of public emergency which threatens the life of the nation';[44] and the Geneva Conventions, which prohibit, as noted, any 'physical or moral coercion' in interrogations, in addition to, *inter alia* 'inhuman treatment',[45] 'cruel treatment',[46] and 'outrages upon personal dignity, in particular, humiliating and degrading treatment'[47] as well as providing for the protection of prisoners

---

Rights Litigation (Oxford: Hart Publishing, 2001) 631–59, 649; M Ignatieff, *The Lesser Evil: Political Ethics in an Age of Terror* (Edinburgh: Edinburgh University Press, 2005) 138–9.

[42] *Supra* n 3, 160, Appendix B, entitled 'Coercive Interrogations' by Tom Lue. Although having a single author, terms such as 'we recommend', used often, suggest that Lue is writing for the Project as a whole.

[43] 'Cruel, inhuman or degrading treatment or punishment' are, in addition, prohibited absolutely at customary international law. This will not be elaborated here, but see eg *infra* n 79 and accompanying text.

[44] Article 4. Article 7 provides, *inter alia*, that '[n]o one shall be subjected to torture or to cruel, inhuman or degrading treatment or punishment'.

[45] Article 130 of the 1949 Geneva Convention III relative to the Treatment of Prisoners of War, Adopted on 12 August 1949, entered into force 21 October 1950; Art 147 of the 1949 Geneva Convention IV relative to the Protection of Civilian Persons in Time of War. For text of international humanitarian law treaties see eg A Roberts and R Guelff (eds), *Documents on the Laws of War* (3rd edn, Oxford: Clarendon, 2000), and the ICRC website <http://www.icrc.org>.

[46] Article 3(1) common to all four Geneva Conventions; Geneva Convention III, *ibid*, Art 87; Geneva Convention IV, Art 118; 1977 Geneva Protocol I Additional to the Geneva Conventions of 12 August 1949, and Relating to the Protection of Victims of International Armed Conflicts, adopted on 8 June 1977, entered into force 7 December 1978, Art 75(1); 1977 Geneva Protocol II Additional to the Geneva Conventions of 12 August 1949 and Relating to the Protection of Victims of Non-International Armed Conflicts, adopted on 8 June 1977, entered into force 7 December 1978, Art 4(2)(a).

[47] Article 3(c) common to all four Geneva Conventions; Additional Protocol I, Art 75(2)(b); Additional Protocol II, Art 4(2)(e).

of war and civilian detainees 'at all time...against all acts of violence or threats thereof and against insults and public curiosity'.[48]

Torture is the focus of this study, and the question of whether torture may ever be practised lawfully under international law as it presently stands is addressed below, in Section D, with some elaboration, and answered in the negative. As the discussion there will show, international statutory provisions, as well as find-ings, rulings and statements prohibiting and criminalizing torture often include prohibitions of cruel, inhuman or degrading treatment and their international humanitarian law equivalents, the same absolute terms applying to both equally. Under both strands of international law, the line separating lawful interroga-tion methods from unlawful ones does not lie between what constitutes torture and what is 'only' cruel, inhuman or degrading. Rather, all forms of torture and ill-treatment are strictly and equally prohibited in all circumstances.

Commenting on the European human rights system, DJ Harris, M O'Boyle and C Warbick explain that:

...the boundary between torture and other forms of ill-treatment is relevant both to the question of compensation that may be awarded...and to a state's reputation.[49]

In other systems it has additional consequences, some of them significant.[50] However, beyond, arguably, the UN Convention Against Torture, as explained above, nothing distinguishes the *absoluteness* of the prohibition of one type of unlawful treatment from another—certainly not a notion that ill-treatment may be resorted to, or justified, in extreme circumstances.

The duty of a state—*any* state—regarding its treatment of detainees—*any* detainees—under international law may be summed up in one short sentence: 'They shall at all times be humanely treated.'[51] It is here that international law has created, through treaty and custom, an obligation that states can never renounce, and a line that must never be crossed.

In *Furundzija*, the ICTY emphasized that:

The essence of the whole corpus of international humanitarian law as well as human rights law lies in the protection of the human dignity of every person...The gen-eral principle of respect for human dignity is...the very *raison d'être* of international humanitarian law and human rights law; indeed in modern times it has become of such paramount importance as to permeate the whole body of international law. This principle is intended to shield human beings from outrages upon their personal dignity, whether

---

[48] Geneva Convention III, Art 13; Geneva Convention IV, Art 27.

[49] DJ Harris, M O'Boyle and C Warbick, *Law of the European Convention on Human Rights* (London: Butterworths, 1995) 56–7.

[50] Including the applicability of universal jurisdiction and admissibility of evidence under the UN Convention Against Torture, and possibly the severity of punishment under international criminal law.

[51] Geneva Convention IV, Art 27. See similarly Art 3(1) common to all four Geneva Conventions; Additional Protocol I, Art 75(1); Additional Protocol II, Art 4(1); Art 10(1) of the ICCPR.

such outrages are carried out by unlawfully attacking the body or by humiliating and debasing the honour, the self-respect or the mental well being of a person.[52]

The pointed words of Lord Gardiner, several decades ago, already quoted in Part I, on the legal and moral repercussions of modifying this position, in our very context (ie interrogating suspected terrorists) may be used again to sum up this discussion; they are as actual now as they were then:

> If it is to be made legal to employ methods not now legal against a man whom the police believe to have, but who may not have, information which the police desire to obtain, I, like many of our witnesses, have searched for, but have been unable to find, either in logic or in morals, any limit to the degree of ill-treatment to be legalised. The only logical limit to the degree of ill-treatment to be legalised would appear to be whatever degree of ill treatment proves to be necessary to get the information out of him, which would include, if necessary, extreme torture.[53]

D. May States Ever Torture Lawfully?

This question will be given short shrift. The subject of discussion here being neither the law as it should be, nor states' actual policies, but rather where international law stands at the time when this study was prepared for publication, in mid-2007, the simple, virtually unanimous answer to the question is no. This is already borne out, *a fortiori*, by the discussion of 'lesser' (or other) forms of ill-treatment in Chapter 18, but some elaboration may nevertheless be helpful.

No state, democratic or otherwise, facing terrorism or otherwise, has so far claimed that torture in a TBS is acceptable under international law. States that torture either deny that they do or, as we have seen, claim that their methods do not constitute torture or (in the case of US administration lawyers) that the President may order torture under a Constitution that supersedes international law; writers who think it *should* be lawful almost invariably call, as we have seen, for changes to that law[54] rather than arguing that torture by states *is* lawful. Even the use of the terms 'virtually' and 'almost' is a generous concession to the few, unconvincing attempts at claiming otherwise. In what follows, I will therefore limit myself to a brief overview of relevant law.

There is extensive agreement among Courts and writers that the prohibition on torture is a rule of customary international law.[55] More importantly for our

---

[52] *Furundzija* ICTY case, *supra* n 1, para 183.

[53] Report of the Committee of Privy Counsellors appointed to consider authorized procedures for the interrogation of persons suspected of terrorism, Cmmd No 4901 (Lord Parker of Wadington, Chairman 1972), Minority report by Lord Gardiner of Kittisford.

[54] See *supra*, Part II, Ch 9, Section D(2)(h).

[55] For courts see eg *Filartiga v Peña-Irala*, 630 F.2d 876, 882 (1980); *Abebe-Jiri v Negewo*, WL 814304 (ND Ga, 1993—only Westlaw citation available), 3; *Kadic v Karadzic* 70 F.3d 232, 245

purposes, this prohibition is widely recognized as a *jus cogens* norm, namely 'a peremptory norm of general international law' which is:

...accepted and recognized by the international community of States as a whole as a norm *from which no derogation is permitted* and which can be modified only by a subsequent norm of general international law having the same character.[56] [Emphasis added.]

Such recognition has been granted by national courts, one of which concluded that there was 'an extraordinary consensus' on this point;[57] international ones;[58] and writers.[59] Some have also considered the prohibition on torture an obligation

C.A.2 (NY 1995); *Estate of Cabello v Fernandez-Larios*, 157 F.Supp.2d 1345, 1360 (SD Fla, 2001). For writers see eg A Cassese, *International Criminal Law* (Oxford: OUP, 2003) 119; C Greenwood, 'International Law and the "War against Terrorism"' 78(2) *International Affairs* 301 (2002); WP Nagan and L Atkins, 'The International Law of Torture: From Universal Proscription to Effective Application and Enforcement' 14 *Harvard Human Rights Journal* 87 (2001) 113; R Wallace, *International Human Rights: Texts and Materials* (London: Sweet & Maxwell, 1997) 310. And see recently Henckaerts and Doswald-Beck, *supra* n 36, 306–8 ('civilians and persons *hors de combat* must be treated humanely'); 315–19 ('torture, cruel or inhuman treatment and outrages upon personal dignity, in particular humiliating and degrading treatment, are prohibited'). For practice see Vol II, Ch 32, sec A and Vol II, Ch 32, sec D, respectively.

Note that as *jus cogens* is a subset of customary international law, all sources below stating that the prohibition on torture is of the former variety accept it, *a fortiori*, as being of the latter.

I have not tapped here a long list of writers arguing that the Universal Declaration on Human Rights reflects, *in totto*, rules of customary international law, or that the same is true for the prohibition of all crimes against humanity.

[56] Vienna Convention on the Law of Treaties, A/CONF.39/27, adopted 22 May 1969, entered into force 23 May 1980, Art 53. 'Non-derogability' within a treaty and for *jus cogens* norms are slightly different concepts, but in this case fully overlap.

[57] *Siderman de Blake v Republic of Argentina*, 965 F.2d 699, 717 (9th Cir 1992), Cert denied. See also eg *Xuncax v Gramajo*, 886 F.Su 162, 189 (D Mass, 1995); *Committee of US Citizens Living in Nicaragua v Reagan*, 859 F.2d 929, 949 (DC Cir, 1988); *Mehinovic v Vuckovic*, 198 F.Supp.2d 1322, 1344 (ND Ga 2002); *R v Bow Street Metropolitan Stipendiary Magistrate And Others, Ex Parte Pinochet Ugarte* (No 3) [2000] 1 AC 147, 174 (per Browne Wilkinson LJ), 247 (per Hope LJ), 260 (per Lord Hutton LJ); *Jones v Ministry of Interior of Saudi Arabia* [2005] 2 WLR 808, para 108. See also *Restatement (Third) of Foreign Relations Law* § 702 (1987), comment o.

[58] See eg *Furundzija* ICTY case, *supra* n 1, paras 146, 153–7; *Delalic* ICTY case, *supra* n 1, para 454; *Prosecutor v Kunarac et al*, ICTY Case No IT-96–23 and IT-96–23/1, Trial Chamber II, Judgment of 22 February 2001, para 466; *Prosecutor v Milan Simic*, ICTY Case No IT-95–9/2-S, Trial Chamber II, Sentencing Judgment of 17 October 2002, para 34. See also in an ECHR case, *Al-Adsani v UK* (Application no 35763/97), Judgment of 21 November 2001, para 61; *Maritza Urrutia v Guatemala*, Inter-Am Ct HR (Ser C) No 103, Judgment of 27 November 2003, para 92; *Caesar v Trinidad and Tobago*, Inter-Am Ct HR (Ser C) No 123, Judgment of 11 March 2005, para 70.

See also comments by human rights monitoring mechanisms, eg Report by Special Rapporteur [on Torture], Mr P Kooijmans, appointed pursuant to Commission on Human Rights resolution 1985/33, UN Doc E/CN.4/1986/15 (1986), para 3; Human Rights Committee, General comment no 29: States of emergency (article 4), UN Doc CCPR/C/21/Rev.1/Add.11, 31 August 2001, para 11; Inter-American Commission on Human Rights, *Report on the Situation of Human Rights of Asylum Seekers within the Canadian Refugee Determination System*, OEA/Ser.L/V/II.106, Doc 40 rev, 28 February 2000, para 154.

[59] See eg JH Burgers and H Danelius, *The United Nations Convention against Torture: A Handbook on the Convention Against Torture and Other Cruel, Inhuman or Degrading Treatment or Punishment* (Dordrecht: M Nijhoff, 1988) 12; Erika De Wet, 'The Prohibition of Torture as an International Norm of jus cogens and Its Implications for National and Customary Law' 15(1) *EJIL* 97

erga omnes, namely one of the rights so important that all states 'have a legal interest in their protection'[60] worldwide.

Most democratic states are bound, in addition, by international human rights treaties which prohibit torture in all circumstances. Notable among these are the International Covenant on Civil and Political Rights (ICCPR) which prohibits torture and other ill-treatment even 'in time of public emergency which threatens the life of the nation';[61] and the UN Convention against Torture, which provides that:

No exceptional circumstances whatsoever, whether a state of war or a threat of war, internal political instability or any other public emergency, may be invoked as a justification of torture.[62]

In November 2001, CAT issued a statement condemning the attacks on the USA on 11 September 2001, both acknowledging 'the terrible threat to international peace and security posed by these acts of international terrorism' and reminding 'State parties to the Convention of the non-derogable nature of most of the obligations undertaken by them in ratifying the Convention', including the 'obligations contained in articles 2...15...and 16 (prohibiting cruel, inhuman or degrading treatment or punishment)...'[63]. CAT has consistently followed this line in its conclusions and recommendations to states parties.[64]

(2004), *passim* (De Wet assumes the existence of this norm without even debating it); Evans and Morgan, *Preventing Torture*, *supra* n 10, 62; T Meron, *Human Rights and Humanitarian Norms as Customary Law* (Oxford: Clarendon, 1991) 23; J Oraá, *Human Rights in States of Emergency in International Law* (Oxford: Clarendon, 1992) 96; Rodley, *The Treatment of Prisoners...*, *supra* n 10, 74.

In addition see Commentaries to the Draft Articles on Responsibility of States for Internationally Wrongful Acts, adopted by the International Law Commission in its fifty-third session (2001), UN Doc A/56/10, Ch. IV.E.2, November 2001, 284.

[60] *Barcelona Traction, Light and Power Company Limited, Second Phase*, I.C.J. Reports 1970, 3, para 33. See eg Evans and Morgan, *supra* n 10, 63; Nagan and Atkins, *supra* n 55, 90; *Restatement (Third) of Foreign Relations Law* §702 (1987), comment o. See also Browne Wilkinson LJ and Lord Hope LJ in the *Pinochet* case, *supra* n 57; *A and others v Secretary of State for the Home Department* [2004] UKHL 56, Judgment of 8 December 2005, para 24 (per Bingham LJ); and the ICTY Trials Camber in *Furundzija*, *supra* n 1, paras 151–2.

[61] See *supra* n 44.

[62] Article 2(2).

[63] See CAT's annual report, UN Doc A/57/44 (2000–2001), para 17.

[64] See eg CAT's annual reports, UN Doc A/51/44 (1996), para 211 (Egypt); UN Doc A/52/44 (1997) para 80 (Algeria); para 258 (Israel); UN Doc A/54/44 (1998–9), para 206 (Egypt); UN Doc A/57/44 (2001–2002), para 40 (Egypt); para 51 (Israel); para 59 (Spain); para 90 (Russian Federation); and UN Doc. CAT/C/USA/CO/2, 18 May 2006, eg paras 5, 19 (USA). The HRC has been more general, consistently urging states, following the declaration of the 'war on terrorism', to ensure that anti-terrorist measures are in conformity with the Covenant. See eg Human Rights Committee's annual reports, UN Doc A/57/40 (Vol I) (2002), paras 79(12)(a) (Sweden); 81(11) (New Zealand); 84(8) (Moldova). See also UN Doc CCPR/CO/79/RUS, 6 November 2003, para 13 (Russian Federation); UN Doc CCPR/CO/79/PHL, 1 December 2003, para 9 (Philippines); UN Doc CCPR/CO/79/LKA, 1 December 2003; para 13 (Sri Lanka); and UN Doc CCPR/C/USA/Q/3/CRP.4, 27 July 2006, para 11 (USA).

Regional human rights treaties also prohibit torture and other ill-treatment in all circumstances.[65] In addition, specific regional treaties have been drawn to prevent,[66] or to 'punish and prevent'[67] torture and other ill-treatment. The Courts established to try cases under the regional human rights conventions have consistently stressed the absolute nature of the prohibition on torture and other ill-treatment, including in the context of anti-terrorist activities.[68]

Torture and other forms of ill-treatment are prohibited absolutely in international humanitarian law treaties as well, as already noted.[69] As also noted, similarly stringent provisions apply to non-international armed conflicts,[70] and to the treatment of civilians under occupation or otherwise under the power of a party to a conflict.[71]

Torture and other ill-treatment are 'grave breaches', namely universally punishable crimes, of the Geneva Conventions.[72] Similarly, they have been deemed war crimes and, where applicable, as crimes against humanity under all *ad hoc* international criminal tribunals established so far.[73] None of these tribunals has,

[65] See the European Convention on Human Rights, Arts 3 and 15(2) (no derogations); American Convention on Human Rights, OAS Treaty Series No 36, 1144, adopted at San José, Costa Rica, on 22 November 1969, entered into force 18 July 1978, Arts 5(1), 5(2), 27(1) and 27(2) (no derogations); African Charter on Human and Peoples' Rights, OAU Doc. CAB/LEG/67/3 rev 5, adopted June 27, 1981, entered into force 21 October 1986, Article 5 (the Charter contains no provisions for derogations).

[66] European Convention for the Prevention of Torture and Inhuman or Degrading Treatment or Punishment, ETS 126, adopted at Strasbourg on 26 November 1987, entered into force 1 February 1989.

[67] Inter-American Convention to Prevent and Punish Torture, OAS Treaty Series No 67, adopted at Cartagena, Columbia, on 9 December 1985, entered into force 28 February 1987. See especially Art 5, which echoes Art 2(2) of the UN Convention Against Torture.

[68] For European cases see eg *Ireland v the UK*, Series A No 25, Judgment of 18 January 1978, para 163; *Tomasi v France*, Series A No 241-A, Judgment of 27 August 1992, para 115; *Chahal v the UK*, Reports 1996-V, Judgment of 15 November 1996, para 79; *Aksoy v Turkey*, Reports 1996-VI, Judgment of 18 December 1996, para 62; *Selmouni v France*, Reports 1999-V, Judgment of 28 July 1999, para 95; *Öcalan v Turkey* (Application no 46221/99), Judgment of 13 March 2003, para 194; *Kmetty v Hungary* (Application no 57967/00), Judgment of 16 December 2003, para 32; For Inter-American cases see eg *Loayza-Tamayo Case* (Peru), (Ser C) No 33, Judgment of 17 September 1997, para 57; *Castillo-Petruzzi et al* (Peru), (Ser C) No 52, Judgment of 30 May 1999, para 197; *Cantoral Benavides case* (Peru), (Ser C) No 69, Judgment of 18 August 2000, para 96; *Maritza Urrutia v Guatemala*, *supra* n 58, para 89.

[69] See *supra*, nn 34–5 and accompanying text. See also additional Protocol I, Arts 75(2)(a)(ii); 75(2)(b); 75(2)(e).

[70] See Art 3(1) common to all four Geneva Conventions; Additional Protocol II, Arts 4(2)(a), 4(2)(e), 4(2)(h).

[71] Geneva Convention IV, Arts 5, 27, 31, 32, 37.

[72] See eg Geneva Convention III, Art 130, Geneva Convention IV, Art 147.

[73] See Nuremberg Charter (Agreement for the Prosecution and Punishment of the Major War Criminals of the European Axis Powers and Charter of the International Military Tribunal, 8 August 1945, 59 Stat. 1544, 82 UNTS 279), Art 6(c) ('inhumane acts' as crimes against humanity), Control Council Law no 10, Punishment of Persons Guilty of War Crimes, Crimes Against Peace and Against Humanity, 20 December 1945, Arts II(1)(b) ('ill treatment' as a war crime), II(1)(c) ('torture, rape, or other inhumane acts' against civilians as crimes against humanity); Statute of the International Tribunal for the Prosecution of Persons Responsible for Serious

to date, accommodated any justifications for torture or other ill-treatment in any circumstances[74] and some, as noted above, have declared the prohibition on torture to be a peremptory rule of international law. Torture and other ill-treatment are also war crimes and crimes against humanity under the ICC Statute.[75]

Violations of International Humanitarian Law Committed in the Territory of the Former Yugoslavia since 1991, UN Doc S/25704 at 36, annex (1993) and S/25704/Add.1 (1993), adopted by Security Council on 25 May 1993, UN Doc S/RES/827 (1993) (henceforth: ICTY), Arts 2(b) ('torture or inhuman treatment' as grave breaches of the Geneva Conventions), 5(f) (torture) and 5(I) ('other inhuman acts'—both as crimes against humanity); Statute of the International Criminal Tribunal for the Prosecution of Persons Responsible for Genocide and Other Serious Violations of International Humanitarian Law Committed in the Territory of Rwanda and Rwandan Citizens Responsible for Genocide and Other such Violations Committed in the Territory of Neighbouring States, between 1 January 1994 and 31 December 1994, UN Doc S/RES 955, adopted by Security Council on 8 November 1994 [henceforth: ICTR]; Arts 3(f) (torture) and 3(i) ('other inhuman acts'—both as crimes against humanity), Arts 4(a) ('cruel treatment such as torture'), 4(e) ('Outrages upon personal dignity') and 4(h) ('Threats to commit any of the foregoing acts'—all three as violations of Art 3 common to all four Geneva Conventions and of Additional Protocol II). See also UNTAET *Regulation 2000/15 on the Establishment of Panels with Jurisdiction over Serious Criminal Offences* [for Timor Leste], UN Doc UNTAET/REG/2000/15, 6 June 2000, Arts 5.1(f) (torture) and 5.1.(i) ('Other inhumane acts'—both as crimes against humanity), Art 6.1(a)(2) ('Torture or inhuman treatment' as war crimes), and note that Art 7 adopts the Art 1(1) of the UN Convention Against Torture definition, and Art 7(3) repeats that Convention's rejection of any justifications for torture, in its Art 2(2). In addition see the Statute of the Special Court for Sierra Leone, established by an Agreement between the United Nations and the Government of Sierra Leone pursuant to Security Council resolution 1315 (2000) of 14 August 2000 (for text see eg the Court's website <http://www.sc-sl.org/scsl-statute.html>, accessed 20 October 2007), Arts 2(f) (torture) and 2(i) ('Other inhumane acts'—both as crimes against humanity), Arts 3(a) ('cruel treatment such as torture'), 3(e) ('Outrages upon personal dignity') and 3(h) ('Threats to commit any of the foregoing acts'—all three as violations of Article 3 common to all four Geneva Conventions and of Additional Protocol II).

I have omitted provisions for other crimes which amount to either torture or other ill-treatment, notably sexual crimes.

[74] In a dissenting opinion to the Court's ruling in *Ireland v UK*, Sir Gerald Fitzmaurice, while conceding that 'Article 3 provides for no exceptions, no special cases and no derogations on emergency grounds' goes on, in what appears to be a protest, to claim that '... there have been cases in which the extraction of information under torture or extreme ill-treatment has led to the saving of hundreds, even thousands of lives' (*Ireland v UK*, Series A No 25, Judgment of 18 January 1978, Separate opinion of Judge Sir Gerald Fitzmaurice, para 33, n 19). No specific 'cases' were cited. In the subsequent *Tyrer* case Fitzmaurice took one step further: 'As regards torture and inhuman treatment, further reflexion on the *Irish* case has led me to doubt whether it is either practicable or right to regard these notions ... as having the absolute and monolithic character which, on the literal reading of Article 3, they appear to have ...'. He goes on to state that '... the gloss that has to be placed upon the literal effect of the Article relates not only to what *constitutes* or amounts to torture etc., but to what may in certain circumstances *justify* its infliction, such as encompassing the greater good of saving the life of the recipient;—or, in certain types of cases, the saving of a great many other lives. This last matter is one of much difficulty and delicacy on which it is all too easy to go wrong' (*Tyrer v UK, supra* n 26, Separate opinion of Judge Sir Gerald Fitzmaurice, paras 3 and 5, respectively).

Not a single judge has, to my knowledge, endorsed this view since; it therefore remains the single argument for possible justification for ant-terrorist torture in an international court.

[75] ICC Statue, Arts 7(1)(f) (torture) and 7(1)(k) (other inhumane acts—both as crimes against humanity), Art 8(1)(ii) ('Torture or inhuman treatment' as war crimes).

Three authoritative statements would, I believe, serve to conclude this brief discussion and portray the current position of international law regarding the obligations of states to refrain from torturing and from accommodating torture, even in a TBS.

The first is the ICTY's succinct summary of the scope of the prohibition on torture in international law:

> The existence of this corpus of general and treaty rules proscribing torture shows that the international community, aware of the importance of outlawing this heinous phenomenon, has decided to suppress any manifestation of torture by operating both at the interstate level and at the level of individuals. *No legal loopholes have been left.*[76] [Emphasis added.]

The second is Rodley's closing comments the issue of 'justifiability':

> The present position on 'justifiability' as an element in the concepts of torture and other ill-treatment may be summarized as follows: the notion is not available as a defence against the charge of violating the prohibition against torture and other ill-treatment; this prohibition is absolute. Nor can it be used to excuse acts of torture or ill-treatment on the general utilitarian grounds that they are intended to serve a greater good.[77]

The third is by Christopher Greenwood who, having argued that the USA's classification of its detainees' status, 'Controversial as it is... is largely in accordance with international humanitarian law',[78] goes on to state the following:

> Status, however, is only part of the story. Whether prisoners of war or not, detainees are not held in legal limbo. Whatever their status, they have a right to humane treatment under customary international law, the relevant principles of which are widely regarded as having been set out in Article 75 of the First Additional Protocol. The use of torture and inhuman or degrading treatment or punishment are prohibited... irrespective of whether the detainees are prisoners of war or not. While the need to interrogate the detainees has frequently been emphasized, the limits within which this may be done are not substantially different for prisoners of war and other detainees—in either case there is complete freedom to question the prisoner but no obligation on the prisoner to answer the questions put (other than the requirement that prisoners of war furnish certain basic information). Moreover, it would be unlawful to use torture, inhuman or degrading treatment as a means of coercing a person to answer questions irrespective of whether he was a prisoner of war.[79]

---

[76] *Furundzija* ICTY case, *supra* n 1, para 146.

[77] Rodley, *The Treatment of Prisoners...*, *supra* n 10, 84.

[78] For a contrasting view on this point see eg 'U.S.: Growing Problem Of Guantanamo Detainees: Human Rights Watch Letter to Donald Rumsfeld' by Kenneth Roth, HRW Executive Director, 29 May 2002 <http://hrw.org/press/2002/05/pentagon-ltr.htm>, accessed 12 August 2003.

[79] Greenwood, *supra* n 55, 316.

E. Do the Israeli and US Methods Amount to Torture?

States have occasionally (and Israel and the USA have consistently) claimed, on various grounds, that measures which their officials have taken against detainees did not amount to torture.[80] States seem, in such cases, to imply what the US August 2002 memorandum stated explicitly, namely that only the harshest forms of physical and mental brutality qualify as torture.

I submit that the question of whether this argument is sound can be addressed without entering any detailed definitional or interpretational discussion of what constitutes torture. In the most general terms, the definition of torture used here, that of Article 1(1) of the UN Convention Against Torture[81] contains four relevant elements:

- *The element of intention.* The act (causing pain and suffering) was intentional.

- *The element of severe pain or suffering.* The act caused the victim severe[82] pain or suffering, whether physical or mental.

- *The element of purpose (or discrimination).*[83] The act was performed for a certain purpose—including obtaining information from the victim.

- *The element of official involvement.* The act was performed or instigated by officials, or at least with official consent or acquiescence.

Discussing the subject more generally, Rodley,[84] Evans[85] and Manfred Nowak[86] argue that there has been a shift, both statutory and jurisprudential, in assessing whether ill-treatment amounts to torture or 'only' to cruel, inhuman or degrading treatment, from a near-exclusive reliance on relative severity to what Evans describes as 'a more nuanced approach',[87] with all three writers stressing

---

[80] In the case of Israel see eg an Israeli delegate's words before the Human Rights Committee: '… before 1999 it had been a practice of the ISA to use moderate physical pressure—though never torture—when interrogating persons suspected of terrorism…' (Human Rights Committee, Summary Record of the 2118th Meeting, 25 July 2003, UN Doc CCPR/C/SR.2118, 6 August 2003, 7). And see also *supra* n 2 and accompanying text.
  In the case of the USA see eg Part III, Ch 15, Section D(3), text accompanying n 450. For European Court of Human Rights cases see eg the French Government's contention in *Selmouni v France*, *supra* n 68, para 94.

[81] For the text of this Article see Ch 7, text accompanying n 7.

[82] All relevant international and regional treaties which define torture require that the pain or suffering be 'severe' in order to constitute torture, with the exception of the definition of torture in Art 2 of the Inter-American Convention to Prevent and Punish Torture.

[83] The latter is not relevant to our discussion.

[84] Rodley, 'The Definition(s) of Torture …' *supra* n 9.

[85] See Evans, 'Getting to Grips with Torture' *supra* n 1.

[86] M Nowak, 'Challenges to the Absolute Nature of the Prohibition on Torture and Ill-treatment' 23 (4) *Netherlands Quarterly of Human Rights* 674 (2005), especially 678–9; *idem*, *supra* n 9, *passim*.

[87] Evans, *supra* n 1, 373.

the rising importance of the existence or absence of a purposive element as the distinguishing factor. Be that as it may, I submit that there is little need to go into this matter here: even according to these writers, the requirement that the pain and suffering be severe for treatment to amount to, or constitute, torture, albeit 'only one element of an increasingly complex matrix',[88] is still very much part of the law as it now stands.[89] This must mean that interrogation methods which cause pain and suffering that are not 'severe', would not amount to torture.

Interrogation methods are, by their very nature, intentional acts performed for the purpose of obtaining information. Nor is it contested that the methods concerned have been, both in the Israeli and US models, applied by officials (or those contracted by the officials and working under their instructions, in the case of the USA). Since therefore the existence of none of the other elements, including the purposive, is disputed, and since the issue of severity is the only non-constant (and contentious) variable, that last element is still the determining one in this particular instance, within this narrow section of the wider definitional debate.

I propose to address the question posed in this section by first citing international jurisprudence on comparable methods, or methods of comparable severity, found to have amounted to torture. I will then cite findings directly concerning the Israeli and US methods. Finally, I will try to arrive at an assessment of a group of methods used by both states, and which have generated much debate about their categorization, an assessment which, I hope, reconciles the various approaches to this question.

1. Jurisprudence on comparable methods amounting to torture

The practice of human rights courts and monitoring bodies shows that they have consistently rejected the 'maximalist' positions on severity cited above. Following, by way of illustrating this rejection, are a number of examples of arguably 'subtler' forms of ill-treatment, drawn from international case-law and reports by human rights monitoring bodies, where they have nevertheless found the ill-treatment to constitute torture. While there is no clear line between pain and suffering which is 'physical' and that which is 'mental', and the two are often intertwined, I have attempted to arrange the material roughly along these lines.

---

[88] *Ibid.*

[89] Evans writes: '... such acts fail to qualify as acts of torture for the purposes of the [UN] Convention [Against Torture] either because they did not involve a sufficiently severe degree of pain or suffering or because they were not inflicted for a purpose' (*ibid*, 375).

Rodley writes: 'The one element of torture that is common to all case law and definitions in legal instruments is that it should involve pain or suffering which, in all but perhaps the Inter-American system should be severe' (*idem, supra* n 9, 489). What Rodley rejects is the concept of 'aggravation' of the pain or suffering, or of its 'relative' severity. However, Rodley does not address the lower, or 'entrance' threshold of ill-treatment; thus I can only surmise from his discussion that he would tend to classify interrogation techniques which cause pain or suffering that is not severe as 'degrading', with 'cruel/inhuman' treatment having the same severity threshold level as torture.

(a) Physical torture

- *Beatriz Weismann de Lanza and Alcides Lanza Perdomo*: the victims were, respectively, '[a]lmost constantly kept blindfolded and with her hands tied', and subjected to various forms of torture, such as 'caballete', 'submarino seco', 'picano' and 'planton'; held incommunicado for nine months and subjected to other forms of torture, such as electric shocks, hanging from his hands, immersion of his head in dirty water, near to asphyxia, and 'submarino seco'.[90]

- *Berterretche*: the victim was subjected to 'beatings, stringing up, asphyxiation, electric shocks and long periods of forced standing in the cold without anything to drink or eat' as well as to 'alleged psychological torture' in that he was told he had been granted freedom, but later this was explained as a 'mistake'.[91]

- *Cariboni*: the victim was kept hooded and made to sit up straight day and night; roused with kicks, injected with hallucinogenic substances, blindfolded with towelling material, which made eyes inflamed and purulent.[92]

- *Aksoy*: the victim was subject to ' "Palestinian hanging", being stripped naked, with arms tied together behind the back and suspended by the arms.'[93]

- *Aydın*: the victim, a 17-year-old girl, was 'subjected to a series of particularly terrifying and humiliating experiences ... having regard to her sex and youth and the circumstances under which she was held. She was detained over a period of three days during which she must have been bewildered and disoriented by being kept blindfolded, and in a constant state of physical pain and mental anguish brought on by the beatings administered to her during questioning and by the apprehension of what would happen to her next.'[94]

---

[90] Human Rights Committee, *Ann Maria Garcia Lanza de Netto v Uruguay, on behalf of Beatriz Weismann de Lanza*, Communication No 8/1977 (3 April 1980), UN Doc CCPR/C/OP/1 at 45 (1984), para 9. The Committee describes these methods consistently as 'torture', the only question being whether they actually took place. The Committee found a violation of Art 7 of the International Covenant on Civil and Political Rights (para 16).
     Explanation of terms: '*caballete*'—forcing prisoners to straddle iron or wooden bars; '*submarino seco*'—near suffocation, for example by placing a plastic bag over the head; '*picano*'—electric shocks from a cattle prod; '*planton*'—being forced to stand upright for long periods.

[91] Human Rights Committee, *Omar Berterretche Acost v Uruguay*, Communication No 162/198325 (25 October 1988), UN GAOR Sup No 40 (A/44/40) at 183 (1989), para 10.2. The Committee concluded that Berterretche 'was subjected to torture and to cruel, inhuman and degrading treatment and punishment' (*ibid*, para 11). It did not specify which physical treatment was considered torture and which was other ill-treatment.

[92] Human Rights Committee, *Raul Cariboni v Uruguay*, Communication No 159/1983 (27 October 1987), UN GAOR Su No 40 (A/43/40) at 184 (1988) para 4. The Committee found a violation of Art 7, because the applicant 'was subjected to torture and inhuman and degrading treatment' (*ibid*, para 10).

[93] *Aksoy v Turkey, supra* n 68, para 64. The Court concluded that 'this treatment was of such a serious and cruel nature that it can only be described as torture' (*ibid*).

[94] *Aydın v Turkey*, European Court of Human Rights, Reports 1997-VI, (Application No 00023178/94), Judgment of 25 September 1997, para 84. Ms Aydın was also raped—an undisputed form of torture (see Part I, Ch 5, Section B). The Court, however, ruled that the other

- *The torture of women*: the UN Special Rapporteur on torture stated that 'Women are subjected to gender-specific forms of torture, including rape, sexual abuse and harassment, virginity testing, forced abortion or forced miscarriage.'[95] Referring, in an earlier report, to the same subject, the Special Rapporteur stated that 'Since it was clear that rape or other forms of sexual assault against women in detention were a particularly ignominious violation of the inherent dignity and the right to physical integrity of the human being, they accordingly constituted an act of torture.'[96]

- *Selmouni*: the victim was subjected to a 'large number of blows' and in addition 'was made to run along a corridor with police officers positioned on either side to trip him up; was made to kneel down in front of a young woman to whom someone said "Look, you're going to hear somebody sing"; one police officer then showed him his penis, saying "Look, suck this", before urinating over him; and he was threatened with a blowlamp and then a syringe.'[97]

- *Sendic*: the victim was 'for three months . . . made to do the "*plantón*" (standing upright with his eyes blindfolded) throughout the day; he was only allowed to sleep for a few hours at a time; he was beaten and given insufficient food'.[98]

- *Detainees in Venezuela*: victims underwent the following: 'David Rodriguez allegedly had his wrists bound and a bag containing tear-gas placed over his head; he was also beaten with a blunt object and received cigarette burns on his ankles. Jose Tores was allegedly severely beaten with blunt objects while handcuffed and had his head banged against the wall repeatedly; Luis Urbano had a bag containing tear-gas placed over his head and was beaten.'[99]

---

ill-treatment to which she was exposed amounted in itself to torture: 'The accumulation of acts of physical and mental violence inflicted on the applicant and the especially cruel act of rape to which she was subjected amounted to torture in breach of Article 3 of the Convention. Indeed the Court would have reached this conclusion on either of these grounds taken separately' (*ibid*, para 86).

[95] Interim Report of the Special Rapporteur on torture to the General Assembly, UN Doc A/55/290 (2000), para 5.

[96] Report of the Special Rapporteur on torture to the Commission on Human Rights, UN Doc E/CN.4/1992/SR.21, para 35.

[97] *Selmouni v France*, *supra* n 68, paras 102–3. The Court concluded: 'Under these circumstances, the Court is satisfied that the physical and mental violence, considered as a whole, committed against the applicant's person caused "severe" pain and suffering and was particularly serious and cruel. Such conduct must be regarded as acts of torture for the purposes of Article 3 of the Convention' (*ibid*, para 104).

For another case, heard in the International Criminal Tribunal for Rwanda, in which a person was convicted of torturing, as he was found responsible for the beatings and threats used against (many) persons see *Prosecutor v Jean-Paul Akayesu*, Case No ICTR-96–4-T, judgment of 2 September 1998.

It should be noted that Akayesu was convicted—separately—of a string of other crimes, including rape (also as torture) and genocide.

[98] *Sendic v Uruguay* (63/1979), Report of the Human Rights Committee, UN GOAR, 37th Session, Supplement No 40 (1982), Annex VIII, para 2.4 (description according to Mr Sendic's wife). The Committee concluded that Sendic had for three months been 'subjected to torture' at paras 16.2 and 20.

[99] Report of visit of the Special Rapporteur on torture to Venezuela, UN Doc E/CN.4/1997/7/Add.3, 13 December 1996, para 18.

- *Methods used in Turkey in 1999*: the UN Special Rapporteur on torture stated the following: 'The pattern of torture appears to have changed in the past few years, with the practice becoming less brutal in some places. Now, owing to shorter custody periods, some security forces carrying out interrogations avoid leaving visible signs on detainees...they use methods such as blindfolding, stripping the victims naked, hosing them with high-pressure cold water and then exposing them to a ventilator, squeezing the testicles, using grossly insulting language and intimidation, such as threats to their life and physical integrity or those of their families. Similarly, instead of outright rape, sexual harassment and threat of rape are used against women. With regard to common criminals, beating is sometimes used, more as a means of correction than of extracting a confession. Falaka (beating on the soles of the feet), "Palestinian hanging" (hands tied behind the back and the body suspended by the tied hands), and electric shocks are reportedly used less frequently...but, nevertheless, still occur in some areas of the country.'[100]
- *Forced feeding of a hunger-striker*: the European Court of Human Rights found that the forced feeding of Ivanovych Nevmerzhitsky, a prisoner on a hunger strike, where 'the Government have not demonstrated that there was a "medical necessity" for such feeding', and where 'restraints applied—handcuffs, a mouth-widener (*роторозширювач*), a special rubber tube inserted into the food channel—in the event of resistance, with the use of force' could amount to torture, and in the specific case did.[101]

(b) Mental torture

- *Miguel Angel Estralla*: For hours upon end, the victim's interrogators put him through a mock amputation with an electric saw, telling that they were going to kill him in a painful way. As a result he suffered, *inter alia*, from a loss of sensitivity in both arms and hands for 11 months, and severe pain in the knees.[102]
- *Cariboni*: the victim could, for many hours at a time, 'hear piercing shrieks which appeared to come from an interrogation under torture; the shrieks were accompanied by loud noises and by music played at a very high volume'. In addition, he was 'repeatedly threatened with torture'.[103]

---

[100] Report of visit of the Special Rapporteur on torture to Turkey, UN Doc E/CN.4/1999/61/Add.1, 27 January 1999, para 14.

[101] *Nevmerzhitsky v Ukraine*, 54825/00 [2005] ECHR 210, Judgment of 5 April 2005, paras 96–98. In principle, however, the Court ruled that 'force-feeding that is aimed at saving the life of a particular detainee who consciously refuses to take food' would not amount to a violation of Art 3, subject to certain conditions. See *ibid*, para 94.

[102] Human Rights Committee, *Miguel Angel Estrella v Uruguay*, Communication No 74/1980 (17 July 1980), UN Doc Su No 40 (A/38/40) at 150 (1983), para 1.6. The Committee found that this constituted 'severe...psychological torture' (*ibid*, para 8.3).

[103] Human Rights Committee, *Raul Cariboni v Uruguay*, Communication No 159/1983 (27 October 1987), UN GAOR Su No 40 (A/43/40) at 184 (1988), para 4. The Committee found a

- *Methods of torture used in Mauritania*: the African Commission on Human and Peoples' Rights referred, *inter alia*, to victims being denied sleep, permanently kept in small, dark or underground cold cells, having their heads plunged into the water to the point of suffocation and held in the 'jaguar position'.[104]

- *Miron Constantin*: the victim, having been severely beaten, 'finally confessed to the murder when the officers allegedly threatened to harm his daughter'.[105]

- *Florin Macovei*: the victim was beaten and in addition, the police 'threatened to kill him and he could hear his friend being ill-treated as well' and later 'threatened to continue the beatings if they did not confess or if they complained about the beatings'.[106]

- *Methods used in Turkey in 1999*: the UN Special Rapporteur on torture described, *inter alia*, 'an isolation room with padded dark walls, called "the dark room" by former detainees the Special Rapporteur had met, and officially used for drug addicts during periods of crisis. This cell was completely dark as it had neither a window facing outside nor artificial light...The only source of light was a powerful lamp, light from which entered the cell through a small window in the wall of an ante-chamber. The only window facing the exterior in this ante-chamber was completely opaque. Therefore, the ante-chamber and cell together could create an environment of total blackness, exactly as alleged by former detainees. According to an international expert consulted by the Special Rapporteur, this kind of room with its extended sensory deprivation effects (deprivation of light and sound) could have a negative impact on the people there detained. Short-term effects would include hallucinations, memory loss, depression and anxiety. There was also a danger of lasting psychiatric effects.'[107]

---

violation of Art 7, because the applicant 'was subjected to torture and inhuman and degrading treatment' (*ibid*, para 10). See also *supra* n 92.

[104] *Malawi African Association v Mauritania*, communication no 54/91, *Amnesty International v Mauritania*, no 61/91, *Ms. Sarr Diop, Union Interafricaine des Droits de l'Homme and RADDHO v Mauritania*, no 98/93, *Collectif des Veuves et Ayants-droit v Mauritania*, no 164/97 à 196/97, *Association Mauritanienne des Droits de l'Homme v Mauritania*, no 210/98, AfCmHPR decision of May 11, 2000, *13th Annual Activity report of the African Commission on Human and Peoples' Rights 1999–2000*, AHG/222 (XXXVI), May 2000, 138–162, paras 10, 12, 22, 23, 115–117. The Commission concluded that all the above acts (and other, harsher ones) '[t]aken together or in isolation...constitute widespread utilisation of torture and of cruel, inhuman and degrading forms of treatment...' (*ibid*, para 118).
Explanation of terms: in the 'jaguar position' the victim's wrists are tied to his or her feet. He or she is then suspended from a bar and thus kept upside down, sometimes over a fire, and is beaten on the soles of his or her feet.

[105] Report of visit of Special Rapporteur on torture to Romania, UN Doc E/CN.4/2000/9/ Add.3, 23 November 1999, para 16.

[106] *Ibid*, para 22.

[107] Report of visit of the Special Rapporteur on torture to Turkey, UN Doc E/CN.4/1999/61/ Add.1, 27 January 1999, para 22.

- *Fatma Tokmak*: the victim, one of those mentioned in the above report, underwent the following torture methods: 'left naked; suspension; squeezing breasts; threats of rape; forced to watch ill-treatment of son; forced to assume sexual position with son'.[108]

- *Detainees from indigenous communities in Mexico*: the UN Special Rapporteur on torture found that they, *inter alia*, 'received death threats to their families, and were placed bound hand and foot under vehicles with the engines running to make them think they were about to be run over'.[109]

- *Abelino Tapia Morales*: another case involving these communities where the victim, aged 70, 'was beaten and subjected to other forms of torture, such as being suspended over a cliff and threatened with being dropped if he did not admit the whereabouts of the weapons and attackers'.[110]

- *Tahir Hussain Khan*: the UN Committee against Torture concluded that deporting the author would expose him to a danger of being tortured. The author claimed he had already undergone what the Committee described as torture, which included sleep deprivation.[111]

- *Maritza Urrutia*: The Inter-American Court of Human Rights concluded that the following constituted torture. She was detained for eight days, during which her head was covered by a hood, she was kept handcuffed to a bed, in a room with the light on and the radio at full volume, which prevented her from sleeping. In addition, she was subjected to very prolonged interrogations, during which she was shown photographs of individuals who displayed signs of torture or had been killed in combat and she was threatened that she would be found by her family in the same way. State agents also threatened to torture her physically or to kill her or members of her family if she did not collaborate. In addition, Maritza Urrutia was obliged to be filmed in a video, which was subsequently broadcast by two Guatemalan television channels, in which she made a statement against her will, the contents of which she was forced to ratify at a press conference held after her release.[112]

- *Solitary confinement*: In his August 2004 interim report to the UN General Assembly, the UN Special Rapporteur on Torture stated that prolonged

---

[108] *Ibid*, Annex: Allegations submitted to the Special Rapporteur by non-governmental organizations between 1 October and 12 December 1998, case 15.

[109] Report of visit of Special Rapporteur on torture to Mexico, UN Doc E/CN.4/1998/38/Add.2, 14 January 1998, para 16.

[110] *Ibid*, para 17.

[111] *Tahir Hussain Khan v Canada*, Communication No 15/1994, decision of 15 November 1994, Report of the Committee against Torture, UN GAOR Su No 4 (A/50/44) (1995), Annex V, para 3.2.

[112] *Maritza Urrutia v Guatemala, supra* n 58, facts as provided in paras 58.4–58.8 and 85. See para 94 for the conclusion that Urrutia had been tortured. Note that in reaching this conclusion, the Court relies, and fully quotes (in para 90) the definition of torture in Art 1(1) of the UN Convention Against Torture.

solitary confinement 'in itself may constitute a violation of the right to be free from torture'.[113]

It is obvious from the foregoing that international bodies have over the years provided extensive jurisprudence to clarify and, as it were, illustrate the definition of torture in general and the concept of severity therein in particular. The result may not be a crystal clear picture of what 'severe' means (especially since it is recognized that individual sensitivities and circumstances play a role), but I believe it may be safely concluded that while a certain, not trivial, level of severity is definitely required for torture to be found, the notion that only acts such as mutilations, death, rape and bone-crushing can amount to torture is firmly rejected.

Writing to the CAT in 2001, when the latter planned to prepare a General Comment on article 1 of the Convention Against Torture,[114] Amnesty International stated that it:

... would urge the Committee to clarify that there neither is, nor should be, an exhaustive list of torture methods, and that the introduction of any 'innovative' means of intentionally inflicting severe pain or suffering for such purposes as those detailed in the definition would be totally rejected, being in violation of this article.[115]

1. Specific jurisprudence (and other findings) on Israeli and US methods

In 1997, the UN Special Rapporteur on torture made the following observations on the methods used by the GSS at that time, namely under the Landau model:

The following forms of pressure during interrogation appear so consistently (and have not been denied in judicial proceedings) that the Special Rapporteur assumes them to be sanctioned under the approved but secret interrogation practices: sitting in a very low chair or standing arced against a wall (possibly in alternation with each other); hands and/or legs tightly manacled; subjection to loud noise; sleep deprivation; hooding; being kept in cold air; violent shaking (an "exceptional" measure, used against 8,000 persons according to the late Prime Minister Rabin in 1995). Each of these measures on its own may not provoke severe pain or suffering. Together—and they are frequently used in combination—they may be expected to induce precisely such pain or suffering, especially if applied on a protracted basis of, say, several hours. In fact, they are sometimes apparently applied for days or even weeks on end. Under those circumstances, they can only be described as torture, which is not surprising given their advanced purpose, namely, to

---

[113] Interim report of the Special Rapporteur on torture to the UN General Assembly, UN Doc A/59/324, 23 August 2004, para 20.

[114] On this intention see eg Evans, *supra* n 1, 368 (especially fn 18). The plan was later dropped, for reasons unknown to me.

[115] Amnesty International letter to Alessio Bruni, Secretary of the Committee against Torture, Ref: UN 9/2001, 7 February 2001, Annex 1.

elicit information, implicitly by breaking the will of the detainees to resist yielding up the desired information.[116]

The CAT echoed this view later that same year:

> ...the methods of interrogation, which were described by non-governmental organizations on the basis of accounts given to them by interrogatees and appear to be applied systematically, were neither confirmed nor denied by Israel. The Committee, therefore, must assume them to be accurate. These methods include: (1) restraining in very painful conditions, (2) hooding under special conditions, (3) sounding of loud music for prolonged periods, (4) sleep deprivation for prolonged periods, (5) threats, including death threats, (6) violent shaking, and (7) using cold air to chill; and are in the Committee's view breaches of article 16 and also constitute torture as defined in article 1 of the Convention. This conclusion is particularly evident where such methods of interrogation are used in combination, which appears to be the standard case.[117]

In 2001, referring to methods used after the HCJ ruling, namely under the HCJ model, the Special Rapporteur observed the following:

> The Special Rapporteur's hope that the 1999 decision of the High Court of Justice would result in an end to the use of interrogation techniques involving torture or cruel, inhuman or degrading treatment...have proved to be ill-founded. The use of 'moderate physical pressure' and other torturous techniques appears still in evidence...[118]

In other words, the Special Rapporteur found (rightly to my mind) a line of continuity between the Landau model methods and those of the HCJ model, and therefore made the same 'definitional' observation concerning the latter as he had done for the former. This view was in effect backed by an Israeli delegate to the CAT, who, looking back in 2001, stated that his:

> ...Government had always maintained that the methods it used for interrogation had never amounted to torture in that they had never amounted to severe pain or suffering;[119]

This, and Israel's view that what it considers 'cruel, inhuman or degrading treatment' are sometimes justifiable, as noted above,[120] indicate that Israel has seen no reason to use, following the HCJ ruling, interrogation methods milder than

---

[116] Report of the Special Rapporteur on torture to the Commission on Human Rights, UN Doc E/CN.4/1997/7, 10 January 1997, para 121.

[117] UN Doc A/52/44 (1997), paras 256–7.

[118] UN Doc E/CN.4/2001/66, 25 January 2001, para 665. The Special Rapporteur added (*ibid*): 'The Special Rapporteur accepts that not all allegations will be well founded. Nevertheless, as long as the Government continues to detain persons incommunicado for exorbitant periods, itself a practice constituting cruel, inhuman or degrading treatment...the burden will be on the Government to prove that the allegations are untrue. This is a burden that it will not generally be able to discharge convincingly.'

[119] UN Press Release, *supra* n 2. See similarly *supra* n 80.

[120] *Supra* n 38 and accompanying text.

those permitted under the Landau model (albeit now, officially, in TBSs only). Nor do the testimonies and official sources[121] indicate otherwise.

The CAT[122] and the Human Rights Committee[123] refrained from making observations defining the HCJ model methods specifically as torture or otherwise.

As for the US interrogation methods under the HVD model, in early 2006 the UN Special Rapporteur on torture, writing within a report by five UN experts on Guantánamo Bay, made the first official assessment by a UN expert on the subject, albeit limited to that detention centre. Having described interrogation techniques approved for use in Guantánamo Bay, and the criteria for assessing whether treatment amounts to torture (the four elements described above in Chapter 18, Section E), the Special Rapporteur cautiously concludes:

On the interviews conducted with former detainees, the Special Rapporteur concludes that some of the techniques, in particular the use of dogs, exposure to extreme temperatures, sleep deprivation for several consecutive days and prolonged isolation were perceived as causing severe suffering. He also stresses that the simultaneous use of these techniques is even more likely to amount to torture.[124]

CAT chose a roundabout way of indicating a finding of torture, and it is only through the reference to Article 1 that this finding can be adduced:

The Committee is concerned that in 2002 the State party authorized the use of certain interrogation techniques, which have resulted in the death of some detainees during interrogation. The Committee also regrets that 'confusing interrogation rules' and techniques defined in vague and general terms, such as 'stress positions', have led to serious abuses of detainees. (articles 11, 1, 2 and 16).[125]

Two additional observations should be mentioned. One, already noted briefly above,[126] is the ICRC's observation on US interrogation methods in Iraq—note that the ICRC is describing *systematic* rather than aberrant 'ill-treatment':

The ill-treatment by the CF [Coalition Forces] personnel during interrogation was not systematic, except with regard to persons arrested in connection with suspected security offences or deemed to have an 'intelligence' value. In these cases, persons deprived of their liberty supervised by the military intelligence were subjected to a variety of

---

[121] See Part III, Ch 14.

[122] The Committee spoke of 'numerous allegations of torture and ill-treatment by law enforcement officials received by the Committee'. See Report of the Committee against Torture, UN Doc A/57/44 (2002), para 52(g).

[123] The Committee stated that it was 'concerned that interrogation techniques incompatible with article 7 of the Covenant are still reported frequently to be resorted to…' UN Doc A/58/40 (Vol. I, 2002–3), para 85(18).

[124] *Situation of detainees at Guantánamo Bay*, UN Doc E/CN.4/2006/120, 15 February 2006, para 52. See paras 49–51 for the description of authorized techniques, described here *supra*, Ch 15, Section B(3)(a).

[125] Conclusions and recommendations on USA, *supra* n 64, para 24.

[126] See Part III, Ch 15.

ill-treatment, ranging from insults and humiliation to both physical and psychological coercion that in some cases might amount to torture, in order to force them to cooperate with their interrogators.[127]

The other one is by Rodley, who spoke in his academic capacity, but we may bear in mind that as UN Special Rapporteur on Torture he had made the two observations on Israeli interrogation methods cited above. Having listed 'a number of techniques approved by the Secretary of Defence for possible use by interrogators',[128] Rodley goes on to state:

Any combination of them, especially over a protracted period of time would certainly 'amount to' torture. Many of these techniques have been used at Guantánamo.[129]

F. 'The Five Techniques'; 'Moderate Physical Pressure'; 'Stress and Duress'; and Similar Methods—the Accumulation Yardstick

I will now turn to the theoretical legal thinking which, I believe, underlies the above findings. To state that when a person dies as a result of violent, painful interrogation methods, he or she has been tortured, can hardly be controversial, although an opposing argument has been put forward.[130] Since such deaths have occurred, as noted, in two of the three models, it was safe to conclude that *some* torture has been practised in both, and by analogy in the third as well.[131]

This is also true of specific, 'instant impact' violent methods used by the two states. 'Waterboarding' has been found by US and international courts and bodies to constitute torture.[132] Similarly, I have argued elsewhere in detail that violent

---

[127] Report of the International Committee of the Red Cross (ICRC) on the Treatment by Coalition Forces of Prisoners of War and Other Protected Persons by the Geneva Conventions in Iraq During Arrest, Internment, and Interrogation, February 2004, para 26.

[128] NS Rodley, 'The Prohibition of Torture: Absolute Means Absolute' 34 *Denver J of Int'l L & Policy* 145 (2006) 148. Rodley names the following: hooding; sleep adjustment; false flag; threat of transfer; isolation for up to 30 days; forced grooming; use of stress positions such as prolonged standing; sleep adjustment; removal of clothing; increasing anxiety by the use of aversions eg presence of dogs; and deprivation of light/auditory stimuli (ie sensory deprivation techniques) (*ibid*, 147).

[129] *Ibid*, 148.

[130] See *supra*, Part III, Ch 15, Section B(4)(a).

[131] As noted, the method of 'shaking' is still being used under the HCJ model and possibly in the CIA program. See *supra*, Part III, Ch 14, Section B(2) and Ch 15, Section B(3)(c).

[132] In the wake of World War II, both the International Tribunal for the Far East and a US Military Commission described as 'torture' (and convicted perpetrators accordingly) acts virtually identical to 'waterboarding'. See *Judgment of the International Military Tribunal for the Far East*, 1 November 1948, Chapter VIII: Conventional War Crimes (Atrocities), 1058. Text available eg at <http://www.ibiblio.org/hyperwar/PTO/IMTFE/>, accessed 31 October 2006. See also eg *United States of America v Hideji Nakamura, Yukio Asano, Seitara Hata, and Takeo Kita,* US Military Commission, Yokohama, 1–28 May, 1947. NARA Records, NND 735027 RG 153, Entry 143 Box 1025.

shaking, a potentially lethal method used by both states, amounts to torture,[133] and the same may be said of the Israeli method of 'bending'.[134]

However, I would like to focus here on the methods of the type listed in the title of this section, which have been at the centre of the debate over what constitutes torture and what is 'only' cruel, inhuman or degrading. Killing an interrogee obviously defeats the purpose of the interrogation, and it is therefore hardly surprising that the 'softer' methods have been, and are being, used far more frequently and systematically.

The paradigmatic international legal case concerning such interrogation techniques was the 1970s case *Ireland v UK* at the European Commission and Court of Human Rights. The case concerned interrogation methods employed by British forces in the interrogation of IRA suspects in Northern Ireland in 1971.

Not only has this case been cited or discussed in virtually every academic work, and dozens of court cases (both too numerous to list here) addressing issues such as what torture is, this case was also cited, and even relied on, in the founding, or otherwise principal, documents of all three models.[135]

The five techniques, employed against altogether 14 detained men in August and October 1971,[136] read now like a (partial) list of methods employed under the Israeli and US models. They were described by the European Court as follows:

(a) *wall-standing*: forcing the detainees to remain for periods of some hours in a 'stress position', described by those who underwent it as being 'spreadeagled against the wall, with their fingers put high above the head against the wall, the legs spread apart and the feet back, causing them to stand on their toes with the weight of the body mainly on the fingers';

(b) *hooding*: putting a black or navy coloured bag over the detainees' heads and, at least initially, keeping it there all the time except during interrogation;

(c) *subjection to noise*: pending their interrogations, holding the detainees in a room where there was a continuous loud and hissing noise;

In the Preface to its 2004–5 annual report, the CPT, giving 'a concrete example' in the 'context of the fight against terrorism', refers directly, though not explicitly, to this US interrogation method (obviously used for a very short period) and the defence its use by the CIA director (described *supra*, Part III, Ch 15, Section B(3)(b)): '… in the CPT's opinion, to immerse persons under water so as to make them believe they might drown is not a professional interrogation technique, it is an act of torture' (15th General Report on the CPT's activities covering the period 1 August 2004 to 31 July 2005, CPT/Inf (2005) 17, 22 September 2005, Preface).

[133] See Y Ginbar, *The Face and the Mirror: Israel's View of its Interrogation Techniques Examined*, LLM Dissertation, University of Essex, 1996, Ch 4.

[134] See *supra*, Part III, Ch 14, Section B(2)(c).

[135] See *Landau Report*, paras 3.22–3.23; *Israel Torture case* ruling, para 30; August 2002 memo, 28–9. The December DOJ 2004 memo only mentions the case in a footnote (14, on p 7).

[136] Twelve arrested on August 9 and two in October (*Ireland v UK*, Series A No 25 (1978), para 96). The Court stresses that the 'techniques were not used in any cases other than the fourteen …' (*ibid*).

(d) *deprivation of sleep*: pending their interrogations, depriving the detainees of sleep;

(e) *deprivation of food and drink*: subjecting the detainees to a reduced diet during their stay at the centre and pending interrogations.[137]

The Court states that the techniques were applied, 'with intermittent periods of respite...during four or possibly five days', noting that it was not possible 'to establish the exact length of the periods of respite'.[138]

The Court, stating first that in its view the distinction between the notions of 'torture' and 'inhuman or degrading treatment...derives principally from a difference in the intensity of the suffering inflicted', went on to clarify that purpose (deliberateness) is nevertheless not immaterial, when stating that by using the term 'torture' the Convention attaches 'a special stigma to *deliberate* inhuman treatment causing very serious and cruel suffering'[139] (emphasis added).

The Court then famously found that the 'five techniques' were unlawful but did not constitute torture (with purpose—'object'—again featuring as a requirement, albeit here insufficient, for a finding of torture):

Although the five techniques, as applied in combination, undoubtedly amounted to inhuman and degrading treatment, although their object was the extraction of confessions, the naming of others and/or information and although they were used systematically, they did not occasion suffering of the particular intensity and cruelty implied by the word torture as so understood.[140]

Did a major jurisprudential shift, of the kind suggested by Rodley, Evans and Nowak, as discussed above, occur between the European Court's findings regarding Northern Ireland in 1978 and those of the CAT regarding Israel in 1997, or else do the two findings reflect different definitional approaches of the two bodies? Perhaps one or the other is true, but I submit that it is not necessary, at least for our present, limited purpose, to pit one against the other.

I believe that Rodley's observations, albeit in different capacities, on the methods used in the Landau and HVD models, offer the most reasonable and convincing approach to this issue. Rodley does not find the interrogation methods in question torturous *prima facie*; rather, he requires a certain accumulation of methods and length of application before describing them as torture. I submit, following what Rodley seems to imply, that unlawful methods of interrogation may be, very roughly, divided in two: those that are inherently torturous, namely whose very use constitutes torture, such as rape, bone-crushing and applying electric shocks to sensitive parts; and those that could in theory be applied so as

---

[137] *Ibid*, para 96. The Court had not conducted any research, and based its conclusions solely on the findings of the Commission, which gives a slightly more detailed description of the techniques. See *Ireland v UK, Yearbook* 1976, 512–949, 784.

[138] *Ibid* (Court), para 104. *cf* Commission (*ibid*, 788).

[139] *Ibid* (Court), para 167.

[140] *Ibid*.

to produce only mild pain and suffering, and it is only through their application over time, alongside other methods, or both, that they would produce severe pain or suffering. Most of the methods discussed in this section belong to that second category.

Incommunicado detention would provide a relevant illustration. It will be recalled that in both models it has been used as an interrogation method[141]—as well as a facilitator for other methods.[142] One needs little more than common sense to expect that, *ceteris paribus*, a prisoner's pain and suffering arising from being totally cut off from the rest of the world would increase the longer he or she is kept in this condition—such suffering is likely to be negligible for a few hours, minimal for a few days, but as weeks and months accumulate it will, at some point, become severe. The particular point may vary, so in the Israeli models that method on its own may not have amounted to torture in many cases.[143] In contrast, persons held incommunicado for years would invariably suffer severely, even setting aside the use of any other methods, therefore the HVDs in the CIA's 'black sites' were clearly tortured, even by that method alone.[144]

This cumulative logic appears to be behind several statements by the UN Commission on Human Rights:

...prolonged incommunicado detention may facilitate the perpetration of torture and can in itself constitute a form of cruel, inhuman or degrading treatment or even torture.[145]

The same logic is expressed, this time explicitly, in a finding of torture by the Human Rights Committee in an individual case:

... the Committee notes, from the information before it, that Mohammed El-Megreisi was detained incommunicado for more than three years, until April 1992, when he was allowed a visit by his wife, and that after that date he has again been detained incommunicado and in a secret location. Having regard to these facts, the Committee finds that Mr. Mohammed Bashir El-Megreisi, by being subjected to prolonged incommunicado detention in an

---

[141] See *supra*, Part III, Ch 12, Sections B(2) and B(4).

[142] The UN Special Rapporteur on torture, recognising that 'torture is most frequently practised during incommunicado detention' has also called for such detention to be made illegal (UN Doc E/CN.4/2002/76, 27 December 2001, Annex 1).

[143] See the UN Special Rapporteur on torture, *supra* n 118.

[144] They were also clearly the victims of enforced disappearance as defined eg in Art 2 of the International Convention for the Protection of All Persons from Enforced Disappearance, adopted by UN General Assembly resolution 61/177 on 20 December 2006 (for text see eg the website of the Office of the High Commissioner for Human Rights <http//:www.ohchr.org>); and (as a crime against humanity) in Art 7(1)(i) of the ICC Statute (although other requirements for such a crime have probably not been met). Exploring the link between enforced disappearances and torture is beyond the scope of this study.

[145] UN Doc E/CN.4Res.2004/41, adopted without vote on 19 April 2004, para 8. See similarly Resolution 2005/39, 19 April 2005, para 9; the Inter-American Court of Human Rights, *Velasquez Rodriguez Case*, Judgment of July 29, 1988, Inter-Am Ct HR (Ser C) No 4 (1988), para 187; repeated in *Godínez Cruz Case*, Judgment of January 20, 1989, Inter-Am Ct HR (Ser C) No 5 (1989), para 197.

unknown location, is the victim of torture and cruel and inhuman treatment, in violation of articles 7 and 10, paragraph 1, of the Covenant.[146]

It is the accumulation of time ('prolonged') that made the incommunicado detention cruel and inhuman, and surely the fact that it was inflicted for years was material in the finding of torture.

Therefore, although the European Court did not explicitly state this, and although it may have been better if it had, it is unreasonable to interpret the *Ireland v UK* ruling as determining that 'the five techniques' were *inherently* non-torturous, namely that no matter how long interrogators deprive a detainee of sleep for, force him to stand, hood him etc—days, weeks or months on end— these methods could never, either separately or in combination, amount to torture.

Although the CAT did not explicitly state this, and although it may have been better if it had, it is unreasonable to interpret its conclusions in 1997 as implying that the Landau methods were *inherently* torturous, namely, that no matter how short the duration—even if interrogators used a single method such as hooding or shackling to a small chair, on its own for a very brief period—it would always constitute torture, just like rape, the breaking of bones, the rack or the screw.

Rather, it may reasonably be suggested that each of these bodies found that specific interrogation methods, which were neither inherently torturous nor inherently non-torturous, amounted to torture *as practised in specific circumstances for specific durations and in specific combinations* (or did not, as the case may be). As seen above, and laid out in greater detail elsewhere,[147] the Israeli methods, even according to official sources, were more numerous, and used in combination for periods several times longer than the 'four or possibly five days' of the British ones. It is not inconceivable, therefore, that the difference between the findings reflects a gap in the perceived severity of the methods used in the two interrogation systems rather than in the definitional approaches of the two bodies.

***

In conclusion, I believe that the following may be described as constituting the international legal principles governing interrogation methods such as 'the five techniques', 'moderate physical pressure', and 'stress and duress':

1. *These methods are always unlawful.* International law prohibits officials from intentionally inflicting pain and suffering on detainees for the purpose of extracting information out of them—under international human rights law they constitute at least acts of 'cruel, inhuman or degrading treatment'; under

---

[146] Human Rights Committee, *El-Megreisi v Libyan Arab Jamahiriya*, Communication No 440/1990, UN Doc CCPR/C/50/D/440/1990 (1994), para 5.4.

[147] In 1997, both the UN Special Rapporteur and the CAT were in possession of a copy of *The Face and the Mirror*, *supra* n 133.

international humanitarian law they constitute at least similarly prohibited acts, including 'physical or moral coercion', 'inhuman treatment', 'cruel treatment', and 'outrages upon personal dignity.'

2. *International law provides no justifications or escape clauses in a TBS or other exceptional circumstances:* the prohibition on such acts is absolute.

3. *These methods may constitute torture.* If officials intentionally inflict pain on detainees for the purpose of extracting information out of them, they are already very close to torturing, the only element left to be established is that the pain inflicted is 'severe'.

4. *Whether or not these methods cause 'severe' pain depends,* inter alia, *on their duration and combination.* Such methods may not be inherently torturous, but used over time, in combination or both they will become exactly that. The particular point at which this happens would depend, *ceteris paribus*, to a large extent on the two cumulative aspects—duration and combination.[148] Unlike in the case of the 'entry level' severity, however, I would emphasize again that at this point the *illegality* of the act has already been firmly established.

This is where the legal formula ends and an assessment of specific methods as applied, their nature, duration and combination—as well as the disposition of the specific victim—must begin. But I submit that it is also here that the hitherto sidelined (albeit necessarily present) element of purpose comes to the fore. Under the three models, the pain and suffering were (or have been) inflicted for a specific purpose, perceived as vital—the extraction of urgently-needed information that would save many innocent lives. It is therefore believed that if the purpose of the interrogation is not achieved, 'disastrous consequences' will follow. It is these very purpose and perceived crucial importance[149] that in all likelihood condemn any 'so-far-and-no-further' mechanisms, legal or otherwise, designed to allow 'coercion' or 'cruel, inhuman or degrading treatment' while stopping short, as it were, at the gates of torture, to failure when milder forms of ill-treatment have not produced the desired results.[150]

Based on the account of the facts (including by officials) and analysis provided here, and on the findings of independent experts and bodies cited, it may be safely concluded that such mechanisms, to the extent that they have existed, did indeed fail, and torture was, or has been, practised under all three models. Therefore, the various officials, academics and others seeking ways of legalizing methods

---

[148] *Cf* the European Court in *Selmouni v France*: 'The Court considers that this "severity" is, like the "minimum severity" required for the application of Article 3, in the nature of things, relative; it depends on all the circumstances of the case, such as the duration of the treatment, its physical or mental effects and, in some cases, the sex, age and state of health of the victim, etc.' (*supra* n 68, para 100).

[149] To which may be added the great practical difficulty in assessing, during a crucial interrogation, where exactly the dividing ill-treatment/torture line lies in the specific case.

[150] See the discussion in Part II, Ch 9, Section D(2)(h).

used within these models are in fact seeking ways of legalizing torture—some inadvertently, perhaps, but most through the inexorable pull of their 'lesser evil' reasoning. They are therefore best described, to use Richard S Weisberg's sharp observation, as 'micromanagers of torture'.[151]

[151] RH Weisberg, 'Loose Professionalism, or Why Lawyers Take the Lead on Torture' in S Levinson (ed), *Torture: A Collection* (Oxford, OUP, 2004), 299–305, 303. Weisberg makes what to my mind is a brilliant comparison of the 'loose professionalism' of French lawyers working within the racist paradigm of the Vichy government's legal system and that of early twenty-first century lawyers working within a torture-justifying paradigm.

19

The 'Defence of Necessity' as Legal Grounds for Torture

Could the 'defence of necessity' (DoN), in its existing forms in national and international legal systems, provide legal grounds for torturing in a TBS? I submit that in order to provide such grounds, the DoN would have to be shown as constituting, at least potentially, what I will call *an uncapped 'choice of evils' justificatory defence*. This formula and its components will be explained in the course of the discussion below. Here we are concerned again, temporarily, with the law as it is rather than how it should be, therefore only possibilities within *existing* law will be explored.

After attempting to show that the DoN in that form may exist in some domestic systems (outside Israel, where this has already been established), I will consider whether a torture-justifying defence of necessity would also apply under international criminal law, which would necessitate an analysis of the DoN in that sphere of the law.

The related question of whether, regardless of its applicability in domestic and international legal systems as they now stand, a torture-justifying DoN would suit the *practicalities* of a state facing terrorism at the beginning of the twenty-first century, will be addressed in the conclusions of this Part.

The reader will quickly realize that the discussion below cannot, by any stretch of the imagination, be considered exhaustive of the DoN and the jurisprudential issues arising from it. Nor is it meant to be—all I wish to do here is to hack, through the thick shrubbery of the legislative, judicial and academic treatment of this subject, a narrow but hopefully clear path towards our specific destination.

A. Domestic Law

1. A preliminary remark: self-defence—a better alternative?

Some writers have suggested that another criminal law defence, 'self-defence', would provide a better (and narrower) defence for officials who torture in a

TBS.[152] Most importantly, they maintain that this defence will prohibit the torture of innocent persons, such as a knowledgeable bystander.[153] Lawyers for the US Justice and Defense Departments have made similar suggestions, alongside claiming the applicability of the DoN.[154]

As these sources themselves recognize, however, the legal[155] notion of self-defence as an individual defence to a crime cannot easily accommodate a situation where a prisoner who is bound and helpless, rather than attacking anyone, is beaten or otherwise deliberately and systematically made to suffer immense pain by one or more officials when neither they nor anyone near them is in any danger, immediate or otherwise.[156] Thus the August 2002 DOJ memo and the Pentagon Working Group concede that:

…this situation is different from the usual self-defense justification, and, indeed, it overlaps with elements of the necessity defense. Self-defense as usually discussed involves using force against an individual who is about to conduct the attack.[157]

Gur-Arye similarly acknowledges that:

Strictly speaking, the use of force in interrogation does not fall within the justification of self-defense.[158]

In order for it to qualify as a defence for torture in a TBS, these writers and officials acknowledge that there is no escape from what Gur-Arye calls 'extending self-defense to include the use of interrogational force'.[159] I submit that such 'extension' would have to be made in one of two directions:

Torture could be considered a measure of what Reichman calls 'collective self-defence.' The August 2002 DOJ memo states that:

…we believe that a claim by an individual of the defense of another would be further supported by the fact that, in this case, the nation itself is under attack and has the right to self-defense.[160]

---

[152] M Gur-Arye, 'Legitimating Official Brutality: Can the War against Terror Justify Torture?' *Center for the Study of Law and Society Faculty Working Papers* (University of California, Berkeley), Year 2003, Paper 11, <http://repositories.cdlib.org/cgi/viewcontent.cgi?article=1010&context=csls>, accessed 13 August 2003; *idem*, 'Can the War against Terror Justify the Use of Force in Interrogations? Reflections in Light of the Israeli Experience' in Levinson (ed), *ibid*, 183–198; Reichman, *supra* n 39. Benvenisti (*supra* n 5) similarly prefers a 'self-defence approach' to the DoN, but unlike the other two writers argues that it would only apply to interrogation methods which fall short of torture.

[153] See Gur-Arye, 'Can the War against Terror…' (*ibid*, 191–5).

[154] See August 2002 DOJ memo, *supra*, Part III, Ch 15, n 283, at 42–6; Pentagon Working Group report, 27–31.

[155] Or for that matter the moral. See Part I, Ch 5, Section B.

[156] See eg Gur-Arye, 'Can the War on Terror…', *supra* n 152, 194; Reichman, *supra* n 39, 44, fn 8.

[157] August 2002 DOJ memo, 44; Pentagon Working Group report, 29. The passage in the latter report is identical to the former, but there is no acknowledgment of this borrowing.

[158] Gur-Arye, 'Can the War on Terror…', *supra* n 152, 194. See also Reichman, *supra* n 39, 44, fn 8.

[159] *Ibid*. Reichman similarly talks of 'a derivative of a self defense' *ibid*.

[160] August 2002 DOJ memo, 44.

A Department of Defense memorandum puts it more generally, and more bluntly:

At the national level, no treaty can override a nation's inherent right to self-defense.[161]

The memorandum cites Article 51 of the UN Charter, which provides for states' right to act in of 'individual or collective' self-defence, in support of this interpretation. However, if states can torture in self-defence, and, as the DoD memorandum seems to suggest, the full gamut of international humanitarian law similarly withdraws before that right—then we are no longer inside the international legal framework within which this discussion takes place. At any rate, torture would then become a legitimate weapon in the defensive armoury of the 'collective', or the 'nation', namely the state. In other words, torture would be inflicted as an act of state, and as such its use must be authorized and regulated by law, just as any other legitimate act of state, including during war. 'Self-defence' in this sense is no longer an individual defence within the criminal law for an otherwise unlawful act, and thereby becomes irrelevant to this particular discussion.[162]

Alternately, 'self-defence' may be kept as an individual defence for the torturer in a TBS; however, to accommodate such torture, the defence of 'self-defence' would inevitably have to 'overlap' with the 'defence of necessity', and acquire its salient characteristics—enough so to make the two virtually indistinguishable. When referring to 'self-defence' in this context, Gur-Arye talks about considering 'what the right balance between the potential harms involved is'[163] while Benvenisti supports a 'net-gain cost-benefit calculus'.[164]

Thus we are back with balancing evils, that is with a DoN in all but name. As will be seen further below, in *Re A (Children)*, Ward LJ, adopted a similar approach, ruling that a plea of 'quasi self-defence' must be available to the doctors who could only save one conjoined twin by killing the other,[165] which, he stated, involves 'choosing the lesser of the two evils'.[166] Even the innocent, then, would not escape harm under that version of 'self-defence', and very little remains of what distinguishes it from the DoN. The conclusion is that this approach does not

---

[161] Memorandum for Alberto R Gonzales, Counsel to the President, and William J Haynes II, General Counsel of the Department of Defense. *Re: Application of treaties and laws to al Qaeda and Taliban detainees*. From Jay S Bybee, Assistant Attorney General, Office of Legal Counsel, US Department of Justice, 22 January 2002, 28.

[162] The question of whether states may lawfully resort to torture is discussed above, in Ch 18, Section D.

[163] Gur-Arye, 'Legitimating Official Brutality...' *supra* n 152, at 33.

[164] Benvenisti, *supra* n 5, 610.

[165] *Re A (Children) (Conjoined Twins: Surgical Separation)* [2000] 4 All ER 961, para 7.7. According to VF Nourse, this is actually a return to the roots of the defence of self-defence: 'Traditionally, self-defense is considered a justification: the defendant is seen as meriting a defense because he had to make a "choice of evils"' (*ibid*, 'Reconceptualizing Criminal Law Defenses' 151(5) *U of Penn L Rev* 1691 (2003) 1703).

[166] *Re A (Children) ibid*, para 7.6.

offer a significant departure from the DoN model and as it is only the latter that has so far been actually applied, we need not be concerned with it any further.

2. The defence of necessity—a short outline

We are concerned here solely with necessity as a general defence in criminal law. General defences cover situations where, in the words of an Anglo-American legal commentary:

[A] defendant may commit the *actus reus* of an offence with the requisite *mens rea* and yet escape liability because he has a 'general defence.'[167]

While most civil law, or 'continental' states do not use the term 'defences',[168] the principle governing parallel legal terms, such as 'grounds of justification and excuse', is the same:

Sometimes it may be that an act or omission is covered by the description of a penal statute, but is nevertheless not punishable by reason of special circumstances, provided for by the law or not: grounds of impunity.[169]

In the case of 'a sober person of reasonable firmness',[170] a general defence typically arises in emergency situations (which a TBS obviously is), as Andrew Ashworth explains:

A well-regulated society will provide a general protection, but it cannot guarantee protection at the very moment when an individual is subjected to sudden attack. The criminal law cannot respect the autonomy of the individual if it does not provide for this dire situation.[171]

This formulation, however, already poses a problem for an official interrogator, who, being himself part of society's general protection, does not fit easily into a formula of individual emergencies.

---

[167] CMV Clarkson and HM Keating (eds), *Criminal Law: Text and Materials* (5th edn, London: Sweet & Maxwell, 2003) 270. See similarly eg Peter Murphy (ed-in-chief), *Blackstone's Criminal Practice: 2003* (Oxford: OUP, 2003) 34 para A3.1; AP Simester and GR Sullivan, *Criminal Law: theory and doctrine* (2nd edn, Oxford–Portland, Oregon: Hart Publishing, 2003) 538–540; J Smith, *Smith & Hogan's Criminal Law: Cases and Materials*, 8th edn (London: Butterworths/LexisNexis, 2002) 308.

[168] See eg J Herrmann, 'The Federal Republic of Germany' in GF Cole, SJ Frankowski and MG Gertz (eds), *Major Criminal Justice Systems: A Comparative Study* (Newbury Park: Sage Publications, 1987) 106–133, 117.

[169] L Dupont and C Fijnaut, 'Belgium' in *International Encyclopaedia of Laws, Volume 1: Criminal Law* (Dventer: Kluwer, 1993) 78 ff, 148.

[170] *R v Martin* [1989] 1 All ER 652, 653.

[171] A Ashworth, *Principles of Criminal Law* (3rd edn, Oxford: OUP, 1999) 138.

(a) Some legal definitions

The Israeli statutory provision for the DoN has already been presented.[172] Following are another three legal definitions from the other states whose law will be referred to often in the discussion:

(i) German penal code (*Strafgesetzbuch*, StGB, 1975):

§ 34. Necessity as justification:

Whoever commits an act in order to avert an imminent and otherwise unavoidable danger to the life, limb, liberty, honour, property or other legal interest of himself or of another does not act unlawfully if, taking into consideration all the conflicting interests, in particular the legal ones, and the degree of danger involved, the interest protected by him significantly outweighs the interest which he harms. This rule applies only if the act is an appropriate means to avert the danger.

§ 35. Necessity as excuse:

(1) Whoever commits an unlawful act in order to avert an imminent and otherwise unavoidable danger to his own life, limb, or liberty, or to that of a relative or person close to him, acts without guilt. This rule does not apply if under the prevailing circumstances the perpetrator could be expected to have assumed the risk, especially because he was himself the cause of the danger or because he found himself in a special legal relationship. If however, the perpetrator did not have to assume the risk with regard to a special legal relationship, the punishment may be reduced in accordance with the provisions of § 49(1).

(2) If, in committing the act, the perpetrator assumes the existence of circumstances which under subparagraph (1) would excuse his conduct, he shall be punished only if he could have avoided the error. The punishment shall be reduced in accordance with the provisions of § 49(1).[173]

(ii) US Model Penal Code

The US Model Penal Code (henceforth MPC, 1985):

Section 3.02 Justification Generally: Choice of Evils

(1) Conduct that the actor believes to be necessary to avoid a harm or evil to himself or to another is justifiable, provided that:

    (a) The harm or evil sought to be avoided by such conduct is greater than that sought to be prevented by the law defining the offense charged; and

    (b) neither the Code nor other law defining the offense provides exceptions or defenses dealing with the specific situation involved; and

    (c) a legislative purpose to exclude the justification claimed does not otherwise plainly appear.

---

[172] *Supra*, Part III, Ch 12, Section B(2), n 37.

[173] 'The Penal Code of the Federal Republic of Germany' trans JJ Darby, *The American Series Of Foreign Penal Codes*, Vol 28 (London: Littleton 1987); §49 concerns 'Special Statutory Mitigating Circumstances.'

(2) When the actor was reckless or negligent in bringing about the situation requiring a choice of harms or evils or in appraising the necessity for his conduct, the justification afforded by this Section is unavailable in a prosecution for any offense for which recklessness or negligence, as the case may be, suffices to establish culpability.[174]

While English and Canadian law contain no statutory provision for the DoN,[175] their courts have provided some of the most interesting cases involving that defence at common law. Stephan's mid-nineteenth century definition of the defence has withstood the ravages of time and, in Brooke LJ's modified version, presented in a end-of-the-twentieth century ruling, seems to encapsulate the principles of that defence at common law at the beginning of the twenty-first century:

(i)   the act is needed to avoid inevitable and irreparable evil;

(ii) no more should be done than is reasonably necessary for the purpose to be achieved;

(iii) the evil inflicted must not be disproportionate to the evil avoided.[176]

This notwithstanding, the lack of clear statutory provisions has created a confusing array of judicial descriptions, opinions and classifications[177] which has, to an extent, spilled over onto international law.

(b) Cases in which the DoN was raised

Cases in which the DoN was raised have spanned sailors, stranded on a drifting boat, who, as a last effort to ward off starvation, killed a cabin boy and ate him;[178] a sailor who threw people off an overcrowded lifeboat;[179] doctors who aborted a

---

[174] The American Law Institute, *Model Penal Code and Commentaries (Official Draft and Revised Comments), Part I—General Provisions §§3.01 to 5.07* (Philadelphia: American Law Institute, 1985). See 8–9 for the text and 9–22 for the commentary. (Henceforth: MPC.)

[175] The same is true of several states within the USA, who have nevertheless recognised the defence in its common law form—Alabama, California, Connecticut, Idaho, Indiana, Iowa, Massachusetts, Mississippi, New Jersey, New Mexico, North Carolina, North Dakota, Ohio, Oklahoma, Rhode Island, South Carolina, South Dakota, Wyoming.

[176] *Re A (Children), supra* n 165, para 26. For Stephan's original formulation, quoted earlier in Brooke LJ's speech, see JF Stephen, *A Digest of the Criminal Law (Crimes and Punishments)* (4th edn, London: Macmillan, 1887) 11. Brooke LJ omitted Stephan's view of the defence as an excuse and its (related) restriction to acts for the sake of self and 'others whom he was bound to protect' (*ibid*).

[177] Not least the confusion among the defences of necessity, duress of circumstances and duress by threats, which need not be addressed here, but cannot be avoided regarding international criminal law. For an attempt at distinguishing the three see eg Smith, *supra* n 167, Ch 11. By contrast, Lord Hailsham LC dismisses any dissimilarity between necessity and duress as '... a distinction without a relevant difference, since ... duress is only that species of the genus of necessity which is caused by wrongful threat' (*R v Howe* [1987] 1 AC 417, 427).

[178] *R v Dudley and Stephens* [1884] 14 QBD 273, defence denied. This case has been discussed in practically every work or court case dealing with the DoN in Anglo-American law. The judgment was endorsed in *Howe, ibid.*

[179] *United States v Holmes*, 26 F Cas 360 (1842), necessity denied.

late-pregnancy foetus to save its mother's life;[180] an anti-war protester who burnt draft records to protest and undermine his country's war effort (claiming this would save lives);[181] prisoners who escaped, fearing violence or molestation;[182] 'pro-life' protesters who broke into abortion clinics (to save the lives of unborn children);[183] cannabis-smugglers who were forced by a storm and mechanical failure to seek shelter in the waters of a state they had not intended to enter;[184] a man being in possession of a gun illegally to hide it from a would-be killer;[185] Iraqis who hijacked a plane to escape being returned to their home country, where, they claimed, they faced torture or execution;[186] a man who killed his quadriplegic daughter who had suffered, in addition, from a severe form of cerebral palsy in 'compassionate homicide';[187] an MI5 agent who revealed state secrets (claiming this would save lives);[188] and more.

One of the most dramatic cases where necessity has been raised is that of 'Mary and Jodie', the conjoined twins,[189]—not least because the judges had to decide what the physicians *must actually do* rather than judge a defendant's action after the fact. They faced a legal/moral dilemma of, essentially, whether to allow doctors to cut off the artery which connected the two (enabling the moribund 'Mary' to live 'off' her twin Jodie's bloodstream, for a while), so that 'Mary' would die but 'Jodie' might live, or order them to let both twins die. In Brooke LJ's words, they had to let the twins die, unless they could 'provide a lawful justification for what would otherwise be an offence of murder'.[190]

The agony of the judges is almost palpable, but all three allowed the life-saving, life-ending operation to proceed. One of them, Brooke LJ, relied explicitly on the 'principle...of necessity'.[191]

---

[180] 16 RGSt 242, Judgment of 11 March 1927, necessity allowed. Cited by GP Fletcher, *Basic Concepts of Criminal Law* (New York: OUP, 1998) 140.

[181] *United States v Simpson*, 420 F.2d 515 (9th Cir, 1972), necessity denied.

[182] Eg *United States v Bailey*, 444 US 394 (1980), necessity denied (on a technicality); *People v Musgrove*, No 3–98-0953 (Ill. 3rd District Ct 2000), necessity allowed.

[183] See eg *City of St Louis v Klocker*, 637 SW 2d 174 (Mo Ct App, 1982); *State v Diener*, 706 SW 2d 582 (Mo Ct App, 1986), necessity denied.

[184] *R v Perka* (1984), 13 DLR (4th), necessity denied. See similarly *R v Salvador, Wannamaker, Campbell and Nunes* (1981), Nova Scotia Supreme Court, 101 ILR 269 (1995).

[185] *Pommell and DPP v Harris* [1995] 1 Cr App R 170, necessity allowed.

[186] *R v Abdul-Hussein and others* [1999] Crim LR 570, necessity allowed.

[187] *R v Latimer* (2001), 39 CR (5th) 1, necessity denied.

[188] *R v Shayler* [2001] EWCA Crim 1977 [2002] UKHL 11, necessity denied.

[189] *Re A (Children), supra* n 165. The facts were presented in Part I, Ch 4, Section B(3). For discussions of this case see eg R Gillon, 'Imposed separation of conjoined twins—moral hubris by the English courts?' 27(3–4) *J of Med. Ethics* (2001); CI Lugosi, 'Playing God: Mary must die so Jodie may live longer' 17 *Issues in Law and Medicine* 123 (2001); VE Munro, 'Square Pegs in Round Holes: The Dilemma of Conjoined Twins and Individual Rights' 10(4) *Social and Legal Studies* 459 (2001).

[190] *Re A (Children), ibid*, para 25. The description of the (proposed) doctors' action as murder may be questioned, but this is beyond the scope of this study.

[191] *Ibid*, para 26. Ward LJ spoke of 'a quasi self-defence' (para 7.7), while Walker LJ relied on the moral-philosophical doctrine of double-effect.

If the law has determined that the DoN may apply, albeit in extremely rare circumstances, even to 'what would otherwise be . . . murder' of a newborn baby—could it not be reasonably argued that it may also apply to the torture of a vile terrorist in a TBS? I would submit that such an argument, at least in an 'atomistic', context-free form, cannot be dismissed offhand. What remains is to examine whether the particular requirements I have set out at the beginning of this section may be fulfilled within the law of necessity, and later add the context—legal, practical and moral—within which a decision on such applicability must be taken.

3. Should the torturer plead the DoN as justification or as excuse?

In this section, the difference between justificatory and excusatory defences will be explained, in particular regarding the DoN, as will its significance for our purposes, before I attempt to answer the question posed in the title.

Defences are sharply divided in civil law systems, and less sharply so in common law systems, into 'justifications' and 'excuses'. The difference is described by Paul Robinson thus:

Justified conduct is correct behaviour which is encouraged or at least tolerated. In determining whether conduct is justified, the focus is on the *act*, not the actor. An excuse represents a legal conclusion that the conduct is wrong, undesirable, but that criminal liability is inappropriate because some characteristic of the actor vitiates society's desire to punish him.[192]

According to the commentators of the MPC:

To say that someone's conduct is 'justified' ordinarily connotes that the conduct is thought to be right, or at least not undesirable; to say that someone's conduct is 'excused' ordinarily connotes that the conduct is thought to be undesirable but that for some reason the actor is not to be blamed for it.[193]

Some defences, such as insanity, intoxication, provocation and mistake of facts are excusatory by nature. In contrast, self-defence is now perceived as justificatory by nature. In the Anglo-American system, the DoN has been claimed to

---

[192] P Robinson, 'Criminal Law Defenses: A Systematic Analysis' 82 *Col L Rev* 199 (1982), 229. *Cf* eg K Greenawalt, 'The Perplexing Borders of Justification and Excuse' 84 *Columbia L Rev* 1897 (1984), 1927: '. . . the central distinction between justification and excuse is between warranted action and unwarranted action for which the actor is not to blame'. See similarly also JC Smith, *Justification and Excuse in the Criminal Law* (London: Stevens & Sons, 1989), *passim*; Clarkson and Keating, *supra* n 167, 270–283, Dupont and Fijnaut, *supra* n 169, 71; Herrmann, *supra* n 168, 117.

[193] MPC, *supra* n 174, 3. The Code, according to its commentators, 'makes a rough analytical distinction between excuse and justification', but does not draw 'a fine line' between the two, as drawing such a line is seen neither as possible nor as desirable (*ibid*, 2–3). *Cf R v Perka*, *supra* n 184, 12–13 (per Dickson CJ).

belong to either category; at any rate, following *Re A (Children)*, as discussed here, it can hardly be argued that it may never apply as justification.[194]

Writers and judges have at times used the concept of 'judicial compassion' to denote the courts' approach in finding a defendant not guilty having accepted his or her excusatory plea.[195]

According to Heribert Schumann, German law requires two conditions for excusable necessity to apply:

First, the actor in an excusing state of necessity will normally be under extreme emotional pressure, which considerably impairs his ability to conform to the requirements of law and thus diminishes his guilt. And second, it must be taken into account that the offender acts with intent to protect highly valued interests.[196]

Crucially, however, Schumann adds that §35(1) precludes the availability of the defence as 'excuse':

...to cases in which the actor is under a special legal duty to withstand the danger (e.g. because he is a police officer or a fireman).[197]

Israeli law similarly provides that the DoN is not available 'where the person was under obligation, either stipulated by law or *ex officio*, to withstand the danger or the threat'.[198] Such provisions already make a strong case for an official interrogator to seek the DoN as justification rather than excuse.

Perhaps, however, an interlude is needed at this point to justify the very posing of the question at issue: If a plea for a DoN in either form is fully accepted by a court, the defendant would be acquitted, with no blemish on his or her name. Why then does it matter which one is applied?

The distinction is of obvious significance for the purposes of this study, which ultimately seeks to answer the question of on whether or not it is *right*, namely justifiable, for officials to torture a suspect in a TBS. But it is equally important for those supporting torture in a TBS, in moral philosophy, in law, in practice or in any combination of the three, who have, to a man (or woman), claimed

---

[194] See the differing views of Dickson CJ and Wilson J in *R v Perka, ibid*. During much of the long history of English law's now-you-see-it-now-you-don't attitude towards the DoN, which is not our concern here, it was viewed as an excuse. However, it has clearly applied as justification as well, at least since Lord Denning's *obiter dictum* in *Buckoke v Greater London Council* [1971] 2 All ER 254, 258, to the effect that a fire-engine driver breaking traffic regulations on his way to save lives in a burning house 'should not be prosecuted. He should be congratulated.'

[195] The term was used by Wilson J in *R v Perka, supra* n 184, 29, and explained at 29–30. See also eg *R v Dudley and Stephens, supra* n 178, 288 (rejecting the applicability of the concept to the particular case); A Brunder, 'A Theory of Necessity' 7(3) *Oxford J of Legal Studies* 339 (1987) 351–2; Fletcher, *Basic Concepts, supra* n 180, 130–1.

[196] H Schumann, 'Criminal Law' in WF Ebke and MW Finkin (eds), *Introduction to German Law* (The Hague: Kluwer, 1996) 383–412, 397. Schumann is referring to a specific (fictional) case where 'the offender's own life or the life of his spouse, child, or close friend is at stake and can only be saved by killing a stranger' (*ibid*).

[197] *Ibid.*

[198] Section 34(15) of the Penal Law 1977 (amendments: 1994, 1995).

such torture to be *justified*, rather than that we should forgive the torturer for acting wrongly due to loss of judgment in difficult circumstances. The distinction has practical implications as well: succumbing to 'extreme emotional pressure' which may result in 'impaired ability', perhaps in more ways than one—these are hardly desirable qualities for a torturer on whom the lives of many depend. Instead the life-saving torturer must be calculated, reasonable, clinical—the kind of qualities needed to make the *right*, or justifiable, decisions, rather than wrong but forgivable ones.

The debate on the issue around Israel's use of torture has demonstrated these points. In Israeli law, the distinction between justification and excuse is not provided for explicitly, the *chapeau* of the provisions for the DoN and other defences stating simply that 'a person shall not be criminally liable for an act'.[199] Nevertheless, the question of what type of DoN would be available to a GSS agent who tortures in a TBS has received some attention. Clearly, under the Landau model, where the DoN was perceived as granting *ab initio* authority to GSS agents to use 'moderate physical pressure', the defence could only be thus perceived in its justificatory form. Has this changed as a result of the HCJ ruling in the *Israel Torture* case?

Gur-Arye claims that it has. She bases this on para 36 of the ruling:

> ... the Supreme Court said: 'the necessity defense has the effect of allowing one who acts under the circumstances of necessity to escape criminal liability. The necessity defense does not posses any additional normative value.' By denying necessity normative value, the Court rejected the notion of necessity as a justification. The Court rather emphasized the personal nature of the necessity, as in the notion of excuse, by ruling that the necessity defense might apply to individual investigators who 'claim to have acted from *a feeling of necessity* (emphasis added).'[200]

The first point is questionable, as the Court refers to 'one who acts under the circumstances of necessity'—clearly placing circumstances above any specific state in which the person involved may be. The point about 'denying necessity normative value' is similarly problematic, as the Court speaks of '*additional* normative value' having already bestowed normative value upon 'circumstances of necessity' generally—and the TBS specifically,[201] as one such set of circumstances which would absolve 'one' from criminal liability. Gur-Arye's final point is weaker once we look at the original Hebrew term used by the Court (in para 38 of the ruling)—*tehushah*—for which (as has already been pointed out) 'sense' is a more precise translation than 'feeling'.

---

[199] Section 34(11) of the Penal Law 1977 (amendments: 1994, 1995), the same formula is used in secs 34(6) through 34(13).

[200] Gur-Arye, 'Can the War against Terror...' *supra* n 152, 188. (Emphasis added in original.) For a similar view see O Gross, 'The Prohibition on Torture and the Limits of the Law' in Levinson (ed), *supra* n 151, 229–253, 248.

[201] See the discussion *supra*, Ch 14, Section B.

Most of all, it should be remembered that the whole case revolved around whether GSS agents could *justifiably* use force in interrogations. The State never claimed that such agents should be excused for understandably committing a wrong. In fact it claimed, in no uncertain terms, that it sees the type of DoN available to interrogators as justificatory, and even that the very nature of the DoN in Israeli law is justificatory.[202] The Court's acceptance of the applicability of the DoN to torturers in TBSs, albeit not in the *a priori*, regulated form for which the State pressed, cannot be divorced from this context.

Finding that torture by officials of a suspected terrorist is 'excused' would also present considerable practical problems in states facing terrorism. An official cannot repeatedly, and *unjustifiably*, disobey instructions, break the letter of the law and remain in office. If Israeli interrogators have to torture dozens annually, as its officials in effect claim, and larger numbers must be tortured in the USA's 'war on terror', and if torture methods must often be applied by several interrogators[203] then dozens, if not hundreds of interrogators in Israel, and possibly more in the USA, may have to be replaced every year, including, presumably, the most experienced, skilled and senior ones.[204] This is a practical impossibility as well as (for torture advocates) an ethical one, not least because the loss of such interrogators would, under the torture-justifying theories, cost human lives (due to subsequent incompetent interrogations), just as refraining from torture would. This issue will be discussed further in the conclusion of this Part.

Problems would also arise for those assisting a torturer, as is inevitably the case in states facing terrorism, where interrogation is part of a complex operation. Unlike justified conduct, it is, in principle, unlawful for others to assist excusable conduct.[205]

Even if a plea of the DoN fails as a justificatory defence for torturers, it may still apply in 'excuse' form where, for instance, an interrogator wrongly believed, having made a reasonable mistake, that the situation was a TBS or that the suspect possessed the life-saving information. This point, which carries considerable 'slippery slope' repercussions, will not be pursued further.

---

[202] See especially the detailed arguments to that effect, HCJ 5100/94 *The Public Committee against Torture in Israel v Government of Israel*, *Principal Arguments by the Respondents*, 17 May 1998, paras 7–13; *Additional Arguments by the Respondents*, 8 June 1999, paras 3–12.

[203] See eg the descriptions of US and Israeli methods, *supra*, Part III, Chs 12, 14 and 15, respectively.

[204] Indeed, Ya'akov Perry relates that in 'exceptionally important cases' he would himself, as Head of the GSS, interrogate suspects. See *idem*, *Strike First* [Hebrew] (Tel Aviv: Keshet, 1999) 148.

[205] See eg George Fletcher, *Rethinking Criminal Law* (Boston: Little, Brown and Co, 1978) 866–7; Greenawalt, *supra* n 192, 1900; Robinson, *supra* n 192, 279–80; JC Smith, *Justification and Excuse*, *supra* n 192, 8. This should be distinguished from cases where the DoN was claimed to apply to accomplices to crimes *directly*, as in eg *Lynch v Director of Public Prosecutions* [1975] All ER 917, *Abbot v R* [1976] All ER 140.

4. The DoN as an uncapped 'choice of evils' defence

Wayne R LaFave states that a justificatory defence (in US law):

... is often expressed in terms of a choice of evils: When the pressure of circumstances presents one with a choice of evils, the law prefers that he avoid the greater evil by bringing about the lesser evil. Thus the evil involved in violating the terms of the criminal law (taking another's property; even taking another's life) may be less than that which would result from literal compliance with the law (starving to death; two lives lost).[206]

The perception of the DoN 'in terms of a choice of evils' is often found in statutes,[207] court judgments,[208] and academic writing.[209] It is not universally accepted as the best view of the defence, nor is it agreed by all that the 'choice of evils' should be perceived in the consequentialist, indeed *act*-consequentialist[210] version which LaFave proposes, and which the torture-justifying position demands.[211] However, my aim here is not to prove that this is the *only* acceptable

---

[206] Wayne R LaFave, *Criminal Law* (3rd edn, St Paul, Minn: West Group, 2000) §5.4(a).

[207] See eg MPC, *supra* n 174, and (for the explicit use of the term) the criminal codes of Arkansas, § 5–2–604; Colorado, CRS § 18–1–702(1), Delaware, Del C § 463, Hawaii, HRS § 703–302; Kentucky, KY ST § 503.030; Nebraska, Rev Stat § 28–1407; Oregon, ORS § 161.200; Pennsylvania, PA CS § 503. See also eg Argentine Penal Code, Art 34(2), exempting from criminal liability: 'Anybody who has caused a harm in order to avert another greater and imminent harm not attributable to him' (translated in *The Argentine Penal Code* (London: Sweet & Maxwell, 1963) 28).

Dupont and Fijnaut, commenting on necessity in Belgium law explain that '[t]he rationale of this justification is that, faced with a choice of evils, it is better to do the lesser evil...' (*idem, supra* n 169, 77).

Section 81 of the Indian Penal Code (identical provisions exist in Malaysia, Singapore and Sri Lanka) provides: 'Nothing is an offence merely by reason of its being done with the knowledge that it is likely to cause harm, if it be done without any criminal intention to cause harm, and in good faith for the purpose of preventing or avoiding other harm to person or property' (cited and discussed by TC Han, 'The General Exception of Necessity under the Singapore Penal Code' 32 *Malaysia L Rev* 271 (1990)). Han argues that its correct interpretation is 'that the harm sought to be averted must be objectively greater than the harm actually caused' (*ibid,* 285).

[208] The term 'choice of evils' is used to describe the DoN in cases too numerous to list exhaustively. See eg *United States v Bailey*, 444 US 394, 410 (1980); *Re A (Children), supra* n 165, para 26; *People v Musgrove*, No 3–98–0953, Ill 3rd District Ct (2000); *State of Hawaii v Larry Ortiz*, Hawaii Interm Ct A (CR NO 95–2198, 2000); *State of Qld v Alyssa Nolan & Anor* [2001] QSC 174, para 19; *R v Shayler supra* n 188, para 49. Even in a Bavarian case where the court stated that the right to protect the Legal Order would in principle justify the use of force to secure a parking space, it went on to rule that this right was abused in the specific case, as 'the harm inflicted was disproportionate to that threatened by the attack' (Judgement of the High State Court in Bavaria, 22 January 1963, 1963 *Neue Juristische Wochenschrift* 824, 825, discussed in Fletcher, *Rethinking Criminal Law, supra* n 205, 864, 873).

[209] See eg, in addition to the sources quoted above, Smith, *Justification and Excuse, supra* n 192, 14 *et seq, passim*; G Williams, *Criminal Law: The General Part* (2nd edn, London: Steven and Sons, 1961) Ch 17, *passim*, eg 729, 734 ('a consequential judgement of value'); *idem, Textbook of Criminal Law* (2nd edn, London: Steven and Sons 1983) 603–8; Robinson, *supra* n 192, 213–215; PH Robinson and JM Darley, 'Testing Competing Theories of Justification' 76 *North Carolina L Rev* 1095 (1998), *passim*.

[210] These terms are discussed in Part I, Ch 2, Section B.

[211] For opposing views see eg Fletcher, *Rethinking Criminal Law, supra* n 205, *passim*, eg 790–793, 857–874; *idem, Basic Concepts..., supra* n 180, 103–6 (and see the discussion of his

view of the DoN, just to show that this view exists within domestic legal systems. I would submit that this is clearly the case, both in logic and in law. If a person burns one (empty) house as the only way to save 50 (empty) houses from burning, she is quite likely to enjoy the DoN,[212] and it would, to my mind, be futile to couch that defence in terms of, say, conflicting rights[213]—the act was justified because property to the value of 50x was saved by destroying property worth 1x, with a net gain of 49x—surely a straightforward consequentialist reasoning. As we have seen, the same reasoning has been used—alongside others—in DoN cases involving much more serious choices. Even in *Re A (Children)*, Ward LJ, while ruling that a plea of 'quasi self-defence' must be available to the doctors,[214] grounds this plea firmly in a 'lesser evil' approach:

> In those circumstances it seems to me that the law must allow an escape [from the principle of the sanctity of life] through choosing the lesser of the two evils. The law cannot say, 'heads I win, tails you lose'. Faced as they are with an apparently irreconcilable conflict, the doctors ... must make that choice along the same lines as the court has done, giving the sanctity of life principle its place in the balancing exercise that has to be undertaken. The respect the law must have for the right to life of each must go in the scales and weigh equally but other factors have to go in the scales as well.[215]

The matter, then, may be considered settled, and I would submit that for our purposes it is the boundaries of utilitarian (or consequentialist) reasoning rather than whether or not the DoN is utilitarian in nature that is the crucial issue. In other words, the real question is not whether the DoN is available in 'choice of evil' form or not, but rather whether that choice is 'capped' or not. The DoN as an uncapped 'choice of evil' defence would be available as justification[216] to a person who has committed *any act whatsoever* as long as, in the circumstances, 'the harm resulting from the act should not be disproportionate to the harm avoided'.[217] In

---

views below); Brunder, *supra* n 195, especially 341–4; GC Christie, 'The Defense of Necessity Considered from the Legal and Moral Points of View' 48 *Duke L J* 975 (1999); M Kremnitzer and R Segev, 'The Legality of Interrogational Torture: A Question of Proper Authorization or a Substantive Moral Issue?' 34 *Israel L Rev* 509 (2000) 545–8.

[212] This is reflected in the law of torts, see eg *Cope v Sharpe* [1912] 1 KB 496; and, in US law, *Restatement (Second) of Torts* § 263 (1965), entitled 'Privilege Created By Private Necessity': '(1) One is privileged to commit an act which would otherwise be a trespass to the chattel of another or a conversion of it, if it is or is reasonably believed to be reasonable and necessary to protect the person *or property* of the actor, the other or a third person from serious harm, unless the actor knows that the person for whose benefit he acts is unwilling that he shall do so.' (Emphasis added.)
For a discussion of the plea of necessity for the destruction of property see eg Christie, *ibid*, 981–1010.

[213] As do, eg, Brunder, *supra* n 195; and Kremnitzer and Segev, *ibid*.

[214] *Re A (Children)*, *supra* n 165, para 7.7.

[215] *Ibid*, para 7.6.

[216] Defences that are excusatory by nature, such as intoxication or insanity, are inherently uncapped; the act, however horrendous, is irrelevant to the plea, which portrays the accused as being incapable of realising its wrongfulness. But see a critique of this conventional approach in CO Finkelstein, 'Duress: A Philosophical Account of the Defense in Law' 37 *Ariz L Rev* 251 (1995).

[217] *R v Shayler supra* n 188, para 64.

contrast, where the law provides for a capped 'choice of evil' justificatory DoN, it places certain acts 'beyond the pale', therefore never justified, whatever the circumstances.

Simester and Sullivan describe the DoN in English law as, ostensibly, being of the capped type:

A balance of harms test may be allowed in some circumstances; whereas in other situations vested legal rights will be given priority, thereby precluding on those occasions a necessity defence based on a balance of evils test. The Devil is in the details.[218]

Their emphasis on 'circumstances', 'situations' and 'details', however, belies an equation of this approach with a 'capped' justificatory DoN, as does Simester and Sullivan's discussion of the evolving English case-law,[219] and their own conclusion:

At the level of principle, where . . . ['certain very stringent conditions'[220]] are met, necessity should be available as a defence *to all crimes*, including murder.[221] [Emphasis added.]

In contrast, a capped view of the DoN subjects certain crimes to a test of vested legal values, or perhaps meta-legal ones, where it is the *acts* themselves rather than circumstances that are at issue, and where such values are applied not on an (at least potentially) flexible scale of 'priorities', but as rigid, indeed *absolute* constraints.[222]

The latter approach could be found in German law.[223] The statutory provision defines the DoN in terms of 'conflicting interests', rather than 'choice of evils', but the latter does exist as an element of the DoN in that system. In the words of Bernsmann:

The characteristic element of justifying necessity is the proportion between the harms involved: the averted harm has to be significantly greater than the harm caused by the actor.[224]

---

[218] Simester and Sullivan, *supra* n 167, 633.

[219] *Ibid*, 632–9.

[220] *Ibid*, 638 (from an earlier passage).

[221] *Ibid*, Simester and Sullivan add that 'Under current law, *Dudley* is regarded as authority that necessity is unavailable to murder. But, on the facts, *Dudley* need not have decided any specific rule for murder.' See also at 637, where they point to Brooke LJ's speech in *Re A (Children)* as enhancing, to a degree, the prospect that the DoN would be available to murder.

[222] Again, this only applies—and, logically, *can* only apply—to the DoN as justification. In its excusatory form, the DoN too would make allowances for the actor's personal circumstances, which impaired his or her ability to act properly, and lawfully. This underlines the importance, for our purposes, of the distinction between the two forms as explained *supra*, Ch 19, Section A(3).

[223] The different roots and evolvement followed by Anglo-American law and German law (and Continental law more generally) is beyond the scope of this study. For discussions see eg Fletcher, *Basic Concepts*, *supra* n 180, Chs 6, 8; MD Dubber, *German Criminal Law: A Critical Introduction* (draft) available on <http://wings.buffalo.edu/law/bclc/web/germanscience.doc>, accessed 6 November 2003.

[224] K Bernsmann, 'Private Self-Defence and Necessity in German Penal Law and in the Penal Law Proposal—Some Remarks' 30 *Israel L Rev* 171 (1996), 181. See similarly Finkelstein, *supra* n 216, 274; Schumann, *supra* n 196, 392.

The crucial point, however, is that, in the words of the same author:

German jurisprudence has recognized *certain absolute limits* to the weighing of interests. [...] In addition to human life, the autonomy over one's bodily spheres is regarded as a supreme interest exempt from deliberation.[225] [Emphasis added.]

Fletcher explains this 'capping' in German law in more philosophical terms:

...the principle of 'appropriate means' signals absolute restraints on pursuing utility maximization.[226]

It appears then that a state wishing to use the DoN as legal grounds for torturing in a TBS would be well advised to cast that defence in the Anglo-American rather than the German mould.

Within the former system, the clearest formulation of an uncapped 'choice of evils' DoN appears in the commentary of the MPC of this defence:

The Model Code rejects any limitations on necessity cast in terms of particular evils to be avoided or particular evils to be justified...[227].

Even more striking, perhaps, is the example that the commentators provide:

While there may be situations, such as rape, where it is hardly possible to claim that greater evil was avoided than that sought to be prevented by the law defining the offense, this is a matter that is safely left to the determination and elaboration of the courts.[228]

In other words, the MPC commentators do not rule out the theoretical possibility that a rapist would enter a plea of 'choice of evils', namely that the rape was *justified*[229] since by raping he had prevented an evil far greater than

---

[225] Bernsmann, *ibid*, 183. See similarly Schumann, *ibid*, 393. Perhaps an even heavier 'capping' may be found in the provision for the DoN in the Criminal Code of Denmark: 'the offence committed through the act of necessity must be such that it can be regarded as only of relatively minor importance' (LB Langsted and V Grade, *Criminal Law in Denmark* (The Hague: Kluwer Law International, 1998) 66). See the discussion in Kremnitzer and Segev, *supra* n 211, 547–8.

[226] Fletcher, *Rethinking Criminal Law*, *supra* n 205, 788. In this context, the concept, or what Dworkin would have termed 'legal principle', of '*Rechtsgut*' (also called *Schutzgut*) in German legal doctrine, may be worth mentioning. It denotes implied legally protected interests, or values, of individuals (*Individualrechtsgüter*) and of society as a whole (*Universalrechtsgüter*). Violations of *Rechtsgüter* may trigger legal consequences, both under the criminal law (grave violations thereof being considered an encroachment on the legal order as a whole) and in torts (for instance under §823 BGB—*Bürgerliches Gesetzbuch*, or Civil Code).

Key individual *Rechtsgüter* (*Universalrechtsgüter*, involving issues such as the right to a clean, healthy environment, are not relevant here) are values protected by the German Constitution, or Basic Law (*Grundgesetz*), in particular the basic rights (*Grundrechte*) provided in Articles 1–19. They include the rights to human dignity, to physical integrity (body and life), to property, honour and sexual self-determination. While in general, *Rechtsgüter* may be waived by the rights holder (acting freely), the *Rechtsgüter* to life and dignity (which would cover torture) may not be waived.

I am grateful to Carolin Hillemanns, PhD, for providing me with this description.

[227] MPC, *supra* n 174, 14.

[228] *Ibid*.

[229] It will be recalled that the section of the MPC (Sec 3.02) commented upon is entitled 'Justifications Generally'.

the evil of rape itself—and succeed. As I have already pointed out, a TBS is perhaps (short of a Noah's-daughters-like apocalyptic scenario) the only situation where such a claim could conceivably be made, and rape has in fact been used as a tool in interrogating suspected terrorists.[230] As such, rape clearly amounts to torture.[231] It follows that the DoN as viewed by the MPC commentators may in theory provide a justificatory defence for interrogational torture, be it by rape or other, comparably severe means. In the USA, as we have seen, lawyers for the Department of Justice and Department of Defense relied directly on the MPC in arguing that torture would be justified under certain circumstances in the interrogation of terrorists,[232] and this assertion has not so far been challenged.

5. Two illustrative cases

Two cases involving scenarios not too far removed from a TBS may illustrate the different approaches of the US and German legal system.

The US case[233] did not concern the legality of torture directly, but rather the admissibility of a confession: police had coerced the defendant to give a statement and he claimed, in appealing, that for this reason, a confession he made later, itself taken properly, should have been suppressed. The case therefore addressed the nexus between the defendant's two statements. The defendant, Leon, had been arrested when he came to collect ransom money from the brother of Louis, whom Leon and an associate, Armand, had kidnapped. What follows was described by the District Court:

For the very good reason that Louis' life was in grave danger from Armand if Leon (or the officers) did not return within a short time, the police immediately demanded that the defendant tell them where he was. When he at first refused, he was set upon by several of the officers. They threatened and physically abused him by twisting his arm behind his back and choking him until he revealed where Louis was being held. The officers went to the designated apartment, rescued Louis and arrested Armand.[234]

Both the District Court and, on further appeal, a Federal Court of Appeals,[235] included *obiter dicta* in their judgments regarding that first interrogation. Neither court referred directly to a DoN (the police officers concerned were not on trial),

---

[230] See the discussion in Part I, Ch 5, Section B, and examples in the Annex and Part II, Ch 9, Section D(2)(f).

[231] See eg *Akayesu* ICTR case, *supra* n 97, paras 597, 687; *Delalic* ICTY case, *supra* n 1, discussion, paras 475–496, and findings, paras 943, 965; *Furundzija* ICTY case, *supra* n 1, paras 264–9; *Fernando and Raquel Mejia v Peru*, Inter-American Commission on Human Rights, Report No 5/96, Case No 10.970, 1 March 1996, para B(3)(a); *Aydın v Turkey, supra* n 94, paras 13, 20, 86.

[232] See *supra*, Part III, Ch 15, Section B(1)(c).

[233] *Leon v State*, 410 So.2d 201 (Fla A 3 Dist, 1982).

[234] *Ibid*, 202, per Schwartz J.

[235] *Leon v Wainwright*, 734 F.2d 770 (CA Fla, 1984).

but nevertheless spoke of an 'immediate necessity'[236] which justified torturing (this term was not used) Leon.

Thus the Court of Appeal stated:

We do not by our decision sanction the use of force and coercion by police officers. Yet this case does not represent the typical case of unjustified force. We did not have an act of brutal law enforcement agents trying to obtain a confession in total disregard of the law. This was instead a group of concerned officers acting in a reasonable manner to obtain information they needed in order to protect another individual from bodily harm or death.[237]

In Germany, a similar case ended differently—in more ways, sadly, than one.[238] In September 2002, Deputy Chief of Frankfurt police Wolfgang Daschner ordered the infliction of pain on a detained kidnapper, Magnus Gaefgen, to make him reveal the whereabouts of Jakob Metzler, 11, the son of Friedrich von Metzler, a rich local banker whom Gafgen had kidnapped for ransom. Dachner first ordered police officer Ortwin Ennigkeit to threaten Gaefgen with torture. Following the threats, Gaefgen admitted that the boy was already dead and his body hidden in a nearby lake.

At their trial in the Frankfurt Regional Court in December 2004,[239] the prosecutor rejected Daschner's claim that his conduct was justified, warning that 'The door to a very dark room was opened and this door needs to be shut again.' However, he requested only that the two be fined and ordered to donate to a charity, owing to the 'very difficult situation' and Daschner's 'honourable' motives.[240] The Court found both defendants guilty: Ennigkeit of coercion[241] and Daschner of instruction to commit coercion.[242] The Court rejected all possible attempts to exempt the two from criminal liability, both in justificatory and excusatory form. The Court ruled that the requirement of justificatory defences were not met, on two grounds: firstly, all other measures had not been

---

[236] *Ibid* at 773, per Fay J; *Leon v State, supra* n 233, 203.

[237] *Leon v Wainwright, supra* n 235, 773.

[238] This account is based mostly on Florian Jessberger, 'Bad Torture—Good Torture? What International Criminal Lawyers May Learn from the Recent Trial of Police Officers in Germany' 3(4) *J of Int'l Crim Justice* 1059 (2005), especially 1061–7. See 1062–4 for a review of the debate within Germany over the case. For media reports see eg Corinna Budras, 'German Policeman's Threat to Killer Merits Penalty, Court, Told' *Bloomberg*, 9 December 2004, <http://www.bloomberg.com/apps/news?pid=10000100&sid=agrRVfgoweRE&refer=germany>; Kristina Merkner, 'Murderer testifies against Frankfurt police' <http://www.faz.net/s/Rub9E75B460C0744F8695B3E0BE5A30A620/Doc~E6964C3B4F0D74F80B232FDBA4CE91624~ATpl~Ecommon~Scontent.html#top>, 26 November 2004, both accessed 13 December 2004.

[239] Landgericht Frankfurt a.M., Judgment of 20 December 2004, Neue Juristische Wochenschrift 2005, 692–696 <http://www.lg-frankfurt.justiz.hessen.de/internet/lg-frankfurt.nsf/vwContentByKey/W269PMLU645JUSZDE>, accessed 20 December 2005.

[240] Budras, *supra* n 238.

[241] *Nöttigung*, under sec 240(1) of the German Penal Code.

[242] *Verleitung eines Untergebenen zu einer Sraftat*, under secs 375(1) and 240(1) of the Code.

exhausted; secondly, the threat to cause pain was an infringement of human dignity, which cannot legitimately be the result of balancing of interests. In the terms used here, the Court reaffirmed that in German law, justificatory defences allow balancing of evils only in 'capped' form, such balancing being *unavailable* to justify the infringement of human dignity and similar core values.

However, the Court did take into account 'massive mitigating circumstances',[243] including Gaefgen's provocative behaviour, the defendants' motivation of saving the child and the great emotional pressure they were under. It imposed fines, but ordered no further punishment. In view of the fact that the Court did not determine that the threat in itself amounted to torture, the judgment is in accord with the approach of the European Commission of Human Rights to 'ticking bomb' and similar cases, discussed below.[244] I believe the Court's combination of a strict principled approach with a lenient punitive one needs to be considered in context, namely in what was perceived as rare and extraordinary circumstances.

On the other hand, Jessberger suggests that the Court's 'guilty, but not to be punished'[245] approach in *Dachner* should apply *as a matter of judicial policy* to torturers in a TBS. If Jessberger's approach is adopted and applied, certainly if Germany were to face the kind of terrorist threat faced by Israel, the US etc it would suffer, once cases of torture in a TBS followed by 'not to be punished' verdicts accumulate, from the same 'slippery slope' and other dangers outlined in Part II, not least the danger of turning the prohibition of torture under Germany's international obligations and in its Basic Law,[246] the criminalization of torture in Germany's Penal Code, as well as the caps on justificatory defences therein, into hollow, toothless, rhetorical exercises. This point is further elaborated in Chapter 20.

6. Conclusion—narrow, theoretical but a possibility

From the foregoing I would conclude that whereas the DoN as a justificatory defence is unavailable to a person who tortures in a TBS in the German and similar legal systems, such availability cannot be ruled out in the Anglo-American legal system.[247] The latter conclusion is precarious, and suffers from a number of weaknesses.

Firstly, this conclusion relies on legal principles, theory and interpretation, whereas there is a dearth, indeed almost total absence, of case-law (outside Israel, of course) specifically concerning the applicability of the DoN to torture in a TBS.

---

[243] Quoted in Jessberger, *supra* n 238, 1965.

[244] Ch 19, Section B(1).

[245] Jessberger, *supra* n 238, 1066. And see his argument in favour of such an approach at 1073.

[246] Article 1(1) of the Basic Law provides that 'The dignity of man is inviolable. To respect and protect it shall be the duty of all state authority.' Article 104 (1)(2) provides that 'Detainees may not be subjected to mental or physical mistreatment.'

[247] Reichman and Kahana reach a similar conclusion, *supra* n 41, 647.

The UK has a law explicitly criminalising torture,[248] and despite its poor wording[249] I have not found any cases in recent UK jurisprudence to support the theoretical claim that the DoN may be available to a torturer in a TBS. Moreover, unlike the USA's treatment of 'illegal combatants', the UK's treatment of its detainees is under close domestic and international (regional) judicial scrutiny, and no claims have been made by officials that torture or other ill-treatment may ever be justified or lawful. In February 2002 the CPT, having visited suspected terrorists detained in the UK, reported that:

The delegation heard no allegations of physical ill-treatment by police officers (or immigration service officials) of persons detained pursuant to the Anti-Terrorism, Crime and Security Act 2001.[250]

The UK, it must be added, was not free of torture scandals in Iraq,[251] but never tried to justify them.

As to US law, Kreimer presents what to my mind is a compelling argument that torture would never be deemed constitutional in the USA, although he does not address the DoJ's idea (exposed after his article was published) that the US Constitution provides the President unlimited powers at war,[252] nor federal courts' reservations as to the applicability of Constitutional guarantees to foreign detainees abroad.[253] Concentrating as he does on rebutting Dershowitz' claim that torture would be constitutional, Kreimer does not deal directly with the issue of whether the DoN would be applicable in this context, and thus falls short of arguing that courts would always deem such torture *unlawful*.[254]

In addition to the theoretical statements cited in the penultimate section, one could claim that the dearth of case-law reflects the indisputable fact that most

---

[248] See also Criminal Justice Act 1988, s 134; Human Rights Act 1998, Sch 1, Art 3.

[249] Criticized by CAT, see *infra* n 260.

[250] *CPT–UK (2002)*, CPT/Inf (2003) 18, para 10.

[251] Notably the case of Baha Musa, a hotelier detained by British troops in September 2003 and 'so brutally beaten by British troops that he died of his injuries'. The 'jurisdictional' aspect of the case reached the House of Lords, see *Al-Skeini and others v Secretary of State for Defence (Consolidated Appeals)* [2007] UKHL 26, judgment of 13 June 2007 (quotation is from para 61, per Lord Rodger of Earlssferry).

[252] See *supra*, Part III, Ch 15, Section E.

[253] See *supra*, Part III, Ch 15, Section E. In contrast to Kreimer, Marcy Strauss argues that the question of the constitutionality of torturing to save lives remains an open question, see *idem*, 'Torture' *Loyola-LA Public Law Research Paper* No 2003–7, January 2003, 225–253. And see a Federal Court's equivocal view *supra*, Ch 15, Section E.

[254] See, in his conclusion, the following: 'Faced with a threat of mass devastation that can be avoided only through torture, could an American official believe, as a matter of morality and public policy, that she should choose the path of the torturer as the lesser evil? On this question, I am prepared to concede that there is room for debate, as there is room for debate as to whether under extraordinary circumstances a public official should choose to violate any provision of the Constitution. But on the question of whether scholars or courts should announce before the fact that the Constitution permits torture, the answer seems clearer: ours is not a Constitution that condones such actions' (SF Kreimer, 'Too Close to the Rack and the Screw: Constitutional constraints on torture' 6 *Univ of Penn J of Const L* 278 (2003) 324–5).

states have so far tortured without taking the trouble of involving their legal system; that, in the words of a high-ranking CIA agent, 'There was a before 9/11, and there was an after 9/11'[255]—put differently, the world has changed and so have its legal needs. This may not as yet be reflected in legal practice; but the *Leon* case may be cited as one which *is* analogous to a TBS, and which appears promising for those supporting the application of the DoN in such cases.

Kreimer's comment regarding *Leon*, namely that it 'appears to acknowledge that a constitutional violation occurred when police choked a kidnapper to determine the location of the kidnap victim',[256] while strengthening his case against the constitutionality of torture, does little to counter any *lawfulness* argument, in view of the strong *dicta* of both courts in favour of that arm-twisting and choking, made 'in a reasonable manner' under an 'immediate necessity'.

To the extent that, in addition to its principled position on justifications, *Leon* is an indication of how an Anglo-American court would treat cases of torture in a TBS (if they ever reach the courts),[257] my assertion, in its 'weak' form, namely that the availability of the DoN in such cases *cannot be ruled out*, stands, for now. A more robust position was expressed by a leading US legal scholar whose work has been quoted in this chapter, LaFave, following the publication of the Pentagon Working Group report; with LaFave using a TBS to illustrate:

Mr. LaFave... said he was unaware that the Pentagon used his textbook in preparing its legal analysis. He agreed, however, that in some cases necessity could be a defense to torture charges. 'Here's a guy who knows with certainty where there's a bomb that will blow New York City to smithereens. Should we torture him? Seems to me that's an easy one,' Mr. LaFave said. But he said necessity couldn't be a blanket justification for torturing prisoners because of a general fear that 'the nation is in danger.'[258]

The other weakness of this assertion, regarding possible conflicts between such availability in domestic law and provisions prohibiting torture in international law, will be discussed in the next section. A third issue, involving the difficulties of applying a defence designed to address extraordinary situations to actions of officials in a state facing terrorism will be addressed in Chapter 20.

---

[255] Cofer Black, then head of the CIA Counterterrorist Center, speaking at a joint hearing of the House and Senate intelligence committees on 26 September 2002, quoted in Priest and Gellman, *supra*, Part III, Ch 15, n 348.

[256] Kreimer, *supra* n 254, p 294, fn 54.

[257] Dershowitz relies heavily on this case in claiming that interrogational torture is not illegal in the USA. See *idem, Why Terrorism Works: understanding the threat, responding to the challenge* (New Haven: Yale University Press, 2002) 124–6; 136.

[258] J Bravin, 'Pentagon Report Set Framework For Use of Torture: Security or Legal Factors Could Trump Restrictions, Memo to Rumsfeld Argued', *Wall Street Journal* (7 June 2004).

B. International Law

Two questions will be addressed in this section. First, whether under current international law, states could use the DoN in their domestic systems to exempt torturers from criminal liability without breaching their international legal obligations; secondly, whether under current international criminal law, the DoN is of the type that could provide a defence for individual officials who torture in a TBS, namely an uncapped justificatory defence, as discussed above.

1. May states use the DoN to exempt TBS torturers from punishment?

It would be quite difficult to construct a positive answer to this question. CAT rejected, as early as 1994, the applicability of the DoN as an exception to the prohibition on torture. Commenting on Israel's initial report, CAT stated the following:

> It is a matter of deep concern that Israeli laws pertaining to the defences of 'superior orders' and 'necessity' are in clear breach of that country's obligations under article 2 of the Convention Against Torture.[259]

CAT has subsequently criticized other states for allowing criminal law justifications to apply, even in theory only, to acts of torture.[260]

The UN Special Rapporteur on torture was quick to make this point in response to the HCJ ruling in the *Israel Torture* case:

> …there is no such defence against torture or similar ill-treatment under international law…[261]

In 2003, the HRC similarly made it clear, having considered Israel's second periodic report, that 'the "necessity defence" argument… is not recognized under the Covenant'.[262]

Thus the idea, advanced by Reichman, that a discretion to allow torture or ill-treatment in a TBS may be left by international bodies to individual states as

---

[259] UN Doc A/49/44 (1994), para 167.
[260] Concerning the UK, UN Doc A/54/44, 17 November 1998, para 76(e); UN Doc CAT/C/CR/33/3, 25 November 2004, para 4(a)(ii); concerning Belgium, UN Doc A/58/44, para 129(b) and 131(b) (2002–3).
[261] UN Doc E/CN.4/2000/9 (2000), para 675.
[262] Concluding observations of the Human Rights Committee: Israel. UN Doc CCPR/CO/78/ISR, 5 August 2003, para 18. Israel had not argued that the DoN is a defence to torture or to other ill-treatment under the Covenant, though its delegate claimed that it was 'an internationally-recognized legal defence' under which 'the use of some force was legitimate in the face of an imminent threat'. See Human Rights Committee, 78th Sess, Summary Record of the 2118th Meeting, 25 July 2003, UN Doc CCPR/C/SR.2118, 6 August 2003, para 34.

falling within what he terms the 'margins of appreciation that international law accords each state'[263] has already been firmly rejected.

Parry and White offer a slightly different position, arguing that:

... the international law ban on torture is primarily a prohibition against state-sponsored torture, not individual acts.[264]

They seem to ignore the fact that HCJ-style *post facto* upholding by domestic prosecutors and courts of the DoN for torturers in TBSs, which they propose, would inevitably turn the torture into an act of state, being both 'inflicted by' officials (interrogators) *and* 'with the consent or acquiescence of' officials (prosecutors and judges), under the definition of torture in Art 1(1) of the UN Convention Against Torture.[265]

Beyond this, the idea that states may be complying with an international legal rule prohibiting torture absolutely while exempting torturers from criminal liability on justificatory grounds clearly defies common sense. The principle underlining the UN bodies' insistence that the duty of states to refrain from torture extends to ensuring that individual torturers are punished had already been laid down by the International Military Court at Nuremberg:

Crimes against international law are committed by men, not by abstract entities, and only by punishing individuals who commit such crimes can the provisions of international law be enforced.[266]

In the *Ireland v UK* case, the now-defunct European Commission of Human Rights addressed directly a TBS and went, I believe, as far as international law, today as then, would (and to my mind *should*) go in accommodating a state's treatment of an official who has ill-treated a detainee in such a situation:

... it is not difficult to take a hypothetical situation, to imagine the extreme strain on a police officer who questions a prisoner about the location of a bomb which has been timed to explode in a public area within a very short while.

In the Commission's view, any such strain on members of the security forces cannot justify the application on a prisoner of treatment amounting to a breach of Art. 3. On the other

---

[263] Reichman, *supra* n 39, 75. Reichman is misusing the term 'margin of appreciation' often invoked by the European Court of Human Rights (see notably, in our context, in *Ireland v UK*, Series A No 25 (1978), para 207 *et sec*), but *never* 'accorded' to states in respect to their non-derogable obligations under the ECHR or any other international human rights treaty.

[264] JT Parry and WS White, 'Interrogating Suspected Terrorists: Should Torture Be An Option?' 63 *Uni of Pittsburgh L Rev* 743 (2002) 765.

[265] Reichman and Kahana make this point, *supra* n 41, 650.

[266] *Judgment of the International Military Tribunal For The Trial of German Major War Criminals* (London: HMSO, 1951) 41. The Court was rejecting the 'act of state' defence, but the statement is equally relevant to the DoN. That the Court's statement still applies in the twenty-first century was illustrated by the International Law Commission's reference to it as an authority in its *Commentaries to the draft articles on Responsibility of States for Internationally Wrongful Acts, adopted by the International Law Commission in its fifty-third session* (2001), UN Doc A/56/10, Ch IV.E.2, November 2001, 279.

hand, as a matter of fact, the domestic authorities are likely to take into account the general situation as a mitigating circumstance in determining the sentence or other punishment to be imposed on the individual in a case which is brought against him before the domestic authorities and courts for acts of ill-treatment. This does not, of course, in proceedings brought under the Convention, affect the responsibility of the High Contracting Party concerned under the Convention for the acts in question. However, where a penalty has been so mitigated by the domestic judicial or disciplinary authorities, having regard to the severity of the acts involved and the necessity of preventing their repetition, this fact cannot in itself be regarded as tolerance on the part of these authorities in determining whether or not the acts involved formed part of a practice in breach of Art. 3 of the Convention. This observation is particularly relevant where no practice is admitted.[267]

The Commission allows a TBS to be taken into account *not* as a defence exempting the interrogator, in whole or in part, from criminal liability but as 'a mitigating circumstance' once 'the severity of the act' and, no less importantly, 'the necessity of *preventing its repetition*' have been taken into account and 'particularly' when 'no practice is admitted'.

The idea that, setting aside states' responsibilities, international criminal law offers the individual torturer in a TBS more than this, namely a full justificatory defence, is the subject of the next section.

2. Can individuals who torture in a TBS successfully plead the DoN under international criminal law?

This section will address international criminal law as it now stands, posing the same question to which domestic law was subjected earlier, namely whether the DoN may be shown as constituting, at least potentially, an uncapped 'choice of evils' justificatory defence, and thus, at least in principle, provide (*post facto*) legal grounds for torturing in a TBS. The principled issues have already been addressed within the domestic context,[268] and so they will not be re-examined here. The Rome Statute of the International Criminal Court (ICC) is central to international criminal law and likely to remain so, therefore its provision for that defence will be considered separately.

(a) Justification or excuse?

This, I believe, is the most difficult hurdle for those seeking to find a viable defence in international criminal law for an official who has efficiently tortured

---

[267] *Ireland v UK*, Yearbook 1976, 512–949, 764.

[268] Domestic statutes and cases are almost invariably relied upon or at least referred to in both judicial and academic discussions of defences in international criminal law. This is chiefly because, in the words of Ilias Bantekas and Susan Nash 'The concept of 'defence' in international criminal law...derives its legal significance as a result of its transplantation from domestic criminal justice systems through the appropriate processes of international law' (*idem, International Criminal Law* (2nd edn, London: Cavendish Publishing, 2003) 127).

a terrorist in a TBS to negotiate. The terms 'necessity' and 'duress' are hopelessly intertwined and interchanged, both in the case-law and in the ICC Statute.[269]

Commentators usually explain, like Cassese, that 'necessity' has a 'broader' scope than 'duress' and covers '*threats to life and limb emanating from objective circumstances* and not from another person'.[270] However, the cases Cassese then discusses[271] *invariably* concern threats 'from another person' and both his commentary and the cases cited use the terms 'duress' and 'necessity' interchangeably. Such a combination of stressing the differences and ignoring them is typical of most writers.

This conflation (or confusion) has forced me to refer to a 'defence of duress/necessity' (DoD/N) rather than to 'necessity' on its own. This is not mere semantics—the resulting defence has a distinct excusatory tilt, reflected in two salient features of the case-law. First, the DoD/N, whatever term is used to describe it, overwhelmingly concerns persons who, having been ordered to commit a crime and facing a threat of imminent death or serious harm if they refuse, went on to commit it. Secondly, that threat is, in all but a few unconvincing pleas (see below), a threat to the individual subjected to duress, the 'duressee', rather than to a third person or persons, leaving less room for calm, rational evaluation. Both these characteristics steer the scenario away from the TBS, and the defence away from 'justification'.

The following, from the US Military Tribunal at Nuremberg, is typical:

> To establish the defense of coercion or necessity in the face of danger there must be a showing of circumstances such that a reasonable man would apprehend that he was in such imminent physical peril as to deprive him of freedom to choose the right and refrain from the wrong.[272]

---

[269] Statutes of previous international tribunals did not provide for the DoN or for any other defence. The closest these statutes came to a defence was in the Nuremberg Charter, *supra* n 73, which provided, in Art 8: 'The fact that the Defendant acted pursuant to order of his Government or of a superior shall not free him from responsibility, but may be considered in mitigation of punishment if the Tribunal determines that justice so requires.' Provisions in subsequent statutes of international tribunals followed this lead very closely. See eg Control Council Law No 10, *supra* n 73, Art II(4)(b); ICTY Statute, *ibid*, Art 7(4); ICTR Statute, *ibid*, Art 6(4). Nevertheless, as will be seen, international tribunals did hold defences to be available to defendants.

[270] Cassese, *International Criminal Law*, *supra* n 55, 243. In his dissenting opinion in the ICTY *Erdemovic* case, Cassese states that '… necessity is a broader heading than duress, encompassing threats to life and limb *generally* and not only when they emanate from another person.' See *Prosecutor v Erdemovic*, Case No IT-96–22-A, Appeals Camber, Judgment of 7 October 1997, (henceforth: *Erdemovic* Appeal) Separate and Dissenting Opinion of Judge Cassese (henceforth: Cassese's dissent), para 14. See similarly Bantekas and Nash, *supra* n 268, 137; MC Bassiouni, *Crimes Against Humanity in International Criminal Law* (The Hague: Kluwer Law International, 1999) 484; M Scaliotti 'Defences Before the International Criminal Court: Substantive Grounds for Excluding Criminal Responsibility—Part 1' 1(1–2) *Int'l Crim L Rev* 111 (2001) 143.

[271] Cassese, *International Criminal Law*, *ibid*, 243–251.

[272] *US v von Leeb et al* (Case 12, the High Command case), in Trials of War Criminals Before the Nuremberg Military Tribunals Under Control Council Law No 10 (henceforth: TWC) Vol XI 462 (1950) 509.

In another case, the Tribunal described that test in terms of whether or not the defendant had 'moral choice', an expression very often repeated subsequently:

…an order of a superior officer or a law or governmental decree will not justify the defence of necessity unless, in its operation, it is of a character to deprive the one to whom it is directed of a moral choice as to his course of action.[273]

In this form a DoD/N was recognized by Nuremberg courts, and even, on occasion, granted.[274]

In a trial before the courts of Norway, three members of the German occupation authorities accused of torturing members of the Norwegian resistance claimed, *inter alia*, that they would have been 'in serious danger from their superiors' had they refused. The Lagmannsrett (lower court) rejected the claim on the facts, adding that it,

…could not believe that a state, even Nazi Germany, could force its subjects, if they were unwilling, to perform such brutal and atrocious acts as those of which the defendants were guilty.[275]

Some defendants in the post-World-War II trials did come close to a justificatory, '*right* moral choice' plea, rather than pleading they were deprived of any,

---

[273] *US v Krauch et al* (Case no 6, the Farben case) TWC Vol VIII 1081 (1950), 1179. See similarly eg *Major War Criminals Judgment, supra* n 266, 77: 'The true test, which is found in varying degrees in the criminal law of most nations is not the existence of the order, but whether moral choice was in fact possible.' For later use of this term see eg Draft Code of Crimes Against the Peace and Security of Mankind, UN Doc A/CN.4/25 (1950), Art 9(d); *R v Finta* (1994) 1 SCR 701, eg 707, 730, 838; both prosecution and defence in *Erdemovic* Appeal, *passim*; *Prosecutor v Tihomir Blaskic*, Case No IT-95–14-T, Trial Chamber, Judgment of 3 March 2000, para 769.

[274] In *US v Friedrich Flick et al* (Case no 5, the Flick case), TWC Vol VI 1187 (1952), four of the six defendants were acquitted of using slave-labour (POWs and concentration camp inmates), as they had acted under the threat of a 'clear and present danger' (*ibid*, 1201). The two superiors, Flick and Weiss, were convicted. However, in the similar case of *US v Alfried Krupp et al* (Case no 9, the Krupp case), TWC Vol IX 1327 (1950), the Tribunal found all defendants guilty of employing slave labour because their will was not overpowered by the Third Reich 'but instead coincided with the will of those from whom the alleged compulsion emanated' (*ibid* at 1439). Moreover, the 'Krupp firm had manifested not only its willingness but its ardent desire to employ forced labor' (*ibid,* 1440). The issue of superior orders *per se* does not concern us here. As Judge Cassese explains '… in the case-law, duress is commonly raised in conjunction with superior orders. However there is no necessary connection between the two. Superior orders may be issued without being accompanied by *any* threats to life or limb. In these circumstances, if the superior order is manifestly illegal under international law, the subordinate is under a duty to refuse to obey the order. If, following such a refusal, the order is reiterated under a threat to life or limb, then the defence of duress may be raised, and superior orders lose any legal relevance. Equally, duress may be raised entirely independently of superior orders, for example, where the threat issues from a fellow serviceman. Thus, where duress is raised in conjunction with manifestly unlawful superior orders, the accused may only have a defence if he first refused to obey the unlawful order and then only carried it out after a threat to life or limb' (*Erdemovic* Appeal —Cassese's dissent, para 15).

[275] *Trial of Kriminalsekretaer Richard Wilhelm Hermann Bruns And Two Others*, (Case no 12) Eidsivating Lagmannsrett and the Supreme Court of Norway (1946), *Law-Reports of Trials of War Criminals, The United Nations War Crimes Commission*, Volume III (London: HMSO, 1948) 15–22, 18.

but used highly strenuous reasoning: Dr Karl Gebhardt, a doctor high in the Nazi medical hierarchy accused of torturous and murderous experiments on prisoners of war and civilians, claimed, *inter alia*, that it was a state's right to experiment on persons in order to combat diseases and alleviate human suffering, which would justify experiments on condemned prisoners. The plea was, unsurprisingly, rejected.[276] Another doctor, Adolf Pokorny, had proposed to Himmler that injections of caladium seginum be tested on 'criminals' as a means of sterilization in lieu of castration. He claimed that he had acted out of a 'lesser evil', damage-minimization motive. This plea was also rejected;[277] the Tribunal held fast to an absolutist position, discussed and defended in Part I,[278] namely that *any* experiments on humans may only be carried out with their informed consent—a position the Tribunal actually went on to codify.[279]

A similarly questionable plea was made in *Aleksovski* in the Appeals Chamber of the ICTY. Aleksovski, convicted *inter alia* of mistreatment of detainees claimed in appealing, *inter alia* that the defence of 'extreme necessity' was available to him. In the Court's words:

> ...the Appellant attempted to establish that by the time the Appellant became warden of Kaonik, he was faced with the *fait accompli* of interned civilians and a raging armed conflict in the region. The Appellant attempted to protect the civilians from the greater harm outside the Kaonik facility by detaining them, proof of which was that none of the interned persons were killed or wounded. On the basis of these facts, the Appellant submits that the defence of extreme necessity should have been applied.[280]

The Court considered these grounds 'entirely misplaced',[281] as the Appellant has been neither accused nor convicted of unlawful detention, only of ill-treating detainees.[282] The Court added:

---

[276] *US v Brandt et al* (Case no 1, the Medical case) TWC Vols. I-II The Tribunal veered somewhat towards the technical, stating that: 'Whatever may be the right of a state with reference to its own citizens it is certain that such legislation may not be extended so as to permit the practice upon nationals of other countries who, held in the most abject servitude, are subjected to experiments without their consent and under the most brutal and senseless conditions' (*ibid*, Vol II, 227).

[277] *Ibid*, 292–4. Due to lack of sufficient proof, the Tribunal acquitted Pokorny, 'not because of the defense tendered, but in spite of it' (*ibid*, 294).

[278] See Part I, Ch 4, Section C(3)(c).

[279] In what became known as the Nuremberg Code. See *ibid*. On these issues see also eg K Ambos, 'Other Grounds for Excluding Criminal Responsibility' in A Cassese, P Gaeta and JRWD Jones (eds), *The Rome Statute of the International Criminal Court: A Commentary*, Vol 1 (Oxford: OUP, 2002) 1003–1048, 1008, where additional cases are discussed; M Lippman, 'The Nazi Doctors Trial and the International Prohibition on Medical Involvement in Torture' 15 *Loyola of Los Angeles Int'l & Comp L J* 395 (1993).

[280] *Prosecutor v Aleksovski*, Case No IT-95–14/1-A, Appeals Court, Judgment of 24 March 2000, para 47.

[281] *Ibid*, para 52.

[282] *Ibid*, para 53.

The Appellant does not and cannot argue, in the present case, that he was faced with only two options, namely, mistreating the detainees or freeing them.[283]

These are rare and feeble exceptions, and have seldom been mentioned thereafter in the DoD/N context.[284] The overwhelming majority of cases considered were of the 'He had to kill or he had to be killed'[285] variety and where upheld, this was done as 'a concession to the instinct of human survival'[286] rather than in approval of a justified act.

On the level of principle, the enormity of the crimes with which defendants in international criminal courts are charged should also be borne in mind. Geert-Jan GJ Knoops states that some crimes, including 'torture...cannot be justified; only the possible exoneration of an excuse can be invoked', and while domestic legal systems have treated duress both (or either) as justification and as excuse, he concludes that 'defenses to war crimes can only have an excusable result, with the exception of self-defense'.[287]

Of relevance here is Jessberger's argument that a 'hierarchy' of applicable law exists, whereby international criminal law must be interpreted in a manner consistent with human rights law.[288] This in turn calls for a 'restrictive interpretation of the grounds for excluding criminal responsibility'[289] so that torturers would not be able to successfully plead the DoN or similar defences.

Alluding to the requirement of acting 'reasonably' for the defences of 'self-defence' and the DoD/N in the ICC Statute and in customary international law to apply, Jessberger concludes:

I would submit that a human rights-oriented interpretation of 'reasonableness' leads to the conclusion that the use of 'preventive torture' to defend against an imminent threat or to avoid a threat of imminent death is always *unreasonable*.[290]

I believe that Jessberger's point should be slightly modified, to take into account that a person may act unreasonably and still claim a defence—including, I submit,

---

[283] *Ibid*, para 54. The Court therefore felt it 'unnecessary' to consider 'whether necessity constitutes a defence under international law' and 'whether it is the same as the defence of duress …' at para 55.

[284] Thus, the 'Medical case' was not mentioned by any of the judges at any stages in the *Erdemovic* case.

[285] *Prosecutor v Erdemovic*, Case No IT-96-T, Trial Chamber II, Sentencing Judgement of 5 March 1998, para 17.

[286] Bassiouni, *supra* n 270, 484. Mathew Lippman, similarly explains 'This rationale recognized that individuals confronting calamities will invariably act in their own self-interest and cannot be deterred by the threat of sanction' (*idem*, 'Conundrums of Armed Conflict: Criminal Defenses to Violations of the Humanitarian Law of War' 15 *Dickinson J Int'l L* 1 (1996) 110).

[287] GJ Knoops, *Defenses in Contemporary International Law* (Ardsley, NY: Transnational Publishers, 2001) 29–30.

[288] This is explicitly provided in the ICC Statute, Art 21(3). Jessberger argues, convincingly to my mind, that this principle applies in customary international law as well. See, *supra* n 238, 1070–3. See similarly A Pellet, 'Applicable Law' in Cassese, Gaeta and Jones (eds), *supra* n 279, Vol II, 1051–1084, 1077–1082. Pellet shares Jessberger's view of such interpretative 'hierarchy' but is less happy about it.

[289] Jessberger, *ibid*.

[290] *Ibid*, 1072.

in accordance with human rights law. Such a defence, however, can clearly be available only in 'excuse' form. [291]

(b) *The DoD/N—an uncapped 'choice of evils' defence?*

According to Bantekas and Nash:

One of the essential elements in a successful plea of duress is that of proportionality (doing that which is the lesser of two evils).[292]

To my mind, the requirement of proportionality, or choice of the 'lesser evil', for the DoD/N rests uneasily with that of lack of moral choice (see above).[293] However, as the (former) requirement has been widely supported by both writers[294] and judges;[295] I will set this point aside and focus on whether or not the 'lesser evil' requirement is perceived as uncapped.

This topic would best be addressed through the much-debated question of whether the DoD/N may be a complete defence to unlawful killing, which was argued at great length in the ICTY Appeals Chamber in the case of *Erdemovic*.

---

[291] As implied in provisions for fair trial, notably Art 14 of the ICCPR. The Human Rights Committee's General Comment on this Article mentions, *inter alia*, the right of '[t]he accused or his lawyer' to 'act diligently and fearlessly in pursuing all available defences'. See CCPR General comment 13: the right to a fair and public hearing by an independent court established by law (Art 14), 13 April 1984, para 11. On the other hand, neither the ICCPR nor the UN Convention against Torture allows for any *justification* for torture in any circumstances. The latter's position is explicitly stated in Art 2(2). The HRC, while stating a rather confused position for our purposes, is probably making the same point regarding the ICCPR: 'The Committee...observes that no justification or extenuating circumstances may be invoked to excuse a violation of article 7 for any reasons...' (General Comment on Article 7, CCPR General comment 20 (1992), para 3).

[292] Bantekas and Nash, *supra* n 268, 136.

[293] In the *Einsatzgruppen* case, the US Tribunal stated: '... it would not be an adequate excuse...if a subordinate...killed a person...because by not obeying it he himself would risk a few days of confinement' (*US v Otto Ohlendorf et al* (Case no 10, *Einsatzgruppen* case), TWC Vol IV, 470 (1949), 471. This, however, is hardly a situation where a defendant can claim to have lost his 'moral choice' so the plea would have fallen on that latter grounds rather than on proportionality. The *Einsatzgruppen* Tribunal itself later set a test of danger to 'life or...serious harm' which must be 'imminent, real and inevitable' (668, 480, respectively) for a plea of duress to be upheld.

[294] See eg, Cassese, *International Criminal Law*, *supra* n 55, 242; Lippman, 'Conundrums of Armed Conflict' *supra* n 286, 66; SR Ratner and JS Abrams, *Accountability for Human Rights Atrocities in International Law: Beyond the Nuremberg Legacy* (Oxford: Clarendon, 1997) 124; Scaliotti, *supra* n 270, 145–7.

[295] See eg *Trial of Gustav Alfred Jepsen et al*, *Law Reports of the Trials of War Criminals*, Vol XV, British Military Court, Luneburg (1946) at 72; *Einsatzgruppen* case), *supra* n 293; *Major War Criminals Judgment*, *supra* n 266, 77; *Erdemovic* Appeal, where all judges referred to the requirement of proportionality. Note eg Joint Separate Opinion of Judge McDonald and Judge Vohrah, who accept proportionality as a component of duress, para 42, but go on to devote most of their opinion to rejecting its applicability to the murder of innocents; see also Separate and Dissenting Opinion of Judge Li, para 5; Separate and Dissenting Opinion of Judge Stephen, paras 19, 22, 52, 67 Cassese's Dissent, paras 17, 41–3, 50. Cassese argues, para 43, that the notion of proportionality '... was manifestly the underlying idea in all the cases where duress was upheld by Italian and German courts after the Second World War'.

Few statements epitomize the plea of duress more acutely than that of Drazen Erdemovic, a self-confessed mass murderer:

Your honour—I had to do this. If I had refused, I would have been killed together with the victims. When I refused, they told me: 'If you are sorry for them, stand up, line up with them and we will kill you too.' I am not sorry for myself but for my family, my wife and son who then had nine months, and I could not refuse because then they would have killed me.[296]

The ICTY Appeals chamber's five judges, while disagreeing on how the question posed here should be answered, were unanimous that post World War II cases had not produced a clear answer, and there is little point in reproducing their lengthy discussions on this issue.[297]

There was a principled argument between the majority and the dissenting judges as to how they should proceed in the absence of a clear rule. The majority went on to find one further afield, applying, in effect, the common law view of duress—or rather of its limits, as reflecting 'general principles of law recognised by civilised nations',[298] and concluding that:

...duress cannot afford a complete defence to a soldier charged with crimes against humanity or war crimes in international law involving the taking of innocent lives.[299]

In the majority's view, considerations of duress in such cases would best be left the sentencing stage, as mitigating factors.[300]

It may be relevant to note that the majority invoked moral as well as legal arguments. Considering Courts' *dicta*, in some post-World War II cases, that where the killing of innocent persons would have proceeded regardless of whether the 'duressee' participated in it or not, the DoD/N will apply,[301] the majority judges responded with a section entitled 'Rejection of utilitarianism and proportionality where human life must be weighed' stating, *inter alia*:

...the [*Masetti* Court's] assertion that the accused is not morally blameworthy where the victim would have died in any case depends entirely again upon a view of morality based on utilitarian logic. This does not, in our opinion, address the true rationale for our rejection of duress as a defence to the killing of innocent human beings.[302]

---

[296] Transcript, *Prosecutor v Drazen Erdemovic*, Case No IT-96–22-T, Trial Court I, 31 May 1996, 9.

[297] *Erdemovic* Appeal—McDonald and Vohrah, para 55; Cassese's dissent (which includes an extensive discussion of that case-law), para 28; Separate and Dissenting Opinion of Judge Li, para 2; Separate and Dissenting Opinion of Judge Stephen, para 24.

[298] See *ibid*, McDonald and Vohrah, paras 56–7 for their justification of this approach.

[299] *Ibid*, para 88.

[300] *Ibid*, paras 82–90.

[301] See eg *Masetti* case, decision of 17 Nov 1947, in *Massimario della Seconda Sezione della Cassazione*, 1947, No 2569, as cited *Ibid*, fn 62. The Italian Court stated: '... the possible sacrifice [of their lives] by Masetti and his men [those who comprised the execution squad] would have been in any case to no avail and without any effect in that it would have had no impact whatsoever on the plight of the persons to be shot, who would have been executed anyway even without him [the accused]' (quoted *ibid*, para 79).

[302] *Ibid*, para 80.

The dissenting judges argued essentially that where there is no clear exception (in this case, regarding killing innocent persons) to a rule (in this case the applicability of the DoD/N to international crimes), the rule must apply.[303] These judges therefore allow in theory for the defence of duress to apply to the killing of innocent persons, and in effect 'to *all* categories of crime, whether or not they involve killing'[304] (obviously including torture). However, they severely limited the scope of such applicability. Judge Cassese summed up his view as follows:

Perhaps—although that will be a matter for a Trial Chamber or a Judge to decide—it will *never* be satisfied where the accused is saving his own life *at the expense of* his victim, since there are enormous, perhaps insurmountable, philosophical, moral and legal difficulties in putting one life in the balance against that of others in this way: how can a judge satisfy himself that the death of one person is a lesser evil that the death of another? Conversely, however, where it is *not* a case of a direct choice between the life of the person acting under duress and the life of the victim—in situations, in other words, where there is a high probability that the person under duress will not be able to save the lives of the victims whatever he does—then duress may succeed as a defence. Again, this will be a matter for the judge or court hearing the case to decide in the light of the evidence available in this regard.[305]

This view leaves the defence of duress uncapped—but only just. A torturer in a TBS does not fit easily into it. I will return to Cassese's portrayal of the DoD/N in the next section because, while he and Judge Stephen lost the battle in *Erdemovic*, they would later, as it were, go on to win the war—for the nature of the defence in the ICC Statute, to which we now turn.

(c) *The DoD/N in the ICC Statute*

There is no explicit provision for a defence of necessity in the ICC Statute. Most defences were grouped together in Article 31 of the Statute under the title 'Grounds for excluding criminal responsibility' and in effect comprise, as William Schabas lists them, 'insanity, intoxication, self-defence, duress and necessity'.[306] However, the latter two are provided for in a single paragraph, as follows:

Art. 31(1). In addition to other grounds for excluding criminal responsibility provided for in this Statute, a person shall not be criminally responsible if, at the time of that person's conduct:
[...]

---

[303] See eg *Erdemovic* Appeal—Cassese's dissent, para 11(i). Cassese and Stephen rejected the majority's resort to domestic jurisprudence, a subject we need not go into here.

[304] *Ibid*, para 41.

[305] *Ibid*, para 42.

[306] WA Schabas, *An Introduction to the International Criminal Court* (2nd edn, Cambridge: CUP, 2004) 110. Bantekas and Nash list, among the defences, 'duress/necessity' *supra* n 268, 130. YS Kim refers to it only as 'duress' *idem*, *The International Criminal Court (A Commentary of the Rome Statute)* (Leeds: Wisdom House, 2003) 323–4.

(d) The conduct which is alleged to constitute a crime within the jurisdiction of the Court has been caused by duress resulting from a threat of imminent death or of continuing or imminent serious bodily harm against that person or another person, and the person acts necessarily and reasonably to avoid this threat, provided that the person does not intend to cause a greater harm than the one sought to be avoided. Such a threat may either be:

    (i) Made by other persons; or

    (ii) Constituted by other circumstances beyond that person's control.

This sets the ICC Statute apart from the statutes of previous international tribunals, none of which had provisions for the DoD/N.

A comprehensive review of the drafting history of the provision for the DoD/N is beyond the scope of this study,[307] which will concentrate instead on the relevant aspects of the 'end product'. Suffice to say generally, following Albin Eser, that like other 'grounds for excluding criminal responsibility', this provision's development 'leads from almost zero to considerable heights, finally ending on a middle level'.[308] The International Law Commission (ILC) draft of 1994[309] does not mention defences at all. Defences appear in detail in an alternative draft compiled by independent experts in 1995 (Siracusa draft),[310] and this approach was subsequently adopted by the *Ad Hoc* Committee,[311] and later by the Preparatory

---

[307] For discussions the drafting history, mostly written by key drafters, see eg Ambos, *supra* n 279, 1003–1048, especially 1015–1018, 1027–1029, 1035–1047; Bantekas and Nash, *supra* n 268, 35–7; A Eser, 'Article 31: Grounds for Excluding Criminal Responsibility' in O Triffterer (ed), *Commentary on the Rome Statute of the International Criminal Court, Observers' Notes, Article by Article* (Baden-Baden: Nomos, 1999) 537–554; P Saland, 'International Criminal Law Principles' in RS Lee (ed), *The International Criminal Court. The Making of the Rome Statute. Issues, Negotiations, Results* (The Hague: Kluwer Law International, 1999) 189–216, especially 191–4, 206–210; Scaliotti, *supra* n 270, especially 150–8.

[308] Eser, *ibid*, 539.

[309] Report of the International Law Commission on the Work of its Forty-Sixth Session Draft Statute for an international Criminal Court, 2 May–22 July, 1994 (GA 49th Sess, Su No 10, UN Doc A/49/10, 1994). I am again following Eser's lead and overlooking earlier drafts. In the parallel process of codifying 'crimes against the peace and security of mankind', a defence of necessity did appear in an early draft, see Draft Convention on the Establishment of an International Penal Tribunal for the Suppression and Punishment of the Crime of *Apartheid* and Other International Crimes, within Study of Ways and Means of Ensuring the Implementation of International Instruments Such as the International Convention on the Suppression and Punishment of the Crime of *Apartheid*, Including the Establishment of the International Jurisdiction Envisaged by the Convention (UN Doc E/CN.4/1326, 1981), 21–45, Art 25(3). In contrast, the Draft Code of Crimes Against the Peace and Security of Mankind, in *ILC Report on the Work of its Forty-Eighth Session* (GA 51st Sess, Su No 10, UN Doc A/51/10 (1996)), included only a general provision (Art 14) for the court to 'determine the admissibility of defences in accordance with the general principles of law, in the light of the character of each crime.'

[310] AIDP, ISISC and MPI, Draft Statute for an International Criminal Court: Alternative to the ILC Draft (Siracusa Draft), Siracusa/Freiburg, July 1995. Article 33(l) provides for 'Necessity/Coercion or Duress'. See also a revised version of that text (but not of the particular provision) in the 'Updated Ciracusa Draft' 15 March 1996, <http://www.iuscrim.mpg.de/forsch/straf/referate/sach/hispint/genpart3.doc>, accessed 27 October 2003, Art 33(l).

[311] See Report of the *Ad Hoc* Committee on the Establishment of an International Criminal Court (GA, 50th Sess, Su No 22, UN Doc A/50/22, 1995), Annex II, para B(5)(b).

Committee. The latter, however, consistently proposed two *separate* provisions for 'necessity' and 'duress/coercion',[312] a separation that was maintained until the actual diplomatic conference in Rome,[313] and the Preparatory Committee's final draft.[314] The final text of Article 31(1)(d) 'was formulated by Canada after informal consultations among delegations during the last stages of the Rome Conference'.[315]

By and large Article 31(1)(d) continues, and to an extent exacerbates, the muddling of the main issues which concern us. This stems from the fact that, in the words of Ambos, this paragraph 'conflates duress and necessity'.[316] Eser puts it somewhat less benevolently:

Among the many compromises which had to be made in order to get this Statute accepted, paragraph 1(d) of this article is one of the least convincing provisions, as in an ill-guided and lastly failed attempt, it tried to combine two different concepts: (justifying) necessity and (merely excusing) duress.[317]

While the justification/excuse distinction is left unaddressed,[318] the nature of the DoD/N in previous international legal fora, as outlined above, the 'conflating' of the two defences, and the fact that both are set out 'within the term "duress" without explicitly mentioning necessity'[319] place the unified defence closer to excuse than to justification. In fact, Cassese, who justifies 'lump[ing]' the two defences, and praises paragraph 31(1)(d) ('to a very large extent this provision

---

[312] See Report of the Preparatory Committee on the Establishment of an International Criminal Court, *Volume 2 (Compilation of Proposals)* (GA, 51st Sess, Su No 22, A/51/22, 1996), 100–101, Art O (necessity), Art P (duress/coercion). Henceforth 'PrepCom' will be used as a shorthand, unless within a title.

[313] See Decisions Taken by the Preparatory Committee at its Session held from 1 to 12 December 1997 (A/AC.249/1997/L.9.Rev1, 1997), Annex II: Report of the Working Group on General Principles of Criminal law, Arts L(d) (duress) and L(e) (necessity)—although those terms are not used as headers here or subsequently; Report of the Intersessional Meeting from 19 to 30 January 1998 in Zutphen, the Netherlands (A/AC.249/1998/L.13, 1998), Arts 25[L](d) (duress) and 25[L](e) (necessity).

[314] Report of the Preparatory Committee on the Establishment of an International Criminal Court, *Draft Statute & Draft Final* Act, (A/Conf.183/2/Add.1, 14 April 1998), Arts 31(1)(d) (duress) and 31(1)(e) (necessity).

[315] Saland, *supra* n 307, 208. Saland chaired the Working Group on the General Principles of Criminal Law both for the PrepCom and on the conference itself.

[316] Ambos, *supra* n 279, 1036. According to Bassiouni, the provision is also 'a synthesis of the various legal approaches on coercion', *supra* n 270, 491.

[317] Eser, *supra* n 307, 550. Bantekas and Nash similarly speak of the 'poor drafting of Art 31(1)(d)', *supra* n 268, 135. See also M Scaliotti 'Defences Before the International Criminal Court: Substantive Grounds for Excluding Criminal Responsibility—Part 2' 2 *Int'l Crim L Rev* 1 (2002) 46.

[318] The two terms appear in Art 33 of the 'Siracusa Draft' (*supra* n 310) at the title of the section on 'Defences'; in the 1995 *Ad Hoc* Committee report (see *supra* n 311), Annex II, para B(5) (b); and in some of the proposals regarding Art O (necessity) in the 1996 Prepcom report (*supra* n 312) whereas in Art P (duress/coercion) only the term 'excuse' appears in one of the proposals. Thereafter, however, both these terms disappear from the relevant provisions in all drafts.

[319] Scaliotti, *supra* n 270, 156.

codifies customary international law'),[320] considers the provision, and the whole issue, under 'Other excuses'.[321] Similarly, Eser, explaining the provision, states that:

…the threat must result in 'duress'; this means that the person concerned *feels unable* to withstand the threat and, thus, is *driven* to the relevant criminal conduct.[322] (Emphases added.)

Nevertheless, the fact that the provision does not explicitly characterize the DoD/N as excusatory leaves open, at least in theory, the possibility that the Court will consider that defence as such, in a particular case. The Court has considerable power, under Article 31(2), to 'determine the applicability of the grounds for excluding criminal responsibility provided for in this Statute to the case before it', a power no doubt enhanced, in the case in point, by the vagueness and uncertainties which the wording of the provision for the DoD/N left behind.[323] As Bantekas and Nash remark:

Whether this intentional omission [of the justification/excuse distinction] has any legal significance remains to be seen, judged on the appropriate sources of the court's jurisdiction.[324]

On the other hand, the Court must also, under its Statute, apply and interpret the law in a manner 'consistent with internationally recognized human rights', the laws of which, as noted, allow for no justification for certain crimes, including torture.[325]

A clearer picture emerges regarding the 'uncapped' nature of the DoD/N as a 'choice of evils' defence. While the actual term ('lesser of evils') appears only in the 'Siracusa Draft'[326] and as an 'item' for discussion in the *Ad Hoc* Committee report (1995),[327] all subsequent drafts, as well as the provision in the Rome Statute itself, include an element of no 'greater harm than the one sought to be avoided', although in the latter, surprisingly, this element becomes totally subjective ('the person does not intend'), which has also attracted some criticism.[328]

Many of the drafting proposals suggested excluding murder, or even 'merely' causing death, from the remit of the DoD/N.[329] The omission of any such

---

[320] Cassese, *International Criminal Law, supra* n 55, 251.

[321] *Ibid*, title of Ch 13 ('Other Excuses: superior order, necessity, duress and mistake').

[322] Eser, *supra* n 307, 551.

[323] According to Saland, the inclusion of this provision was important for 'those who were particularly unhappy with the definition of a certain ground', *supra* n 307, 208. See also Ambos, *supra* n 279, 1028; Eser, *supra* n 307, 552–3, Scaliotti, *supra* n 270, 157.

[324] Bantekas and Nash, *supra* n 268, 129.

[325] See *supra*, Ch 19, Section B(1). The provision quoted is from Art 21(3).

[326] *Supra* n 310, Art 33, under 'Open questions and elements to be regulated in a General Part'.

[327] See *Supra* n 311, Annex II, para B(5)(b).

[328] See eg Scaliotti, *supra* n 270, 156.

[329] See eg 'Siracusa Draft', *supra* n 310, Art 33(l)(1) – for necessity but not for duress, *cf* Art 33(l)(2); 1996 PrepCom report, *supra* n 312, in Arts O (necessity), Proposal 1 para 3, and P(1)(c)

exclusion from the Statute's provision was therefore significant and its result, in the word of Scaliotti, is that:

...the defence was available also to a charge of murder, as the intention not to cause death as requirement for duress/necessity had been deleted.[330]

Scaliotti and others specifically point out that the Statute thus 'put aside the ICTY jurisprudence'.[331]

If indeed, as Ambos similarly declares, 'Cassese's answer [in *Erdemovic* re killing innocents] has been confirmed and complemented by Article 31(1)(d) of the Rome Statute',[332] and if, as Cassese himself declares, 'the right to life is the most fundamental human right',[333] could we safely assume that the Court may *a fortiori* exclude from criminal liability a violation of what is implicitly, according to this view, a 'less' fundamental right, that of freedom from torture, under extreme circumstances such as a TBS?

The answer can only be given by the Court itself. It must be emphasized again, however, that if a torturer would attempt to *justify* her action, she is quite likely to encounter strong opposition, maybe especially from judges like Cassese who, as already noted, considers the DoD/N strictly as an excuse. In fact, it may be the very categorization of the defence as excuse that allows Cassese and others to justify its 'uncapped' nature, or even its very applicability to international crimes. As Ambos explains, while arguing against punishing 'duressees' strictly as a means of expressing the law's disapproval of an act:

The law's disapproval may be sufficiently expressed by the verdict of wrongfulness of an act committed under duress, exempting the actor—on a personal level—from culpability. This also answers the question about the theoretical classification of duress in general and subparagraph (d) in particular: it is an excuse, since the commission of the atrocious crimes 'within the jurisdiction of the Court' can never be justified on the basis of a balancing of interests but can only be excused on the basis of compassion for an understanding of the actor's human weakness.[334]

(duress/coercion); 1997 PrepCom report, *supra* n 313, in Arts L(d) (duress) and L(e) (necessity); report of the Zutphen intersessional meeting, *supra* n 313, in Arts 25[L](d) (duress) and in Art 25[L](e) (necessity); the PrepCom's Draft Statute of April 1998, *supra* n 314, in Arts 31(1) (d) (duress) and 31(1)(e) (necessity). Well into the diplomatic conference, the Working Paper on Article 31, A/CONF.183/C.1/WGGP/L.6, 22 June 1998, proposed to exclude murder or the intention to cause death from the remit of the DoD/N.

[330] Scaliotti, *supra* n 270, 153–4. See similarly Cassese's (approving) words: '... this provision... *does not exclude in principle* the plea of duress in the event of a person under duress killing another person' (*idem, International Criminal Law, supra* n 55, 251).

[331] Scaliotti, *supra* n 317 (Part II) 46. See similarly Schabas, *supra* n 306, 113, Bantekas and Nash, *supra* n 268, 391: 'The characterisation of duress [in the ICC Statute] as a full defence that is capable of excluding liability has clearly been influenced by the dissenting opinion of Cassese J in the *Erdemovic* case before the ICTY.'

[332] Ambos, *supra* n 279, 1044.

[333] Cassese, *International Criminal Law, supra* n 55, 250.

[334] Ambos, *supra* n 279, 1045–6.

As already discussed above, this study, and the vast majority of the fast-expanding literature, are concerned with the justifiability of torture in a TBS, rather than the possibility that persons who torture unjustifiably for certain (personal) reasons could nevertheless be forgiven. No less importantly, states resorting to such torture would use it in order to obtain what is perceived as crucial information from hardened terrorists, a task they are unlikely to entrust to weaklings who deserve compassion.

3. Conclusion—a very distant possibility, if at all

As international criminal law in general, and the ICC Statute in particular, now stand, pending the development of (especially the latter's) jurisprudence, the defence of necessity seems to be either merged with, or submerged under, the defence of duress. While this union seems, in pure theory, to afford protection for a wide—indeed possibly unlimited—range of crimes, and thus may be characterized as 'uncapped', the protection it offers perpetrators of acts such as murder, and possibly torture, is itself very limited. Moreover, the availability of the defence is closely—inextricably, it may be argued—linked to the *unavailability* of justifications for such acts.

No person accused of torture has as yet stood in front of an international criminal tribunal and pleaded a justificatory defence of necessity (or duress), arguing that the tortured person was a terrorist suspect and the situation a TBS. There are no judgements, nor are there provisions in the ICC Statute explicitly ruling out the applicability of this type of DoN in such circumstances. However, in view of the above, international criminal law appears, at present, to offer an extremely narrow margin indeed, if at all, for an international court to uphold such a defence, and only in this excusatory form.

20

Part IV—Conclusions

A. Recapitulation

In this Part, I have examined some questions involving the legality of interrogation methods and of means of ensuring exemption from criminal responsibility for officials applying them, as used under the three 'working' models described in Part III.

Both states concerned, Israel and the USA, have denied that the methods they have used amounted to torture under international law, or even to 'cruel, inhuman or degrading treatment' (ill-treatment). Officials for both states, as well as academic and other writers, have also suggested that methods of 'coercion' or 'moderate physical pressure' may be used which are below the 'threshold' of ill-treatment, while others argued that international law does not prohibit ill-treatment in the same absolute way that it does torture, and it therefore may be lawful to 'ill-treat' in extreme situations, such as TBSs, or, alternately, to keep these acts unlawful while exempting perpetrators from criminal liability by applying the defence of necessity (DoN).

An examination of the relevant international principles, rules and jurisprudence refuted these claims. Not only torture, but all 'coercive interrogation' are unlawful at all times, unless methods used are so mild—for instance less than a threat or an insult—as to be trivial (and in all likelihood ineffective); international law contains no 'opt out' clauses for extraordinary circumstances, such as a TBS. Under international law, states may never torture or otherwise ill-treat detainees, nor may they ever exempt perpetrators of such acts from prosecution or punishment by justifying an individual act in case of a TBS, and accepting the perpetrator's plea of the DoN.

The methods at the centre of the claims for legality, such as incommunicado detention, sleep deprivation and painful positions, while not inherently torturous, are not only 'inherently' unlawful, but also, when combined and used over time (as they almost invariably are) may amount to torture. Indeed, international monitoring bodies and independent experts have found that both states' interrogation methods have constituted torture. This is not surprising in view of the justification for their use—the need to obtain urgently-needed, life-saving information. This justification, and the utilitarian moral reasoning behind it, discussed in Part I, can hardly allow for interrogations to stop abruptly somewhere between 'suffering' and 'severe suffering' when a terrorist suspect still refuses to talk, and the suffering of hundreds, thousands or more are perceived to hang in the balance.

The DoN is the only legal basis for the only fully-legalized torture models applied to date; it is a (so far latent) component of the legal basis suggested for the HVD model; it is often recommended by academic and other supporters of torture in TBSs; and its 'lesser evil' rationale fully reflects the torture-justifying moral view discussed in Part I. For those reasons, I undertook an in-depth analysis of the DoN as a putative legal basis for torture in a TBS. This was done in Chapter 19, regarding both domestic and international criminal law.

It was noted that there is a dearth, indeed almost total absence, of case-law (outside Israel, of course) specifically concerning the applicability of the DoN to torture in a TBS, in both domestic and international criminal law, and the discussion was often in the abstract, or by analogy. I submitted that in order to qualify as a defence for torture in a TBS, the DoN must be a justificatory (as opposed to excusatory), uncapped 'lesser evil' defence. In other words, the act must be deemed right and proper, as opposed to the actor being forgiven for acting wrongly, particularly to allow for acts by officials; and the defence must be perceived as a choice of lesser harm, applicable to all crimes, without exception, to include torture. I have found that the DoN in the Anglo-American system could, with some effort, be interpreted as having those qualities, therefore its availability for individual torturers in a TBS in domestic legal systems cannot be ruled out. On the other hand, I found in the German system a DoN that, while allowing 'lesser evil' calculations, 'caps' them with absolute prohibitions on acts undermining basic values, torture being one such act.

In international criminal law, the DoN has, to a large extent, blended into the defence of duress which, while of late (including in the ICC Statute) having possibly acquired an 'uncapped' nature (namely, applicability to all crimes), it assumes, by and large, an excusatory nature. Individual perpetrators of all war crimes and crimes against humanity may in certain, very limited circumstances (largely of the 'kill or die' variety), be forgiven, but in all probability none would ever be justified. This leaves an extremely narrow margin indeed, if at all, for an international court to uphold even this—excusatory—type of defence for a torturer in a TBS.

In sum, a state facing terrorism applying a torture-legalizing DoN model may 'get away with it' within its own domestic system, if the nature of the defence is, or is rendered, an uncapped justificatory 'lesser evil' one. However, states would run into a brick wall when it comes to their international legal obligations, and the chances that their torturing agents would escape conviction and punishment by an international criminal court (if they face one) are very slim indeed, if they exist at all. The chances of an Israel-style *routine* escape from prosecution and punishment for torturers in international courts are nonexistent.

B. The DoN Model in Light of Current Reality

I will submit that beyond all of the above, the DoN model, and all other 'ex post' models, suffer from two fundamental and, I believe, fatal conceptual flaws, which I would call the requirement of amateurism and the requirement of rarity.

First,[335] the models both consider the stakes in a TBS to be high enough to justify sacrificing a universally recognized fundamental value, in allowing the torture of human beings; *and* dictate, by denying prior authorization, that this torture only be carried out by an untrained, inexperienced, unequipped, improvising amateur.[336] This begs the question: if it is so crucially important to torture in such situations, why risk failure and not assign it to professionals? If, on the other hand, torture can be left to fallible amateurs, why not dispense with it altogether? There is no way around this contradiction[337] which does not involve compromising, indeed undermining, the rule of law—a state under the rule of law cannot train or equip its law-enforcement officials to perform acts which its laws prohibit absolutely. A state whose laws prohibit torture and, for instance, acts of genocide cannot train its law enforcement officials to torture any more that it can train (and equip) them to exterminate humans in gas chambers.

Secondly, the DoN and other 'ex post' models depend, crucially, on TBSs to be rare occurrences, otherwise torture would become in practice routine, authorized and institutionalized—for which the DoN can no longer form a legal basis.[338]

Torture-justifying writers consistently state, as a matter of fact, that, to use one of many formulations, that of M Gross, 'Circumstances justifying torture do come together in very rare instances'.[339] The notion of rarity is also vital in

---

[335] On this issue see the incisive comments of H Shue, 'Torture in Dreamland: Disposing of the Ticking Bomb' 37 *Case West Res J Int'l L* 231 (2006).

[336] See eg the HCJ ruling in the *Israel Torture* case, para 36. This point is discussed in Part II, Ch 9, Section D(2).

[337] It has been suggested to me that this could be circumvented by appointing as interrogators persons previously involved in training soldiers to withstand harsh interrogations. However, this would create, in effect, a variation of the 'hypocrisy model' discussed in Part III, Ch 11. For law enforcement officials to be trained to break the law, then ordered not to do it, then be exempted once they have, would turn that law into a farce. A rule-of-law approach to this issue was revealed in early 2006 during a court case in Denmark involving an officer charged with ill-treating detainees in Iraq. According to press reports, the Danish army did indeed train soldiers to withstand harsh treatment, unlawful under international humanitarian law, in case they were captured by an unscrupulous enemy. However, soldiers who had undergone such training *were not allowed to conduct interrogations*, for fear that 'in stressful situations they easily could use the inhuman tricks which they learn during the exercises'. See 'The Hommel Case: The Command of the Danish Military Failed Hommel', *Politiken*, 13 January 2006. I am indebted to the Danish section of Amnesty International for translating this article.

[338] See *supra*, Part III, Ch 14, Section B(1)(a).

[339] ML Gross, 'Regulating Torture in a Democracy: Death and Indignity in Israel' 36(3) *Polity* 367 (2004) 387. See similarly eg O Gross, 'The Prohibition on Torture ...' *supra* n 167, 234; *idem*, 'Are Torture warrants warranted? Pragmatic absolutism and official disobedience' 88 *Minn L Rev*

order to avoid the disastrous society-wide repercussions of routine state brutality that may undermine the utilitarian justification for torture, on which their view ultimately rests.[340]

I submit, however, that while it was safe for Brooke LJ, to predict that the medical operation which was at the heart of the conjoined twins case 'is, and is always likely to be, an exceptionally rare event',[341] the same is not true regarding the struggle against terrorism at the beginning of the twenty-first century. For such a rarity to be a constant fact, cooperation is needed from the terrorists to keep the frequency or scale of their operations down; this kind of cooperation has not, of late, been forthcoming.

As these conclusions were first written, during the evening of 16 May 2004, Israeli news media were reporting that security forces in Jerusalem had been placed on 'very high alert' because of intelligence information on an imminent terrorist attack. Roadblocks were erected at the city's entrances. Altogether, security forces 'had 43 warnings on plans to launch attacks within Israel' and its Defence Minister, Shaul Mofaz, told a Cabinet meeting on the same day that two suicide attacks had been thwarted 'within the last few days'.[342]

This was by no means a rare occasion. During 2001, 2002, 2003 and 2004, hardly a week passed by without similar incidents and announcements.[343] In most cases, alert-levels were later reduced,[344] often because the would-be perpetrators had been caught. In other cases—not seldom enough, unfortunately, to be considered rare either—a deadly terrorist attack was indeed launched. This was reflected in official data, which in effect claimed that at the height of the *Intifadah* hardly a week passed by without a TBS—or without torture.

Other democracies facing terrorism may not have experienced the same frequency of real, imminent threats.[345] It should be remembered, however,

---

1481 (2004) 1501; *idem* and FN Aoláin, *Law in Times of Crisis: Emergency Powers in Theory and Practice* (Cambridge: CUP, 2006) 125; Gur-Arye, 'Legitimating Official Brutality...' *supra* n 152, 6; Stanford Levinson, ' "Precommitment" and "Post-Commitment": The Ban on Torture in the Wake of September 11' 81 *Texas L Rev* 2013 (2003) 2048; Parry, *supra* n 41, 258; Parry and White, *supra* n 264, 766; LS Sheleff, *Ultimate Penalties: Capital Punishment, Life Imprisonment, Physical Torture* (Columbus, Ohio: State University Press, 1987) 305.

[340] This justification is discussed in Part I.

[341] *Re A (Children), supra* n 165, para 26.

[342] Y Lis, G Alon and A Reguler, ' "Very high" alert in Jerusalem due to intelligence warnings' *Haaretz* website <http://www.haaretz.co.il/hasite/spages/428114.html>, accessed 16 May 2004.

[343] See eg E Weiss, 'High alert in Jerusalem because of fears of a terrorist attack' <http://www.ynet.co.il/articles/0,7340,L-2277114,00.html>, posted, accessed 27 November 2002; ' "Hot intelligence warnings" of terrorist attacks' <http://images.maariv.co.il/cache/ART433023.htm>, posted, accessed 11 February 2003; R Singer and the agencies, 'IDF imposes total closure over the Territories because of intelligence warnings of terrorist attacks on Peshach Eve' <http://www.haaretz.co.il/hasite/spages/284590.html>, posted, accessed 16 April 2003.

[344] As was the case on 16 May 2004 (same website as *supra* n 342, two hours later).

[345] The situation in Iraq between the summer of 2003 and mid-2007, when these conclusions were being finalized, was far worse than in Israel and the USA (see immediately below), but I am not sure that Iraq may safely be described as a democracy during the period.

that the USA suffered far more casualties on 9/11 than Israel has, as a result of terrorist attacks, not only during the last *Intifadah* but throughout its history of some six decades. According to US Secretary of State for Defence at the time, Donald Rumsfeld, the main terrorist enemy the USA faces, *al-Qa'idah*, has a global reach, with 'cells in 50–60 countries'.[346] In November 2006 the head of the UK's MI5, Dame Eliza Manningham-Buller, stated that the agency had identified 30 'major terrorist plots' being planned by some 200 UK-based networks.[347] At any time, any of these may be plotting, or actually be at various stages of putting into action plans for heinous acts of 'mega-terrorism'[348] against US or UK targets—or others. In Iraq, where the US army was, between May 2003 and June 2004 the main occupying force, and thereafter the main component of the Multinational Forces, one of whose task is to protect Iraqi citizens' security, many thousands of innocent civilians have been killed in thousands of terrorist attacks since.[349] Thus, the numbers of terrorists, their global dispersion and the enormity of their real and planned attacks create, for those states too, a situation where *the rarity of TBSs cannot be taken for granted*. This is especially true when, inevitably, it is governments and their intelligence services who would define, at the crucial (and anxious) moment, the existence of a TBS, based on information that is, and likely to remain, confidential.

It is in this factual light that arguments for the restraining effects of a DoN (and other 'ex post') models—in this case as provided by Parry and White—should be viewed:

If interrogators know that they act at their peril, because the law provides no authority for torture under any circumstances, then they are likely to be deterred from acting except when the choice—however distasteful—seems obvious.

Even if interrogators know that the necessity defense is available, they will not be able to predict with certainty before they act whether the defense would be successful, and the resulting uncertainty would also foster deterrence.[350]

---

[346] I found this data on the website of the Embassy of the United States, Caracas, Venezuela, Public Affairs Office, 'Press Release, Campaign Against Terrorism: Secretary Rumsfeld, General Myers Briefing on Afghan Military Campaign' 9 October 2001 <http://embajadausa.org.ve/wwwh695. html>, accessed 23 January 2004. See similarly eg a CNN transcript of a Pentagon briefing, aired 20 May 2002 10:04 ET <http://www.cnn.com/TRANSCRIPTS/0205/20/se.01.html>, accessed 23 January 2004.

[347] R Norton-Taylor, 'MI5: 30 terror plots being planned in UK', *The Guardian* (10 November 2006).

[348] See Part II, Ch 10, Conclusions.

[349] As emphasised in the previous Parts, we are not concerned here with the legality, or morality, of this or that occupation, nor of armed operations such as shooting at soldiers. However, many attacks clearly aimed at civilians and thus falling within the 'hard core of settled meaning' (see Part I, Ch 1, Section B) of terrorism as used here, have undoubtedly occurred in Iraq.

[350] Parry and White, *supra* n 264, 763–4. See similarly Gur-Arye, 'Legitimating Official Brutality...' *supra* n 152, 25–6; O Gross, in both articles cited *supra* n 339, *passim*; Reichman, *supra* n 41, 68; O Gross and Aoláin, *supra* n 339, 147–8.

In reality though, however 'apprehensive' the first GSS interrogator may have been, believing he or she was facing the first TBS after the HCJ ruling, a few months and a dozen or so such cases later, interrogators would have learned the rules of the game. With time, GSS interrogators came to know that the Attorney General would always grant immunity from prosecution under the DoN, no matter what they did or what the circumstances were. Even if Israel, the USA or other states facing terrorism were to introduce a much stricter 'ex post' system, the accumulation of cases which the reality of the 'war on terror' (or at least its perception by governments) provides would sooner or later mean that patterns would emerge, procedures would form and rules set, whether officially or through nods and winks.

For the would-be torturer facing a perceived TBS after the first 10, 20 or 50 terrorists have been tortured and the authorities have reacted (or not), what O Gross calls 'the uncertain prospect' becomes a tried, tested and predictable procedure, and his 'ex-post facto ratification' becomes an *ex ante, carte blanche*, go-ahead;[351] Meir Dan-Cohen's 'price tag on the option of violating the law' becomes a 'freebie', in the case of torture, and so the relevant 'decision rules' (those available to the general public) become 'conduct rules' (available to officials);[352] Levinson's 'precommitment' to the general prohibition on torture[353] becomes hollow and meaningless.[354]

Such an eventuality may be hinted at by Gross and Aoláin, who argue the following:

> ...the sequence of extra-legal action and subsequent public ratification may bring about an eventual change in the law, turning a political precedent into a legal one...[355]

In our case in point, this would mean the abandonment of an 'ex post ratification' system in favour of explicit legalization of torture.

Torture in Israel has once again become 'institutionalized' to the extent that in late 2005, an Israeli judge spoke of 'an interrogation procedure...that GSS interrogators called the "necessity interrogation" procedure'[356]—surely an absurd oxymoron in a system based on a ruling that outlawed any reliance on the

---

[351] See O Gross, eg 'Chaos and Rules...' *supra* n 339, 1124; *idem*, 'Are Torture warrants warranted?...' *ibid*, 1530; *idem* and Aoláin, *ibid*, 137–142.

[352] M Dan-Cohen, 'Decision Rules and Conduct Rules: On Acoustic Separation in Criminal Law' 97 *Harvard LR* 625 (first quotation is from 638), reprinted in *idem*, *Harmful Thoughts: Essays on Law, Self, and Morality* (Princeton: Princeton University Press, 2000) 37–93. Gur-Arye bases her argument that the HCJ ruling in the *Israel Torture* case allowed the DoN for torturing in a TBS only as an excuse on Cohen's analysis. See Gur-Arye, 'Legitimating Official Brutality...' *supra* n 152, 20–4.

[353] Levinson, *supra* n 339.

[354] For similar criticism see E A Posner and A Vermeule, 'Should Coercive Interrogation Be Legal?' *U of Chicago Public Law Working Paper No 84*, March 2005, 22–3.

[355] Gross and Aoláin, *supra* n 339, 159.

[356] PH 775/04 (Jerusalem Dist Court), *The State of Israel v Amer 'Abd al-'Aziz*, Verdict, 29 December 2005, para 5 (per Noam J).

DoN for 'general directives governing the use of physical means'.[357] For reasons outlined above I submit that these are not all 'slippery slope' problems of Israel's HCJ model. Rather, they also represent, in the circumstances, a flaw intrinsic to *any* such model, an *inevitable* outcome of the combination of a belief that torture in extreme situations is justified and the intensity of the 'war on terror'.

Therefore, since:

1. in a state facing the volume of terrorism, or terrorist threat, which at the beginning of the twenty-first century plagues Afghanistan, Israel, Iraq, the Russian Federation, Saudi Arabia, the UK, the USA, and a long string of other states, the introduction of torture, even if only in TBSs, would inevitably entail its institutionalized practice;

2. as Israel's Supreme Court has determined, rightly by an almost wall-to-wall consensus among writers, the 'defence of necessity' cannot be a basis for such institutionalization; and

3. the same would apply to any other relevant individual defence, such as self-defence and any other 'ex post' mechanism;

it may safely be concluded that the DoN (and *mutatis mutandis* any other individual defence or 'ex post' mechanism) cannot provide a workable framework for legalized torture of terrorist suspects in TBSs in such states. This would add to the total unacceptability of torture—as well as all 'lesser' types of 'coercive interrogation'—in any circumstances under international law, the fact that interrogation methods used in the DoN models (as well as the HVD one) have amounted to torture, the insurmountable problems that a DoN-seeking torturer, certainly one seeking justification, would encounter in an international criminal court, and the considerable difficulties such a torturer would meet in many, if not most domestic ones.

In the case of the USA the facts are not as clear, nor is the question of whether the DoN was initially behind the general immunity which CIA interrogators of senior *al-Qa'idah* suspects seemed to enjoy. More likely it was just some sweeping assumption of legality. A blanket immunity was, however, granted by law *ex post facto*, and subsequent abductors, jailors in secret prisoners and sleep-depriving (etc) interrogators will be acting in accordance with US law—at least as understood by the administration.

One conclusion must not be drawn, however. It is highly unlikely that interrogators from the USA, Israel and other democracies will ever force a rat into a detainee's rectum. However, it would be a grave mistake to view this as applying 'a principled break',[358] let alone marking an absolutist 'pale'. As long as much of these countries' professional efforts, at the beginning of the twentieth century (especially in the wake of Abu Ghraib), go into devising ways of inflicting on

---

[357] HCJ ruling in the *Israel Torture* case, para 36.
[358] Dershowitz, *supra* n 257, 147.

detainees excruciating agony without 'shocking' the (TV) viewer, or voter, and into putting in place legislation that would allow that—such countries are no better morally, and no less violative, nay criminal, legally, than their Argentinean counterparts of the last century.[359] International legal definitions wisely avoid distinguishing the physical from the mental, the immediate from the cumulative, the active from the passive. They teach our conscience to be shocked by that which does not create shocking images on our screens. Torture is torture is torture.

∗∗∗

My further conclusion is therefore that, in view of current state of international law and the realities of the 'war on terror', democratic states facing terrorism have only two real—or at least only two honest—options:

1. *Openly legalize torture.* Torture would then be carried out professionally by trained, authorized officials acting under legally-issued (in the legal positivist sense) orders. This would necessitate changes not only to domestic law, including constitutional provisions, but radical, I would say earth-shattering changes to international human rights law, international humanitarian law and international criminal law, including upsetting customary and even *jus cogens* norms. Alternately, it would entail one or several states breaking away from, and possibly breaking down, those strands of the international legal system.

2. *Never torture detainees,* not even terrorists, not even in a TBS, nor ever attempt to 'only' ill-treat them.

I would, unsurprisingly, support the latter option.

---

[359] Perhaps, on a level, worse. I once heard Adv Leah Tzemel remark, concerning non-democratic states that torture: 'at least they have the decency to lie about it'.

PART V

CONCLUSIONS

21

Conclusions

[Ivan Karamazov, talking to his brother Alyosha] *'Tell me honestly, I challenge you—answer me: imagine that you are charged with building the edifice of human destiny, whose ultimate aim is to bring people happiness, to give them peace and contentment at last, but that in order to achieve this it is essential and unavoidable to torture just one little speck of creation, that same little child beating her breast with her little fists, and imagine that this edifice has to be erected on her unexpiated tears. Would you agree to be the architect under those conditions? Tell me honestly!'*

'No, I wouldn't agree,' said Alyosha quietly.[1]

...torture is a microcosm, raised to the highest level of intensity, of the tyrannical political relationships that liberalism hates the most.[2]

The links between the three 'limbs' of this study—the moral, the practical and the legal—are almost self-explanatory.

The consequentialist (and, specifically, utilitarian) morality of extreme situations discussed in Part I, as advocated by those ethicists who justify resort to interrogational torture in a 'pure' theoretical 'ticking bomb situation' (TBS), is reflected in the legal positions and actual practices of states facing terrorism that have chosen to inflict such torture on suspected knowledgeable terrorists in (real or perceived) situations of this kind, as seen in Part III.

In particular, the consequentialist 'lesser evil' approach to the TBS dilemma transforms directly into the interpretation of the 'defence of necessity' (DoN) as an 'uncapped' lesser evil justificatory defence to all crimes—or indeed to the interpretation of the powers of war-time leaders as being 'uncapped'. Since torture involves the infliction of unlimited harm by one person (or more) on another, what I call 'an absolutist anti-absolutist' moral position—one denying that there are *any* acts that are always morally prohibited—must be adopted to grant interrogators the kind of unlimited, unrestrained power over detainees that such infliction requires.

Once this morality and the legal corollaries thereof are accepted in and adopted by a state, all that remains is for that state to find ways of torturing effectively while limiting torture to those instances—such as TBSs—in which a consequentialist cost-benefit calculus would deem it justified. This means finding

---

[1] F Dostoevsky, *The Karamazov Brothers*, trans I Avsey (Oxford: OUP, 1994) 308.
[2] D Luban, 'Liberalism, Torture, and the Ticking Bomb' 91 *Virginia L Rev* 1425 (2005) 1425.

ways of avoiding 'slippery slope' dangers discussed in Part II, which unless dealt with would bring about results that are altogether worse than those of not torturing at all.

On all these fronts, however, there are problems. Some of those, I have tried to show, are well-nigh insurmountable, while others are totally so. On the legal front these include the absolute, 'no-exceptions' (*jus cogens*, 'non-derogable') prohibition on torture and other ill-treatment in international law; the very narrow margins that some domestic systems (outside Israel) would allow for a torturer in a TBS to enjoy the 'defence of necessity'; the absolute rejection of any uncapped 'lesser evil' justificatory rationale that would facilitate such enjoyment in other systems; and the all-but-bolted-gates in front of those wishing to rely on this rationale in international criminal law, although formally it may still be up to the International Criminal Court to turn the final key.

On the practical, 'societal' front the difficulties include the dangers of expansion, escalation and institutionalization of torture, once it has been allowed in a TBS 'only'. Even the basic justification for torture—that it is an essential, and *effective* 'weapon' in the 'war on terror'—is not problem-free. Torture does not always work, and this study shows that even torturers have admitted as much. And where it has worked, torture may have won battles but has not won wars. In all likelihood torture would, and in fact actually has, intensified wars and other conflicts, prolonged them, deepened dehumanization and hatred of the 'enemy' and impeded efforts at reconciliation.

For me, the ultimate monument to the practical failure of torture is clearly visible in the hills and valleys of the occupied West Bank—the barrier (part fence, part wall) erected there by Israel is the diametrical opposite of torture (although it has caused suffering). It relies on physically blocking would-be terrorists from reaching their target, rather than finding out their plots and thwarting them. As noted, the construction of this barrier was recommended as the best solution by the head of the GSS, the intelligence (and torturing) arm of the Israeli security forces, who acknowledged his organization's failure to stop terrorist attacks by other means.

The fact that torture comes with no guarantee of success, whereas the dangers it entails for a society—those mentioned here and others discussed in Part II—are very real, has led several ethicists to call for an absolute ban on torture on consequentialist grounds.

Others however, including states, officials, journalists and ethicists, have gone in different directions. Aware of the special stigma attached to torture, they have sought 'eat-your-cake-and-have-it' solutions to the TBS problem in the legal sphere, and ostensibly the moral one. If one can coerce the terrorist into providing the life-saving information while maintaining the legally and morally required 'humane treatment' of him, or at least while ill-treating him without resort to 'outright torture', then actually there is no reason to face the 'torture-or-people-will-die' dilemma posed in this study. However, 'humane coercion' is an oxymoron—physical and psychological coercion are inherently inhumane; they are so defined in international law, which wisely placed the line of illegality firmly between 'humane treatment' and 'cruel, inhuman or degrading treatment', or 'coercion', rather than between 'outright' torture and 'outright-minus-one' torture. Thus international law prohibits these and all other forms of ill-treatment 'short of torture'. Moreover, 'stress and duress', 'moderate physical pressure', 'torture lite', and similar techniques become torturous over time and when used cumulatively. The 'lesser evil' rationale will not allow interrogators to stop at the not-always-clear line between what is 'cruel, inhuman or degrading' and what is torture, if they fail to convince the terrorist to speak in a TBS. This study shows that this, again, is not merely a sound logical conclusion—it has translated into reality: such barriers have not worked, if they have been erected at all; torture was found by independent experts to have been perpetrated in all models established by states and discussed in this study.

In effect, the 'defence of necessity' (DoN) models examined in this study stem from a similar 'eat-your-cake-and-have-it' rationale, that is supported by ethicists who propose models combining an absolute prohibition on torture in law with some kind of after-the-fact exoneration for perpetrators. The state can thereby both allow its agents to torture and refrain from itself torturing; it can both save numerous lives in TBSs and preserve its legal and moral integrity. This enterprise, we have seen, is in logic flawed and in practice unworkable for the situation in which states facing terrorism at the beginning of the twenty-first century find themselves.

In practice, once a DoN (or other 'ex post') system is in place, any envisaged deterrent effect that punishments stipulated in law against torturers may have on (non-TBS) torturers is eroded to the point of vanishing in real situations now facing real states. TBSs, actual or perceived, come, if not thick and fast, then at least too often to fulfil the requirement of rarity—an essential ingredient of the models, both legal and theoretical, which shift responsibility onto the individual interrogator. Once rarity disappears and routine settles in, the interrogator's initial fears of unknown prosecution and punishment are allayed by his progressively extensive knowledge of prosecutorial and judicial (or possibly legislative) patterns emerging out of past cases. The corresponding public perception of torture as a rare occasion for consideration and possible *post facto* 'ratification' is equally eroded when the accumulated past 'ratifications' eat away at the 'precommitment' to the absolute prohibition of torture, to create what is in effect a system of *ab initio* 'ratification' for torture. The negligent effect which torture in rare cases is supposed to have on the system—interrogators, interrogation policies, the prison system, courts and society as a whole—becomes progressively more substantial as cases accumulate.

Thus in the case of Israel, the attempt by the Supreme Court to allow torture (not so named) in TBSs only while avoiding its legitimation as a policy through rules, regulations and prior authorization has failed when, during the second *Intifadah*, the advent of (real of perceived) dozens of TBSs a year, officially admitted (and many more cases of torture according to other sources), have meant that would-be torturers know what to expect; they have no fear of criminal punishment, or even prosecution, and officially acknowledged procedures (including of authorization) and methods have emerged (or re-emerged), to render Israel once more a torturing state. A similar pattern may have initially emerged for CIA agents interrogating 'high-value detainees' in the USA's 'war on terror', though this was not clear at that time the study was concluded. Later, in 2006, the US Congress ensured an equivalent of Israel's 100 per cent immunity policies, through retroactive legislation, and the President's interpretation of this legislation has ensured that torture will continue.

The alternative view defended here, was described succinctly by Nigel S Rodley as 'absolute means absolute'.[3] Absolutism, at least in the minimal version defended here, is not the 'fanatic' morality of purists, it is part of international, and often national laws which prohibit, and practices which never involve, not only torture but also acts and policies such as genocide, slavery, rape, cruel forms of the death penalty and waiving informed consent to expedite the development of a vaccine to HIV/AIDS which would save millions. It is borne of the belief, well-grounded in practice, that to be realistic does not preclude being 'humanistic'.

I believe that this is illustrated in the clear similarities between the international community's attitude to terrorism and its attitude towards torture. In a 'declaration on the issue of combating terrorism' adopted unanimously by the UN Security Council in early 2003, the Council 'reaffirms', *inter alia*, that:

…any acts of terrorism are criminal and unjustifiable, regardless of their motivation, whenever and by whomsoever committed and are to be unequivocally condemned, especially when they indiscriminately target or injure civilians;[4]

Article 2(2) of the UN Convention against Torture, already quoted in this study, states that:

No exceptional circumstances whatsoever, whether a state of war or a threat of war, internal political instability or any other public emergency, may be invoked as a justification of torture.

I believe that both these statements not only reflect international law correctly—they are also morally right, but they are right only when understood exactly as they appear—as *absolutist* prohibitions, and as part of a moral-cum-legal view of how individuals, groups and states should behave; a view that includes, among many other things, what I have called minimal absolutist prohibitions. Otherwise I submit that morally, legally or logically, if torture is to be justified, or legalized, as a 'lesser evil' means of preventing some horrendous catastrophe such

---

[3] NS Rodley, 'The Prohibition of Torture: Absolute Means Absolute' 34 *Denver J of Int'l L & Policy* 145 (2006).

[4] Security Council Resolution 1456 (2003), adopted 20 January 2003, Annex.

as a terrorist attack, this cannot be done without similarly also justifying terrorist attacks—certainly small ones costing 'only' a few, or a few dozen lives, if they are shown to be the only way to prevent some greater evil, or catastrophe. For many in states facing terrorism, the latter scenario is neither likely nor convincing, but any attempt to disassociate one type of moral prohibition from another cannot succeed, as the two share an unavoidable 'slippery surface'. And for terrorists, as we have seen, no difference exists—few of those supporting terrorism seem to consider the intentional killing of civilians as valuable for its own sake; rather, such killing is justified as a necessary evil in the face of greater ones, including, so they say, murder and torture (by the USA, Israel etc) on a large scale. This point will be illustrated below.

In conclusion, I will bring the story of two different individuals, from two different contexts, who to my mind personify the minimal absolutist approach to the key questions raised in this study, and the views of one who does not.

The first is the story of Mr FS Cocks, involved in the drafting of a human rights treaty. It appears from the *travaux preparatoires* of the European Convention for the Protection of Human Rights and Fundamental Freedoms that a version of what I called here 'minimal absolutism'—the idea that certain rights may *never* be violated or, in legal terms, are non-derogable, was first expressed by Mr Cocks, a UK representative, at the meeting of the Consultative Assembly on 7 September 1949.[5]

Mr. Cocks proposed the following wording to be included in the Convention:

The Consultative Assembly takes this opportunity of declaring that all forms of physical torture...are inconsistent with civilized society, are offences against heaven and humanity and must be prohibited.

It declares that this prohibition must be absolute and that torture cannot be permitted for any purpose whatsoever, either for extracting evidence, to save life or even for the safety of the state.

The Assembly believes that it would be better even for society to perish than for it to permit this relic of barbarism to remain.[6]

The proposal was, in Antonio Cassese's words, 'cast in lofty and eloquent language, better suited for political or moral declaration than for a legal text'[7] and was 'withdrawn after discussion'.[8] However, it is clear from the present structure of the Convention that its essential, 'moral' elements were preserved:[9] torture and

---

[5] The draft before the Consultative Assembly at the time did not include provisions either for derogations from or for the non-derogability of rights, but only a qualifying article, applicable to all rights and freedoms protected by the proposed Convention. See *Collected Edition of the 'Travaux Preparatoires'*, Vol 1 (The Hague: Martinus Nijhoff, 1975) 230.

[6] Document No 91, 236, *ibid*, Vol 1, 252–4.

[7] A Cassese, 'Prohibition of Torture and Inhuman or Degrading Treatment or Punishment' in R St J Macdonald, F Matscher and H Petsold (eds), *The European System for the Protection of Human Rights* (Dordrecht: Martinus Nijhoff, 1993) 225–261, 227.

[8] *ECHR Travaux Preparatoires*, *supra* n 5, 252, fn 4.

[9] See Cassese, *supra* n 7, 227–8.

'inhuman or degrading treatment or punishment' are never allowed, not even in the face of 'war or other public emergency threatening the life of the nation'.[10] In turn, the International Covenant on Civil and Political Rights was adopted as a worldwide agreement, and includes an identical two-tier system, which provides for the same absolute prohibition on torture and ill-treatment.[11] In other words, Mr Cocks' minimal absolutism has prevailed, and on a global scale.

The second story is of 'Arin Ahmad, and concerns a real TBS which transpired in the Spring of 2002, when a murderous terrorist attack was thwarted not days or hours but literally minutes before it was to take place. I bring this story as it was told by the would-be suicide bomber, 'Arin 'Awwad Hussein Ahmad, a young Palestinian woman. 'Arin's fiancé, an activist for the *Tanzim* (a Palestinian group involved in terrorism), was killed by Israeli forces in March 2002. The following month Israeli forces conducted a wide-ranging operation in Bethlehem, where 'Arin was studying, causing death and destruction, as she observed. In response, 'Arin volunteered for a suicide bombing mission inside Israel. She was coached by *Tanzim* activists for the mission and videotaped, gun in hand. She wrote a will and a letter to her parents. On 22 May 2002 'Arin Ahmad purified herself and prayed. She was then dressed in modern clothes, provided with a bag full of explosives and fitted with a triggering device attached to her body. She was driven to the Israeli city of Rishon le-Tzion, together with another would-be suicide bomber, 'Issa, with the operation's commander, Ibrahim, in another vehicle. Their mission was to kill as many (innocent) civilians as possible, at a location chosen for maximum effect. This is how 'Arin described what happened next:

> Me and 'Issa got off [the car] each with a bag and the explosives inside, ready for activation. I went to my [designated] place and 'Issa went to the place where he was supposed to blow himself up with the explosives. I saw that there were two zebra crossings at the place... and I stood by a wall on my own. I started thinking, why do I need to carry out a suicide bombing, this is suicide, and suicide is prohibited in the Qur'an, and I saw people just like me, they hadn't done me any harm, why do I have to carry out a suicide bombing. The Mirs [two way radio] was with me, and I contacted Ibrahim, who had already left the area. I told him that I'd changed my mind, and I don't want to do anything.[12]

Like the fictional Ethica of Part I, the real 'Arin Ahmad had to make a crucial decision in extreme circumstances. But this story shows, I believe, the ability to

---

[10] Article 15(1) of the European Convention on Human Rights, which renders Art 3 (prohibiting torture and inhuman or degrading treatment) non-derogable.

[11] In Arts 7 and 4.

[12] A/156, Adorayim Mil Ct file 1419/02 *'Arin Awwad Hussein Ahmad*, hearing of 29 May 2002, 5–6. The rest of the story was taken from 'Arin Ahmad's testimony *ibid*, 1–5. 'Arin's version was cited by the Court without any claims that she was distorting the truth. The Court also found her change of heart to be genuine. It nevertheless convicted 'Arin of attempted murder, citing the military laws which do not recognize remorse as grounds for acquittal. Following an appeal, she was sentenced to seven years' imprisonment and two years' suspended sentence. See A [appeal] Judea and Samaria 2746/04+1001/05 *re 'Arin Ahmad*.

be truly free, and as such to be a moral agent in the fullest sense of the term, even in the face of great adversity, oppression, suffering and danger, and with choice seemingly narrowing down to 'greater' and 'lesser' evils. 'Arin was certainly wrong to give in to her fears and hatred when she opted for terrorism in the first place—she would have been equally wrong, I submit, had she decided to become a terrorist suicide bomber on the basis of a perfectly sound utilitarian calculus. But staring at the moral abyss, she chose to step back. I believe that 'Arin shunned terrorism absolutely, once and for all—she certainly did so on the personal, practical level (no terrorist would ever recruit *her* again)—and to that extent she was more courageous, and adopted a more wholesome morality on the pavement in Rishon le-Tzion than have the Supreme Court judges in Jerusalem or the leaders (and their lawyers) in Washington.

The particular case is probably very rare, but individuals and groups at the beginning of the twenty-first century do face the lure of terrorism, just as governments face the lure of torture. Ultimately, as discussed in this study, it does boil down to a personal question: will you attack civilians in the quest for freedom, independence or an ideal regime? Will you torture a terrorist to save many innocent lives? A terrorist organization must recruit the suicide bomber, a state must recruit the torturer, both types of would-be agents must, like 'Arin, face their would-be victims and make their choice.

Diametrically opposed to both Mr Cocks and Ms Ahmad stand individuals like Khalid Sheikh Muhammad, the self-confessed mastermind of the 9/11 terrorist attacks. They have deliberately killed people, including children, who clearly 'hadn't done them any harm'. However, Mohammad's words to the 'Combatant Status Review Tribunal' in Guantánamo in March 2007, spoken in broken English, reveal that he too had thought of this, and his justification for his actions is relevant here:

I don't like to kill people. I feel very sorry they have been killed kids in 9/11...I know American people are torturing us from seventies. [REDACTED] I know they talking about human rights. And I know it is against American Constitution, against American laws. But they said every law, they have exceptions, this is your bad luck you been part of the exception to our laws.[13]

Fashionable though it may be in some quarters at the time this is written, I believe that to equate the morality of terrorists like Mohammad with that of the USA in its 'war on terror' is preposterous. However, by opting for torture, the USA, Israel and other states have rejected the (minimal) absolutist view as to what means are legitimate in fighting terrorism: if the law prohibiting torture has exceptions, then so does, in effect, 'every law' governing (at least small-scale) human behaviour,

---

[13] Verbatim Transcript of Combatant Status Review Tribunal Hearing for ISN 10024, 10 March 2007, on board U.S. Naval Base Guantanamo Bay, Cuba <http://www.defenselink.mil/news/transcript_ISN10024.pdf>, accessed 17 April 2007, 24.

since no act is so 'bad' as to be beyond torture. And here Muhammad has a point: *to that extent* the terrorists and the anti-terrorist torturers and torture-justifiers are, morally, one and the same.

I believe that it is Mr Cocks and Ms Ahmad who chose the right course—essentially the same one—and that we should follow. Because, while most of us concentrate on the possibility of becoming, at any time, victims of terrorist attacks, we are all also, at all times, would-be torturers, would-be terrorists, unless in freedom we decide otherwise.

I am hardly breaking new grounds in claiming that nations, groups and individuals will never agree unanimously on what goals they should pursue—the ideal form of government, the ideal life, the true faith etc.

What I believe humans *may* be able to agree, indeed should agree—although this too is neither new nor likely to materialize anytime soon—is that in pursuing *any* goals whatsoever, they maintain, to paraphrase Dostoevsky's words, *that little speck of humanity* at all times.

Therefore I have a simple conclusion and recommendation as to what we should do in a TBS—when we hold a knowledgeable prisoner who will not talk, and innocent lives are at risk, or what we should demand that our neighbours, our government, our courts and legislature, our liberation movement, our international community do in such a situation: *they—we—must do anything humanly possible to save the lives at risk.*

Which means doing everything in our power that does not involve losing our own humanity. Which in turn means never to torture or otherwise ill-treat another human being, whatever the circumstances.

Annex

The 'Ticking Bomb' Scenario—a Few Examples

The 'ticking bomb situation' (TBS) is at the heart of this study, and I thought it useful to illustrate further what officials, courts and writers have meant when invoking this term. Below are 'ticking bomb' scenarios in addition to those already described in the study itself. Most are imagined, but some are real (or described as such). They are arranged in chronological order.

Jeremy Bentham

Jeremy Bentham envisaged a situation devoid of bombs, but nevertheless very much the precursor of and inspiration to subsequent 'ticking bomb situations':

Suppose an occasion, to arise, in which a suspicion is entertained, as strong as that which would be received as a sufficient ground for arrest and commitment as for felony—a suspicion that at this very time a considerable number of individuals are actually suffering, by illegal violence inflictions equal in intensity to those which if inflicted by the hand of justice, would universally be spoken of under the name of torture. For the purpose of rescuing from torture these hundred innocents, should any scruple be made of applying equal or superior torture, to extract the requisite information from the mouth of one criminal, who having it in his power to make known the place where at this time the enormity was practising or about to be practised, should refuse to do so? To say nothing of wisdom, could any pretence be made so much as to the praise of blind and vulgar humanity, by the man who to save one criminal, should determine to abandon a 100 innocent persons to the same fate?[14]

Paul Teitgen

Paul Teitgen described to Alistair Horne a situation he had faced in 1956, during the 'Battle of Algiers', when he served as secretary-general at the Algiers' prefecture, with special responsibilities for overseeing police. Horne writes:

In November [1956] he [Teitgen] was confronted with an appalling moral dilemma. Fernarnd Yveton, the Communist, had been caught red-handed placing a bomb in the

---

[14] J Bentham, Mss Box 74.b, 429 (27 May 1804), cited in WL Twining and PE Twining, 'Bentham on Torture' 24(3) *Northern Ireland Legal Quarterly* 305 (1973) 347.

gasworks where he was employed. But a second bomb had not been discovered, and if it exploded and set off the gasometers thousands of lives might be lost. Nothing would induce Yveton to reveal its whereabouts, and Teigten was pressed by his Chief of Police to have Yveton *passé à la question*. 'But I refused to have him tortured. I trembled the whole afternoon. Finally the bomb did not go off. Thank God I was right. Because if you once get into the torture business, you're lost.'[15]

Anthony Quinton

Anthony Quinton provided the earliest 'ticking bomb' example as an argument for the *morality* of torturing in extreme circumstances that I have found. He places the bomb in a hospital:

Consider a man caught planting a bomb in a large hospital, which no one but he knows how to defuse and no one dare touch for fear of setting it off. This was the kind of extreme situation that I had in mind when I said earlier that I thought torture could be justifiable.[16]

William and P Twining

William and P Twining describe in detail a case of an atomic TBS:

It is believed that an atomic bomb has been placed somewhere in a major city with a timing device attached to it. X, who is believed to have information about the location of the bomb, has been captured. The following conditions are satisfied:

(1) The evidence in support of the contention that he has the relevant information would satisfy the requirement of evidence for convicting him of an offence.
(2) There are reasonable grounds for believing that he is likely to tell the truth if severe torture is threatened, and, if necessary, applied to him.
(3) There are reasonable grounds for believing that no other means would have the effect of compelling him to tell the truth.
(4) There are reasonable grounds for believing that if the information is obtained quickly, there is a good chance of defusing the bomb before it goes off.
(5) There are reasonable grounds for believing that the likely damage to be caused by the bomb will include death of many citizens, the maiming of others, including the infliction of much more severe pain *on others* with much more lasting effect than will be the effect of the infliction of torture on the person who has been captured.
(6) There are reasonable grounds for believing that the torturing will not have consequences (e.g. retaliation by X's friends) which would be worse than the damage likely to result from the bomb going off.[17]

---

[15] A Horne, *A Savage War of Peace: Algeria 1954–1962* (revised edn, London: Papermac, 1996), 204. It may be relevant to add that Teigten, a hero of the Résistance, had been tortured by the Gestapo in Dachau 14 years before this event.

[16] Anthony Quentin, *The Listener*, 2 December 1971, 757–8, at 758, cited by Twining and Twining, *supra* n 1, 346, fn 2.

[17] WL Twining and PE Twining, 'Bentham on Torture' 24(3) *Northern Ireland Legal Quarterly* 305 (1973) 346–7.

Michael Levin

In 1982, Michael Levin placed the bomb on Manhattan Island:

There are situations in which it is note merely permissible, but morally mandatory, to torture. Suppose a terrorist has hidden a bomb on Manhattan Island, which will detonate at noon on 4 July—unless...Suppose, further, that he is caught at 10 am that fateful day, but—preferring death to failure—won't disclose where the bomb is...If the only way to save those lives is to subject the terrorist to the most excruciating possible pain, what grounds can there be for not doing so? I suggest that there are none...Torture only the obviously guilty, and only for the sake of saving innocents, and the line between Us and Them will remain clear. There is little danger that the western democracies will lose their way if they choose to inflict pain as one way of preserving order.[18]

Adrian Zuckerman

In 1987, the *Landau Commission of Inquiry* in Israel quoted the following passage by Adrian Zuckerman to describe the classic TBS:

This is not to say that it is impossible to envisage situations where the organs of the State may excusably resort to torture. Where it is known that a bomb has been planted in a crowded building, it is perhaps justifiable to torture the suspect so that lives may be saved by discovering its location.[19]

The Commission went on to express the view that:

This is an extreme example of actual torture, the use of which would perhaps be justified in order to uncover a bomb about to explode in a building full of people.[20]

Antonio Cassese

Antonio Cassese provides two examples to the kind of 'problems that have to be faced head on' by democratic countries. The first is a real, the second a fictitious one:

A few years ago, at the Geneva Diplomatic talks (1974–7) to update the 1949 Geneva Conventions, one colonel from a Western Great Power told another negotiator off the record that he had sometimes found himself in the position of having an enemy prisoner tortured, knowing that that prisoner could supply essential information for saving a whole battalion. 'I was aware of the inhumanity of what I had ordered,' said the Colonel, 'but against that one man's suffering, an enemy into the bargain, was the safety of hundreds of my men. For me they weighed heavier in the balance.'

[18] Michael Levin, 'The Case for Torture' *Newsweek* (17 June 1982) at 13.

[19] AAS Zuckerman, 'The Right against Self-Incrimination: An Obstacle to the Supervision of Interrogation' 102 *Law Quarterly Rev* 45 (1986), n 4, quoted at para 3.15 of the Landau report.

[20] *Report of the Commission of Inquiry in the matter of Interrogation Methods of the General Security Service regarding Hostile Terrorist Activity*, First Part [Hebrew] (Jerusalem: October, 1987) para 3.15.

[...] Should a person suspected of having placed (or knowing where there has been placed) a time bomb due to go off soon in a public building be caught, can the urgency of the situation justify the infliction of torture or other mistreatment in order to obtain the information?[21]

Israeli Supreme Court

In its ruling in the *Israel Torture case*, the Israeli Supreme Court described a TBS twice. Here is the second, more detailed one:

In the course of their argument, the State's attorneys submitted the 'ticking time bomb' argument. A given suspect is arrested by the GSS. He holds information respecting the location of a bomb that was set and will imminently explode. There is no way to diffuse the bomb without this information. If the information is obtained, however, the bomb may be diffused. If the bomb is not diffused, scores will be killed and maimed. Is a GSS investigator authorized to employ physical means in order to elicit information regarding the location of the bomb in such instances? The State's attorneys answer in the affirmative.[22]

Henry Shue

In Henry Shue's example, the bomb is nuclear:

There is a standard philosopher's example which someone always invokes: suppose a fanatic, perfectly willing to die rather than collaborate in the thwarting of his own scheme, has set a hidden nuclear device to explode in the heart of Paris. There is no time to evacuate the innocent people or even the movable art treasures—the only hope of preventing tragedy is to torture the perpetrator, find the device, and deactivate it.[23]

Alan Dershowitz

In 2002, Following the terrorist attacks on the USA on 11 September 2001, Alan Dershowitz, who had already used the TBS, suggested a version in which a TBS is imagined in the eve of those attacks:

Several weeks before September 11, 2001, the Immigration and Naturalization Service detained Zacarias Moussaoui after flight instructors reported suspicious statements he had made while taking flying lessons and paying for them with large amounts of cash. The government decided not to seek a warrant to reach his computer. Now imagine that they had, and that they discovered he was part of a plan to destroy large occupied buildings, but without any further details. They interrogated him, gave him immunity

---

[21] A Cassese, 'The Savage States: Torture in the 1980s' in *idem, Human Rights in a Changing World* (Cambridge: Polity Press, 1990) 105.

[22] HCJ 5100/94 *The Public Committee Against Torture in Israel v the Government of Israel et al*, PD 53(4) 817, Judgment of 6 September 1999, para 33.

[23] H Shue, 'Torture' 7 *Philosophy and Public Affairs* 124 (1978) 141.

from prosecution, and offered him large cash rewards and a new identity. He refused to talk. They then threatened him, tried to trick him, and employed every lawful technique available. He still refused. They even injected him with sodium pentothal and other truth serums, but to no avail. The attack now appeared to be imminent, but the FBI still had no idea what the target was or what means would be used to attack it. We could not simply evacuate all buildings indefinitely. An FBI agent proposes the use of nonlethal torture—say, a sterilized needle inserted under the fingernails to produce unbearable pain without any threat to health or life, or the method used in the film *Marathon Man*, a dental drill through an unanaesthetized tooth.[24]

Bruce Hoffman

Burce Hoffman recounts the following tale of a real TBS, told to him by 'a much decorated, battle-hardened Sri Lankan army officer charged with fighting the LTTE [also known as the "Tamil Tigers"] and protecting the lives of Colombo's citizens'. Hoffman, who says he could not use the officer's real name, calls him 'Thomas', adding that he 'had another name, one better known to his friends and enemies alike: Terminator'.

Thomas had little confidence that I understood what he was saying. I was an academic, he said, with no actual experience of the life-and-death choices and the immense responsibility borne by those charged with protecting society from attack. Accordingly, he would give me an example of the split-second decisions he was called on to make. At the time, Colombo was on 'code red' emergency status, because of intelligence that the LTTE was planning to embark on a campaign of bombing public gathering places and other civilian targets. Thomas's unit had apprehended three terrorists who, it suspected, had recently planted somewhere in the city a bomb that was then ticking away, the minutes counting down to catastrophe. The three men were brought before Thomas. He asked them where the bomb was. The terrorists—highly dedicated and steeled to resist interrogation—remained silent. Thomas asked the question again, advising them that if they did not tell him what he wanted to know, he would kill them. They were unmoved. So Thomas took his pistol from his gun belt, pointed it at the forehead of one of them, and shot him dead. The other two, he said, talked immediately; the bomb, which had been placed in a crowded railway station and set to explode during the evening rush hour, was found and defused, and countless lives were saved.[25]

Mirko Bagaric and Julie Clarke

Mirko Bagaric and Julie Clarke place the ticking bomb in a plane:

A terrorist network has activated a large bomb on one of hundreds of commercial planes carrying over three hundred passengers that is flying somewhere in the world at any

---

[24] AM Dershowitz, *Why Terrorism Works: understanding the threat, responding to the challenge* (New Haven: Yale University Press, 2002) 142–3.
[25] B Hoffman, 'A nasty business' 289 (1) *The Atlantic Monthly* 49 (January 2002) 52.

point in time. The bomb is set to explode in thirty minutes. The leader of the terrorist organization announces this intent via a statement on the Internet. He states that the bomb was planted by one of his colleagues at one of the major airports in the world in the past few hours. No details are provided regarding the location of the plane where the bomb is located. Unbeknown to him, he was under police surveillance and is immediately apprehended by police. The terrorist leader refuses to answer any questions of the police, declaring that the passengers must die and will do so shortly.[26]

They add:

Who in the world would deny that all possible means should be used to extract the details of the plane and the location of the bomb?[27]

Schlesinger report

In an appendix entitled 'Ethical Issues', the Schlesinger report, not unlike the Israeli Supreme Court ruling in the *Israel Torture case*, put the TBS at the heart—indeed the *moral* heart—of the USA's 'harsh interrogation' policies:

For the U.S., most cases for permitting harsh treatment of detainees on moral grounds begin with variants of the 'ticking time bomb' scenario. The ingredients of such scenarios usually include an impending loss of life, a suspect who knows how to prevent it—and in most versions is responsible for it—and a third party who has no humane alternative to obtain the information in order to save lives.[28]

This is followed by an example:

An excellent example is the case of a 4th Infantry Division battalion commander who permitted his men to beat a detainee whom he had good reason to believe had information about future attacks against his unit. When the beating failed to produce the desired results, the commander fired his weapon near the detainee's head. The technique was successful and the lives of U.S. servicemen were likely saved. However, his actions clearly violated the Geneva Conventions and he reported his actions knowing he would be prosecuted by the Army. He was punished in moderation and allowed to retire.[29]

'24'

Fox's popular TV thriller '24' has featured several TBSs and several torture sessions. Here is the description of a scene combining the two. The TBS is

---

[26] M Bagaric and J Clarke, 'Not Enough Official Torture in the World? The Circumstances in which Torture is Morally justifiable' 39 *U of San Francisco L Rev* 581 (2005) at 583.

[27] *Ibid.*

[28] *Final Report of the Independent Panel To Review DoD Detention Operations*, August 2004, Appendix H, at 2, <http://www.defense.gov/news/Aug2004/d20040824finalreport.pdf>, accessed 25 August 2004. The Panel had been appointed by Secretary of Defence Donald Rumsfeld in May of that year, following the exposure of the Abu Ghraib scandal.

[29] *Ibid*, 2–3.

nuclear—the nuclear bomb stolen in this episode is planned to be detonated in a US city:

12:24 AM

Everyone at CTU [Counter-Terrorist Unit] watches the television as Logan addresses the nation. Audrey [of the CTU] interrupts with news that one of the convoys headed for Iowa is missing and hasn't called in at its checkpoint. The convoy was carrying a nuclear warhead.

12:30 AM

[...]

At the site of the torched, ambushed convoy, a group of men put the crated warhead onto their flatbed truck and throw a tarp over it. They drive off.

12:33 AM

[...]

Michelle warns Curtis that Prado [captured minutes ago, who is party to the nuclear plot and knows where its leader, Marwan, plans to be] is a Marine who won't cave easily. Curtis wants to use Richards, the torture specialist.

12:35 AM

[...]

[enter] a lawyer from Amnesty Global [who had been alerted by the terrorists]. The attorney has a signed court order protecting Prado.

[...]

12:43 AM

Jack enters the interrogation room and pulls the attorney aside. He points out that millions of lives are at stake, but the lawyer won't budge.

12:54 AM

Marwan speaks to the driver of the truck holding the nuclear warhead. The man the truck is to meet will have the bomb's detonation codes. Marwan does not want to give the Americans time to start evacuations. Marwan hangs up. He is near downtown Los Angeles.

12:49 AM

Jack wants to resign and let Prado go free. He plans to take him on as a private citizen, and then no agency will be held liable.

[...]

12:58 AM

[...] Jack tasers the Marshall and slaps handcuffs on Prado. 'Now we're gonna talk', Jack says as he slams the door of the car.

12:59 AM

When Prado claims that he doesn't know Marwan, Jack breaks the man's fingers one by one. Prado finally relents, and confesses that Marwan will be at a place just east of downtown. 'This will help you with the pain', Jack says as he knocks Prado out with a punch.[30]

---

[30] '24', season 4, episode 18, Day 4: 12:00 AM–1:00 AM, originally aired by Fox on 18 April 2005. The quotations are collated from 'episode guide' <http://www.fox.com/24/episodes/season4/12pm.htm>, and 'episode information' <http://www.tvrage.com/24/episodes/679>, both accessed 24 March 2006. This TV serialised drama was created by Joel Surnow and Robert Cochran. Each season covers 24 hours in the life of Jack Bauer (Kiefer Sutherland), a counter-terrorist agent working for the Counter Terrorist Unit in Los Angeles.

Himma

Finally, Himma envisage what is well-nigh a doomsday scenario:

Suppose that US officials have as much evidence as anyone could have for believing that: (1) there are ten hydrogen bombs hidden in the ten most populous US cities; (2) the bombs are powerful enough to decimate each city leaving no survivors and extensive radioactive fallout; (3) the bombs are set to go off in 24 hours; (4) it is not possible to evacuate any of the cities within 24 hours; (5) a conspirator in custody knows where each of the bombs is and will reveal this information quickly enough, if tortured, for officials to find and disarm each of the bombs; and (6) there is no other way to avoid having the bombs detonate. [...] these bombs will kill hundreds of millions of people.[31]

---

[31] KE Himma, 'Assessing the Prohibition Against Torture,' in SP Lee (ed), *Intervention, Terrorism, and Torture: Contemporary Challenges to Just War Theory* (Dordrecht: Springer, 2007) 235–248, 237–8.

Bibliography

A. Books and Articles

'3 in Al-Qaeda missile plot extradited to US: report', *Philippine Daily Enquirer*, 6 March 2003 <http://www.inq7.net/brk/2003/mar/06/brkafp_11–1.htm>, citing Agence France-Presse, accessed 30 July 2003

'20 al-Qaeda men handed over to US', *Dawn/The News International*, Karachi (1 April 2002) <http://www.karachipage.com/news/Apr_02/040102.html>, accessed 10 July 2003

Ackroyd, Carol, Margolis, Karen, Rosenhead, Jonathan and Shallice, Tim, *The Technology of Political Control* (2nd edn, London: Pluto Press, 1980)

Adams, Lorraine, 'Terrorism and the English Language: This year's crop of terrorism books offers thrills over insight' *The Washington Monthly* (September 2002)

Aeschylus, 'Agamemnon' (ca 458 BC) in *iden The Oresteia*, trans Ian Johnston (Arlington, Va: Richer Resource Publication 2007) 7–70

Alexander, Larry, 'Deontology at the Threshold' 37 *San Diego Law Review* 893 (2000)

Al-Haq, Palestinian Victims of Torture Speak Out (Ramallah: Al-Haq, 1993)

—— Torture for Security: The Systematic Torture and Ill-Treatment of Palestinians by Israel (Ramallah: Al-Haq, 1995)

Alleg, Henri, *The Question*, trans John Calder (London: John Calder, 1958)

Allison, Lincoln, 'The Utilitarian Ethics of Punishment and Torture' in *idem* (ed), *The Utilitarian Response: The Contemporary Viability of Utilitarian Political Philosophy* (London: Sage, 1990) 9–29

Alter, Jonathan, 'Time To Think About Torture' *Newsweek* (5 November 2001), reproduced on <http://www.sweetliberty.org/issues/war/safety/torture1.htm>, accessed 3 July 2003

Amand, Matthew G St, 'Public Committee Against Torture in Israel v. the State of Israel et al: Landmark Human Rights Decision by the Israeli High Court of Justice or Status Quo Maintained?' 25 *NC J Int'l L and Comm Reg* 655 (2000)

Amann, Diane Marie, 'Abu Ghraib' 153 *U Pennsylvania L Rev* 2085

Amar, Akhil Reed, 'Fourth Amendment First Principles' 107 *Harv L Rev* 757 (1994)

—— *The Constitution and Criminal Procedure: First Principles* (New Haven: Connecticut, Yale University Press, 1997)

Ambos, Kai, 'Other Grounds for Excluding Criminal Responsibility' in Cassese, Antonio, Gaeta, Paula and Jones, John RWD (eds), *The Rome Statute of the International Criminal Court: A Commentary*, Vol 1 (Oxford: Oxford University Press, 2002) 1003–1048

Amnesty International, *Afghanistan: Cruel, inhuman or degrading treatment or punishment*, AI Index: ASA 11/015/1999 (London: Amnesty International, 1 November 1999)

—— *Broken bodies, shattered minds: Torture and ill-treatment of women*, AI Index: ACT 40/001/2001 (London: Amnesty International, 2001)

—— Cageprisoners, the Center for Constitutional Rights, the Center for Human Rights and Global Justice at NYU School of Law, Human Rights Watch and Reprieve, *Off the Record: U.S. Responsibility for Enforced Disappearances in the 'War on Terror'*, AI Index: AMR 51/093/2007 (7 June 2007)

—— *Crimes of hate, conspiracy of silence: Torture and ill-treatment based on sexual identity*, AI Index: ACT 40/016/2001 (London: Amnesty International, 2001)

—— *Death by Shaking: the Case of 'Abd al-Samad Harizat*, AI Index: MDE 15/23/95 (London: Amnesty International, October 1995)

—— 'Guantánamo Bay: a coercive regime' Amnesty International website, <http://web.amnesty.org>, accessed 12 August 2003

—— *Hidden scandal, secret shame: Torture and ill-treatment of children*, AI Index: ACT 40/38/00 (London: Amnesty International, 2000)

—— *Iran: Death Sentences of juvenile offenders and stoning sentences continue to be passed*, Press release (20 October 2005) <http://news.amnesty.org/index/ENGMDE130632005>, accessed 25 November 2005

—— *Iran: stonings should stop*, AI Index MDE 13/024/2001, 11 July 2001

—— *Israel and the Occupied Territories: The Military Justice System in the Occupied Territories; Detention, Interrogation and Trial Procedures* (London: Amnesty International, 1991)

—— *Israel, the Occupied Territories and the Palestinian Authority: Without distinction— attacks on civilians by Palestinian armed groups*, AI Index: MDE 02/002/2002 (London: Amnesty International, 2002)

—— *Racism and the administration of justice*, AI Index: ACT 40/020/2001 (London: Amnesty International, 2001)

—— *Report on Torture* (2nd edn, London: Duckworth, 1975)

—— *Sri Lanka: Extrajudicial Executions, 'Disappearances' and Torture, 1987 to 1990*, AI Index ASA 37/21/90 (London: Amnesty International, 1990)

—— *Torture in the Eighties*, AI Index: ACT 04/01/84 (London: Amnesty International, 1984)

—— *Under constant medical supervision: Torture, ill-treatment and the health professions in Israel and the Occupied Territories*, AI Index: MDE 15/037/1996 (London: Amnesty International, August 1996)

—— *United States of America: Law and executive disorder*, AI Index: AMR 51/135/2007 (London: Amnesty International, 17 August 2007)

—— *United States of America: Memorandum to the US Government on the rights of people in US custody in Afghanistan and Guantánamo Bay*, AI Index: AMR 51/053/2002 (London: Amnesty International, 15 April 2002)

—— *Urgent Action (on a 15-year-old Iranian girl sentenced to stoning)*, AI Index: MDE 13/006/2001 (London: Amnesty International, 18 January 2001)

—— *When the State kills . . . : The Death Penalty v. Human Rights*, AI Index: ACT 51/07/89 (London: Amnesty International, 1989)

Anderson, Kenneth, 'What to Do with Bin Laden and Al Qaeda Terrorists?: A Qualified Defense of Military Commissions and United States Policy on Detainees at Guantanamo Bay Naval Base' 25 *Harv J of L & Pub Policy* 591 (2002)

Annan, Kofi, 'No Letting Up on AIDS' *Washington Post* (29 November 2001)

Annas, George and Grodin, Michael (eds), *The Nazi Doctors and the Nuremberg Code: Human Rights in Human Experimentation* (Oxford: Oxford University Press, 1992)

Anscombe, Elizabeth, 'War and Murder' in Haber, Joram Graf (ed), *Absolutism and its Consequentialist Critics* (Lanham, Maryland: Rowan and Littlefield, 1994) 29–40

Anscombe, GEM, 'Modern Moral Philosophy' 33 *Philosophy* 1 (1958)

Argentine National Commission of the Disappeared, *Nunca Mas (Never Again)* (London: Faber and Faber, 1986)

Aristophanes, 'Frogs' (ca 405 BC, trans RH Webb) in Hadas, Moses (ed), *The Complete Plays of Aristophanes* (New York: Bantam Books, 1962) 366–415

Aristotle, *The Nichomachean Ethics*, trans David Ross, revised by JL Ackrill and JO Urmson (Oxford: Oxford University Press, 1998)

Arrigo, Jean Maria, 'A Utilitarian Argument Against Torture Interrogation of Terrorists' 10(3) *Science and Engineering Ethics* 543 (2004)

Ashworth, Andrew, *Principles of Criminal Law* (3rd edn, Oxford: Oxford University Press, 1999)

Associated Press, 'Military says Tamil rebel captured by army kills himself by taking cyanide' <http://news.aol.com/topnews/articles/_a/military-says-tamil-rebel-captured-by/n20070419042109990007>, 18 April 2007, accessed 20 April 2007

Austin, John, *The Province of Jurisprudence Determined* (1832) ed Wilfrid E Rumble (Cambridge: Cambridge University Press, 1995)

Aquinas, St Thomas (1225–1274), *Summa Theologica*, Second and Revised Edition, 1920. Literally translated by Fathers of the English Dominican Province, <http://www.newadvent.org/summa/>, accessed 21 October 2007

Bagaric, Mirko and Clarke, Julie, 'Not Enough Official Torture in the World? The Circumstances in which Torture is Morally justifiable' 39 *U of San Francisco L Rev* 581 (2005)

Baier, Kurt, 'Egoism' in Singer, Peter (ed), *A Companion to Ethics* (Oxford: Blackwell, 1999) 197–204

Bailey, James Wood, *Utilitarianism, Institutions and Justice* (New York: Oxford University Press, 1997)

Bailey, SH, Ching, Jane, Gunn, MJ and Ormerod, David, *Smith, Bailey and Gunn on the Modern English Legal System* (4th edn, London: Sweet & Maxwell, 2002)

Bantekas, Ilias and Nash, Susan, *International Criminal Law* (2nd edn, London: Cavendish Publishing, 2003)

Barak, Aharon, 'A Judge on Judging: the Role of a Supreme Court in a Democracy' 116 *Harv L Rev* 16 (2002)

Barcalow, Emmett, *Moral Philosophy: Theories and Ethics* (2nd edn, Belmont, Ca: Wadsworth Publishing Company, 1998)

Bash, Tami and Ginbar, Yuval, *The Death of Mustafa Barakat in the Interrogation Wing of the Tulkarm Prison* (Jerusalem: B'Tselem, September, 1992)

Basoglu, Metin, Jaranson, Mollica, James M, Richard and Kastrup, Marianne, 'Torture and Mental Health: A Research Overview' in Gerrity, Ellen, Keane, Terence M and Tuma, Farris (eds), *The Mental Health Consequences of Torture* (New York: Kluwer Academic/Plenum Publishers, 2001) 35–62

—— Livanou, Maria and Crnobarić, Cvetana, 'Torture vs Other Cruel, Inhuman, and Degrading Treatment: Is the Distinction Real or Apparent?' 64 *Arch Gen Psych* 277 (2007)

Bassiouni, M Cherif, *Crimes Against Humanity in International Criminal Law* (The Hague: Kluwer Law International, 1999)

BBC Website, 'Profile: Abd al-Hadi al-Iraqi' <http://news.bbc.co.uk/1/hi/world/middle_east/6601087.stm>, accessed 28 April 2007

Beauchamp, Tom L and Childress, James F, *Principles of Biomedical Ethics* (4th edn, New York: Oxford University Press, 1994)

Bedau, Hugo Adam (ed), *The Case against Death Penalty*, <http://www.soci.niu.edu/~critcrim/dp/dppapers/aclu.antidp>, accessed 25 October 2007

Beecher, Henry K, 'Ethics and Clinical Research' in Kuhse, Helga and Singer, Peter (eds), *Bioethics: An Anthology* (Oxford: Blackwell, 1999) 421–6

Benn, Stanley I, 'Private and Public Morality: Clean Living and Dirty Hands' in *idem* and Gaus, GF (eds), *Public and Private in Social Life* (London: Croom Helm, 1983) 155–181

Bennett, Jonathan, 'Whatever the Consequences' in Thomson, Judith Jarvis and Dworkin, Gerald (eds), *Ethics* (New York: Harper and Row, 1968) 211–236

Bentham, Jeremy, *An Introduction to the Principles of Morals and Legislation* (new edn, 1823) (Oxford: Clarendon, 1879)

—— Mss Box 74.b (27 May 1804), reprinted in Twining, WL and Twining, E, 'Bentham on Torture' 24(3) *Northern Ireland Legal Quarterly* 305 (1973) 347

—— 'Of Compulsion and herein of Torture, *Bentham Manuscripts, University College London* 46/56–62, reprinted by Twining, WL and Twining, E, 'Bentham on Torture' 24(3) *Northern Ireland Legal Quarterly* 305 (1973) 320–337

—— 'Of Torture' *Bentham Manuscripts, University College London* 46/63–70, reprinted in Twining, WL and Twining, E, 'Bentham on Torture' 24(3) *Northern Ireland Legal Quarterly* 305 (1973) 308–320

Benvenisti, Eyal, 'The Role of National Courts in Preventing Torture of Suspected Terrorists' 8 *EJIL* 596 (1997)

Beqer, Avihai, 'An Enlightened Demolition' [Hebrew] *Haaretz Weekly* (26 December 2002)

Bernsmann, Klaus, 'Private Self-Defence and Necessity in German Penal Law and in the Penal Law Proposal—Some Remarks' 30 *Israel L Rev* 171 (1996)

Bhagavad Gita, trans Huan Mascaró (London: Penguin Books, 1962)

Bible, The, eg *The Bible: Authorised King James Version with Apocryph* (Oxford: Oxford University Press, 1997)

Biletzki, Anat, 'The Judicial Rhetoric of Morality: Israel's High Court of Justice on the Legality of Torture' January 2001, Paper no 9, Occasional Papers of the School of Social Science, Princeton, NJ <http://www.sss.ias.edu/publications/papers/papernine.pdf>, accessed 21 October 2007

'Binalshibh to go to third country for questioning', CNN website (16 September 2002) <http://www.cnn.com>, accessed 10 July 2003

Blair, Tony, Speech at the Labour Party conference, 2 October 2001, 'Full text: Tony Blair's speech' *The Guardian* website <http://www.guardian.co.uk/>, accessed 12 November 2001

Blanchard, Lynn, 'Community Assessment and Perception: Preparation for HIV Vaccine Efficacy Trials' in King, Nancy MP, Henderson, Gail E and Stein, Jane (eds), *Beyond Regulations: Ethics in Human Subjects Research* (Chapel Hill, NC and London: University of North Carolina Press, 1999) 85–94

Borum, Randy, 'Approaching Truth: Behavioral Science Lessons on Educing Information from Human Sources' in Intelligence Science Board, *Educing Information Interrogation: Science and Art* (Washington, DC: National Defense Intelligence College, 2006) <http://www.fas.org/irp/dni/educing.pdf>, accessed 16 January 2007, 17–44

Bosley, Sarah, 'Aids vaccine for Africa to begin human trials' *The Guardian* (12 July 2000)

Bowden, Mark, 'The Dark Art of Interrogation' *The Atlantic Monthly* (October 2003)

Boyd, Kenneth M, Higgs, Roger and Pinching, Anthony J, 'An AIDS lexicon' 26(1) *J Med Ethics* 66 (2000)

Brandt, RB, 'Utilitarianism and the Rules of War' in Cohen, Marshall, Nagel, Thomas and Scanlon, Thomas (eds), *War and Moral Responsibility* (Princeton: Princeton University Press, 1974) 25–45

Bravin, Jess and Fields, Gary, 'How Do Interrogators Make Terrorists Talk' *Wall Street Journal*, 4 March 2003 <http://online.wsj.com>, accessed 6 March 2003

Brock, Dan W, 'Recent Work in Utilitarianism' 10 *Am Phil Quart* 241 (1973)

Browder, J Pat, 'Can Community Consultation Substitute for Informed Consent in Emergency Medicine Research? A Response' in King, Nancy MP, Henderson, Gail E and Stein, Jane (eds), *Beyond Regulations: Ethics in Human Subjects Research* (Chapel Hill and London: University of North Carolina Press, 1999) 204–212

Brower, Charles H II, 'The Lives of Animals, the Lives of Prisoners, and the Revelations of Abu Ghraib' 37 *Vanderbilt J of Transnat'l L* 1353 (2004)

Brown, David, 'U.N. Warns of African AIDS Toll' *Washington Post* (28 June 2000)

Brunder, Alan, 'A Theory of Necessity' 7(3) *Oxford J of Legal Studies* 339 (1987)

Buckler, Steve, *Dirty Hands: The Problem of Political Morality* (Aldershot, Hants: Avebury, 1993)

Budras, Corinna, 'German Policeman's Threat to Killer Merits Penalty, Court Told' *Bloomberg* (9 December 2004) <http://www.bloomberg.com/apps/news?pid=10000100&sid=agrRVfgoweRE&refer=germany>, accessed 10 December 2004

Burgers, J Herman and Danelius, Hans, *The United Nations Convention against Torture: A Handbook on the Convention Against Torture and Other Cruel, Inhuman or Degrading Treatment or Punishment* (Dordrecht: M Nijhoff, 1988)

Burt, Robert A, 'Judicial Supremacy, Judicial Impotence and the Rule of Law in Times of Crisis' unpublished manuscript, June 2000, <http://islandia.law.yale.edu/sela/eburt.pdf>, accessed 25 October 2007

Caplan, Arthur L (ed), *When Medicine Went Mad: Bioethics and the Holocaust* (Totowa, NJ: Humana Press, 1992)

Cargile, James, 'On Consequentialism' 29 *Analysis* 78 (1969)

Carrington, Frank, *Neither Cruel nor Unusual: The Case for Capital Punishment* (New Rochelle, NY: Arlington, 1978)

Cassese, Antonio, *International Criminal Law* (Oxford: Oxford University Press, 2003)

—— 'Prohibition of Torture and Inhuman or Degrading Treatment or Punishment' in Macdonald, R St J, Matscher, F and Petsold, H (eds), *The European System for the Protection of Human Rights* (Dordrecht: Martinus Nijhoff, 1993)

—— 'The Savage States: Torture in the 1980s' in *idem, Human Rights in a Changing World* (Cambridge: Polity Press, 1990)

Chapman, Steve, 'Should we use torture to stop terrorism?' *Chicago Tribune* (1 November 2001)

Chen, Joie, host, CNN Talkback Live: Torture: Should It Be an Option When Dealing With Terrorists? aired 7 November 2001 15:08 ET, CNN website, <www.cnn.com/transcripts>, accessed 12 September 2002

Chippaux, Jean-Philippe, 'Pharmaceutical colonialism in Africa' *Le Monde Diplomatique* (English Edition), August 2005

Christie, George C, 'The Defense of Necessity Considered from the Legal and Moral Points of View' 48 *Duke L J* 975 (1999)

'Clarification', *Haaretz* (12 November 2006)

Clark, Melissa L, 'Israel's High Court of Justice Ruling on the General Security Service Use of 'Moderate Physical Pressure': An End to the Sanctioned Use of Torture?' 11 *Indiana Int'l and Comp L Rev* 145 (2000)

Clarkson, CMV and Keating, HM (eds), *Criminal Law: Text and Materials* (5th edn, London: Sweet & Maxwell, 2003)

Clover, Jonathan (ed), *Utilitarianism and Its Critics* (New York and London: Macmillan, 1990)

Coady, CAJ, 'Politics and the Problem of Dirty Hands' in Singer, Peter (ed) *A Companion to Ethics* (Malden, Mass: Blackwell, 1993) 373–383

Cobain, Ian, 'Secrets of the London Cage' *The Guardian* (12 November 2005)

Cohen, Barak, 'Democracy and the Mis-Rule of Law: The Israeli Legal System's Failure to Prevent Torture in the Occupied Territories' 12 *Ind Int'l & Comp L Rev* 75 (2001)

Cohen, Richard, 'Using Torture to Fight Terrorism' *Washington Post* (6 March 2003)

Cohen, William and Danelski, David J, *Cohen and Danelski's Constitutional Law Civil Liberty and Individual Rights* (5th edn, Westbury, NY: Foundation Press, 2002)

Craig, Olga, ' "They will do what is needed to get the information—and fast" ' The *Daily Telegraph* (9 March 2003)

Crelinsten, Ronald D, and Schmid, Alex J, *The Politics of Pain: Torturers and Their Masters* (Boulder, Col: Westview Press, 1995)

Cummiskey, David, *Kantian Consequentialism* (New York and Oxford: Oxford University Press, 1996)

Dan-Cohen, Meir, 'Decision Rules and Conduct Rules: On Acoustic Separation in Criminal Law' in *idem, Harmful Thoughts: Essays on Law, Self, and Morality* (Princeton: Princeton University Press, 2000) 37–93

Davis, Nancy (Ann), 'Contemporary Deontology' in Singer, Peter (ed), *A Companion to Ethics* (Oxford: Blackwell, 1999) 205–218

'Defending an Open Society' with Nina Totenberg, Michael Horowitz, Nancy Gertner, Philip Heymann and John Shattuck, John F Kennedy Library and Foundation: Responding to Terrorism (14 November 2001) John F Kennedy Library and Museum website < http://www.jfklibrary.org/Education+and+Public+Programs/Kennedy+Library+Forums/default.htm?view=historical >, accessed 21 October 2007

Dershowitz, Alan M, 'Commentary' *Los Angeles Times*, 8 November 2001

—— 'Is It Necessary to Apply 'Physical Pressure' to Terrorists—and to Lie about it?' 23 *Israel L Rev* 192 (1989)

—— 'Israel: The Jew among Nations' in Kellermann, Alfred E *et al* (eds), *Israel among the Nations* (The Hague: Kluwer, 1998) 129–136

—— 'Tortured Reasoning' in Levinson, Sanford (ed), *Torture: A Collection* (Oxford: Oxford University Press, 2004) 257–280

—— *Why Terrorism Works: understanding the threat, responding to the challenge* (New Haven: Yale University Press, 2002)

De Wet, Erika, 'The Prohibition of Torture as an International Norm of jus cogens and Its Implications for National and Customary Law' 15(1) *EJIL* 97 (2004)

De Zulueta, Felicity, 'The Torturers' in Forest, Duncan (ed), *A Glimpse of Hell* (London: Cassell and Amnesty International, 1996) 87–103

Dine, Janet and Watt, Bob, 'The Transmission of Disease during Consensual Sexual Activity and the Concept of Associative Autonomy' [1998] 4 *Web JCLI*, <http://webjcli.ncl.ac.uk/1998/issue4/watt4.html>, accessed 12 October 2001

Djabali, Leila, 'For My Torturer, Lieutenant D...' trans Anita Barrows, in Cronyn, Hume, McKane, Richard and Watts, Stephen (eds), *Voices of Conscience: Poetry from Opposition* (North Shield, Northumberland: Iron Press 1995) 193

Djilas, Milovan, *Of Prisons and Ideas*, trans Michael Boro Petrovitch (San Diego, Cal: Harcourt Brace Jovanovich Publishers, 1986)

Donagan, Alan, *The Theory of Morality* (Chicago: University of Chicago Press, 1977)

Dostoevsky, Fyodor, *The Karamazov Brothers*, trans Ignat Avsey (Oxford: Oxford University Press, 1994)

Dotan, Yoav, 'General Petition and Judicial Policy in the High Court of Justice' [Hebrew] 20(1) *Iyunei Mishpat* 193 (1996)

Dubber, Markus Dirk, *German Criminal Law: A Critical Introduction* (draft) available on <http://wings.buffalo.edu/law/bclc/web/germanscience.doc>, accessed 6 November 2003

DuBois, Page, *Torture and Truth* (New York: Routledge, 1991)

Duffy, Helen, *The 'War on Terror' and the Framework of International Law* (Cambridge: Cambridge University Press, 2005)

Dupont, Lieven and Fijnaut, Cyrille, 'Belgium' in *International Encyclopaedia of Laws*, Vol 1: Criminal Law (Dventer: Kluwer, 1993)

Dworkin, Gerald (eds), *Ethics* (New York: Harper and Row, 1968) 211–236

Dworkin, Ronald, *Life's Dominion: An Argument about Abortion and Euthanasia* (London: HarperCollins, 1993)

—— 'Rights as Trumps' in Waldron, Jeremy (ed), *Theories of Rights* (Oxford: Oxford University Press, 1984) 153–167

—— *Taking Rights Seriously* (London: Duckworth, 1978)

Dwyer, Jim, Lipton, Eric, Flynn, Kevin, Glanz, James and Fessenden, Ford, 'Fighting to Live as the Towers Died' *New York Times* (26 May 2002)

Eban, Katherine, 'Rorschach and Awe' *Vanity Fiar website*, <http://www.vanityfair.com/politics/features/2007/07/torture200707?printable=true&currentPage=all>, 17 July 2007, accessed 18 July 2007

Elliott, Michael, 'The Next Wave' *Time Magazine* (17 June 2002)

'Ends, Means and Barbarity' *The Economist* (9 January 2003)

Enker, Aharon and Kanai, Ruth, 'Self-Defence and Necessity following Amendment no 37 to the Penal Law' [Hebrew] 3 *Plilim* 5 (1992)

Eser, Albin, 'Article 31: Grounds for Excluding Criminal Responsibility' in Triffterer, Otto (ed), *Commentary on the Rome Statute of the International Criminal Court, Observers' Notes, Article by Article* (Baden-Baden: Nomos, 1999) 537–554

Euripides, 'Iphigenia at Aulis' in *Euripides: 10 Plays*, trans Paul Roche (New York: Signet Classics, 1998) 215–276

Evans, Malcolm and Morgan, Rod, *Combating Torture in Europe* (Strasbourg: Council of Europe Publishing, 2001)

—— *Preventing Torture: A Study of the European Convention for the Prevention of Torture and Inhuman or Degrading Treatment or Punishment* (Oxford: Clarendon, 1998)

—— 'The European Convention for the Prevention of Torture: Operational Practice' 41 *ICLQ* 590 (1992)

—— 'The European Convention for the Prevention of Torture: 1992–1997' 46 *ICLQ* 663 (1997)

—— (eds), *Protecting Prisoners: The Standards of the European Committee for the Prevention of Torture in Context* (Oxford: Oxford University Press, 1999)

Finkelstein, Claire O, 'Duress: A Philosophical Account of the Defense in Law' 37 *Ariz L Rev* 251 (1995)

Finnis, John, *Aquinas: Moral, Political and Legal Theory* (Oxford: Oxford University Press, 1998)

Fisher, Louis, *Constitutional Structures: Separated Powers and Federalism*, vol 1 (New York: McGraw-Hill 1995)

Fishkin, James, 'Utilitarianism versus Human Rights' 1(2) *Social Philosophy and Policy* 103 (Spring 1984)

Fletcher, George P, *Basic Concepts of Criminal Law* (New York: Oxford University Press, 1998)

—— *Rethinking Criminal Law* (Boston: Little, Brown and Co, 1978)

Foot, Philippa, 'The Problem of Abortion and the Doctrine of Double Effect' in *idem, Virtues and Vices and Other Essays on Moral Philosophy* (Oxford: Basil Blackwell 1978) 19–32

—— 'Virtues and Vices' in *idem, Virtues and Vices and Other Essays on Moral Philosophy* (Oxford: Basil Blackwell 1978) 1–18

Fost, Norman, 'Waived Consent for Emergency Research' 24(2&3) *Am J Law & Medicine* 163 (1998)

Freedland, Jonathan, 'Use brains, not brawn' *The Guardian* (4 December 2002)

Frey, RG, 'Introduction: Utilitarianism and Persons' in *idem* (ed), *Utility and Rights* (Oxford: Basil Blackwell, 1985)

—— 'What a Good Man Can Bring Himself to Do' in Haber, Joram Graf (ed), *Absolutism and its Consequentialist Critics* (Lanham, Maryland: Rowan and Littlefield, 1994) 109–117

Fried, Charles, *Right and Wrong* (Cambridge, Mass: Harvard University Press, 1978)

Garrett, Stephen A, *Conscience and Power: An Examination of Dirty Hands and Political Leadership* (New York: St Martin's Press, 1996)

—— 'Political Leadership and "Dirty Hands": Winston Churchill and the City Bombing of Germany' in Nolan, Cathal J (ed), *Ethics and Statecraft: The Moral Dimension of International Affairs* (Westport, Conn: Greenwood Press, 1995) 75–91

Gerstein, Robert S, 'Do Terrorists Have Rights?' in Rapoport, David C and Alexander, Yonah (eds), *The Morality of Terrorism* (New York: Pergamon Press, 1982) 290–307

Gertz, Bill, 'Most prisoners in Iraq jails called "threat to security"' *Washington Times* (4 May 2004)

Gewirth, Alan, 'Are There Any Absolute Rights?' 31(122) *Phil Quart* 1 (January 1981)

Gez, Sassi and Ronen, Moshe, *Criminal law: A Guide to Criminal Law in Israel*, [Hebrew] (Tel-Aviv: Hemed, 2001)

Gil'ad, Amihud, 'An Absolute Moral Imperative: Torturing is Prohibited' [Hebrew] 4 *Mishpat u-Mimshal* 425 (1998)

Gillon, Raanan, 'Imposed separation of conjoined twins—moral hubris by the English courts?' 27(3–4) *J Med Ethics* (2001)

Gilon, Carmi, *Shin-Beth between the Schisms*, [Hebrew] Rami Tal, ed (Tel-Aviv: Miskal, 2000)

Ginbar, Yuval, *Back to a Routine of Torture: Torture and Ill-treatment of Palestinian Detainees during Arrest, Detention and Interrogation, September 2002–April 2003*, trans Jessica Bonn (Jerusalem: Public Committee Against Torture in Israel, 2003)

—— *Detention and Interrogation of Salem and Hanan 'Ali, Husband and Wife, Residents of Bani Na'im Village* (Jerusalem: B'Tselem, June 1995)

—— *Flawed Defense: Torture and Ill-Treatment in GSS interrogations Following the Supreme Court Ruling, 6 September 1999–6 September 2001*, trans Jessica Bonn (Jerusalem: Public Committee Against Torture in Israel, September 2001)

—— *Legitimizing Torture: The Israeli High Court of Justice Rulings in the Bilbeisi, Hamdan, and Mubarak Cases* (Jerusalem: B'Tselem, January 1997)

—— *Routine Torture* (Jerusalem: B'Tselem, May 1998)

—— *The Face and the Mirror: Israel's View of its Interrogation Techniques Examined* LLM Dissertation (University of Essex, 1996)

—— *The 'New Procedure' in GSS Interrogation: The Case of 'Abd a-Nasser 'Ubeid* (Jerusalem: B'Tselem, November 1993)

—— and Stein, Yael, *Torture during Interrogations: Testimony of Palestinian Detainees, Testimony of Interrogators* (Jerusalem: B'Tselem, November 1994)

Giv'on, 'Oded, 'The Use of Violence in GSS Interrogations or the Element of Immediacy in the "Necessity" Defence' [Hebrew] 10 *Mishpat ve-Tzava* 93 (1989–90)

Glover, Jonathan, *Humanity: a moral history of the twentieth century* (London: Pimlico, 2001)

Golan, Daphna and Cohen, Stanley, *The Interrogation of Palestinians during the Intifada: Ill-Treatment, 'Moderate Physical Pressure' or Torture?* (Jerusalem: B'Tselem, March 1991)

Goodspeed, Peter, 'Leader of Tamil Tigers known for ruthless warfare: Rebel group has fight-to-the-death determination' *The Toronto Star* (21 August 1994) reproduced on <http://www.tamiltigers.net/tamilcanadian/canada9405.html>, accessed 24 February 2003

Gorali, Moshe, 'What is the Punishment for Someone who Prepared a Sandwich for the Terrorist?' [Hebrew] *Haaretz* (1 September 2002)

Gordon, Neve and Marton, Ruchama (eds), *Torture: Human Rights, Medical Ethics and the Case of Israel* (London: Zed Books, 1995)

Górecki, Jan, *Capital Punishment: Criminal Law and Social Evolution* (New York: Columbia University Press, 1983)

Gormley, Ken, 'One Hundred Years of Privacy' 1992 *Wis L Rev* 1335 (1992)

Grady, Christine, *The Search for an AIDS Vaccine: Ethical Issues in the Development and Testing of a Preventive HIV Vaccine* (Bloomington and Indianapolis: Indiana University Press, 1995)

Greaty, Conor (ed) *Terrorism* (Aldershot, Hants: Dartmouth, 1996)

Greenawalt, Kent, 'The Perplexing Borders of Justification and Excuse' 84 *Columbia L Rev* 1897 (1984)

Greenberg, Karen J and Dratel, Joshua L, *The Torture Papers: The road to Abu Ghraib* (Cambridge: CUP, 2005)

Greenwood, Christopher, 'International Law and the "War against Terrorism"' 78(2) *International Affairs* 301 (2002)

Griffin, James, 'Toward a Substantive Theory of Rights' in Haber, Joram Graf (ed), *Absolutism and its Consequentialist Critics* (Lanham, Maryland: Rowan and Littlefield, 1994) 137–160

Grisez, Germain and Shaw, Russell, 'Persons, Means and Ends' in Haber, Joram Graf (ed), *Absolutism and its Consequentialist Critics* (Lanham, Maryland: Rowan and Littlefield, 1994) 21–28

Grondona, St Clare, Letter to *The Times* (27 November 1971)

Gross, Michael L, 'Regulating Torture in a Democracy: Death and Indignity in Israel' 36(3) *Polity* 367 (2004)

Gross, Oren, 'Are Torture Warrants Warranted? Pragmatic absolutism and official disobedience' 88 *Minn L Rev* 1481 (2004)

—— 'Chaos and Rules: Should Responses to Violent Crises Always be Constitutional?' 112 *Yale L J* 1011 (2003)

—— 'The Prohibition on Torture and the Limits of the Law' in Levinson, Sanford (ed), *Torture: A Collection* (Oxford: Oxford University Press, 2004) 229–253

—— and Aoláin, Fionnuala Ní, *Law in Times of Crisis: Emergency Powers in Theory and Practice* (Cambridge: Cambridge University Press, 2006)

Grosso, Catherine M, 'International Law in the Domestic Arena: The Case of Torture in Israel' 86 *Iowa L Rev* 305 (2000)

Guggenheim, Ken AP, 'Rumsfeld Backs Iraq Interrogation Methods' (12 May 2004) <http://news.findlaw.com/ap_stories/a/w/1152/5–12-2004/20040512100009_36.html>, accessed 13 May 2004

Gur-Arye, Miriam, 'Can the War against Terror Justify the Use of Force in Interrogations? Reflections in Light of the Israeli Experience' in Levinson, Sanford (ed) *Torture: A Collection* (Oxford: Oxford University Press, 2004) 183–198

—— 'Legitimating Official Brutality: Can the War against Terror Justify Torture?' *Center for the Study of Law and Society Faculty Working Papers* (University of California, Berkeley), Year 2003, Paper 11, <http://repositories.cdlib.org/cgi/viewcontent.cgi?article=1010&context=csls>, accessed 13 August 2003

Haber, Joram Graf, 'Introduction' in *idem* (ed), *Absolutism and its Consequentialist Critics* (Lanham, Maryland: Rowan and Littlefield 1994) 1–13

Haines, Herbert H, *Against Capital Punishment: The Anti-Death Penalty Movement in America, 1972–1994* (New York: Oxford University Press, 1996)

Hale, Steven, 'Resources on Nonconsensual Human Experimentation' <http://www.gpc.edu/~shale/humanities/composition/assignments/experiment.html>, accessed 25 October 2007

Halfi, Avraham, 'Because maybe you' in *idem*, *New and Old* [Hebrew] (Tel-Aviv: 'Eqed, 1977) 83

Hampshire, Stuart, *Innocence and Experience* (Cambridge, Mass: Harvard University Press, 1989)

—— 'Public and Private Morality' in *idem* (ed) *Public and Private Morality* (Cambridge: Cambridge University Press, 1978) 23–53

Hampson Françoise, 'Torture' in Clarke, Paul Barry and Linzey, Andrew (eds), *Dictionary of Ethics, Theology and Society* (London and New York: Routledge, 1996) 829–831

Han, Tan Cheng, 'The General Exception of Necessity under the Singapore Penal Code' 32 *Malaysia L Rev* 271 (1990)

Hansen, Suzy, 'Why terrorism works' <http://www.salon.com/books/int/2002/09/12/dershowitz/index.html> 12 September 2002, accessed 22 November 2002

Hare, RM, *Moral Thinking: Its Levels, Method, and Point* (Oxford: Clarendon, 1981)
—— 'Rules of War and Moral Reasoning' in Cohen, Marshall, Nagel, Thomas, and Scanlon, Thomas (eds), *War and Moral Responsibility* (Princeton: Princeton University Press, 1974) 46–61
—— *Sorting Out Ethics* (Oxford: Clarendon Press, 1997)
Harel, Amos, 'GSS Has Used "Exceptional Interrogation Means" 90 Times Since 1999 HCJ Ruling' *Haaretz* (25 July 2002)
Harris, DJ, O'Boyle, M and Warbick, C, *The Law of the European Convention of Human Rights* (London: Butterworth, 1995)
Harris, Paul and Wazir, Burhan, 'Briton tells of ordeal in Bush's torture jail' *The Observer* (29 December 2002) <http://observer.guardian.co.uk>, accessed 30 December 2002
Harris, Sheldon, *Factories of Death: Japanese Biological Warfare 1932–45 and the American Cover-up* (New York: Routledge, 1994)
Harrison, Jonathan, 'Utilitarianism, Universalisation, and Our Duty to be Just' in Thomson, Judith Jarvis and Dworkin, Gerald (eds), *Ethics* (New York: Harper and Row, 1968) 76–103
Hart, HLA, 'Positivism and the Separation of Law and Morals' in RM Dworkin (ed) *The Philosophy of Law* (Oxford: Oxford University Press, 1977) 17–37
Hay, Peter, *Ordinary Heroes: The Life and Death of Chana Szenesh, Israel's National Heroine* (New York: Paragon House, 1989)
Herrmann, Johachim, 'The Federal Republic of Germany' in Cole, George F, Frankowski, Stanislav J and Gertz, Marc G (eds), *Major Criminal Justice Systems: A Comparative Study* (Newbury Park: Sage Publications, 1987)
Hill, Thomas E Jr, 'Moral Purity and the Lesser Evil' 66 *The Monist* 213 (1983)
Himma, KE, 'Assessing the Prohibition Against Torture' in Lee, SP (ed), *Intervention, Terrorism, and Torture: Contemporary Challenges to Just War Theory* (Dordrecht: Springer, 2007) 235–248,
Hobbes, Thomas, *The Leviathan* (1651) ed JCA Gaskin (New York: Oxford University Press, 1996)
Hodgkinson, Peter and Rutherford, Andrew (eds), *Capital Punishment: Global Issues and Prospects* (Winchester: Waterside Press, 1996)
Hoffman, Bruce, 'A nasty business' 289(1) *The Atlantic Monthly* (January 2002) 49–52
Hoffstater, Noam *"Ticking Bombs": Testimonies of Torture Victims in Israel*, trans Jessica Bonn (Jerusalem: Public Committee Against Torture in Israel, 2007) <http://www.stoptorture.org.il//eng/images/uploaded/publications/140.pdf>, accessed 23 June 2007
Horne, Alistair, *A Savage War of Peace: Algeria 1954–1962* (London: Papermac, 1987)
' "Hot intelligence warnings" of terrorist attacks' <http://images.maariv.co.il/cache/ART433023.htm>, posted, accessed 11 February 2003
Human Rights Watch, *Torture and Ill-Treatment: Israel's Interrogation of Palestinians from the Occupied Territories* (New York: Human Rights Watch, 1994)
—— *World Report 2003* (New York: Human Rights Watch, 2003)
—— and the American Civil Liberties Union, *Witness to Abuse: Human Rights Abuses under the Material Witness Law since September 11* (New York: HRW and ACLU, June 2005)
Hume, David, *A Treatise of Human Nature* (1739–1740) (2nd edn, Oxford: Clarendon, 1978)

Hunke, Heinz and Ellis, Justine, *Torture—a Cancer in Our Society* (London: the Catholic Institute for International Relations and the British Council of Churches, 1978)

Ibsen, Henrik, *A Doll's House*, trans William Archer (Studio City, Ca: Players Press, 1993)

Ignatieff, Michael, *The Lesser Evil: Political Ethics in an Age of Terror* (Edinburgh: Edinburgh University Press, 2005)

Imseis, Ardi, ' "Moderate" Torture On Trial: Critical Reflections on the Israeli Supreme Court Judgment Concerning the Legality of General Security Service Interrogation Methods' 19 *Berk J Int'l Law* 328 (2001)

Inbar, Eitan, *Constitutional Law as Reflected in Judicial Rulings* [Hebrew] (Tel-Aviv: Karmel, 2001)

Innes, Brian, *A History of Torture* (New York: St Martin's Press, 1998)

International Committee of the Red Cross, (Jean-Marie Henckaerts and Louise Doswald-Beck, eds), *Customary International Humanitarian Law* (Cambridge: Cambridge University Press, 2005)

'Is Torture Ever Justified?' *The Economist* (9 January 2003)

Isenberg, Arnold, 'Deontology and the Ethics of Lying' in Thomson, Judith Jarvis and Dworkin, Gerald (eds), *Ethics* (New York: Harper and Row, 1968) 163–185

Jacoby, Jeff, 'How Not to Win the War' *The Boston Globe* (26 January 2003) H11

Jehl, Douglas and Johnston, David, 'Within C.I.A., Growing Worry of Prosecution for Conduct' *New York Times* (27 February 2005)

Jempson, Mike, 'Torture Worldwide' in Forest, Duncan (ed), *A Glimpse of Hell* (London: Cassell and Amnesty International, 1996) 46–86

Jessberger, Florian, 'Bad Torture—Good Torture? What International Criminal Lawyers May Learn from the Recent Trial of Police Officers in Germany' 3(4) *J Int'l Crim Justice* 1059 (2005)

Johnson, Steve, 'Unravelling the psyche of al-Qaida: Experts say painful torture is wrong method for questioning Mohammed' MSNBC news website, <http://www.msnbc.com/news/881132.asp>, 5 March 2003, accessed 21 May 2003

Jones, James H, *Bad Blood: The Tuskegee Syphilis Experiment* (New York: Free Press, 1993)

Kagan, Shelly, *Normative Ethics* (Boulder, Colorado: Westview, 1998)

—— and Kahana, Tsvi, 'Israel and the Recognition of Torture: Domestic and International Aspects' in Scott, Carig (ed), *Torture as Tort: Comparative Perspectives on the Development of Transnational Human Rights Litigation* (Oxford: Hart Publishing, 2001) 631–659

Kant, Immanuel, *Critique of Practical Reason*, trans Lewis White Beck (3rd edn, New York: Macmillan 1993)

—— 'Ethical Duties towards Others: Truthfulness' in *idem*, *Lectures on Ethics*, trans Louis Infield (Indianapolis, Indiana: Hackett Publishing, 1980) 224–235

—— 'On the Common Saying: "This May be True in Theory, but it does not Apply in Practice" ' in *idem*, *Political Writings*, trans HB Nisbet, ed Hans Reiss (2nd edn, Cambridge, Cambridge University Press, 1991)

—— 'On the Supposed Right to Lie from Altruistic Motives' in *idem*, *Critique of Practical Reason and Other Writings in Moral Philosophy*, trans and ed Lewis White Beck (Chicago: University of Chicago Press, 1967) 346–350

—— 'Perpetual Peace: A Philosophical Sketch' [1795] in *idem*, *Political Writings*, trans HB Nisbet, ed Hans Reiss (2nd edn, Cambridge: Cambridge University Press, 1991) 93–130

—— *Political Writings*, trans HB Nisbet, ed Hans Reiss (2nd edn, Cambridge: Cambridge University Press, 1991)

—— *The Metaphysics of Morals*, trans M Gregor (Cambridge: Cambridge University Press, 1991)

—— *The Moral Law: Groundwork for the Metaphysics of Morals*, 2nd edn, trans HJ Paton (London: Routledge, 1991)

Kaspit, Ben, 'A Fence Now' [Hebrew] *Maariv* (17 December 2003)

Kierkegaard, Søren, *Purity of Heart is to Will One Thing* (1847) trans Douglas Steere (New York: Harper & Row, 1958)

Kedmi, Yaacov, *On Criminal Procedure* (Part 1) [Hebrew] (Tel-Aviv: Dyunon, 1997)

Kerns, Thomas, *Ethical Issues in HIV Vaccine Trials* (London: Macmillan, 1997); also available in online edition <http://home.myuw.net/tkerns/MyUWsite/evtsite/evt-toc.html>, accessed 4 December 2001

Kim, Young Sok, *The International Criminal Court (A Commentary of the Rome Statute)* (Leeds: Wisdom House Publications, 2003)

Kleinman, Steven M, 'Barriers to Success: Critical Challenges in Developing a New Educing Information Paradigm' in Intelligence Science Board, *Educing Information Interrogation: Science and Art* (Washington, DC: National Defense Intelligence College, 2006) <http://www.fas.org/irp/dni/educing.pdf>, accessed 16 January 2007, 235–266

Knoops, Geert-Jan GJ, *Defenses in Contemporary International Law* (Ardsley, NY: Transnational Publishers, 2001)

Koh, Hongju, 'Can the President Be Torturer in Chief?' 81 *Indiana L J* 1145 (2006)

Kois, Lisa M, 'Dance, Sister, Dance!' in Dunér, Bertil (ed), *An End to Torture: Strategies for its Eradication* (London: Zed Books, 1998) 85–108

Kommers, Donald P and Finn, John E, *American Constitutional Law: Essays, Cases and Comparative Notes* (Belmont, CA: West/Wadsworth, 1998)

Krauthammer, Charles, 'It's time to be honest about doing terrible things' *The Weekly Standard* (5 December 2006)

Kraybill, Ernest N and Bauer, B Susan, 'Can Community Consultation Substitute for Informed Consent in Emergency Medicine Research?' in King, Nancy MP, Henderson, Gail E and Stein, Jane (eds), *Beyond Regulations: Ethics in Human Subjects Research* (Chapel Hill and London: University of North Carolina Press, 1999) 191–198

Kreimer, Seth F, 'Too Close to the Rack and the Screw: Constitutional constraints on torture' 6 *Univ of Penn J of Const L* 278 (2003)

Kremnitzer, Mordechai, 'The Landau Commission Report—Was the Security Service Subordinated to the Law, or the Law to the "Needs" of the Security Service?' 23 *Israel L Rev* 216 (1989)

—— and Segev, Re'em, 'The Application of Force in the Course of GSS Interrogations—A Lesser Evil?' [Hebrew] 4 *Mishpat u-Mimshal* 667 (1998)

—— and Segev, Re'em, 'The Legality of Interrogational Torture: A Question of Proper Authorization or a Substantive Moral Issue?' 34 *Israel L Rev* 509 (2000)

Kuhn, Thomas S, *The Structure of Scientific Revolutions* (rev 3rd edn, Chicago, University of Chicago Press, 1996)

LaCroix, Wilfred Laurence, *War and International Ethics: Tradition and Today* (Lahmand, MD: University Press of America, 1988)

LaFave, Wayne R, *Criminal Law* (3rd edn, St Paul, Minn: West Group, 2000)

—— *Search and Seizure: A Treatise on the Forth Amendment* (3rd edn, St Paul, Minn: West Publishing Company, 1995)

Langsted, Lars Bo and Grade, Vagn, *Criminal Law in Denmark* (The Hague: Kluwer Law International, 1998)

Laurence, John, *A History of Capital Punishment: with Special Reference to Capital Punishment in Great Britain* (London: Sampson Low, Marston & Co, no date)

Lawyers Committee for Human Rights, *Imbalance of Powers: How Changes to U.S. Law & Policy Since 9/11 Erode Human Rights and Civil Liberties* (New York: LCHR, 2003)

Lefkovits, Etgar, 'Suicide bomber kills nine in Jerusalem' *Jerusalem Post* (3 March 2002)

'Legal Torture?' 60 Minutes, CBS News, 20 September 2002; for the full transcript see <http://www.midnightspecial.net/FBIttorturearticle.htm>, accessed 3 July 2003

Lein, Yehezkel, *Absolute Prohibition: The Torture and Ill-treatment of Palestinian Detainees*, trans Shaul Vardi and Zvi Shulman (Jerusalem: B'Tselem and Hamoked, May 2007), <http://www.btselem.org/Download/200705_Utterly_Forbidden_eng.doc>, accessed 23 June 2007

Lemov, Rebecca, 'The Birth of Soft Torture: CIA interrogation techniques—a history' *Slate* (16 November 2005) <http://www.slate.com/id/2130301/>, accessed 18 November 2005

Levin, Michael, 'The Case for Torture' *Newsweek* (17 June 1982) 13

—— 'Torture and Other Extreme Measures Taken for the General Good: Further Reflections on a Philosophical Problem' in Suedfeld, Peter (ed), *Psychology and Torture* (New York: Hemisphere Publishing, 1990) 89–98

Levinson, Stanford, '"Precommitment" and "Post-Commitment": The Ban on Torture in the Wake of September 11' 81 *Texas L Rev* 2013 (2003)

—— 'Brutal Logic' *Village Voice* 11 May 2004

Lichtblau, Eric with Liptak, Adam, 'Questioning to be Legal, Humane and Aggressive, The White House Says' *New York Times* (4 March 2003)

Lifton, Robert Jay, *The Nazi Doctors: Medical Killing and the Psychology of Genocide* (London: Macmillan, 1986)

Lippman, Mathew, 'Conundrums of Armed Conflict: Criminal Defenses to Violations of the Humanitarian Law of War' 15 *Dickinson J Int'l L* 1 (1996)

—— 'The Nazi Doctors Trial and the International Prohibition on Medical Involvement in Torture' 15 *Loyola of Los Angeles Int'l & Comp L J* 395 (1993)

Lis, Yonatan, Alon, Gid'on and Reguler, Arnon, '"Very high" alert in Jerusalem due to intelligence warnings' *Haaretz* website, <http://www.haaretz.co.il/hasite/spages/428114.html>, accessed 16 May 2004

Lithwick, Dahlia, 'Tortured Justice' *MSN Slate Magazine*, 24 October 2001, <http://www.slate.com/id/2057099/>, accessed 22 October 2007

Locke, John, *Two Treatises of Government* (1690) (Cambridge: Cambridge University Press, 1988)

Luban, David, 'Eight Fallacies About Liberty and Security' in Richard Ashby Wilson (ed), *Human Rights in the 'War on Terror'* (Cambridge: Cambridge University Press, 2005) 242–257

—— 'Liberalism, Torture, and the Ticking Bomb' 91 *Virginia L Rev* 1425 (2005)

Loue, Sana, *Legal and Ethical Aspects of HIV-Related Research* (New York and London: Plenum Press, 1995)

Lueck, Thomas J with Kocieniewski, David, 'Youths' Arrest Said to Foil Killing Spree' *New York Times* website, 7 July 2003 <http://www.nytimes.com>, accessed 7 July 2003

Lugosi, Charles I, 'Playing God: Mary must die so Jodie may live longer' 17 *Issues in Law and Medicine* 123 (2001)

Lukes, Steven, 'Liberal Democratic Torture' 36 *British Journal of Political Science* 1 (2005)
—— *Marxism and Morality* (Oxford: Clarendon Press, 1985)

Maass, Peter, 'If a Terror Suspect Won't Talk, Should He Be Made To?' *New York Times Week in Review* (9 March 2002)

Machiavelli, Niccoló, *The Prince* (1532) trans P Bondanella (Oxford: Oxford University Press, 1984)

MacIntyre, Alasdair, *After Virtue* (2nd edn, Notre Dame: University of Notre Dame Press, 1984)

Mackie, JL, *Ethics: Inventing Right and Wrong* (London, Penguin Books, 1990)

'Man shot wife to end their misery' *Colchester and North Essex Evening Gazette*, (20 September 2000)

Mangakis, Georgios-Alexandros, *Letter to Europeans* (1973) Quoted in Twining, WL and Twining E, 'Bentham on Torture' 24(3) *Northern Ireland Legal Quarterly* 305 (1973) 355

Mann, Kenneth, 'Criminal Procedure' In Shapira, Amos and DeWitt-Arar, Keren C (eds), *Introduction to the Law of Israel* (The Hague: Klower Law International 1995) 267–294

Maran, Rita, *Torture: the Role of Ideology in the French-Algerian War* (New York: Praeger, 1989)

'Martyrdom-Seeking Operations between Israeli Conspiracies and Palestinian Successes' [Arabic] 'Izz al-Din al-Qassam Brigades website <http://www.qassam.net/tagrer/taqreer2002/05_2002/taqree25_05_02.htm>, accessed 31 May 2002

Massu, Jacques, *La Vraie Bataille d'Alger* (Paris: Plon, 1971)
—— *Le Torrent et la Digue* (Paris: Plon, 1972)

Mattox, Major John Mark, US Army, 'The Moral Status of Military Deception' *Joint Services Conference on Professional Ethics*, Springfield, Virginia, 27–28 January 2000 <http://www.usafa.af.mil/jscope/JSCOPE00/Mattox00.html#_ednref1>, accessed 12 May 2001

McCloskey, HJ, 'An Examination of Restricted Utilitarianism' 66 *Philosophical Review* 466 (1957)
—— 'Respect for Human Moral Rights versus Maximizing Good' in Frey, RG (ed), *Utility and Rights* (Oxford: Basil Blackwell, 1985) 121–136

McManners, Hugh, 'The truth about torture and interrogation' *The Independent* (12 May 2004)

Merkner, Kristina, 'Murderer testifies against Frankfurt police' <http://www.faz.net/s/Rub9E75B460C0744F8695B3E0BE5A30A620/Doc~E6964C3B4F0D74F80B232FDBA4CE91624~ATpl~Ecommon~Scontent.html#top>, 26 November 2004, accessed 13 December 2004

Meron, Theodor, *Human Rights and Humanitarian Norms as Customary Law* (Oxford: Clarendon 1991)

'Midweek' BBC Radio 4 (5 March 2003)

Mill, John Stuart, *Utilitarianism* (1863) in *Utilitarianism, Liberty, Representative Government*, ed HB Acton (London: JM Dent & Sons, 1972) 1–61

Millett, Kate, *The Politics of Cruelty: An essay on the literature of political* imprisonment (London: Penguin Books, 1995)

Minow, Martha, 'What Is the Greatest Evil?' 118 *Harv L Rev* 2134 (2005)

Moore, George Edward, *Principia Ethica* (Cambridge: Cambridge University Press 1960)

Moore, Michael S, 'Torture and the Balance of Evils' 23 *Israel L Rev* 280 (1989)

—— 'Torture and the Balance of Evils' in *idem, Placing Blame: A General Theory of the Criminal Law* (Oxford: Clarendon Press, 1997) 669–736

Morgan, Rod, 'The utilitarian justification of torture: Denial, desert and disinformation' 2(2) *Punishment and Society* 181 (1999) 184–6

Mulcahy, Leigh-Ann, *Human Rights and Civil Practice* (London: Sweet & Maxwell, 2001)

Munro, Vanessa E, 'Square Pegs in Round Holes: The Dilemma of Conjoined Twins and Individual Rights' 10(4) *Social and Legal Studies* 459 (2001)

Murphy, Peter (ed-in-chief), *Blackstone's Criminal Practice: 2003* (Oxford: Oxford University Press, 2003)

Nagel, Thomas, *Mortal Questions* (Cambridge: Cambridge University Press, 1985)

—— 'Ruthlessness in Public Life' in Hampshire, Stuart (ed), *Public and Private Morality* (Cambridge: Cambridge University Press, 1978) 75–91

—— 'World Poverty' in Peter Singer (ed), *A Companion to Ethics* (Oxford: Blackwell, 1999) 273–283

Nagan, Winston P and Atkins, Lucie, 'The International Law of Torture: From Universal Proscription to Effective Application and Enforcement' 14 *Harv Hum Rts J* 87 (2001)

Navon, Amit, 'Stories from the Interrogation Rooms' [Hebrew] *Maariv Weekend Supplement* (5 July 2002)

Nielsen, Kai, 'Against Moral Conservatism' in Haber, Joram Graf (ed), *Absolutism and its Consequentialist Critics* (Lanham, Maryland: Rowan and Littlefield, 1994) 161–173

Noble Qur'an, The, eg The Noble Qur'an [Arabic] (Beirut: Dar al- 'Arabiyyah, nd)

Norton-Taylor, Richard, 'MI5: 30 terror plots being planned in UK' *The Guardian* (10 November 2006)

Nourse, VF, 'Reconceptualizing Criminal Law Defenses' 151(5) *U of Penn L Rev* 1691 (2003)

Nowak, Manfred, 'Challenges to the Absolute Nature of the Prohibition on Torture and Ill-treatment' 23(4) *Netherlands Quarterly of Human Rights* 674 (2005)

—— 'What Practices Constitute Torture?: US and UN Standards' 28(4) *Human Rights Quarterly* 809 (2006)

Nozick, Robert, *Anarchy, State and Utopia* (Oxford: Blackwell, 1974)

Office of the United Nations High Commissioner for Human Rights, *Human Rights: A Compilation of International Instruments*, Vol 1 (First Part) (New York: UN, 2002)

—— *Human Rights: A Compilation of International Instruments*, Vol 1 (Second Part) (New York: UN, 2002)

'Opinion: Is torture ever justified?' *The Economist* (9 January 2003)

Oraá, Jaime, *Human Rights in States of Emergency in International Law* (Oxford: Clarendon, 1992)

Orecklin, Michele, 'Why They Crack' *Time Magazine* (24 June 2003)

'ORSF' posting at the *New York Daily News Yankees Webforum*, <http://www.webforums.com/forums/f-read/msa110.11.html> on Saturday, 15 September 2001 at 14:24; accessed 20 September 2001

Pacheco, Allegra (ed and trans), *The Case Against Torture in Israel: A Compilation of Petitions, Briefs and Other Documents Submitted to the Israeli High Court of Justice* (Jerusalem: The Public Committee Against Torture in Israel, 1999)

—— *Torture by the Israeli Security Services: The Case of Abdel Rahman Ahmar* (Jerusalem: The Public Committee Against Torture in Israel, 1996)

'Pakistan Illegally hands over 440 to US' <http://www.khilafah.com/home/category.php?DocumentID=6445&TagID=6>, 10 March 2003, citing ANI (Asian News International), accessed 30 July 2003

Parra, Alan M, 'U.S. Interrogation of Al Qaeda and Taliban Suspects: Is it Torture?' *International Organizations Bulletin* 9 (Spring 2003)

Parry, John T, 'Judicial Restraints on Illegal State Violence: Israel and the United States' 35 *Vand J Transnat'l L* 73 (2002)

—— 'What is Torture, Are We Doing It, and What if We Are?' 64 *University of Pittsburgh L Rev* 237 (2003)

—— and White, Welsh S, 'Interrogating Suspected Terrorists: Should Torture Be An Option?' 63 *University of Pittsburgh L Rev* 743 (2002)

Paskins, Barrie, 'What's Wrong with Torture?' 2 *Brit J Int'l Studies* 138 (1976)

Passow, Judah, 'Warlord of the Jihad' *The Sunday Times Magazine* (26 January 2003) 25–29

Pellet, Allain, 'Applicable Law' in Cassese, Antonio, Gaeta, Paula and Jones, John RWD (eds), *The Rome Statute of the International Criminal Court: A Commentary*, Vol II (Oxford: Oxford University Press, 2002), Vol II, 1051–1084

Pence, Greg, 'Virtue Theory' in Peter Singer (ed), *A Companion to Ethics* (Oxford: Blackwell, 1999) 249–258

Perry, Yaacov, *Strike First* [Hebrew] (Tel Aviv: Keshet, 1999)

Peters, Edward, *Torture*, expanded edition (Pennsylvania: University of Pennsylvania Press, 1996)

Pettit, Philip, 'Consequentialism' in Singer, Peter (ed), *A Companion to Ethics* (Oxford: Blackwell, 1999) 230–240

—— 'The Consequentialist Perspective' in *idem*, Baron, Marcia W and Slote, Michael, *Three Methods of Ethics* (Malden, Mass: Blackwell, 1997) 92–174

—— Baron, Marcia W and Slote, Michael, *Three Methods of Ethics* (Malden, Mass: Blackwell, 1997)

Physicians for Human Rights, *Break them down: systematic use of psychological torture by US forces* (Cambridge, Mass: Physicians for Human Rights, 2005)

Physicians for Human Rights and Human Rights First, *Leave No Marks: Enhanced Interrogation Techniques and the Risk of Criminality*, August 2007, <http://physiciansforhumanrights.org/library/documents/reports/leave-no-marks.pdf>, accessed 14 August 2007

Pojman, Louis P and Reiman, Jeffrey, *The Death Penalty: For and Against* (Lanham, Maryland: Rowman & Littlefield, 1998)

Pollack, Andrew and Broad, William J, 'Bioterrorism: Anti-Terror Drugs Get Test Shortcut' *New York Times* (31 May 2002)

Posner, Eric A and Vermeule, Adrian, 'Should Coercive Interrogation Be Legal?' *U of Chicago Public Law Working Paper No 84*, March 2005

Posner, Richard A, 'The Best Offense' *The New Republic* (2 September 2002)

—— 'Torture, Terrorism and Interrogation' in Levinson, Sanford (ed), *Torture: A Collection* (Oxford: Oxford University Press, 2004) 291–298

Préfontaine, Daniel C, 'Implementing International Standards in Search and Seizure: Striking the Balance between Enforcing the Law and Respecting the Rights of the Individual' paper presented at the Sino Canadian International Conference on the Ratification and Implementation of Human Rights: Beijing, China, October 2001, <http://www.icclr.law.ubc.ca/Publications/Reports/International_Standards.pdf>, accessed 11 March 2003

Press, Eyal, 'In Torture We Trust?' *The Nation* (31 November 2003)

Priest, Dana, 'CIA Puts Harsh Tactics On Hold: Memo on Methods Of Interrogation Had Wide Review' *Washington Post* (27 June 2004) <http://www.washingtonpost.com/wp-dyn/articles/A8534–2004Jun26.html>, accessed 21 October 2007

—— 'Memo Lets CIA Take Detainees Out of Iraq. Practice Is Called Serious Breach of Geneva Conventions' *Washington Post* (24 October 2004) <http://www.washingtonpost.com/wp-dyn/articles/A57363–2004Oct23.html>, accessed 21 October 2007

—— and Gellman, Barton, 'U.S. Decries Abuse but Defends Interrogations: "Stress and Duress" Tactics Used on Terrorism Suspects Held in Secret Overseas Facilities', *Washington Post,* 26 December 2002 <http://www.washingtonpost.com/ac2/wp-dyn/A37943–2002Dec25?language=printer>, accessed 21 October 2007

Proceedings of a seminar on Israel and international human rights law: the issue of torture, 9 June 1995 (Jerusalem: Center for Human Rights, the Hebrew University, 1995)

Proctor, Robert, *Racial Hygiene: Medicine under the Nazis* (Cambridge, Mass: Harvard University Press, 1989)

Public Committee Against Torture in Israel and IMUT—Mental Health Workers for the Advancement of Peace, *Dilemmas of Professional Ethics as a Result of the Involvement of Doctors and Psychologists in Interrogations and Torture: A Symposium* (Jerusalem: PCATI and IMUT, 1993)

Quigley, John, 'International Limits on Use of Force to Elicit Confessions: A Critique of Israel's Policy on Interrogation' 14 *Brook J of Int'l L* 485 (1988)

Rabinovich-Te'omim, RB, 'Extradition to the Custody of Gentiles' [Hebrew] 7 *Noam* 366 (1973–4)

Rachels, James, 'On Moral Absolutism' in Haber, Joram Graf (ed), *Absolutism and its Consequentialist Critics* (Lanham, Maryland: Rowan and Littlefield, 1994) 199–215

Raphael, DD, *Moral Philosophy* (2nd edn, Oxford: Oxford University Press, 1994)

Raskin, Jef, 'The Flawed Calculus of Torture' *Toronto Globe & Mail* (11 April 2002)

Ratner, Steven R and Abrams, Jason S, *Accountability for Human Rights Atrocities in International Law: Beyond the Nuremberg Legacy* (Oxford: Clarendon, 1997)

Rawls, John, *A Theory of Justice* (rev edn, Oxford: Oxford University Press, 1999)

Regan, Tom, 'Introduction' in *idem* (ed), *Matters of Life and Death* (3rd edn, New York: McGraw-Hill, 1993) 1–29

Reichman, Amnon, 'When We Sit to Judge Are We Being Judged: The Israeli GSS Case, Ex Parte Pinochet, and Domestic/Global Deliberation', G Cardozo J, *Int'l & Comp L UI* (2001)

—— and Kahana, Tsvi, 'Israel and the Recognition of Torture: Domestic and International Aspects' in Scott, Carig (ed), *Torture as Tort: Comparative Perspectives on the Development of Transnational Human Rights Litigation* (Oxford: Hart Publishing, 2001) 631–659

Reuters report, 12 June 2001, 6:03 AM PT <http://www.zdnet.com/zdfeeds/msncobrand/news/0,13622,2773428-hud00025nshm3,00.html>, accessed 17 September 2001

Risen, James, Johnston, David and Lewis, Neil A, 'Harsh C.I.A. Methods Cited in Top Qaeda Interrogations' *New York Times* (13 May 2004)

Rivabella, Omar, *Requiem for a Woman's Soul* (Hammondsworth, Middlesex: Penguin Books, 1987)

Robinson, Paul H, 'Letter to the Editor' 23 *Israel L Rev* 189 (1989)

—— 'Criminal Law Defenses: A Systematic Analysis' 82 *Col L Rev* 199 (1982)

—— and Darley, John M, 'Testing Competing Theories of Justification' 76 *North Carolina L Rev* 1095 (1998)

Rodley, Nigel S, 'The Definition(s) of Torture in International Law' 55 *Current Legal Problems* 465 (2002)

—— 'The Prohibition of Torture: Absolute Means Absolute' 34 *Denver J of Int'l L & Policy* 145 (2006)

—— 'The Prohibition of Torture and How to Make it Effective' *Proceedings of a seminar on Israel and international human rights law: the issue of torture*, 9 June 1995 (Jerusalem: Center for Human Rights, the Hebrew University of Jerusalem, 1995) 5–32

—— *The Treatment of Prisoners under International Law* (2nd edn, Oxford: Clarendon, 1999)

Ross, David, *The Right and the Good* (Oxford: Clarendon, 1930)

Roy, Benjamin, 'The Tuskegee Syphilis Experiment: Biotechnology and the Administrative State' 87(1) *J Nat Med Assoc* 56 (1995)

Rudolph, Harold, *Security, Terrorism, Torture: Detainees' Rights in South Africa and Israel: A Comparative Study* (Cape Town, Juta:1984)

Rutenberg, Jim, 'Media Stoke Debate on Torture as U.S. Option' *New York Times* (6 November 2001)

Ruthven, Malise, *Torture: The Grand Conspiracy* (London: Weidenfeld and Nicolson, 1978)

Saland, Per, 'International Criminal Law Principles' in Lee, Roy S (ed), *The International Criminal Court: The Making of the Rome Statute—Issues, Negotiations, Results* (The Hague: Kluwer Law International, 1999) 189–216.

Sartre, Jean-Paul, 'A Victory' (originally 'Une Victoire' published in *L'Express*), preface in Alleg, Henri, *The Question*, trans John Calder (London: John Calder, 1958) 11–28

—— *Les Mains Sales* (1948); for an English translation (by Lionel Abel) see eg in *idem*, *No Exit and Other Plays: Dirty Hands, The Flies, The Respectful Prostitute* (New York: Vintage Books, 1989)

'Saudi interrogators use Koran to connect with captives' CNN website (1 December 2003) <http://www.cnn.com>, accessed 2 December 2003

Scaliotti, Massimo, 'Defences Before the International Criminal Court: Substantive Grounds for Excluding Criminal Responsibility—Part 1' 1(1–2) *Int'l Crim L Rev* 111 (2001)

—— 'Defences Before the International Criminal Court: Substantive Grounds for Excluding Criminal Responsibility—Part 2' 2 *Int'l Crim L Rev* 1 (2002)

Scarry, Elaine, 'Five Errors in the Reasoning of Alan Dershowitz' in Levinson, Sanford (ed), *Torture: A Collection* (Oxford: Oxford University Press, 2004) 281–290

—— *The Body in Pain* (New York: Oxford University Press, 1985)

Schabas, William A, *An Introduction to the International Criminal Court* (2nd edn, Cambridge: Cambridge University Press, 2004)

—— *The Death Penalty As Cruel Treatment and Torture: Capital Punishment Challenged in World Courts* (Boston: Northeastern University Press, 1996)

Scheffler, Samuel (ed), *Consequentialism and its Critics* (Oxford: Oxford University Press, 1988)

—— *The Rejection of Consequentialism: A Philosophical Investigation of the Considerations Underlying Rival Moral Conceptions* (Oxford: Clarendon, 1982)

Schmetzer, Uli, 'Pakistan's scientists under scrutiny' *Chicago Tribune* (1 November 2001)

Schüklenk, Udo, 'Protecting the Vulnerable: Testing Times for Clinical Research Ethics' <http://www.wits.ac.za/bioethics/res.htm>, accessed 10 November 2001

—— and Hogan, Carlton, 'Patient Access to Experimental Drugs and AIDS Clinical Trial Designs: Ethical Issues' in Kuhse, Helga and Singer, Peter (eds), *Bioethics: An Anthology* (Oxford: Blackwell, 1999) 441–448

Schumann, Heribert, 'Criminal Law' in Ebke, Werner F and Finkin, Matthew W (eds), *Introduction to German Law* (The Hague: Kluwer, 1996) 383–412

Sen, Amartya, 'Plural Utility' 81 *Proceedings of the Aristotelian Society* 193 (1980–1981)

—— 'Rights and Agency' in Scheffler, Samuel (ed), *Consequentialism and its Critics* (Oxford: Oxford University Press, 1988) 188–223

Shalgi, Moshe and Cohen, Zvi, *Criminal Procedure* [Hebrew] (2nd edn, Jerusalem: Din, 2000)

Shamsi, Hina, *Command's Responsibility: Detainee Deaths in U.S. Custody in Iraq and Afghanistan*, ed Deborah Pearlstein (New York: Human Rights First February, 2006) <http://www.humanrightsfirst.info/pdf/06221-etn-hrf-dic-rep-web.pdf>, accessed 14 April 2006

Shavit, Ari, 'A State on Board the Titanic' [Hebrew] *Haaretz Weekly* (5 October 2000)

Shaw, William H, *Contemporary Ethics: Taking Account of Utilitarianism* (Malden: Mass: Blackwell, 1999)

Sheleff, Leon, 'Maximising Good and Minimising Evil—On the Landau Commission's Report, Terrorism and Torture' [Hebrew] 1 *Plilim* (1990)

—— 'The Need to Defend the Honest Truth: Legal Agonies on the Subject of the Use of Torture' [Hebrew] 17 *Mehqarei Mishpat* 459 (2002)

—— *Ultimate Penalties: Capital Punishment, Life Imprisonment, Physical Torture* (Columbus: Ohio State University Press, 1987)

Shenon, Phillip and Risen, James, 'Terrorist Yields Clues to Plots, Questioners Say' *New York Times* (12 June 2002)

Shue, Henry, 'Torture' 7 *Philosophy and Public Affairs* 124 (1978)

—— 'Torture in Dreamland: Disposing the Ticking Bomb' 37 *Case Western Reserve J. Int'l L* 231 (2006)

Sidgwick, Henry, *The Methods of Ethics* (4th edn, London: Macmillan, 1890)

Silverglate, Harvey A, 'Torture Warrants?' *The Boston Phoenix* (6–13 December 2001) <http://bostonphoenix.com/boston/news_features/other_stories/multipage/documents/02042267.htm>, accessed 21 October 2007

Silverman, Lisa, *Tortured Subjects: Pain, Truth and the Body in Early Modern France* (Chicago and London: the University of Chicago Press, 2001)

Simester, AP and Sullivan, GR, *Criminal Law: theory and doctrine* (2nd edn, Oxford–Portland, Oregon: Hart Publishing, 2003)

Simon, Pierre-Henry, *Contre la Torture* (Paris: 1957)

Singer, Roni and the agencies, 'IDF imposes total closure over the Territories because of intelligence warnings of terrorist attacks on Peshach Eve' <http://www.haaretz.co.il/hasite/spages/284590.html>, posted, accessed 16 April 2003

Sipress, Alan and Nakashima, Ellen, 'Death Toll in Bali Attack Rises to 188; Most Victims Were Foreigners; Terror Network Suspected' *Washington Post* (14 October 2002)

Slote, Michael, *From Morality to Virtue* (New York: Oxford University Press, 1992)

—— 'Virtue Ethics' in Pettit, Philip, Baron, Marcia W and Slote, Michael, *Three Methods of Ethics* (Malden, Mass: Blackwell, 1997) 175–238

Smart, JJC, 'An Outline of a System of Utilitarian Ethics' in *idem* and Williams, Bernard (eds), *Utilitarianism: For and Against* (Cambridge: Cambridge University Press, 1973) 1–76

Smilansky, Saul, 'Who Should a Utilitarian Be?' No 44 *Iyyun, The Jerusalem Philosophical Quarterly* 91 (1995)

Smith, David, '"I don't blame them but I hope they mourn the dead"' *The Observer* (24 July 2005)

Smith, JC, *Justification and Excuse in the Criminal Law* (London: Stevens & Sons, 1989)

Smith, John, *Smith & Hogan's Criminal Law: Cases and Materials* (8th edn, London: Butterworths/LexisNexis, 2002)

Solomon, Alisa, 'A New U.S. Threat to Human Rights: The Case Against Torture' *The Village Voice* (week of 28 November – 4 December 2001)

Sorell, Tom, *Moral Theory and Anomaly* (Oxford: Blackwell, 2000)

—— *Moral Theory and Capital Punishment* (Oxford: Basil Blackwell, 1987)

Sorensen, Harley, 'As You Wave The Flag, Wave Goodbye To Our Freedoms' *San Francisco Chronicle* (12 November 2001) <http://www.commondreams.org/views01/1113–04.htm>, accessed 25 October 2007

Sottas, Eric, 'Perpetrators of Torture' in Dunér, Bertil (ed), *An End to Torture: Strategies for its Eradication* (London: Zed Books, 1998) 62–84

Statman, Daniel, 'Hard Cases and Moral Dilemmas' 15 *Law and Philosophy* 117 (1996)

—— 'The Absoluteness of the Prohibition Against Torture' [Hebrew] 4 *Mishpat u-Mimshal* 161 (1997)

Staub, Ervin, 'The Psychology and Culture of Torture and Torturers' in Suedfeld, Peter (ed), *Psychology and Torture* (New York: Hemisphere Publishing, 1990) 49–88

Stephen, James Fitzjames, A *Digest of the Criminal Law (Crimes and Punishments)* (4th edn, London: Macmillan, 1887)

Stimson, Henry L, 'The Decision to Use the Atomic Bomb' in Gutmann, Amy and Thompson, Dennis (eds), *Ethics & Politics: Cases and Comments* (Chicago: Nelson-Hall Publishers, 1984) 4–15

Stone, Richard, *Entry, Search and Seizure: A Guide to Civil and Criminal Powers of Entry* (London: Sweet & Maxwell, 1997)

Strauss, Marcy, 'Torture' *Loyola-LA Public Law Research Paper* No 2003–7, January 2003

Strauss, Ronald P, 'Community Advisory Board—Investigator Relationships in Community-Based HIV/AIDS Research' in King, Nancy MP, Henderson, Gail E and Stein, Jane (eds), *Beyond Regulations: Ethics in Human Subjects Research* (Chapel Hill, NC and London: University of North Carolina Press, 1999) 94–101

Suedfeld, Peter, 'Torture: A Brief Overview', in *idem* (ed), *Psychology and Torture* (New York: Hemisphere Publishing 1990) 1–11

Sumner, LW, *The Moral Foundation of Rights* (Oxford: Clarendon, 1987)

The American Series of Foreign Penal Codes, Vol 28 (London: Littleton, 1987)

The Digest of Justinian (6th Century AD); for English text see Watson, A (ed), *The Digest of Justinian* (Philadelphia: University of Pennsylvania Press, 1998). For the Latin text see eg <http://www.thelatinlibrary.com/justinian.html> accessed 21 February 2003

'The Hommel Case: The Command of the Danish Military Failed Hommel' [Danish] *Politiken* (13 January 2006)

'The ICRC and the International Day in Support of Victims of Torture' ICRC website <http://www.icrc.org>, 26 June 2002, accessed 21 November 2002

Thomson, Judith Jarvis, 'A Defence of Abortion' in Singer, Peter (ed) *Applied Ethics* (Oxford: Oxford University Press, 1986) 37–56

—— *The Realm of Rights* (Cambridge, Mass: Harvard University Press, 1990)

—— 'The Trolley Problem' 94 *Yale L J* 1395 (1985)

Trianosky, Gregory, 'What is Virtue Ethics All About?' *27 Am Phil Quart* 335 (1990)

Trinquier, Roger, *Modern Warfare: A French View of Counterinsurgency*, trans Daniel Lee (London: Pall Mall Press, 1964)

Twining, William and Paskins, Barrie, 'Torture and Philosophy' 52 (Supp) *Proceedings of the Aristotelian Society* 143 (1978)

Twining, WL and Twining, E, 'Bentham on Torture' 24(3) *Northern Ireland Legal Quarterly* 305 (1973)

'U.S. Constitution: Fourth Amendment: Annotations' FindLaw <http://caselaw.lp.findlaw.com/data/constitution/amendment04>, accessed 11 March 2003

Van den Haag, Ernest, 'The Death Penalty Once More' in Bedau, Hugo Adam (ed), *The Death Penalty in America: Current Controversies* (New York: Oxford University Press, 1997) 445–456

Van Fraassen, Bas C, 'Values and the Heart's Command' in Gowans, Christopher W (ed) *Moral Dilemmas* (New York and Oxford: Oxford University Press, 1987) 138–153

Videl-Naquet, Pierre, *Torture: Cancer of Democracy, France and Algeria, 1954–62*, trans Barry Richard (Baltimore: Penguin Books, 1963)

Walker, Clive, *The Prevention of Terrorism in British Law* (Manchester: Manchester University Press, 1992)

Wailoo, Keith A, 'Research Partnerships and People 'at Risk': HIV Vaccine Efficacy Trials and African American Communities' in King, Nancy MP, Henderson, Gail E and Stein, Jane (eds), *Beyond Regulations: Ethics in Human Subjects Research* (Chapel Hill, NC and London: University of North Carolina Press, 1999) 102–107

Wallace, Rebecca, *International Human Rights: Texts and Materials* (London: Sweet & Maxwell, 1997)

Walzer, Michael, *Just and Unjust Wars: A Moral Argument with Historical Illustrations* (New York: Basic Books, 1997)

—— 'Political Action: The Problem of Dirty Hands' in Cohen, Marshall, Nagel, Thomas and Scanlon, Thomas (eds), *War and Moral Responsibility* (Princeton: Princeton University Press, 1974) 62–82

Wastell, David, 'Rumsfeld: My plans for our British prisoners' *Daily Telegraph* (25 February 2002) 4–5

Weisbard, Alan J, Comments on Biletzki, Anat, 'The Judicial Rhetoric of Morality: Israel's High Court of Justice on the Legality of Torture' January 2001, Paper no 9,

Occasional Papers of the School of Social Science, Princeton, NJ, <http://www.sss.ias. edu/publications/papers/papernine.pdf>, accessed 21 October 2007

Weisberg, Richard H Weisberg, 'Loose Professionalism, or Why Lawyers Take the Lead on Torture' in Levinson, Sanford (ed), *Torture: A Collection* (Oxford: Oxford University Press, 2004) 299–305

Weiss, Efrat, 'High alert in Jerusalem because of fears of a terrorist attack' <http://www. ynet.co.il/articles/0,7340,L-2277114,00.html>, posted, accessed 27 November 2002

Weissbrodt, David, Fitzpatrick, Joan & Newman, Frank, *International Human Rights— Law, Policy and Process* (3rd edn, Cincinnati, Ohio: Anderson Publishing, 2001)

Welsome, Eileen, *The Plutonium Files: America's Secret Medical Experiments During the Cold War* (New York: Delacorte Press, 1999)

Wendel, W Bradley, 'Legal Ethics and the Separation of Law and Morals' *91 Cornell L Rev* 67 (2005)

White, Josh, 'Detainee in Photo With Dog Was "High-Value" Suspect' *Washington Post* (13 March 2006) <http://www.washingtonpost.com/wp-dyn/content/article/2006/03/12/ AR2006031200962.html>, accessed 21 October 2007

Williams, Bernard, 'A Critique of Utilitarianism' in *idem* and Smart, JJC (eds), *Utilitarianism: For and Against* (Cambridge: Cambridge University Press, 1973) 77–150

—— *Ethics and the Limits of Philosophy* (London: Fontana, 1985)

—— 'Politics and Moral Character' in Hampshire, Stuart (ed), *Public and Private Morality* (Cambridge: Cambridge University Press, 1978) 55–73

Williams, Glanville, *Criminal Law: The General Part* (2nd edn, London: Steven and Sons, 1961)

—— *Textbook of Criminal Law* (2nd edn, London: Steven and Sons 1983)

Williams, Patricia J, 'Any Means Necessary' *The Nation* (26 November 2001)

Williams, Peter and Wallace, David, *Unit 731: Japan's Secret Biological Warfare in World War II* (New York: The Free Press, 1989)

Wolf, Susan, 'Moral Saints' 79(8) *Journal of Philosophy* 419 (August 1982)

Žižek, Slavoj, *Welcome to the Desert of the Real* (London: Verso, 2002)

Zuckerman, Adrian AS, 'Coercion and the Judicial Ascertainment of Truth' 23 *Israel L Rev* 146 (1989)

B. Other Documents

Note: the order is alphabetical, but documents relating to international treaty-monitoring bodies are grouped together.

Addameer, press release, 17 April 2003; available on <http://www.addameer.org>

Affidavit of 'Azzam Yusuf, taken by Adv Muhammad Darawshah at the Kishon detention center on 13 January 2002

Affidavit of Khalil Abu Dush, taken by Adv Fida' Qa'war at the Sharon prison on 9 April 2003

Affidavit of Walid Abu Khdeir, taken by Adv Hanan Khatib at his home in East Jerusalem on 30 May 2001

Alan Baker Legal Adviser, Ministry of Foreign Affairs, Second Periodic Report of Israel to CAT, Opening Statement, 15 May 1998

American Forces Press Service, 'Defense Department Takes Custody of al Qaeda Leader' 27 April 2007, <http://www.defenselink.mil/news/newsarticle.aspx?id=32969>, accessed 28 April 2007

Amnesty International letter to Alessio Bruni, Secretary of the Committee against Torture, Ref: UN 9/2001 (7 February 2001)

AR 15–6 Investigation of the Abu Ghraib Prison and 205th Military Intelligence Brigade LTG Anthony R Jones; *AR 15–6 Investigation of the Abu Ghraib Detention Facility and 205th Military Intelligence Brigade* MG George R Fay, nd (published August 2004), <http://www.defenselink.mil/news/Aug2004/d20040825fay.pdf>, accessed 25 August 2004

Army Regulation 15–6: Final Report: Investigation into FBI Allegations of Detainee Abuse at Guantanamo Bay, Cuba Detention Facility, 1 April 2005 (amended 9 June 2005) (written by Lieutenant General Randall M Schmidt and Brigadier General John T Furlow), <http://www.defenselink.mil/news/Jul2005/d20050714report.pdf>, accessed 23 June 2006

Association Internationale de Droit Pénal (AIDP)/International Institute of Higher Studies in Criminal Sciences (ISISC)/Max Planck Institute for Foreign and International Criminal Law (MPI) *et al, 1994 ILC Draft Statute for an International Criminal Court with suggested modifications (updated Siracusa-Draft)*, prepared by a committee of experts, Siracusa/Freiburg/Chicago, 15 March 1996, <www.iuscrim. mpg.de/forsch/straf/referate/sach/hispint/genpart3.doc>, accessed 27 October 2003

Avert (Website of), UK-based international HIV and AIDS charity, <http://www.avert. org/worldstats.htm>, accessed 25 April 2007

B'Tselem, the Israeli Information Centre for Human Rights in the Occupied Territories website <www.btselem.org>, accessed 21 January 2003

B'Tselem and the Association for Civil Rights in Israel, *Comments on the Second Periodic Report of the State of Israel on the Implementation of the UN Convention Against Torture and Other Cruel, Inhuman or Degrading Treatment or Punishment*, Jerusalem, May 1998

Bush, George W, The National Security Strategy of the United States, signed by Bush on 17 September 2002 For full text see White House website <http://www.whitehouse. gov/>, accessed 11 November 2002; *New York Times* website <http://www.nyt.com>, 20 September 2002, accessed 20 September 2002

Catholic Educator's Resource Centre website <http://www.catholiceducation.org/>, accessed 13 January 2003

CIA document entitled 'KUBARK Counterintelligence Interrogation' July 1963, see eg <http://www.kimsoft.com/2000/kubark.htm>, accessed 27 October 2007

CNN transcript of a Pentagon briefing, aired 20 May 2002, 10:04 ET, <http://edition. cnn.com/TRANSCRIPTS/0205/20/se.01.html>, accessed 23 January 2004

Comments by the Government of Israel on the concluding observations of the Human Rights Committee, UN Doc CCPR/CO/78/ISR/Add.1 (24 January 2007)

Committee on Legal Affairs and Human Rights, Parliamentary Assembly, Council of Europe, *Secret detentions and illegal transfers of detainees involving Council of Europe member states: second report*, 11 June 2007, <http://assembly.coe.int/Documents/ WorkingDocs/Doc07/edoc11302.pdf>, accessed 25 October 2007

Department of the Army, the Inspector General, *Detainee Operations Inspection*, 21 July 2004, available eg on <http://www.globalsecurity.org/military/library/report/2004/ daig_detainee-ops_21jul2004.pdf>, accessed 30 December 2004

Department of Defense, *Memorandum for Record, ICRC Meeting with MG Miller on 9 October 2003*, <http://www.washingtonpost.com/wp-srv/nation/documents/GitmoMemo10–09–03.pdf>, accessed 4 September 2004

Deputy Inspector General for Intelligence, *Review of DoD-Directed Investigations of Detainee Abuse*, Report No 06-INTEL-10, 25 August 2006, <http://www.fas.org/irp/agency/dod/abuse.pdf>, accessed 30 May 2007

Directorate of Human Rights, *Explanatory Report on the European Convention for the Prevention of Torture and Inhuman and Degrading Treatment or Punishment* (Strasbourg: Council of Europe, 1989)

Email from REDACTED to MC Briese, Gary Bald, TJ Harrington, Frankie Battle and other redacted parties Re Request for Guidance regarding OGC EC dated 19 May 2004, signed [REDACTED], 'On scene Commander—Baghdad' <http://www.aclu.org/torturefoia/released/FBI.121504.4940_4941.pdf>, accessed 22 December 2004

Embassy of the United States, Caracas, Venezuela, Public Affairs Office, 'Press Release, Campaign Against Terrorism: Secretary Rumsfeld, General Myers Briefing on Afghan Military Campaign' 9 October 2001, <http://embajadausa.org.ve/wwwh695.html>, accessed 23 January 2004

European Committee for the Prevention of Torture and Inhuman or Degrading Treatment or Punishment (CPT), reports and other documents:

—— *15th General Report on the CPT's activities covering the period 1 August 2004 to 31 July 2005*, CPT/Inf (2005) 17, (22 September 2005)

—— *1st General Report on the CPT's Activities Covering the Period November 1989 to December 1990*, CPT/Inf (91) 3

—— *Public statement concerning the Chechen Republic of the Russian Federation,* (10 July 2003), CPT/Inf (2003) 33

—— *Public statement on Turkey,* (15 December 1992), CPT/Inf (93) 12, Appendix 4

—— *Public Statement on Turkey,* (6 December 1996), CPT/Inf (96) 34

—— *Report to the Austrian Government on the visit to Austria carried out by the European Committee for the Prevention of Torture and Inhuman or Degrading Treatment or Punishment (CPT) from 14 to 23 April 2004*, CPT/Inf (2005) 13

—— *Report to the Azerbaijani Government on the visit to Azerbaijan carried out by the European Committee for the Prevention of Torture and Inhuman or Degrading Treatment or Punishment (CPT) from 24 November to 6 December 2002*, CPT/Inf (2004) 36

—— *Report to the Bulgarian Government on the visit to Bulgaria carried out by the carried out by the European Committee for the Prevention of Torture and Inhuman or Degrading Treatment or Punishment (CPT) from 26 March to 7 April 1995*, CPT/Inf (97) 1

—— *Report to the Georgian Government on the visit to Georgia carried out by the European Committee for the Prevention of Torture and Inhuman or Degrading Treatment or Punishment (CPT) from 18 to 28 November 2003 and from 7 to 14 May 2004*, CPT/Inf (2005) 12

—— *Report to the Government of Bosnia and Herzegovina on the visit to Bosnia and Herzegovina carried out by the European Committee for the Prevention of Torture and Inhuman or Degrading Treatment or Punishment (CPT) from 27 April to 9 May 2003*, CPT/Inf (2004) 40

—— *Report to the Government of Greece on the visit to Greece carried out by the carried out by the European Committee for the Prevention of Torture and Inhuman or Degrading Treatment or Punishment (CPT) from 14 to 26 March 1993*, CPT/Inf (94) 20

—— *Report to the Government of Slovenia on the visit to Slovenia carried out by the carried out by the European Committee for the Prevention of Torture and Inhuman or Degrading Treatment or Punishment (CPT) from 19 to 28 February 1995*, CPT/Inf (96) 18

—— *Report to the Government of the Federal Republic of Germany on the visit to Germany carried out by the carried out by the European Committee for the Prevention of Torture and Inhuman or Degrading Treatment or Punishment (CPT) from 8 to 20 December 1991*, CPT/Inf (93) 13

—— *Report to the Government of the United Kingdom on the visit to Northern Ireland carried out by the carried out by the European Committee for the Prevention of Torture and Inhuman or Degrading Treatment or Punishment (CPT) from 20 to 29 July 1993*, CPT/Inf (94) 17

—— *Report to the Government of the United Kingdom on the visit to the United Kingdom carried out by the European Committee for the Prevention of Torture and Inhuman or Degrading Treatment or Punishment (CPT) from 17 to 21 February 2002*, CPT/Inf (2003) 18

—— *Report to the Government of the United Kingdom on the visit to the United Kingdom and the Isle of Man carried out by the European Committee for the Prevention of Torture and Inhuman or Degrading Treatment or Punishment (CPT) from 12 to 23 May 2003*, CPT/Inf (2005) 1

—— *Report to the Latvian Government on the visit to Latvia carried out by the European Committee for the Prevention of Torture and Inhuman or Degrading Treatment or Punishment (CPT) from 25 September to 4 October 2002*, CPT/Inf (2005) 8

—— *Report to the Maltese Government on the visit to Malta carried out by the carried out by the European Committee for the Prevention of Torture and Inhuman or Degrading Treatment or Punishment (CPT) from 1 to 9 July 1990*, CPT/Inf (92) 5

—— *Report to the Norwegian Government on the visit to Norway carried out by the European Committee for the Prevention of Torture and Inhuman or Degrading Treatment or Punishment (CPT) from 13 to 23 September 1999*, CPT/Inf (2000) 15

—— *Report to the Portuguese Government on the visit to Portugal carried out by the carried out by the European Committee for the Prevention of Torture and Inhuman or Degrading Treatment or Punishment (CPT) from 20 to 24 October 1996*, CPT/Inf (98) 1

—— *Report to the Spanish Government on the visit to Spain carried out by the carried out by the European Committee for the Prevention of Torture and Inhuman or Degrading Treatment or Punishment (CPT) from 10 to 14 June 1994*, CPT/Inf (96) 9

—— *Report to the Spanish Government on the visit to Spain carried out by the carried out by the European Committee for the Prevention of Torture and Inhuman or Degrading Treatment or Punishment (CPT) from 21 to 28 April 1997*, CPT/Inf (98) 9

European Convention for the Protection of Human Rights and Fundamental Freedoms, *Collected Edition of the 'Travaux Preparatoires'* Vol 1 (The Hague: Martinus Nijhoff, 1975)

Final Report of the Independent Panel to Review DoD Detention Operations, August 2004, <http://www.defense.gov/news/Aug2004/d20040824finalreport.pdf>, accessed 25 August 2004

GSS document: To: interrogation file, re: Husam 'Ataf 'Ali Badran, signed 'alias "Oz" ', Head of Interrogations Department, Samaria, no date

Hayden, General Michael V, 'Director's Statement on Executive Order on Detentions, Interrogations' (20 July 2007) <https://www.cia.gov/news-information/press-releases-statements/statement-on-executive-order.html>, accessed 13 August 2007

International AIDS Vaccine Initiative (IAVI) website, <http://www.iavi.org/viewpage.cfm?aid=12>, accessed 6 April 2007

International Law Commission, *Commentaries to the Draft Articles on Responsibility of States for Internationally Wrongful Acts,* adopted by the International Law Commission in its fifty-third session (2001), UN Doc A/56/10, Ch IV.E.2 (November 2001)

'Interrogation Log, Detainee 063' obtained by *Time* magazine, <http://www.time.com/time/2006/log/log.pdf>, accessed 22 June 2006

Hanna Senesh Legacy Foundation website, <http://www.hannahsenesh.org.il/>, accessed 13 January 2003

Headquarters, Department of the Army, *FM 34–52 Intelligence Interrogation,* Washington, DC, 8 May 1987, <http://www.globalsecurity.org/intell/library/policy/army/fm/fm34–52/>, accessed 6 March 2005

—— *FM 34–52 Intelligence Interrogation,* Washington, DC, 28 September 1992, <http://www.fas.org/irp/doddir/army/fm34–52.pdf>, accessed 8 April 2005

—— *FMI 3–63.6, Command and Control of Detainee Operations, September 2005, Expires September 2007,* available eg on <http://www.fas.org/irp/doddir/army/fmi3–63-6.pdf>, accessed 24 October 2005

Hearing of the Senate Armed Services Committee. Subject: Threats to U.S. National Security (17 March 2005). The Transcript is available at <http://www.humanrights-first.org/us_law/etn/docs/fedwires125g.htm>, accessed 9 April 2005

House of Commons Hansard debate for 11 July 2005, cols 565–7, <http://www.publications.parliament.uk/pa/cm200506/cmhansrd/cm050711/debtext/50711–06.htm>, accessed 15 July 2005

[UN] Human Rights Committee, reports and other documents:

—— Annual report: UN Doc A/57/40 (2002)

—— CCPR General comment 13: the right to a fair and public hearing by an independent court established by law (Art 14), 13 April 1984

—— Concluding observations of the Human Rights Committee: Israel. UN Doc CCPR/C/79/Add.93, 18 August 1998

—— Concluding observations of the Human Rights Committee: Israel. UN Doc. CCPR/CO/78/ISR, 5 August 2003

—— Concluding observations of the Human Rights Committee: Philippines UN Doc. CCPR/CO/79/PHL, 1 December 2003

—— Concluding observations of the Human Rights Committee: Russian Federation UN Doc CCPR/CO/79/RUS, 6 November 2003

—— Concluding observations of the Human Rights Committee: Sri Lanka.UN Doc CCPR/CO/79/LKA, 1 December 2003

—— General Comment on Article 7, CCPR General comment 20 (1992)

—— General Comment no 29: States of emergency (article 4), UN Doc CCPR/C/21/Rev.1/Add.11, 31 August 2001

—— 78th Sess, Summary Record of the 2118th Meeting, 25 July 2003, UN Doc CCPR/C/SR.2118, 6 August 2003

[UN] **Human Rights Committee, reports to the Committee**

—— Combined Second and Third Periodic reports of the United States of America to the Human Rights Committee, UN Doc CCPR/C/USA/3, 28 November 2005

—— Israel's Initial Report to the UN Human Rights Committee, UN Doc CCPR/C/81/Add.13, 9 April 1998

Inter-American Commission on Human Rights, *Report on the Situation of Human Rights of Asylum Seekers within the Canadian Refugee Determination System*, OEA/Ser.L/V/II.106, Doc 40 rev, 28 February 2000

IAVI (International Aids Vaccine Initiative) website <http://www.iavi.org/viewpage.cfm?aid=12>, accessed 6 April 2007

ICRC Operational update, 'US detention related to the events of 11 September 2001 and its aftermath—the role of the ICRC' <http://www.icrc.org/Web/Eng/siteeng0.nsf/html/66FGEL?OpenDocument>, 29 March 2005, accessed 13 April 2005

International AIDS Vaccine Initiative (IAVI) petition, prepared for presentation at the XIV International AIDS Conference, July 2002 in Barcelona, <http://www.iavi.org/callforaction/>, accessed 10 January 2002

International Criminal Court (ICC) website <http://www.icc-cpi.int/home.html&l=en>

Interview with Prime Minister Yitzhaq Rabin in 'Weekly Diary' *Kol Yisrael* (Israel's state-owned radio station), 29 July 1995, quoted in both *Haaretz* and *Davar* daily newspapers (30 July 1995)

Israel Supreme Court's website <http://www.court.gov.il>

Joint Chiefs of Staff, 'Joint Doctrine for Detainee Operations: Joint Publication 3–63' (JP 3–63) (23 March 2005) <www.dtic.mil/doctrine/jel/pd/3_63pd.pdf>, accessed 10 April 2005

Joint United Nations Programme on HIV/AIDS (UNAIDS) and World Health Organization (WHO), *AIDS epidemic update, December* 2005, <http://www.unaids.org/epi/2005/doc/EPIupdate2005_pdf_en/epi-update2005_en.pdf>, accessed 23 January 2006

15th Knesset, 291st meeting, 6 March 2002, Response of Minister Dani Naveh to Interpellation No 3074

16th Knesset, First Session, 'Minutes no. 12 of Meeting of the Constitution, Law and Justice Committee, 19 May 2003' minutes/Constitution Committee/6485, at 17. Available (in Hebrew) at <http://www.knesset.gov.il/protocols/data/html/huka/2003–05-19.html>, accessed 29 October 2003

—— First Session, 'Minutes [number missing] of Meeting of the Constitution, Law and Justice Committee, 8 June 2003' minutes/Constitution Committee/6610, at 13. Available (in Hebrew) at <http://www.knesset.gov.il/protocols/data/html/huka/2003–06-08.html>, accessed 29 June 2003

Letter dated 2 April 2003 from the Permanent Mission of the United States of America to the United Nations Office at Geneva addressed to the secretariat of the Commission on Human Rights, UN Doc E/CN.4/2003/G/73 (7 April 2003)

Letter from Barbara Olshansky *et al* of the Center for Constitutional Rights re: Request submitted under the Freedom of Information Act to Scott A Kotch, Information and Privacy Coordinator, Central Intelligence Agency (21 December 2004)

Letter from TJ Harrington, FBI Deputy Assistant Director, Counterterrorism to Major General Donald J Ryder, Department of the Army's Criminal Investigation Command re Suspected Mistreatment of Detainees (14 July 2004) <http://www.aclu.org/torturefoia/released/FBI_4622_4624.pdf>, accessed 7 May 2005

Letter no 6585 from Major Nitzan Sultani, Deputy Attorney for Judea and Samaria and the Gaza Area to Att. Labib Habib, (1 August 2004)

Letter from William J Haynes II of the [USA] General Counsel of the Department of Defense to Kenneth Roth, Executive Director of Human Rights Watch (2 April 2003) available on HRW website, <http://www.hrw.org/press/2003/04/dodltr040203.pdf>, accessed 29 July 2003

Levin, Daniel, Acting Assistant Attorney General, Memorandum for James B Comey, Deputy Attorney General, *Regarding Legal Standards Applicable Under 18 USC §§ 2340–2340A*, 30 December 2004, available eg in KJ Greenberg and JL Dratel, *The Torture Papers: The road to Abu Ghraib* (Cambridge: Cambridge University Press, 2005)

Memorandum for Alberto R Gonzales, Counsel to the President, from Jay S Bybee, Assistant Attorney General, US Department of Justice, Office of the Legal Counsel, *Re: Standards of Conduct for Interrogation under 18 U.S.C. §§ 2340–2340A* (1 August 2002)

[Secretary For Defense] Memo for Commander, SOUTHCOM: *Counter Resistance Technique in the War on Terrorism*, dated 16 April 2003

[Thomas M Pappas, COL, MI] Memorandum for Commander, CJTF-7, LTG Sanchez, Subject: *Request for Exception to CJTF-7 Interrogation and Counter Resistance Policy*, 30 November 2003, <http://www.publicintegrity.org/docs/AbuGhraib/Abu7.pdf>, accessed 28 March 2005

[US President] Memorandum for the Vice President, the Secretary of State, the Secretary of Defense, the Attorney General, the Chief of Staff to the President, the Director of Central Intelligence, the Assistant to the President for National Security Affairs, the Chairman of the Joint Chiefs of Staff. Subject: Humane treatment of al Qaeda and Taliban detainees. The White House, 7 February 2002, available eg on <http://pegc.no-ip.info/archive/White_House/bush_memo_20020207_ed.pdf>, accessed 8 October 2004

Memorandum to Counsel to the President. Subject: Comments on your paper on the Geneva Conventions. From: William H Taft, IV (2 February 2002)

Mission Permanente d'Israël auprès de l'Office des Nations Unies et des Organisations internationales à Genève, *Statement by Ms. Nili ARAD … and Mr. Shai NITZAN*, 18th Session of the Committee Against Torture (CAT), Geneva (7 May 1997)

National Bioethics Advisory Commission [USA], *Ethical and Policy Issues in Research Involving Human Participants, Volume I: Report and Recommendations of the National Bioethics Advisory Commission*, April 2001, <http://bioethics.georgetown.edu/nbac/pubs.html>, accessed 15 December 2001

Office for Human Research Protection, U.S. Department of Human Health and Services, *Institutional Review Board Guidebook*, <http://ohrp.osophs.dhhs.gov/irb/irb_guidebook.htm>, accessed 21 December 2001

Office of the Director of National Intelligence (DNI) *Summary of the High Value Terrorist Detainee Program*, nd, published in October 2006, <http://www.defenselink.mil/pdf/thehighvaluedetaineeprogram2.pdf>, accessed 6 October 2006

'President Bush Signs Military Commissions Act of 2006' <http://www.whitehouse.gov/news/releases/2006/10/20061017–1.html#>, posted, accessed 17 October 2006

'President Discusses Creation of Military Commissions to Try Suspected Terrorists' 6 September 2006, <http://www.whitehouse.gov/news/releases/2006/09/20060906–3.html>, accessed 10 October 2006

Report of the International Committee of the Red Cross (ICRC) on the Treatment by Coalition Forces of Prisoners of War and Other Protected Persons by the Geneva Conventions in Iraq During Arrest, Internment, and Interrogation, February 2004. The report was not published officially by the ICRC. See eg <http://www.stopwar.org.uk/Resources/icrc.pdf>, accessed 11 August 2004

Report of the Commission of Inquiry in the Matter of Interrogation Methods of the General Security Service regarding Hostile Terrorist Activity, First Part (Jerusalem: October, 1987). For extensive excerpts of the Government Press Office translation (not used here) see 23 Is L Rev 146 (1989)

Report of the Committee of Privy Counsellors appointed to consider authorized procedures for the interrogation of persons suspected of terrorism, Cmmd No 4901 (Lord Parker of Wadington, Chairman, 1972)

Rocky the Reactionary, website dedicated to Captain Humbert Roque ('Rocky') Versace, <http://www.homeofheroes.com/profiles/profiles_versace.html>, accessed 13 January 2003

Rubinstein, Elyakim, 'GSS Interrogations and the Defence of Necessity—a Framework for the Attorney General's Considerations (following the HCJ ruling)' [Hebrew] 28 October 1999 press release, later published, under the same title, in 44 *Ha-Praklit* 409 (1999)

Security Council Resolution 1456 (2003), adopted 20 January 2003

Situation of detainees at Guantánamo Bay, Report of the Chairperson of the Working Group on Arbitrary Detention, Ms Leila Zerrougui; the Special Rapporteur on the independence of judges and lawyers, Mr Leandro Despouy; the Special Rapporteur on torture and other cruel, inhuman or degrading treatment or punishment, Mr Manfred Nowak; the Special Rapporteur on freedom of religion or belief, Ms Asma Jahangir and the Special Rapporteur on the right of everyone to the enjoyment of the highest attainable standard of physical and mental health, Mr Paul Hunt, UN Doc E/CN.4/2006/120 (15 February 2006)

State Comptroller [Israel], *Summary of the Audit Report on the Interrogation System in the General Security Service (GSS) for the years 1988–1992*, Report No 1/year 2000, Jerusalem, 2000

Statement by 'Izz al-Din al-Qassam Brigades following 1 June 2001 attack, 'Izz al-Din al-Qassam Brigades website, <http://www.qassam.org/byanat/byanat2001/04_06_2001.htm>, accessed 18 February 2002

Statement by the [US] President [George W Bush] in His Address to the Nation, 11 September, 8:30 PM EDT, White House website <http://www.whitehouse.gov/>, accessed 11 November 2002

'Statement of the Joint United Nations Programme on HIV/AIDS (UNAIDS) at the Fourth WTO Ministerial Conference' Doha, Qatar, 9–13 November 2001, <http://www.unaids.org/publications/documents/health/access/WTOstatement2001.html>, accessed 27 November 2001

Taguba, Maj Gen Antonio M, *Article 15–6 investigation of the 800th Military Police Brigade*, March 2004, available eg on <http://news.findlaw.com/hdocs/docs/iraq/tagubarpt.html>, accessed 11 August 2004

——— Annex 28 'Interrogation Rules of Engagement' (according to the Annexes list it pertains to the 205th MI Brigade), undated <http://www.aclu.org/torturefoia/released/a28.pdf>, accessed 28 March 2005

—— Annex 93, '800th Military Police Rules of Engagements for Operations in Iraq' undated <http://www.aclu.org/torturefoia/released/a93.pdf>, accessed 29 March 2005

—— Annex (no unclear), Thomas M Pappas, COL, MI, Memorandum for Commander, CJTF-7, LTG Sanchez, Subject: Request for Exception to CJTF-7 Interrogation and Counter Resistance Policy, 30 November 2003, <http://www.publicintegrity.org/docs/AbuGhraib/Abu7.pdf>, accessed 28 March 2005

Terrorism Research Centre website <www.terrorism.com>, accessed 28 May 2002

Testimony as Prepared by Secretary of Defense Donald H Rumsfeld, before the Senate and House Armed Services Committees (Friday, 7 May 2004) <http://www.defenselink.mil/speeches/2004/sp20040507-secdef1042.html>, accessed 11 August 2004

Testimony of Avidgodr Eskin, taken by Yuval Ginbar at Eskin's home in Jerusalem on 12 June 1998. B'Tselem interrogations testimony no 64, on file at B'Tselem, the Israeli Information center for Human Rights in the Occupied Territories and with the author

Testimony of Dr Jamal Muhammad Mussa 'Amer, taken by Yuval Ginbar and Marwah Jabara-Tibi at Bir Zeit University in the West Bank on 25 March 1998 and by Yuval Ginbar at 'Orient House' East Jerusalem, on 2 April 1998. B'Tselem interrogation testimony no 62 on file at B'Tselem, and with the author

Transcript of Conference Call With Senior Administration Officials on the Executive Order Interpreting Common Article Three, Washington, 20 July 2007, see eg <http://www.prnewswire.com/cgi-bin/stories.pl?ACCT=104&STORY=/www/story/07-20-2007/0004629772&EDATE=>, accessed 23 July 2007

Transcript of the Senate Judiciary Committee's hearings on the nomination of Alberto R Gonzales to be attorney general as transcribed by Federal News Service, 6 January 2005, <http://www.nytimes.com/2005/01/06/politics/06TEXT-GONZALES.html?oref=login&pagewanted=print&position=>, accessed 7 January 2005

Tri-Council Policy Statement: Ethical Conduct for Research Involving Humans, prepared jointly by the Canadian Medical Research Council (MRC), the Natural Sciences and Engineering Research Council (NSERC), and the Social Sciences and Humanities Research Council (SSHRC), <http://www.ncehr.medical.org/english/code_2/apdx02.html>, accessed 12 November 2007

UN Committee Against Torture, reports and related documents

—— Annual reports: UN Doc A/49/44 (1994); UN Doc A/51/44 (1996); UN Doc A/52/44 (1997); UN Doc A/53/44 (1998); UN Doc A/54/44 (1998–9); UN Doc A/57/44 (2001–2); UN Doc A/58/44 (2002–3)

—— Conclusion and Recommendations of the Committee against Torture: Israel. UN Doc CAT/C/SR.297/Add.1, 9 May 1997

—— Conclusions and Recommendations of the Committee against Torture: Israel. UN Doc CAT/C/SR.339, 25 May 1998

—— Conclusion and Recommendations of the Committee against Torture: Israel. UN Doc CAT/C/XVII/Concl.5, 23 November 2001

—— Conclusions and recommendations of the Committee Against Torture: United Kingdom of Great Britain and Northern Ireland—Dependent Territories, UN Doc CAT/C/CR/33/3, 25 November 2004

—— Conclusions and recommendations of the Committee Against Torture: United States of America, UN Doc CAT/C/USA/CU/2, 18 May 2006

—— Summary record of the public part of the 337th meeting [15 May 1998]: Israel. UN Doc CAT/C/SR.337 (Summary Record), 22 May 1998

—— UN Press Release, 'CAT, 27th Session, 21 November 2001, Afternoon' <http://www.unhchr.ch/huricane/huricane.nsf/NewsRoom?OpenFrameSet>, accessed 30 November 2001

UN Committee Against Torture, reports to the Committee

—— Israel's Special Report to the UN Committee Against Torture, UN Doc CAT/C/33/Add.2/Rev.1, 18 February 1997

—— Israel's Second Periodic Report to the UN Committee Against Torture, UN Doc CAT/C/33/Add.3, March 1998

—— United States of America's Initial Report to the UN Committee Against Torture, [15 October 1999], UN Doc CAT/C/28/Add.5, 9 February 2000

—— Second Periodic Report of the United States of America to the Committee Against Torture, UN Doc CAT/C/48/Add.3, 6 May 2005

UN Commission on Human Rights, resolutions

—— UN Doc E/CN.4Res.2003/32, adopted without vote on 23 April 2003

—— UN Doc E/CN.4/2004/127, adopted without vote on 19 April 2004

—— UN Doc E/CN.4Res.2004/41, adopted without vote on 19 April 2004

—— UN Doc E/CN.4/Res.2005/39, adopted without vote on 19 April 2005

UN High Commissioner for Human Rights website <http//:www.ohchr.org>

UN Security Council's Anti-Terrorism Committee, established under resolution 1373 of 28 September 2001, website <http://www.un.org/sc/ctc/>, accessed 21 October 2007

UN Special Rapporteur on Torture, reports

—— Annual reports: UN Doc E/CN.4/1986/15 (1986); UN Doc E/CN.4/1992/SR.21 (1992); UN Doc RE/CN.4/1996/35 (1996); UN Doc E/CN.4/1997/7 (1997); UN Doc E/CN.4/1998/38 (1998); UN Doc E/CN/1999/61 (1999); UN Doc E/CN.4/2000/9 (2000); Interim Report of the Special Rapporteur on torture to the General Assembly, UN Doc A/55/290 (2000); UN Doc E/CN.4/2001/66 (2001); UN Doc E/CN.4/2002/76 (2002)

—— Report of the Special Rapporteur on torture, Sir Nigel Rodley, submitted pursuant to Commission on Human Rights resolution 2000/43, Addendum: Visit to Brazil, UN Doc E/CN.4/2001/66/Add.2 (30 March 2001)

—— Report of the Special Rapporteur on torture, Addendum: Summary of cases transmitted to Governments and replies received, UN Doc E/CN.4/2002/76/Add.1 (14 March 2002)

—— Report of visit of Special Rapporteur on torture to Mexico, UN Doc E/CN.4/1998/38/Add.2 (14 January 1998)

—— Report of visit of Special Rapporteur on torture to Romania, UN Doc E/CN.4/2000/9/Add.3 (23 November 1999)

—— Report of visit of the Special Rapporteur on torture to Turkey, UN Doc E/CN.4/1999/61/Add.1 (27 January 1999)

—— Report of visit of the Special Rapporteur on torture to Venezuela, UN Doc E/CN.4/1997/7/Add.3 (13 December 1996)

UNAIDS/WHO, 'AIDS epidemic update December 2006' <http://data.unaids.org/pub/EpiReport/2006/2006_EpiUpdate_en.pdf>, accessed 26 April 2007

UNAids website <http://www.unaids.org>, accessed 12 July 2000

UNAIDS Sponsored Regional Workshops to Discuss Ethical Issues in Preventative HIV Vaccine Trials: *UNAIDS Report*, UNAIDS/00.036 E, Geneva, September 2000. Also available on <http://www.unaids.org/publications/documents/vaccines/vaccines/una00036e_.pdf>, accessed 18 October 2007

US Department of Defense News Release, 'Guantanamo Provides Valuable Intelligence Information' <http://www.defenselink.mil/releases/2005/nr20050612–3661.html>, accessed 23 June 2006

'U.S.: Growing Problem Of Guantanamo Detainees: Human Rights Watch Letter to Donald Rumsfeld' by Kenneth Roth, HRW Executive Director, 29 May 2002, <http://hrw.org/press/2002/05/pentagon-ltr.htm>, accessed 12 August 2003

US Holocaust Memory Museum website <http://www.ushmm.org/museum>

USA Food and Drug Administration regulations, 21 CFR 50.23 [revised as of April 1, 2000], <http://www.access.gpo.gov/nara/cfr/waisidx_00/21cfr50_00.html>, accessed 11 December 2001

Verbatim Transcript of Combatant Status Review Tribunal Hearing for ISN 10024, 10 March 2007, on board U.S Naval Base Guantanamo Bay, Cuba <http://www.defenselink.mil/news/transcript_ISN10024.pdf>, accessed 17 April 2007

Vice Admiral Albert T Church III, [US] Department of Defense, Review of Detention Operations and Interrogation Techniques—Executive Summary, <http://www.dod.mil/cgi-bin/dlprint.cgi?http://www.dod.mil/transcripts/2005/tr20050310–2262.html>, accessed 16 March 2005

'Visrusmyth: a Rethinking AIDS Website' <http://www.virusmyth.net/aids/>, accessed 12 December 2001

White House Fact Sheet, 'Status of Detainees at Guantanamo' Office of the Press Secretary, February 7, 2002, <http://www.whitehouse.gov/news/releases/2002/02/20020207–13.html>, accessed 9 February 2002

White House, The, 'Statement by the President: United Nations International Day in Support of Victims of Torture' 26 June 2003, <http://www.whitehouse.gov/news/releases/2003/06/20030626–3.html>, accessed 29 July 2003

—— 'Statement on United Nations International Day in Support of Victims of Torture' 40 Weekly Comp Pres Doc 1167–68 (5 July 2004), <http://www.findarticles.com/p/articles/mi_m2889/is_27_40/ai_n6148650>, accessed 3 January 2005

[Pentagon] Working Group Report on Detainee Interrogations in the Global War on Terrorism: Assessment of Legal, Historical, Policy, and Operational Considerations, 4 April 2003 <http://www.defenselink.mil/news/Jun2004/d20040622doc8.pdf>, accessed 14 June 2004

World AIDS Day website <http://www.worldaidsday.org/difference/findout.cfm>, accessed 27 November 2001

'24', season 4, episode 18, Day 4: 12:00 AM–1:00 AM originally aired by Fox TV on 18 April 2005. See 'episode guide' <http://www.fox.com/24/episodes/season4/12pm.htm>; 'episode information' <http://www.tvrage.com/24/episodes/679>, both accessed 24 March 2006

Index